Snapshots of Evolving Traditions

Berlin-Brandenburgische Akademie der Wissenschaften

Texte und Untersuchungen zur Geschichte der altchristlichen Literatur (TU)

Archiv für die Ausgabe der Griechischen Christlichen Schriftsteller der ersten Jahrhunderte

Begründet von
O. von Gebhardt und A. von Harnack

Herausgegeben von
Christoph Markschies

Band 175

berlin-brandenburgische
AKADEMIE DER WISSENSCHAFTEN

Snapshots of Evolving Traditions

Jewish and Christian Manuscript Culture,
Textual Fluidity, and New Philology

Edited by
Liv Ingeborg Lied & Hugo Lundhaug

DE GRUYTER

Herausgegeben durch die
Berlin-Brandenburgische Akademie der Wissenschaften
von Christoph Markschies

ISBN 978-3-11-034418-9
e-ISBN (PDF) 978-3-11-034805-7
e-ISBN (EPUB) 978-3-11-038397-3
ISSN 0082-3589

Library of Congress Cataloging-in-Publication Data
A CIP catalog record for this book has been applied for at the Library of Congress.

Bibliografische Information der Deutschen Nationalbibliothek
Die Deutsche Nationalbibliothek verzeichnet diese Publikation in der
Deutschen Nationalbibliografie; detaillierte bibliografische Daten sind im Internet über
http://dnb.dnb.de abrufbar.

© 2017 Walter de Gruyter GmbH, Berlin/Boston
Druck und Bindung: Hubert & Co. GmbH & Co. KG, Göttingen
♾ Gedruckt auf säurefreiem Papier
Printed in Germany

www.degruyter.com

Dedicated to
Jostein Børtnes, Ingvild Sælid Gilhus, Tomas Hägg[†], Tor Hauken, Geir Hellemo,
Lisbeth Mikaelsson, Halvor Moxnes, Turid Karlsen Seim[†] and Einar Thomassen
for demonstraiting the value of stimulating networks and environments
for research and innovation

Preface

The present volume aims to provide a broad introductory exploration of the applicability of the perspective of New Philology to late-antique Christian and Jewish texts in their manuscript contexts, and to inspire further studies along these lines. It springs from our longstanding common interest in methodological issues related to the study of ancient texts, an interest that has been fueled in part by many years of trying to make sense of texts as they appear in their manuscripts, as well as fruitful discussions with, and the groundbreaking studies of, this book's contributors.

We would like to thank series editor Christoph Markschies and the publisher, Walter de Gruyter, in particular project editor Stefan Selbmann and production editor Sabina Dabrowski. Most of all, we would like to thank the contributors of the volume for all the work that has gone into these essays and for their patient accommodation to the editors' various requests.

Thanks are also due to the European Research Council (ERC), whose generous support of the NEWCONT-project[1] has contributed to making this volume possible. Some of the articles published here were first presented at the NEWCONT-workshop "Textual Transmission and Manuscript Culture: Textual Fluidity, 'New Philology,' and the Nag Hammadi (and Related) Codices," held at the University of Oslo, 11–12 December 2012.

Oslo, April 2016

Liv Ingeborg Lied and Hugo Lundhaug

[1] New Contexts for Old Texts: Unorthodox Texts and Monastic Manuscript Culture in Fourth- and Fifth-Century Egypt. ERC Grant agreement no 283741, under the European Community's Seventh Framework Programme (FP7/2007–2013).

Table of Contents

List of contributors

Katrine Brix is PhD-student at the Divinity School of Humboldt University in Berlin.

Jeff W. Childers is Professor of New Testament and Early Christianity in the Graduate School of Theology, Abilene Christian University.

James R. Davila is Professor of Early Jewish Studies at the University of St Andrews.

René Falkenberg is Assistant Professor of Theology at Aarhus University.

J. Gregory Given is PhD-student at Harvard Divinity School.

Lance Jenott is a Post-doctoral Research Fellow at the University of Oslo, Faculty of Theology.

Lillian I. Larsen is Chair of Religious Studies at the University of Redlands.

Liv Ingeborg Lied is Professor of Religious Studies at MF Norwegian School of Theology.

Hugo Lundhaug is Professor of Biblical Reception and Early Christian Literature at the University of Oslo, Faculty of Theology.

Eva Mroczek is Assistant Professor in the Department of Religious Studies at the University of California, Davis.

Michael Penn is Professor in the Department of Religious Studies at Stanford University.

Samuel Rubenson is Professor of Church History at the Centre for Theology and Religious Studies at Lund University.

Images

Abbreviations

1 Apoc. Jas.	The *(First) Apocalypse of James* (NHC V,3)
2 Apoc. Jas.	The *(Second) Apocalypse of James* (NHC V,4)
Acts Pet. 12 Apost.	The *Acts of Peter and the Twelve Apostels* (NHC VI,1)
AJP	*American Journal of Philology*
APF.B	Archiv für Papyrusforschung und Verwandte Gebiete, Beiheft
Ap. Jas.	The *Apocryphon of James* (NHC I,2)
Ap. John	The *Apocryphon of John* (NHC II,1; III,1; IV,1; PB 8502,2)
Apoc. Adam	The *Apocalypse of Adam* (NHC V,5)
Apoc. Paul	The *Apocalypse of Paul* (NHC V,2)
Apoc. Pet.	*Apocalypse of Peter* (NHC VII,3)
ARKEN	Akademische Reden und Kolloquien: Friedrich-Alexander-Universität Erlangen-Nürnberg
ArTS	University of Pennsylvania Armenian Texts and Studies
Asclepius	*Asclepius 21–29* (NHC VI,8)
ATDan	Acta Theologica Danica
Auth. Teach.	*Authoritative Teaching/Authentikos Logos* (NHC VI,3)
BASP	*Bulletin of the American Society of Papyrologists*
BCNH.C	Bibliothèque copte de Nag Hammadi: Section "Concordances"
BCNH.É	Bibliothèque copte de Nag Hammadi: Section "Études"
BCNH.T	Bibliothèque copte de Nag Hammadi: Section "Textes"
BETL	Bibliotheca ephemeridum theologicarum lovaniensium
BGAM	Beiträge zur Geschichte des alten Mönchtums und des Benediktinerordens
BH	*Book History*
BHS	*Biblia Hebraica Stuttgartensia*
Bib	*Biblica*
BJRL	*Bulletin of the John Rylands Library*
BL	British Library
BL Add.	British Library Additional
BL Or.	British Library Oriental
BM	British Museum
BPl	Bibliothèque de la Pléiade
ByzF	*Byzantinische Forschungen*
ByzZ	*Byzantinische Zeitschrift*
CBET	Contributions to Biblical Exegesis and Theology
CBQ	*Catholic Biblical Quarterly*
CHRC	*Church History and Religious Culture*
CP	*Classical Philology*
CPG	*Clavis patrum graecorum*
CSCO	Corpus Scriptorum Christianorum Orientalium

CSML	Cambridge Studies in Medieval Literature
CSQ	*Cistercian Studies Quarterly*
CT	Codex Tchacos
CurBR	*Currents in Biblical Research*
Dial. Sav.	The *Dialogue of the Savior* (NHC III,5)
Disc. 8–9	The *Discourse on the Eighth and Ninth* (NHC VI,6)
DJD	Discoveries in the Judean Desert
DRev	*Downside Review*
EAW	Einleitung in die Altertumswissenschaft
ECF	Early Church Fathers
EMTC	Eastern Mediterranean Texts & Contexts
Ep. Pet. Phil.	The *Letter of Peter to Philip* (NHC VIII,2)
ErIsr	*Eretz Israel*
ETLC	Editorial Theory and Literary Criticism
EVO	*Egitto e Vicino Oriente*
Exeg. Soul	The *Exegesis on the Soul* (NHC II,6)
ExpTim	*Expository Times*
FAT	Forschungen zum Alten Testament
GBS	Guides to Biblical Scholarship
GCS	Die griechischen christlichen Schriftsteller der ersten Jahrhunderte
Gos. Eg.	The *Gospel of the Egyptians/Holy Book of the Great Invisible Spirit* (NHC III,2; IV,2)
Gos. Phil.	The *Gospel of Philip* (NHC II,3)
Gos. Thom.	The *Gospel of Thomas* (NHC II,2)
Gos. Truth	The *Gospel of Truth* (NHC I,3)
GQ	*Ginzei Qedem*
Great Pow.	The *Concept of Our Great Power* (NHC VI,4)
HDR	Harvard Dissertations in Religion
HSS	Harvard Semitic Studies
HTR	*Harvard Theological Review*
HTS	Harvard Theological Studies
Hug	*Hugoye: Journal of Syriac Studies*
Hyp. Arch.	The *Hypostasis of the Archons* (NHC II,4)
Hypsiph.	*Hypsiphrone* (NHC XI,4)
ICS	*Illinois Classical Studies*
IFAO	Institut français d'archéologie orientale du Caire
Interp. Know.	The *Interpretation of Knowledge* (NHC XI,1)
ISBL	Indiana Studies in Biblical Literature
JA	*Journal Asiatique*
JAC	*Jahrbuch für Antike und Christentum*
JAJ	*Journal of Ancient Judaism*

JAOS	*Journal of the American Oriental Society*
JCH	*Journal of Cognitive Historiography*
JCoptS	*Journal of Coptic Studies*
JCTCRS	Jewish and Christian Texts in Contexts and Related Studies
JEastCS	*Journal of Eastern Christian Studies*
JECS	*Journal of Early Christian Studies*
JETS	*Journal of the Evangelical Theological Society*
JJS	*Journal of Jewish Studies*
JNES	*Journal of Near Eastern Studies*
JSJ	*Journal for the Study of Judaism in the Persian, Hellenistic, and Roman Periods*
JSJS	Supplements to the Journal for the Study of Judaism
JSOT	*Journal for the Study of the Old Testament*
JSP	*Journal for the Study of the Pseudepigrapha*
JSPSup	Supplements to the Journal for the Study of the Pseudepigrapha
JSSSup	Journal of Semitic Studies Supplement Series
JTS	*Journal of Theological Studies*
LAI	Library of Ancient Israel
LCL	Loeb Classical Library
LDAB	Leuven Database of Ancient Books
LHBOTS	Library of Hebrew Bible/Old Testament Studies
Lit. Frag.	The *Liturgical Fragments* (NHC XI,*2a–e*)
LNTS	Library of New Testament Studies
LSJ	Liddell, Scott, and Jones, *A Greek-English Lexicon*, 9th ed.
MCPL	*Meddelanden från Collegium Patristicum Lundense*
Melch.	*Melchizedek* (NHC IX,*1*)
MGH	Monumenta Germaniae Historica
MONB	Monasterio Bianco (White Monastery)
MOPAI	Early Monasticism and Classical Paideia
MPER	Mitteilungen aus der Sammlung der Papyrus Erzherzog Rainer
MPIL	Monographs of the Peshiṭta Institute Leiden
MSR	*Mélanges de science religieuse*
MThSt	Marburger theologische Studien
Mus	*Le Muséon: Revue d'études orientales*
NA[27]	*Novum Testamentum Graece*, Nestle-Aland, 27th ed.
NAPSPatMS	North American Patristic Society Patristic Monograph Series
NETS	*A New English Translation of the Septuagint*
NEWCONT	New Contexts for Old Texts: Unorthodox Texts and Monastic Manuscript Culture in Fourth- and Fifth-Century Egypt
NHC	Nag Hammadi Codex
NHMS	Nag Hammadi and Manichaean Studies
NHS	Nag Hammadi Studies

NLH	*New Literary History*
Norea	The *Thought of Norea* (NHC IX,2)
NovT	*Novum Testamentum*
NovTSup	Supplements to *Novum Testamentum*
NPNF²	*Nicene and Post-Nicene Fathers*, Series 2
NRSVA	New Revised Standard Version, Anglicised
NTS	*New Testament Studies*
NTTSD	New Testament Tools, Studies and Documents
OCA	Orientalia Christiana Analecta
OCP	*Orientalia Christiana Periodica*
OECGT	Oxford Early Christian Gospel Texts
OECS	Oxford Early Christian Studies
OHS	Publications of the Oxford Historical Society
OLA	Orientalia Lovaniensia Analecta
OLZ	*Orientalistische Literaturzeitung*
On Anoint.	*On the Anointing* (NHC XI,2a)
On Bap. A	*On Baptism A* (NHC XI,2b)
On Bap. B	*On Baptism B* (NHC XI,2c)
On Euch. A	*On the Eucharist A* (NHC XI,2d)
On Euch. B	*On the Eucharist B* (NHC XI,2e)
OrChr	*Oriens Christianus*
Orig. World	*On the Origin of the World* (NHC II,5; XIII,2)
OTE	*Old Testament Essays*
Paraph. Shem	The *Paraphrase of Shem* (NHC VII,1)
ParOr	*Parole de l'orient*
PB	Papyrus Berolinensis
PBA	Proceedings of the British Academy
PETSE	Papers of the Estonian Theological Society in Exile
PG	Patrologia Graeca
PL	Patrologia Latina
PLAL	Perspectives on Linguistics and Ancient Languages
Plato Rep.	*Plato, Republic 588b–589b* (NHC VI,5)
PO	Patrologia Orientalis
P. Oxy.	Papyrus Oxyrhynchus
PV	Papyrologica Vindobonensia
Pr. Paul	The *Prayer of the Apostle Paul* (NHC I,1)
Pr. Thanks.	The *Prayer of Thanksgiving* (NHC VI,7)
PTS	Patristische Texte und Studien
R&T	*Religion and Theology*
RAC	*Reallexicon für Antike und Christentum*
RevQ	*Revue de Qumran*
RGRW	Religions in the Graeco-Roman World

SA	Studia Anselmiana
SAC	Studies in Antiquity and Christianity
SALL	Studies in Arabic Language and Literature
SBLDS	Society of Biblical Literature Dissertation Series
SBLEJL	Society of Biblical Literature Early Judaism and Its Literature
SBLMS	Society of Biblical Literature Monograph Series
SBLRBS	Society of Biblical Literature Resources for Biblical Study
SBLSCS	Society of Biblical Literature Septuagint and Cognate Studies
SBLTCS	Society of Biblical Literature Text-Critical Studies
SC	Sources chrétiennes
SEAug	Studia Ephemeridis Augustinianum
SecCent	*Second Century*
Sem	*Semitica*
Sent. Sext.	The *Sentences of Sextus* (NHC XII,*1*)
SHG	Subsidia Hagiographica
SJJTP	Supplements to the Journal of Jewish Thought and Philosophy
SKCO	Sprachen und Kulturen des christlichen Orients
SNTSMS	Society for New Testament Studies Monograph Series
Soph. Jes. Chr.	The *Wisdom of Jesus Christ* (NHC III,*4*; PB 8502,*3*)
SpOr	Spiritualité Orientale
SSLJM	Sources and Studies in the Literature of Jewish Mysticism
ST	*Studia Theologica*
STAC	Studien und Texte zu Antike und Christentum
STDJ	Studies on the Texts of the Desert of Judah
Steles Seth	The *Three Steles of Seth* (NHC VII,*5*)
StPatr	Studia Patristica
SWGS	Schriften der Wissenschaftlichen Gesellschaft in Straßburg
Teach. Silv.	The *Teachings of Silvanus* (NHC VII,*4*)
TENTS	Texts and Editions for New Testament Study
Testim. Truth	The *Testimony of Truth* (NHC IX,*3*)
Thom. Cont.	The *Book of Thomas* (NHC II,*7*)
Thund.	The *Thunder: Perfect Mind* (NHC VI,*2*)
TLZ	*Theologische Literaturzeitung*
TPL	Textus patristici et liturgici
Treat. Res.	The *Treatise on the Resurrection* (NHC I,*4*)
Treat. Seth	The *Second Treatise of the Great Seth* (NHC VII,*2*)
Tri. Trac.	The *Tripartite Tractate* (NHC I,*5*)
Trim. Prot.	*Trimorphic Protennoia* (NHC XIII,*1*)
TS	Texts and Studies
TSAJ	Texte und Studien zum antiken Judentum
TUGAL	Texte und Untersuchungen zur Geschichte der altchristlichen Literatur

TzF	Texte zur Forschung
Val. Exp.	*A Valentinian Exposition* (NHC XI,2)
VC	*Vigiliae Christianae*
VT	*Vetus Testamentum*
VTSup	Supplements to Vetus Testamentum
WUNT	Wissenschaftliche Untersuchungen zum Neuen Testament
WZ(H)	Wissenschaftliche Zeitschrift der Martin-Luther-Universität Halle-Wittenberg
ZAC	*Zeitschrift für Antikes Christentum*
ZÄS	*Zeitschrift für ägyptische Sprache und Altertumskunde*
ZAW	*Zeitschrift für die alttestamentliche Wissenschaft*
ZfdPh	*Zeitschrift für deutsche Philologie*
ZGRS	Zondervan Greek Reference Series
ZKT	*Zeitschrift für katholische Theologie*
Zost.	*Zostrianos* (NHC VIII,1)
ZPE	*Zeitschrift für Papyrologie und Epigraphik*

Hugo Lundhaug and Liv Ingeborg Lied

Studying Snapshots:
On Manuscript Culture, Textual Fluidity,
and New Philology

Confronted with the plethora of variants encountered in the manuscripts of the New Testament, textual critic David Parker has argued that "the attempt to produce an original form of a living text is worse than trying to shoot a moving target, it is turning a movie into a single snapshot, it is taking a single part of a complex entity and claiming it to be the whole."[1] This volume, which explores Coptic, Syriac, Hebrew, and Greek texts and manuscripts, argues that when scholars of early Christian and Jewish literature acknowledge the fact that our surviving textual witnesses constitute exactly such snapshots, and that these snapshots are not necessarily representative of the entire movie, it is pertinent to approach the interpretation of these texts from a perspective inspired by New Philology, taking textual fluidity and manuscript culture fully into consideration. Thus the essays included in this book represent new points of departure in the study of Jewish and Christian texts from Late Antiquity by focusing on the primary medium that contains them, namely the manuscripts, and explore various methodological tools with which to do so.

During the last twenty-five years there has been increasing interest in various aspects of late-antique media culture,[2] that is, the technological, cognitive, and communicative contexts of late-antique literary production, distribution, and consumption. As a result, our knowledge about scribes and scribal practices; manuscript production; copying, circulation and transmission of texts and manuscripts; literacy, reading and memorization; orality and aurality; and other contexts of use of ancient texts have increased remarkably. After the turn of the century, these aspects have engaged scholars of Early Christian, and Early Jewish, studies widely, and discussions are currently taking place among scholars of the Hebrew Bible and Septuagint studies, in studies of the Dead Sea Scrolls and the Old Testament Pseudepigrapha,[3]

---

1 David C. Parker, "Textual Criticism and Theology," *ExpTim* 118:12 (2007): 583–89 at 586.

2 Cf. the definition of "media culture" in Anthony Le Donne and Tom Thatcher, eds., *The Fourth Gospel in First Century Media Culture* (LNTS 426; London: T&T Clark, 2011), 2. We have extended their definition by the addition of the aspect of technology.

3 See, e.g., Robert A. Kraft, "The Pseudepigrapha in Christianity," in *Tracing the Threads: Studies in the Vitality of the Jewish Pseudepigrapha* (ed. John C. Reeves; SBLEJL 06; Atlanta: Scholars Press, 1994), 55–86; Philip R. Davies, *Scribes and Schools: The Canonization of the Hebrew Scriptures* (LAI; London: SPCK, 1998); Liv Ingeborg Lied, "*Nachleben* and Textual Identity: Variants and Variance in the Reception History of 2 Baruch," in *Fourth Ezra and Second Baruch: Reconstructions after the Fall* (ed. Matthias Henze and Gabriele Boccaccini; JSJS 164; Leiden: Brill, 2013), 403–28; Hindy Najman and Eibert Tigchelaar, eds., *Composition, Rewriting and Reception of the Book of Jubilees* (Special

in New Testament scholarship,[4] Nag Hammadi studies,[5] and Rabbinics,[6] to mention only a few of the fields involved.

In the study of the textual transmission of the New Testament, for instance, recent research on these various aspects of ancient media culture and editorial practices, with its ongoing revision and discussion of the dominating historical-critical paradigm, has been described as a sea change.[7] Others have described such changes in scholarly paradigms as parts of a broader shift within the general study of texts and writings in Late Antiquity – from a focus on origins to a focus on practice.[8] In other words, scholars are taking increasing interest in the ways in which people engaged with manuscripts and textual contents over time, and how the texts that have come down to us are the results of such complicated processes of engagement.[9]

---

issue; *RevQ* 104:26 [2014]); Matthew P. Monger, "4Q216 and the State of Jubilees at Qumran," *RevQ* 104:26 (2014): 595–612; Seth L. Sanders, *From Adapa to Enoch: Scribal Culture and Religious Vision in Judea and Babylonia* (TSAJ; Tübingen: Mohr Siebeck, forthcoming).

4 See below.

5 See, e.g., Karen L. King, "Approaching the Variants of the *Apocryphon of John*," in *The Nag Hammadi Library After Fifty Years: Proceedings of the 1995 Society of Biblical Literature Commemoration* (ed. John D. Turner and Anne McGuire; NHMS 44; Leiden: Brill, 1997), 105–37; Stephen Emmel, "Religious Tradition, Textual Transmission, and the Nag Hammadi Codices," in *The Nag Hammadi Library after Fifty Years: Proceedings of the 1995 Society of Biblical Literature Commemoration* (ed. John D. Turner and Anne McGuire; NHMS 44; Leiden: Brill, 1997), 34–43; Hugo Lundhaug, "The Nag Hammadi Codices: Textual Fluidity in Coptic," in *Comparative Oriental Manuscript Studies: An Introduction* (ed. Alessandro Bausi; Hamburg: COMSt, 2015), 419–23.

6 Cf. Carol Bakhos, ed., *Current Trends in the Study of Midrash* (JSJS 106; Leiden: Brill, 2006); Peter Schäfer and Chaim Milikowsky, "Current Views on Editing of Rabbinic Texts of Late Antiquity: Reflections on a Debate after Twenty Years," in *Rabbinic Texts and the History of Late-Roman Palestine* (eds. Martin Goodman and Philip S. Alexander; PBA 165; Oxford: Oxford University Press, 2010), 79–88.

7 Bart D. Ehrman, *The Orthodox Corruption of Scripture: The Effect of Early Controversies on the Text of the New Testament* (Rev. ed.; New York: Oxford University Press, 2011), esp. 352–62.

8 See, e.g., King, "Approaching the Variants"; Michael Philip Penn, "Monks, Manuscripts, and Muslims: Syriac Textual Changes in Reaction to the Rise of Islam," *Hug* 12:2 (2009): 235–57; Michael Philip Penn, "Moving Beyond the Palimpsest: Erasure in Syriac Manuscripts," *JECS* 18:2 (2010): 261–303.

9 See, e.g., Eldon Jay Epp, *The Theological Tendency of Codex Bezae Cantabrigiensis in Acts* (SNTSMS 3; Cambridge: Cambridge University Press, 1966); Penn, "Monks, Manuscripts, and Muslims"; Philip R. Davies, "Biblical Studies: Fifty Years of a Multi-Discpline," *CurBR* 13:1 (2014): 34–66; John S. Kloppenborg and Judith H. Newman, eds., *Editing the Bible: Assessing the Task Past and Present* (SBLRBS 69; Atlanta: Society of Biblical Literature, 2012); Liv Ingeborg Lied, "Text – Work – Manuscript: What Is an 'Old Testament Pseudepigraphon'?" *JSP* 25:2 (2015): 150–65; Lundhaug, "Textual Fluidity in Coptic"; Emmel, "Religious Tradition"; Menahem Kister et al., eds. *Tradition, Transmission, and Transformation from Second Temple Literature through Judaism and Christianity in Late Antiquity* (STDJ 113; Leiden: Brill, 2015).

New Philology

Since the late 1980s New Philology has provided a timely corrective to the broader field of editorial theory, addressing one of the main issues discussed by editors and interpreters of ancient and medieval texts since at least the late nineteenth century: the problem of manuscript variation and the contradictory objectives of retrieving the authentic form of a text while taking seriously the available manuscript evidence. The goal of most published critical editions is to get as close as possible to an assumed early text, presenting a highly polished text, believed to be an approximation of as early a text-form as possible – certainly earlier than that preserved in the earliest extant manuscripts. In other words, the text presented as "the text" in a modern edition is typically, although to varying degrees, foreign to the pool of existing manuscripts and the texts presented there.

It is an important characteristic of late-antique and medieval manuscripts, indeed all manuscripts prior to the printing press, that all copies of a text are unique. Although the level of variance differs, the textual variation witnessed in manuscripts is at times massive. In addition, critical editions have tended to overlook paratextual information, such as texts sharing the page with the main text block, like marginalia and other interventions made by the scribe or later readers. The typical modern edition does not try to make sense of the breadth of variation and unruliness displayed by actual manuscripts – it more commonly attempts to move behind and beyond it, disregarding the crucial fact that the variation and unruliness of the texts as they have been preserved in manuscripts are not extrinsic to late-antique and medieval writing, but are constitutive of it.[10]

Background

In a bold challenge to the common practices of textual criticism, Bernard Cerquiglini argued in 1989 that traditional philology, indebted to print culture, regarded variants simply as deviations from the norm, rather than as a natural product of scribal culture,

---

[10] See, e.g., Bernard Cerquiglini, *Éloge de la variante: Histoire critique de la philologie* (Paris: Seuil, 1989); English translation: Bernard Cerquiglini, *In Praise of the Variant: A Critical History of Philology* (trans. Betsy Wing; Parallax: Re-Visions of Culture and Society; Baltimore: Johns Hopkins University Press, 1999); Paul Zumthor, *Essai de poétique médiévale* (Paris: Seuil, 1972); English translation: Paul Zumthor, *Toward a Medieval Poetics* (trans. Philip Bennett; Minneapolis: University of Minnesota Press, 1992); Stephen G. Nichols, "The New Philology: Introduction: Philology in a Manuscript Culture," *Speculum* 65:1 (1990): 1–10; John Dagenais, *The Ethics of Reading in Manuscript Culture: Glossing the* Libro de Buen Amor (Princeton: Princeton University Press, 1994), xv–xvi; Andrew Taylor, *Textual Situations: Three Medieval Manuscripts and Their Readers* (Material Texts; Philadelphia: University of Pennsylvania Press, 2002).

where textual variants should rather be seen *as* the norm.[11] In manuscript cultures, that is, in cultures where literature is written down and copied by hand,[12] texts are constantly in a process of change, both through scribal reworking and copying, and through the work of active readers taking notes in the margins and otherwise interfering with the text. Texts are adapted, translated, interpolated and supplemented. Earlier glosses become part of the text block of the next copy, and new glosses affect the way readers encounter and understand the text. Cerquiglini thus famously concluded that "medieval writing does not produce variants; it is variance."[13] This fact, he claimed, had not been sufficiently taken into consideration. Traditional critical editions, he argued, disguise the variance of medieval texts by printing an ideal text and hiding the variants in the apparatus, where they subsequently languish as in a prison.[14] He consequently advocated a shift in scholarly focus from a quest for originals and constructed hypothetical texts, to the variants themselves as found in actual manuscripts.

The so-called "New Philology" thus grew out of the study of medieval vernacular literature.[15] Scholars working on such texts found that the principles and methods of traditional textual criticism[16] did not make as much sense in their field as for schol-

---

11 Cerquiglini, *Éloge de la variante*; idem, *In Praise of the Variant*.

12 The term "manuscript culture" is applied here to grasp the commonalities between cultures where literature is transmitted chirographically, in rhetorical contrast to a culture where literature is reproduced in print. On the other hand, though, it is important to note also the geographical and historical differences between the various milieus and traditions that have recorded and copied their literature by hand. There is of course no such thing as one, singular, manuscript culture. Thus, manuscripts and their texts must be studied in the context of the culture that produced and used them.

13 Cerquiglini, *In Praise of the Variant*, 77–78.

14 Cerquiglini, *In Praise of the Variant*, e.g., 73. Eldon Jay Epp makes a similar argument regarding New Testament textual criticism in his article "It's All about Variants: A Variant-Conscious Approach to New Testament Textual Criticism," *HTR* 100:3 (2007): 275–308.

15 Especially the fields of French and Norse medieval studies saw many early adopters. New Philology also drew explicitly on developments taking place since the 1960s in adjacent fields, for instance discussions and finds in fields like book history (e.g., Donald F. McKenzie, *Bibliography and the Sociology of Texts* [London: British Library, 1986]); media studies (Elizabeth Eisenstein, *The Printing Press as an Agent of Change: Communications and Cultural Transformations in Early-modern Europe*. 2 vols. [Cambridge: Cambridge University Press, 1979]); developments in studies on memory, orality, and literacy in a number of fields, e.g., Walter J. Ong, *Orality and Literacy: The Tecnologizing of the Word* (New York: Methuen, 1982); Mary Carruthers, *The Book of Memory: A Study of Memory in Medieval Culture* (CSML 70; Cambridge: Cambridge University Press, 1990); reception history (e.g., Hans-Georg Gadamer, *Warheit und Methode* (Tübingen: Mohr Siebeck, 1960); material culture studies (Arjun Appadurai, ed., *The Social Life of Things: Commodities in Cultural Perspective* [Cambridge: Cambridge University Press, 1986]).

16 New Philology constitutes a challenge to both the "Bédierist" and "Lachmannian" schools of editing. The latter is well represented by, and described in, such works as Paul Maas, *Textkritik* (EAW 1.2; Leipzig: Teubner, 1927); Giorgio Pasquali, *Storia della tradizione e critica del testo* (Florence: Le Monnier, 1952); Martin L. West, *Textual Criticism and Editorial Technique* (Stuttgart: Teubner, 1973); Sebastiano Timpanaro, *The Genesis of Lachmann's Method* (ed. and trans. Glenn W. Most; Chicago:

ars working on more stable textual traditions.[17] The challenges posed by the often considerable variance observed between textual witnesses simply demanded a different approach. With a literature characterized by an abundance of textual variants, the perspective that came to be known as "New Philology" thus constituted a much needed alternative to the quest for origins that had characterized the dominant philological paradigms, suggesting as it did a radically different way of editing and studying such unstable textual traditions.

The term "New Philology" itself, in the sense we are using it here, was not an invention of Cerquiglini, but was first coined by Stephen Nichols in his influential introduction to the 1990 special issue on "New Philology" in the medievalist journal *Speculum*,[18] an issue which was greatly inspired by Cerquiglini's book, published in French the year before.[19] Already in 1972, however, another French medievalist, Paul Zumthor, had emphasized the fluidity, or *mouvance* as he chose to label it, of medieval texts,[20] thus foreshadowing the later "New Philology" by quite a few years.[21]

University of Chicago Press, 2005); Michael D. Reeve, *Manuscripts and Methods: Essays on Editing and Transmission* (Rome: Edizioni di Storia e Letteratura, 2011); Paolo Trovato, *Everything You Always Wanted to Know about Lachmann's Method: A Non-Standard Handbook of Genealogical Textual Criticism in the Age of Post-Structuralism, Cladistics, and Copy-Text* (Storie e linguaggi; Padova: Libreriauniversitaria.it, 2014). Karl Lachmann himself never created a stemma in his own editorial work, and the designation "Lachmann's method" for genealogical textual editing was in fact coined by the theory's most influential detractor, Joseph Bédier, in his highly influential article "La tradition manuscrite du Lai de l'Ombre: Réflections sur l'art d'éditer les anciens textes," *Romania* 54 (1928): 161–98, 321–56. Bédier's alternative solution, which has also been exceedingly influential, was to edit the best text, based on a single manuscript judged by the scholar to be the best one available, and only emend the text if absolutely necessary. Like genealogical criticism, however, "Bédierist" editing also privileges one version of the text above all the others, albeit one that has not been (re)constructed. On the differences between these approaches, cf., e.g., G. Thomas Tanselle, "Classical, Biblical, and Medieval Textual Criticism and Modern Editing," *Studies in Bibliography* 36 (1983): 21–68; Nadia Altschul, "The Genealogy of Scribal Versions: A 'Fourth Way' in Medieval Editorial Theory," *Textual Cultures* 1:2 (2006): 114–36. Cf. also Jerome J. McGann, *A Critique of Modern Textual Criticism* (Chicago: University of Chicago Press, 1983).

17 Cf. Hans Ulrich Gumbrecht, *The Powers of Philology: Dynamics of Textual Scholarship* (Urbana, Ill.: University of Illinois Press, 2003), 39.

18 Nichols, "Philology in a Manuscript Culture."

19 The English translation was published ten years later, in 1999, in the series Parallax, edited by Nichols.

20 Zumthor, *Essai de poétique médiévale*; idem, *Toward a Medieval Poetics*.

21 As Richard Trachsler has pointed out, Cerquiglini's focus on variants was both similar to and different from Paul Zumthor's notion of *mouvance* (Zumthor, *Essai de poétique médiévale*; idem, "Intertextualité et mouvance," *Littérature* 41 (1981): 8–16). While Zumthor in a sense painted a picture of a medieval work that was always in motion and did not really exist anywhere in particular, from Cerquiglini's perspective, on the other hand, it existed everywhere, in each and every variant (Richard Trachsler, "How to Do Things with Manuscripts: From Humanist Practice to Recent Textual Criticism," *Textual Cultures* 1:1 [2006]: 5–28).

While it may thus be argued that "New Philology" was not really all that "new" when the term was coined in 1990, let alone now,[22] it is not the label that matters, but the perspectives it signals. And certainly with regard to the fields of Coptic and Syriac Studies, perspectives informed by "New Philology," whether under that name or other monikers such as "*mouvance*," "textual fluidity," "Scribal Versionism," "Material Philology," "Artefactual Philology," "New Medievalism" or similar, have so far not received the attention they deserve.[23]

Manuscripts and Their Texts

At the heart of New Philology is a focus on the material artifact constituted by the manuscript. As an alternative way of dealing with medieval manuscript variance, New Philology pinpoints the fact that a literary work does not exist independently of its material embodiment, and that this physical form is part of the meaning of the text.[24] This means that when studying a text, it is important to also study the manuscript, the relationship between the text and for instance the form and layout of the manuscript, as well as other features of the material text carrier: other texts collected in the same manuscript, front-matter, colophons and marginal notes, bindings, and cartonnage, etc. Material artifacts come into being at particular times, in particular places, for particular purposes.[25] The production of the artifact is determined by social, economic, and intellectual factors, and importantly, as these physical objects continue to exist over time, they are circulated and consumed in ways that are also socially, economically, and intellectually determined. Signs of use will occasionally show in the artifacts themselves, and these signs of use are interesting in their own

---

22 What is new in "new philology," states Stephen Nichols in his introductory article to the special "new philology" issue of the journal *Speculum*, is a desire to return to philology's "roots in a *manuscript* culture." The other sense in which the new philological enterprise could be said to be "new" was in its attempt to align philology with postmodernist literary and cultural studies (Nichols, "Philology in a Manuscript Culture"; cf. Trachsler, "How to Do Things," 21).
23 "Scribal Versionism": Altschul, "Genealogy of Scribal Versions"; "Material Philology": Stephen G. Nichols, "Why Material Philology? Some Thoughts," *ZfdPh* 116 (1997): Sonderheft, 10–30; "Artefactual Philology": Matthew James Driscoll, "The Words on the Page: Thoughts on Philology, Old and New," in *Creating the Medieval Saga: Versions, Variability, and Editorial Interpretations of Old Norse Saga Literature* (ed. Judy Quinn and Emily Lethbridge; Odense: University Press of Southern Denmark, 2010); "New Medievalism": e.g. Marina Scordilis Brownlee, Kevin Brownlee, and Stephen G. Nichols, eds., *The New Medievalism* (Baltimore: Johns Hopkins University Press, 1991).
24 Driscoll, "Words on the Page," 90.
25 Driscoll, "Words on the Page," 91.

right.[26] In other words, texts should not be studied as abstract texts divorced from the physical form of their presentation.

A perspective informed by New Philology has several consequences when applied to the study of Christian and Jewish Texts from Late Antiquity and the Middle Ages. Rather than speculating regarding hypothetical original texts and *their* contexts, the emphasis is on the production, use, and historical context of each individual copy. Paratextual features and other evidence of the contexts of the manuscripts' production must be taken into consideration since a preserved text's primary context is constituted by its manuscript,[27] and various forms of wear and tear are important, since they indicate how the manuscripts were actually used. By so doing, we may be able to shed light on the people who produced and owned the manuscripts, those who read the texts, and their socio-historical, cultural, and religious contexts.[28]

Production and use are indeed key terms in this enterprise. In relation to traditional philology, New Philology constituted a shift in focus from hypothetical originals or archetypes to manuscripts and manuscript cultures. It also brought with it certain postmodern sensibilities,[29] including a turning away from an emphasis on origins, authorship, and authorial intention, to that of reception and reading, and

---

26 Driscoll, "Words on the Page," 90–91.

27 On paratexts, see esp. Gérard Genette, *Paratexts: Thresholds of Interpretation* (trans. Jane E. Lewin; Literature, Culture, Theory 20; Cambridge: Cambridge University Press, 1997). Cf. also Driscoll, "Words on the Page"; Larry W. Hurtado, *The Earliest Christian Artifacts: Manuscripts and Christian Origins* (Grand Rapids, Mich.: Eerdmans, 2006). For a study of Nag Hammadi texts that takes paratextual features fully into consideration, see René Falkenberg's essay in the present volume. For a study of the paratextual features of the so-called Codex Tchacos and *Gos. Jud.*, see Lance Jenott, *The Gospel of Judas: Coptic Text, Translation, and Historical Interpretation of "The Betrayer's Gospel"* (STAC 64; Tübingen: Mohr Siebeck, 2011). Cf. also the essays of Eva Mroczek and Liv Ingeborg Lied for further studies of paratexts in Syriac, Greek and Hebrew manuscripts.

28 For a study of the producers and owners of the Nag Hammadi Codices utilizing a thorough analysis of the codices themselves, including their colophons, cartonnage, and codicology, see Hugo Lundhaug and Lance Jenott, *The Monastic Origins of the Nag Hammadi Codices* (STAC 97; Tübingen: Mohr Siebeck, 2015).

29 On New Philology's background in postmodern literary theory, see, e.g., Susan Yager, "New Philology," in *Handbook of Medieval Studies: Terms – Methods – Trends* (ed. Albrecht Classen; 3 vols.; Berlin: Walter de Gruyter, 2010), 2:999–1006. The postmodern indulgencies of some "New Philological" scholarship have indeed also garnered some criticism. John Dagenais, otherwise sympathetic to those aspects of "New Philology" that are drawn upon in the present essay, laments what he in some "New Medievalist" studies regards as "the last gasp of the verbal iconolatry that has characterized so much of twentieth-century thinking about literature" (*Ethics of Reading*, xv–xvi). At the same time he also lambasts those criticisms of "New Philology" that merely amount to "pronouncing the words 'trendy' or 'fashionable,' uttering 'Derrida' in a hoarse whisper, and reaching for the nearest cruciform object" (*Ethics of Reading*, xvi). Dagenais' main criticism of the proponents of "New Philology," however, is that many are still to a certain degree stuck in the "old philology" paradigm and do not really embrace the full implications of a focus on manuscript culture (*Ethics of Reading*, 12–13).

manuscripts in use.[30] As Michael Penn has aptly observed on the basis of his work on Syriac manuscripts, "the works we study are not so much the product of individual authors as the accumulation of a series of readers."[31] Penn here draws on the insights of John Dagenais, who posits that medieval manuscript culture can best be understood from the perspective of the reader. Even the scribes should be regarded primarily as readers, he argues, and medieval literature should be thought of more as "lecturature" than as literature.[32] He thus advocates "a shift from a view that privileges the author and/or his text ... to one that privileges the individual reader and the multitude of medieval literary activities, such as commentary and copying, that mirror reading."[33] This implies a shift in focus from origins and originals to transmission history, where the study of texts in their manuscript-contexts can reveal "an evolving, frequently contested, multi-layered process of meaning making," as Penn puts it.[34] Dagenais vividly describes his own eye-opening encounter with the manuscripts, stating that the literature he found there "was far more fluid and dynamic. It had rough edges, not the clean, carefully pruned lines of critical editions."[35] This realization then lead him to the insight that "it is at the edges of manuscripts and in the various activities by which medieval people transformed one manuscript into another ... that the most important part of 'medieval literature' happens."[36]

---

30 Altschul, "Genealogy of Scribal Versions," 122–23. Commenting on Zumthor's concept of *mouvance*, Roy Rosenstein remarks that it "was the logical next leap to be taken in confiscating the legacy of the author after his long-awaited and much-touted death. ... the post-authorial written tradition constitutes the work's ongoing creation, in which by now the long dead and buried author is denied authority and authorship" ("Mouvance," in *Handbook of Medieval Studies: Terms – Methods – Trends* [ed. Albrecht Classen; 3 vols.; Berlin: Walter de Gruyter, 2010], 3:1540).
31 Penn, "Monks, Manuscripts, and Muslims," 251.
32 Dagenais, *Ethics of Reading*, 20–26, 28–29. Karen King also reflects on this phenomenon, observing that "insofar as scribes were free from the constraints of an ideal of verbatim transmission and authorial 'copyright,' they were able to function as editors and even authors." While she feels that "the categories of author, editor, and scribe are still useful," she rightly points out that "the clear distinctions among these categories in print culture can obscure the fluid practices of ancient chirography" (King, "Approaching the Variants," 114).
33 Dagenais, *Ethics of Reading*, xvii.
34 Penn, "Monks, Manuscripts, and Muslims," 251; cf. Penn, "Moving Beyond the Palimpsest," 301. Or, as John Bryant states it, "Texts in revision – that is, 'fluid texts' or any work that exists in multiple versions – provide concrete evidence of writers writing and readers reading and can be of use in overcoming problems related to witnessing the otherwise unwitnessable process of production and consumption in a culture" (John Bryant, "Witness and Access: The Uses of the Fluid Text," *Textual Cultures* 2:1 [2007]: 17).
35 Dagenais, *Ethics of Reading*, xvi.
36 Dagenais, *Ethics of Reading*, xvi.

Textual Fluidity

The second major implication of New Philology relates directly to this picture of textual transmission and how it may impact our view of the texts. It has to do with how, as a consequence, we should treat textual variants and what implications we should draw from this view of textual transmission in our studies of the texts themselves. First and foremost, this has to do with the phenomenon of textual fluidity, i.e., the fact that in a manuscript culture, texts are inevitably changed, both intentionally and unintentionally, when they are copied, and so they develop, sometimes in major and significant ways, along their histories of transmission.[37]

The shift suggested by New Philology is significant. Traditional Source and Redaction Criticism have implied, explicitly or implicitly, that at a certain point the text is "finished" (some scholars even use the term "published," drawing on a terminology borrowed from print culture). Whereas it is held that a text may have developed along diverse lines, drawing on older sources, and may still display phases of early revision and editing, it is assumed that once the text has left the hand of the author, or alternatively the final editor, it starts circulating as a distinct entity, and changes made to the text after this point are regarded primarily as corruptions. From this perspective, the text may well have become corrupt through the inherently flawed process of scribal copying, but the text essentially remains a distinct entity throughout its transmission. Once this idea of textual fixation is abandoned, however, it opens up for significantly new perspectives. The changes introduced to the text in its transmission and use may now be studied as interesting and important aspects of the life of a text. The circulation of the text may be seen as an extended continuum of a development of which the texts attested in individual manuscripts provide us with snapshots. Likewise, seeing texts as fluid also opens up for the insight that textual traditions are never linear, but sometimes broken, interrupted and fundamentally transformed along the way.

---

37 It is important to note, however, that the differences between manuscript culture and print culture should not be exaggerated. The textual fluidity research by John Bryant, for instance, is focused on writings that are firmly embedded in a print culture. Although it has often been pointed out that print culture has been instrumental in creating the impression that textual fluidity is an anomaly, an impression that has influenced modern scholars' approach to texts produced in the far more unstable textual environment of a manuscript culture, research by Bryant and others have shown that fluidity is an inherent feature of textual production and transmission also after the onset of the printing press. Indeed, while New Philology arose on the basis of editorial problems related specifically to manuscript culture, textual fluidty is a broader phenomenon. See, e.g., John Bryant, *The Fluid Text: A Theory of Revision and Editing for Book and Screen* (Editorial Theory and Literary Criticism; Ann Arbor: University of Michigan Press, 2002); Peter L. Shillingsburg, *Resisting Texts: Authority and Submission in Constructions of Meaning* (Ann Arbor: University of Michigan Press, 1997), 165–80. As G. Thomas Tanselle argues, "Editing ancient texts and editing modern ones are not simply related fields; they are essentially the same field. The differences between them are in details; the similarities are in fundamentals" ("Classical, Biblical, and Medieval," 68).

New works grow out of older ones, writings are re-identified, and excerpted passages start circulating autonomously. These insights matter to our evaluation and analysis of copies that have hitherto primarily been used in textual criticism as "witnesses" to an earlier text. It may for instance well be that such copies have never been associated with the earlier writing by anyone other than their modern editors. To those who engaged with the texts in their manuscript contexts they may have been regarded quite differently.

From this follow several important questions regarding the status of the preserved texts and what we can learn from them. To what degree do the preserved texts, with all their variants, reflect the interests and concerns of the manuscripts' manufacturers and owners? Is it at all possible to reach an approximation of the "original"? Or how close to it is it possible to get? What degree of fluidity can we expect with regard to the text or texts under scrutiny? These are questions that will be dealt with in detail throughout the present volume, with case studies focusing on different types of manuscripts and text traditions deriving from different geographical and chronological contexts.

Current Developments in Related Fields

Perspectives akin to those promoted by New Philology have gained a foothold in several disciplines. The post-1980s developments in New Testament textual criticism provides us with a pertinent example. While few texts have been more the focus of traditional reconstructionist philology than the texts of the New Testament, where for obvious reasons the aim has always been to get back as close to the original, archetype, or initial texts as possible, there has in recent years also been an increased focus on textual transmission. Although the term "New Philology" and its foundational studies are seldom referred to in this field, the inherent instability of the biblical texts, especially in their earliest phases of transmission, has garnered increasing attention.[38] There has also been a markedly increased emphasis on scribes and scribal practices.[39] As Juan Hernández describes it, "no longer are contemporary textual critics concerned

---

[38] See, e.g., Ehrman, *Orthodox Corruption of Scripture*; Kim Haines-Eitzen, *Guardians of Letters: Literacy, Power, and the Transmitters of Early Christian Literature* (Oxford: Oxford University Press, 2000); David C. Parker, *The Living Text of the Gospels* (Cambridge: Cambridge University Press, 1997); Wayne C. Kannaday, *Apologetic Discourse and the Scribal Tradition: Evidence of the Influence of Apologetic Interests on the Text of the Canonical Gospels* (SBLTCS 5; Atlanta: Society of Biblical Literature, 2004).
[39] See, e.g., Harry Y. Gamble, *Books and Readers in the Early Church: A History of Early Christian Texts* (New Haven: Yale University Press, 1995); Haines-Eitzen, *Guardians of Letters*; Hurtado, *Earliest Christian Artifacts*.

primarily with the quest for the *Urtext*."[40] Instead, "the very habits of the scribe, once used to get back to the original wording of a passage and construct critical editions of the NT, are used to 'reconstruct' the scribe and inform our understanding of his/her? scribal habits, including theological tendencies."[41] The increased focus on variants that reflect intentional changes to the texts, rather than simply unintentional scribal errors, is noteworthy, as is the heightened emphasis on the variants themselves and what they may tell us concerning their own contexts.[42]

Today New Testament textual critics may pursue either the initial text, or the history of its transmission. And yet, to many scholars, the history of the text and the importance of establishing the texts and contexts of the actual manuscripts are still primarily regarded as stepping stones, although methodologically important ones, on the way to the goal of understanding the earliest possible retrievable version of the text. The ultimate goal is still to gain access to the text in its earliest possible form.

The New Philological perspectives presented in this volume also have much in common with studies in the field of Reception History, where the history of engagement with texts in circulation is also explored.[43] While the perspectives overlap in several respects, New Philology is particularly apt when it comes to studying the use and transmission of the texts in their manuscript contexts, as well as highlighting the media cultures in which texts have been transmitted and transformed. In other words, studies inspired by New Philology always privileges the primary, material context of the texts, the manuscripts, and focus on the signs of use and engagement

---

40 Juan Hernández, *Scribal Habits and Theological Influences in the Apocalypse: The Singular Readings of Sinaiticus, Alexandrinus, and Ephraemi* (WUNT^2 218; Tübingen: Mohr Siebeck, 2006), 28.

41 Hernández, *Scribal Habits*, 28; He adds that "Such issues have become so much a part of the current scholarly mainstream that monograph treatments of scribal tendencies constitute their own genre today" (ibid.). Cf. Epp, *Theological Tendency*; Ehrman, *Orthodox Corruption of Scripture*; Kannaday, *Apologetic Discourse*; Dirk Jongkind, *Scribal Habits of Codex Sinaiticus* (Texts and Studies, Third Series 5; Piscataway: Gorgias Press, 2007); James R. Royse, *Scribal Habits in Early Greek New Testament Papyri* (NTTSD 36; Leiden: Brill, 2008).

42 According to Ehrman, "Arguably the most significant conceptual development in the field of NT textual studies of the past fifty years, and especially in the past twenty (at least in the English-speaking world), has been the widespread realization that an exclusive concentration on the autographs is myopic, as it overlooks the value of variant forms of the text for historians interested in matters other than exegesis" (Bart D. Ehrman, "The Text as Window: New Testament Manuscripts and the Social History of Early Christianity," in *The Text of the New Testament in Contemporary Research: Essays on the Status Quaestionis* [2nd ed.; ed. Bart D. Ehrman and Michael W. Holmes; NTTSD 42; Leiden: Brill, 2013], 803). Variants, Ehrman points out, "provide data for the social history of early Christianity." Since "Changes that scribes made in their texts frequently reflect their own sociohistorical contexts," he argues, "variant readings are not merely chaff to be discarded en route to the original text," but valuable historical evidence for later periods and contexts in its transmission history (ibid., 804).

43 Cf., recently, Brennan W. Breed, *Nomadic Text: A Theory of Biblical Reception History* (ISBL; Bloomington: Indiana University Press, 2014); John W. Lyons and Emma England, eds., *Reception History and Biblical Studies: Theory and Practice* (LHBOTS, Scriptural Traces; London: T&T Clark, 2015).

visible there. Furthermore, these materially existing remnants are interpreted in light of the technological, cognitive, and communicative contexts of literary production, distribution, and consumption in the particular cultures in which the manuscripts were embedded.

Perspectives promoted by Book History also provide many insights similar to those of New Philology. Both perspectives focus on the material text-bearing artifact, and both emphasize their production, circulation, engagement and use.[44] One might say that the main difference between the two lies in Book History's primary focus on early print cultures, while New Philology arose from the problems of grasping chirographically transmitted literature. Hence, studies informed by Book History have typically focused on the period after the advent of the printing press, and their main objects of study have been early printed books and their environments of production and circulation, primarily (but not exclusively) in pre-modern Europe. Currently, however, scholars are successfully applying insights from Book History to the study of book culture also prior to the printing press, and scholars are increasingly willing to approach historical textual artifacts in terms of a continuum across the technological divide.[45]

In our view, neither the difference between the approaches, nor the differences between a manuscript culture and print culture should be exaggerated, and there is here much to learn across scholarly disciplines. While we should certainly be vary of applying concepts and vocabulary arising from print culture to a scribal culture, we also need to be aware of the many processual, social, and cognitive continuities between the two. What is of primary importance is that we in our studies of the ancient texts and their manuscripts are cognizant of how we conceptualize texts, textual transmission, and manuscript culture.

Outline of the volume

The essays in this volume deal specifically with manuscripts from the Christian East, as well as some manuscripts of Jewish provenance. Within this general area, the book has two main foci: Coptic literature, first and foremost represented by the

---

44 Cf., e.g., the classic contributions by Roger Chartier, *The Order of Books: Readers, Authors, and Libraries in Europe between the Fourteenth and the Eighteenth Centuries* (Stanford: Stanford University Press, 1992); McKenzie, *Bibliography and the Sociology of Texts*.
45 Cf., e.g., Liv Ingeborg Lied, "Manuscript Culture and the Myth of Golden Beginnings," in *Religion across Media: From Early Antiquity to Late Modernity* (ed. Knut Lundby; New York: Peter Lang, 2013), 54–70; Eva Mroczek, *The Literary Imagination in Jewish Antiquity* (New York: Oxford University Press, 2016).

Nag Hammadi Codices,[46] and Syriac writings. In addition, however, the volume also covers Hebrew and Greek, as well as some Latin and Georgian writings. The texts discussed in this volume cover a wide spectrum of genres. Apocalypses, epistles, psalms and "gospels" (canonical and non-canonical), commentary literature, mystical texts, school exercises, stories, sayings and sermons. The manuscripts also stem from a variety of locations and linguistic traditions, dating from the first to the fifteenth century, although the main bulk of manuscripts discussed in the present volume were produced and used in the period from the fourth to the thirteenth century.

The main goal of this volume is to explore the relevance and value of applying a perspective inspired by New Philology to these texts. It is not a volume on New Philology per se, but rather a collection of studies exploring the implications of taking seriously a range of implications arising from it, suggesting new and exciting arenas of research. From this perspective the book has three main foci: (1) The study of texts in their manuscript contexts. (2) Textual fluidity and its implications. (3) Discussion and evaluation of modern editorial practices. The volume thus aims to show how perspectives inspired by New Philology can provide us with additions, constructive alternatives, and critical correctives to a historical-critical paradigm and its privileged models of interpretation which are still dominant in those academic fields that have made early Jewish and Christian texts their main topic of study.

The studies presented in this volume provide a wealth of examples of how perspectives inspired by New Philology may open up new vistas in the study of texts in their manuscript contexts, while taking seriously the attestation of the texts in particular manuscripts, and allowing knowledge about the manuscripts and their contexts of production and use to inform the understanding of both texts and manuscripts, as well as the people who copied and read them.

The first four chapters focus on the Nag Hammadi Codices. In the first one, Hugo Lundhaug discusses the implications of textual fluidity for the interpretation of the Nag Hammadi texts. Extrapolating insights from those cases where we have more than one copy of a text to those cases where we have only single witnesses, it is argued that the illusion of textual stability that is created by the lack of witnesses should not lead us to use the texts uncritically as evidence of contexts far removed chronologically and geographically from that of the extant manuscripts. A shift in emphasis from origins and original contexts to the context of the users and producers of the manuscripts is consequently advocated.

---

46 This focus betrays the fact that several of the articles were originally presented at the workshop "Textual Transmission and Manuscript Culture: Textual Fluidity, 'New Philology,' and the Nag Hammadi (and Related) Codices," organized by the ERC-funded project NEWCONT (New Contexts for Old Texts: Unorthodox Texts and Monastic Manuscript Culture in Fourth- and Fifth-Century Egypt) at the University of Oslo, 11–12 December 2012.

Lance Jenott follows with a case-study of the textual variants of the two extant Coptic manuscript witnesses of a text we used to know as the *(First) Apocalypse of James* when we only knew it from one of the Nag Hammadi manuscripts, but which recently turned up in another manuscript simply under the name of *James*. Jenott shows that while the two copies are not wildly different, even minor textual variants may carry significant theological implications.

In the following contribution, René Falkenberg shows the benefits of a New Philological approach to the Nag Hammadi manuscripts, focusing specifically on Nag Hammadi Codex III on which he presents an in-depth study, showing how a detailed focus on the codicological and paratextual features of this particular manuscript may give us new insights into the editing, copying, and reading of the manuscript and its texts.

Where Jenott analyzes the differences between two versions of a text, where one is preserved in the Nag Hammadi Codices, and Falkenberg presents an analysis of an entire Nag Hammadi Codex as a whole, Katrine Brix focuses on a text that is preserved in different versions, in different dialects, in two separate Nag Hammadi Codices, namely the so-called *Gospel of Truth*, attested in Nag Hammadi Codices I and XII. While scholars have largely ignored the textual variants between these witnesses due to the damaged state of one these manuscripts, Brix shows the importance of taking both witnesses equally seriously.

Moving away from the Nag Hammadi Codices, Samuel Rubenson's essay presents a broad vista of textual fluidity in the transmission of the collection of monastic texts known as the *Apophthegmata Patrum*, the sayings of the desert fathers, across many centuries and a multitude of linguistic and geographical areas. This contribution forcefully brings out the high level of textual fluidity of these sayings and the problems inherent in utilizing them as historical sources for the earliest phases of monasticism.

The *Apophthegmata Patrum* also feature in Lillian Larsen's essay on late-antique paedagogical materials deriving from the Egyptian monastic tradition. Larsen shows how the monks reused classical paedagogical texts and principles in their own context, and highlights how scholars have often glossed over the implications of these particular sources owing to traditional practices of editing and interpreting such materials.

With Greg Given's essay, the spotlight is moved from textual fluidity as such, to generic fluidity, looking at the genre of the letter in the Coptic manuscript tradition, focusing on the exegetical payoff for readers of four selected texts from the Nag Hammadi Codices. Utilizing a comparative approach and taking paratextual features seriously into consideration, Given discusses such questions as the relationship between literary letters and "real" letters, and the rhetorical function of framing texts as letters, and argues that scholars need to be aware of the generic fluidity common in Coptic manuscripts, acknowledging the fact that features that may appear bizarre to us may not have done so to the intended readers of the manuscripts.

In the essay "Know Thy Enemy: The Materialization of Orthodoxy in Syriac manuscripts" Michael Philip Penn explores how the Christological controversies affected the way Syriac speaking Christians engaged with manuscripts containing works attesting to their adversaries' beliefs. Penn studies the strategies employed by scribes and active readers, such as narrative framing, reading marks and marginalia, still extant as materializations of differences in the manuscripts preserved in the British Library. These interventions reflect a culture of disputation, showing the urgent need to know the beliefs of the enemy whilst reassuring the faithful, and illustrate how manuscript pages may become spaces of ongoing meaning-making.

Jeff Childers' essay "'You Will Find What You Seek:' the Form and Function of a Sixth-Century Divinatory Bible in Syriac" explores British Library Add. 17,119, a manuscript that resists the standard classification of textual artifacts. This codex contains the Gospel of John, but also includes a system of *hermeneia* to the Gospel text, provided for the purpose of offering divinatory guidance. Whereas Add. 17,119 has so far primarily been used as a text witness to the Gospel of John, hence detaching the ancient text from the artifact in which it resides, Childers deals with the codex itself as a material object, synthesizing Gospel text and divinatory apparatus, exploring it as a "diving gospel." From this point of departure and building on the traits observable in the manuscript, Childers studies the dynamic history of the manuscript, the possible functions and shifting evaluations of its divinatory contents, the relationship between Gospel text and *hermeneia*, and the continuing reverence of the material artifact itself.

Liv Ingeborg Lied's essay deals with the attestation of the so-called Epistle of Baruch in Syriac manuscripts. This systematic study of paratextual features in these manuscripts, such as titles and end titles, shows that the Epistle appears as two distinct literary entities in the Syriac manuscript material and that it was probably engaged with as such by those who produced the manuscripts, and copied and read the Epistle. Based on this exploration of the manuscript material, Lied discusses trajectories in the history of editing the Epistle of Baruch, arguing that the paradigms and methods that have guided this history have created editions of the Epistle that systematically disregard key features in the manuscript attestation of this writing.

Eva Mroczek's essay, "The End of the Psalms in the Dead Sea Scrolls, Greek Codices, and Syriac Manuscripts," explores the enumeration and ending of the Book of Psalms in extant manuscripts from three different linguistic milieus. These manuscripts show how the content and the numbering of psalms were variable, and how the conception of the limits and shape of the Book of Psalms was not necessarily fixed. Mroczek explores the varying expressions of awareness of the canonical number of 150 psalms, as well as the paratextual framing of psalms beyond that number in the Hebrew, Greek and Syriac manuscripts, showing how a study of the presentations of boundaries to textual collections – boundaries that the manuscripts themselves transgress – may provide a new take on the longstanding discussions about scripture and canon.

In the final essay, "Translating the Hekhalot Literature: Insights from New Philology," James R. Davila provides a retrospective reflection upon his own process of translating and editing the Hekhalot literature. Davila explores the theoretical background to the translation and the practical constraints involved in producing it, discussing both traditional textual criticism and New Philology with a critical, analytical edge.

Summary

The New Philology-inspired studies presented in this volume show how we may choose to privilege texts as they have been preserved in actual manuscripts, in all their idiosyncratic glory, over the wish to get back to an approximation of earlier text-forms. The emphasis is placed firmly on extant texts as they are found in actual manuscripts, with no intention of using them to reconstruct a hypothetical prior text, or to make them serve as stand-ins for such a text. Texts as they appear in manuscripts are not seen as mere stepping-stones, or obstacles to be overcome, on the way to the ideal text, but are instead the primary focus. By this shift in focus, texts can be studied in the context of the manuscripts containing them, taking seriously the various media cultures that shaped the way readers engaged with texts in their material context, and emphasizing the interpretation of texts in the context of their use.

Bibliography

Altschul, Nadia. "The Genealogy of Scribal Versions: A 'Fourth Way' in Medieval Editorial Theory." *Textual Cultures* 1:2 (2006): 114–36.

Appadurai, Arjun, ed. *The Social Life of Things: Commodities in Cultural Perspective*. Cambridge: Cambridge University Press, 1986.

Bakhos, Carol, ed. *Current Trends in the Study of Midrash*. Supplements to the Journal for the Study of Judaism 106. Leiden: Brill, 2006.

Bédier, Joseph. "La tradition manuscrite du Lai de l'Ombre: Réflections sur l'art d'éditer les anciens textes." *Romania* 54 (1928): 161–98, 321–56.

Breed, Brennan W. *Nomadic Text: A Theory of Biblical Reception History*. Indiana Series in Biblical Literature. Bloomington & Indianapolis: Indiana University Press, 2014.

Brownlee, Marina Scordilis, Kevin Brownlee, and Stephen G. Nichols, eds. *The New Medievalism*. Baltimore: Johns Hopkins University Press, 1991.

Bryant, John. *The Fluid Text: A Theory of Revision and Editing for Book and Screen*. Editorial Theory and Literary Criticism. Ann Arbor: University of Michigan Press, 2002.

–. "Witness and Access: The Uses of the Fluid Text." *Textual Cultures* 2:1 (2007): 16–42.

Carruthers, Mary. *The Book of Memory: A Study of Memory in Medieval Culture*. Cambridge Studies in Medieval Literature 70. Cambridge: Cambridge University Press, 1990.

Cerquiglini, Bernard. *Éloge de la variante: Histoire critique de la philologie*. Paris: Seuil, 1989.

–. *In Praise of the Variant: A Critical History of Philology*. Translated by Betsy Wing. Parallax: Re-Visions of Culture and Society. Baltimore: Johns Hopkins University Press, 1999.

Chartier, Roger. *The Order of Books: Readers, Authors, and Libraries in Europe between the Fourteenth and the Eighteenth Centuries*. Stanford: Stanford University Press, 1992.

Dagenais, John. *The Ethics of Reading in Manuscript Culture: Glossing the Libro de Buen Amor*. Princeton: Princeton University Press, 1994.

Davies, Philip R. *Scribes and Schools: The Canonization of the Hebrew Scriptures*. Library of Ancient Israel. London: SPCK, 1998.

–. "Biblical Studies: Fifty Years of a Multi-Discpline." *Currents in Biblical Research* 13:1 (2014): 34–66.

Driscoll, Matthew James. "The Words on the Page: Thoughts on Philology, Old and New." Pages 87–104 in *Creating the Medieval Saga: Versions, Variability, and Editorial Interpretations of Old Norse Saga Literature*. Edited by Judy Quinn and Emily Lethbridge. Odense: University Press of Southern Denmark, 2010.

Ehrman, Bart D. *The Orthodox Corruption of Scripture: The Effect of Early Controversies on the Text of the New Testament*. Revised edition. New York: Oxford University Press, 2011.

–. "The Text as Window: New Testament Manuscripts and the Social History of Early Christianity." Pages 803–30 in *The Text of the New Testament in Contemporary Research: Essays on the Status Quaestionis*. Second Edition. Edited by Bart D. Ehrman and Michael W. Holmes. New Testament Tools, Studies and Documents 42. Leiden: Brill, 2013.

Eisenstein, Elizabeth. *The Printing Press as an Agent of Change: Communications and Cultural Transformations in Early-Modern Europe*. 2 Volumes. Cambridge: Cambridge University Press, 1979.

Emmel, Stephen. "Religious Tradition, Textual Transmission, and the Nag Hammadi Codices." Pages 34–43 in *The Nag Hammadi Library after Fifty Years: Proceedings of the 1995 Society of Biblical Literature Commemoration*. Edited by John D. Turner and Anne McGuire. Nag Hammadi and Manichaean Studies 44. Leiden: Brill, 1997.

Epp, Eldon Jay. *The Theological Tendency of Codex Bezae Cantabrigiensis in Acts*. Society for New Testament Studies Monograph Series 3. Cambridge: Cambridge University Press, 1966.

–. "It's All about Variants: A Variant-Conscious Approach to New Testament Textual Criticism." *Harvard Theological Review* 100:3 (2007): 275–308.

Gadamer, Hans-Georg. *Warheit und Methode*. Tübingen: Mohr Siebeck, 1960.

Gamble, Harry Y. *Books and Readers in the Early Church: A History of Early Christian Texts*. New Haven: Yale University Press, 1995.

Genette, Gérard. *Paratexts: Thresholds of Interpretation*. Translated by Jane E. Lewin. Literature, Culture, Theory 20. Cambridge: Cambridge University Press, 1997.

Gumbrecht, Hans Ulrich. *The Powers of Philology: Dynamics of Textual Scholarship*. Urbana, Ill.: University of Illinois Press, 2003.

Haines-Eitzen, Kim. *Guardians of Letters: Literacy, Power, and the Transmitters of Early Christian Literature*. Oxford: Oxford University Press, 2000.

Hernández, Juan. *Scribal Habits and Theological Influences in the Apocalypse: The Singular Readings of Sinaiticus, Alexandrinus, and Ephraemi*. Wissenschaftliche Untersuchungen zum Neuen Testament, 2. Reihe 218. Tübingen: Mohr Siebeck, 2006.

Hurtado, Larry W. *The Earliest Christian Artifacts: Manuscripts and Christian Origins*. Grand Rapids, Mich.: Eerdmans, 2006.

Jenott, Lance. *The Gospel of Judas: Coptic Text, Translation, and Historical Interpretation of "The Betrayer's Gospel."* Studien und Texte zu Antike und Christentum 64. Tübingen: Mohr Siebeck, 2011.

Jongkind, Dirk. *Scribal Habits of Codex Sinaiticus*. Texts and Studies, Third Series 5. Piscataway: Gorgias Press, 2007.

Kannaday, Wayne C. *Apologetic Discourse and the Scribal Tradition: Evidence of the Influence of Apologetic Interests on the Text of the Canonical Gospels*. Society of Biblical Literature Text-Critical Studies 5. Atlanta: Society of Biblical Literature, 2004.

King, Karen L. "Approaching the Variants of the *Apocryphon of John*." Pages 105–37 in *The Nag Hammadi Library After Fifty Years: Proceedings of the 1995 Society of Biblical Literature Commemoration*. Edited by John D. Turner and Anne McGuire. Nag Hammadi and Manichaean Studies 44. Leiden: Brill, 1997.

Kister, Menahem, Hillel I. Newman, Michael Segal and Ruth A. Clements, eds. *Tradition, Transmission, and Transformation from Second Temple Literature through Judaism and Christianity in Late Antiquity*. Studies on the Texts of the Desert of Judah 113. Leiden: Brill, 2015.

Kloppenborg, John S., and Judith H. Newman, eds. *Editing the Bible: Assessing the Task Past and Present*. Society of Biblical Literature Resources for Biblical Study 69. Atlanta: Society of Biblical Literature, 2012.

Kraft, Robert A. "The Pseudepigrapha in Christianity." Pages 55–86 in *Tracing the Threads: Studies in the Vitality of the Jewish Pseudepigrapha*. Edited by John C. Reeves. Society of Biblical Literature Early Judaism and Its Literature 06. Atlanta: Scholars Press, 1994.

Le Donne, Anthony, and Tom Thatcher, eds. *The Fourth Gospel in First Century Media Culture*. Library of New Testament Studies 426. London: T&T Clark, 2011.

Lied, Liv Ingeborg. "Manuscript Culture and the Myth of Golden Beginnings." Pages 54–70 in *Religion across Media: From Early Antiquity to Late Modernity*. Edited by Knut Lundby. New York: Peter Lang, 2013.

–. "*Nachleben* and Textual Identity: Variants and Variance in the Reception History of 2 Baruch." Pages 403–28 in *Fourth Ezra and Second Baruch: Reconstructions after the Fall*. Edited by Matthias Henze and Gabriele Boccaccini; Supplements to the Journal for the Study of Judaism 164. Leiden: Brill, 2013.

–. "Text – Work – Manuscript: What is an 'Old Testament Pseudepigraphon'?" *Journal for the Study of the Pseudepigrapha*, 25:2 (2015): 150–65.

Lundhaug, Hugo. "The Nag Hammadi Codices: Textual Fluidity in Coptic." Pages 419–23 in *Comparative Oriental Manuscript Studies: An Introduction*. Edited by Alessandro Bausi. Hamburg: COMSt, 2015.

Lundhaug, Hugo, and Lance Jenott. *The Monastic Origins of the Nag Hammadi Codices*. Studien und Texte zu Antike und Christentum 97. Tübingen: Mohr Siebeck, 2015.

Lyons, John W., and Emma England, eds. *Reception History and Biblical Studies: Theory and Practice*. Library of Hebrew Bible/Old Testament Studies, Scriptural Traces. London: T&T Clark, 2015.

Maas, Paul. *Textkritik*. Einleitung in die Altertumswissenschaft 1.2. Leipzig: Teubner, 1927.

McGann, Jerome J. *A Critique of Modern Textual Criticism*. Chicago: University of Chicago Press, 1983.

McKenzie, Donald F. *Bibliography and the Sociology of Texts*. London: British Library, 1986.

Monger, Matthew P. "4Q216 and the State of Jubilees at Qumran." *Revue de Qumran* 104:26 (2014): 595–612.

Mroczek, Eva. *The Literary Imagination in Jewish Antiquity*. New York: Oxford University Press, 2016.

Najman, Hindy and Eibert Tigchelaar, eds. *Composition, Rewriting and Reception of the Book of Jubilees*. Special issue. *Revue de Qumran* 104:26 (2014).

Nichols, Stephen G. "The New Philology: Introduction: Philology in a Manuscript Culture." *Speculum* 65:1 (1990): 1–10.

–. "Why Material Philology? Some Thoughts." *Zeitschrift für deutsche Philologie* 116 (1997): Sonderheft, 10–30.

Ong, Walter J. *Orality and Literacy: The Tecnologizing of the Word*. New York: Methuen, 1982.

Parker, David C. *The Living Text of the Gospels*. Cambridge: Cambridge University Press, 1997.

–. "Textual Criticism and Theology." *Expository Times* 118:12 (2007): 583–89.

Pasquali, Giorgio. *Storia della tradizione e critica del testo*. Florence: Le Monnier, 1952.

Penn, Michael Philip. "Monks, Manuscripts, and Muslims: Syriac Textual Changes in Reaction to the Rise of Islam." *Hugoye: Journal of Syriac Studies* 12:2 (2009): 235–57.

–. "Moving Beyond the Palimpsest: Erasure in Syriac Manuscripts." *Journal of Early Christian Studies* 18:2 (2010): 261–303.

Reeve, Michael D. *Manuscripts and Methods: Essays on Editing and Transmission*. Rome: Edizioni di Storia e Letteratura, 2011.

Rosenstein, Roy. "Mouvance." Pages 3:1538–47 in *Handbook of Medieval Studies: Terms – Methods – Trends*. Edited by Albrecht Classen. 3 Vols. Berlin: Walter de Gruyter, 2010.

Royse, James R. *Scribal Habits in Early Greek New Testament Papyri*. New Testament Tools, Studies and Documents 36. Leiden: Brill, 2008.

Sanders, Seth L. *From Adapa to Enoch: Scribal Culture and Religious Vision in Judea and Babylonia*. Texte und Studien zum antiken Judentum. Tübingen: Mohr Siebeck, forthcoming.

Schäfer, Peter, and Chaim Milikowsky. "Current Views on Editing of Rabbinic Texts of Late Antiquity: Reflections on a Debate After Twenty Years." Pages 79–88 in *Rabbinic Texts and the History of Late-Roman Palestine*. Edited by Martin Goodman and Philip S. Alexander. Proceedings of the British Academy 165. Oxford: Oxford University Press, 2010.

Shillingsburg, Peter L. *Resisting Texts: Authority and Submission in Constructions of Meaning*. Ann Arbor: University of Michigan Press, 1997.

Tanselle, G. Thomas. "Classical, Biblical, and Medieval Textual Criticism and Modern Editing." *Studies in Bibliography* 36 (1983): 21–68.

Taylor, Andrew. *Textual Situations: Three Medieval Manuscripts and Their Readers*. Material Texts. Philadelphia: University of Pennsylvania Press, 2002.

Timpanaro, Sebastiano. *The Genesis of Lachmann's Method*. Edited and Translated by Glenn W. Most. Chicago: University of Chicago Press, 2005.

Trachsler, Richard. "How to Do Things with Manuscripts: From Humanist Practice to Recent Textual Criticism." *Textual Cultures* 1:1 (2006): 5–28.

Trovato, Paolo. *Everything You Always Wanted to Know about Lachmann's Method: A Non-Standard Handbook of Genealogical Textual Criticism in the Age of Post-Structuralism, Cladistics, and Copy-Text*. Storie e linguaggi. Padova: Libreriauniversitaria.it, 2014.

West, Martin L. *Textual Criticism and Editorial Technique*. Stuttgart: Teubner, 1973.

Yager, Susan. "New Philology." Pages 2:999–1006 in *Handbook of Medieval Studies: Terms – Methods – Trends*. Edited by Albrecht Classen. 3 Vols. Berlin: Walter de Gruyter, 2010.

Zumthor, Paul. *Essai de poétique médiévale*. Paris: Editions du Seuil, 1972.

–. "Intertextualité et mouvance." *Littérature* 41 (1981): 8–16.

–. *Toward a Medieval Poetics*. Translated by Philip Bennett. Minneapolis: University of Minnesota Press, 1992.

Hugo Lundhaug*

An Illusion of Textual Stability: Textual Fluidity, New Philology, and the Nag Hammadi Codices

Despite the fact that readers are inclined to regard textual fluidity as textual corruption and to look upon fluid texts as anomalies, textual fluidity is, as John Bryant has pointed out, in fact the norm across "all linguistic cultures."[1] Here I look closer at the Nag Hammadi Codices,[2] which constitute some of the earliest examples of Coptic manuscript culture, and argue that the mechanisms of chirographic textual transmission need to be taken fully into consideration in any study of the contents and contexts of this material. As Stephen Emmel reminds us, most Coptic literature "was composed either for, or in the act of, public declamation in the context of Christian worship. In so far as it was transmitted, it was transmitted as 'living (liturgical) literature', which could be altered in the course of transmission to suit new times, places, and needs."[3] Whether the Nag Hammadi Codices were used liturgically or not, there is certainly considerable evidence for the fluidity of the transmission of their texts. Here I will highlight evidence for such fluidity and its crucial, but frequently overlooked, implications and show how insights from New Philology may fruitfully be applied to the study of the Nag Hammadi Codices.

Since the discovery of the Nag Hammadi Codices in 1945,[4] the most commonly assumed interpretive context for the texts contained in them has been that of second-

---

* This article has been written under the aegis of project NEWCONT (New Contexts for Old Texts: Unorthodox Texts and Monastic Manuscript Culture in Fourth- and Fifth-Century Egypt) at the University of Oslo. The project is funded by the European Research Council (ERC) under the European Community's Seventh Framework Programme (FP7/2007–2013) / ERC Grant agreement no 283741. Some of the materials in this essay have previously appeared in Hugo Lundhaug, "The Nag Hammadi Codices: Textual Fluidity in Coptic," in *Comparative Oriental Manuscript Studies: An Introduction* (ed. Alessandro Bausi et al.; Hamburg: COMSt, 2015), 419–23.

1 John Bryant, "Witness and Access: The Uses of the Fluid Text," *Textual Cultures* 2:1 (2007): 18–19. Bryant defines a fluid text as "any written work that exists in multiple material versions due to revisions (authorial, editorial, cultural) upon which we may construct an interpretation" (Bryant, "Witness and Access," 17).

2 These codices derive from the fourth and/or fifth centuries CE. On the dating of these manuscripts, see Hugo Lundhaug and Lance Jenott, *The Monastic Origins of the Nag Hammadi Codices* (STAC 97; Tübingen: Mohr Siebeck, 2015), 9–11.

3 Stephen Emmel, "Coptic Literature in the Byzantine and Early Islamic World," in *Egypt in the Byzantine World, 300–400* (ed. Roger S. Bagnall; Cambridge: Cambridge University Press, 2007), 94.

4 On the discovery of the Nag Hammadi Codices, see James M. Robinson, *The Nag Hammadi Story* (2 Vols.; NHMS 86; Leiden: Brill, 2014), 1:1–40, 77–92; Lundhaug and Jenott, *Monastic Origins*, 11–21.

or third-century "Gnosticism."[5] Scholarly interpretations of the texts have generally been made, and evaluated, on the basis of the assumption that this is the context of their authorship. However, the major impact this wide-ranging consensus has had on the understanding of the texts hides the fact that it rests on a number of presuppositions that are less well-grounded than generally assumed. Most notably, scholarship on the Nag Hammadi writings has typically relied on an implicit assumption of textual stability and a correspondingly exaggerated faith in the possibility of gaining some kind of access to the original texts and the contexts of their composition.

As Michael Williams has pointed out, there has been a tendency among scholars of the Nag Hammadi tractates "to equate rather too facilely or thoughtlessly the 'text' of a given writing only with what is after all our own modern text-critical 'guesstimate' about the 'original,' skipping past on our way perfectly real, physical copies of that writing that someone did use."[6] Simply put, the contexts of the production and use of the manuscripts have generally not been the contexts in which the texts have been interpreted. Stephen Emmel notes that Nag Hammadi scholars have generally taken for granted "that the Nag Hammadi tractates bear some more or less close relationship to a hypothetical original composition," while moving "back and forth between the Coptic text we have and the original we would *like* to have, keeping careful lookout for signs of corruption, redaction, and so on, in an effort to minimize being led astray by such a long and complex history of transmission."[7] As Emmel points out, doing so is highly difficult and the results intrinsically hypothetical.[8] An obvious way to counter these difficulties, however, is to focus primarily on the texts as we have them in the manuscripts, without trying to get back to an earlier form of the text, i.e., an approach informed by New Philology.

---

5 For critical discussions of the problems inherent in the scholarly reception of the Nag Hammadi Codices as evidence of "Gnosticism," see esp. Michael A. Williams, *Rethinking "Gnosticism": An Argument for Dismantling a Dubious Category* (Princeton, N. J.: Princeton University Press, 1996); idem, "Was There a Gnostic Religion? Strategies for a Clearer Analysis," in *Was There a Gnostic Religion?* (ed. Antti Marjanen; Publications of the Finnish Exegetical Society 87; Helsinki: Finnish Exegetical Society, 2005), 55–79; idem, "A Life Full of Meaning and Purpose: Demiurgical Myths and Social Implications," in *Beyond the Gnostic Gospels: Studies Building on the Work of Elaine Pagels* (ed. Eduard Iricinschi et al.; STAC 82; Tübingen: Mohr Siebeck, 2013), 19–59. Karen L. King, *What is Gnosticism?* (Cambridge, Mass.: Belknap Press of Harvard University Press, 2003).
6 Michael A. Williams, "Response to the papers of Karen King, Frederik Wisse, Michael Waldstein and Sergio La Porta," in *The Nag Hammadi Library After Fifty Years: Proceedings of the 1995 Society of Biblical Literature Commemoration* (ed. John D. Turner and Anne McGuire; NHMS 44; Leiden: Brill, 1997), 209.
7 Stephen Emmel, "Religious Tradition, Textual Transmission, and the Nag Hammadi Codices," in *The Nag Hammadi Library After Fifty Years: Proceedings of the 1995 Society of Biblical Literature Commemoration* (ed. John D. Turner and Anne McGuire; NHMS 44; Leiden: Brill, 1997), 40–41.
8 Emmel, "Religious Tradition," 41–42.

When applied to the study of the Nag Hammadi texts, New Philology has several notable consequences.[9] Most importantly, the emphasis is changed from hypothetical original texts and *their* contexts, to the texts in the form in which they have actually come down to us. Since a preserved text's primary context is constituted by its manuscript, it is pertinent to gain as solid an understanding as possible of the context of the production and use of the manuscript, which can then subsequently inform our analyses of how the texts may have been received in that context. Information concerning the production and use of the codices may be reached by means of codicological and palaeographical analysis, studies of documents reused as cartonnage in the codices' covers, and through an investigation of paratextual features such as titles, colophons, punctuation, etc., as well as the selection and sequence of the texts themselves in each individual codex.[10] By doing so, we may be able to shed light on the socio-historical, cultural, and religious context of the people who produced and owned the manuscripts, who presumably also read the texts contained in them.[11]

It is highly likely that those who produced the Nag Hammadi Codices, and for whom they were made, were Christian monks who in the fourth and fifth centuries were active in Upper Egypt, close to the cliffs of the Jabal al-Tarif and the Jabal Abu Mana.[12] What does this insight imply for our interpretation of the texts? If the texts had remained completely stable from the time of their authorship, throughout their history of transmission, and up to the production of our extant manuscripts it may arguably have been of marginal relevance for our understanding of the texts themselves. In that case it would have been easy to argue that the original context of composition would be far more relevant than the context of the preserved manuscripts. Since this kind of stability cannot be taken for granted, however, we need to take the

---

9 For a brief introduction to New Philology, see Hugo Lundhaug and Liv Ingeborg Lied, "Studying Snapshots: On Manuscript Culture, Textual Fluidity, and New Philology," in the present volume.

10 On paratexts see esp. Gérard Genette, *Paratexts: Thresholds of Interpretation* (trans. Jane E. Lewin; Literature, Culture, Theory 20; Cambridge: Cambridge University Press, 1997). Cf. also Matthew James Driscoll, "The Words on the Page: Thoughts on Philology, Old and New," in *Creating the Medieval Saga: Versions, Variability, and Editorial Interpretations of Old Norse Saga Literature* (ed. J. Quinn and E. Lethbridge; Odense: University Press of Southern Denmark, 2010), 87–104; Larry W. Hurtado, *The Earliest Christian Artifacts: Manuscripts and Christian Origins* (Grand Rapids, Mich.: Eerdmans, 2006). For a study of texts from the Nag Hammadi Codices that takes paratextual features fully into consideration, see René Falkenberg's essay in the present volume. Cf. also the essays of Eva Mroczek and Liv Ingeborg Lied for further studies of paratextual features in Syriac, Greek, and Hebrew manuscripts.

11 For a study of the producers and owners of the Nag Hammadi Codices utilizing a thorough analysis of the codices themselves, including their colophons, cartonnage, and codicology, see Lundhaug and Jenott, *Monastic Origins*.

12 On the monastic provenance of the Nag Hammadi Codices, see Lundhaug and Jenott, *Monastic Origins*.

manuscripts and their context seriously into consideration if we wish our analyses of the Nag Hammadi texts to be historically plausible.

When we take textual fluidity fully into consideration, we should expect many of the texts to have been reworked to various extents up until the end of their transmission histories. Several questions may thus be asked. Why were the Nag Hammadi texts read in Egyptian monasteries, and what happened to them when they were transmitted in this particular context?[13] To what degree do the Nag Hammadi texts reflect the interests and concerns of the codices' owners? What degree of editing or rewriting can we expect the texts to have undergone in order to make them fit such a context? What degree of textual fluidity should we expect?

Texts in Multiple Manuscripts

An indication of the fluidity we might expect from the singularly attested texts may be had from a look at some of the texts that are preserved in multiple copies within the Nag Hammadi Codices themselves.[14]

The Apocryphon of John

The most obvious example is constituted by the *Apocryphon of John*. It has been preserved in three copies within the Nag Hammadi Codices alone, in Codices II, III, and IV, as well as in Papyrus Berolinensis 8502. Since three of these manuscripts, NHC II and III and PB 8502, are relatively well-preserved, we here have a wonderful opportunity to compare multiple versions of the text and get a glimpse of the fluidiy of its transmission.

Working on the basis of a traditional text-critical paradigm, Michael Waldstein and Frederik Wisse, the editors of the major English-language edition of the text, initially wanted to create a single critical Coptic text, or at least a single critical English

---

13 As Michel Desjardins has put it, "The emphasis on asceticism which we find throughout the entire Nag Hammadi corpus, for instance, could tell us as much about the predilections of fourth century monks as it does about second century Gnosticism" ("The Sources for Valentinian Gnosticism: A Question of Methodology," *VC* 40:4 [1986]: 344; cf. idem, "Rethinking the Study of Gnosticism." *R&T* 12:3/4 [2005]: 380).

14 The following texts are, at least partly, attested in one or more additional manuscripts within or outside the Nag Hammadi Codices themselves: Multiple attestation within the NHC: *Gos. Truth* (partly), *Ap. John*, *Gos. Eg.*, *Eugnostos*; NHC texts also attested outside the NHC: *Ap. John*, *Gos. Thom.* (partly), *Orig. World* (partly), *Soph. Jes. Chr.*, *1 Apoc. Jas.*, *Plato Rep.*, *Pr. Thanks.*, *Asclepius, Teach. Silv.* (partly), *Zost.* (partly), *Ep. Pet. Phil.*, *Sent. Sext.* For details, see the list in Lance Jenott's contribution in the present volume.

translation, on the basis of all the extant witnesses.[15] Due to the nature of the differences between these witnesses, however, they not only had to give up the attempt to
establish a single critical text, but even the attempt to make a single critical translation.[16] Instead they settled for a synoptic presentation of all surviving witnesses in
parallel columns, with separate translations.[17]

The relationship between the four versions of *Ap. John* is indeed complicated.
Although they can be grouped into a long (NHC II and IV) and a short (PB 8502 and
NHC III) recension, the differences run deeper than the simple addition of material
in the long in relation to the short recension, such as a several pages long section on
the creation of the various parts of Man by different angels. A good example of the
more subtle, but still important, differences between the versions can be seen in the
following passage:[18]

PB 8502:	ⲁⲥϭⲱ{ⲱ}ϣⲧ ⲉϩⲟⲩⲛ ⲉⲣⲟϥ ⲉⲙⲁⲧⲉ ⲛϭⲓⲧⲃⲁⲣⲃⲏⲗⲱ ⲡⲓⲧⲃⲃⲟ ϩⲛⲟⲩⲟⲓ̈ⲛ
NHC III:	ⲁⲩⲱ ⲁϭⲥⲱϣⲧ ⲉⲙⲁϣⲟ ⲛ̄ϭⲓⲧⲃⲁⲣⲃⲏⲗⲟⲛ ⲉϩⲟⲩⲛ ⲉⲡϩⲓⲗⲓⲕⲣⲓⲛⲉⲥ ⲛ̄ⲟⲩⲟⲉⲓⲛ·
NHC II:	ⲁⲩⲱ ⲁϥϭⲱϣⲧ· ⲉϩⲟⲩⲛ ϩⲛ̄ⲧⲃⲁⲣⲃⲏⲗⲱ ⲙ̄ⲡⲟⲩⲟⲉⲓⲛ· ⲉ[ⲧ]ⲧⲃⲃⲏⲩ
	ⲉⲧⲕⲧⲏⲩ ⲁⲡⲁϩⲟⲣⲁⲧⲟⲛ· ⲙ̄ⲡⲛ̄ⲁ̄ ⲙⲛ̄ⲡⲉϥⲡⲣⲣⲉ
PB 8502:	Barbelo gazed intensely into him, the pure light,
NHC III:	And Barbelon gazed intensely into the pure light,
NHC II:	And he gazed into Barbelo in/with the pure light
	surrounding the invisible spirit and its shining,
PB 8502:	ⲁⲥ[ⲕ]ⲟⲧⲥ ⲉϩⲟⲩⲛ ⲉⲣⲟϥ ⲁⲥϫⲡⲟ ⲛ̄ⲛⲟⲩⲥⲡⲓⲛⲑⲏⲣ ⲛⲟⲩⲟⲓ̈ⲛ ⲙ̄ⲙⲁⲕⲁⲣⲓⲟⲛ
NHC III:	ⲁⲩⲱ ⲁⲥⲧⲕⲁⲧⲟ ⲉϩⲟⲩⲛ ⲉⲣⲟϥ ⲁⲥϫⲡⲟ ⲛ̄ⲟⲩⲥⲡⲓⲛⲑⲏⲣ ⲛ̄ⲟⲩⲟⲉⲓⲛ ⲉϥⲉⲓⲛⲉ ⲙ̄ⲡⲟⲩⲟⲉⲓⲛ ⲉⲧⲉⲛⲁⲉⲓⲁⲧϥ̄·
NHC II:	ⲁⲩⲱ ⲁⲥϫⲉⲟⲩⲱ [ⲉⲣⲟϥ ⲁ]ϥϫⲡⲟ ⲛⲟⲩⲧⲕ̄ ⲛ̄ⲟⲩⲟⲉⲓⲛ ϩⲛⲟⲩⲟⲉⲓ[ⲛ]ⲉ ⲙⲙⲛ̄ⲧⲙⲁⲕⲁⲣⲓ[ⲟⲥ] ⲛ̄ⲉⲓⲛⲉ·
PB 8502:	and she turned to him and begot a spark of blessed light,
NHC III:	and she turned to him and begot a spark of light resembling the blessed light,
NHC II:	and she conceived [from him]. He begot a spark of light in light of blessed like-
	ness,

---

15 Michael Waldstein and Frederik Wisse, *The Apocryphon of John: Synopsis of Nag Hammadi Codices
II,1; III,1; and IV,1 with BG 8502,2* (NHMS 33; Leiden: Brill, 1995).

16 Frederik Wisse, "After the *Synopsis*: Prospects and Problems in Establishing a Critical Text of the
Apocryphon of John and in Defining its Historical Location," in *The Nag Hammadi Library After Fifty
Years: Proceedings of the 1995 Society of Biblical Literature Commemoration* (ed. John D. Turner and
Anne McGuire; NHMS 44 Leiden: Brill, 1997), 141–42.

17 Cf. Wisse, "After the *Synopsis*," 141–42. Despite choosing this solution, they nevertheless ended
up reconstructing a considerable amount of text in each version on the basis of the others. On their
emendation policy, see Wisse, "After the *Synopsis*," 139–41. The earlier attempt to produce a single
translation into English can also be detected in the final translations of the individual texts.

18 PB 8502 29.18–30.9; NHC III 9.10–19; NHC II 6.10–18. Coptic text from Waldstein and Wisse, *Apocryphon of John*, 40–41. Since the badly damaged NHC IV here (NHC IV 9.11–23) seems to be very close
to NHC II, I have not included NHC IV in this example.

PB 8502:	ⲛⲉϥϣⲟ̅ϣ̅ ⲇⲉ ⲟⲩⲃⲏⲥ ⲁⲛ ϩ̅ⲛⲧⲙ̅ⲧ̅ⲛⲟϭ
NHC III:	ⲁⲗⲗⲁ ⲛ̅ϥϣⲟ̅ϣ̅ ⲁⲛ ϩ̅ⲛⲧⲙ̅ⲧ̅ⲛⲟϭ
NHC II:	ⲉϥϣⲟ̅ϣ̅ ⲇⲉ [ⲁⲛ] ⲙⲛ̅ⲧⲉϥⲙⲛ̅ⲧⲛ[ⲟ]ϭ
PB 8502:	but it was not equal to her in greatness.
NHC III:	but it was not equal in greatness.
NHC II:	but it was [not] equal to his greatness.

PB 8502:	ⲡⲁⲓ̈ ⲡⲉ ⲡⲙⲟⲛⲟⲅⲉⲛⲏⲥ ⲛ̅ⲧⲁϥⲟⲩⲱⲛϩ ⲉⲃⲟⲗ ⲙ̅ⲡⲓⲱⲧ
NHC III:	ⲡⲉⲉⲓ ⲡⲉ ⲡⲙⲟⲛⲟⲅⲉⲛⲏⲥ ⲉⲣⲟⲩⲱⲛϩ ⲉⲃⲟⲗ ϩ̅ⲙ̅ⲡⲓⲱⲧ
NHC II:	ⲡⲁⲓ̈ ⲛⲉⲟⲩϣⲣ̅ⲟⲩⲱⲧ [ⲡⲉ] ⲛ̅ⲧⲙⲏⲧⲣⲟⲡⲁⲧⲱⲣ ⲉⲁϥⲟⲩⲱⲛϩ ⲉⲃⲟⲗ
PB 8502:	This is the only-begotten one who appeared from the father,
NHC III:	This is the only-begotten one appearing from the father,
NHC II:	This one who had appeared was an only son of the mother-father,

PB 8502:	ⲡⲁⲩⲧⲟⲅⲉⲛⲏⲧⲟⲥ ⲛⲛⲟⲩⲧⲉ ⲡϣⲏⲣⲉ ⲛϣⲣ̅ⲡⲙ̅ⲙⲓⲥⲉ ⲙ̅ⲡⲧⲏⲣϥ ⲛⲧⲉⲡⲉⲓⲡ̅ⲛ̅ⲁ̅ ⲙⲡⲟⲩⲟⲓⲛ <ⲛ>ⲁⲗ[ⲓ]ⲕⲣⲓⲛⲉⲥ
NHC III:	ⲡⲁⲩⲧⲟⲅⲉⲛⲏⲥ ⲛ̅ⲛⲟⲩⲧⲉ ⲡϣⲏⲣⲉ ⲛ̅ϣⲁⲙⲓⲥⲉ ⲛ̅ⲧ̅ⲛ̅ⲛⲁⲡⲓⲱⲧ ⲧⲏⲣⲟⲩ ⲡⲓⲗⲓⲕⲣⲓⲛⲉⲥ ⲛ̅ⲟⲩⲟⲉⲓⲛ
NHC II:	ⲉⲧⲉ[ⲡⲁⲓ̈] ⲡⲉ ⲡⲉϥϫⲡ[ⲟ] ⲟⲩⲁⲁⲧϥ⳿ ⲡϣⲣ̅ⲟⲩⲱⲧ⳿ ⲛ̅[ⲧ]ⲉ[ⲡ]ⲉⲓⲱⲧ [ⲡⲟⲩ]ⲟⲉⲓⲛ⳿ ⲉⲧⲧⲃ̅ⲃⲏⲩ⳿
PB 8502:	the divine self-generated, the first-born son of the universe of the spirit of the pure light.
NHC III:	the divine self-generated, the first-born son of all of those of the father, the pure light.
NHC II:	namely his only-begotten, the only son of the father, [the] pure light.

As is readily apparent from this example, even minor differences between versions may carry major theological implications,[19] and illustrate the perilously tricky nature of extrapolating an original text on the basis of these surviving witnesses. It goes without saying that it makes for a significantly different text, with markedly different interpretive possibilities, whether Barbelo(n) looks into the Father (8502 and NHC III) or whether the Father looks into her (NHC II); whether he is active in begetting (NHC II) or not (8502 and NHC III); whether the spark of light is referred to as not equal to *her* (8502 and perhaps NHC III) or to *him* (NHC II and perhaps III) in greatness; or whether the son is described as "an only son of the mother-father" (NHC II) or not.

How, then, do we account for such variation? On the basis of traditional methodology, Waldstein and Wisse explain the variants either in terms of different translations from Greek into Coptic, translations of different Greek *Vorlagen*, or as errors introduced in the Coptic phase of transmission. Interestingly, they explain the differences between the two copies of the shorter recension (NHC III,1 and PB 8502,2) as the result of different translations of the same Greek work, while the two ver-

---

19 Good examples of cases where small differences between manuscripts may carry large implications for textual interpretation can be seen in Lance Jenott's analysis of differences between the two surviving witnesses to the text known as *1 Apoc. Jas.* (in NHC V) or simply *Jas.* (In Codex Tchacos), and in René Falkenberg's analysis of the epilogue of *Ap. John*, both in the present volume.

sions of the longer text (NHC II,*1* and IV,*1*), which they regard as copies of the same translation of a longer Greek text, still contain differences that lead them to the conclusion that they "do not appear to stand in a 'sister' or 'mother-daughter' relationship."[20]

Waldstein and Wisse thus conclude that the four copies represent two independent Coptic translations from the original Greek of a shorter version of the *Apocryphon of John*, and two copies of a Coptic translation of a longer Greek version. Going even further back, they believe that the *Urtext* behind these hypothetical Greek versions was composed in the early third century, and then "underwent a major redaction, represented by the longer version" later in the third century. Then, sometime in the late third or early fourth century, these Greek versions were independently translated into Coptic, the shorter version at least twice. To account for the remaining differences between the extant versions, they propose that these Coptic versions were then copied multiple times before eventually ending up in our four preserved codices.[21] While this is a plausible scenario, the problem with such an elaborate explanation is that there is no solid evidence to back it up, and it must therefore remain merely one possible solution among many.[22]

Indeed, even in all its complexity this picture is probably too simple. Waldstein and Wisse's reasoning is based on the premise that the variants are primarily to be explained by differences of translation and errors of transmission,[23] and although they briefly discuss the question of redaction with regard to the differences between the short and long recensions, they do not take intentional rewriting and the broader phenomenon of textual fluidity fully into consideration when considering the whole breadth of variance among all four witnesses. Despite the major differences between the surviving Coptic witnesses, the primary focus for most scholars working on the *Apocryphon of John* has remained the hypothetical Greek original, pure and uncontaminated by the errors introduced in its later transmission. It is the hypothetical Greek original and *its* historical and sociocultural context, as well as the sources that may have been utilized by its equally hypothetical author that has been the focus of most studies.[24] Thus an imagined second-century context, such as an urban school

---

20 Waldstein and Wisse, *Apocryphon of John*, 1.

21 Waldstein and Wisse, *Apocryphon of John*, 1.

22 See also the discussion of various earlier suggestions in Andrew K. Helmbold, "The *Apocryphon of John*: A Case Study in Literary Criticism," *JETS* 13:3 (1970): 173–79.

23 See, e.g., Waldstein and Wisse, *Apocryphon of John*, 7; cf. Wisse, "After the *Synopsis*," 145–46.

24 Notable exceptions, however, include Bernard Barc and Louis Painchaud, "La réécriture de l'Apocryphon de Jean à la lumière de l'hymne final de la version longue," *Mus* 112 (1999): 317–33; Louis Painchaud, "La classification des textes de Nag Hammadi et le phénomène des réécritures," in *Les textes de Nag Hammadi et le problème de leur classification: Actes du colloque tenu à Québec du 15 au 19 septembre 1993* (ed. Louis Painchaud and Anne Pasquier; BCNH.É 3; Québec: Les presses de l'Université Laval, 1995), 51–85.

setting in Alexandria,[25] rather than the fourth-/fifth-century contexts of the extant manuscripts, has usually been privileged in scholarly interpretations of the text, despite the fact that we may reasonably suspect that the contexts through which the text has passed in its transmission may have significantly influenced those versions that are actually available to us.[26]

If, on the contrary, we regard our four Coptic witnesses as snapshots of a fluid text, without privileging the original, each witness becomes important in itself as evidence of the text's reception and use by those who manufactured and owned the codices, and since the context of the production and use of the Nag Hammadi Codices, and PB 8502, is most likely that of Upper Egyptian monasticism,[27] the preserved copies of the text may profitably be read in light of that context, rather than that of, e.g., a hypothetical urban school-setting in Alexandria, at a time long before the production of the preserved manuscripts.

The Gospel of Truth

The *Gospel of Truth* provides us with a second example. It is attested in two of the Nag Hammadi Codices. Unfortunately one of them, the Codex XII version, has suffered significant damage,[28] leaving only the one in Codex I well preserved.[29] Despite the fact that we are thus left with only a few parallel passages, it is nevertheless clear from what has been preserved that there are substantial differences between them.

One obvious difference is linguistic. The version in Codex I is in the Lycopolitan dialect of Coptic, while the Codex XII version is in the Sahidic dialect. But there are also important textual differences that cannot easily be explained by reference to the dialectal differences or by postulating different translations from the Greek. Moreover, although it is readily apparent that the two scribes were not equally skilled – the

---

25 Karen L. King, *The Secret Revelation of John* (Cambridge, Mass.: Harvard University Press, 2006), 9–13, 244.

26 On the perils of overemphasising the hypothetical original, see the insightful comments of Karen L. King, "Approaching the Variants of the *Apocryphon of John*," in *The Nag Hammadi Library After Fifty Years: Proceedings of the 1995 Society of Biblical Literature Commemoration* (ed. John D. Turner and Anne McGuire; NHMS 44; Leiden: Brill, 1997), 105–37, esp. 130–37.

27 For an extended argument in favor of the monastic provenance of the Nag Hammadi Codices, see Lundhaug and Jenott, *Monastic Origins*.

28 In Nag Hammadi Codex XII, *Gos. Truth* is fragmentarily preserved in just three severely damaged leaves (six manuscript pages). See Frederik Wisse, "NHC XII, 2: The Gospel of Truth," in *Nag Hammadi Codices XI, XII, XIII* (ed. Charles W. Hedrick; NHS 28; Leiden: Brill, 1990), 329–47.

29 In Nag Hammadi Codex I, *Gos. Truth* has been preserved in an almost complete form in twenty-eight manuscript pages. See Harold W. Attridge and George W. MacRae, "The Gospel of Truth," in *Nag Hammadi Codex I (The Jung Codex): Introductions, Texts, Translations, Indices* (ed. Harold W. Attridge; NHS 22; Leiden: Brill, 1985), 55–117.

scribe of the Codex I version being by far the least accomplished of the Nag Hammadi scribes – the variants are not adequately accounted for by errors of transmission.[30]

What conclusions may be drawn on the basis of these differences? It is notable that most scholars working on the *Gospel of Truth*, or who have made reference to the *Gospel of Truth* in studies of early Christianity or "Gnosticism," have simply based their studies on the Codex I version of the text, and have either explicitly or implicitly dismissed the version contained only fragmentarily in Codex XII,[31] thus concealing the inherent fluidity of the text. However, as Frederik Wisse has noted, "the differences between the two versions of the *Gospel of Truth* go far beyond those expected for independent translations into different dialects." Not only does the Codex XII version represent "a somewhat shorter text" that often differs in substance from Codex I, but "the many serious problems of syntax in [Codex I] are not evident in [Codex XII]."[32] To account for this, Wisse suggests that either the Coptic translator of the Codex XII text "produced a version that was a simplification of the Greek," or "the Coptic of Codex I is awkward and at times corrupt."[33] He thus suggests that the Codex I version may be "an inferior Coptic translation of a corrupted Greek text."[34]

This has not prevented other scholars from drawing quite different conclusions based on the same evidence. Contrary to Wisse, Einar Thomassen, for instance, claims that "the text transmitted in Codex XII was significantly inferior to that of Codex I."[35] Moreover, while Thomassen admits that "the text of Codex I may have been reworked in places," he nevertheless asserts that "in substance" we are "justified in treating NHC I,3 as representing a Valentinian document dating from before the time of Irenaeus' work of the 180s."[36] Michel Tardieu, for his part, prefers the other version to be closer to the original text. Noting the major differences between the two codices, he argues that the Sahidic version in Codex XII "provides evidence of a non-glossed [*Gospel of Truth*], that is, the writing of Valentinus himself."[37] For Tardieu the Codex I version "belongs to a later stage of development of a school which calls itself Valentinian, but whose theological interests were very different from those of its

---

30 For detailed comparison of the versions, see Katrine Brix' article in the present volume.
31 See, e.g., Jacqueline A. Williams, *Biblical Interpretation in the Gnostic Gospel of Truth from Nag Hammadi* (SBLDS 79; Atlanta: Scholars Press, 1988); Einar Thomassen, *The Spiritual Seed: The Church of the 'Valentinians'* (NHMS 60; Leiden: Brill, 2006), 147.
32 Wisse, "NHC XII, 2," 330.
33 Wisse, "NHC XII, 2," 330
34 Wisse, "NHC XII, 2," 331
35 Thomassen, *Spiritual Seed*, 147.
36 Thomassen, *Spiritual Seed*, 147–148. Thomassen refers to Irenaeus' anti-heretical work *Adversus Haereses*.
37 Michel Tardieu in Raoul Mortley, "'The Name of the Father is the Son' (Gospel of Truth 38) [with Afterword by Michel Tardieu]," in *Neoplatonism and Gnosticism* (ed. Richard T. Wallis and Jay Bregman; Albany, N. Y.: State University of New York Press, 1992), 250.

founder." In Tardieu's opinion, the Codex I version seems to be a commentary on a shorter Greek text of which the Codex XII version is a translation.

Despite acknowledging the differences between the two preserved versions of the *Gospel of Truth*, both Thomassen and Tardieu are willing to treat one of them as a relatively accurate representation of a hypothetical original text composed in Greek by the heresiarch Valentinus himself, long before the production of our surviving Coptic witnesses. Even bracketing the question of Valentinus' authorship,[38] there are important questions that need to be asked. How confident can we be that either of the two versions of the *Gospel of Truth* preserved in the Nag Hammadi Codices is a reasonably accurate representation of the original? How confident can we be that the original was composed in Greek? How confident can we be that the original was composed in the second century? How much of what constitutes the preserved texts go back to the original, and how much should be attributed to later redaction and rewriting? A scholar who has come to a very different conclusion to those mentioned above is Raoul Mortley, who argues on the basis of parallels with fourth-century theological debates that the *Gospel of Truth*, as preserved in Codex I, presupposes the Arian debate, which thus situates at least this version of the text firmly in a fourth century context, close to the time of the production of Codex I itself.[39] If Mortley is right, it at the very least becomes problematic to use this version of the text as evidence of second-century theology.

Yet a significant number of scholars have continued to regard the Codex I version as essentially identical to an original second-century composition, simply, it seems, because this is the best preserved copy.[40] Even those who recognize the substantial differences between the two versions still work from the assumption of a stable textual tradition where textual variation is explained away as scribal errors rather than as an endemic quality of textual transmission in a manuscript culture. I would argue that it is more accurate to describe the two witnesses to the *Gospel of Truth* as "snapshots" of a far more complex history of transmission, and that we stand on firmer ground reading the preserved texts as they have been preserved, trying primarily to understand them in light of their manuscript contexts. It should be acknowledged that trying to get back to the "original" text or even to its essential qualities or original context on the basis of these very different preserved versions must remain highly speculative.

---

38 Valentinus' authorship of *Gos. Truth* has been argued by, e.g., Benoit Standaert, "'L'Évangile de Vérité': Critique et lecture," *NTS* 22 (1976): 243–75; J. A. Williams, *Biblical Interpretation*, 4–5; Thomassen, *Spiritual Seed*.
39 Mortley, "Name of the Father."
40 E.g., J. A. Williams, *Biblical Interpretation*; Hans-Martin Schenke, "Evangelium Veritatis (NHC II, 3/XII, 2," in in *Nag Hammadi Deutsch* (ed. Hans-Martin Schenke, Hans-Gebhard Bethge, and Ursula Ulrike Kaiser; 2 vols.; GCS, Neue Folge 8; Koptisch-Gnostische Schriften 2; Berlin: Walter de Gruyter, 2001–3), 1:27–44; Thomassen, *Spiritual Seed*.

The Prayer of Thanksgiving

Another example is the *Prayer of Thanksgiving*. While it is only attested once within the Nag Hammadi corpus itself, it is also attested in Greek and Latin manuscripts.[41] Again, there is a number of notable textual and contextual differences between the surviving versions. The Coptic text, preserved only in Nag Hammadi Codex VI, is introduced by a phrase that is found in neither the Greek nor the Latin version of the text.[42] In Nag Hammadi Codex VI, the *Prayer of Thanksgiving* follows the otherwise unattested Hermetic *Discourse on the Eighth and the Ninth*, and seems to have been added on at the end of that text in order to serve as a direct continuation of it. The introductory phrase of the *Prayer of Thanksgiving*, "This is the prayer that they said,"[43] is easily understood as a reference to a prayer performed by Hermes Trismegistus and his pupil as referred to in the preceding *Discourse on the Eighth and the Ninth*. The end of the *Prayer of Thanksgiving* is equally interesting. While the Nag Hammadi version ends by stating that "When they had said these things in prayer, they kissed each other (ⲁⲩⲣ̄ⲁⲥⲡⲁⲍⲉ ⲛ̄ⲛⲉⲩⲉⲣⲏⲟⲩ·) and went to eat their holy bloodless food,"[44] the Latin version has "Wishing these things, we turn to a pure meal without any flesh of animals,"[45] and the Greek text has no comparable ending at all.

How do we account for these differences? The different manuscript contexts may give us a clue. It is not difficult to imagine how, in its current form, the Coptic version might have been received by the fourth- or fifth-century monks reading Nag Hammadi Codex VI as a prayer very much akin to a common Christian prayer. Indeed, its ending might even be seen to provide the prayer with what can be interpreted as a Eucharistic setting. In this light it is worth noting that a kiss, or embrace, was a common component of fourth- and fifth-century Eucharistic celebrations,[46] and that the Eucharist

---

41 See the convenient edition of all three versions in Jean-Pierre Mahé, *Hermès en Haute-Égypte: Les textes hermétiques de Nag Hammadi et leurs parallèles grecs et latins: Tome I* (BCNH.T 3; Québec: Les Presses de l'Université Laval, 1978), 160–67; Peter Dirkse and James Brashler, "The Prayer of Thanksgiving," in *Nag Hammadi Codices V,2–5 and VI with Papyrus Berolinensis 8502,1 and 4* (ed. Douglas M. Parrott; NHS 11; Leiden: Brill, 1979), 378–87.

42 The Greek text is preserved in Papyrus Mimaut, currently kept in the Louvre as Papyrus 2391, a magical papyrus. The Latin text is part of *Asclepius* in the *Corpus Hermeticum*.

43 *Pr. Thanks.* 63.33: ⲡⲁⲓ̈ ⲡⲉ ⲡϣⲗⲏⲗ ⲛ̄ⲧⲁⲩϫⲟⲟϥ.

44 *Pr. Thanks.* 65.2–7: ⲛ̄ⲧⲁⲣⲟⲩϫⲉ ⲛⲁⲓ̈ ⲉⲩϣⲗⲏⲗ' ⲁⲩⲣ̄ⲁⲥⲡⲁⲍⲉ ⲛ̄ⲛⲉⲩⲉⲣⲏⲟⲩ· ⲁⲩⲱ ⲁⲩⲃⲱⲕ ⲉⲩⲛⲁⲟⲩⲱⲙ ⲛ̄ⲧⲉⲩⲧⲣⲟⲫⲏ ⲉⲥⲟⲩⲁⲁⲃ· ⲉⲙⲛ̄ⲥⲛⲟϥ ⲛ̄ϩⲏⲧⲥ̄ (Dirkse and Brashler, "The Prayer of Thanksgiving," 384, 386).

45 *haec optantes conuertimus nos ad puram et sine animalibus cenam* (text and trans. Dirkse and Brashler, "Prayer of Thanksgiving," 384–87).

46 See L. Edward Phillips, *The Ritual Kiss in Early Christian Worship* (Alcuin/Grow Liturgical Studies 36; Cambridge: Grove Books: 1996); Michael Philip Penn, *Kissing Christians: Ritual and Community in the Late Ancient Church* (Divinations: Rereading Late Ancient Religion; Philadelphia: University of Pennsylvania Press, 2005).

is commonly referred to as a bloodless sacrifice.[47] The ending of the Coptic text may thus indicate that, unlike the Greek and Latin versions, it has been adapted to fit a late-antique Christian context. The Greek text, on the other hand, is preserved in a magical codex, while the Latin version is in a manuscript of the *Corpus Hermeticum*, providing the *Prayer of Thanksgiving* with very different manuscript contexts.[48]

The *Prayer of Thanksgiving* in Codex VI is not the only originally non-Christian Nag Hammadi text that may have been rewritten to fit a Christian context. An excerpt from Plato's *Republic*, found in the same codex, has clearly been rewritten to suit interests and tastes decidedly different from those of its originally intended audience. Like the final text of the codex, an excerpt from *Asclepius*, it seems to have been adapted to fit an Egyptian monastic context.[49]

Similarly it is not difficult to imagine how not only the *Prayer of Thanksgiving* itself, but also the prayers in the *Discourse on the Eighth and the Ninth*, to which it has been appended in Nag Hammadi Codex VI, might have resonated with Christian readers.[50] In the latter case, however, we have no way of knowing the degree to which the text may have been adapted to fit its new context, since it is only attested in this single manuscript. However, based on the evidence of the Nag Hammadi texts that are attested in multiple versions, it is likely that the *Discourse on the Eighth and the Ninth* may have been adapted as well.

Implications

The examples above, which are representative also of the other Nag Hammadi texts with multiple attestation, show that there is often considerable variance between the various copies both within and outside the corpus. Although both the extent of attestation and the degree of absolute and observable fluidity vary from case to case, the situation is similar in the sense that the differences are significant enough to warrant

---

47 In the Sacramentary of Serapion, for instance, the *Prayer of Offering* states that "to you (i.e., to God) we offered this living sacrifice (τὴν ζῶσαν θυςίαν), the unbloody offering (τὴν προσφορὰν τὴν ἀναίμακτον)" (Serapion, *Pr.* 1; Maxwell E. Johnson, *The Prayers of Sarapion of Thmuis: A Literary, Liturgical, and Theological Analysis* [OCA 249; Rome: Pontificio Istituto Orientale, 1995], 46 [text], 47 [trans.]).

48 See note 42 above.

49 For the Plato fragment, see Christian Bull, "An Origenistic Adaptation of Plato in Nag Hammadi Codex VI," in *Papers Presented at the Seventeenth International Conference on Patristic Studies held in Oxford 2015* (ed. Markus Vinzent; StPatr; Leuven: Peeters, forthcoming); for the Coptic *Asclepius* excerpt, see idem, "Demons of the Air in the *Perfect Discourse* (NHC VI,8) and Monastic Literature," in *Nag Hammadi at 70: What Have We Learned?* (ed. Louis Painchaud et al.; BCNH.É; Québec: Les Presses de l'Université Laval, forthcoming).

50 Compare, e.g., *Disc. 8–9* 55.10–14 with Horsiesios, *Test.* 33 and 35 or *Exeg. Soul* 135.4–7.

closer attention to textual transmission and to an interpretation of the texts in the contexts in which they have been preserved, than has hitherto been the norm in Nag Hammadi scholarship.

There is no doubt that the textual transmission of the Nag Hammadi texts can be characterized as fluid, but just how fluid is it compared to other relevant corpora? Is it closer to the relative stability of the New Testament texts,[51] for example, or to the inherently far more fluid apocryphal acts of the apostles? In the latter case, François Bovon points out, "each scribe achieved an individual performance," and it is often impossible to establish a single critical text.[52] The situation is comparable to that of Medieval literature in the vernacular, which, in Paul Zumthor's words, "appears as if it is made up of a tangled intertwining of texts, each one of which barely lays claim to its own autonomy."[53] The fluidity encountered by scholars of such literature is certainly of a different magnitude to that confronted by the New Testament textual critics, but where do the Nag Hammadi texts belong in this picture? In general terms it seems safe to place them somewhere in the middle, but certainly closer to the apocryphal acts of the apostles and similar literature than to the New Testament.[54]

Textual fluidity is also a salient feature of texts that deal with, or refer to, liturgical practices. As Paul Bradshaw has argued, "documents dealing with liturgical

---

51 It is important to note that the New Testament is stable only relative to other more fluid corpora, it is certainly nowhere near absolute stability. As David C. Parker points out, "the wealth of textual variation in our manuscripts of the Gospels is proof enough that the early Christian users of the Gospels treated them as *living texts*, which were re-worded, expanded or reduced, to bring out what these users believed to be the true meaning of the text" ("Textual Criticism and Theology," *ExpTim* 118:12 [2007]: 585, emphasis original). Elsewhere he states that "there is a sense in which there is no such thing as either the New Testament or the Gospels. What is available to us is a number of reconstructions of some or all of the documents classified as belonging to the New Testament ... Textual criticism makes it clear that the text is in a sense inaccessible to us" (*The Living Text of the Gospels* [Cambridge: Cambridge University Press, 1997], 204).

52 François Bovon, "Beyond the Canonical and the Apocryphal Books, the Presence of a Third Category: The Books Useful for the Soul," *HTR* 105:2 (2012): 134. For an argument in favour of the application of Paul Zumthor's concept of *mouvance* (see his *Essai de poétique médiévale* [Paris: Editions du Seuil, 1972]) to the editing of apocrypha, see Rémi Gounelle, "Editing a Fluid and Unstable Text: The Example of the *Acts of Pilate* (or *Gospel of Nicodemus*)," *Apocrypha* 23 (2012): 81–97. On the fluidity of the apocryphal acts, see also Christine M. Thomas, *The Acts of Peter, Gospel Literature, and the Ancient Novel: Rewriting the Past* (Oxford: Oxford University Press, 2003).

53 Paul Zumthor, "The Text and the Voice," *NLH* 16:1 (1984): 77, quoting in translation his own article "Intertextualité et mouvance," *Littérature* 41 (1981): 15.

54 Here it should be mentioned that the canonical Acts of the Apostles is in fact the most fluid of the New Testament texts. As David C. Parker points out, "The Acts of the Apostles is a book which was so thoroughly revised and expanded in the course of the second and third centuries that it is customary to refer to two editions of Acts, the 'old uncial' and the 'western' (Parker, "Textual Criticism and Theology," 585–86).

matters are particularly prone to editorial corrections so as to give authoritative status to current worship practices."[55] This, he stresses, includes all phases of transmission, including the translation of works from one language to another.[56] We are here dealing with "material which circulates within a community and forms a part of its heritage and tradition but which is constantly subject to revision and rewriting to reflect changing historical and cultural circumstances."[57] As Bradshaw describes it, such "living literature" is characterized by the existence of many recensions with qualitative and/or quantitative differences, "often with no clear reflection of a single *Urtext*."[58] As we have seen, these features are salient characteristics of many of the Nag Hammadi texts too.

Most importantly, the evidence from those Nag Hammadi texts that have been preserved in multiple copies, such as the *Apocryphon of John*, the *Gospel of Truth*, and the *Prayer of Thanksgiving*, discussed above, indicate that in terms of textual fluidity we should expect the Nag Hammadi texts to be closer to this type of literature than to the New Testament. When we take a closer look at those Nag Hammadi texts that have been preserved in multiple copies, it soon becomes evident that it is highly unlikely that any of the Nag Hammadi texts are fundamentally stable. It is thus safer to treat them as snapshots of fluid textual traditions rather than as stable evidence of the original form of the texts. They certainly do not provide direct access to the originals or the intentions of their authors, and should therefore not be treated as such.

Singularly Attested Texts

Unfortunately, the illusion of textual stability may often be sustained without significant challenge in those cases where we have no other witnesses, and thus no direct evidence of fluidity.[59] In this regard most of the Nag Hammadi texts are indeed noticeably different from both the texts of the New Testament and the apocryphal acts. While, as mentioned above, researchers of medieval textual traditions and New

---

55 Paul F. Bradshaw, *The Search for the Origins of Christian Worship: Sources and Methods for the Study of Early Liturgy* (2nd rev. ed., London: SPCK, 2002), 91.

56 Bradshaw, *Search for the Origins*, 91.

57 Bradshaw, *Search for the Origins*, 5; cf. idem, "Liturgy and 'Living Literature,'" in *Liturgy in Dialogue: Essays in Memory of Ronald Jasper* (ed. Paul F. Bradshaw and Bryan Spinks; London: SPCK, 1993), 138–53.

58 Bradshaw, *Search for the Origins*, 5.

59 This is the case with *Pr. Paul, Ap. Jas., Treat. Res., Tri. Trac., Gos. Phil., Hyp. Arch., Exeg. Soul, Thom. Cont., Dial. Sav., Apoc. Paul, 2 Apoc. Jas., Apoc. Adam, Acts Pet. 12 Apost., Thund., Auth. Teach., Great Pow., Disc. 8–9, Paraph. Shem, Treat. Seth, Apoc. Pet., Steles Seth, Melch., Norea, Testim. Truth, Marsanes, Interp. Know., Val. Exp., Lit. Frag.* (*On Anoint., On Bap. A* and *B, On Euch. A* and *B), Allogenes, Hypsiph., Trim. Prot.,* and the unidentified *Fragments* in Codex XII.

Testament textual critics are confronted with a profusion of textual witnesses and a multitude of variants, Nag Hammadi scholars often have to make do with a text as it is found in a single, often badly preserved, manuscript. While this may in one sense provide the scholar with a simpler situation, with no attested variant readings, there is an inherent risk of letting the paucity of evidence create the impression that the text under scrutiny is a stable entity. For even in cases where we have only a single witness, it is still necessary to consider the likely relationship of the extant text to all the other, now lost, copies of the text that were produced throughout its period of circulation. It cannot be overemphasized that even though variation is not readily apparent from a single copy, singularly attested texts are not inherently more stable than texts with multiple attestation, although one may often get that impression from modern scholarship on such texts. The challenges of textual fluidity do not disappear when there is only a single version of a text that has survived up until our time, they are just less apparent.

This is of course not to say that parts of these Nag Hammadi texts are not in many cases likely to derive from times significantly earlier than the preserved manuscripts, but we have no way of knowing how far back in time, or exactly which parts those might be. Moreover, since the transmission of texts not only involve the aggregation of additional materials, but also deletions and reformulations, it becomes very difficult to assess what these texts may have looked like in their original form, especially when we have no direct evidence of their transmission history.

While in cases of multiple attestation the study of textual variants may provide us with specific clues regarding a literary work's history of transmission and the historical and sociological context of its preserved witnesses, the situation is less straightforward when we do not have the luxury of this kind of evidence. Nevertheless, there is, as already mentioned, no reason to believe that the transmission of these texts were characterized by greater stability than that of the texts where we can observe the textual fluidity directly, such as the *Gospel of Truth*, the *Apocryphon of John*, and the *Prayer of Thanksgiving*. As with the witnesses to those texts, there is good reason to treat them as snapshots, or single frames, of fluid textual traditions, and it is therefore methodologically sound to begin our interpretive efforts by trying to understand the texts in their most secure context, namely that from which each preserved snapshot derives.

Both Tito Orlandi[60] and Stephen Emmel have called for readings of the Nag Hammadi texts within the context of Coptic literature. Such a task, Emmel points out, involves reading "the texts exactly as we have them in the Nag Hammadi Codices in an effort to reconstruct the reading experience of whoever owned each of the Codi-

---

60 Tito Orlandi, "Nag Hammadi Texts and the Coptic Literature," in *Colloque international "l'Évangile selon Thomas et les textes de Nag Hammadi": Québec, 29–31 mai 2003* (ed. Louis Painchaud and Paul-Hubert Poirier; BCNH.É 8; Québec: Les Presses de l'Université Laval, 2007), 323–34.

ces."[61] One may well argue that such readings should not only constitute a supplement to the usual practice of interpreting the texts in the context of their hypothetical originals, but that they should indeed constitute the primary approach. One could argue that it is only when we grasp the significance of the Nag Hammadi texts within their fourth- and/or fifth-century context(s) that we may be able to use them responsibly as evidence of earlier periods as well.

When reading the texts in their manuscript contexts it is pertinent to look for traits that connect them to the religio-historical context of their manuscripts, moving cautiously back in time *only* when the text has been thoroughly surveyed for such features, and being aware of the fact that the further back we move from the time of the extant manuscripts, the more hypothetical our analyses become. This approach implies that we should start by exploring contextual evidence from a time considerably later than the second- or third-century contexts that have most commonly been the default starting point in Nag Hammadi studies. Moreover, it also implies a shift in geographical focus from hypothetical locations of origin spread across the Roman world, to an area much closer to the upper-Egyptian location of production and discovery of the manuscripts.

Looking at fourth- to fifth-century Upper Egypt, there are certain historical factors we may reasonably expect to have influenced the transmission of the Nag Hammadi texts. We know, for instance, that debates over Origenism erupted in Egypt at the turn of the fifth century, and that this controversy had both a pre-history and an aftermath in Egypt and beyond.[62] Scholars have indeed detected the influence of Origen or "Origenism" in several Nag Hammadi tractates, including such singularly attested texts

---

61 Emmel, "Religious Tradition," 42.

62 On the Origenist controversy in Egypt, see, e.g., Elizabeth A. Clark, *The Origenist Controversy: The Cultural Construction of an Early Christian Debate* (Princeton: Princeton University Press, 1992); Aloys Grillmeier, "La 'Peste d'Origène': Soucis du patriarche d'Alexandrie dus à l'apparition d'origénistes en Haute Egypte (444–451)," in *Alexandrina: Hellénisme, judaïsme et christianisme à Alexandrie: Mélanges offerts au P. Claude Mondésert* (Paris: Cerf, 1987), 221–37; Jon F. Dechow, *Dogma and Mysticism in Early Christianity: Epiphanius of Cyprus and the Legacy of Origen* (NAPSPatMS 13; Macon, Ga.: Mercer University Press, 1988); Samuel Rubenson, "Origen in the Egyptian Monastic Tradition of the Fourth Century," in *Origeniana Septima: Origenes in den Auseinandersetzungen des 4. Jahrhunderts* (ed. W. A. Bienert and U. Kühneweg; BETL 13; Leuven: Peeters, 1999), 319–37; Mark Sheridan, "The Modern Historiography of Early Egyptian Monasticism," in *Il monachesimo tra eredità e aperture: Atti del simposio "Testi e temi nella tradizione del monachesimo cristiano" per il 50° anniversario dell'Instituto Monastico di Sant'Anselmo, Roma, 28 maggio – 1° giugno 2002* (ed. Maciej Bielawski and Daniël Hombergen; SA 140, Analecta Monastica 8; Rome: Pontificio Ateneo S. Anselmo, 2004), 197–220; Hugo Lundhaug, "Origenism in Fifth-Century Upper Egypt: Shenoute of Atripe and the Nag Hammadi Codices," in *Ascetica, Liturgica, Orientalia, Critica et Philologica* (vol. 12 of *Papers Presented at the Sixteenth International Conference on Patristic Studies held in Oxford 2011*, ed. Markus Vinzent. StPatr 64; Leuven: Peeters, 2013), 217–28; idem, "The Body of God and the Corpus of Historiography: The *Life of Aphou of Pemdje* and the Anthropomorphite Controversy," in *Bodies, Borders, Believers: Ancient Texts and Present Conversations: Essays in Honor of Turid Karlsen Seim on Her 70th Birthday* (ed. Anne Hege

as the *Tripartite Tractate*,[63] the *Teachings of Silvanus*,[64] the *Treatise on the Resurrection*,[65] the *Exegesis on the Soul*,[66] and the *Gospel of Philip*.[67] The Origenist traits range from terminology to metaphors and theological concepts, and include the idea of the pre-existence and fall of souls due to sin, a concept of the resurrection that excludes the material flesh, the concept of the ascent of the soul, or mind, back to heaven, the *apokatastasis*, and transforming vision of Christ.[68] Such similarities have of course triggered questions concerning the direction of influence,[69] but from the perspective of New Philology, when reading the texts as they appear in the manuscripts, this is no longer an important question. Instead, what is relevant is the very fact that these issues were points of contention at the time the manuscripts were manufactured and read, and that they are reflected in the preserved texts.

One scholar who has taken textual fluidity seriously with regard to the Nag Hammadi Codices is Alberto Camplani, who warns against trying to use hypothetical original versions of these texts, often projected back onto the second century, as sources for the reconstruction of the earliest forms of the doctrines or ideas witnessed in the extant manuscripts.[70] Referring to several instances of apparent reworking and interpolation, Camplani rightly points out that in processes of constant textual revision, we should also expect theological corrections.[71] Camplani stresses that his point

---

Grung et al.; Eugene, Or.: Pickwick, 2015), 40–56; Krastu Banev, *Theophilus of Alexandria and the First Origenist Controversy: Rhetoric and Power* (OECS; Oxford: Oxford University Press, 2015).

63 See Alberto Camplani, "Per la cronologia di testi valentiniani: il *Trattato Tripartito* e la crisi ariana," *Cassiodorus* 1 (1995): 171–95; idem, "Sulla trasmissione di testi gnostici in copto," in *L'Egitto cristiano: Aspetti e problemi in età tardo-antica* (ed. Alberto Camplani; SEAug 56; Rome: Institutum Patristicum Augustinianum, 1997), 153–54.

64 See Roelof van den Broek, "The Theology of the Teachings of Silvanus," *VC* 40:1 (1986): 1–23.

65 See Camplani, "Per la cronologia."

66 See Hugo Lundhaug, *Images of Rebirth: Cognitive Poetics and Transformational Soteriology in the* Gospel of Philip *and the* Exegesis on the Soul (NHMS 73; Leiden: Brill, 2010); idem, "Origenism."

67 See Hugo Lundhaug, "Begotten, Not Made, to Arise in This Flesh: The Post-Nicene Soteriology of the *Gospel of Philip*," in *Beyond the Gnostic Gospels: Studies Building on the Work of Elaine Pagels* (ed. Eduard Iricinschi et al.; STAC 82; Tübingen: Mohr Siebeck, 2013), 235–71.

68 See Lundhaug, "Origenism."

69 Was Origen inspired by the Nag Hammadi texts, or *vice versa*? On this question Alberto Camplani ("Per la cronologia," 195) has argued convincingly that the direction of influence is more likely to be *from* Origen *to* the Nag Hammadi texts, than the other way around, as argued by Holger Strutwolf (*Gnosis als System: Zur Rezeption der valentinianischen Gnosis bei Origenes* [Forschungen zur Kirchen- und Dogmengeschichte 56; Göttingen: Vandenhoeck & Ruprecht, 1993]) and others (e.g., Jean-Daniel Dubois, "Le *Traité Tripartite* (Nag Hammadi I, 5): Est-il antérieur à Origène?" in *Origeniana Octava: Origen and the Alexandrian Tradition: Papers of the Eighth International Origen Congress, Pisa, 27–31 August 2001* [ed. Lorenzo Perrone, P. Bernardino, and D. Marchini; BETL 164; Leuven: Peeters, 2003], 303–16).

70 Camplani, "Per la cronologia," 174.

71 Camplani, "Per la cronologia," 173.

is not to re-date all the Nag Hammadi texts, but rather to insist that these codices may contain older works that may have been significantly altered up until shortly before the production of the codices, while at the same time other texts may have suffered less alteration in their history of transmission.[72] As an example of late rewriting he has drawn attention to the *Tripartite Tractate*, in Nag Hammadi Codex I, which he argues shows an awareness of the Arian controversy.[73]

The Dialogue of the Savior

The *Dialogue of the Savior* provides us with another example of a text that may fruit-fully be read in the historical context of its manuscript. It is a fascinating text featuring a post-resurrection dialogue between Jesus and his disciples that is only known from Nag Hammadi Codex III. As with most other Nag Hammadi texts, scholars have usually taken for granted a second-century Greek original, and have focused on this second-century context in their analyses of the text.[74] Considering the great detail in which scholars have analyzed the redactional history leading up to that hypothetical text,[75] the silence regarding possible changes introduced to the text in its later phases of transmission is striking.[76]

---

72 Camplani, "Per la cronologia," 176.

73 Camplani, "Per la cronologia"; idem, "Sulla trasmissione," 153–54.

74 See, e.g., Helmut Koester and Elaine H. Pagels, "The Dialogue of the Savior (III,5): Introduction," in *The Nag Hammadi Library in English* (ed. James M. Robinson; 3rd ed.; New York: HarperSanFrancisco, 1990), 244; Silke Petersen, "Zitate im Dialog des Erlösers (NHC III,5)," in *Ägypten und Nubien in spätantiker und christlicher Zeit: Akten des 6. Internationalen Koptologenkongresses Münster, 20.–26. Juli 1996* (ed. Stephen Emmel et al.; 2 vols.; SKCO 6; Wiesbaden: Reichert, 1999), 2:521; Silke Petersen and Hans-Gebhard Bethge, "Der Dialog des Erlösers (NHC III,5)," in *Nag Hammadi Deutsch* (ed. Hans-Martin Schenke, Hans-Gebhard Bethge, and Ursula Ulrike Kaiser; 2 vols.; GCS, Neue Folge 8; Koptisch-Gnostische Schriften 2; Berlin: Walter de Gruyter, 2001–3), 1:382; Julian V. Hills, "The Dialogue of the Savior," in *The Complete Gospels: Annotated Scholars Version* (ed. Robert J. Miller; Rev. and exp. ed.; Sonoma, Cal.: Polebridge Press, 1994), 343–56.

75 Scholars have speculated in considerable detail concerning its redactional history. See, e.g., Helmut Koester and Elaine H. Pagels, "Introduction," in *Nag Hammadi Codex III,5: The Dialogue of the Savior* (ed. Stephen Emmel; NHS 26; Leiden: Brill, 1984), 1–17; idem, "*Dialogue of the Savior (CG III, 5)*: Brief Report on Introduction," in *Nag Hammadi and Gnosis: Papers read at the First International Congress of Coptology (Cairo, December 1976)* (ed. Robert McL. Wilson; NHS 14; Leiden: Brill, 1978), 73–74; Pierre Létourneau, *Le Dialogue du Sauveur (NH III, 5): Texte établi, traduit et présenté* (BCNH.T 29; Québec: Les Presses de l'Université Laval, 2003), 18–41.

76 Létourneau pays some attention to later revisions, but his main focus is on the sources and composition of the original (see *Le Dialogue du Sauveur*, 18–41). He also argues that the final editing of the document took place in the Greek phase of transmission, before the translation of the work into Coptic (ibid., 40). Elsewhere he argues against any major influence of rewriting on the preserved ver-

It is also striking how different the text appears when we read it in light of the fourth or fifth centuries rather than the first or second. Jesus' statement that "when I came I opened the way and I taught them about the crossing which the elect and the ⲙⲟⲛⲁⲭⲟⲥ shall cross,"[77] carries significantly different connotations to a fourth-century audience than to a second-century one. Since most scholars have read the text in light of the latter context, the term ⲙⲟⲛⲁⲭⲟⲥ, which here appears in the plural, has been rendered as the "solitary,"[78] "die Einzelnen,"[79] or "les solitaires."[80] In a fourth-century context, however, a better translation of the term would simply be "monks."[81] And

---

sion of the text, on the basis of its theological coherence ("The *Dialogue of the Savior* as a Witness to the Late Valentinian Tradition," *VC* 65 [2011]: 86).

77 *Dial. Sav.* 120.23–26. All translations of *Dial. Sav.* are my own, based on the Coptic text of Stephen Emmel, ed., *Nag Hammadi Codex III,5: The Dialogue of the Savior* (NHS 26; Leiden: Brill: 1984). The spelling used in *Dial. Sav.* is in fact ⲙⲟⲛⲟⲭⲟⲥ as in one of the monastic letters (fragment C8) found in the cover of Nag Hammadi Codex VII (J. W. B. Barns, G. M. Browne, and J. C. Shelton [eds.], *Nag Hammadi Codices: Greek and Coptic Papyri from the Cartonnage of the Covers* [NHS 16; Leiden: Brill, 1981], 143). The spelling ⲙⲟⲛⲟⲭⲟⲥ for ⲙⲟⲛⲁⲭⲟⲥ is also attested elsewhere. Cf., e.g., the only preserved copy of Pachomius' first *Instruction* (*Instr.* 1.39, 51, 60) in manuscript BL Or. 7024 discovered at Edfu (Coptic text in E. A. Wallis Budge [ed.], *Coptic Apocrypha in the Dialect of Upper Egypt* [London: British Museum, 1913], 146–76; Louis Théophile Lefort [ed.], *Oeuvres de S. Pachôme et ses Disciples*, CSCO 150, Scriptores Coptici 23 [Leuven: L. Durbecq, 1956], 1–24); the Pachomian *Prophecy of Apa Charour*, preserved in a ninth-century manuscript from the monastery of the Archangel Michael at Phantoou (P. Morgan M. 586, 100) (Coptic text in Lefort, *Oeuvres* [1956], 100–4); and MONB.FM, a manuscript of Shenoute's Canon 9 (*God Who Alone Is True*) from the White Monastery (see Johannes Leipoldt, *Sinuthii Archimandritae: Vita et Opera Omnia*, 3 vols., CSCO 41, 42, 73, Scriptores Coptici 1, 2, 5 [Paris: Typographeo reipublica, 1906–1913], 4:163, 165, 166).

78 Emmel, *Dialogue of the Savior*, 43.

79 Petersen and Bethge, ""Der Dialog des Erlösers," 387.

80 Létourneau, *Le Dialogue du Sauveur*, 51.

81 On the term ⲙⲟⲛⲁⲭⲟⲥ see esp. E. A. Judge, "The Earliest Use of Monachos for 'Monk' (P. Coll. Youtie 77) and the Origins of Monasticism," *JAC* 20 (1977): 72–89; Malcolm Choat, "The Development and Usage of Terms for 'Monk' in Late Antique Egypt," *JAC* 45 (2002): 5–23. For further references to the scholarly literature on this point, see ibid., 5 n. 4; 8 n. 20. Dmitrij F. Bumazhnov takes the presence of the term ⲙⲟⲛⲁⲭⲟⲥ in *Dial. Sav.* as evidence for the 'Gnostic reception and orthodox non-reception' of the term in the second century ("Zur Bedeutung der Targume bei der Herausbildung des ΜΟΝΑΧΟΣ-Konzeptes in den Nag Hammadi-Texten," *ZAC* 10 [2007]: 252–59; idem, "Einige Beobachtungen zur Geschichte des Begriffs ΜΟΝΑΧΟΣ (Mönch)," in *Historica, Biblica, Ascetica et Hagiographica: Papers Presented at the Fourteenth International Conference on Patristic Studies held in Oxford 2003* [ed. Frances M. Young, Mark J. Edwards, and Paul M. Parvis; StPatr 39; Leuven: Peeters, 2006], 293–99; idem, "Some Ecclesiological Patterns of the Early Christian Period and Their Implications for the History of the Term ΜΟΝΑΧΟΣ (Monk)," in *Einheit der Kirche im Neuen Testament: Dritte europäische orthodox-westliche Exegetenkonferenz in Sankt Petersburg 24.–31. August 2005* [ed. Anatoly A. Alexeev, Christos Karakolis, and Ulrich Luz; WUNT 218; Tübingen: Mohr Siebeck, 2008], 251–64, esp. 252), but does not consider the possibility that the term may have been introduced into the text at a later stage, or the possibility that the text as a whole may be a product of the fourth or fifth, rather than the second century.

once the text is analyzed in light of fourth- and fifth-century monastic literature it becomes clear that the text's descriptions of the post-mortem ascent of the soul and the necessary separation from material concerns dovetail nicely with what we find in such texts as Pachomius' *First Instruction*, the *Life of Pachomius*, and Athanasius' *Life of Antony*, to mention only a few examples.[82] When the text is read in light of a hypothetical second-century context for the supposed original, comparative texts such as these are not relevant, and the translation of ⲙⲟⲛⲁⲭⲟⲥ as "monk" does not make sense. It is clear that we lose much potentially valuable information when the manuscript-context is ignored.

The Teachings of Silvanus

The *Teachings of Silvanus* is also an interesting case. Scholars have assigned dates to its hypothetical original ranging from the first to the fourth century.[83] Roelof van den Broek, who placed the text as late as the second or third decades of the fourth century[84] and concluded that the *Teachings of Silvanus* "gives us an idea of what a mediocre orthodox contemporary of Eusebius and Athanasius thought important enough to collect and put together in a book,"[85] seems to have been on the right track when he placed the text as late as he did, but looking at the preserved Coptic text, there are aspects that may seem to fit better into an even later context.[86]

---

82 For an analysis of *Dial. Sav.* in light of monastic literature, see Hugo Lundhaug, "The *Dialogue of the Savior* (NHC III,5) as a Monastic Text," in *Papers Presented at the Seventeenth International Conference on Patristic Studies held in Oxford 2015* (ed. Markus Vinzent; StPatr; Leuven: Peeters, forthcoming).

83 See, e.g., Yvonne Janssens, *Les Leçons de Silvanos (NH VII, 4): Texte établi et présenté* (BCNH.T 13; Québec: Les Presses de l'Université Laval, 1983): first, second, or early third century; Malcolm Peel, "Introduction to VII,4: The Teachings of Silvanus," in *Nag Hammadi Codex VII* (ed. Birger Pearson; NHMS 33; Leiden: Brill, 1996), 272–73: late third or early fourth century; van den Broek: "The Theology," *VC* 40:1 (1986): 17: second or third decades of the fourth century. According to Birger A. Pearson, it is "no earlier than the end of the second century, but it preserves some very ancient material" ("Cracking a Conundrum: Christian Origins in Egypt" *ST* 57 [2003]: 66). On the grounds of what he characterizes as "monism ... linked with Gnosticizing motifs," Schoedel suggests "a milieu like that of third century Alexandrian Christianity" (William R. Schoedel, "Jewish Wisdom and the Formation of the Christian Ascetic," in *Aspects of Wisdom in Judaism and Early Christianity* [ed. Robert L. Wilken; University of Notre Dame Center for the Study of Judaism and Christianity in Antiquity 1; Notre Dame, Ind.: University of Notre Dame Press, 1975], 170–71).

84 Broek, "The Theology," 17.

85 Broek, "The Theology," 17.

86 For some reason van den Broek argued that the mid-fourth century dates on some of the cartonnage fragments from the cover of Codex VII provide us with a *terminus ante quem* for the composition of *Teach. Silv.* (Broek, "The Theology," 1). This is puzzling, since it is clear that the dates on the carton-

One passage, only briefly mentioned by van den Broek, calls for further analysis in this regard, a Christological statement on page 99 of the manuscript, where we are told that "Christ has one hypostasis" (пєхс оүгупостасіс ноүшт тєтєоүнтаҁс).[87] In a Christological, rather than Trinitarian, context, the statement that Christ "has one hypostasis" does not refer to the relationship between the second person and the rest of the Trinity, but rather to the relationship between the divine and human in Christ. The term hypostasis seems to have been first used in such a Christological sense by Apollinaris of Laodicea[88] in an attempt to safeguard the divinity of the incarnated Son against Arianism. It was then later taken up by Cyril of Alexandria against Nestorius, to argue in favor of one, rather than two subjects in Christ.[89] Ironically, Cyril believed the phrase to be of Athanasian provenance[90] and his formulation was later appropriated by the defenders of a two-nature Christology and thus became part of the Chalcedonian definition, which established as dogma that Christ was to be regarded as two natures in one hypostasis.

The statement that Christ "has one hypostasis," is thus highly significant in the context of the late fourth century onwards. To mention just one example from Coptic literature, Proklos, bishop of Cyzicus, states in a homily against Nestorius, preserved in papyrus codex Oriental 5001 in the British Library, that "We do not separate the natures into two hypostases, but the two natures are one hypostasis (оүгупостасіс ноүшт) from the divinity and the humanity."[91]

So how do we evaluate the significance of this statement in the *Teachings of Silvanus*? If we want to keep reading this text, including this passage, in a first-, second-, third-, or early fourth-century context we will have to regard the fact that the text

---

nage fragments can only provide us with a *terminus post quem* for the production of the manuscript, which thus in fact allows for a potentially *later* date of composition for the text.

87 *Teach. Silv.* 99.13–14 (Coptic text from Malcolm Peel [ed. and trans.] and Jan Zandee [trans.], "NHC VII,4: The Teachings of Silvanus," in *Nag Hammadi Codex VII* [ed. Birger Pearson; NHMS 33; Leiden: Brill, 1996], 316).

88 See István Pásztori-Kupán, *Theodoret of Cyrus* (ECF; London: Routledge, 2006), 61; J. N. D. Kelly, *Early Christian Doctrines* (4th ed.; London: Adam & Charles Black, 1968), 293; Marcel Richard, "L'introduction du mot *hypostase* dans la théologie de l'incarnation," *MSR* 3 (1945): 5–32, 243–70.

89 Cyril of Alexandria, *Twelve Anathemas*, 3–4: "If any one in the one Christ divides the persons [ὑποστάσεις] after their union, conjoining them with a mere conjunction in accordance with worth, or a conjunction effected by authority or power, instead of a combination according to a union of natures [καθ᾽ νωσιν φυσίκην], let him be anathema. If any one distributes between two characters [πρόσωπα] or persons [ὑποστάσεις] the expressions used about Christ in the Gospels etc. ... applying some to the man, conceived of separately, apart from the Word, ... others exclusively to the Word ..., let him be anathema." (Henry Bettenson and Chris Maunder, *The Documents of the Christian Church* [4th ed.; Oxford: Oxford University Press, 2011], 49).

90 Pásztori-Kupán, *Theodoret*, 62.

91 Proklos of Cyzicus, *Homily Against Nestorius*, 126b (E. A. Wallis Budge, ed., *Coptic Homilies in the Dialect of Upper Egypt* [London: British Museum, 1910], 100).

uses a Christological expression that was not used before the late fourth century as a mere coincidence, unrelated to the discussions concerning the relationship between Christ's humanity and divinity in the late fourth and early fifth centuries. The statement could be explained as a late interpolation, but at the same time, how can we be certain that it was not part of the original composition of the text? That is, how can we be sure that the text was not originally composed in the late context in which the statement on Christ's single hypostasis carried a particular christological meaning, or at least that significant portions of the text were changed to reflect the concerns of this period? We know that Codex VII may well have been produced late enough to accommodate a text that was not only changed, but even composed, as late as the fifth century. Are there, then, any good reasons to date the original composition of this text any earlier than a time when the statement that "Christ has one hypostasis" would fit right in, as would have been the case during the Christological debates of the fourth and fifth centuries? Or is it even worthwhile to speak about an original composition at all?

When considering these questions it is worth remembering that although as a whole the Teachings of Silvanus is only attested in a single manuscript, we do have direct evidence of significant textual fluidity in the transmission of a part of it, in the form of a parchment leaf in the British Museum preserving a section of the text transmitted under the name of St. Antony.[92] The two witnesses are parallel, but by no means identical, and Funk and Schenke aptly concluded that the *Teachings of Silvanus* can be characterized as "gewachsen, nicht geschaffen."[93] It is, in other words, a fluid text, but this does not necessarily mean that it is not to be regarded as a reasonably coherent text in its current form. Van den Broek, for example, has argued that even though the text has lost some of its coherence due to what he terms "the insertion of irrelevant materials and the omission of vital arguments," it still reflects "a coherent train of thought,"[94] and a similar conclusion has been reached in a recent study by Dmitrij Bumazhnov.[95] In any case, one would at least expect those who copied and read the text in Nag Hammadi Codex VII to have approached it as a textual unity of some coherence.

---

92 This text was identified as a parallel to the *Teachings of Silvanus* by Wolf-Peter Funk, "Ein doppelt überliefertes Stück spätägyptischer Weisheit," *ZÄS* 103 (1976): 8–21.

93 Hans-Martin Schenke and Wolf-Peter Funk, "Die Lehren des Silvanus [NHC VII,4]," in *Nag Hammadi Deutsch* (ed. Hans-Martin Schenke, Hans-Gebhard Bethge, and Ursula Ulrike Kaiser; 2 Vols.; GCS, Neue Folge 8, Koptisch-Gnostische Schriften 2; Berlin: Walter de Gruyter, 2001–3), 2:606.

94 Broek, "The Theology," 5.

95 Dmitrij F. Bumazhnov, "'Be Pleasing to God, and You Will Need No One': The Concept of Religiously Motivated Self-Sufficiency and Solitude in *The Teachings of Silvanus* 97,3–98,22 (NHC VII,4) in Its Late Antiquity Context," in *Bibel, Byzanz und Christlicher Orient: Festschrift für Stephen Gerö zum 65. Geburtstag* (ed. D. Bumazhnov et al.; OLA 187; Peeters: Leuven, 2011), 83–113.

Looking at the text while being open to a late context, we see that there are also other parts of it that may reflect a similarly late date or that would have made good sense in such a context. The text argues, for instance, that "It is not right for us to say that God is a body" (ογⲇικⲁιоⲛ ⲅⲁⲣ ⲁⲛ ⲡⲉ ⲉⲧⲣⲉⲛϫⲟⲟⲥ ϫⲉογⲥⲱⲙⲁ ⲡⲉ ⲡⲛⲟγⲧⲉ).[96] And, similarly, two manuscript pages later: "do not confine the God of everything to mental images" (ογⲧⲉ ⲡⲛⲟγⲧⲉ ⲙ̄ⲡⲧⲏⲣϥ̄ ⲙ̄ⲡⲣ̄ⲕⲁⲁϥ ⲛⲁⲕ ⲛ̄ϩⲉⲛⲉⲓⲛⲉ ⲛ̄ϩⲏⲧ·).[97] Such statements would certainly make sense in light of the antropomorphite controversy around the turn of the fifth century (399), when Theophilus of Alexandria clamped down on the popular belief among certain Egyptian monks that God had a human form, most vividly described by John Cassian in his famous story about the old monk Serapion who had trouble praying without a mental image of God in a human form (*Conferences* 10.3).

Several other Christological statements in the *Teachings of Silvanus* also make very good sense in fourth- and fifth-century Egypt, and the text's many thematic affinities with early Egyptian monasticism, most recently brought out by Bumazhnov,[98] add important additional layers when we read the text in the context of the time and place of the manuscript's production and use.

The Gospel of Philip

A further issue concerns the phenomenon of translation literature. In an article on philological method and the Nag Hammadi Codices, Bentley Layton once noted that "it is crucially important to observe that the original language (Greek) is precisely what we do *not* have."[99] For Layton the goal of the philological enterprise was to get as close as possible to the lost original text. With great confidence in modern scholars' ability to bypass the preserved translation and get a sense of the hypothetical original, Layton argued that "if we cannot reconstruct that lost Greek original on paper, still we can hope to approximate the ancient author's own culture and thought through a recovery of its meaning in a sympathetic English translation keyed to a commentary oriented above all towards Greek usage."[100] Such an English translation based on the hypothetical Greek, he argued, would in fact be a better text than the one actually preserved in Coptic.[101]

---

96 *Teach. Silv.* 100.6–8 (Coptic text from Peel and Zandee, "Teachings of Silvanus," 318).
97 *Teach. Silv.* 102.9–11 (Coptic text from Peel and Zandee, "Teachings of Silvanus," 324).
98 Bumazhnov, "Be Pleasing to God."
99 Bentley Layton, "The Recovery of Gnosticism: The Philologist's Task in the Investigation of Nag Hammadi," *SecCent* 1 (1981): 97.
100 Layton, "Recovery of Gnosticism," 97
101 Layton argues that "conceivably the ancient Coptic version might be substituted for the English translation: but since ancientness in itself is no virtue, and since Coptic diction is notoriously non-philosophical, modern 'classicist's English' (provided that it is accurate) will probably be in closer

While few have followed Layton's suggestion that one should translate the hypo-thetical Greek texts rather than the preserved Coptic, many have shared his general goals and presuppositions. Frederik Wisse, for instance, commenting on his work on the *Apocryphon of John*, agrees with Layton that the ideal would be to create a criti-cal English translation that would "bypass the Coptic translations to get as close as possible to the common Greek text behind them."[102] When we take textual fluidity seriously into the equation, however, such an approach is problematic. When the pre-served Coptic text is seen mostly as an obstacle to be overcome on the way to a more important underlying Greek text, there is a danger of missing, or dismissing, aspects that may be highly significant for the interpretation of the text.

This is the case when allusions or wordplays that make sense only in Coptic are dismissed based on the presumption that the original language was Greek, and any features of the text relying on its specifically Coptic aspects are regarded as secondary and hence irrelevant. One such case can be seen in the *Gospel of Philip*, where editors have emended the Coptic word for "door" (ро) to "king" (р̄ро), thus ruining the Coptic wordplay in a passage stating that one needs to see the door (ро) in order to enter in to the king (р̄ро):

ⲙ̄ⲡⲣ̄ⲕⲁⲧⲁⲫⲣⲟⲛⲉⲓ ⲙ̄ⲡϩⲓⲉⲓⲃ	Do not despise the lamb,
ⲁ.ⲭⲛ̄ⲧϥ ⲅⲁⲣ ⲙ̄ⲛ̄ϭⲟⲙ ⲉⲛⲁⲩ ⲉⲡⲣⲟ	for it is impossible to see the *door* without it.
ⲙ̄ⲛ̄ⲗⲁⲁⲩ ⲛⲁϣ̄ϯⲡⲉϥⲟⲩⲟⲉⲓ ⲉϩⲟⲩⲛ ⲉⲡⲣ̄ⲣⲟ	No one will be able to enter in to the *king*
ⲉϥⲕⲏⲕⲁϩⲏⲩ[103]	naked.

Instead of interpreting this as a Coptic wordplay, editors have sometimes emended the passage. Since the wordplay is not possible in Greek, the appearance of "door" (ро) has simply been regarded as a mistake and emended to "king" (<р̄>ро), a word that appears on the very next line in the manuscript.[104] A Coptic wordplay, which nicely explains the appearance of this pair of words, is ruled out from the outset. Reading

---

touch with the ancient author's Hellenistic thought than ancient Coptic, whose nuances of diction, philosophical or otherwise, are largely lost upon us and in any case are certainly not Greek" (Layton, "Recovery of Gnosticism," 97); implemented most clearly in Bentley Layton, *The Gnostic Treatise on Resurrection from Nag Hammadi* (HDR 12; Missoula, Mont.: Scholars Press, 1979). For the opposite position, cf., Robert McL. Wilson, "The Trials of a Translator: Some Translation Problems in the Nag Hammadi Texts," *Les textes de Nag Hammadi: Colloque du Centre d'Histoire des Religions (Strasbourg, 23–25 octobre 1974)* (ed. Jacques-É. Ménard; NHS 7; Leiden: Brill, 1975), 38.

102 Wisse, "After the *Synopsis*," 141–42.

103 *Gos. Phil.* 58.14–17 (Coptic text from Lundhaug, *Images of Rebirth*, 482).

104 Bentley Layton, ed., Wesley W. Isenberg, trans, "The Gospel According to Philip," in *Gospel Ac-cording to Thomas, Gospel According to Philip, Hypostasis of the Archons, and Indexes.* Vol. 1 of *Nag Hammadi Codex II,2–7 Together with XIII,2, Brit. Lib. Or.4926(1), and P. Oxy. 1, 654, 655* (ed. Bentley Lay-ton; NHS 20; Leiden: Brill, 1989), 156. Hans-Martin Schenke, *Das Philippus-Evangelium (Nag-Hamma-di-Codex II,3): Neu herausgegeben, übersetzt und erklärt* (TUGAL 143; Berlin: Akademie Verlag, 1997),

"king" instead of "door," however, significantly diminishes the sophistication and rhetorical effect of the passage. Not only does the emendation dissolve the wordplay, it also removes an important allusion to John 10:9, "I am the door; if any one enters by me, he will be saved" (RSV). This allusion connects the passage with two important themes elsewhere in the *Gospel of Philip*, namely the necessity of participating in the Eucharist (the lamb) in order to become like Christ, and the necessity of becoming like Christ to be able to truly see Christ (the door).[105] Thus, in order to properly understand this passage it needs to be read in Coptic, a fact which highlights the unfortunate consequences of regarding the Coptic text as a mere stepping-stone on the way to the hypothetical Greek original.

This is also not the only place in the *Gospel of Philip* where we may speak of Coptic wordplays. In another passage there is a rhetorical play on the similarity between the Coptic words for "water" (ⲙⲟⲟⲩ) and "death" (ⲙⲟⲩ) which works only in this language:

> ⲛ̄ⲑⲉ ⲛ̄ⲧⲁⲓ̅ⲥ̅ ϫⲱⲕ ⲉⲃⲟⲗ ⲙ̄ⲡⲙⲟⲟⲩ ⲙ̄ⲡⲃⲁⲡⲧⲓⲥⲙⲁ
> ⲧⲁⲉⲓ ⲧⲉ ⲑⲉ ⲁϥⲡⲱϩⲧ ⲉⲃⲟⲗ ⲙ̄ⲡⲙⲟⲩ
> ⲉⲧⲃⲉⲡⲁⲉⲓ ⲧⲛ̄ⲃⲏⲕ ⲙⲉⲛ ⲉⲡⲓⲧⲛ̄ ⲉⲡⲙⲟⲟⲩ
> ⲧⲛ̄ⲃⲏⲕ ⲇⲉ ⲁⲛ ⲉⲡⲓⲧⲛ̄ ⲉⲡⲙⲟⲩ
> ϣⲓⲛⲁ ϫⲉⲛⲟⲩⲡⲁϩⲧⲛ̄ ⲉⲃⲟⲗ ϩⲙ̄ⲡⲡⲛ̄ⲁ̄ ⲙ̄ⲡⲕⲟⲥⲙⲟⲥ[106]

> As Jesus perfected the water (ⲡⲙⲟⲟⲩ) of baptism,
> thus he poured out death (ⲡⲙⲟⲩ).
> Therefore we go down into the water (ⲡⲙⲟⲟⲩ),
> but we do not go down into death (ⲡⲙⲟⲩ),
> so that we may not be poured out in the spirit of the world.

In his own baptism Jesus "perfected the water" (ϫⲱⲕ ⲉⲃⲟⲗ ⲙ̄ⲡⲙⲟⲟⲩ) and "poured out death" (ⲡⲱϩⲧ ⲉⲃⲟⲗ ⲙ̄ⲡⲙⲟⲩ). Therefore, the text tells us, "we go down into the water" (ⲧⲛ̄ⲃⲏⲕ ⲙⲉⲛ ⲉⲡⲓⲧⲛ̄ ⲉⲡⲙⲟⲟⲩ), "but we do not go down into death" (ⲧⲛ̄ⲃⲏⲕ ⲇⲉ ⲁⲛ ⲉⲡⲓⲧⲛ̄ ⲉⲡⲙⲟⲩ). While the connection between baptism and death may here ultimately derive from Romans 6, the manner in which the connection is made in this passage of the *Gospel of Philip* certainly works better rhetorically in Coptic than in Greek.

26–27, simply regards ⲣⲟ as an irregular way of writing ⲣ̄ⲣⲟ, and translates "König," without directly emending the Coptic text.

105 For a detailed analysis and interpretation of the passage, see Lundhaug, *Images of Rebirth*, 281–84.

106 *Gos. Phil.* 77.7–12 (Lundhaug, *Images of Rebirth*, 520).

A similar point may be made with regard to two deceptively similar phrases found on pages 82 and 86 of the manuscript. The first states that

ⲉϥⲏⲡ ⲁⲛ ⲉⲡⲕⲁⲕⲉ ⲏ ⲧⲟⲩϣⲏ ⲁⲗⲗⲁ ⲉϥⲏⲡ ⲉⲡⲉϩⲟⲟⲩ ⲙⲛ̄ⲡⲟⲩⲟⲉⲓⲛ[107]

It does not belong (ⲏⲡ) to the darkness or the night, but it belongs (ⲏⲡ) to the day and the light.

The second phrase, which also functions as the end of the *Gospel of Philip*, substitutes ϩⲏⲡ ("hidden") for ⲏⲡ ("belong"), while keeping the structure of the sentence:

ⲉϥϩⲏⲡ ⲁⲛ ϩⲙ̄ⲡⲕⲁⲕⲉ ⲙⲛ̄ⲧⲟⲩϣⲏ ⲁⲗⲗⲁ ⲉϥϩⲏⲡ ϩⲛ̄ⲛⲟⲩϩⲟⲟⲩ ⲛ̄ⲧⲉⲗⲉⲓⲟⲛ ⲙⲛ̄ⲟⲩⲟⲉⲓⲛ ⲉϥⲟⲩⲁⲁⲃ[108]

It is not hidden (ϩⲏⲡ) in the darkness or the night, but it is hidden (ϩⲏⲡ) in a perfect day and a holy light.

Again the full rhetorical effect is dependent on the Coptic language. I would therefore argue, firstly, that when taken together it is unlikely that these wordplays do not amount to more than mere coincidences, and secondly, that these features should be taken into consideration in the interpretation of the text. However, if the hypothetical Greek original is the focus, wordplays like these, which depend on the Coptic language, must be dismissed as coincidences or as something added later by a creative translator.[109] They certainly cannot be regarded as significant for the interpretation of the text. As is readily apparent from these examples,[110] with such an approach, when the only preserved version of the text must yield to an unattested hypothetical version, important aspects of the extant text are lost.

Moreover, can we really be confident that such a procedure brings us closer to the original text? The common assumption that the Nag Hammadi texts are ultimately translations of Greek originals should not simply be taken for granted, but should be investigated on a text-by-text basis. The possibility that at least some of the Nag Hammadi texts were originally composed in Coptic cannot be dismissed out of hand, and when we take textual fluidity fully into account, acknowledging the likelihood of the texts being subject to several stages of editorial activity in their transmission, in Coptic as well as in their hypothetical earlier Greek phase(s) of transmission, it is not always clear what practical consequences we should draw from the assess-

---

107 *Gos. Phil.* 82.8–10 (Lundhaug, *Images of Rebirth*, 530).

108 *Gos. Phil.* 86.16–18 (Lundhaug, *Images of Rebirth*, 538).

109 Cf. Johannes B. Bauer, "Zum Philippus-Evangelium Spr. 109 und 110," *TLZ* 7 (1961): 554; Søren Giversen, *Filipsevangeliet*, 12.

110 More examples could be added. See, e.g., the juxtaposition of ⲥⲱ ("drink") and ϩⲃⲥⲱ ("garment") at *Gos. Phil.* 57.8 (cf. Lundhaug, *Images of Rebirth*, 252 n. 373); and the play on the various meanings of the word ϫⲡⲟ at *Gos. Phil.* 58.22–26 (cf. Lundhaug, *Images of Rebirth*, 192–93).

ment that a document's original language was Greek.[111] In order to give a proper assessment of the text as we have it, all aspects should be taken into consideration, including those features that may have been added in the translation phase or in the transmission of the translation.

Conclusion

There is a need to pay even closer attention to the Nag Hammadi texts as they have actually been preserved in the manuscripts, and to focus less on their earlier and increasingly hypothetical phases of textual transmission. As David Parker has argued on the basis of the plethora of variants in Greek New Testament manuscripts, "the attempt to produce an original form of a living text is worse than trying to shoot a moving target, it is turning a movie into a single snapshot, it is taking a single part of a complex entity and claiming it to be the whole."[112] It is no less problematic to regard the snapshot constituted by singularly attested texts as practically identical with a hypothetical original, and thus to treat the former as if it were the latter. What is needed with regard to the Nag Hammadi Codices is for scholars to acknowledge the fact that our surviving textual witnesses constitute exactly such snapshots, and that these snapshots are not necessarily representative of the entire movie.

As we have seen, there is good reason to take seriously the implications of textual fluidity also for the singularly attested Nag Hammadi texts, even though the paucity of evidence has in many cases created an illusion of textual stability, and evidence of textual fluidity has often been dismissed as, indeed, deviations from the norm, which may safely be ignored in the quest for the original and the context of its authorship. This has been the case despite the evidence of fluidity from those Nag Hammadi texts where we do in fact have several witnesses preserved. These display many differences that cannot simply be explained away as errors of transmission or different translations of a Greek Vorlage.

Importantly, an awareness of the phenomenon of textual fluidity should caution us against the uncritical use of the Nag Hammadi texts as stand-ins for their unattested earlier versions, not to mention their hypothetical originals. Since the textual traditions that are attested in the form of snapshots in the Nag Hammadi Codices are characterized by a high level of fluidity, I would suggest that the texts ought to be read primarily in the context of their manuscripts, and only secondarily, and with great caution, in earlier and increasingly hypothetical contexts.[113] While this may consti-

---

111 Lundhaug, *Images of Rebirth*, 357–58.
112 Parker, "Textual Criticism and Theology," 586.
113 There is also a need for greater caution in the dating of texts and manuscripts, and fort the entire range of possible datings to be seriously considered when trying to understand them, and not only the

tute an unfamiliar way of treating the Nag Hammadi texts, the burden of proof should be on those who would like to use them as evidence of contexts far removed from that of the extant manuscripts, and not the other way around.

An alternative to the common approach of focusing on hypothetical, usually Greek, originals[114] is of course to read the texts in the versions in which they have been preserved to us in the manuscripts, in the contexts of the production and use of the manuscripts. In the case of the Nag Hammadi Codices, this context is most likely that of Upper Egyptian monasteries of the fourth and fifth centuries. If the implications of the perspectives outlined here were to be taken fully into consideration with regard to the Nag Hammadi collection as a whole, the way in which the texts are used as sources for the history of early Christianity would have to be radically reconsidered, as they can no longer be used uncritically as sources for the second and third centuries, as is often the case, but instead of the later, but no less interesting, period of early Egyptian monasticism. For this context, often far removed from that of the hypothetical originals, they may indeed prove to be highly valuable. Textual fluidity should therefore not be ignored in studies of the Nag Hammadi texts, it should be taken fully into account. As John Bryant puts it "We cannot cure the condition, for fluidity is not a disease and requires no cure. Rather, our obligation is to understand the causes and currents of fluidity. And find out what it means."[115]

The textual fluidity evident in the Nag Hammadi texts also raises important questions for our understanding of the way in which these texts were received, and the underlying attitudes of their scribes and readers toward textual variation. Did they embrace textual variation, as Cerquiglini famously argued that the people of the Middle Ages did?[116] It has been argued against Cerquiglini's position that "the awareness of the very fertile variability of medieval and modern texts does not by any means imply unbridled enthusiasm for variability as such."[117] According to Alberto Varvaro, "medieval variability (variance) is never the simultaneous presence of variants, but rather of the instability of a text in different locations, environments, and

---

earliest possible ones. It is too often the case that although a significant possible chronological range is mentioned, subsequent interpretations tend to stick closely to the context of the earliest possible date, often without any further argument. For an excellent example of the fruitfulness of being aware of later contexts, see, e.g., Dylan M. Burns' convincing demonstration of fourth-century rewriting of *Allogenes* in his "Apophatic Strategies in *Allogenes* (NHC XI,3)," *HTR* 103:2 (2010): 161–79.

114 Cf., e.g., Layton, "Recovery of Gnosticism."

115 John Bryant, *The Fluid Text: A Theory of Revision and Editing for Book and Screen* (ETLC; Ann Arbor: University of Michigan Press, 2002), 174.

116 Bernard Cerquiglini, *Éloge de la variante: Histoire critique de la philologie* (Paris: Seuil, 1989); English translation: *In Praise of the Variant: A Critical History of Philology* (trans. Betsy Wing; Parallax: Re-Visions of Culture and Society; Baltimore: Johns Hopkins University Press, 1999).

117 Alberto Varvaro, "The 'New Philology' from an Italian Perspective," *Text* 12 (1999): 57; cf. Keith Busby, "Variance and the Politics of Textual Criticism," in *Towards a Synthesis? Essays on the New Philology* (ed. Keith Busby; Amsterdam: Rodopi, 1993), 29–45.

times."[118] This may well in many cases be a useful distinction, but it is should be noted that the claim that there is never the simultaneous presence of variants does not fit the evidence of the Nag Hammadi Codices, where we do indeed have several cases of different versions of the same works preserved side by side in roughly contemporaneous codices deriving from the same community.[119] This is the case with the *Gospel of Truth* (NHC I,4; XII,2), the *Apocryphon of John* (NHC II,1; III,1; IV,1), *Eugnostos the Blessed* (NHC III,3; V,1), the *Gospel of the Egyptians* (NHC III,2; IV,2), and the untitled treatise *On the Origin of the World* (NHC II,5; XIII,2). We even have the curious case of Nag Hammadi Codex III, where *Eugnostos the Blessed* is found side-by-side with the *Wisdom of Jesus Christ*, a text that incorporates, within a different frame narrative, large portions of *Eugnostos the Blessed*.[120] The full implications of this simultaneous presence of variants within the Nag Hammadi Codices for the status of the Nag Hammadi texts among the producers and users of these codices, and for their textual culture and attitudes, still remain to be explored.

In summary, an approach to the Nag Hammadi texts inspired by the perspectives of New Philology brings with it a significant change in focus from hypothetical originals to preserved texts, from authors to readers and scribes, from composition to transmission, and from stability to fluidity – in short, from a view of the manuscripts as (more or less) erroneous witnesses to autographs, to manuscripts as snapshots of fluid texts. By doing so it helps dispel the illusion of textual stability that is often the biproduct of the traditional philological paradigm.

Bibliography

Attridge, Harold W., and George W. MacRae. "The Gospel of Truth." Pages 55–117 in *Nag Hammadi Codex I (The Jung Codex): Introductions, Texts, Translations, Indices*. Edited by Harold W. Attridge. Nag Hammadi Studies 22. Leiden: Brill, 1985.

Banev, Krastu. *Theophilus of Alexandria and the First Origenist Controversy: Rhetoric and Power*. Oxford Early Christian Studies. Oxford: Oxford University Press, 2015.

Barc, Bernard, and Louis Painchaud. "La réécriture de l'Apocryphon de Jean à la lumière de l'hymne final de la version longue." *Le Muséon* 112 (1999): 317–33.

Barns, J. W. B., G. M. Browne, and J. C. Shelton, eds. *Nag Hammadi Codices: Greek and Coptic Papyri from the Cartonnage of the Covers*. Nag Hammadi Studies 16; Leiden: Brill, 1981.

Bauer, Johannes B. "Zum Philippus-Evangelium Spr. 109 und 110." *Theologische Literaturzeitung* 7 (1961): 551–54.

Bettenson, Henry, and Chris Maunder. *The Documents of the Christian Church*. Fourth Edition. Oxford: Oxford University Press, 2011.

---

118 Varvaro, "New Philology," 57.
119 See Lundhaug and Jenott, *Monastic Origins*.
120 On Nag Hammadi Codex III, se René Falkenberg's contribution in the present volume.

Bovon, François. "Beyond the Canonical and the Apocryphal Books, the Presence of a Third Category: The Books Useful for the Soul." *Harvard Theological Review* 105:2 (2012): 125–37.

Bradshaw, Paul F. "Liturgy and 'Living Literature.'" Pages 138–53 in *Liturgy in Dialogue: Essays in Memory of Ronald Jasper*. Edited by Paul F. Bradshaw and Bryan Spinks. London: SPCK, 1993.

–. *The Search for the Origins of Christian Worship: Sources and Methods for the Study of Early Liturgy*. Second Revised Edition. London: SPCK, 2002.

Broek, Roelof van den. "The Theology of the Teachings of Silvanus." *Vigiliae Christianae* 40:1 (1986): 1–23.

Bryant, John. *The Fluid Text: A Theory of Revision and Editing for Book and Screen*. Editorial Theory and Literary Criticism. Ann Arbor: University of Michigan Press, 2002.

–. "Witness and Access: The Uses of the Fluid Text." *Textual Cultures* 2:1 (2007): 16–42.

Budge, E. A. Wallis. *Coptic Homilies in the Dialect of Upper Egypt*. London: British Museum, 1910.

–. *Coptic Apocrypha in the Dialect of Upper Egypt*. London: British Museum, 1913.

Bull, Christian. "An Origenistic Adaptation of Plato in Nag Hammadi Codex VI." In *Papers Presented at the Seventeenth International Conference on Patristic Studies held in Oxford 2015*. Edited by Markus Vinzent. Studia Patristica. Leuven: Peeters, forthcoming.

–. "Demons of the Air in the *Perfect Discourse* (NHC VI,8) and Monastic Literature." In *Nag Hammadi at 70: What Have We Learned?* Edited by Louis Painchaud, Eric Crégheur, and Tuomas Rasimus. Bibliothèque copte de Nag Hammadi: Section "Études". Québec: Les Presses de l'Université Laval, forthcoming.

Bumazhnov, Dmitrij F. "Einige Beobachtungen zur Geschichte des Begriffs ΜΟΝΑΧΟΣ (Mönch)." Pages 293–99 in *Historica, Biblica, Ascetica et Hagiographica: Papers Presented at the Fourteenth International Conference on Patristic Studies held in Oxford 2003*. Edited by Frances M. Young, Mark J. Edwards, and Paul M. Parvis. Studia Patristica 39. Leuven: Peeters, 2006.

–. "Zur Bedeutung der Targume bei der Herausbildung des ΜΟΝΑΧΟΣ-Konzeptes in den Nag Hammadi-Texten." *Zeitschrift für Antike und Christentum* 10 (2007): 252–59.

–. "Some Ecclesiological Patterns of the Early Christian Period and Their Implications for the History of the Term ΜΟΝΑΧΟΣ (Monk)." Pages 251–64 in *Einheit der Kirche im Neuen Testament: Dritte europäische orthodox-westliche Exegetenkonferenz in Sankt Petersburg 24.–31. August 2005*. Edited by Anatoly A. Alexeev, Christos Karakolis, and Ulrich Luz. Wissenschaftliche Untersuchungen zum Neuen Testament 218. Tübingen: Mohr Siebeck, 2008.

–. "'Be Pleasing to God, and You Will Need No One': The Concept of Religiously Motivated Self-Sufficiency and Solitude in *The Teachings of Silvanus* 97,3–98,22 (NHC VII,4) in Its Late Antiquity Context." Pages 83–113 in *Bibel, Byzanz und Christlicher Orient: Festschrift für Stephen Gerö zum 65. Geburtstag*. Edited by D. Bumazhnov, E. Grypeou, T. B. Sailors, and A. Toepel. Orientalia Lovaniensia Analecta 187. Peeters: Leuven, 2011.

Burns, Dylan M. "Apophatic Strategies in *Allogenes* (NHC XI,3)." *Harvard Theological Review* 103:2 (2010): 161–79.

Busby, Keith. "Variance and the Politics of Textual Criticism." Pages 29–45 in *Towards a Synthesis? Essays on the New Philology*. Edited by Keith Busby. Amsterdam: Rodopi, 1993.

Camplani, Alberto. "Per la cronologia di testi valentiniani: il *Trattato Tripartito* e la crisi ariana," *Cassiodorus* 1 (1995): 171–95.

–. "Sulla trasmissione di testi gnostici in copto." Pages 121–75 in *L'Egitto cristiano: Aspetti e problemi in età tardo-antica*. Edited by Alberto Camplani. Studia Ephemeridis Augustinianum 56. Rome: Institutum Patristicum Augustinianum, 1997.

Cerquiglini, Bernard. *Éloge de la variante: Histoire critique de la philologie*. Paris: Seuil, 1989.

–. *In Praise of the Variant: A Critical History of Philology*. Translated by Betsy Wing. Parallax: Re-Visions of Culture and Society. Baltimore: Johns Hopkins University Press, 1999.

Choat, Malcolm. "The Development and Usage of Terms for 'Monk' in Late Antique Egypt." *Jahrbuch für Antike und Christentum* 45 (2002): 5–23.

Clark, Elizabeth A. *The Origenist Controversy: The Cultural Construction of an Early Christian Debate*. Princeton: Princeton University Press, 1992.

Dechow, Jon F. *Dogma and Mysticism in Early Christianity: Epiphanius of Cyprus and the Legacy of Origen*. North American Patristic Society Patristic Monograph Series 13. Macon, Ga.: Mercer University Press, 1988.

Desjardins, Michel R. "The Sources for Valentinian Gnosticism: A Question of Methodology." *Vigiliae Christianae* 40:4 (1986): 342–47.

–. "Rethinking the Study of Gnosticism." *Religion and Theology* 12:3/4 (2005): 370–84.

Dirkse, Peter, and James Brashler. "The Prayer of Thanksgiving." Pages 375–87 in *Nag Hammadi Codices V,2–5 and VI with Papyrus Berolinensis 8502,1 and 4*. Edited by Douglas M. Parrott. Nag Hammadi Studies 11. Leiden: Brill, 1979.

Driscoll, Matthew James. "The Words on the Page: Thoughts on Philology, Old and New." Pages 87–104 in *Creating the Medieval Saga: Versions, Variability, and Editorial Interpretations of Old Norse Saga Literature*. Edited by J. Quinn and E. Lethbridge. Odense: University Press of Southern Denmark, 2010.

Dubois, Jean-Daniel. "Le *Traité Tripartite* (Nag Hammadi I, 5): Est-il antérieur à Origène?" Pages 303–16 in *Origeniana Octava: Origen and the Alexandrian Tradition: Papers of the Eighth International Origen Congress, Pisa, 27–31 August 2001*. Edited by Lorenzo Perrone, P. Bernardino, and D. Marchini. Bibliotheca ephemeridum theologicarum lovaniensium 164. Leuven: Peeters, 2003.

Emmel, Stephen. *Nag Hammadi Codex III,5: The Dialogue of the Savior*. Nag Hammadi Studies 26. Leiden: Brill: 1984.

–. "Religious Tradition, Textual Transmission, and the Nag Hammadi Codices." Pages 34–43 in *The Nag Hammadi Library After Fifty Years: Proceedings of the 1995 Society of Biblical Literature Commemoration*. Edited by John D. Turner and Anne McGuire. Nag Hammadi and Manichaean Studies 44. Leiden: Brill, 1997.

–. "Coptic Literature in the Byzantine and Early Islamic World." Pages 83–102 in *Egypt in the Byzantine World, 300–400*. Edited by Roger S. Bagnall. Cambridge: Cambridge University Press, 2007.

Funk, Wolf-Peter. "Ein doppelt überliefertes Stück spätägyptischer Weisheit." *Zeitschrift für ägyptische Sprache und Altertumskunde* 103 (1976): 8–21.

Genette, Gérard. *Paratexts: Thresholds of Interpretation*. Translated by Jane E. Lewin. Foreword by Richard Macksey. Literature, Culture, Theory 20. Cambridge: Cambridge University Press, 1997.

Grillmeier, Aloys. "La 'Peste d'Origène': Soucis du patriarche d'Alexandrie dus à l'apparition d'origénistes en Haute Egypte (444–451)." Pages 221–37 in *Alexandrina: Hellénisme, judaïsme et christianisme à Alexandrie: Mélanges offerts au P. Claude Mondésert*. Paris: Cerf, 1987.

Gounelle, Rémi. "Editing a Fluid and Unstable Text: The Example of the *Acts of Pilate* (or *Gospel of Nicodemus*)." *Apocrypha* 23 (2012): 81–97.

Helmbold, Andrew K. "The *Apocryphon of John*: A Case Study in Literary Criticism." *Journal of the Evangelical Theological Society* 13:3 (1970): 173–79.

Hills, Julian V. "The Dialogue of the Savior." Pages 343–56 in *The Complete Gospels: Annotated Scholars Version*. Edited by Robert J. Miller. Revised and expanded edition. Sonoma, Cal.: Polebridge Press, 1994.

Hurtado, Larry W. *The Earliest Christian Artifacts: Manuscripts and Christian Origins*. Grand Rapids, Mich.: Eerdmans, 2006.

Janssens, Yvonne. *Les Leçons de Silvanos (NH VII, 4): Texte établi et présenté*. Bibliothèque Copte de Nag Hammadi, Section "Textes" 13. Québec: Les Presses de l'Université Laval, 1983.

Johnson, Maxwell E. *The Prayers of Sarapion of Thmuis: A Literary, Liturgical, and Theological Analysis*. Orientalia Christiana Analecta 249. Rome: Pontificio Istituto Orientale, 1995.

Judge, E. A. "The Earliest Use of Monachos for "Monk" (P. Coll. Youtie 77) and the Origins of Monasticism." *Jahrbuch für Antike und Christentum* 20 (1977): 72–89.

Kelly, J. N. D. *Early Christian Doctrines*. Fourth Edition. London: Adam & Charles Black, 1968.

King, Karen L. "Approaching the Variants of the *Apocryphon of John*." Pages 105–37 in *The Nag Hammadi Library After Fifty Years: Proceedings of the 1995 Society of Biblical Literature Commemoration*. Edited by John D. Turner and Anne McGuire. Nag Hammadi and Manichaean Studies 44. Leiden: Brill, 1997.

–. *What is Gnosticism?* Cambridge, Mass.: Belknap Press of Harvard University Press, 2003.

–. *The Secret Revelation of John*. Cambridge, Mass.: Harvard University Press, 2006.

Koester, Helmut, and Elaine H. Pagels. "*Dialogue of the Savior* (CG III, 5): Brief Report on Introduction." Pages 73–74 in *Nag Hammadi and Gnosis: Papers read at the First International Congress of Coptology (Cairo, December 1976)*. Edited by Robert McL. Wilson. Nag Hammadi Studies 14. Leiden: Brill, 1978.

–. "Introduction." Pages 1–17 in *Nag Hammadi Codex III,5: The Dialogue of the Savior*. Edited by Stephen Emmel. Nag Hammadi Studies 26. Leiden: Brill, 1984.

–. "The Dialogue of the Savior (III,5): Introduction." Pages 244–46 in *The Nag Hammadi Library in English*. Edited by James M. Robinson. 3rd edition. New York: HarperSanFrancisco, 1990.

Layton, Bentley. *The Gnostic Treatise on Resurrection from Nag Hammadi*. Harvard Dissertations in Religion 12. Missoula, Mont.: Scholars Press, 1979.

–. "The Recovery of Gnosticism: The Philologist's Task in the Investigation of Nag Hammadi." *Second Century* 1 (1981): 85–99.

Layton, Bentley, ed., Wesley W. Isenberg, trans. "The Gospel According to Philip." Pages 142–215 in *Gospel According to Thomas, Gospel According to Philip, Hypostasis of the Archons, and Indexes*. Vol. 1 of *Nag Hammadi Codex II,2–7 Together with XIII,2, Brit. Lib. Or.4926(1), and P. Oxy. 1, 654, 655*. Edited by Bentley Layton. Nag Hammadi Studies 20. Leiden: Brill, 1989.

Lefort, Louis Théophile, ed. *Oeuvres de S. Pachôme et ses Disciples*. Corpus Scriptorum Christianorum Orientalium 150, Scriptores Coptici 23. Leuven: L. Durbecq, 1956.

Leipoldt, Johannes. *Sinuthii Archimandritae: Vita et Opera Omnia*. 3 Vols. Corpus Scriptorum Christianorum Orientalium 41, 42, 73, Scriptores Coptici 1, 2, 5. Paris: Typographeo reipublica, 1906–1913.

Létourneau, Pierre. *Le Dialogue du Sauveur (NH III, 5): Texte établi, traduit et présenté*. Bibliothèque Copte de Nag Hammadi, Section "Textes" 29. Québec: Les Presses de l'Université Laval, 2003.

–. "The *Dialogue of the Savior* as a Witness to the Late Valentinian Tradition." *Vigiliae Christianae* 65 (2011): 74–98.

Lundhaug, Hugo. *Images of Rebirth: Cognitive Poetics and Transformational Soteriology in the* Gospel of Philip *and the* Exegesis on the Soul. Nag Hammadi and Manichaean Studies 73. Leiden: Brill, 2010.

–. "Begotten, Not Made, to Arise in This Flesh: The Post-Nicene Soteriology of the *Gospel of Philip*." Pages 235–71 in *Beyond the Gnostic Gospels: Studies Building on the Work of Elaine Pagels*. Edited by Eduard Iricinschi, Lance Jenott, Nicola Denzey Lewis and Philippa Townsend. Studien und Texte zu Antike und Christentum 82. Tübingen: Mohr Siebeck, 2013.

–. "Origenism in Fifth-Century Upper Egypt: Shenoute of Atripe and the Nag Hammadi Codices." Pages 217–28 in *Ascetica, Liturgica, Orientalia, Critica et Philologica*. Vol. 12 of *Papers Presented at the Sixteenth International Conference on Patristic Studies held in Oxford 2011*. Edited by Markus Vinzent. Studia Patristica 64. Leuven: Peeters, 2013.

–. "The Nag Hammadi Codices: Textual Fluidity in Coptic." Pages 419–23 in *Comparative Oriental Manuscript Studies: An Introduction*. Edited by Alessandro Bausi, Pier Giorgio Borbone, Françoise Briquel-Chatonnet, Paola Buzi, Jost Gippert, Caroline Macé, Marilena Maniaci, Zisis Melissakis, Laura E. Parodi, and Witold Witakowski. Hamburg: COMSt, 2015.

–. "The Body of God and the Corpus of Historiography: The *Life of Aphou of Pemdje* and the Anthropomorphite Controversy." Pages 40–56 in *Bodies, Borders, Believers: Ancient Texts and Present Conversations: Essays in Honor of Turid Karlsen Seim on Her 70ᵗʰ Birthday*. Edited by Anne Hege Grung, Marianne Bjelland Kartzow, and Anna Rebecca Solevåg. Eugene, Or.: Pickwick, 2015.

–. "The *Dialogue of the Savior* (NHC III,5) as a Monastic Text." In *Papers Presented at the Seventeenth International Conference on Patristic Studies held in Oxford 2015*. Edited by Markus Vinzent. Studia Patristica. Leuven: Peeters, forthcoming.

Lundhaug, Hugo, and Lance Jenott. *The Monastic Origins of the Nag Hammadi Codices*. Studien und Texte zu Antike und Christentum 97. Tübingen: Mohr Siebeck, 2015.

Mahé, Jean-Pierre. *Hermès en Haute-Égypte: Les textes hermétiques de Nag Hammadi et leurs parallèles grecs et latins: Tome I*. Bibliothèque Copte de Nag Hammadi, Section "Textes" 3. Québec: Les Presses de l'Université Laval, 1978.

Mortley, Raoul. "'The Name of the Father is the Son' (Gospel of Truth 38) [with Afterword by Michel Tardieu]." Pages 239–52 in *Neoplatonism and Gnosticism*. Edited by Richard T. Wallis and Jay Bregman. Albany, N.Y.: State University of New York Press, 1992.

Orlandi, Tito. "Nag Hammadi Texts and the Coptic Literature." Pages 323–34 in *Colloque international "l'Évangile selon Thomas et les textes de Nag Hammadi": Québec, 29–31 mai 2003*. Edited by Louis Painchaud and Paul-Hubert Poirier. Bibliothèque copte de Nag Hammadi: Section "Études" 8. Québec: Les Presses de l'Université Laval, 2007.

Painchaud, Louis. "La classification des textes de Nag Hammadi et le phénomène des réécritures." Pages 51–85 in *Les textes de Nag Hammadi et le problème de leur classification: Actes du colloque tenu à Québec du 15 au 19 septembre 1993*. Edited by Louis Painchaud and Anne Pasquier. Bibliothèque copte de Nag Hammadi, Section "Études" 3. Québec: Les presses de l'Université Laval, 1995.

Parker, David C. *The Living Text of the Gospels*. Cambridge: Cambridge University Press, 1997.

–. "Textual Criticism and Theology." *Expository Times* 118:12 (2007): 583–89.

Pásztori-Kupán, István. *Theodoret of Cyrus*. The Early Church Fathers. London: Routledge, 2006.

Peel, Malcolm. "Introduction to VII,4: The Teachings of Silvanus." Pages 249–76 in *Nag Hammadi Codex VII*. Edited by Birger Pearson. Nag Hammadi and Manichaean Studies 33. Leiden: Brill, 1996.

Peel, Malcolm (ed. and trans.), and Jan Zandee (trans.). "NHC VII,4: The Teachings of Silvanus." Pages 278–369 in *Nag Hammadi Codex VII*. Edited by Birger Pearson. Nag Hammadi and Manichaean Studies 33. Leiden: Brill, 1996.

Penn, Michael Philip. *Kissing Christians: Ritual and Community in the Late Ancient Church*. Divinations: Rereading Late Ancient Religion. Philadelphia: University of Pennsylvania Press, 2005.

Petersen, Silke. "Zitate im Dialog des Erlösers (NHC III,5)." Pages 2:512–27 in *Ägypten und Nubien in spätantiker und christlicher Zeit: Akten des 6. Internationalen Koptologenkongresses Münster, 20.–26. Juli 1996*. Edited by Stephen Emmel, Martin Krause, Siegfried G. Richter, and Sofia Schaten. 2 Vols. Sprachen und Kulturen des christlichen Orients 6. Wiesbaden: Reichert, 1999.

Petersen, Silke, and Hans-Gebhard Bethge. "Der Dialog des Erlösers (NHC III,5)." Pages 1:381–97 in *Nag Hammadi Deutsch*. Edited by Hans-Martin Schenke, Hans-Gebhard Bethge, and Ursula Ulrike Kaiser. 2 Vols. Die Griechischen Christlichen Schriftsteller der ersten Jahrhunderte, Neue Folge 8, Koptisch-Gnostische Schriften 2. Berlin: Walter de Gruyter, 2001–3.

Phillips, L. Edward. *The Ritual Kiss in Early Christian Worship*. Alcuin/Grow Liturgical Studies 36.
Cambridge: Grove Books: 1996.

Richard, Marcel. "L'introduction du mot *hypostase* dans la théologie de l'incarnation." *Mélanges de science religieuse* 3 (1945): 5–32, 243–70.

Robinson, James M. *The Nag Hammadi Story*. 2 Vols. Nag Hammadi and Manichaean Studies 86.
Leiden: Brill, 2014.

Rubenson, Samuel. "Origen in the Egyptian Monastic Tradition of the Fourth Century." Pages 319–37
in *Origeniana Septima: Origenes in den Auseinandersetzungen des 4. Jahrhunderts*. Edited
by W. A. Bienert and U. Kühneweg. Bibliotheca ephemeridum theologicarum lovaniensium 13.
Leuven: Peeters, 1999.

Schenke, Hans-Martin. *Das Philippus-Evangelium (Nag-Hammadi-Codex II,3): Neu herausgegeben,
übersetzt und erklärt*. Texte und Untersuchungen zur Geschichte der altchristlichen Literatur
143. Berlin: Akademie Verlag, 1997.

–. "Evangelium Veritatis (NHC II, 3/XII, 2)." Pages 1:27–44 in *Nag Hammadi Deutsch*. Edited by
Hans-Martin Schenke, Hans-Gebhard Bethge, and Ursula Ulrike Kaiser. 2 Vols. Die Griechischen
Christlichen Schriftsteller der ersten Jahrhunderte, Neue Folge 8; Koptisch-Gnostische Schrif-
ten 2; Berlin: Walter de Gruyter, 2001–3.

Schenke, Hans-Martin, and Wolf-Peter Funk. "Die Lehren des Silvanus [NHC VII,4]." Pages 2:601–24
in *Nag Hammadi Deutsch*. Edited by Hans-Martin Schenke, Hans-Gebhard Bethge, and Ursula
Ulrike Kaiser. 2 Vols. Die Griechischen Christlichen Schriftsteller der ersten Jahrhunderte, Neue
Folge 8; Koptisch-Gnostische Schriften 2; Berlin: Walter de Gruyter, 2001–3.

Schoedel, William R. "Jewish Wisdom and the Formation of the Christian Ascetic." Pages 169–99 in
Aspects of Wisdom in Judaism and Early Christianity. Edited by Robert L. Wilken. University of
Notre Dame Center for the Study of Judaism and Christianity in Antiquity 1. Notre Dame, Ind.:
University of Notre Dame Press, 1975.

Sheridan, Mark. "The Modern Historiography of Early Egyptian Monasticism." Pages 197–220
in *Il monachesimo tra eredità e aperture*: *Atti del simposio "Testi e temi nella tradizione del
monachesimo cristiano" per il 50° anniversario dell'Instituto Monastico di Sant'Anselmo,
Roma, 28 maggio – 1° giugno 2002*. Edited by Maciej Bielawski and Daniël Hombergen. Studia
Anselmiana 140, Analecta Monastica 8. Rome: Pontificio Ateneo S. Anselmo, 2004.

Standaert, Benoit. "'L'Évangile de Vérité': Critique et lecture." *New Testament Studies* 22 (1976):
243–75.

Strutwolf, Holger. *Gnosis als System: Zur Rezeption der valentinianischen Gnosis bei Origenes*.
Forschungen zur Kirchen- und Dogmengeschichte 56. Göttingen: Vandenhoeck & Ruprecht,
1993.

Thomas, Christine M. *The Acts of Peter, Gospel Literature, and the Ancient Novel: Rewriting the Past*.
Oxford: Oxford University Press, 2003.

Thomassen, Einar. *The Spiritual Seed: The Church of the 'Valentinians'*. Nag Hammadi and Manichaean Studies 60. Leiden: Brill, 2006.

Varvaro, Alberto. "The 'New Philology' from an Italian Perspective." *Text* 12 (1999): 49–58.

Waldstein, Michael, and Frederik Wisse, eds. *The Apocryphon of John: Synopsis of Nag Hammadi
Codices II,1; III,1; and IV,1 with BG 8502,2*. Nag Hammadi and Manichaean Studies 33. Leiden:
Brill, 1995.

Williams, Jacqueline A. *Biblical Interpretation in the Gnostic Gospel of Truth from Nag Hammadi*.
Society of Biblical Literature Dissertation Series 79. Atlanta: Scholars Press, 1988.

Williams, Michael A. *Rethinking "Gnosticism": An Argument for Dismantling a Dubious Category*.
Princeton, N. J.: Princeton University Press, 1996.

–. "Response to the papers of Karen King, Frederik Wisse, Michael Waldstein and Sergio La Porta."
Pages 208–20 in *The Nag Hammadi Library After Fifty Years: Proceedings of the 1995 Society of*

Biblical Literature Commemoration. Edited by John D. Turner and Anne McGuire. Nag Hammadi and Manichaean Studies 44. Leiden: Brill, 1997.

–. "Was There a Gnostic Religion? Strategies for a Clearer Analysis." Pages 55–79 in *Was There a Gnostic Religion?* Edited by Antti Marjanen. Publications of the Finnish Exegetical Society 87. Helsinki: Finnish Exegetical Society, 2005.

–. "A Life Full of Meaning and Purpose: Demiurgical Myths and Social Implications." Pages 19–59 in *Beyond the Gnostic Gospels: Studies Building on the Work of Elaine Pagels*. Edited by Eduard Iricinschi, Lance Jenott, Nicola Denzey Lewis, and Philippa Townsend. Studien und Texte zu Antike und Christentum 82. Tübingen: Mohr Siebeck, 2013.

Wilson, Robert McL. "The Trials of a Translator: Some Translation Problems in the Nag Hammadi Texts." Pages 32–40 in *Les textes de Nag Hammadi: Colloque du Centre d'Histoire des Religions (Strasbourg, 23–25 octobre 1974)*. Edited by Jacques-É. Ménard. Nag Hammadi Studies 7. Leiden: Brill, 1975.

Wisse, Frederik. "NHC XII, 2: The Gospel of Truth." Pages 329–47 in *Nag Hammadi Codices XI, XII, XIII*. Edited by Charles W. Hedrick. Nag Hammadi Studies 28. Leiden: Brill, 1990.

–. "After the *Synopsis*: Prospects and Problems in Establishing a Critical Text of the Apocryphon of John and in Defining its Historical Location." Pages 138–53 in *The Nag Hammadi Library After Fifty Years: Proceedings of the 1995 Society of Biblical Literature Commemoration*. Edited by John D. Turner and Anne McGuire. Nag Hammadi and Manichaean Studies 44. Leiden: Brill, 1997.

Zumthor, Paul. *Essai de poétique médiévale*. Paris: Editions du Seuil, 1972.

–. "Intertextualité et mouvance," *Littérature* 41 (1981): 8–16.

–. "The Text and the Voice." *New Literary History* 16:1 (1984): 67–92.

Lance Jenott*

Reading Variants in *James* and the *Apocalypse of James*: A Perspective from New Philology

> The differences among the manuscripts have become great, either through the negligence of some copyists or through the perverse audacity of others; they either neglect to check over what they have transcribed, or, in the process of checking, they make additions or deletions as they please. (Origen, *Comm. Matt.* 15.14)[1]

The fact that scribes altered the text of the New Testament in the process of copying it anew has long been recognized as an obstacle to recovering the original, or at least an older, reading of the biblical texts.[2] In recent years, the sociohistorical contexts of copyists and their motivations for intentionally changing the texts have become the focus of study in their own right, apart from the quest to recover the original words of the author.[3] In the field of patristic literature too, the phenomenon of textual fluidity has been duly noted. As Herbert Musurillo has observed, "With the patristic texts there are always two serious hazards to look out for: the tendency [among ancient scribes] to correct and normalize the Greek, and the tendency to change the text in a theological direction, either towards orthodoxy or towards heterodoxy."[4] In the field of medieval textual criticism, where manuscripts abound in plentitude, variant readings between texts of the same literary work are the norm rather than the exception.[5]

---

* This essay has been written under the aegis of project NEWCONT at the University of Oslo, which is funded by the European Research Council (ERC) under the European Community's Seventh Framework Programme (FP7/2007–2013) / ERC Grant agreement n° 283741.
1 Trans. Bruce M. Metzger, "Explicit References in the Works of Origen of Alexandria to Variant Readings in New Testament Manuscripts," in *Biblical and Patristic Studies in Memory of Robert Pierce Casey* (ed. J. Neville Birdsall and Robert W. Thomson; Freiburg: Herder, 1963), 78.
2 Burnett Hillman Streeter, *The Four Gospels: A Study of Origins, Treating of the Manuscript Tradition, Sources, Authorship, and Dates* (4th rev. ed.; London: MacMillan and Co., 1930), 139, 306–7, 328–29; cf. Bruce M. Metzger and Bart D. Ehrman, *The Text of the New Testament: Its Transmission, Corruption, and Restoration* (4th ed.; New York: Oxford University Press, 2005), 250–71.
3 E.g., Bart D. Ehrman, *The Orthodox Corruption of Scripture: The Effect of Early Christological Controversies on the Text of the New Testament* (New York: Oxford University Press, 1993); David C. Parker, *The Living Text of the Gospels* (Cambridge: Cambridge University Press, 1997). For references to similar studies written from the 1940s onward, see Metzger and Ehrman, *Text of the New Testament*, 259 n. 12.
4 Herbert Musurillo, "Some Textual Problems in the Editing of the Greek Fathers" in *Introductio, Editiones, Critica, Philologica: Papers Presented to the Third International Conference on Patristic Studies Held at Christ Church, Oxford, 1959* (ed. Frank L. Cross; TUGAL 78; StPatr 3; Berlin: Akademie-Verlag, 1961), 86.
5 Els Rose, "*Virtutes Apostolorum*: Editorial Problems and Principles," *Apocrypha* 23 (2012): 11–45.

In the case of the Coptic manuscripts discovered near Nag Hammadi, a collection of largely ancient Christian apocrypha and other important theological works, scholars have observed that here too we are dealing with texts which have been subjected to a complex history of transmission, alteration, and rewriting. The result of redactional activity can be seen most clearly in the many variant readings, both large and small, found in those tractates for which more than one manuscript has survived, a fact which, as James Robinson has pointed out, "leads one to wonder about the bulk of the texts that exist only in a single version."[6] While the redactional histories underlying the latter group of tractates must remain speculative, and based on internal evidence,[7] actual text-critical work involving a comparison of variant readings can be, and to some extent has been, performed on those tractates for which more than one manuscript exists, even if only in fragments. These tractates constitute about one-third of the Nag Hammadi collection:

1. *The Gospel of Truth* (NHC I,3; XII,2)[8]
2. *The Apocryphon of John* (NHC II,1; III,1; IV,1; PB 8502,2)[9]

---

6 James M. Robinson, "Introduction," in *The Nag Hammadi Library in English* (ed. Robinson; San Francisco: HarperSanFrancisco, 1988), 2.

7 Cf. Louis Painchaud and Timothy Janz, "The 'Kingless Generation' and the Polemical Rewriting of Certain Nag Hammadi Texts," in *The Nag Hammadi Library After Fifty Years: Proceedings of the 1995 Society of Biblical Literature Commemoration* (ed. John D. Turner and Anne McGuire; NHMS 44; Leiden: Brill, 1997), 440.

8 For a comparison of the two versions of *Gos. Truth*, see the contribution by Katrine Brix in this volume. Geoffrey S. Smith also delivered an insightful paper entitled "Ecclesiastical Politics and the Transmission of Early Christian Literature: Origenism and the *Gospel of Truth*" at the 2014 annual meeting of the Society of Biblical Literature in San Diego, with a detailed comparison of the variants between NHC I,3 and XII,2. See also Raoul Mortley, "The Name of the Father is the Son (Gospel of Truth 38)," in *Neoplatonism and Gnosticism* (ed. Richard T. Wallis and Jay Bregman; Studies in Neoplatonism 6; Albany: State University of New York Press, 1992), 239–52, who argued that the text of NHC I had been rewritten in light of the Arian controversy.

9 For attention to variant readings in *Ap. John*, see Søren Giversen, *Apocryphon Johannis: The Coptic Text of the Apocryphon Johannis in the Nag Hammadi Codex II with Translation, Introduction, and Commentary* (ATDan 5; Copenhagen: Munksgaard, 1963), 276–82; Michael Waldstein and Frederik Wisse, *The Apocryphon of John: Synopsis of Nag Hammadi Codices II,1; III,1; and IV,1 with BG 8502,2* (NHMS 33; Leiden: Brill, 1995), 6–8; Karen L. King, "Approaching the Variants of the Apocryphon of John," in Turner and McGuire, *Nag Hammadi Library After Fifty Years*, 105–37; Michael A. Williams, "Response to papers by Karen King, Frederik Wisse, Michael Waldstein and Sergio La Porta," in Turner and McGuire, *Nag Hammadi Library After Fifty Years*, 208–22; Karen L. King, *The Secret Revelation of John* (Cambridge, Mass.: Harvard University Press, 2006), 25–81, in which Waldstein and Wisse's synoptic translations of PB 8502 and NHC II are reproduced, and "significant variant readings" in NHC III are noted; Bernard Barc and Louis Painchaud, "La réécriture de l'Apocryphon de Jean á la lumière de l'hymne final de la version longue," *Mus* 112 (1999): 317–33; Bernard Barc and Wolf-Peter Funk, *Le livre des Secrets de Jean: Recension brève (NH III, 1 et BG, 2)* (BCNH.T 35; Quebec: Les Presses de l'Université Laval, 2012), 3–7.

3. *The Gospel of Thomas* (NHC II,*2*; P. Oxy. 1, 654, 655)[10]
4. *On the Origin of the World* (NHC II,*5*; XIII,*2*; BL Or. 4926[1])[11]
5. *The Gospel of the Egyptians* (NHC III,*2*; IV,*2*)[12]
6. *Eugnostos the Blessed* (NHC III,*3*; V,*1*)[13]
7. *The Wisdom of Jesus Christ* (NHC III,*4*; PB 8502,*3*; P. Oxy. 1081)[14]
8. *The (First) Apocalypse of James* (NHC V,*3*; CT,*2*)[15]
9. Plato, *Republic* 588b–589b (NHC VI,*5*; Greek text)[16]

---

10 Miroslav Marcovich, "Textual Criticism on the Gospel of Thomas," *JTS* 20 (1969): 53–74; Harold W. Attridge, "The Greek Fragments," in *Nag Hammadi Codex II,2–7 together with XIII,2*, Brit. Lib. Or. 4926(1), and P. Oxy. 1, 654, 655*, vol. 1: *Gospel According to Thomas, Gospel According to Philip, Hypostasis of the Archons, and Indexes* (ed. Bentley Layton; NHS 20; Leiden: Brill, 1989), 99–102.
11 Christian Oeyen, "Fragmente einer subachmimischen Version der gnostischen 'Schrift ohne Titel,'" in *Essays on The Nag Hammadi Texts In Honour of Pahor Labib* (ed. Martin Krause; NHS 6; Leiden: Brill, 1975), 125–44, esp. 132–35; Bentley Layton, "The British Library Fragments," in *Nag Hammadi Codex II,2–7 together with XIII,2*, Brit. Lib. Or. 4926(1), and P. Oxy. 1, 654, 655*, vol. 2: *On the Origin of the World, Expository Treatise on the Soul, Book of Thomas the Contender* (ed. Layton; NHS 21; Leiden: Brill, 1989), 95–134.
12 Alexander Böhlig and Frederik Wisse, *Nag Hammadi Codices III,2 and IV,2: The Gospel of The Egyptians (The Holy Book of the Great Invisible Spirit)* (NHS 4; Leiden: Brill, 1975), 8–17.
13 Surprisingly, very little work has been published on the variant readings between the two MSS of *Eug.* See Douglas M. Parrott, *The Nag Hammadi Codices III,3–4 and V,1 with Papyrus Berolinensis 8502,3 and Oxyrhynchus Papyrus 1081: Eugnostos and The Sophia of Jesus Christ* (NHS 27; Leiden: Brill, 1991), 16–18, who points out that "In comparison with *Eug*-III, *Eug*-V appears to have undergone considerable expansion. ... there are fourteen instances where it has more text" (17); cf. Deirdre J. Good, *Reconstructing the Tradition of Sophia in Gnostic Literature* (SBLMS 32; Atlanta: Scholars Press, 1987), xvi–xviii.
14 Martin Krause, "Das literarische Verhältnis des Eugnostosbriefes zur Sophia Jesu Christi," in *Mullus: Festschrift Theodor Klauser* (ed. Alfred Stuiber and Alfred Hermann; Münster: Aschendorff, 1964), 215–23; Catherine Barry, *La sagesse de Jésus-Christ (BG, 3; NH III, 4)* (BCNH.T 20; Quebec: Les Presses de l'Université Laval, 1993), 18–20.
15 Antti Marjanen, "The Seven Women Disciples in the Two Versions of the *First Apocalypse of James*," in *The Codex Judas Papers: Proceedings of the International Congress on the Tchacos Codex Held at Rice University, Houston, Texas, March 13–16, 2008* (ed. April D. DeConick; NHMS 71; Leiden: Brill, 2009), 535–46, esp. 541–43 on the significance of variant readings for how the women disciples of Jesus are presented; Wolf-Peter Funk, "The Significance of the Tchacos Codex for Understanding the *First Apocalypse of James*," in DeConick, *Codex Judas Papers*, 509–33; Funk, "Die erste Apokalypse des Jakobus (NHC V,3 / CT 2)," in *Antike christliche Apokryphen in deutscher Übersetzung*, Band *I: Evangelien und Verwandtes, Teilband 2* (ed. Christoph Markschies and Jens Schröter; Tübingen: Mohr Siebeck, 2012), 1152–80, with annotated synoptic translations.
16 Hans-Martin Schenke, "Zur Faksimile-Ausgabe der Nag-Hammadi-Schriften," *OLZ* 69 (1974), cols. 235–242; E. G. Matsagouras, "Plato Copticus, Republic 588b–589b: Translation and Commentary" (M. A. thesis, Delhousie University, 1976); Matsagouras, "Plato Copticus," *Platon* (1977): 191–99; Tito Orlandi, "La traduzione copta di Platone, *Resp*. IX, 588b–589b: problemi critici ed esegetici," in *Atti della Accademia Nazionale dei Lincei* (Rendiconti morali, Serie VIII, vol. 22, fasc. 1–2; Rome: 1977), 45–62; James Brashler, "Plato, Republic 588b–589b," in *Nag Hammadi Codices V,2–5 and VI*

10. *The Prayer of Thanksgiving* (NHC VI,7; P. Mimaut, col. XVIII,591–611; Latin *Asclepius* 41b)[17]

11. *Asclepius 21–29* (NHC VI,8; Latin *Asclepius*; Greek fragments from Lactantius, Cyril of Alexandria, and Stobaeus)[18]

12. *The Teachings of Silvanus* (NHC VII,4; BL Or. 6003; Arabic MS)[19]

13. *Zostrianos* (NHC VIII,1; P. Bodmer XLIII)[20]

14. *The Letter of Peter to Philip* (NHC VIII,2; CT,1)[21]

15. *The Sentences of Sextus* (NHC XII,1; Greek, Latin, Syriac, Armenian, Georgian recensions)[22]

---

with *Papyrus Berolinensis 8502, 1 and 4* (ed. Douglas M. Parrott; NHS 11; Leiden: Brill, 1979), 325–39; Louis Painchaud, "Fragment de la république de Platon (NH VI, 5)" in Paul-Hubert Poirier and Louis Painchaud, *Les sentences de Sextus (NH XII, 1); Fragment de la république de Platon (NH VI, 5)* (BC-NH.T 11; Quebec: Les Presses de l'Université Laval, 1983), 117–22.

17 Jean-Pierre Mahé, "La Prière d'actions de grâces du Codex VI de Nag-Hammadi et Le Discours parfait," *ZPE* 13 (1974): 40–60; Jean-Pierre Mahé, *Hermès en Haute-Égypte, Tome I: Les textes hermétique de Nag Hammadi et leurs parallèles grecs et latins* (BCNH.T 3; Quebec: Les Presses de l'Université Laval, 1978), 15–23, 141–67; Peter Dirkse and James Brashler, "The Prayer of Thanksgiving," in Parrott, *Nag Hammadi Codices V,2–5 and VI*, 375–87, esp. 375–76.

18 Mahé, *Hermès en Haute-Égypte, Tome I*, 15–23, concludes that the Coptic version is superior to the Latin and closer to the Greek original of the *Perfect Discourse* (23); synoptic texts and detailed analysis are given in Mahé, *Hermès en Haute-Égypte, Tome II: Le fragment du Discourse parfait et les Définitions hermétiques arméniennes* (BCNH.T 7; Quebec: Les Presses de l'Université Laval, 1982), 145–272.

19 Wolf-Peter Funk, "Ein doppelt überliefertes Stück spätägyptischer Weisheit," *ZÄS* 103 (1976): 8–21, devotes some attention to the redaction of the Arabic version and BL Or. 6003 in monastic settings (18–19). On the Arabic MS, see Walter E. Crum, *Catalogue of the Coptic Manuscripts in the British Museum* (London: British Museum, 1905), 407 no. 979 n. 1. A Latin translation of the Arabic text is published in Migne, PG 40:1073–1080, which Funk uses as the basis of his comparison.

20 Rodolphe Kasser and Philippe Luisier, "P. Bodmer XLIII: Un feuillet de *Zostrien*," *Mus* 120 (2007): 251–72.

21 Hans-Gebhard Bethge, "'Der Brief des Petrus an Philippus' als Bestandteil von NHC VIII und Codex Tchacos: Beobachtungen und Überlegungen zum überlieferungsgeschichtlichen und inhaltlich-sachlichen Verhältnis beider Paralleltexte," in *Judasevangelium und Codex Tchacos: Studien zur religionsgeschichtlichen Verortung einer gnostischen Schriftsammlung* (ed. Enno Edzard Popkes and Gregor Wurst; WUNT[1] 297; Tübingen: Mohr Siebeck, 2012), 173–88.

22 Paul-Hubert Poirier, "Les Sentences de Sextus (NH XII, 1)," in Poirier and Louis Painchaud, *Les sentences de Sextus (NH XII, 1); Fragment de la république de Platon (NH VI, 5)*, esp. 22–24, with further comparisons made on specific passages throughout the commentary; cf. Frederik Wisse, "The Sentences of Sextus: Introduction," in *Nag Hammadi Codices XI, XII, XIII* (ed. Charles W. Hedrick; NHS 28; Leiden: Brill, 1990), 295–327, esp. 300 for a brief discussion of the theological significance of some variants.

In addition to this list of Nag Hammadi texts for which there are duplicate witnesses, we can also mention the three witnesses to the *Gospel of Mary* (PB 8502,*1*; P. Ryl. 463; P. Oxy. 3525).[23]

As the preceding footnotes show, attention has been paid to the variant readings found in duplicates to Nag Hammadi texts. However, the bulk of these efforts have followed the principles of traditional textual criticism aimed at recovering the "original" or "better" version of the text. As a corollary, variant readings which are deemed to be secondary become regarded as "corruptions" which can be ignored, corrected, or explained away based on the text which is deemed more accurate. So, for example, the editors of the *Gospel of the Egyptians* (NHC III,*2*; IV,*2*) conclude that "there are in III a considerable number of misinterpretations, secondary expansions as well as omissions. In light of this, III must be considered the inferior version."[24] Sometimes this mode of analysis even leads to heavy-handed criticism of the persons responsible for producing the texts as we have them. In the case of the small Coptic fragment of Plato's *Republic* found in NHC VI, a detailed comparison with the parallel Greek version led one scholar to disregard the Coptic translation as "a disastrous failure" and the "hopelessly confused" product of "an intellectually unsophisticated person who has lost contact with a living philosophical tradition."[25]

In response to this trend, Louis Painchaud has drawn attention to the potential historical significance of those passages which traditional text critics are wont to judge as corruptions:

> Avant d'être considérées comme des fautes ou des mélectures qui corrompent le texte, les divergences textuelles entre les versions et les aspérités rencontrées dans les textes doivent être envisagées comme les traces possibles de corrections intentionnelles qui attestent la vie des textes, traces à travers lesquelles on peut lire dans un texte l'identité de ses lecteurs successifs et la réception qu'ils lui ont réservée.[26]

---

23 Colin H. Roberts, *Catalogue of the Greek and Latin Papyri in the John Rylands Library* (Manchester: Manchester University Press, 1938), 3:18–23; Anne Pasquier, *L'Évangile selon Marie (BG,1)* (BCNH.T 10; Quebec: Les Presses de l'Université Laval, 1983), 2–3, 42–43, 97; Karen L. King, *The Gospel of Mary of Magdala: Jesus and the First Woman Apostle* (Santa Rosa, Calif.: Polebridge Press, 2003), 7–11, 14–18 (synoptic translation); Erika Mohri, *Maria Magdalena: Frauenbilder in Evangelientexten des 1. bis 3. Jahrhunderts* (MThSt 63; Marburg: Elwert, 2000), 261–65; Dieter Lührmann, *Die Apokryph gewordenen Evangelien: Studien zu neuen Texten und zu neuen Fragen* (NovTSup 112; Leiden: Brill, 2004), 105–24; Christopher Tuckett, *The Gospel of Mary* (OECGT; Oxford: Oxford University Press, 2007), 119–33.
24 Böhlig and Wisse, *Gospel of The Egyptians*, 17.
25 Brashler, "Plato, Republic 588b–589b," 325–26.
26 Louis Painchaud, "La classification des textes de Nag Hammadi et la phénomène des réécritures," in *Les textes de Nag Hammadi et le problème de leur classification: Actes du colloque tenu à Québec du 15 au 19 Septembre 1993* (BCNH.E 3; Quebec: Les Presses de l'Université Laval, 1995), 76.

This sympathetic approach to interpreting the variants in the Nag Hammadi texts dovetails nicely with the so-called "new philology" current among scholars of medieval manuscript cultures, which "urges scholars to take seriously the variety that characterizes manuscript transmission, instead of chopping one's way through the jungle of variants in search of a common ancestor or archetype."[27] Here we can fruitfully draw on Matthew Driscoll's distinction between a literary "work," a "text," and an "artifact": a work being an abstract concept, such as "the" *Apocryphon of John* (regardless of how many versions of it exist); a text being the actual words on the page; and an artifact being the physical object (in our case, the manuscript) in which the text is recorded, along with paratextual features such as format, titles, punctuation and other sense divisions, artwork, colophons, as well as other tractates in the codex, all of which frame the way text is read and contribute to the creation of meaning by the reader.[28] This approach regards each manuscript and its texts as having a history of their own, and attempts to understand their idiosyncrasies as part of that history; passages which traditionally would be regarded as corruptions are instead seen as part of the living text which would have made sense to (or elicited sense from) its readers.[29] Accordingly, the aim of comparing variant readings among duplicates of the Nag Hammadi texts would be first and foremost to see how differences in, for example, the text's emphasis, ideology, theology, and narrative appear if the text reads one way or another, and secondly, when possible, to contextualize those variants in known theological trends and controversies from the history of the early Church.

The focus on reading the Nag Hammadi artifacts just as we have them also helps avoid some of the methodological difficulties inherent in the traditional quest for the "original" versions. As Stephen Emmel has put it,

---

27 Rose, "*Virtutes Apostolorum*," 12; cf. Stephen G. Nichols, "Philology in a Manuscript Culture," *Speculum* 65:1 (1990): 1–10, esp. 7–9; and for an application to the Nag Hammadi Codices: Hugo Lundhaug, "The Nag Hammadi Codices: Textual Fluidity in Coptic," in *Comparative Oriental Manuscript Studies: An Introduction* (ed. Alessandro Bausi; Hamburg: COMSt, 2015), 419–23.
28 Matthew J. Driscoll, "Words on the Page: Thoughts on Philology Old and New," *Creating the Medieval Saga: Versions, Variability, and Editorial Interpretations of Old Norse Saga Literature* (ed. Judy Quinn and Emily Lethbridge; Odense: Syddansk Universitetsforlag, 2010), 87–104.
29 Cf. Bernard Cerquiglini, *In Praise of the Variant: A Critical History of Philology* (trans. Betsy Wing; Baltimore: Johns Hopkins University Press, 1999). A similar view of the potential for readers to find meaning in texts which modern critics deem corrupt was expressed by Waldstein and Wisse in their introduction to *The Apocryphon of John: Synopsis* (7): "faulty translations were copied and recopied a number of times in spite of the fact that the sense was obscured in many places. This only makes some sense if the translators, the copyists and the intended readers did not require a clear sense to find religious benefit. The meaning they expected was apparently not compromised by unfamiliarity with the lexical meaning of certain words, or by garbled syntax. Perhaps it was even enhanced."

> For the most part, I think we take it for granted that the Nag Hammadi texts do bear some more
> or less close relationship to a hypothetical original composition, and we move back and forth
> between the Coptic text we have and the original we would *like* to have, keeping careful out-
> look for signs of corruption, mistranslation, redaction, and so on, in an effort to minimize being
> led astray by such a long and complex history of transmission. But we move through a mine-
> field. ... It is not yet clear to what extent we can even recover the original texts of the Coptic
> translations.[30]

Most studies of the Nag Hammadi treatises tend to bracket the issue of textual fluidity altogether, proceeding with a seeming ease to discussions of an original version,
assigning it, by guess-work, to a time and place, and reconstructing the circumstances of the person who composed it. I am partly sympathetic to that approach,
since as a historian my curiosity naturally includes the who, what, why, when, and
where of these curious texts (the social and intellectual "dynamics" underlying
their initial production). Still, it remains a serious question of how far we can go
in discussing the original versions, that is, to what extent our Coptic copies represent what the authors once wrote, and to what extent that writing has been altered
in the course of transmission (think again of the Coptic fragment of Plato with its
far-reaching divergences from the Greek text). It seems to me that asking questions
about an author's historical circumstances is warranted, at least in principle, as is
any historical question; but it is when we attempt to answer those questions that we
must remember how increasingly speculative our answers probably are as we move
further away from the extant copies, going back in time into the hypothetical layers
of the text's transmission, composition, and even the Neighborhood of Make-Be-
lieve that is "pre-composition."

An alternative to the traditional approach to studying the Nag Hammadi texts is,
as Emmel has recommended,

> to read the Nag Hammadi Codices as part of Coptic literature ... to read the texts exactly as we
> have them in the Nag Hammadi Codices in an effort to reconstruct the reading experience of
> whoever owned each of the Codices. This reading would have to be undertaken in full cogni-
> zance of contemporary Coptic literature, and the culture of Upper Egypt during, say, the third to
> the seventh centuries.[31]

One utility of this approach is that we have a fairly specific idea of where and when
the codices were produced and read, namely in Egypt in the fourth and fifth centuries
(and perhaps later, depending on when they were discarded). Furthermore, an even
thicker historical context for these codices is provided by the fact that, in all likeli-

---

30 Stephen Emmel, "Religious Tradition, Textual Transmission, and the Nag Hammadi Codices," in
Turner and McGuire, *Nag Hammadi Library After Fifty Years*, 41 (the emphasis is Emmel's).
31 Emmel, "Religious Tradition," 42.

hood, they were produced and read by Christian monks.[32] This information, based on the codices themselves as artifacts, supplies a certain degree of historical context which we simply do not have when it comes to answering questions about the original versions of the individual tractates. It is not surprising, then, that more studies of the codices in their Egyptian context have been published in recent years (though still from quite different theoretical positions: e.g., whether or not the category of Gnosticism is assumed in the analysis).

In what follows, I present a comparative reading of Jesus' introductory discourse in the "work" conventionally entitled *The (First) Apocalypse of James* (hereafter *James*),[33] texts of which are preserved in two manuscripts, namely Nag Hammadi Codex V (NHC V) and Codex Tchacos (CT), the latter published as late as 2007.[34] In keeping with the purpose of the present volume, my comparison of readings in *James* will treat each manuscript as a different "snapshot" of the work, the divergent texts of which evidently took on lives of their own in different Christian communities. The copy in NHC V was evidently produced and read by monks in Upper Egypt (probably no earlier than the second half of the fourth century).[35] In the case of CT, we are unfortunately in the dark about its geographical and sociohistorical provenance, though the evidence from codicology, dialect, paleography, and radiocarbon testing points, on the balance, to a fourth-century date of production somewhere in Middle to Upper Egypt.[36] Whether it too was produced and read by Christian monks,

---

32 See Hugo Lundhaug and Lance Jenott, *The Monastic Origins of the Nag Hammadi Codices* (STAC 97; Tübingen: Mohr Siebeck, 2015).

33 The actual title on the version in NHC V is *The Apocalypse of James*, but the qualification *"(First)"* was added by modern editors to distinguish the treatise from another work in the codex which bears the same title. Further attention will be paid to the actual titles in the two manuscripts below.

34 Rodolphe Kasser and Gregor Wurst, eds., in collaboration with Marvin Meyer and François Gaudard, *The Gospel of Judas: Critical Edition, Together with the Letter of Peter to Philip, James, and a Book of Allogenes from Codex Tchacos* (Washington, D. C.: National Geographic Society, 2007), 120–61 (hereafter cited as *Critical Edition*).

35 Lundhaug and Jenott, *Monastic Origins*, 11, 120.

36 The geographic placement is based on the Coptic dialects found in the codex, which can be classified as largely Sahidic with traces of other dialects from Middle Egypt (Kasser, "Étude dialectale," in *Critical Edition*, 35–78). As for the date of production, radiocarbon tests performed by Timothy Jull at the University of Arizona placed CT in the third or fourth century CE (for a summary of Jull's report, see the "Publisher's Note" in Rodolphe Kasser, Marvin Meyer, and Gregor Wurst, *The Gospel of Judas from Codex Tchacos* [Washington, D. C.: National Geographic Society, 2006], 184). Although National Geographic journalist Herbert Krosney initially reported an average date of 280 CE ± 60 for CT, Christian Askeland has recently clarified, based on his own review of Jull's report, that Krosney misrepresented the results with a marked preference for the third century, while a more accurate interpretation of the data yields an equally plausible date-range anywhere between 250 to 400 CE. See Krosney, *The Lost Gospel: The Quest for the Gospel of Judas Iscariot* (Washington, D. C.: National Geographic Society, 2006), 274; Askeland, "Carbon Dating and the Gospel of Judas," paper delivered at the 2014 annual meeting of the Society of Biblical Literature in San Diego. The codicology and paleography of

we do not know. I am less concerned with explaining how the variant readings were generated, whether by deliberate or accidental alteration, than with discussing how they, though often quite small, create what are essentially two different texts, with their unique emphases, and how the texts might have made sense to readers in late antique Egypt.

Jesus' Introductory Discourse in *James*

The copy of James in NHC V has always been regarded as an especially good example of a text which must have fallen victim to "corruption" as it was recopied again and again. Even before the text of CT became available, Wolf-Peter Funk had commented on "certain roughnesses" in the text from NHC V, which in his opinion resulted from the process of transmission, perhaps beginning already in the Greek phase, but certainly continuing in Coptic. According to Funk,

> We have in any case to reckon with the fact that as a copy our present text is the product of a process of transmission within Coptic, and that a large part of its unevenness is rooted in this process. So long as we have no other witnesses to the text available, it is at many places not possible to decide with certainty whether the text is really in order or, when it does not seem to be in order, how it is to be improved.[37]

A comparison of manuscript witnesses became possible with the publication of CT in 2007. Thus in the recently revised edition of the Antike christliche Apocryphen, Funk presents German translations of the two versions in synopsis, and attempts to improve the text of NHC V with greater reliability on the basis of the parallel text in CT.[38] Yet Funk also concludes that the two versions are sufficiently different from each other – not only in their word choice and Coptic diction, but also in their meaning and quantity of text – that any attempt to reconstruct an "original" version would be futile. Rather, "Das Hauptinteresse muß darin be-

---

CT square nicely with a fourth- or even fifth-century date as well. Cartonnage papyri from CT's leather cover may someday tell us more about the date and provenance, but they remain unpublished (Wurst, "Introduction," in *Critical Edition*, 27).

37 Wolf-Peter Funk, "The First Apocalypse of James," in *New Testament Apocrypha*, vol. 1: *Gospels and Related Writings* (ed. Wilhelm Schneemelcher; trans. Robert McL. Wilson; Westminster: John Knox Press, 1990), 314–15.

38 Funk, "Die erste Apokalypse des Jakobus," 1153: "Der erste Schritt nach Kenntnisnahme des Tchacos-Textes … muß naturgemäß darin bestehen, den Text von NHC V,3 mit größerer Zuverlässigkeit wiederherzustellen, als dies vorher möglich war."

stehen, beide Texte vergleichen zu können."[39] Let us do just that, starting at the beginning.[40]

Title and Incipit

NHC V 24	CT 10
[10]ⲧⲁⲡⲟⲕⲁⲗⲩⲯⲓⲥ ⲛ̄ⲓ̈ⲁⲕⲱⲃⲟⲥ	
[11]ⲡϫⲟⲉⲓⲥ ⲇⲉ ⲡⲉⲛⲧⲁϥϣⲁϫⲉ ⲛⲙ̄ⲙⲁⲓ̈ [12]ϫⲉ	
ⲉⲛⲁⲩ ϭⲉ ⲉⲡϫⲱⲕ ⲛ̄ⲧⲉ ⲡⲁⲥⲱⲧⲉ [13]ⲁⲓ̈ϯⲙⲁⲉⲓⲛ ⲛⲁⲕ ⲉⲛⲁⲓ̈ ⲓ̈ⲁⲕⲱⲃⲟⲥ [14]ⲡⲁⲥⲟⲛ· ⲉⲓⲕⲏ ⲅⲁⲣ ⲁⲛ ⲁⲓ̈ⲙⲟⲩⲧⲉ [15]ⲉⲣⲟⲕ ϫⲉ ⲡⲁⲥⲟⲛ· ⲉⲛⲧⲟⲕ ⲡⲁⲥⲟⲛ [16]ⲉ̇ⲣⲁⲓ̈ ϩⲛ̄ ⲟⲩⲗⲏ ⲁⲛ·	[1]ⲉⲉⲓⲛⲉⲩ ⲇⲉ ⲉⲑⲁⲛ ⲙ̄ⲡⲁⲥⲱⲧⲉ [2]ϯⲛⲁⲧⲁⲙⲟⲕ ⲉⲛⲁⲓ̈ ⲓ̈ⲁⲕⲕⲱⲃⲉ̣ [3]ⲡⲁⲥⲟⲛ ⲉⲓⲕⲏ ⲅⲁⲣ ⲁ[ⲛ] ⲉⲩⲙ̣ⲟⲩ̣[4]ⲧⲉ ⲉⲣⲟⲕ ϫⲉ ⲥⲟⲛ ⲁⲗⲗⲁ ⲛ̣[ⲧⲕ̄] [5]ⲟⲩⲥⲟⲛ ⲁⲛ ϩ̄ⲛ ⲟⲩⲗⲏ:
ⲟⲩⲧⲉ ⲛ̄ϯⲉ ⲛ̄[17]ⲛⲁⲧⲉⲓⲙⲉ ⲉⲣⲟⲕ ⲁⲛ· ϫⲉⲕⲁⲁⲥ ⲉⲓ̈[18]ϣⲁⲛϯⲙⲁⲉⲓⲛ ⲛⲁⲕ ⲉⲓⲙⲉ ⲁⲩⲱ [19]ⲥⲱⲧⲙ̄·	ⲕⲟ̣ ⲇⲉ [6]ⲛ̣ⲁ̣ⲧⲥⲟⲟⲩⲛⲉ ⲉⲣⲁⲕ ϫⲉⲕⲁ̣[ⲁⲥ [7]ⲉⲉⲓ]ⲛ̣ⲁⲧⲁⲙⲟⲕ ϫⲉ ⲁⲛⲟⲕ ⲛⲓⲙ̣ [8]ⲥ̣ⲱⲧⲙ̄

---

39 Funk, "Die erste Apokalypse des Jakobus," 1154: "Das Verhältnis der beiden Versionen zueinander ist durchaus problematisch. Sie sind nicht bloß in Wortwahl und koptischer Diktion, oft auch im Verständnis, sehr verschieden, sondern auch hinsichtlich des quantitativen Textbestandes – und zwar nicht bloß bezüglich der Redeeinführungen, wo dieser Tatbestand zunächst am deutlichsten hervortritt, sondern auch in zahlreichen anderen Sätzen und Satzteilen. Inwieweit diese Divergenzen auf unterschiedliche griechische Ausgangstexte zurückgehen (was zweifellos gelegentlich der Fall ist), auf unterschiedliche Gewohnheiten der koptischen Übersetzer oder auch auf innerkoptische Entwicklungen und/oder Textverderbnisse – und welcher der beiden Versionen im jeweiligen Einzelfall der Vorzug zu geben ist – läßt sich oft nicht (oder noch nicht) mit Bestimmtheit sagen. Unter diesen Umständen wäre (zumal in diesem frühen Stadium der Erforschung) der Versuch aussichtslos, einen einheitlicheren, der „ursprünglichen" Fassung nahekommenden Text zu rekonstruieren. Das Hauptinteresse muß darin bestehen, beide Texte vergleichen zu können ..."
40 The Coptic texts which follow are my own transcriptions made from photographs of the manuscripts. This was necessary to avoid certain reconstructions and emendations made by previous editors. In those places where the text is reconstructed, I follow the editions of William R. Schoedel, "(First) Apocalypse of James," in Parrott, *Nag Hammadi Codices V,2–5 and VI*, 65–103, and Kasser and Wurst, *Critical Edition*. In the translations, significant variant readings are set in italics to facilitate comparison.

The Apocalypse of James

It was the Lord who spoke with me:

| "*Now then, to see* the fulfilment of my redemption, I *have shown* you these things, my brother James. For it is not without reason that *I have called you my* brother, though you are not *my* brother materially. | "Now *as I see* the fulfillment of my redemption, I *shall teach* you about these things, my brother James. For it is not without reason that *you are called* brother, though [you] are not *a* brother materially. |
| *And I am not* ignorant about *you,* so *when* I show you, *understand and* listen." | *You are* ignorant about *yourself,* so [I] will teach you *who I am.* Listen." |

Right from the outset one sees a significant difference in the way the two texts are presented, with the version in NHC V bearing a superscript title "The Apocalypse of James" not found in CT. The title of "apocalypse" in NHC V's version may be due to the scribe's deliberate organization of the codex as a special collection of revelations,[41] perhaps comparable to the rationale underlying the selection of treatises in the so-called *Codex Visionum* discovered (not far from Nag Hammadi) among the Dishna Papers.[42] Four of the five tractates in NHC V are entitled apocalypses: *The Apocalypse of Paul*, a first *Apocalypse of James* followed by a second *Apocalypse of James* (the two tractates bear the same title), and *The Apocalypse of Adam*.[43] Furthermore, in each of the four apocalypses of NHC V, the title "apocalypse" appears at the beginning of the tractate in a superscript (pages 17, 24, 44, 64) and in at least three of them (if not all four) it is repeated at the end of the text in a subscript (pages 24, 44, 85).[44] At the beginning of the first *Apocalypse of James* on page 24, the superscript is

---

41 Fraçoise Morard, "Les Apocalypses du Codex V de Nag Hammadi" in Painchaud and Pasquier, *Les textes de Nag Hammadi*, 341–57; Michael A. Williams, "Interpreting the Nag Hammadi Library as 'Collection(s)' in the History of 'Gnosticism(s),'" in Painchaud and Pasquier, *Les textes de Nag Hammadi*, 33; more recently, Julio Cesar Dias Chaves, "Scribal Intervention in the Titles of Nag Hammadi Codex V," forthcoming in *Judaïsme Ancien / Ancient Judaism* 4 (2016).

42 The *Codex Visionum* includes the *Vision of Dorotheus* (P. Bodmer XXIX), hexameter poems on such biblical figures as Abraham, Cain, Abel, and Jesus (P. Bodmer XXX–XXXVII), and the first three visions from the *Shepherd of Hermas* (P. Bodmer XXXVIII). See André Hurst et al., eds., *P. Bodmer XXIX: Vision de Dorotheus* (Bibliotheca Bodmeriana; Geneva: Fondation Martin Bodmer, 1984); Hurst and Jean Rudhardt, eds., *P. Bodmer XXX–XXXVII: «Codex des Visions», Poèmes divers* (Munich: K. G. Saur, 1999); cf. James M. Robinson, *Story of the Bodmer Papyri: From the First Monastery's Library in Upper Egypt to Geneva and Dublin* (Eugene, Or.: Cascade, 2011), 189–90.

43 The title of NHC V,1 is mostly lost in a lacuna on p. 17, but might have read simply ⲉⲩⲅⲛⲱⲥⲧⲟⲥ, with no designation as an apocalypse. See Douglas M. Parrott, *Nag Hammadi Codices III,3–4 and V,1*, 166.

44 It remains unclear whether there was a subscript title following 2 *Apoc. Jas.* on page 63. Alexander Böhlig posits that there was a subscript which is now lost in a lacuna except for the initial *tau* (*Koptisch-gnostische Apokalypsen aus Codex V von Nag Hammadi im Koptischen Museum zu Alt-Kairo* [Son-

written in smaller letters than the rest of the text and is crammed into a small frame below the decorated paragraph marker which separates it from the previous tractate. This may reflect a scribal habit of sometimes writing superscripts in smaller letters when they follow subscripts on the same page (a similar phenomenon appears in at least two other roughly contemporaneous manuscripts),[45] or perhaps the scribe added the superscript as an afterthought, as some researchers have suggested.[46] In any event, the fact that the superscript introduces the text as an apocalypse, and not merely as a dialogue, grounds the narrative in early traditions about James' reception of special revelation from the risen Lord.[47] The function of the term "apocalypse" in the title can therefore be understood as a mode of religious advertising insofar as it promises to offer the reader secret truths, now revealed, which Jesus had originally delivered to James, and which were later recorded and transmitted for posterity. Simultaneously, the title enhances the religious self-esteem of the reader as someone privileged enough to receive such revelation him- or herself.[48]

---

derband, WZ(H); Halle-Wittenberg, 1963]). Alternatively, Wolf-Peter Funk maintains that the title "The Apocalypse of James" is absent from the end of the tractate, and that the ink traces below the textual column are of a long paragraph marker (*Die Zweite Apokalypse des Jakobus aus Nag-Hammadi-Codex V* [TUGAL 119; Berlin: Akademie-Verlag, 1976], 54, 192). If so, 2 *Apoc. Jas.* would be the only tractate in the codex without a subscript. In my estimation, the possibility remains that a subscript written in smaller characters could have appeared below the paragraphus, comparable to the superscript of 1 *Apoc. Jas.* on page 24. Cf. Paul-Hubert Poirier, "Titres et sous-titres, incipit et desinit dans les codices coptes de Nag Hammadi et Berlin: description et éléments d'analyse" in *Titres et articulations du texte dans les oeuvres antiques: Actes du Colloque International de Chantilly 13–15 décembre de 1994* (ed. Jean-Claude Fredouille et al.; Collection des études augustiniennes, Série Antiquité 152; Paris: Institut d'Études Augustiniennes, 1997), 371.

45 See the superscript title of Jonah in BL Or. 7594, following the much more prominent subscript of Deuteronomy and a colophon with decorative marks; and in Chester Beatty XII, the title of Melito's *Peri Pascha* (simply ⲙⲉⲗⲉⲧⲱⲛ) after the more prominent subscript of the Epistle of Enoch and decorative *diplai*.

46 Schoedel, "(First) Apocalypse of James," 65; Armand Veilleux, *La Première Apocalypse de Jacques (NH V,3); La Second Apocalypse de Jacques (NH V,4)* (BCNH.T 17; Quebec: Les Presses de l'Université Laval, 1986), 64; Paul-Hubert Poirier, "Titres et sous-titres," 349, 370. The other superscript titles in NHC V (pp. 17 and 44), though partially damaged, do not appear to be written in a smaller letters than the rest of the text.

47 E.g., the tradition known to Paul in 1 Cor 15:3–8, that the resurrected Jesus first appeared to Cephas, then to the Twelve, then to more than five-hundred brothers at one time, then to James, then to all the apostles, and finally to Paul himself. According to another tradition quote by Eusebius from Clement of Alexandria's lost *Hyptotyposes*, "After the resurrection, the Lord gave the tradition of knowledge to James the Just and John and Peter, these gave it to the other Apostles, and the other Apostles to the Seventy, of whom Barnabas was also one" (*Hist. Eccl.* 2.1.4, Lake).

48 Cf. Michael A. Williams, "Secrecy, Revelation, and Late Antique Demiurgical Myths," *Rending the Veil: Concealment and Secrecy in the History of Religions* (ed. Elliot R. Wolfson; Chappaqua, N. Y.: Seven Bridges Press, 1998), 31–58.

In contrast to NHC V, the version in CT has no superscript title to frame the tractate in a special way from the beginning, and only a shorter title, simply the name *James* (ïⲁⲕⲕⲱⲃⲟⲥ), appears at the end of the tractate on page 29. The brief title of *James* in CT is consistent with a practice, witnessed in, for example, codices Sinaiticus, Vaticanus, and Alexandrinus, of abbreviating the titles of canonical texts to the name of the apostolic author, with no specification of the genre: e.g., simply ïⲟⲩⲇⲁ for the Epistle of Jude.[49] It thus recalls Athanasius' criticism of heretics who try to lead simple-minded Christians astray with apocryphal books that bear "the same names as the authentic books" (τῇ ὁμωνυμίᾳ τῶν ἀληθῶν βιβλίων), and are endowed with a false sense of antiquity so as to appear "as if they were ancient."[50]

In addition to the title "Apocalypse of James," the version in NHC V includes a helpful incipit ("It was the Lord who spoke with me") which clarifies the identity of the initial speaker. In contrast, the much more elliptical text of CT begins in *media res* ("Now as I see the fulfillment of my redemption ..."), and the reader must wait to find out to whom the voice of the anonymous "I" in the opening lines belongs. The speaker's reference to "my brother James" at the end of the first sentence suggests that he is Jesus, but in CT, that impression is not explicitly confirmed until two pages into the dialogue (CT 12.18).

In both versions Jesus addresses his interlocutor as "my brother James," but then goes on to affirm that he is not his brother "materially" (ϩⲛ ⲑⲩⲗⲏ, a phrase perhaps comparable to κατὰ σάρκα in the NT, with its biological connotations).[51] The denial of James' biological relationship to Jesus may be interpreted along the lines of formula-

---

49 In Codex Sinaiticus, all subscript titles of the Catholic Epistles (with the exception of the Epistle of James) are entitled by the name of the apostle without specification of the genre: i.e., ⲡⲉⲧⲣⲟⲩ ⲁ, ⲡⲉⲧⲣⲟⲩ ⲃ, ïⲱⲁⲛⲛⲟⲩ ⲁ, ïⲱⲁⲛⲛⲟⲩ ⲃ, ïⲱⲁⲛⲛⲟⲩ ⲅ, and ïⲟⲩⲇⲁ; only the Epistle of James bears the longer form as ⲉⲡⲓⲥⲧⲟⲗⲏ ïⲁⲕⲱⲃⲟⲩ. Some variation occurs in the superscript titles, however: First Peter and First John bear the longer form (ⲡⲉⲧⲣⲟⲩ ⲉⲡⲓⲥⲧⲟⲗⲏ ⲁ, ⲉⲡⲓⲥⲧⲟⲗⲏ ïⲱⲁⲛⲛⲟⲩ ⲁ), while the rest of the Catholic Epistles (except James, which has no superscript) bear the short form (ⲡⲉⲧⲣⲟⲩ ⲃ, ïⲱⲁⲛⲛⲟⲩ ⲃ, ïⲱⲁⲛⲛⲟⲩ ⲅ, and ïⲟⲩⲇⲁ). In Codex Vaticanus too, all the Catholic Epistles bear the short form in superscript, running headers, and subscript, except, again, for the Epistle of James, which bears the longer form ïⲁⲕⲱⲃⲟⲩ ⲉⲡⲓⲥⲧⲟⲗⲏ in the superscript (but the short form ïⲁⲕⲱⲃⲟⲩ in the subscript and running headers). In Codex Alexandrinus, one finds the short forms ⲡⲉⲧⲣⲟⲩ ⲁ (subscript 80r, no superscript), ⲡⲉⲧⲣⲟⲩ ⲃ (subscript 81v, no superscript), ïⲱⲁⲛⲛⲟⲩ ⲁ (superscript 81v and subscript 83v), ïⲱⲁⲛⲛⲟⲩ ⲃ (83v subscript, no superscript), ïⲱⲁⲛⲛⲟⲩ ⲅ (84r subscript, no superscript), except, again, on the Epistle of James, which has the long form ïⲁⲕⲱⲃⲟⲩ ⲉⲡⲓⲥⲧⲟⲗⲏ in the subscript (78r) and no superscript. Though here too, the Epistle of Jude has the longer form ïⲟⲩⲇⲁ ⲉⲡⲓⲥⲧⲟⲗⲏ in both superscript and subscript (84r/84v). One might be tempted to speculate that the unique persistence of the longer form ⲉⲡⲓⲥⲧⲟⲗⲏ ïⲁⲕⲱⲃⲟⲩ found in codices Sinaiticus, Vaticanus, and Alexandrinus was intended to readily distinguish it from other such "James" texts in circulation such as ïⲁⲕⲕⲱⲃⲟⲥ in CT.
50 Athanasius, *Thirty-Ninth Festal Letter*, ed. Perikles-Petros Joannou, *Fonti, Fasciolo IX: Discipline générale antique (IIᵉ–IXᵉ s.)*, vol. 2: *Les canons des pères grecs* (Rome: Tipographia Italo-Orientale S. Nilo, 1963), 72.
51 E.g., Acts 2:30, Rom 1:3, 9:3.

tions concerning the perpetual virginity of Mary, which were already well developed in the fourth century when our manuscripts were copied and read.[52] In language quite similar to that of *James*, Epiphanius argues that James "was *called a brother* (καλεῖται) of the Lord because of their common upbringing, not *by nature* (κατὰ φύσιν) but rather by grace (κατὰ χάριν)."[53] The small variant reading "you are called brother" in CT (cast in the passive voice), in contrast to "I have called you my brother" in NHC V (in the active voice), subtly distances James even further from a biological relationship with Jesus.

At the end of the text's introduction, Jesus explains to James why he needs to be instructed, and here too the divergences in wording, though superficially similar, provide two different reasons, both concerned with the problem of James' self-ig-norance. In NHC V, Jesus tells James that "I am not ignorant about you, so when I show you, understand and listen." Here, Jesus does not clarify what he will "show" James precisely, but the context ("I am not ignorant about you") suggests that it is knowledge of James himself. Quite oppositely in CT, Jesus tells James that "You are ignorant about yourself ..." and, contrary to what one might expect – that Jesus will teach James about James – the solution is to learn about Jesus: "... so [I] will teach you *who I am*. Listen." Whereas NHC V is ambiguous as to what James needs to learn, the version in CT states that the solution to his self-ignorance is to learn about Jesus.[54] Thus the version in CT underscores the fact that Jesus is the model for James (and the reader) to imitate in bodily suffering and death, but also in subsequent victory into eternal life, as one reads later in the narrative. Both versions then continue with Jesus' Christological discourse concerning his relationship to the preexistent Father, named He Who Is, in good biblical fashion.[55]

---

52 Luigi Gambero, *Mary and the Fathers of the Church: The Blessed Virgin Mary in Patristic Thought* (San Francisco: Ignatius Press, 1999). Epiphanius championed the perpetual virginity of Mary and criticized the so-called Antidicomarians for teaching that she had sexual intercourse with Joseph after Jesus' birth (*Pan*. 78). The siblings of Jesus mentioned in the Gospels (Mark 6:3 etc.), he maintained, had been born to Joseph in a previous marriage (*Pan* 78.7.1–9).

53 Epiphanius, *Pan* 78.7.9 (Holl, *Epiphanius*, 3:458): ἀδελφὸς δὲ τοῦ κυρίου οὗτος καλεῖται διὰ τὸ ὁμότροφον, οὐχὶ κατὰ φύσιν, ἀλλὰ κατὰ χάριν. Similarly Eusebius (*Hist. Eccl.* 2.1.4, Lake): James "was called the brother of the Lord, inasmuch as the latter too was styled the child of Joseph ..." (Ἰάκωβον, τὸν τοῦ κυρίου λεγόμενον ἀδελφόν, ὅτι δὴ καὶ οὗτος τοῦ Ἰωσήφ ὠνόμαστο παῖς).

54 At this point, Funk unnecessarily emends his translation of CT to read "Du aber bist unwissend über <mich>," commenting that the text in the MS would not be irregular, if it were not for the fact that what follows is teaching about Jesus' identity ("Die erste Apokalypse des Jakobus," 1159). He specu-lates that the "original" text of *James* might have included both variants ("I am not ignorant about you, but you are ignorant about me ..."). Cf. Funk, "Significance of the Tchacos Codex," 517.

55 The name He Who Is (ⲡⲉⲧϣⲟⲟⲡ) is comparable to the God of Israel's moniker "I Am Who I Am" in Exod 3:14 (אֶהְיֶה אֲשֶׁר אֶהְיֶה / ἐγώ εἰμι ὁ ὤν / ⲁⲛⲟⲕ ⲡⲉ ⲡⲉⲧϣⲟⲟⲡ [P. Bodmer XVI]). In *James*, the name is bestowed upon the preexistent Father of Jesus. In the text of CT, there is a clear distinction between the preexistent Father and the God of Israel ("the god who dwells in Jerusalem" [23.18–19; cf. 18.17]). However, in the parallel text at NHC V 36, a fascinating variant reading – "when you depart ... [*weep*] *for him who dwells in Jerusalem* (cf. Luke 19:41–44) – complicates this distinction, and might even

Christology I: Jesus and God

NHC V 24	CT 10
ⲛⲉⲙⲛ̄ ⲗⲁⲁⲩ ϣⲟⲟⲡ ⲛ̄ⲥⲁ ²⁰ⲡⲉⲧϣⲟⲟⲡ· ⲟⲩⲁⲧϯⲣⲁⲛ ⲉⲣⲟϥ ²¹ⲙ̄ⲛ̄ ⲟⲩⲁⲧϣⲁϫⲉ ⲙ̄ⲙⲟϥ ⲡⲉ·	ⲛⲉⲙⲛ ⲗⲁⲟⲩⲉ ϣⲟⲟⲡ ⁹[ⲉⲓ]ⲙⲏⲧⲓ ⲡⲉⲧϣⲟⲟⲡ ⲟ[ⲩⲁⲧ¹⁰ϯ]ⲣⲁⲛ ⲉⲣⲟϥ ⲡⲉ [ⲁⲩⲱ ⲟⲩⲁⲧ¹¹ϣⲁϫ[ⲉ ⲉ]ⲣⲟϥ ⲡⲉ [ϩⲛ ⲛⲁⲉⲓ ⲉⲧ]¹²ϣⲟⲟ[ⲡ] ⲏ ⲛⲉⲧⲛⲁϣⲱ[ⲡⲉ]
²²ⲁⲛⲟⲕ ϩⲱ ⲁⲛⲟⲕ ⲟⲩⲁⲧϯⲣⲁⲛ ⲉⲣⲟϥ ²³ⲉⲃⲟⲗ ϩⲙ̄ ⲡⲉⲧϣⲟⲟⲡ·	ⲁⲛⲟⲕ ¹³ⲇⲉ ⲁⲛⲕⲟⲩⲉⲃⲟⲗ ϩⲙ̄ ⲡⲉ[ⲧ]ϣⲟ¹⁴ⲟⲡ· ⲁⲩⲱ ⲟⲩⲁⲧϯⲣⲁⲛ ⲉⲣⲟϥ ⲡ[ⲉ]
ⲛ̄ⲑⲉ ⲉⲧⲁⲩ²⁴[ϯ ⲛ̄ⲟⲩ]ⲏⲡⲉ ⲛ̄ⲣⲁⲛ ⲉⲣⲟⲉⲓ ϩⲛ̄ ⲥⲛⲁⲩ ²⁵[ⲉⲃ]ⲟⲗ ϩⲙ̄ ⲡⲉⲧϣⲟⲟⲡ·	¹⁵ⲉⲁⲩⲙⲟⲩⲧⲉ ⲇⲉ ⲉ[ⲣⲟ]ⲓ̈ [ⲛ̄ⲟⲩⲏⲡⲉ ⲛ̄]¹⁶ⲣⲁⲛ ⲉⲛⲛⲟ[ⲩ]ⲉⲓ ⲁⲛ ⲛⲉ [ϩⲛ̄ϣ]¹⁷ⲙⲟ ⲉⲣⲟⲓ̈ ⲛⲉ:
ⲁⲛⲟⲕ ⲇⲉ ²⁶[ϯ]ϣⲟⲟⲡ ϩⲁⲧⲉⲕϩⲏ·	ⲉⲉⲓⲟ ⲇⲉ ⲛ̄ϣ[± ...] ¹⁸ⲉⲁⲛⲕⲟⲩⲙⲉ ⲉ̄ⲥⲛⲁⲩ ⲉⲃⲟⲗ [ϩ]ⲙ̄ ¹⁹ⲡⲉⲧϣⲟⲟⲡ
Nothing existed except He Who Is. He is unnamable and ineffable.	Nothing existed except He Who Is. He is [un]nameble *and he is* ineffable [*among those that*] *are or will be.*
I too, *I am* unnamable, from He Who Is.	Now I, I am from He Who Is, *and he* is unnamable.
Even as many names have been given to me, † *in two from He Who Is.* †	Although I have been called by [many] names, *they are not mine; they are foreign to me.*
But [I] am prior to you.	But I [...]; *I am second from He Who Is.*

In distinction to the prologue of the Gospel of John (ϩⲛ̄ ⲧⲉϩⲟⲩⲉⲓⲧⲉ ⲛⲉϥϣⲟⲟⲡ ⲛ̄ϭⲓ ⲡϣⲁϫⲉ ⲁⲩⲱ ⲡϣⲁϫⲉ ⲛⲉϥϣⲟⲟⲡ ⲛ̄ⲛⲁϩⲣⲙ̄ ⲡⲛⲟⲩⲧⲉ, "In the beginning was the Word and the Word was with God"; John 1:1), the two versions of *James* agree that "nothing was existing" (ⲛⲉⲙⲛ̄ ⲗⲁⲁⲩ ϣⲟⲟⲡ) but God, who is unnamable and ineffable, while CT includes the additional qualification "[among those things that] are or will be," adding a more biblical tone to the passage (cf. Eccl 3:15; Rev 1:4, 8).[56]

The two texts start to diverge, however, as Jesus describes his relationship to God. In both versions, Jesus teaches that he "comes" from He Who Is, yet whereas in NHC

---

lead the reader to maintain the identification of the God of Israel with the preexistent Father, despite the antipathy to Jerusalem and its inhabitants expressed elsewhere in the text. The archon named *Adonaios* in NHC V 39.11 may refer to the God of Israel, though it could also be understood to refer to another heavenly ruler depending on the reader's cosmological presuppositions.

56 The restoration follows the *Critical Edition*, which also suggests [ⲡⲁⲣⲁ ⲛⲉⲧ]ϣⲟⲟⲡ, "[in comparison with those who] are ..."

V Jesus clearly says that "I too, *I am unnamable*, from He Who Is," the version in CT reverses the sequence of statements, and affirms, again, that it is God who cannot be named: "I, I am from He Who Is, and *he is unnamable*" (ⲁⲛⲟⲕ ⲇⲉ ⲁⲛⲕⲟⲩⲉⲃⲟⲗ ϩⲙ̄ ⲡⲉⲧϣⲟⲟⲡ ⲁⲩⲱ ⲟⲩⲁⲧ†ⲣⲁⲛ ⲉⲣⲟϥ ⲡ[ⲉ]). Funk attributes this discrepancy to a mistake on the part of the Coptic translator of the text in CT, and emends his German translation of CT to read "Ich aber stamme aus dem Seienden und <bin> unbenennbar," thus bringing it into conformity with NHC V.[57] Yet the text of CT is perfectly intelligible without emendation. As Funk notes, it actually reads "and *he is* unnamable," as indeed it is understood in the English *Critical Edition* ("For my part, I am from the One Who Is and is unnamable").[58] Thus the text of NHC V creates a higher Christology than that of CT: Jesus is portrayed as more like God insofar as he shares with him the attribute of being unnameable; in CT, only God is unnameable.

The topic of unnameability then leads into Jesus' next statement concerning the fact that he has been called by many names. Both versions agree on this point, but then diverge regarding the nature and veracity of his names. In CT Jesus disavows these names, claiming that "they are not mine; they are foreign to me." Such a renunciation is absent in the text of NHC V, however, which at this point appears to be somewhat garbled: here Jesus does not say that the names are foreign to him, but rather that "Even as many names have been given to me, *in/by* two from He Who Is" (ϩⲛ̄ ⲥⲛⲁⲩ [ⲉⲃ]ⲟⲗ ϩⲙ̄ ⲡⲉⲧϣⲟⲟⲡ). This difficult crux in NHC V has been construed in various ways by modern commentators. William Schoedel understands it to mean that Jesus has received two names from God: "... just as I have been given a number of names – two from Him-who-is."[59] Quite differently, Armand Veilleux interprets ϩⲛ̄ ⲥⲛⲁⲩ to refer not to the names, but to Jesus and James themselves. He therefore glosses his translation to read "tous deux (nous sommes sortis) [de] Celui-qui-est," and explains that the passage underscores a special relationship between James and Jesus insofar as "both" have come from He Who Is.[60] According to Funk, the text remains a riddle "und ist sicherlich keine regelrechte Wiedergabe des Originaltextes." Given the newly

---

57 Funk, "Die erste Apokalypse des Jakobus," 1159 n. 23: "falsche Zuordnung des koordinierten prädikativen Adjektivs des griech(ische) Ausgangstextes durch den Übersetzer."
58 The grammatical issue is that the copula ⲡⲉ/ⲧⲉ/ⲛⲉ is not used in nominal sentences in which the predicate is indefinite and the subject is a first- or second-person personal pronoun. See "Nominal Sentence Patterns," in Bentley Layton, *A Coptic Grammar* (Wiesbaden: Herrassowitz Verlag, 2000), §§ 259–64 (esp. § 264, which represents the pattern into which CT 10.12–14 falls); cf. Thomas O. Lambdin, *Introduction to Sahidic Coptic* (Macon, Ga.: Mercer University Press, 1983), 18. Hence the similar syntax of CT 10.18–19 (ⲉⲁⲛⲕⲟⲩⲙⲉϩⲥⲛⲁⲩ ⲉⲃⲟⲗ [ϩ]ⲙ̄ ⲡⲉⲧϣⲟⲟⲡ) where no copula is required.
59 Schoedel, "(First) Apocalypse of James," 69. This translation evidently suppresses the preposition ϩⲛ̄, or reads it as a plural indefinite article modifying a cardinal number (a construction which would be unprecedented in Coptic; see Layton, *A Coptic Grammar*, §§ 66, 70).
60 Veilleux, *La Première Apocalypse de Jacques*, 68 (cf. 24), following the interpretation of Rodolphe Kasser, "Bibliothèque gnostique VI: Les deux Apocalypses de Jacques," *RTP* 18 (1968): 163–86.

available parallel in CT, in which Jesus goes on to say that "I am second from He Who Is," Funk proposes that the meaning of NHC V should probably be interpreted in an ontological way as well, "Jesus als Dyade."[61]

We might pause for a moment to consider this crux from more of a reader-oriented perspective, not asking what its "original" or "inherent" sense is (i.e., the point the author hoped to communicate in the now lost original composition), but rather how a reader of Coptic in late antique Egypt might have attempted to make sense of it. Although we may deem the passage as an obvious corruption, the fact remains that ancient readers of NHC V would have encountered it as it currently stands and evidently made no attempt to correct it (whereas corrections and explanatory glosses were made elsewhere in the codex).[62]

For a reader who belonged to an interpretive community thoroughly informed by Christian Scripture, the interpretive strategy employed to make sense of the passage (to borrow Stanley Fish's formulation)[63] might have included biblical passages concerning the names of Jesus, such as Heb 1:4–5 (ESV), where Jesus is said to have become "superior to the angels *as the name he has inherited* is more excellent than theirs," that is, the name of "Son" given to him by the Father; or John 17:11, in which Jesus states that he is one with the Father, having received the name of the Father ("your name, which you have given me").[64] The point in such conjectures is of course not to determine how ancient readers actually understood the passage (that information is inaccessible to us without their commentaries on the text) but to underscore the fact that what appears to modern scholars as a textual crux might also have been experienced as such by readers of NHC V in antiquity. In contexts where reading for pietistic purposes (edification, instruction, etc.) was the norm, such puzzles probably served as especially powerful catalysts for theological reflection and exegesis, as indeed the "difficult" passages in Scripture always have.[65]

---

61 Funk, "Die erste Apokalypse des Jakobus," 1160 n. 25.

62 E.g., NHC V 2.18; 6.6; 7.7; 7.26; 7.33; 9.1; 10.3; 14.4; 26.6; 26.7; 26.18; 28.8; 28.22; 31.9; 31.13; 33.11 (cf. 34.23, another marginal gloss?); 41.22; 51.10; 56.23; 72.8; 73.7; 73.15; 77.3; 78.6; 78.10; 78.27; 79.10; 79.28; 80.4; 81.16; 81.18; 81.19; 81.24; 82.7; 82.12; 85.5.

63 See, e.g., Stanley Fish, "Interpreting the *Variorum*," in Fish, *Is There A Text in This Class? The Authority of Interpretive Communities* (Cambridge, Mass.: Harvard University Press, 1980), esp. 167–73.

64 Cf. Phil 2:9–10: "Therefore God has highly exalted him and bestowed on him *the name that is above every name*, so that at the name of Jesus every knee should bow, in heaven and on earth and under the earth"; Rev 19:12–16: "he has a name written which no one knows but himself ... and the name by which he is called is The Word of God. ... On his robe and on his thigh he has a name written, King of kings and Lord of lords"; and Matt 1:23: "they shall call his name Immanuel, which means God with us."

65 See Michael Williams' discussion of "problem passages" and "scriptural chestnuts" in *Rethinking "Gnosticism": An Argument for Dismantling a Dubious Category* (Princeton: Princeton University Press, 1996), 63–79.

While the version in NHC V presents a higher Christology by making Jesus more like God (he shares with God the attribute of unnameability and, perhaps, has received two names from God), the version in CT presents a more subordinationist Christology: Jesus does not share God's attribute of being unnameable, and also clearly states that "I am second from He Who Is."[66] CT's affirmation that Jesus is "second" (мег̄с̄наγ) probably relates to the ambiguous language of "in/by two" (г̄н снаγ) found in NHC V, though what the "original" reading was, and how it arrived in its current shape in the two manuscripts, is beyond our reach. As the two versions currently stand, the emphasis in NHC V is placed on Jesus' temporal superiority to James ("But I am prior to you"); in CT, the emphasis is on Jesus' subordination to God ("I am second from He Who Is").

Christology II: Femaleness, Jesus, and the Image of God

NHC V 24–25	CT 10–11
епідн аксд[²⁷н]е н̄ҫа ⳁм̄нтҫⲅⲓⲙⲉ·	епеідн [а]кс̣[ине] ²⁰ⲉⲧⲃⲉ ⲧⲙⲛⲧⲥⲅⲓⲙⲉ: ⲥⲱⲧ[м̄]
неcϣⲟⲟⲡ ²⁸[н̄]ⳝⲓ ⳁм̄нтⲥⲅⲓⲙⲉ· алла неcⲣ̄ ϣⲟ²⁹[ⲣп̄ н̄ⳝⲓ] ⳁм̄нтⲥⲅⲓⲙⲉ ан· аγⲱ ³⁰[аⲥ]ⲥⲟⲃⲧⲉ наⲥ н̄г[е]нⳝ ⲟⲙ мн̄ ноγⲧⲉ	²¹ⲧⲙⲛⲧⲥⲅⲓⲙⲉ неcϣⲟⲟⲡ ⲡ[е] ²²алла неⲥϣⲟⲟⲡ ан пе ⲭн̄ н̄²³ϣⲟⲣⲡ аⲥⲧⲁⲙⲓⲟ наⲥ н̄г̄нⳝ[ом] ²⁴мн̄ г̄нⲛⲟⲩⲧⲉ:
³¹[.]е[.]ϣⲟⲟⲡ ⲇⲉ ан	ⲡⲉⲧϣⲟ[ⲟⲡ] ²⁵ⳝⲉ ⲉ ⲩϣⲟⲟⲡ ⲭⲛ̄ ⲛⲁϣⲟⲣ[ⲡ] ²⁶ⲧⲙⲛⲧⲥⲅⲓⲙⲉ г̄ⲱⲱⲥ ⲥϣ²⁷ⲟⲡ ⲙⲉⲛ алла ⲭⲛ̄ ⲛ̄ϣⲟⲣⲡ ан
[н̄ⲧ²]а̣ⲓ̈ⲉ̄ⲓ̄ ⲉⲃⲟλ (25) ⲉⲁⲛⲟⲕ ⲟⲩⲅ̄ⲓ̄ⲕⲱⲛ н̄ⲧⲉ ⲡⲉⲧϣⲟ[ⲟⲡ]	(11) ⲁⲛⲟⲕ ⲇⲉ н̄ⲧⲁⲉⲓⲉⲓ ⲉⲃⲟλ г̄ⲛ ⲑⲓ²ⲕⲱⲛ м̄ⲡⲉⲧϣⲟⲟⲡ ⲉⲧⲁⲙⲱⲧⲛ̄ ³ⲉⲡⲉⲧϣⲟⲟⲡ·
²а̄ⲓ̈ⲉⲓⲛⲉ ⲇⲉ ⲉⲃⲟλ н̄ⳁⲅ̄ⲓⲕⲱⲛ н̄ⲧⲉ[± …?]	н̄ⲧⲁⲉⲓⲉⲓ ⲇⲉ ⲟⲛ ⲉ⁴[ⲧ]а̣м̣[ⲱⲧ]н̄ ⲉⲑⲓⲕⲱⲛ н̄ⲛ ⳝ ⲟⲙ

---

66 A lacuna CT 10.17 distorts the full context of the statement: ⲉⲉⲓⲟ ⲇⲉ н̄ϣ[± …] ⲉⲁⲛⲕ ⲟⲩⲙⲉⲅ̄ⲥⲛⲁⲩ ⲉⲃⲟλ [г̄]м̄ ⲡⲉⲧϣⲟⲟⲡ, "But I [...]; I am second from He Who Is." The *Critical Edition* reconstructs the passage as ⲉⲉⲓⲟ ⲇⲉ н̄ϣ[ⲟⲣⲡ ⲁⲛ] and translates "I am [not first]; I am second, from the One Who Is." That is a sensible restoration, though the negative modifier is rather uncertain and would extend the line well into the right-hand margin of the manuscript (making it the longest line on page 10). Funk suggests that with a few extra character spaces at the end of line 17, the text of CT could have read "Ich bin aber eher [du], da ich ein Zweiter aus dem Seienden bin," thus conflating the variants in CT and NHC V ("Die erste Apokalypse des Jakobus," 1160 n. 26). Both suggestions are difficult because of the length of character spaces required. I would suggest the restoration ⲉⲉⲓⲟ ⲇⲉ н̄ϣ[ⲟⲟⲡ], ⲉⲁⲛⲕ ⲟⲩⲙⲉⲅ̄ⲥⲛⲁⲩ ⲉⲃⲟλ [г̄] м̄ ⲡⲉⲧϣⲟⲟⲡ, "Although I [am], I am second from He Who Is." The latter restoration preserves the same theological significance as the negated sentence in the *Critical Edition* (namely that Jesus exists, but God existed prior to him) but fits better the space of the lacuna.

³ⲝⲉⲕⲁⲁⲥ ⲉⲣⲉ ⲛ̣ⲓ̣ϣⲏⲣⲉ ⲛ̄ⲧⲉ ⲡⲉⲧϣ[ⲟⲟⲡ]
⁴ⲝⲉ ⲉⲩⲉⲉⲓⲙⲉ ⲝⲉ ⲁϣ ⲛⲉ ⲛⲉⲧⲉ ⲛⲟⲩⲟⲩ
⁵ⲁⲩⲱ ⲝⲉ ⲁϣ ⲛⲉ ⲛ̄ϣⲙ̄ⲙⲟ·

ⲉⲓⲥ ϩⲏⲧⲉ ⁶ϯⲛⲁϭⲱⲗⲡ ⲛⲁⲕ ⲉⲃⲟⲗ
ⲛ̄ϩⲱⲃ ⲛⲓⲙ ⁷ⲙ̄ⲡⲓⲙⲩⲥⲧⲏⲣⲓⲟⲛ· (etc.)

Now since you have asked about femaleness:

Femaleness existed, but femaleness was not
at the beginning. And [it] prepared for itself
powers and deities.

But [...] not existing [...]

[It is I who] came forth as an image of
He Who Is.

And I have *brought forth*
the image of [...]

so that the children of He Who Is may know
what belongs to them
and what is foreign.

Behold, I *shall reveal*
each part of this mystery to you.

---

⁵ⲝⲉⲕⲁⲁⲥ ⲉⲣⲉ ⲛ̄ϣⲏⲣⲉ ⲙⲡⲉⲧϣⲟ⁶ⲟⲡ
ⲉⲩⲛⲁⲙ̄ⲙⲉ ⲉⲛⲟⲩⲟⲩ:
ⲁⲩ⁷ⲱ ⲛⲉⲧⲉ ⲛⲟⲩⲟⲩ ⲁⲛ ⲛⲉ̣ [>>]>>>

⁸ⲉⲓⲥ ϩⲏⲧⲉ ⲁⲓ̈ϭⲱⲗⲡ ⲛⲁⲕ ⲉⲃⲟⲗ
⁹[ⲙ̄]ⲡⲓⲙⲩⲥⲧⲏⲣⲓⲟⲛ: (etc.)

Now since you have asked about femaleness,
listen:

Femaleness existed, but it did not exist from the
beginning. And it created for itself [powers] and
deities.

Again, He Who Is exists from the beginning. As
for femaleness, it does exist, but not from the
beginning.

But it is I who came forth in the image of
He Who Is
to inform you about He Who Is.

And *also*, I have *come forth to [inform] you about*
the image of *the powers*,

so that the children of He Who Is may know
what belongs to them
and what does not belong to them.

Behold, I *have revealed*
the mystery to you.

Although both versions begin with an allusion to an earlier question posed by James concerning femaleness, no such question appears in the narrative. This may be a genuine literary seam, reflecting the incorporation of older materials into the text either in its compositional phase or subsequent transmission.[67] Or perhaps the allusion to James' prior question is a literary device[68] meant to create the impression that the present conversation is only one part of a longer history of dialogue between Jesus and James.

In any event, the reference to femaleness which made for itself "powers and deities" (cf. 1 Cor 8:5) anticipates the more detailed account found later in the narrative concerning Achamoth "the female" who created cosmic powers apart from the

---

67 Schoedel, "(First) Apocalypse of James," 65.
68 Veilleux, *La Première Apocalypse de Jacques*, 68.

preexistent Father (CT 21–22; NHC V 34–35). These demonic powers oppress people in this life, and three of them act as "toll collectors" who interrogate souls as they ascend to heaven after bodily death (CT 21; NHC V 33). Thus in the current pericope, the fact that femaleness did not exist "from the beginning" emphasizes God's superiority to the malicious powers responsible for human suffering. Both manuscripts agree on this point, but CT includes an entire sentence not found in NHC V which reiterates the point a second time: "Again, He Who Is exists from the beginning. As for femaleness, it does exist, but not from the beginning." The parallel text in NHC V 24.31 is much shorter and is unfortunately obscured by three small lacunae ([.]є[.]ϣoon ⲇє ⲁⲛ [...] ⲁ̣ⲓⲉ̄ⲓ єⲃoⲗ) for which various reconstructions have been proposed.[69]

That Jesus has come forth in the image of He Who Is follows the biblical precedent that Christ is the εἰκὼν τοῦ θεοῦ (2 Cor 4:4; Col. 1:15; cf. John 14:9), but the two versions present Jesus' mission to the world in somewhat different terms. In NHC V, the purpose of Jesus' mission is much more abbreviated than in CT, and here too, it is obscured by a short lacuna: Jesus has come forth as the image of He Who Is, and has "brought forth the image of [...]" (ⲁⲓⲉⲓⲛє ⲇє єⲃoⲗ ⲛ̄ϯⲉ̄ⲓⲕⲱⲛ ⲛ̄ⲧє [± ...]). Modern editors have traditionally restored this passage as "the image of [Him]" (ϯⲉ̄ⲓⲕⲱⲛ ⲛ̄ⲧє[ϥ]), i.e., the image of God (though the newly available text in CT could point to a different restoration).[70] If one were to follow this restoration, the focus of the passage in NHC V would be entirely on the importance of the image of God revealed by Jesus. For readers in the fourth century and beyond, this focus may have resonated with the soteriological theory, already formulated by Irenaeus,[71] and central to Athanasius'

---

69 Böhlig, Schoedel, and Veilleux reconstruct NHC V 24.31 as [ⲛ]є[ⲥ]ϣoon ⲇє ⲁⲛ [є]ⲁ̣ⲓⲉ̄ⲓ єⲃoⲗ, "But [it (femaleness) did] not exist [when] I came forth ..." Hans-Martin Schenke suggests [ⲛ]є[ⲩ]ϣoon ⲇє ⲁⲛ, "But [they (the powers and dieties)] were not existing ..." (review of Böhlig, *Koptisch-gnostische Apokalypsen* in *OLZ* 61 1/2 [1966]: col. 28); and Rodolphe Kasser suggests [є]є[ⲓ]ϣoon ⲇє ⲁⲛ[oⲕ ⲁ]ⲓⲉⲓ єⲃoⲗ, "But as I exist, I myself have come forth ..." ("Textes gnostiques: remarques à propos des éditions récentes du Livre Secret de Jean et des Apocalypses de Paul, Jacques et Adam," *Mus* 78 [1965]: 81). In the case of the third lacuna, however, the gap before ⲁⲓⲉ̄ⲓ is at least two character spaces long (cf. Kasser's suggestion), so that a single *epsilon* is insufficient. I would therefore adopt Schenke's proposal, and add the II Perfect conjugation in the third lacuna (as in CT), thus [ⲛ]є[ⲩ]ϣoon ⲇє ⲁⲛ [ⲛ̄ⲧ]ⲁ̣ⲓⲉ̄ⲓ єⲃoⲗ, "But [they] (the powers and deities) did not exist (i.e., from the beginning). It is I who came forth ..."

70 Schoedel and Veilleux reconstruct ϯⲉ̄ⲓⲕⲱⲛ ⲛ̄ⲧє[ϥ], which is also assumed by Funk in his translation "Ich brachte [sein] Abbild hervor." Böhlig's ϯⲉ̄ⲓⲕⲱⲛ ⲛ̄ⲧє [ⲡⲉⲧϣooⲡ] is not impossible, since the lacuna is at the end of the line, but would extend unusually far into the margin. But now with the parallel text in CT, according to which Jesus has come to teach about the "image of the powers" (ⲉⲓⲕⲱⲛ ⲛ̄ⲛ̄ϭoⲙ) one might be tempted to reconstruct NHC V 25.2 accordingly as "I have brought forth the image of [the powers]" (ϯⲉ̄ⲓⲕⲱⲛ ⲛ̄ⲧє [ⲛ̄ϭoⲙ]). Both ⲛ̄ⲧє[ϥ] and ⲛ̄ⲧє [ⲛ̄ϭoⲙ] would fit within the fluctuating length of lines on the textual column's right-hand side. At any rate, this lacuna raises an important methodological question: Where two manuscripts of the same work display so many variant readings, how sound is it to reconstruct lacunae in one manuscript according to the text in the other?

71 Irenaeus, *Haer.* III.18.1; V.1.3. Cf. Mary Ann Donovan, *One Right Reading? A Guide to Irenaeus* (Collegeville, Minn.: Liturgical Press, 1997), 82–83.

theology, that the image of God in which humanity was originally created (Gen 1:26) had become so intractably tarnished after the Fall that it could not be restored in any other way than by the incarnation of the Savior.[72]

The parallel version in CT presents a somewhat expanded version in which Jesus' mission is given a two-fold purpose: first, to teach about God ("to inform you about He Who Is"; as in John 1:18, "he has made him known"), and secondly, to teach about demons ("to [inform] you about the image of the powers," ⲉⲓⲕⲱⲛ ⲛ̄ⲛ̄ϭⲟⲙ). Thus the version in CT has more of a demonological focus than NHC V, that in addition to knowledge of God, one needs also to know about the "image of the powers."

For ancient Christian apologists, the images of demonic powers were the physical statues of the gods, which were hand-crafted and erroneously worshipped by heathens.[73] While CT's *James* is clearly not addressing the problem of pagan idolatry, it does share with the apologists a concern that demons have misled humanity into blindness, ignorance, and forgetfulness of the true God (CT 13.17–24; 14.8–15.11). The "image of the powers," then, which Jesus has come to reveal, may refer to the illusory influence demons exercise over humanity. Jesus has come forth as the image of He Who Is, so that the "children of He Who Is" may distinguish what is theirs and what is not theirs, that is, so that they might understand that their lineage is not from the demonic powers but from the preexistent Father (cf. CT 20.12–18). To come to this realization, one needs to learn the nature of the demons and their ranks in the heavens (CT 12.4–13.23) and to understand how they stupefy humanity by means of the "weak" flesh (CT 13.20–23; 15.8–9; 19.13–14). Jesus has come forth to obliterate the forgetfulness and ignorance they have wrought in humanity (CT 14.21–25), not only by his teaching, but also through his passion and death. While Jesus' human body of flesh suffered and died, the impassible divinity within him remained unharmed, thus marking a victory over the demonic powers by proving to them that he cannot be seized (CT 16.16–21; 18.4–9).[74]

---

72 Athanasius, *C. Gent.* 34; *Inc.* 13–14. On interpretations of Gen 1:26 by Jews and Christians up to the time of Origen, see Robert McL. Wilson, "The Early History of the Exegesis of Gen. 1:26," in *Editiones, Critica, Philologica, Biblica, Iudaica, Historica: Papers Presented to the Second International Conference on Patristic Studies, Held at Christ Church, Oxford, 1955* (ed. Frank L. Cross and Kurt Aland; TUGAL 63; StPatr 1; Berlin: Akademie-Verlag, 1957), 420–37.

73 E.g., Athenagoras, *Leg.* 18, 23, 26; Tertullian, *Apol.* 22; Athanasius, *C. Gent.* 11.

74 The notion that only Jesus' flesh suffered, but not his divinity, has often been confused with Docetism in the analysis of texts traditionally classified as "Gnostic." But to regard this interpretation of the crucifixion as docetic obscures the fact that it was also advocated by patristic authors who are regarded as orthodox in later Christian tradition (e.g., Melito, *Peri Pascha* 66–67; Tertullian, *Prax.* 27, *Carn. Chr.* 5; Athanasius, *Inc.* 8–9; cf. J. N. D. Kelly, *Early Christian Doctrines* [5th ed.; London: A & C Black, 1977], 142–58, esp. 152). The point of the distinction was not to deny the reality of Jesus' suffering or its soteriological significance, but to resolve the paradox of a god who could die, yet live. By the fifth century, the "orthodox" position (against the Nestorians) was simply to maintain the paradox

The Christology, demonology, and interpretation of the crucifixion as an *exposé* and victory over demonic powers expressed in *James* therefore resonates with the Pauline Letter to the Colossians, according to which Christ is the image of God and superior to every dominion and power (Col 2:10). On the cross, he has "stripped off (ἀπεκδυσάμενος / ⲁϥⲕⲁⲁϥⲕⲁϩⲏⲩ) the principalities and powers and made a public example (ἐδειγμάτισεν / ⲁϥⲟⲩⲟⲛϩⲟⲩ ⲉⲃⲟⲗ) of them, triumphing over them in it" (Col 2:15). Since those who are in Christ have metaphorically discarded their bodies of flesh (Col 2:11), they should mortify their bodily passions as well, "stripping off the old human being with its acts, and putting on the new one which is being renewed in knowledge according to the image of its creator" (Col 3:5, 9–10).

Finally, at the conclusion to the Christological discourse appears a small but highly significant variant reading which frames the meaning of the two texts quite differently. In NHC V, Jesus tells James that "I *shall* reveal each part of this mystery to you," whereas in CT he states that "I *have* revealed" it. The future tense in NHC V casts Jesus' opening discourse as an introduction to the rest of the treatise, so that the reader expects to learn "each part" of the mystery in what follows. In contrast, the past tense in CT's version identifies "the mystery" with the foregoing Christological discourse itself. Most interesting is that the special focus CT places upon this discourse as "the mystery" is amplified by paratextual features in the manuscript. At the beginning of the discourse, just where Jesus says "Listen" (CT 10.8), the scribe marked the passage with a paragraphus in the left-hand margin, and on the next page punctuated its logical conclusion with a series of *diplai* (>>>) inside the textual column (CT 11.7), thus demarcating the entire passage in an inclusio.[75] Because of the infrequency of the paragraphus in CT (there are only three extant instances in the codex: pp. 10, 61, 63) it was apparently used to mark passages which the scribe regarded as especially significant.[76]

What might the scribe of CT have found particularly important in this passage? As we have seen, both NHC V and CT state that "nothing existed except He Who Is,"

---

that "the Impassible suffered"; see Paul L. Gavrilyuk, *The Suffering of the Impassible God: The Dialectics of Patristic Thought* (Oxford: Oxford University Press, 2004), 133–34, 172–73.

75 It is also possible that a later reader of CT added the paragraphus at 10.8, but I find it more likely that it was the scribe since the logical conclusion to the passage is marked with *diplai* within the textual column on 11.7. The same *diplai* marks are used elsewhere in the codex to mark the end of sub-sections. See Lance Jenott, *The Gospel of Judas: Coptic Text, Translation, and Historical Interpretation of the 'Betrayer's Gospel'* (STAC 64; Tübingen: Mohr Siebeck, 2011), 224.

76 In contrast to the irregular usage of the paragraphus in CT, the scribe of NHC V used it in a much more routine way to divide the passages in *Apoc. Adam* in which each of the thirteen kingdoms make pronouncements about the origins of the messianic illuminator (NHC V 79–82); in some instances, a number inscribed in the right hand margin accompanies the paragraphus (80.9; 81.14; 82.4; 82.10). The scribe of NHC V, or a later reader, also inscribed at least one paragraphus in 1 *Apoc. Jas.*, to mark a passage (now rather lacunous) which seems to describe the descent of Jesus past the archon Adonaios (39.8).

and CT's variant reading "I am second from He Who Is" would only make the text's subordinationist Christology more emphatic. In fourth century Egypt, such theology could easily have been understood in terms of Arian doctrine, which maintained that the Father alone existed in the beginning, and that the Son was temporally subordinate to him. Hence the famous catch-phrase associated with the Arians, "There was a time when he was not."[77] A brief summary of Arius' doctrine is preserved in his letter to Bishop Alexander:

> For (the Son) is not eternal or co-eternal or co-unoriginate with the Father, nor has he his being together with the Father, as some speak of relations, introducing two ingenerate beginnings, but God is before all things as being Monad and Beginning of all. Wherefore also he is before the Son. ... For he is above him as being his God and before him. But if the terms *from him* (ἐξ αὐτοῦ, Rom 11:36),[78] and *from the womb* (Ps 110:3), and *I came forth from the Father* (John 16:28) be understood by some to mean as a part of him, one in essence or as an issue, then the Father is according to them compounded and divisible and alterable and material ...[79]

Given that these theological questions incited so much controversy in the Church at the time when our two texts of *James* were copied and read, it is probably not a coincidence that the scribe of CT marked off this particular Christological discourse as "the mystery" Jesus has revealed. While the Christological discourse of *James* is certainly not a straightforward summary of Arius' credo, its theology would lend itself to discussions of this important Christological question. Indeed, Jesus' affirmation that "I am *from* He Who Is" (ⲉⲃⲟⲗ ⲅ̄ⲙ ⲡⲉⲧϣⲟⲟⲡ) would have raised the same theological questions which Arius says were aroused by the terminology of Rom 11:36 (ἐξ αὐτοῦ) when applied to the Son's generation from the Father.

Conclusion

From the foregoing analysis of the introductory discourse in *James* (CT,2) and its parallel version in the *Apocalypse of James* (NHC V,2) we can see that both texts have been altered in the course of transmission. The variations between the two are not necessarily large in terms of the amount of text; they are not as large as, for example, variations on the ending of Mark's gospel, or the short and long versions of the *Apocryphon of John*, in which the differences between manuscripts constitute entire par-

---

77 On Arian controversy see, e.g., Richard P. C. Hanson *The Search for the Christian Doctrine of God: The Arian Controversy, 318–381* (Edinburgh: T&T Clark, 1988); C. Wilfred Griggs, *Early Egyptian Christianity from its Origins to 451 CE* (Leiden: Brill, 1993), 133–56.
78 Rom 11:36: "For from him (ἐξ αὐτοῦ) and through him and to him are all things."
79 *Letter of Arius to Alexander* (trans. *A New Eusebius: Documents Illustrating the History of the Church to AD 337* [2nd rev. ed.; ed. J. Stevenson and W. H. C. Frend; London: SPCK, 1987], 326–27).

agraphs or even several pages of text. Rather, the variations between *James* and the *Apocalypse of James* are found in smaller points of vocabulary and syntax. Yet these are also significant insofar as they can create interesting points of difference in the theology and meaning of the texts. They are thus more comparable to the subtle but theologically loaded reading variants in, for example, Mark 6:3 ("Is this not the carpenter, the son of Mary ...?" versus "Is this not the *son of* the carpenter *and of* Mary ...?"), or John 1:18 ("the only-begotten *God*" versus "the only-begotten *Son*").[80] For purposes of practicality, I have limited the present study to *James'* opening dialogue and its Christological teaching. But much more study remains to be done on variant readings found in the remainder of the two texts, and their potential theological significance.[81]

Such an examination raises an important methodological question: To what extent can we talk about the "original" versions of literary works such as *James* when it appears that they were subjected to so much revision during transmission?[82] It seems to me that we cannot rely much on the conventional criteria applied in the field of New Testament textual criticism.[83] We cannot rely on the *age of the witness* (not to mention *text types*), since the manuscripts are roughly contemporaneous. We cannot rely on the *geographic distribution* of a particular reading, since the texts come from the same place (or approximately the same place, Egypt, in the case of the Nag Hammadi Codices, PB 8502, and CT). Few decisions can probably be made regarding the originality of a reading based on the *style, vocabulary, and theology* of an author, since points of style are elusive when dealing with Coptic translations of lost *Vorlagen*, and presuppositions about an author's theology run the risk of circular reasoning. It may be that in some cases, the *more difficult reading* is preferable, though there remains the possibility that the original reading is not preserved in any of the witnesses.

The assumption of textual fluidity may lead to the more traditional approach of *Quellenforschung*, by positing the existence of hypothetical sources underlying the preserved text, and focusing on the history of each source as a discrete unit.[84] Or,

---

80 Cf. Bruce M. Metzger, *A Textual Commentary on the Greek New Testament: A Companion Volume to the United Bible Societies' Greek New Testament* (3rd ed.; London: United Bible Societies, 1971), 88–89, 198.

81 Compare, e.g., NHC V 25.7–8 with CT 11.9–14; NHC V 27.8–12 with CT 13.24–14.5; NHC V 28.16–20 with CT 15.5–7; NHC V 30.13–17 with CT 16.27–17.5; NHC V 36.15–19 with CT 23.13–19.

82 For further consideration of this question, see the contribution to this volume by Hugo Lundhaug, "An Illusion of Textual Stability."

83 On these criteria and their application, see Metzger and Ehrman, *Text of the New Testament*, 300–15.

84 Einar Thomassen has offered an analysis of the *(First) Apocalypse of James* along these lines, concluding that the text is not Valentinian in origin, but incorporates material which had been used by Valentinians in earlier periods (e.g., the formulae spoken to the heavenly toll-collectors); see Thomas-

from the perspective of material philology, the assumption of fluidity may lead to a focus on the composition as a whole, understood as the final product of the transmission process. It is easier to ignore the reality of textual fluidity in the case of literary works which are preserved in only one manuscript, since no direct evidence of fluidity appears before our eyes. Nevertheless, it is quite likely that these texts have also been redacted in the course of transmission (as suggested by the evidence from works preserved in more than one manuscript).

In the case of literary works such as *James*, for which different textual witnesses can be compared, a sensible approach would be to treat each text as its own entity, as a unique "snapshot" of the work, with all its idiosyncrasies, the accumulation of which reflects the various periods and places through which the text has passed in the course of transmission. The natural starting point for understanding the text would be the social and intellectual circumstances of the period from which the manuscript comes (though other contexts could theoretically be posited based on other evidence, if available, such as references to the work in earlier periods). The degree to which texts vary from one manuscript to another could even lead to the larger question of whether they should be considered as distinct works in their own right.[85]

Bibliography

Attridge, Harold W. "The Greek Fragments." Pages 95–128 in *Nag Hammadi Codex II,2–7 together with XIII,2*, Brit. Lib. Or. 4926(1), and P. Oxy. 1, 654, 655*, vol. 1: *Gospel According to Thomas, Gospel According to Philip, Hypostasis of the Archons, and Indexes*. Edited by Bentley Layton. Nag Hammadi Studies 20. Leiden: Brill, 1989.

Barc, Bernard and Louis Painchaud, "La réécriture de l'Apocryphon de Jean á la lumière de l'hymne final de la version longue," *Le Muséon* 112 (1999): 317–33.

Barc, Bernard and Wolf-Peter Funk. *Le livre des Secrets de Jean: Recension brève (NH III, 1 et BG, 2)*. Bibliothèque copte de Nag Hammadi, Textes 35. Quebec: Les Presses de l'Université Laval, 2012.

Barry, Catherine. *La sagesse de Jésus-Christ (BG, 3; NH III, 4)*. Bibliothèque copte de Nag Hammadi, Textes 20. Quebec: Les Presses de l'Université Laval, 1993.

Bethge, Hans-Gebhard. "'Der Brief des Petrus an Philippus' als Bestandteil von NHC VIII und Codex Tchacos: Beobachtungen und Überlegungen zum überlieferungsgeschichtlichen und inhaltlich-sachlichen Verhältnis beider Paralleltexte." Pages 173–88 in *Judasevangelium und Codex Tchacos: Studien zur religionsgeschichtlichen Verortung einer gnostischen Schriftsammlung*. Edited by Enno Edzard Popkes and Gregor Wurst. Wissenschaftliche Untersuchungen zum Neuen Testament I 297. Tübingen: Mohr Siebeck, 2012.

---

sen, "The Valentinian Materials in *James* (NHC V,3 and CT,2)," in *Beyond the Gnostic Gospels: Studies Building on the Work of Elaine Pagels* (ed. Eduard Iricinschi et al.; STAC 82; Tübingen: Mohr Siebeck, 2013), 79–90.

85 See the contribution to this volume by Liv Ingeborg Lied, who treats this question with regard to the extant versions of the *Epistle of Baruch*.

Böhlig, Alexander. *Koptisch-gnostische Apokalypsen aus Codex V von Nag Hammadi im Koptischen Museum zu Alt-Kairo.* Sonderband, Wissenschaftliche Zeitschrift der Martin-Luther-Universität. Halle-Wittenberg, 1963.

Böhlig, Alexander and Frederik Wisse, *Nag Hammadi Codices III,2 and IV,2: The Gospel of The Egyptians (The Holy Book of the Great Invisible Spirit).* Nag Hammadi Studies 4. Leiden: Brill, 1975.

Brashler, James. "Plato, Republic 588b–589b." Pages 325–39 in *Nag Hammadi Codices V,2–5 and VI with Papyrus Berolinensis 8502, 1 and 4.* Edited by Douglas M. Parrott. Nag Hammadi Studies 11. Leiden: Brill, 1979.

Cerquiglini, Bernard. *In Praise of the Variant: A Critical History of Philology.* Translated by Betsy Wing. Baltimore: Johns Hopkins University Press, 1999.

Chaves, Julio Cesar Dias. "Scribal Intervention in the Titles of Nag Hammadi Codex V." *Judaïsme Ancien / Ancient Judaism* 4 (2016): forthcoming.

Crum, Walter E. *Catalogue of the Coptic Manuscripts in the British Museum.* London: British Museum, 1905.

Dirkse, Peter and James Brashler. "The Prayer of Thanksgiving." Pages 375–87 in *Nag Hammadi Codices V,2–5 and VI with Papyrus Berolinensis 8502, 1 and 4.* Edited by Douglas M. Parrott. Nag Hammadi Studies 11. Leiden: Brill, 1979.

Donovan, Mary Ann. *One Right Reading? A Guide to Irenaeus.* Collegeville, Minn.: Liturgical Press, 1997.

Driscoll, Matthew J. "Words on the Page: Thoughts on Philology Old and New." Pages 87–104 in *Creating the Medieval Saga: Versions, Variability, and Editorial Interpretations of Old Norse Saga Literature.* Edited by Judy Quinn and Emily Lethbridge. Odense: Syddansk Universitets-forlag, 2010.

Ehrman, Bart D. *The Orthodox Corruption of Scripture: The Effect of Early Christological Controversies on the Text of the New Testament.* New York: Oxford University Press, 1993.

Emmel, Stephen. "Religious Tradition, Textual Transmission, and the Nag Hammadi Codices." Pages 34–43 in *The Nag Hammadi Library After Fifty Years: Proceedings of the 1995 Society of Biblical Literature Commemoration.* Edited by John D. Turner and Anne McGuire. Nag Hammadi and Manichaean Studies 44. Leiden: Brill, 1997.

Fish, Stanley. "Interpreting the *Variorum*," Pages 147–73 in *Is There A Text in This Class? The Authority of Interpretive Communities.* Edited by Stanley Fish. Cambridge, Mass.: Harvard University Press, 1980.

Funk, Wolf-Peter. *Die Zweite Apokalypse des Jakobus aus Nag-Hammadi-Codex V.* Texte und Unter-suchungen zur Geschichte der altchristlichen Literatur 119. Berlin: Akademie-Verlag, 1976.

–. "The First Apocalypse of James." Pages 314–15 in *New Testament Apocrypha*, vol. 1: *Gospels and Related Writings.* Edited by Wilhelm Schneemelcher. translated by Robert McL. Wilson. Westminster: John Knox Press, 1990.

–. "The Significance of the Tchacos Codex for Understanding the *First Apocalypse of James*." Pages 509–33 in *The Codex Judas Papers: Proceedings of the International Congress on the Tchacos Codex Held at Rice University, Houston, Texas, March 13–16, 2008.* Edited by April D. DeConick. Nag Hammadi and Manichaean Studies 71. Leiden: Brill, 2009.

–. "Die erste Apokalypse des Jakobus (NHC V,3 / CT 2)." Pages 1152–80 in *Antike christliche Apokryphen in deutscher Übersetzung*, Band I: *Evangelien und Verwandtes, Teilband 2.* Edited by Christoph Markschies and Jens Schröter. Tübingen: Mohr Siebeck, 2012.

–. "Ein doppelt überliefertes Stück spätägyptischer Weisheit." *Zeitschrift für ägyptische Sprache und Altertumskunde* 103 (1976): 8–21.

Gambero, Luigi. *Mary and the Fathers of the Church: The Blessed Virgin Mary in Patristic Thought.* San Francisco: Ignatius Press, 1999.

Gavrilyuk, Paul L. *The Suffering of the Impassible God: The Dialectics of Patristic Thought*. Oxford: Oxford University Press, 2004.

Giversen, Søren. *Apocryphon Johannis: The Coptic Text of the Apocryphon Johannis in the Nag Hammadi Codex II with Translation, Introduction, and Commentary*. Acta Theologica Danica 5. Copenhagen: Munksgaard, 1963.

Good, Deirdre J. *Reconstructing the Tradition of Sophia in Gnostic Literature*. Society of Biblical Literature Monograph Series 32. Atlanta: Scholars Press, 1987.

Griggs, C. Wilfred. *Early Egyptian Christianity from its Origins to 451 CE*. Leiden: Brill, 1993.

Hanson, Richard P. C. *The Search for the Christian Doctrine of God: The Arian Controversy, 318–381*. Edinburgh: T&T Clark, 1988.

Hurst, André, ed. *P. Bodmer XXIX: Vision de Dorotheus*. Bibliotheca Bodmeriana. Geneva: Fondation Martin Bodmer, 1984.

Hurst, André and Jean Rudhardt, eds. *P. Bodmer XXX–XXXVII: «Codex des Visions», Poèmes divers*. Munich: K. G. Saur, 1999.

Jenott, Lance. *The Gospel of Judas: Coptic Text, Translation, and Historical Interpretation of the 'Betrayer's Gospel'*. Studien und Texte zu Antike und Christentum 64. Tübingen: Mohr Siebeck, 2011.

Joannou, Perikles-Petros. *Fonti, Fasciolo IX: Discipline générale antique (IIᵉ–IXᵉ s.)*, vol. 2: *Les canons des pères grecs*. Rome: Tipographia Italo-Orientale S. Nilo, 1963.

Kasser, Rodolphe. "Bibliothèque gnostique VI: Les deux Apocalypses de Jacques." *Revue de Théologie et de Philosophie* 18 (1968): 163–86.

–. "Textes gnostiques: remarques à propos des éditions récentes du Livre Secret de Jean et des Apocalypses de Paul, Jacques et Adam." *Le Muséon* 78 (1965): 71–98.

Kasser, Rodolphe, Marvin Meyer, and Gregor Wurst. *The Gospel of Judas from Codex Tchacos*. Washington, D. C.: National Geographic Society, 2006.

Kasser, Rodolphe and Philippe Luisier. "P. Bodmer XLIII: Un feuillet de *Zostrien*." *Le Muséon* 120 (2007): 251–72.

Kasser, Rodolphe and Gregor Wurst, eds., in collaboration with Marvin Meyer and François Gaudard. *The Gospel of Judas: Critical Edition, Together with the Letter of Peter to Philip, James, and a Book of Allogenes from Codex Tchacos*. Washington, D. C.: National Geographic Society, 2007.

Kelly, J. N. D. *Early Christian Doctrines*. 5ᵗʰ edition. London: A & C Black, 1977.

King, Karen L. "Approaching the Variants of the Apocryphon of John." Pages 105–37 in *The Nag Hammadi Library After Fifty Years: Proceedings of the 1995 Society of Biblical Literature Commemoration*. Edited by John D. Turner and Anne McGuire. Nag Hammadi and Manichaean Studies 44. Leiden: Brill, 1997.

–. *The Gospel of Mary of Magdala: Jesus and the First Woman Apostle*. Santa Rosa, Calif.: Polebridge Press, 2003.

–. *The Secret Revelation of John*. Cambridge, Mass.: Harvard University Press, 2006.

Krause, Martin. "Das literarische Verhältnis des Eugnostosbriefes zur Sophia Jesu Christi." Pages 215–23 in *Mullus: Festschrift Theodor Klauser*. Edited by Alfred Stuiber and Alfred Hermann. Münster: Aschendorff, 1964.

Krosney, Herbert. *The Lost Gospel: The Quest for the Gospel of Judas Iscariot*. Washington, D. C.: National Geographic Society, 2006.

Lambdin, Thomas O. *Introduction to Sahidic Coptic*. Macon, Ga.: Mercer University Press, 1983.

Layton, Bentley. "The British Library Fragments." Pages 95–134 in *Nag Hammadi Codex II,2–7 together with XIII,2*, *Brit. Lib. Or. 4926(1), and P. Oxy. 1, 654, 655*, vol. 2: *On the Origin of the World, Expository Treatise on the Soul, Book of Thomas the Contender*. Edited by Bentley Layton. Nag Hammadi Studies 21. Leiden: Brill, 1989.

–. *A Coptic Grammar*. Wiesbaden: Herrassowitz Verlag, 2000.

Lührmann, Dieter. *Die Apokryph gewordenen Evangelien: Studien zu neuen Texten und zu neuen Fragen*. Supplements to Novum Testamentum 112. Leiden: Brill, 2004.

Lundhaug, Hugo. "The Nag Hammadi Codices: Textual Fluidity in Coptic." Pages 419–23 in *Comparative Oriental Manuscript Studies: An Introduction*. Edited by Alessandro Bausi. Hamburg: COMSt, 2015.

Lundhaug, Hugo and Lance Jenott. *The Monastic Origins of the Nag Hammadi Codices*. Studien und Texte zu Antike und Christentum 97. Tübingen: Mohr Siebeck, 2015.

Mahé, Jean-Pierre. "La Prière d'actions de grâces du Codex VI de Nag-Hammadi et Le Discours parfait." *Zeitschrift für Papyrologie und Epigraphik* 13 (1974): 40–60.

–. *Hermès en Haute-Égypte, Tome I: Les textes hermétique de Nag Hammadi et leurs parallèles grecs et latins*. Bibliothèque copte de Nag Hammadi, Textes 3. Quebec: Les Presses de l'Université Laval, 1978.

–. *Hermès en Haute-Égypte, Tome II: Le fragment du* Discourse parfait *et les Définitions* hermétiques arméniennes. Bibliothèque copte de Nag Hammadi, Textes 7. Quebec: Les Presses de l'Université Laval, 1982.

Marcovich, Miroslav. "Textual Criticism on the Gospel of Thomas." *Journal of Theological Studies* 20 (1969): 53–74.

Marjanen, Antti. "The Seven Women Disciples in the Two Versions of the *First Apocalypse of James*." Pages 535–46 in *The Codex Judas Papers: Proceedings of the International Congress on the Tchacos Codex Held at Rice University, Houston, Texas, March 13–16, 2008*. Edited by April D. DeConick. Nag Hammadi and Manichaean Studies 71. Leiden: Brill, 2009.

Matsagouras, E. G. "Plato Copticus, Republic 588b–589b: Translation and Commentary." M. A. thesis, Delhousie University, 1976.

–. "Plato Copticus," *Platon* (1977): 191–99.

Metzger, Bruce M. "Explicit References in the Works of Origen of Alexandria to Variant Readings in New Testament Manuscripts." Pages 78–95 in *Biblical and Patristic Studies in Memory of Robert Pierce Casey*. Edited by J. Neville Birdsall and Robert W. Thomson. Freiburg: Herder, 1963.

–. *A Textual Commentary on the Greek New Testament: A Companion Volume to the United Bible Societies' Greek New Testament*. 3rd edition. London: United Bible Societies, 1971.

Metzger, Bruce M. and Bart D. Ehrman. *The Text of the New Testament: Its Transmission, Corruption, and Restoration*. 4th edition. New York: Oxford University Press, 2005.

Mohri, Erika. *Maria Magdalena: Frauenbilder in Evangelientexten des 1. bis 3. Jahrhunderts*. Marburger theologische Studien 63. Marburg: Elwert, 2000.

Morard, Fraçoise. "Les Apocalypses du Codex V de Nag Hammadi." Pages 341–57 in *Les textes de Nag Hammadi et le problème de leur classification: Actes du colloque tenu à Québec du 15 au 19 Septembre 1993*. Edited by Louis Painchaud and Anne Pasquier. Bibliothèque copte de Nag Hammadi, Études 3. Quebec: Les Presses de l'Université Laval, 1995.

Mortley, Raoul. "The Name of the Father is the Son (Gospel of Truth 38)." Pages 239–52 in *Neoplatonism and Gnosticism*. Edited by Richard T. Wallis and Jay Bregman. Studies in Neoplatonism 6. Albany: State University of New York Press, 1992.

Musurillo, Herbert. "Some Textual Problems in the Editing of the Greek Fathers." Pages 85–96 in *Introductio, Editiones, Critica, Philologica: Papers Presented to the Third International Conference on Patristic Studies Held at Christ Church, Oxford, 1959*. Edited by Frank L. Cross. Texte und Untersuchungen zur Geschichte der altchristlichen Literatur 78. Studia Patristica 3. Berlin: Akademie-Verlag, 1961.

Nichols, Stephen G. "Philology in a Manuscript Culture." *Speculum* 65:1 (1990): 1–10.

Oeyen, Christian. "Fragmente einer subachmimischen Version der gnostischen 'Schrift ohne Titel.'" Pages 125–44 in *Essays on The Nag Hammadi Texts In Honour of Pahor Labib*. Edited by Martin Krause. Nag Hammadi Studies 6. Leiden: Brill, 1975.

Orlandi, Tito. "La traduzione copta di Platone, *Resp.* IX, 588b–589b: problemi critici ed esegetici." Pages 45–62 in *Atti della Accademia Nazionale dei Lincei*. Rendiconti morali, Serie VIII, 22, fasc. 1–2. Rome: 1977.

Painchaud, Louis. "Fragment de la république de Platon (NH VI, 5)." In *Les sentences de Sextus (NH XII, 1). Fragment de la république de Platon (NH VI, 5)*. Edited by Paul-Hubert Poirier and Louis Painchaud. Bibliothèque copte de Nag Hammadi, Textes 11. Quebec: Les Presses de l'Université Laval, 1983.

–. "La classification des textes de Nag Hammadi et la phénomène des réécritures." Pages 51–85 in *Les textes de Nag Hammadi et le problème de leur classification: Actes du colloque tenu à Québec du 15 au 19 Septembre 1993*. Edited by Louis Painchaud and Anne Pasquier. Bibliothèque copte de Nag Hammadi, Études 3. Quebec: Les Presses de l'Université Laval, 1995.

Painchaud, Louis and Timothy Janz. "The 'Kingless Generation' and the Polemical Rewriting of Certain Nag Hammadi Texts." Pages 439–60 in *The Nag Hammadi Library After Fifty Years: Proceedings of the 1995 Society of Biblical Literature Commemoration*. Edited by John D. Turner and Anne McGuire. Nag Hammadi and Manichaean Studies 44. Leiden: Brill, 1997.

Parker, David C. *The Living Text of the Gospels*. Cambridge: Cambridge University Press, 1997.

Parrott, Douglas M., ed. *The Nag Hammadi Codices III,3–4 and V,1 with Papyrus Berolinensis 8502,3 and Oxyrhynchus Papyrus 1081: Eugnostos and The Sophia of Jesus Christ*. Nag Hammadi Studies 27. Leiden: Brill, 1991.

Pasquier, Anne. *L'Évangile selon Marie (BG,1)*. Bibliothèque copte de Nag Hammadi, Textes 10. Quebec: Les Presses de l'Université Laval, 1983.

Poirier, Paul-Hubert. "Les Sentences de Sextus (NH XII, 1)." Pages 1–108 in *Les sentences de Sextus (NH XII, 1): Fragment de la république de Platon (NH VI, 5)*. Edited by Paul-Hubert Poirier and Louis Painchaud. Bibliothèque copte de Nag Hammadi, Textes 11. Quebec: Les Presses de l'Université Laval, 1983.

–. "Titres et sous-titres, incipit et desinit dans les codices coptes de Nag Hammadi et Berlin: description et éléments d'analyse." Pages 339–83 in *Titres et articulations du texte dans les oeuvres antiques: Actes du Colloque International de Chantilly 13–15 décembre de 1994*. Edited by Jean-Claude Fredouille, Marie-Odile Goulet-Cazé, Philippe Hoffmann, Pierre Petitmengin, and Simone Deléani. Collection des études augustiniennes, Série Antiquité 152. Paris: Institut d'Études Augustiniennes, 1997.

Roberts, Colin H. *Catalogue of the Greek and Latin Papyri in the John Rylands Library*. Manchester: Manchester University Press, 1938.

Robinson, James M., ed. *The Nag Hammadi Library in English*. San Francisco: HarperSanFrancisco, 1988.

–. *Story of the Bodmer Papyri: From the First Monastery's Library in Upper Egypt to Geneva and Dublin*. Eugene, Ore.: Cascade, 2011.

Rose, Els. "*Virtutes Apostolorum*: Editorial Problems and Principles." *Apocrypha* 23 (2012): 11–45.

Schenke, Hans-Martin. Review of Alexander Böhlig, *Koptisch-gnostische Apokalypsen* in *Orientalistische Literaturzeitung* 61 1/2 (1966): cols. 23–34.

–. "Zur Faksimile-Ausgabe der Nag-Hammadi-Schriften." *Orientalistische Literaturzeitung* 69 (1974): cols. 235–42.

Schoedel, William R. "(First) Apocalypse of James." Pages 65–103 in *Nag Hammadi Codices V,2–5 and VI with Papyrus Berolinensis 8502, 1 and 4*. Edited by Douglas M. Parrott. Nag Hammadi Studies 11. Leiden: Brill, 1979.

Stevenson, James and William H. C. Frend, eds. *A New Eusebius: Documents Illustrating the History of the Church to AD 337*. 2nd revised edition. London: SPCK, 1987.

Streeter, Burnett Hillman. *The Four Gospels: A Study of Origins, Treating of the Manuscript Tradition, Sources, Authorship, and Dates*. 4th revised edition. London: MacMillan and Co., 1930.

Thomassen, Einar. "The Valentinian Materials in *James* (NHC V,*3* and CT,*2*)." Pages 79–90 in *Beyond the Gnostic Gospels: Studies Building on the Work of Elaine Pagels*. Edited by Eduard Iricinschi, Lance Jenott, Nicola Denzey Lewis, and Philippa Townsend. Studien und Texte zu Antike und Christentum 82. Tübingen: Mohr Siebeck, 2013.

Tuckett, Christopher. *The Gospel of Mary*. Oxford Early Christian Gospel Texts. Oxford: Oxford University Press, 2007.

Veilleux, Armand. *La Première Apocalypse de Jacques (NH V,3): La Second Apocalypse de Jacques (NH V,4)*. Bibliothèque copte de Nag Hammadi, Textes 17. Quebec: Les Presses de l'Université Laval, 1986.

Waldstein, Michael and Frederik Wisse, eds. *The Apocryphon of John: Synopsis of Nag Hammadi Codices II,1; III,1; and IV,1 with BG 8502,2*. Nag Hammadi and Manichaean Studies 33. Leiden: Brill, 1995.

Williams, Michael A. "Interpreting the Nag Hammadi Library as 'Collection(s)' in the History of 'Gnosticism(s).'" Pages 3–50 in *Les textes de Nag Hammadi et le problème de leur classification: Actes du colloque tenu à Québec du 15 au 19 Septembre 1993*. Edited by Louis Painchaud and Anne Pasquier. Bibliothèque copte de Nag Hammadi, Études 3. Quebec: Les Presses de l'Université Laval, 1995.

–. *Rethinking "Gnosticism": An Argument for Dismantling a Dubious Category*. Princeton: Princeton University Press, 1996.

–. "Response to Papers by Karen King, Frederik Wisse, Michael Waldstein and Sergio La Porta." Pages 208–22 in *The Nag Hammadi Library After Fifty Years: Proceedings of the 1995 Society of Biblical Literature Commemoration*. Edited by John D. Turner and Anne McGuire. Nag Hammadi and Manichaean Studies 44. Leiden: Brill, 1997.

–. "Secrecy, Revelation, and Late Antique Demiurgical Myths." Pages 31–58 in *Rending the Veil: Concealment and Secrecy in the History of Religions*. Edited by Elliot R. Wolfson. Chappaqua, N. Y.: Seven Bridges Press, 1998.

Wilson, Robert McL. "The Early History of the Exegesis of Gen. 1:26." Pages 420–37 in *Editiones, Critica, Philologica, Biblica, Iudaica, Historica: Papers Presented to the Second International Conference on Patristic Studies, Held at Christ Church, Oxford, 1955*. Edited by Frank L. Cross and Kurt Aland. Texte und Untersuchungen zur Geschichte der altchristlichen Literatur 63. Studia Patristica 1. Berlin: Akademie-Verlag, 1957.

Wisse, Frederik. "The Sentences of Sextus: Introduction." Pages 295–327 in *Nag Hammadi Codices XI, XII, XIII*. Edited by Charles W. Hedrick. Nag Hammadi Studies 28. Leiden: Brill, 1990.

René Falkenberg

The Making of a Secret Book of John: Nag Hammadi Codex III in Light of New Philology

Codex III stands out among the Nag Hammadi Codices. It was received by scholars separately and earlier than the other twelve codices.[1] The production of its leather cover does not readily conform to any of the main scribal or codicological subgroups of the Nag Hammadi Codices.[2] The scribal hand of Codex III is unique compared to the other codices, and there is no scribal overlap with any of them.[3] The Coptic dialect of the Codex III texts is also closer to standard Sahidic than the rest of the Nag Hammadi texts.[4] While Codex III stands out with regard to these features, its contents do not: Four of its five texts are attested by parallel Coptic versions, not only in other Nag Hammadi Codices (NHC), but also in Papyrus Berolinensis 8502 (Berlin Codex). The first Codex III text, the *Apocryphon of John* in its short recension, is also found in the Berlin Codex.[5] The second text, the *Gospel of the Egyptians*, is found in NHC IV.[6] The third text, *Eugnostos the Blessed*, is found in NHC V; the fourth text, the

---

1 Codex III was therefore studied before any larger collection of Nag Hammadi scriptures appeared, cf. Togo Mina, "Le papyrus gnostique du Musee Copte," *VC* 2 (1948): 129–36; Jean Doresse, "Trois livres gnostiques inedits: Evangelie des Egyptiens. – Epître d'Eugnoste. – Sagesse de Jésus Christ," *VC* 2 (1948): 137–60. At first the codex was numbered I by Henri-Charles Puech and only later, in 1957, received its current number III, cf. James M. Robinson, ed., *The Facsimile Edition of the Nag Hammadi Codices: Codex III* (Leiden: Brill, 1976), ix. Today Codex III is preserved in the Coptic Museum in Cairo.
2 James M. Robinson, ed., *The Facsimile Edition of the Nag Hammadi Codices: Introduction* (Leiden: Brill, 1984), 85–86. Analysis of the cover and its lining suggests that quire, straps, cartonnage, and cover may have been manufactured at the same time, cf. Robinson, *The Facsimile Edition ... Codex III*, xi–xii. Most of the lining and the straps are lost and only small scraps of blank cartonnage remain inside the cover.
3 From a comparison of scribal hand and style, the Nag Hammadi codices can be categorized into three different groups: A: Codices I, VII, and XI; B: IV, V, VI, VIII, and IX; C: II and XIII; whereas the remaining codices, III, X, and XII, were inscribed by three other scribes, cf. Michael A. Williams, *Rethinking "Gnosticism": An Argument for Dismantling a Dubious Category* (Princeton N. J.: Princeton University Press, 1996), 242–43.
4 Wolf-Peter Funk, "The Linguistic Aspect of Classifying the Nag Hammadi Codices," in *Les textes de Nag Hammadi et le problem de leur classification: Actes du colloquetenu à Québec du 15 au 19 septembre 1993* (ed. Louis Painchaud and Anne Pasquier; BCNH.E 3; Québec: Les presses de l'Université Laval, 1995), 121–22, 136–39.
5 The long recension of *Ap. John* exists in NHC II and IV.
6 Even if the extant subtitle of *Gos. Eg.* is "The Holy Book of the Great Invisible Spirit" (69.18–20), *Gos. Eg.* is the most commonly used title and is taken from the first line of the colophon (69.6), restored as "The gospel of <the> Egyptians" (ⲡⲉⲩⲁⲅⲅⲉⲗⲓⲟⲛ <ⲛ̄>ⲛ̄ⲣ̄ⲙⲛ̄ⲕⲏⲙⲉ; lit. [without the emendation]: "The Egyptian gospel") in the *editio princeps* of Alexander Böhlig and Frederik Wisse, eds., *Nag Hammadi*

Wisdom of Jesus Christ, is found in the Berlin Codex; while the fifth and last text, the *Dialogue of the Savior*, is only attested in Codex III.

In earlier scholarship all texts of Codex III were viewed as later Coptic versions of Greek texts that originated from the first to the third centuries. Literary, source, and redaction criticism was, and still is, applied in an effort to retrieve the earliest possible form of the Nag Hammadi texts. In its focus on *variance* in wording between a given text's different witnesses (if available), this "old philology" approach is not contrary to "new philology."[7] In this sense, the task of "old" and "new" philology is closely related.[8] There is, however, a major difference between the two in the interpretation of the results: Traditional philology aims to strip off later textual redactions of a text in order to reach, as far as possible, the composition of its original author; new philology instead embraces these 'accretions' (variant readings) in order to study the work of its later redactors and scribes. In the present article I refer simply to 'the scribe' – even if that person probably did more with the texts than merely copying them into the codex. According to the approach of new philology, the scribe is also understood as an active reader and interpreter of the texts transmitted. But how did this scribe intend to present the codex to contemporary fellow readers and how were the codex texts interpreted at this final stage?

In order to answer such questions, the current study aims to analyse the work of the scribe of Codex III on the basis of the physical traces and textual variance to be detected from the production of the codex in the fourth or fifth century.[9] Inspired by the methodology of new philology I will first describe the physical evidence of Codex III and the handiwork of its scribe, and argue for a deliberate choice of the five texts and their sequence.[10] Second, I will analyse the prologue and epilogue of the

---

Codices III,2 and IV,2: The Gospel of the Egyptians (The Holy Book of the Great Invisible Spirit) (NHS 4; Leiden: Brill, 1975), 166.

7 In our earliest manuscripts exact one-to-one copies were not produced. The best example of *verbatim* consistency between two copies in the Nag Hammadi codices is found among the two versions of the long recension of *Ap. John*, but even if they are highly similar, many differences can be detected as well, cf. Michael Waldstein and Frederik Wisse, eds., *The Apocryphon of John: Synopsis of Nag Hammadi Codices II,1; III,1; and IV,1 with BG 8502,2* (NHMS 33; Leiden: Brill, 1995), 5–6. So, variance in wording of the Nag Hammadi texts is a given for the modern scholar.

8 One important difference, though, lies in the fact that "new philology" treats each and every manuscript as important in itself, whereas "old philology" mainly focuses on the end product, namely the best possible approximation to an original *Urtext*.

9 We do not know the exact production date of Codex III, but if the codex is to be associated with the other Nag Hammadi codices it is generally assumed that they all can be dated on the basis of the NHC VII cartonnage that provides the mid-fourth century (i.e. the year 348) as a secure *terminus post quem*, cf. John W. B. Barns, Gerald M. Browne, and John C. Shelton, *Nag Hammadi Codices: Greek and Coptic Papyri from the Cartonnage of the Covers* (NHS 16; Leiden: Brill, 1981), 3–5.

10 Roelof van den Broek, "[Review of] Nag Hammadi Codices III,2 and IV,2. The Gospel of the Egyptians (The Holy Book of the Great Invisible Spirit), eds. A. Böhlig, F. Wisse, P. Labib, Leiden: Brill 1975,"

first text (*Apocryphon of John*) in order to determine whether editorial activity reveals any central themes, and see if they are shared by some, or all, of the other Codex III texts, which would allow us to determine whether the scribe sought to amplify certain topics throughout the codex. Third, on the basis of these shared themes, I will see if the use of paratextual features (e.g. titles, *paragraphi cum corone*, and the colophon) attest a 'master plan' for the codex as a whole. Of special interest is the first title in the codex and also an intriguing colophon which may have been authored by the scribe of Codex III. Throughout this examination of the work of the scribe, the shared themes, the paratextual features, and the message of the colophon, I assume a fourth or fifth century date of manuscript production and a monastic context.

The Scribe's Handiwork and Text Disposition

Codex III originally consisted of a single quire of 78 leaves (= 156 pages) containing one front flyleaf with a blank recto (= p. A) and a title on its verso (= p. B), 147 numbered pages where p. 148 was left blank (= p. C), and some leaves that are missing.[11] Severe deterioration is attested at the beginning and end, and throughout the codex as well, but approximately half of the extant leaves (= 78 pages) are in a fairly well-preserved state.[12]

The cover, when opened, measures in height 26,0–26,2 cm and in width 34,5–35,0 cm.[13] The codex folios measure a height up to 25,8 cm (pp. 99/100), and at the centre of the quire a folio width of 28,7 cm (pp. 74–75), that is a page width of 14,4 cm; the beginning and end of the codex attest a page width of 15,6 cm (pp. 9/10) and

---

VC 31 (1977): 234, was the first to suggest that the choice of texts and their sequence in Codex III was deliberate.

11 Three back flyleafs (pp. D/E; F/G; H/I) and two stubs (pp. a/b; c/d) are missing, cf. Stephen Emmel, ed., *Nag Hammadi Codex III,5: The Dialogue of the Savior* (NHS 26; Leiden: Brill, 1984), 20–26. Additionally, pp. 1–4 are only witnessed by two small fragments, while six of the 74 inscribed leaves are entirely lost (pp. 19/20; 45/46; 47/48; 79/80; 109/110; 115/116). These may have become detached from the manuscript soon after its discovery. On the discovery and trafficking of the codex, cf. Robinson, *The Nag Hammadi Story, Volume I: The Discovery and Monopoly* (NHMS 86; Leiden: Brill, 2014), 66–70.

12 Until now only one of the lost fragments of the deteriorated leaves has been retrieved (almost half of pp. 145/146), cf. Stephen Emmel, "A Fragment of Nag Hammadi Codex III in the Beinecke Library: Yale Inv. 1784," *BASP* 17 (1980): 53–60. As a fortunate consequence of blotting and running ink (visible mainly in pp. 1–7, 128–147) large parts of the text of p. 1 are attested by mirror blotting on p. B, cf. Wolf-Peter Funk, "Die ersten Seiten des Codex III von Nag Hammadi," in *Divitiae Aegypti: Koptologische und verwandte Studien zu Ehren von Martin Krause* (ed. Cäcilia Fluck et al.; Wiesbaden: Reichert, 1995), 99–104. The mirror blotting on p. B can be seen in fig. 1.

13 Robinson, *The Facsimile Edition ... Codex III*, xi.

16,1 cm (pp. 143/144).[14] The text of the codex pages is inscribed in single columns that vary 20,1–22,6 cm in height and 10,2–12,0 cm in width.[15]

It is clear that the scribe did not copy the five Codex III texts from memory or dictation but from extant Coptic models in other codices. This is strongly suggested, for instance, by two occurrences of *homoioteleuton* which the scribe corrected.[16] It has been suggested that one of these corrections was made by another scribe but such a conclusion seems unwarranted.[17] Nevertheless, compared to the other Nag Hammadi codices, the number of scribal corrections in Codex III are striking (e.g. erasure, overwriting, adding of missing letters above the line).[18]

The scribe wrote with a skilled hand in a non-cursive unimodular Coptic script. A straight left column margin is maintained throughout the codex and also a relatively straight right margin, sometimes upheld with diples as linefillers. Not only the scribal hand, but also the scribe's disposition of lines, columns, and texts in the codex display considerable skill. This impression is supported by the data in Table 1, where the number of lines per page (single column) is displayed.

---

14 Robinson, *The Facsimile Edition ... Codex III*, xvii.

15 Emmel, *The Dialogue of the Savior*, 26. The column height and width for each Codex III text: *Ap. John* (20,0–20,5 × 10,2–8 cm); *Gos. Eg.* (21,5 × 10,5–11,3 cm); *Eugnostos* (21,5 × 10,3–11,0 cm); *Soph. Jes. Chr.* (21,5 × 9,8–10,8 cm); *Dial. Sav.* (21,5 × 10,6–11,6 cm), cf. Frederik Wisse, "Nag Hammadi Codex III: Codicological Introduction," in *Essays on the Nag Hammadi Texts: In Honour of Pahor Labib* (ed. Martin Krause; NHS 6; Leiden: Brill, 1975), 233. However, the precise column width is difficult to measure out since the right margin is not fully straight in the codex pages.

16 In p. 24 (line 17), the scribe marked and inserted three missing lines at the bottom of the page; and in p. 37 (line 14), erasure of wet ink letters indicates that the scribe instantly wrote new letters over the text erased. All in all some 13 possible occurrences of *homoioteleuton* can be found in the codex: 12.23 (ⲁⲩⲧⲟⲅⲉⲛⲛⲥ = Berlin Codex 34.15–18); 13.13 (ⲛⲓⲙ = Berlin Codex 35.15–16); 16.13 (ⲇⲩⲛⲁⲙⲓⲥ = Berlin Codex 39.13–16); 21.5 (ⲡⲛⲁ) = Berlin Codex 46.19–47.1); 24.17 (ⲇⲩⲛⲁⲙⲓⲥ = Berlin Codex 52.5–8); 37.14 (ⲡⲉ/ϣⲱⲡⲉ = Berlin Codex 72.12–13); 44.18 (ⲛⲣⲟⲟⲩⲧ ⲛⲅⲉⲛ[ⲉⲁ] = IV 55.4–[7]); 55.21 (ⲡⲁⲣⲑⲉⲛⲓⲕⲏ = IV 67.7–[9]); 83.10 (ⲛⲗⲟⲅⲟⲥ = V 11.14–20); 94.24 (ⲛⲕⲉⲟⲩⲁ ⲡⲉ = 72.3–6; Berlin Codex 84.13–17); 98.7 (ⲁⲧⲧⲁⲕⲟ = Berlin Codex 89.15–17); 105.14 (ⲟⲩⲟⲉⲓⲛ = Berlin Codex 100.15–17); 111.2 (ⲉⲕⲕⲗⲏⲥⲓⲁ = Berlin Codex 111.3–7). We need to notice that, since none of the remaining 11 instances of *homoioteleuton* causes any grammatical problems in the Coptic text, the missing text might already have been lacking in the scribe's exemplar(s).

17 Waldstein and Wisse, *The Apocryphon of John*, 2. But if we compare the hand of the inserted text in the bottom of p. 24 with the scribal hand of the codex, the corrected text seems to have been written by the codex scribe as well; see selected letters in the second line of the inserted passage at the bottom of the page (esp. ⲥ, ⲩ, and ⲉ) compared with p. 24, lines 19 (ⲩ) and 25 (ⲥ and ⲉ), cf. Robinson, *The Facsimile Edition ... Codex III*, 28.

18 Wisse, "Nag Hammadi Codex III," 236; Emmel, *The Dialogue of the Savior*, 29. This, on the one hand, could suggest a sloppy scribe; on the other hand, as Emmel rightly points out, "the quality of the final copy must be judged not by the number of his corrections, but by the number of errors which he failed to notice and correct," cf. Emmel, *The Dialogue of the Savior*, 30. A study of these scribal corrections remains a *desideratum*.

Table 1: Lines per page (l/p) in Codex III.[19]

	Ap. John 1.[1]–40.11	Gos. Eg. 40.12–69.20	Eugnostos 70.1–90.13	Soph. Jes. Chr. 90.14–119.18	Dial. Sav. 120.1–147.23
22 l/p				101	
23 l/p	13, 23, 25		72, 73, 74, 75, 83, 87, 88	96, 100, 103	123, 125, 126, 127, 128, 129, 130, 135, 137, 139
24 l/p	1, 5, 7, 8, 9, 11, 14, 15, 17, 21, 22, 27, 29, 31, 37	41, 42, 43, 51, 55	70, 71, 76, 77, 78, 81, 82, 84, 85, 86, 89	91, 92, 93, 94, 95, 99, 102, 104, 111, **112**, 117	121, 122, 124, 131, 132, 133, 136, 138, **140**, 141, **143**, **144**, **145**, **146**
25 l/p	6, 10, 16, 18, 24, 26, 28, 33, 35, 36, 39	50, 53, 54, 59, 61, **63**		97, 98, 105, 106, 107, 108, **113**, **114**, **118**	**134**, **142**
26 l/p	12, 30, 32, 34, 38	49, 52, 56, 57, 58, 60, **62**, **65**, **67**, **68**			120
27 l/p		**64**, **66**			
28 l/p		44			

From Table 1 it appears that the scribe preferred a codex average of 24–25 lines per page, but variance can be detected as well, up to a difference of seven lines if we compare p. 101 (22 l/p) with p. 44 (28 l/p). The most remarkable variance is found in the last seven pages of the *Gospel of the Egyptians*, where it seems as if the scribe inserted an increasing number of lines (pp. 62–68). The same phenomenon may be discernable at the end of both the *Wisdom of Jesus Christ* (pp. 112–118 [115/116 are lost]) and the *Dialogue of the Savior* (pp. 140–146), though not as clearly as in the *Gospel of the Egyptians*.[20] The scribe may here have sought to structure his writing so that texts began at the top of a page (i.e. *Eugnostos the Blessed* and *Dialogue of the Savior*) and ended at the bottom of a page (i.e. *Gospel of the Egyptians*, *Wisdom of Jesus Christ*, and *Dialogue of the Savior*).[21] The same tendency is indicated by the data given in Table 2 which displays the average number of letters per line in the Codex III pages.

---

19 Table 1 does not include pages 40, 69, 90, 119, and 147 which all contain elaborate titles, and it does not include deteriorated pages where entire lines are missing.

20 This could perhaps be due to the need to make room for the colophon at the end of *Gos. Eg.*, and may point in the direction of this colophon actually being added to the scribe's plan after he had started copying the Codex III texts.

21 The scribe was certainly not short of space since the last extant page (p. 148 = p. C) was blank and probably also the six following pages of the three lost back flyleafs, cf. note 11.

Table 2: Characters per line (ch/l) in each of the Codex III pages.[22]

	Ap. John 1–40	Gos. Eg. 40–69	Eugnostos 70–90	Soph. Jes. Chr. 90–119	Dial. Sav. 120–147
18 ch/l				96, 100, 104	
19 ch/l		50	72, 90	90, 92, 93, 98, 101, 102, 103, 106	
20 ch/l		52, 53, 54	70, 71, 73, 74, 75, 86	94, 97, 99, 105, 108, 111, **114, 117, 118, 119**	120, 122, 134
21 ch/l	18	51, **68, 69**	76, 77, 78, 81, 82, 84, 85, 87, 88, 89	91, 95, 107, **112, 113**	**141**
22 ch/l	5, 15	55, 56, 59, 60, 61, **66, 67**	83		135, 136, 138, **140, 144**
23 ch/l	12, 13, 14, 16, 17, 30, 36	49, **62, 64**			133, 139, **142**
24 ch/l	6, 9, 11, 31, 32, 34, 35	**63**			
25 ch/l	10, 29, 33	**65**			137

Again, crowded text is detected in the *Gospel of the Egyptians* where the scribe clearly uses more characters per line towards the end of the text (pp. 62–65); this crowding is not that visible in the very last pages (pp. 66–69), but possibly at this stage the scribe realised that it was no longer necessary to crowd the text in order to fit the end of the *Gospel of the Egyptians*.[23] Once more, a similar tendency may possibly be found in the last pages of the *Wisdom of Jesus Christ* (pp. 112–119) and the *Dialogue of the Savior* (pp. 140–142 and 144 [143 and 145–147 are too damaged]).[24]

---

22 Table 2 only includes pages where three or more lines are fully visible. Diples are included in the counting.

23 A good guess would be that the scribe here aimed to insert the colophon (69,6–17) at the end of *Gos. Eg.*

24 May Table 1 and 2 also provide us with information on the number of Coptic models (exemplars) from which the scribe copied? In Table 1 a change of exemplar could be indicated since the average lines per page in *Gos. Eg.* (≈ 25,5 l/p) is reduced two whole lines in *Eugnostos* (≈ 23,5 l/p). In Table 2 a similar change could be indicated since the average characters per line in *Ap. John* (≈ 23,5 ch/l) is reduced by one and a half letter in *Gos. Eg.* (≈ 22,0 ch/l), even if the column width is narrower in the former (10,2–8 cm) than in the latter (10,5–11,3 cm). However, the data still remain inconclusive: The first four pages of *Gos. Eg.* (pp. 40–43) follow the column height of *Ap. John* (20,0–20,5 cm), and it is only from p. 44, and throughout the rest of Codex III, that the column height is increased by 1,0–1,5 cm up to an average of 21,5 cm.

The scribe's rationale could have been purely aesthetic, but it could also point to a deliberate tripartite division of the codex.[25] If the latter is the case, we have three separate text blocks: [1] The *Apocryphon of John* begins the codex and ends in the middle of p. 40, where the *Gospel of the Egyptians* commences. The latter runs until the bottom of p. 69. The coupling of these two texts in Codex III may be due to the fact that they have many *mythologoumena* in common.[26] [2] *Eugnostos the Blessed* begins at the top of p. 70 and ends in the middle of p. 90, where the *Wisdom of Jesus Christ* takes over and runs until the bottom of p. 119. These two texts not only share *mythologoumena*, but are in fact almost identical, and seem to be placed together in Codex III for this reason.[27] [3] Finally we have the *Dialogue of the Savior* beginning at the top of p. 120 and ending at the bottom of p. 147.

To evaluate the hypothesis of three intentional text blocks we need to have a look at the other four codices where we find parallel versions of the Codex III texts (see Table 3).

Table 3: Codex III texts and their parallel versions in other codices.[28]

Codex III	Codex II	Codex IV	Codex V	Berlin Codex
				Gos. Mary
***Ap. John*, SR**	***Ap. John*, LR**	***Ap. John*, LR**		***Ap. John*, SR**
Gos. Eg.	*Gos. Thom.*	***Gos. Eg.***		
Eugnostos	*Gos. Phil.*		***Eugnostos***	
Soph. Jes. Chr.	*Hyp. Arch.*		*Apoc. Paul*	***Soph. Jes. Chr.***
Dial. Sav.	*Orig. World*		*1 Apoc. Jam.*	*Act Pet.*
	Exeg. Soul		*2 Apoc. Jam.*	
	Book Thom.		*Apoc. Adam*	

---

25 If we count the number of characters per page and its variance (e.g. p. 65 [26 l/p x 25 ch/l = 650 ch/p] and p. 100 [23 l/p x 18 ch/l ≈ 410 ch/p]), it is easy to see that a deliberate structure and placement of texts in the codex certainly was within the capability of the codex scribe. At least we need to notice that the codex potentially could be structured as the scribe pleased.

26 Böhlig and Wisse, *Nag Hammadi Codices III,2 and IV,2*, 32–34; and also the many mythological names shared only by *Ap. John* and *Gos. Eg.* in Codex III; e.g. Adamas, Barbelon, Belias, Eleleth, and Seth, cf. Régine Charron, *Concordance des textes de Nag Hammadi. Le codex III* (BCNH.C 3; Sainte-Foy, Québec: Les presses de l'Université Laval, 1995), 506–19.

27 It seems *Soph. Jes. Chr.* is a rewriting of *Eugnostos* into a dialogue between Christ and his disciples. Certain parts of *Eugnostos* were not reused in *Soph. Jes. Chr.*, but as much as two thirds of the text of *Soph. Jes. Chr.* correspond almost verbatim with *Eugnostos*.

28 In a similar list, Williams also includes NHC XIII, since it earlier was suggested (by Yvonne Janssens) that *Ap. John* was the first, and now lost, text of that codex, cf. Michael A. Williams, "Interpreting the Nag Hammadi Library as Collection(s) in the History of 'Gnosticism(s),'" in *Les textes de Nag Hammadi et le problem de leur classification: Actes du colloquetenu à Québec du 15 au 19 septembre 1993* (ed. Louis Painchaud and Anne Pasquier; BCNH.É 3; Québec: Les presses de l'Université Laval, 1995), 20–21. Due to the speculative nature of this suggestion, Codex XIII is not included here.

As for the first text block (*Apocryphon of John* and *Gospel of the Egyptians*), a similar coupling and sequence is found in Codex IV, even though it has the long recension (LR) of the *Apocryphon of John*, whereas Codex III has the short recension (SR).[29] Apparently our scribe was not the only one who felt that the two texts made a nice pairing.

The two texts of the second block (*Eugnostos the Blessed* and *Wisdom of Jesus Christ*) are not attested together elsewhere, but since these texts are to a large extent identical, it is evident why they were placed next to each other in Codex III. A similar pairing of two related texts is attested in Codex V where the identical titled apocalypses of James are found together (*1 Apoc. Jam. and 2 Apoc. Jam.*) and also in Codex II where the *Hypostasis of the Archons* (*Hyp. Arch.*) and the untitled text *On the Origin of the World* (*Orig. World*) are placed side by side.[30] The best example in the fourth or fifth century of such an assemblage of similar texts is, of course, the grouping of the gospels in the New Testament.

The third text block consists only of the *Dialogue of the Savior*, which is only witnessed in Codex III. The reason why the scribe included it may be that it is of the same revelation dialogue genre as both the preceding text (*Wisdom of Jesus Christ*) and the first text in the codex (*Apocryphon of John*). This genre is characterised by a discourse between Christ and his disciples before or after the resurrection. In the *Apocryphon of John*, John is the single interlocutor, whereas in the *Wisdom of Jesus Christ* and the *Dialogue of the Savior* we find a larger group of disciples in conversation with the Saviour. Two of these revelation dialogues are also found together in the Berlin Codex, where the short recension of the *Apocryphon of John* is followed by the *Wisdom of Jesus Christ*. At the end of that version of the *Apocryphon of John*, we find a sentence that is missing from the long recension, which may shed light on why the two texts were paired in that codex: "I will teach you (pl.) about what will happen" (Berlin Codex 76.5–6).[31] Here, in the *Apocryphon of John*, Christ promises not only John, but all his disciples, that he will give another teaching in the future. In the context of the Berlin Codex this sentence makes good sense, since the following text (*Wisdom of Jesus Christ*) can be understood to constitute this teaching.

The parallel sentence at the end of the *Apocryphon of John* in Codex III also promises future teaching, but the two following texts (*Gospel of the Egyptians* and *Eugnostos the Blessed*) are not revelation dialogues. For this we have to wait until the last two texts of the codex (*Wisdom of Jesus Christ* and *Dialogue of the Savior*). This

---

29 On the differences between the long and short recensions of *Ap. John*, cf. Waldstein and Wisse, *The Apocryphon of John*, 7–8.

30 For similarities between *Hyp. Arch.* and *Orig. World*, cf. Francis T. Fallon, *The Enthronement of Sabaoth: Jewish Elements in Gnostic Creation Myths* (NHS 10; Leiden: Brill, 1978), 7, *passim*.

31 Translated from Coptic text in Bernard Barc and Wolf-Peter Funk, *Le livre des secrets de Jean: Recension brève (NH III,1 et BG,2)* (BCNH.T 35; Québec: Les presses de l'Université Laval, 2012), 170. All translations in the present contribution are my own.

could be the reason why the parallel sentence in Codex III is formulated differently from the one in the Berlin Codex: "I will [teach yo]u (pl.), once again (ⲟⲛ), about what is coming" (Codex III 39.21–22).[32] The adverb ⲟⲛ ("again/further" < πάλιν) may be taken to signal that the promise of such a future teaching is not fulfilled immediately after the *Apocryphon of John* (in *Gospel of the Egyptians* and *Eugnostos the Blessed*), but only further on in the codex in the two other revelation dialogues (in *Wisdom of Jesus Christ* and *Dialogue of the Savior*).

The two texts that, at first sight, do not seem to fit into a deliberate codex disposition are the *Gospel of the Egyptians* and *Eugnostos the Blessed*, which separate the first two text blocks, i.e. the first text block (*Apocryphon of John* and *Gospel of the Egyptians*) from the second (*Eugnostos the Blessed* and *Wisdom of Jesus Christ*). Upon closer inspection these two text blocks are actually strongly held together by the colophon at the end of the *Gospel of the Egyptians*, where a person called "Eugnostos" is mentioned (see below). The scribe most likely assumed this person to be the same as the implied author of the following text, *Eugnostos the Blessed*.

So, there are strong indications that the sequence of texts in Codex III follows a deliberate and coherent pattern, where the *Apocryphon of John* is paired with the *Gospel of the Egyptians* since they share a similar mythological system. The third text follows since the scribe, in the colophon at the end of the *Gospel of the Egyptians*, mentions a person called "Eugnostos" who may have been thought to be identical with the author of the following text, *Eugnostos the Blessed*. The fourth text is chosen since the *Wisdom of Jesus Christ* appears to develop the philosophical system of *Eugnostos the Blessed* even further, and since the *Apocryphon of John* earlier promised to give his disciples additional teaching. As the fifth text, the *Dialogue of the Savior* simply continues and concludes that teaching.

Additionally, Table 3 shows that there was an inclination to place the *Apocryphon of John* at the beginning of a codex, as is the case in NHC II, III, and IV. This might be an indication of its special role in the overall text disposition of these three codices in the sense that it prominently presents themes that are central to all of the codex texts.[33] As we will see below, the *Apocryphon of John* as the first and longest text in Codex III seems indeed to introduce themes that are central to the four other texts and thus to the codex as a whole.

---

32 Translated from the Coptic text in Barc and Funk, *Le livre des secrets de Jean*, 171.

33 In Codex V, *Eugnostos* is also placed as the first text. The other four codex texts are each entitled an "apocalypse" (one of Paul, two of James, and one of Adam) and deal mainly with the transmission between earthly and heavenly existence. Because *Eugnostos* only deals with the heavenly world, the scribe of Codex V might have preferred it as the first codex text, since *Eugnostos* thus comes to represent the ultimate goal strived for in the four texts following.

Shared Themes

I will focus on the common ground and main themes in the prologue and epilogue of the *Apocryphon of John* in comparison with the other four texts. As such the analysis can be no more than a *prolegomenon* to a full study of the common themes of the Codex III texts.[34]

The prologue of the *Apocryphon of John* closely ties in with material from the canonical gospels, especially the Gospel of John, which forms the basis, more or less, for four specific questions raised at the beginning of the *Apocryphon of John* to be unfolded and answered in that text as well as in the other Codex III texts.

In the epilogue of the *Apocryphon of John*, the Saviour's teaching is secretly given to John and the disciples and mainly concerns the immovable race of the elect and the fallen state of the created world. When comparing the epilogue of the *Apocryphon of John* in the two extant versions of the short recension, it becomes clear that the Codex III version is directed more towards describing an acute problem with femininity than the version in the Berlin Codex. Indeed, the meaning of the correlation between the elect race and the deficiency of femininity is, arguably, the most central theme in Codex III.

Prologue of the *Apocryphon of John*: Four Johannine Questions

At the very beginning of the first Codex III text we hear that "John, the [br]other [of James ... s]ons [of Zebed]ee, went up to the Temple" (1.2–4), where a Pharisee claims that Jesus "has lead you (pl.) astray" and "turned you (pl.) away from the [trad]itions of your fathers" (1.11–15).[35] John responds emotionally to the accusation: "An[d when] I heard this, I turned away from [the Te]mple to a mountainous place [... I] grieved greatly" (1.15–18).[36] Thereafter he poses four questions central not only to the *Apocryphon of John*, but also to the other texts in Codex III.

---

34 A full analysis would not only need to compare the five texts with each other, but also with the different versions of these texts in the other codices.

35 Translated from Coptic text in Barc and Funk, *Le livre des secrets de Jean*, 61. The gospel connection is not Johannine here, but rather synoptic since the post-resurrection setting is the Temple (e.g. Luke 24:53) and the teaching of Christ is presented as opposed to Jewish tradition (e.g. Matt 15:2). Remarkable here is the very last sentence in Codex III at the end of *Dial. Sav.*, where it is explicitly stated, almost as a correction to the charge of the Pharisee in *Ap. John* 1.11 (Christ "has lead you astray"), that "I say to [you: ...] that you (pl.) do not lead astray [your] spirits and your souls" (147.20–22; text translated from Coptic text in Létourneau, *Le Dialogue du Sauveur (NH III,5): Texte établi, traduit et présenté* (BCNH.T 29; Québec: Les presses de l'Université Laval, 2003), 104.

36 Translated from Coptic text in Barc and Funk, *Le livre des secrets de Jean*, 63. At this unspecified "mountainous place" John receives the revelatory speech from Christ during the rest of *Ap. John*.

Codex III (1.19–[?])[37]	Berlin Codex (20.8–19)
How [... was] he sent to the world by [his] Father [... ...] we will g[o to? ... ...]	[1] How was the Saviour appointed; [2] why was he sent to the world by his Father who sent him; [3] who is his Father; and [4] how is that realm we will go to? He said to us that this realm received the form of that incorruptible realm; he did not teach us about that one, of what sort it is.

These four questions partially resonate with the Gospel of John.[38] At least the first two questions in the *Apocryphon of John* seem easily answered by that Gospel: [1] "How was the Saviour appointed"? Even if an explicit election of Christ is absent in John, the question could allude to the Johannine prologue where the unique status of Christ as God's own creative Word (John 1:1–3) and only Son (1:14) is pointed out. [2] "Why was he sent to the world by his Father who sent him"? This question is answered directly in the Gospel of John where it is said that God gives his Son to provide believers with eternal life, and to save the world (3:16–17). In the overall context of Codex III, these two questions concern a Christian salvation history where Christ, by divine election in primordial time, was sent to the world for the salvation of humankind. A broader presentation of salvation history is important in order to understand not only the *Apocryphon of John* but also the rest of Codex III, since all the texts deal with issues of protology, cosmogony, anthropogony, and eschatology.[39]

Such a theological mountain places are entailed in the gospels in order to stress the elevated status of the divine teaching (e.g. Matt 17:1 par.; 28:16), which also is the case with mountains mentioned in the epilogue of *Gos. Eg.* (68.2–3, 12–14) and the prologue of *Soph. Jes. Chr.* (90.19–91.2; 91.18–20). A mountain place is perhaps mentioned in *Dial. Sav.* (123.1–2) as well: ⲡⲧⲟ[ⲟⲩ ⲡⲉⲉⲓ]ⲙⲁ in Emmel, *The Dialogue of the Savior*, 46 (in note); however, reconstructed as ⲡⲧⲟ[ⲡⲟⲥ· ⲡ]ⲙⲁ in Pierre Létourneau, *Le Dialogue du Sauveur*, 56.

37 Both versions translated from Coptic text in Barc and Funk, *Le livre des secrets de Jean*, 62–63. Since the prologue of *Ap. John* in Codex III is so fragmentary we must here rely on the parallel in the Berlin Codex which, actually, does not readily apply to the methodology of new philology. However, since the passage also is attested in the two longer versions of *Ap. John* (II 1.21–28; IV 2.1–[?]) we can be sure that it, in whatever form, was part of our text.

38 It is commonly held that *Ap. John* functions to complete the teachings given in the canonical Gospel, cf. John Turner, "The Johannine Legacy: The Gospel and the *Apocryphon of John*," in *The Legacy of John: Second-Century Reception of the Fourth Gospel* (ed. Tuomas Rasimus; NovTSup 132; Leiden: Brill, 2010), 139, cf. his note 39 where Turner also refers to Karen L. King, Titus Nagel, and Zlatko Pleše.

39 We even have the "salvation plan" (ⲟⲓⲕⲟⲛⲟⲙⲓⲁ) explicitly mentioned in the prologue of *Soph. Jes. Chr.* (91.4, 9; 92.5–6) and possibly in the *incipit* of *Gos. Eg.* (40.12), if we follow the translation of Régine Charron, "Livre sacré du Grand Esprit invisible (NH III,2; IV,2)," in *Écrits gnostiques: La bibliothèque de Nag Hammadi* (ed. Jean-Pierre Mahé and Paul-Hubert Poirier; BPl 538; Paris: Gallimard, 2007), 523. The reason for preferring the restoration of Charron to the one of Böhlig and Wisse is that they unnecessarily emend the text: ⲡϫⲱⲱⲙⲉ ⲛ̄{ⲧ}ⲉ̈[ⲓⲉ]ⲣ[ⲁ ⲛ̄ⲧⲉ ⲛ̄ⲣⲙ̄ⲛ̄ⲕⲏⲙⲉ] ("The [holy] book [of the Egyptians]), cf. Böhlig and Wisse, *Nag Hammadi Codices III,2 and IV,2*, 52.

The following question – [3] "who is his Father"? – is also dealt with in the Gospel of John, but there theology is mainly entailed in order to defend the authority of the Christ figure.[40] So, theology (the Father) in John chiefly aims to shed light on the Christ figure (the Son) and, accordingly, we find no interest in explaining the deeper nature of the fatherly godhead there. However, all Codex III texts, with the exception of the *Dialogue of the Savior*, transcend these scanty descriptions of the godhead in the Gospel of John, since they present, in negative discourses, lengthy sections on the very nature of God.[41] So, the answer to the question of who the Father is (stating what he is not) is central to the first four texts of Codex III.

On the final question – [4] "how is that realm we will go to?" – the Gospel of John is less specific, even if it is stated in the *Apocryphon of John* that the Saviour has already informed his disciples about the nature of this world ("He said to us that this realm received the form of that incorruptible realm"). Nevertheless, a parallel may be found in the Gospel of John in the saying about the heavenly dwelling places in the house of the Father (14:2–3).[42] But still the John of the *Apocryphon of John* complains about the lack of teaching ("he did not teach us about that one [= the incorruptible realm], of what sort it is."). Indeed, wording associated with "incorruption" as related to the nature of the divine world and also the notion of "realm" (ⲁⲓⲱⲛ) as a designation of heavenly dwellings or entities are attested extensively throughout Codex III.[43]

The heavenly world, both referred to as a single realm and as multiple realms, is an important and shared theme of Codex III. All the texts concern the hierarchies of the divine world, from the godhead down to the lower angels, as well as the heavenly dwelling places of the divine entities together with the elect ones. The nomenclature of such dwellings, angelic inhabitants, and chosen ones could easily relate,

---

40 Especially in John 5–8 ('the court speeches') where Christ, owing to his divine sonship, almost programmatically is charged of making himself equal with the godhead (John 5:18), cf. also the Christological use of the ἐγώ εἰμι-formula (e.g. 8:24, 28, 58), well-known as a self-designation of God in the Septuagint (e.g. Deut 32:39; Isa 41:4).

41 Cf. *Ap. John* (3.[?]–7.[12] = Berlin Codex 22.[17]–27.4); *Gos. Eg.* (40.[13]–41.7); *Eugnostos* (71.13–73.8); and *Soph. Jes. Chr.* (94.5–96.3).

42 The Gospel of John does not operate with the divine world as a "realm" but rather as a "kingdom" (cf. 3:3–5; 18:36).

43 ⲁⲓⲱⲛ is found 106 times in Codex III: 35 in *Ap. John*; 38 in *Gos. Eg.*; 21 in *Eugnostos*; eleven in *Soph. Jes. Chr.*; and once in *Dial. Sav.*; words related to "incorruption" (ⲁⲧⲧⲁⲕⲟ, ⲁⲫⲑⲁⲣⲧⲟⲥ and the like) are attested 69 times: eight in *Ap. John*; 36 in *Gos. Eg.*; eleven in *Eugnostos*; 13 in *Soph. Jes. Chr.*; and once in *Dial. Sav.*, cf. Charron, *Concordances*. Compared to the New Testament, αἰών appears rather frequently with some 172 occurrences, where two thirds (approx. 112) attest a temporal use (e.g. "forever"), whereas a spatial or personalised use is less common, cf., however, Heb 1:2; 1 Tim 1:17; Rev 15:3 (spatial use); and perhaps Eph 2:2; 3:9; Col 1:25 (as divine entities); ἄφθαρτος and ἀφθαρσία are found 14 times in the letters of the New Testament but never in a spatial use, cf. John R. Kohlenberger III, Edward W. Goodrick, and James A. Swanson, *The Greek-English Concordance to the New Testament* (ZGRS; Grand Rapids, Mich.: Zondervan, 1997).

somehow, to the self-understanding of the scribe and the intended readers of Codex III and therefore, I will argue, to a monastic background. In fourth- and fifth-century Egypt, the notion of 'living an angelic life' was often applied to monks and nuns.[44] The possibility of such a context for Codex III is strengthened by the fact that "elect ones" and "monks" are explicitly mentioned in the prologue of the *Dialogue of the Savior*.[45]

Epilogue of the *Apocryphon of John*: Secrecy, Race of Elect, Deficiency of Femininity

Immediately after the Saviour has finished the teaching of the revelation dialogue, he gives John instruction to write down his words (here: "the myster[y]") and transmit them to the other disciples (here: "your fellow spirits") and, by implication, also to the readers of Codex III.

Codex III (39.14–24)[46]	Berlin Codex (75.15–76.9)
[I tell the]se things to you	But I am telling these things to you
so that you may writ[e them down and	so that you may write them down and
give th]em to your fellow spirits [secretly,	give them to your fellow spirits in secret,
for this] is the myster[y of the]	for this mystery belongs to the
immovable [race] ([ⲛ̄ⲧⲅⲉⲛⲉⲁ ⲉ]ⲧⲉⲙⲉⲥⲕⲓⲙ):	immovable race (ⲛⲁⲧⲅⲉⲛⲉⲁ ⲉⲧⲉⲙⲁⲥⲕⲓⲙ ⲡⲉ).
This mother came bef[ore me another ti]me,	But the mother came another time before me.
as for [every]thing [she did]	Once more, this is what she did
in the world, she was [establish]ing[47]	in the world: She established
the deficiency (ⲉⲩⲥⲧⲉⲣⲏⲙⲁ);	the seed (ⲥⲡⲉⲣⲙⲁ).
I will [teach yo]u, once again,	I will teach you
about what (fem.) is coming (ⲉⲧⲉⲧⲛ̄ⲛⲏⲟⲩ),	about what will happen,
for [I gave you these things] to write down	for I gave you these things to write down
and keep [se]curely.	and keep securely.

---

44 A fine introductory study on the monastic *bios angelikos* is found in Ellen Muehlberger, "Ambivalence about the Angelic Life: The Promise and Perils of an Early Christian Discourse of Asceticism," *JECS* 16 (2008): 447–78.

45 "But when I came, I laid open the way and taught them about the Passover that they will pass through, namely the elect ones (ⲥⲱⲧⲡ) and the monks (ⲙⲟⲛⲟⲭⲟⲥ)" (120.21–26); "You are the monks' (ⲙⲟⲛⲟⲭⲟⲥ) thought and total freedom from anxiety. Again, [hear] us just as you heard your chosen ones (ⲥⲱⲧⲡ) who by your sacrifice enter because of their [go]od works" (121.16–22); both passages translated from the Coptic text in Létourneau, *Le Dialogue du Sauveur*, 50–54.

46 Both texts translated from Coptic text in Barc and Funk, *Le livre des secrets de Jean*, 168–71.

47 The Coptic verb used in both versions is ⲧⲁϩⲟ ⲉⲣⲁⲧ⸗, "set on feet, make to stand, establish," in line with ἱστάναι and ἀνορθοῦν ("set up again, restore, rebuild"; LSJ 147b), cf. Walter E. Crum, *A Coptic Dictionary* (Oxford: Clarendon Press, 1939), 456a–b. However, most translators prefer to translate ⲧⲁϩⲟ ⲉⲣⲁⲧ⸗ with "rectify, correct, instruct" (or the like), e.g. Waldstein and Wisse, *The Apocryphon of John*,

In the first sentence the Saviour stresses, in both versions, that his teaching is to be given "[secretly (or: hidden, ⲉ̄ⲛⲟⲩⲡⲉⲑⲏⲡ̄)]" since it is characterised as a "myster[y] (ⲙⲩⲥⲧⲏⲣⲓ[ⲟⲛ])," which is in agreement with the very title of the *Apocryphon of John*: "The Secret Book (ⲁⲡⲟⲕⲣⲩⲫⲟⲛ) of John."[48] Thus is created an overall atmosphere of secrecy which can be detected in all five Codex III texts.[49] This vocabulary also seems related to a ritual, and even baptismal, setting.[50] In fact, a wide range of ritualistic formulae of praise and prayer are found throughout all five texts.[51]

However, the main theme here is not secrecy, but rather the elect race and the identity of the mother figure. Even if the *Apocryphon of John* in Codex III is riddled with lacunae, it seems that "the myster[y]" given to John *concerns* "[the] immovable [race]" ([ⲛ̄ⲧⲅⲉⲛⲉⲁ ⲉ]ⲧⲉⲙⲉⲥⲕⲓⲙ).[52] The Berlin Codex, on the other hand, uses a subjective, rather than objective, genitive (i.e. ⲡⲁⲧⲅⲉⲛⲉⲁ ⲉⲧⲉⲙⲁⲥⲕⲓⲙ ⲡⲉ), hence emphasising that everything John writes down ("this mystery") he gives to his fellow disciples since it rightfully belongs to them. Thus the disciples, in the Berlin Codex, are to be counted among the elect of "the immovable race" and "the seed (ⲥⲡⲉⲣⲙⲁ)" earlier brought forth by "the mother" who is mentioned just before the present passage:

224; Barc and Funk, *Le livre des secrets de Jean*, 365. Here we need to notice, that the short recension of *Ap. John* prefer to use ⲧⲁϩⲟ ⲉⲣⲁⲧ⸗, where the parallels in the long recension uses ⲥⲟⲟϩⲉ ("reprove, correct"; Crum, *Coptic Dictionary*, 380b), cf. Michael Allen Williams, *The Immovable Race: A Gnostic Designation and the Theme of Stability in Late Antiquity* (NHS 29; Leiden: Brill, 1985), 122. Therefore the choice of translation is deeply dependent on the context where ⲧⲁϩⲟ ⲉⲣⲁⲧ⸗ occurs in Codex III or the Berlin Codex, cf. note 55.

48 In the superscript title (p. B.1–2) and subscript title (40.10–11); translated from Coptic text in Barc and Funk, *Le livre des secrets de Jean*, 61, 171.

49 ⲙⲩⲥⲧⲏⲣⲓⲟⲛ: *Ap. John* (27.16–17; 30.26; 39.17–18; 40.5); *Gos. Eg.* (44.1–2; 51.24; 63.12); *Soph. Jes. Chr.* (91.8–9); *Dial. Sav.* (128.6; 143.8). ϩⲱⲡ (ϩⲏⲡ†): *Ap. John* (25.18; 39.[17]); *Gos. Eg.* (44.2; 52.1; 63.15; 69.8); *Eugnostos* (74.15); *Soph. Jes. Chr.* (97.3); *Dial. Sav.* (134.17).

50 In *Gos. Eg.*, baptism (ⲃⲁⲡⲧⲓⲥⲙⲁ) is associated with the body of Seth given "secretly (ⲉ̄ⲛⲟⲩⲙⲩⲥⲧⲏⲣⲓⲟⲛ) through a virgin for the begetting of the holy ones by means of invisible secret (ϩⲏⲡ) symbols (ⲥⲩⲙⲃⲟⲗⲟⲛ) in reconciliation of the world with the world by rejecting the world" (63.10–17); "this one (= the godhead) whose name came [forth] in an in[visible] symbol (ⲥⲩⲙⲃⲟⲗⲟⲛ), [a] secret (ϩⲏⲡ) in[visible my]stery ([ⲙⲩ]ⲥⲧⲏⲣⲓⲟⲛ)" (43.24–44.3); both translations from Coptic text in Böhlig and Wisse, *Nag Hammadi Codices III,2 and IV,2*, 66, 144. A related baptismal use of ⲥⲩⲙⲃⲟⲗⲟⲛ may be found in *Soph. Jes. Chr.* (117.8–118.3 = Berlin Codex 123.2–124.9), cf. René Falkenberg, "Matthew 28:16–20 in the Nag Hammadi Library. Reception of the Great Commission in the *Sophia of Jesus Christ*," in *Mark and Matthew II: Comparative Readings: Reception History, Cultural Hermeneutics, and Theology* (ed. Eve-Marie Becker and Anders Runesson; WUNT 304; Tübingen: Mohr Siebeck, 2013), 100–2.

51 Giving praise or glory (†ⲥⲙⲟⲩ, †ⲉⲟⲟⲩ or the like): 13 times in *Ap. John*; eight times in *Gos. Eg.*; eight times in *Dial. Sav.*, cf. Charron, *Concordance*. Prayers ending with an "amen" are found in *Gos. Eg.* (55.11–16) and *Dial. Sav.* (121.5–122.1). The conclusion of *Gos. Eg.* and its colophon is marked with "amen" three times (69.5, 17, 20), and also the end of *Soph. Jes. Chr.* (119.17). Longer proclamations of joy are mainly found in *Eugnostos* (75.23–76.10; 81.12–21; 89.15–90.3) and *Soph. Jes. Chr.* (100.4–16; 105.19–106.4; 113.19–114.5).

52 I.e., interpreting the restored ⲛ̄ⲧⲅⲉⲛⲉⲁ as an objective genitive.

"Now, the fatherly mother, rich in mercy, is the blessed one who takes form in her seed (cпєрма)" (Berlin Codex 75.10–13).[53]

In the Berlin Codex, the mother seems to be either Barbelō, the androgynous spouse (the aforementioned "fatherly mother") of the highest god, or perhaps the Wisdom figure.[54] But in Codex III we have to rule Barbelō out and instead vote for Wisdom as this mother figure, since she is the one who manifests "the deficiency (ᵧⲥⲧⲉⲣⲏⲙⲁ)" instead of "the seed" that the Berlin Codex attests. Deficient nature in the *Apocryphon of John* is, in fact, closely connected to that Wisdom figure.[55] Wisdom is, in both versions of the *Apocryphon of John*, responsible for bringing forth the evil world creator in the so-called myth of Wisdom's fall.[56]

In the following sentence (dealt with above), the masculine gender in the Berlin Codex's "I will teach you about *what* will happen (ⲡⲉⲧⲛⲁϣⲱⲡⲉ)," is in Codex III stated in the feminine: "I will [teach yo]u, once again, about *what* is coming (or: *she* who is coming) (ⲉⲧⲉⲧⲛ̄ⲛⲏⲟⲩ)." Above we concluded that the *Apocryphon of John*, in both versions, here refers to the following revelation dialogue, the *Wisdom of Jesus Christ*, and it is implied that John is the composer of that text too ("for [I gave you (= John) these things] to write down and and keep [se]curely"). Also the very title of the *Wisdom of Jesus Christ* strengthens such a connection to the epilogue of the *Apocryphon of John*, especially in the Codex III version, since the title presents the same mother figure: "The Wisdom (ⲥⲟⲫⲓⲁ) of Jesus (Christ)."[57] Accordingly, comparing the epilogue of the *Apocryphon of John* in the Berlin Codex version with that in Codex III, the latter seems more interested in femininity ("This mother" and "what [fem.] is coming") and adds a stronger connection than the former to the fallen Wisdom figure, owing to the emphasis on her creation of deficient nature ("she was [establish]ing the deficiency").

This might also explain the peculiarity that the partner of the godhead in Codex III is not called Barbelō (ⲃⲁⲣⲃⲏⲗⲱ, fem.) as in the Berlin Codex, but rather Barbelon (ⲃⲁⲣⲃⲏⲗⲟⲛ, Greek neut.),[58] which is odd since the neuter gender does not exist in

---

53 Translated from Coptic text in Barc and Funk, *Le livre des secrets de Jean*, 168.
54 The expression "fatherly mother" would point to Barbelō since she belongs to the masculine pantheon of Father (the godhead), Mother (Barbelō), and Son (the Saviour), cf. the triadic formulae in Berlin Codex 21.19–22.1; 35.19. Another indication of Barbelō as the mother figure in the Berlin Codex is the fact that this triadic formula is associated with the revelation of "the seed (cпєрма) of Seth" (Berlin Codex 35.13–36.5; translated from the Coptic text in Barc and Funk, *Le livre des secrets de Jean*, 96–97).
55 Strengthened by a close parallel earlier in *Ap. John*: "... so that our fellow sister who is li[ke u]s, Wisdom (ⲥⲟⲫⲓⲁ), will establish (or: restore/rectify; cf. note 47) her deficienc[ies] (ᵧⲥⲧⲉⲣⲏⲙⲁ)" (Codex III 25.20–22); translated from Coptic text in Barc and Funk, *Le livre des secrets de Jean*, 131.
56 Codex III 14.9–16.11; Berlin Codex 36.16–39.10.
57 This subscript title of *Soph. Jes. Chr.* (119.18) is abbreviated in comparison with the *incipit* title (90.14): "The Wisdom of Jesus Christ (ⲧⲥⲟⲫⲓⲁ ⲛ̄ⲓ̄ⲥ̄ ⲡⲉⲭⲣ̄ⲥ̄)"; translated from the Coptic text in Catherine Barry, *La Sagesse de Jésus-Christ (BG,3; NH III,4): Texte établi, traduit et commenté* (BCNH.T 20; Québec: Les presses de l'Université Laval, 1993), 116, 160.
58 I.e. eleven times in *Ap. John*; three times in *Gos. Eg.*, cf. Charron, *Concordance*.

Coptic. An explanation is perhaps that the scribe of Codex III, by retaining the Greek neuter, wanted to disassociate the spouse of God (roaming the higher levels of existence) with the deficiency of femininity brought forth by Wisdom in the lower spheres of creation.

Editorial activity in Codex III in connection with the deficiency of femininity is not only detected in the epilogue of the *Apocryphon of John*. Elsewhere in that text we find two separate descriptions of Wisdom's fall (14.14–19; 15.4–9), where only one of these exists in the Berlin Codex parallel (37.12–18). In Codex III's version of the *Wisdom of Jesus Christ* we also find a similar depiction of the fall (114.14–18), which is absent from the version in the Berlin Codex.[59]

In all five Codex III texts, a shared theme does not alone concern the fallen Wisdom, but primarily the outcome of her fall, "the deficiency."[60] In Codex III, deficient nature is also related to a generally negative view of "the female (ᴄϩιмє)" or "femininity (ⲙⲛⲧⲥϩιмє)."[61] This presentation of femininity functions to heuristically divide the heavenly from the earthly, which in contemporary religio-philosophical discourse is often presented in terms of the polarisation of gender (masculinity vs. femininity, or even genderlessness vs. androgynity [double gender]), of ontology (being vs. becoming), and of ethical behaviour, in terms of emotional stability (rest) vs. changeability (movement). This last dualistic pair brings us back to "[the] immovable [race]" from the epilogue of the *Apocryphon of John* in the Codex III version.

I argued above that the Saviour's teaching ("the myster[y]") given to John *concerns* "[the] immovable [race]" in Codex III, rather than *belongs* to that race as is the case in the Berlin Codex (that is the objective vs. subjective genitive). Thus, "the myster[y of (or: concerning) the] immovable [race]" in Codex III is given a more explicit content in the following description of the dire status of femininity (i.e. "This mother" [= fallen

---

59 Besides these three passages of Wisdom's fall, we find three other negative descriptions of Wisdom in Codex III, cf. 25.21–22 (*Ap. John*); 57.1 (*Gos. Eg.*); 107.24–108.1 (*Soph. Jes. Chr.*). The Wisdom figure is found in the first four of the Codex III texts: Four times in *Ap. John*; twice in *Gos. Eg.*; twelve times in *Eugnostos*; thirteen times in *Soph. Jes. Chr.* (cf. Charron, *Concordance*). In most of these instances, Wisdom is paired with other divine figures from the highest pantheon and therefore portrayed positively there.

60 The "deficiency" (ϩⲩⲥⲧⲉⲣⲏⲙⲁ and ϣⲱⲱⲧ [nouns] or ϣⲧⲁ [verb]), privative expressions included (e.g. ⲁⲧϣⲱⲱⲧ): Nine times in *Ap. John*; three times in *Gos. Eg.*; three times in *Eugnostos*; six times in *Soph. Jes. Chr.*; four times in *Dial. Sav.* (cf. Charron, *Concordance*).

61 E.g. in *Eugnostos* (85.7–9): "And thus appeared the deficiency of femininity" (translated from Coptic text in Anne Pasquier, *Eugnoste. Lettre sur le Dieu transcendant (NH III,3 et V,1): Texte établi et présenté* [BCNH.T 26; Québec: Les presses de l'Université Laval, 2000], 52–54); due to one missing folio in Codex III (pp. 109/110), the *Eugnostos* parallel in *Soph. Jes. Chr.* only exists in the Berlin Codex (107.10–13): "By means of these appeared the deficiency in the female" (translated from Coptic text in Barry, *La Sagesse de Jésus-Christ*, 86); *Dial. Sav.* (144.17–20): "Matthew said: 'He tells us, pray where there is n[o fem]ale, destroy the works of femininity!'" (translated from Coptic text in Létourneau, *Le Dialogue du Sauveur*, 98).

Wisdom], who "was [establish]ing the deficiency"). According to this interpretation, the topic of the immovable race is somehow related to the deficiency brought forth by the Wisdom figure.

In the *Apocryphon of John*, we have what has elsewhere been labelled "an etiology of movement" which is closely connected to the deficiency of Wisdom.[62] Earlier in the revelation dialogue, we read that the Saviour tells John about the whereabouts of the evil world creator and his dark rulers who resulted from Wisdom's fall; afterward the Saviour says: "Now, the mother began to 'rush about' (επιφερ[ε]) [since] she recognised her deficiency"; John then asks what 'rush about' means, and the Saviour answers: "Are you thinking as Moses said: 'over the waters'?" (Berlin Codex 44.19–45.10).[63] This passage clearly alludes to Gen 1:2 (LXX: πνεῦμα θεοῦ ἐπεφέρετο ἐπάνω τοῦ ὕδατος, Rahlfs).[64] But the Saviour instead interprets the 'rushing about' (επιφερ[ε]) as related to the mother's emotional reaction to the wrongdoings of her evil son and his dominions: When the mother begins to 'rush about' she reacts with repentance, shame, and fear. Thus the etiology comes to represent Wisdom's deficiency as referring to the fallen state of the created world, and her restlessness (or: her 'rushing about') as referring to how this fallen world effects the movement (emotions) of the soul.

However, the allusion to Gen 1:2 with the πνεῦμα θεοῦ is, in fact, related to the solution of the problem with the deficiency: "Spirit (πνα)" and other "spiritual (πνευματικος)" figures are the heavenly principle most often referred to in all of the Codex III texts.[65] As an antidote to deficiency this Spirit is, in the *Apocryphon of John*, provided by "the race (γενεα) above," who "sent to the mother her own Spirit (πνα) to raise up those who are like it," and this "Holy Spirit [comes forth] fr[om] the mighty realm and will estab[lish] from their deficiencies the [resto]ration of the realm so th[at it will] become a fullness; accordingly, they will no longer be deficient" (Codex III 32.8–22).[66]

Possibly "the race above" is related to, if not identical with, the immovable race. Instead of viewing this race as reflecting some kind of social reality, I am more inclined to understand the designation as an idealised 'higher spiritual reality' the reader can look forward to take part in.[67] The people "who are like it (= the Spirit)"

---

62 The following observations on this etiology are based on Williams, *The Immovable Race*, 111–13. Unfortunately the Codex III version misses a folio here (pp. 19/20), so we must here rely on the Berlin Codex version which, by the way, is fully supported by the two long recensions of *Ap. John*.

63 Both translations from Coptic text in Barc and Funk, *Le livre des secrets de Jean*, 114.

64 Cf. the analysis of the passage in Louis Painchaud, "The Use of Scripture in Gnostic Literature," *JECS* 4 (1996): 129–46, 136–38.

65 Most prominently in *Ap. John* (fifty six times); eighteen times in *Gos. Eg.*; four times in *Eugnostos*; eleven times in *Soph. Jes. Chr.*; eight times in *Dial. Sav.*, cf. Charron, *Concordance*.

66 All translations from the Coptic text in Barc and Funk, *Le livre des secrets de Jean*, 149–51.

67 In has been argued, with due caution though, that the phrase functions as a self-designation of one or more social communities in Late Antiquity, cf. Williams, *The Immovable Race*, 186–203.

are most likely worldly and spiritual (probably baptised) persons who are affected by the consequences of Wisdom's fall, thus the mention of "their deficiencies" which by the agency of the Spirit are to be annulled ("accordingly, they will no longer be deficient").

After this mythological explanation of the spiritual cure for deficient nature, John asks if every soul can attain salvation, and the Saviour replies affirmatively, saying: "Those whom the Spirit of Life enters ... will be saved," thus "they are purified from everything evil (κακιа)" and are "from now on without anger (οргн), envy (κως), [jealousy (φθονος)], desire (επιθγμιλ), and gree[d] (πλнсмо[νн]); [by] all [the]se things they are [un]controlled" (33.4–[15]).[68] This passage is not mythological, but rather ethically oriented. Here it becomes clear what is meant by the mythological description of deficiency and its evil influence on humankind who was formerly controlled by "everything evil" (i.e. "anger, envy, [jealousy], desire, and gree[d]"). The antidote is "the Spirit of Life" that sets humankind free and enables them to transcend these negative passions. Thus one can argue that they live a life "[un]controlled" by evil passions: the emotions of their souls are unmoved by bad influence and as such they can ultimately expect to join the heavenly and immovable race. In short, this spiritual race of elect consists of people whose souls are free from evil thoughts and dark passions.

We need to notice that the designation "the immovable race" is quite rare and only attested in five Nag Hammadi texts, of which three are found in Codex III: the *Apocryphon of John*, the *Gospel of the Egyptians*, and the *Wisdom of Jesus Christ*.[69] Additionally we find in Codex III another phrase closely related to our concept of a heavenly and elect race, namely "the race (гєнєл) which has no kingdom over it" in *Eugnostos the Blessed* (75.17–18) and the *Wisdom of Jesus Christ* (99.18–19).[70] This heavenly race is presented as kingless and therefore not ruled by any earthly influence which, in the context of the other Codex III texts, means that it is free from the control exercised by the evil world rulers.

But if the elect race is one of the most prominent themes in Codex III, how come it does not show up in the *Dialogue of the Savior*? In order to answer this question we need to look at wording closely associated with the theme of divine immovability, that is, for instance, "(heavenly) rest (йтон; ληληλγcιc)" which is found in all Codex III texts.[71] Related is also the concept of "standing (still) (ωρє [λρєт] єρλτ=)" which

---

68 Both translations from the Coptic text in Barc and Funk, *Le livre des secrets de Jean*, 153.

69 Four times in *Ap. John* (33.3; 36.24–25; 38.2–3; 39.18) and probably also once in a lacuna (Berlin Codex 22.15); three times in *Gos. Eg.* (51.8–9; 59.13–14; 61.19–20); and once in *Soph. Jes. Chr.* (97.9). The other occurrences of the phrase are in *Steles Seth* (NHC VII 118.12–13) and *Zost.* (NHC VIII 6.[27]; 51.16).

70 Translation from the Coptic text in Pasquier, *Eugnoste*, 42; Barry, *La Sagesse de Jésus-Christ*, 130.

71 йтон and ληληλγcιc: Twice in *Ap. John* (6.20; 35.1); six times in *Gos. Eg.* (43.16, 23; 55.9; 65.4, 22; 67.17); three times in *Eugnostos* (76.3; 86.14; 89.23); five times in *Soph. Jes. Chr.* (100.8; 114.1; 117.11, 14; 118.14); eight times in *Dial. Sav.* (120.6, 7 (twice); 121.8; 141.3, 11, 16; 147.18).

is found only in the *Apocryphon of John* and the *Dialogue of the Savior*.[72] It is not unlikely that the prominent use of ⲙ̄ⲧⲟⲛ, ⲁⲛⲁⲡⲁⲩⲥⲓⲥ, and ⲱϩⲉ (ⲁϩⲉ†) ⲉⲣⲁⲧ⸗ in the *Dialogue of the Savior* was the main reason why the scribe included the text in Codex III. The likelihood of this is strengthened when we take the prologue of the *Dialogue of the Savior* into consideration.

Codex III (120.2–23)
The Saviour said to his disciples: "Already the time has come, brothers, for us to abandon our labour and stand at rest (ⲁϩⲉ ⲉⲣⲁⲧⲛ̄ ⲛ̄ⲧⲁⲛⲁⲡⲁⲩⲥⲓⲥ), for he who will stand at rest will rest eternally. But I tell you: Always dwell above [...] time [... I tell] you [... do not] fear (ⲣ̄ϩⲟⲧⲉ) [it ...] you, [for] I [tell you]: Anger (ⲟⲣⲅⲏ) is fear [and he who] arouses anger [is] a [...] but as you have [...] they received these words concerning it (= the anger, probably) with fear and trembling (ⲥⲧⲱⲧ), and it established them with rulers (ⲁⲣⲭⲱⲛ), for from it nothing comes forth."[73]

Here at the very beginning of the *Dialogue of the Savior*, the Saviour says that he and his disciples should no longer concern themselves with worldly affairs ("the time has come, brothers, for us to abandon our labour"), but rather enter into a passionless state ("stand at rest"). Entering such a condition will allow them to participate in the eternal reality ("for he who will stand at rest will rest eternally"), which is also connected with heavenly existence ("Always dwell above"). Even though the passage following is badly damaged, it is possible to see that the Saviour addresses the problem of negative emotions (e.g. "Anger is fear" and "fear and trembling"). He ends up concluding that anyone controlled by such passions will partake in the emptiness of the fallen and demonic world ("it [= the anger] established them with rulers, for from it nothing comes forth"), rather than the fullness of the eternal and heavenly world mentioned just before ("Always dwell above").

Thus the *Dialogue of the Savior*'s prologue fits well with descriptions of the immovable race and its connection to the worldly deficiency in the other four Codex III texts. Again, if we apply a new philology perspective and compare with a fourth- or fifth-century context, the abovementioned ideas relating to race and deficiency is likely to have been attractive for persons who exercised asceticism in Late Antiquity. Indeed, the battle against demons and the ability to control evil emotions are central *topoi* in early Egyptian monasticism.[74] Another ascetic *topos* closely related

---

72 ⲱϩⲉ (ⲁϩⲉ†) ⲉⲣⲁⲧ⸗ occurs fourteen times in *Ap. John* and eleven times in *Dial. Sav.*, cf. Charron, *Concordance*. "To stand still," in a literary sense, is also attested as an ascetic form of practice in early anchoritic and cenobitic monasticism, cf. Williams, *The Immovable Race*, 86–92.

73 Text translated from the Coptic text in Létourneau, *Le Dialogue du Sauveur*, 50.

74 As has been formulated by Williams in connection with *Ap. John* (but applicable to the other Codex III texts too): "The effort to identify these 'loose powers' of instability [= the rulers] and thwart their attacks is an enterprise which *ApocryJn* shares with other literature of the era." He then gives an example from the *Life of Antony* 38 and concludes: "It is easy to see how a document such as *ApocryJn*, which also presented a weaponry against the relentless assaults of the cosmic powers of instability,

to monastic practice is a negative view on sexuality and procreation, which is also directly addressed in the three revelation dialogues of Codex III.[75]

Summing up the Shared Themes

We have seen that the *Apocryphon of John* has a special role to play in Codex III, both as the first and longest text in the codex, and by treating central themes shared by the remaining four texts.

In the prologue and epilogue, John ("the [br]other [of James ... s]ons [of Zebed]ee") is presented as the receiver, transmitter, and writer of the *Apocryphon of John*. This is in accordance with church tradition where the same John, thought to be identical with the beloved disciple, is also said to be the writer of the fourth Gospel (John 21:24).[76] That the *Apocryphon of John* actually aims to fulfil the teaching of the Gospel of John is implied by the Johannine questions posed by John in the *Apocryphon of John*'s prologue. Most central are two questions on the nature of the godhead ("who is his Father"?) and of the heavenly world ("how is that realm we will go to?"). The latter focuses on the "incorruptible realm" which in all Codex III texts is described as inhabited by divinities and angelic creatures in complex heavenly hierarchies. The former question focuses on the divine nature of the godhead, which in the first four texts is described in lengthy negative discourses. In Codex III, however, God is also described in positive terms, where the most important is the description of the godhead as the highest form of Spirit. We even have such a name of God in the subtitle of the *Gospel of the Egyptians*: "The Holy Book of the Great Invisible Spirit (ⲡⲛⲉⲩⲙⲁ)" (69.18–20).[77]

In the epilogue of the *Apocryphon of John*, this spiritual principle is also important, albeit implicitly. The epilogue concerns the heavenly race of elect ("[the] immovable [race]") and its relation to "the deficiency" which is associated with the "mother"

---

would still have been attractive to monastic athletes in fourth-century Egypt, long after its original composition." Both quotations from Williams, *The Immovable Race*, 131.

75 E.g. in *Ap. John* (23.19–21; 28.20–22; 31.21–32.3), *Soph. Jes. Chr.* (93.19–21; 108.10–15), and *Dial. Sav.* (144.15–[21]).

76 "The manuscript tradition [of the Gospel of John] is unanimous: no one other than 'John' appears as the author in the titles. Likewise, the church tradition is practically unanimous: ... all ancient witnesses assigned the Fourth Gospel to John the apostle," cf. Tuomas Rasimus, "Introduction," in *The Legacy of John: Second-Century Reception of the Fourth Gospel* (ed. Tuomas Rasimus; NovTSup 132; Leiden: Brill, 2010), 3–4.

77 Translated from the Coptic text in Böhlig and Wisse, *Nag Hammadi Codices III,2 and IV,2*, 166. The divine spiritual principle is important in all five texts (cf. note 65). The godhead is explicitly called "the invisible Spirit" (or the like) in *Ap. John* seventeen times, in *Gos. Eg.* eight times, and in *Soph. Jes. Chr.* twice, cf. Charron, *Concordance*.

(= fallen Wisdom). Throughout Codex III heavenly reality is linked with masculinity and stability (i.e. immovability/ [heavenly] rest/ standing [still]), and earthly existence with femininity and changeability (i.e. deficiency/ mother/ Wisdom). Such a dualistic scheme is presented in a mythological form (= the myth of Wisdom's fall) and in relation to ethics, i.e. to the movement (emotions) of the soul: The fallen world of demonic powers is thought to influence the soul in a bad way, but the cure is given by means of the spiritual principle that frees humankind from the control of the evil forces, thus enabling the elect to be part of "[the] immovable [race]" being wholly free from dark emotions.

We also noticed that the shared themes in the Codex III texts shows strong points of contact with fourth and fifth century Egyptian monasticism. The heavenly and angelic hierarchies displayed in all Codex III texts could also be understood as referring to holy monks and nuns who were said to 'live an angelic life' and who were therefore regarded as part of such an angelic reality. Additionally, the ethical profile of Codex III fits well with the asceticism practiced in anchoritic and cenobitic monasticism: Contemporary monks and nuns were said to battle demons, to be free from evil passions, and to practice abstinence from the world, especially with regard to sexuality.

The above insights on the shared themes are, to a certain extent, highlighted throughout the codex by means of paratextual features, especially concerning the scribe's presentation of codex titles, the use of *paragraphus cum corone*, and the Codex III colophon.

Paratextual Features

Paratextual elements can be characterised as text or marking that is added to, but not part of, the main text in order to present it to the reader.[78] The paratextual elements added to the Codex III texts include superscript and subscript titles and a colophon,

---

78 The theory of paratext has been dealt with by Gérard Genette, and even if he analyses literature and books from late medieval to modern times, his considerations readily applies to manuscripts from Late Antiquity as well: "Most often, then, the paratext is itself a text: if it is still not *the* text, it is already some text. But we must at least bear in mind the paratextual value that may be vested in other types of manifestation: these may be iconic (illustrations), material (for example, everything that originates in the sometimes very significant typographical choices that go into making a book), or purely factual. By *factual* I mean the paratext that consists not of an explicit message (verbal or other) but of a fact whose existence alone, if known to the public, provides some commentary on the text and influences how the text is received"; "the paratext in all its forms is a discourse that is fundamentally heteronomous, auxiliary, and dedicated to the service of something other than itself that constitutes its raison d'être. This something is the text. Whatever aesthetic or ideological investment the author makes in a paratextual element …, the paratextual element is always subordinate to "its" text, and this functionality determines the essence of its appeal and its existence," cf. Gérard Genette,

as well as markings in the form of *paragraphi cum corone*, punctuation (raised dots, dicolon, and tricolon), diples, and blank spaces.[79] All paratextual elements supplement the main text either for communicative or aesthetical purposes, in often overlapping ways. I define these as follows:

[1] The communicative purpose: The best example of this characteristic is the colophon which basically gives information from scribe to readers. Titles also belong to this category since they inform readers of which texts the codex contains. Punctuation (i.e. the raised dot) has a communicative purpose as well, since it helps readers separate or amplify wording or sentences in the main text. Finally, the *paragraphus* belongs here too, since it marks the end of texts or specific passages within the running text (adding to the use of, e.g., dicolon, tricolon, and blank spacing). This latter use of the *paragraphus* can be difficult to interpret: Even if a certain paragraph was marked in a specific text, that specific text itself does not necessarily provide enough information on why the marking was made, but applying a wider scope (i.e. the shared themes in the whole of Codex III) might provide the additional information needed.

[2] The aesthetical purpose: In Codex III, aesthetics relate to the formatting of the titles, which are written in enlarged letters and decorated with one or more *paragraphi*. Other decorative elements include rows of diples, decorative "twisted ropes," and horizontal lines. The diple, which is found in the running text, also belongs in this category, but when used, it is always placed as the last character of a line, probably in order to uphold a straight right column margin.[80]

Below we will analyse the scribe's use of the paratextual elements in relation to the communicative and aesthetical purposes attested in Codex III, as it is displayed in figs. 1–5.

Paratexts: Thresholds of Interpretation (trans. J. E. Lewin; Literature, Culture, Theory 20; Cambridge: Cambridge University Press, 1997 [1987]), 7, 12.

79 Paratextual elements can be "a title, a subtitle, intertitles; prefaces, postfaces, notices, forewords, etc.; marginal, infrapaginal, terminal notes; epigraphs; illustrations; blurbs, book covers, dustjackets, and many other kinds of secondary signals, whether allographic or autographic," cf. Gérard Genette, *Palimpsests: Literature in the Second Degree* (trans. C. Newman and C. Doubinsky; Stages 8; Lincoln: University of Nebraska Press, 1997 [1982]), 3.

80 In the extant text of Codex III we have seventy two attestations of the diple: Ten times in *Ap. John*; six in *Gos. Eg.*; thirteen in *Eugnostos*; thirteen in *Soph. Jes. Chr.*; and thirty times in *Dial. Sav.* It has been suggested that the use of diples in *Eugnostos* amplifies central divinities, wording or passages (cf. Pasquier, *Eugnoste*, 7–8). In Codex III, the diple can mark divinities or demons (i.e. 17.22; 18.2; 41.24; 69.14; 82.6, 22; 83.23; 85.14; 117.10; 118.25), and in *Dial. Sav.*, it particularly marks the λοгос (121.14; 129.23; 135.12–13). Even if more interesting examples can be found, the majority of diple occurrences hardly seem to point in any deliberate direction, but if it would be the case, the use of the diple then belongs to the communicative purpose of the paratextual elements.

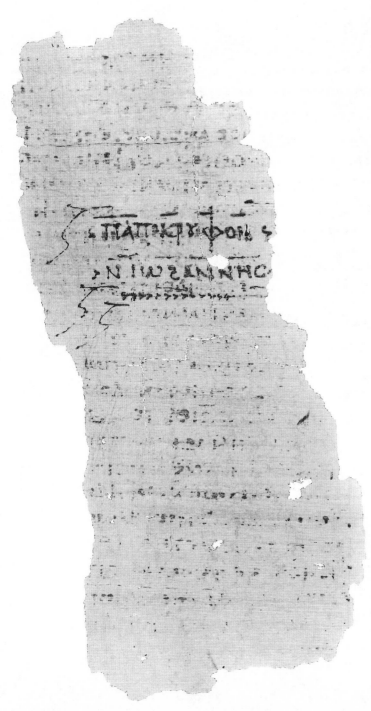

Fig. 1: The *Apocryphon of John* (back of front flyleaf, NHC III B). Three *paragraphi cum corone* [at the left] decorate the supertitle.

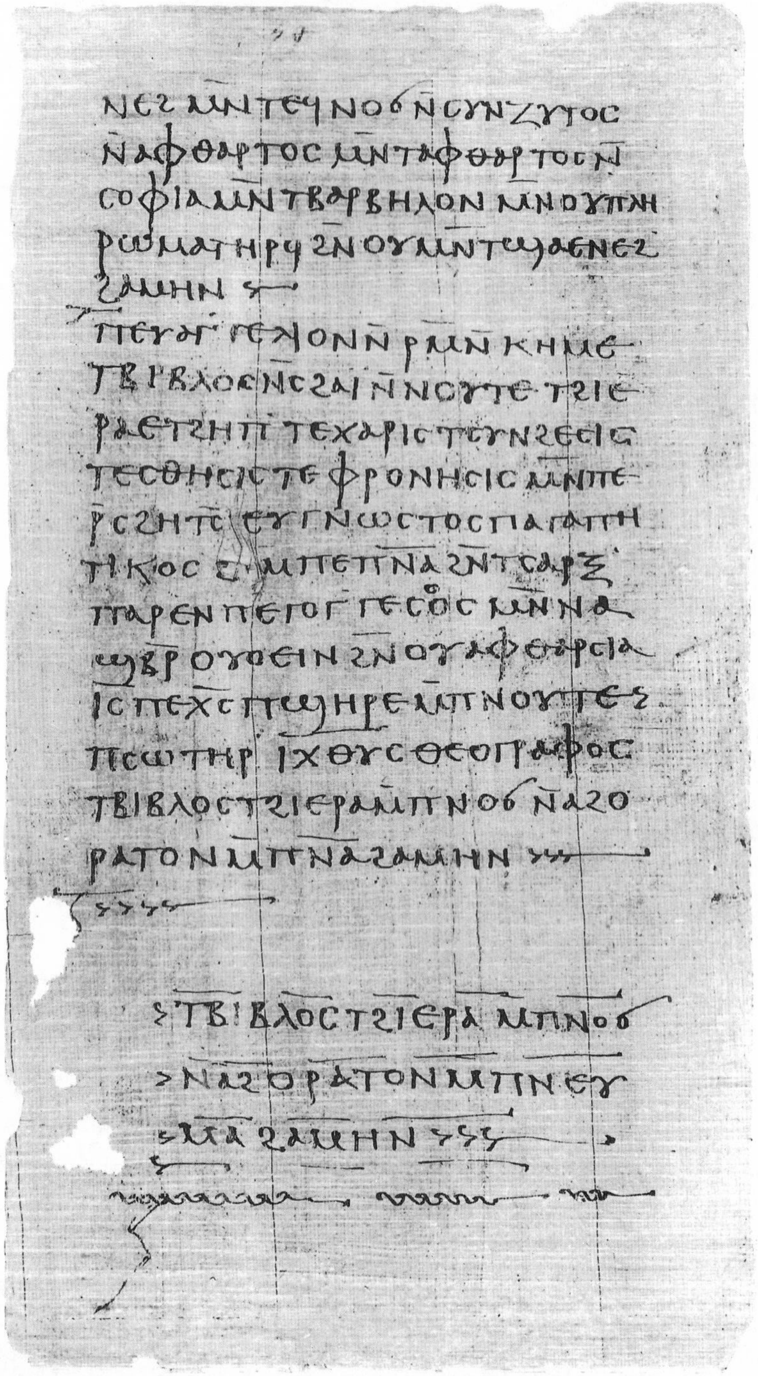

Fig. 2: The *Gospel of the Egyptians* (NHC III.69). Three *paragraphi cum corone* [below lines 5, 17, and 20 at the left], Codex III colophon [lines 6–17], and subtitle [lines 18–20].

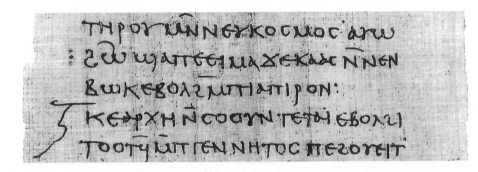

Fig. 3: *Eugnostos the Blessed* (NHC III 76.10–14). Marking with tricolon [line 11, in left margin], dicolon and blank space [line 12, after ⲁⲧⲓⲣⲟⲛ], and *paragraphus cum corone* [below line 12, in left margin].

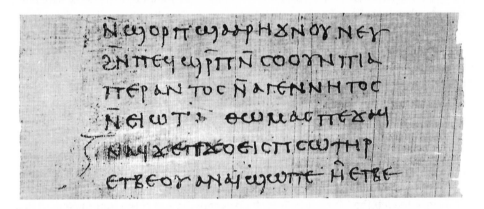

Fig. 4: The *Wisdom of Jesus Christ* (NHC III 96.11–16). Marking with tricolon [lines 11–12, in left margin], dicolon [line 14, after ⲉⲓⲱⲧ], and *paragraphus cum corone* [below line 14, in left margin].

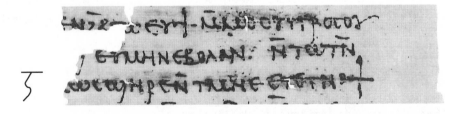

Fig. 5: The *Dialogue of the Savior* (NHC III 143.17–19). Marking with dicolon [line 18, after ⲉⲃⲟⲗ ⲁⲛ] and perhaps *paragraphus cum corone* [below line 18, in destroyed left margin].

Titles and *Paragraphi cum Corone*

The primary, and aesthetic, function aesthetic purpose of the *paragraphus* is clearly displayed in fig. 1 where three *paragraphi*, together with enlarged letters, single diples, a row of diples, and horizontal strokes, decorate the superscript title of the *Apocryphon of John*. At the bottom of fig. 2, the subscript title of the *Gospel of the Egyptians* (69.18–20) is decorated almost identically with single diples, horizontal strokes, and three decorative "twisted ropes" where the first rope is combined with a *paragraphus cum corone*. The subscript titles of the *Apocryphon of John* (40.10–11) and *Eugnostos the Blessed* (90.12–13) are adorned in a similar manner, and most likely also the subscript title of the *Wisdom of Jesus Christ* (119.18) and the *Dialogue of the Savior* (bottom of p. 147), even if both texts miss a large part of papyrus at the left side.[81] Of notice is also the undecorated and centred superscript title of the *Dialogue of the Savior* (120.1) which on the left (between lines 1–2) is marked by a plain *paragraphus* (i.e. a short horizontal stroke without the *coronis*).[82] In addition to the decorative *paragraphus* beneath the subscript title of the *Gospel of the Egyptians*, fig. 2 shows two other uses of the *paragraphus* which are related to the communicative purpose.

The second use is found just above the subscript title, where a *paragraphus* marks the end of the text at the left (between lines 17–18) together with two rows of diples, both ending with a stroke. The first diple-stroke fills out line 17, the other is drawn just beneath the *paragraphus*. Almost identical markings are found at the end of the *Apocryphon of John* (40.9–10), *Eugnostos the Blessed* (90.11–12), and also the *Wisdom of Jesus Christ* (119.17–18) where only part of the *paragraphus* is visible. The end of the *Dialogue of the Savior* (bottom, p. 147) attests some decorative "twisted ropes" and probably a *paragraphus* in the left margin as well (the papyrus is damaged here).

The third use of the *paragraphus* is as a mark within the main text. In fig. 2 it can be seen at the left (between lines 5–6). It may mark the end of the running text of the *Gospel of the Egyptians*, but it could also mark the beginning of a text, in this case, the beginning of the colophon. Here it is accompanied by a diple with a short stroke and also a blank space (line 5) which did not occur in the second use of the *paragraphus*.

So, apparently three different uses of the *paragraphus* are attested in Codex III: [1] As a decorative element (aesthetic purpose), [2] as a marking of the end of a text, and [3] as a marking of the beginning (or the end) of a pericope in the running text.

---

81 We also have three instances of titles within the running text of Codex III, namely *incipit* titles in *Eugnostos* (70.1) and *Soph. Jes. Chr.* (90.14). In *Gos. Eg.* (40.12–13) we have a paraphrased *incipit* title: "The Book of the H[oly Salvation Plan] of the Great Invisible [Spirit]," if we follow the translation of Charron, "Livre sacré du Grand Esprit invisible," 523, cf. note 39.

82 This simple kind of *paragraphus* marking is attested in a Coptic biblical manuscript from the fourth century (i.e. BL Or. 7594), cf. Theodore Petersen, "The Paragraph Mark in Coptic Illuminated Ornament," in *Studies in Art and Literature for Belle da Costa Greene* (ed. Dorothy Miner; Princeton, N. J.: Princeton University Press, 1954), 297.

The latter two uses are related to the communicative purpose.[83] The final use seems to come with supplementary marking (here: diple with stroke and blank spacing). In addition to fig. 2, figs. 3–5 are, most likely, three more examples of this use of the *paragraphus*. But why did the scribe mark such passages? One may think that it was later readers, rather than the codex scribe, who used the *paragraphus* to mark important passages for future reading, but as we shall see, it was in fact the scribe himself who made them during the process of inscribing the codex.

Leaving fig. 2 with the colophon aside for a moment, we will now focus on the third use of the *paragraphus* in figs. 3–5 and study why the scribe wanted to highlight exactly these passages in Codex III. Intuitively, one has the impression that this third kind of *paragraphus* marks the text following, but when a marking is found within a running text, it marks, by implication, both the end *and* the beginning of a train of thought in that text. This becomes especially clear when we look into the passage from *Eugnostos the Blessed* marked in fig. 3.

Fig. 3 context: Codex III (76.10–24)
And [tricolon] enough until this point so that we will not go on endlessly [dicolon, blank space, and *paragraphus*]. This is another beginning of knowledge from the begotten one (ⲅⲉⲛⲛⲏⲧⲟⲥ), the first who was revealed before the universe: ... Immediately, the beginning of that light revealed an immortal, androgynous (ⲛ̅ϩⲟⲟⲩⲧⲥϩⲓⲙⲉ) man.[84]

The extensive paratextual marking here (tricolon, dicolon, space, and *paragraphus*) is by no means accidental, since we, in this passage of *Eugnostos the Blessed*, now shift from the highest heavenly reality (described before the marking) down to a lower reality (described afterwards). In the passage, a Christ figure ("the begotten one, the first who was revealed before the universe") provides readers with the basic information ("beginning of knowledge") needed to understand how anthropological existence came to be ("an immortal, androgynous man"). Philosophically speaking, we are here presented with the transition from oneness to duality, from being to becoming, and from the divine world characterised by genderlessness down to the empirical world characterised by gender polarity.[85] Hence, the passage concerns the ultimate beginning of male and female gendered nature, and thus the beginning of the defi-

---

83 In contemporary Greek manuscripts we find a similar use of the *paragraphus*: "fairly regularly a paragraphus will divide the main text from the *subscriptio*"; "A paragraphus accompanied by a blank space in the text serves to mark a period (sometimes also colon)"; quotations taken from William A. Johnson, "The Function of the Paragraphus in Greek Literary Prose Texts," *ZPE* 100 (1994): 65, 66 n. 4.
84 Translated from Coptic text in Pasquier, *Eugnoste*, 42–44.
85 Actually, the divinities of the highest heavenly world in *Eugnostos* are characterised as "Father" (= God; 73.2; 75.23) and "sons" (= race of elect; 75.22), thus entailing the masculine grammatical gender. However, the point here is the relationship, i.e. parent ("Father") and children ("sons"), and not the gender, except for the fact that femininity is presented as non-existing in the highest heavenly reality.

ciency of femininity, which is a close parallel to the myth of Wisdom's fall and as well a primary theme in the *Apocryphon of John* and the rest of Codex III.[86]

The use of the tricolon is a bit puzzling. It seems to highlight the first sentence quoted ("And enough until this point so that we will not go on endlessly"), and it could, in fact, mark Codex III's scribe's addition to the main text, since this sentence is absent from the other versions of *Eugnostos the Blessed*.[87] This assumption seems to be confirmed by a similar use of the tricolon in the next marked passage from the *Wisdom of Jesus Christ* in fig. 4.

> Fig. 4 context: Codex III (96.3–17)
> "For that one (= God) is entirely mind, and he is thought, prudence, reflection, reasoning, and power. They are all equal in power and the sources of the universes, and their whole kind, from the beginning (ϫⲓⲛⲛ̄ϣⲟⲣⲡ̄) to the end, were [tricolon] in the foreknowledge of him, the infinite unbegotten Father [dicolon]." Thomas said [*paragraphus*] to him: "Lord, Saviour, why did they come to be, or why were they revealed?"[88]

This passage is marked with tricolon, dicolon and *paragraphus*, but not with blank space as we saw in figs. 2 and 3. The tricolon from fig. 3 is also attested here (as the second of the only two occurrences in Codex III), where it may mark the wording "from the beginning (ϫⲓⲛⲛ̄ϣⲟⲣⲡ̄)" which is not found in the *Eugnostos the Blessed* parallel. Therefore the use of the two tricolons in figs. 3 and 4 could, perhaps, indicate the conscious editorial activity of the scribe.

The missing blank space is rather interesting. At some point, during inscription, the spacing actually was there. If we look closely at the beginning of line 15, we are able to see parts of the erased text, ⲑⲱⲙⲁⲥ ⲡⲉ(ϫⲁϥ) ("Thomas said"), underneath the text written, ⲛⲁϥ ϫⲉⲡϫ(ⲟⲉⲓⲥ) ("to him: Lord"). This erased text ("Thomas said") is afterwards inscribed above, in the formerly blank space of line 14. Evidently the scribe at first wanted to mark this passage with a space, like the markings in figs. 2 and 3, but seems to have changed his mind in order to inscribe fully the partly empty line above. We do not know why the scribe had this change of heart, but what we do know is that while erasing the former text of line 14 the scribe also partially erased the *paragraphus* (more fainted than the one in fig. 3). It must therefore have been drawn before the erasure and hence by the scribe of Codex III, and not added later by someone else.

---

86 Even if humankind is symbolised by a double gendered reality in *Eugnostos*, the paradigmatic human being is still presented with the potential to attain undying existence ("an *immortal*, androgynous man").

87 I.e. *Eugnostos* in Codex V and the two versions of *Soph. Jes. Chr.* in Codex III and the Berlin Codex, cf. note 27.

88 Translated from Coptic text in Barry, *La Sagesse de Jésus-Christ*, 124–26.

The question is, of course, if the scribe wanted to retract the evident marking of this passage or not. I think not, because this passage is central both to the *Wisdom of Jesus Christ* and to the rest of the texts in the codex. In the marked passage, the text describes the completely noetical nature of the godhead ("For that one is entirely mind, and he is thought, prudence, reflection, reasoning, and power") which forms the foundation for all of existence ("They are ... the sources of the universes"). Thus it comes quite naturally that Thomas asks the Saviour how these noetic faculties of God were revealed to humankind ("why did they come to be, or why were they revealed?"). The Saviour's following answer is central to the *Wisdom of Jesus Christ* and an important addition to *Eugnostos the Blessed* where it is absent, but also central to all Codex III texts since the subsequent pericope in the *Wisdom of Jesus Christ* concerns the spiritual principle of the godhead and the immovable race of the elect (96.17–97.16). Thus, the scribal marking here hits two of the main themes of the whole codex.

So, in fig. 4, the scribe deleted, *in media res*, one of the formerly preferred paratextual elements, namely the blank space attested in figs. 2 and 3. The tricolon, if our interpretation is correct, is not necessarily part of the cluster of paratextual features preferred by the scribe to highlight specific thematic passages, since it instead could concern the editorial activity of the scribe. What we are left with, then, are the *paragraphus* and the dicolon. Like the tricolon, the dicolon also is rare in Codex III and only found four times: in 76.12 (fig. 3), 96.14 (fig. 4), 119.17 (the end of *Wisdom of Jesus Christ*), and in 143.18 (fig. 5). In the first three passages, the dicolon is always accompanied by a *paragraphus*.[89] In the fourth passage (fig. 5), the left margin of the page is missing, so there we have no visible *paragraphus*. However, since dicolon in Codex III always is accompanied with a *paragraphus*, we are justified in proposing that such a marking was drawn also in the lost margin of p. 147, between lines 18–19. Accordingly, this passage in the *Dialogue of the Savior* (fig. 5) was possibly highlighted by the scribe as well.

Fig. 5 context: Codex III (143.15–24)
The Lord said: "The rulers (ⲁⲣⲭⲱⲛ) and the administrative powers (ⲇⲓⲟⲓⲕⲏⲧⲏⲥ) have garments given for a time and not lasting [dicolon[90]]. You [*paragraphus*, possibly], however, as sons of the truth, shall not clothe yourselves with these temporary garments; instead I say to you that you will become bles[se]d (ⲙⲁⲕⲁ[ⲣⲓ]ⲟⲥ) when you strip yourselves."[91]

---

89 The *paragraphus* is only partially visible in *Soph. Jes. Chr.* (between lines 17–18) due to destroyed papyrus.
90 Even if the dicolon looks a bit strange here, probably owing to spilled ink, its presence is confirmed by the editors of the Coptic text, cf. Emmel, *The Dialogue of the Savior*, 86; Létourneau, *Le Dialogue du Sauveur*, 96.
91 Translated from Coptic text in Létourneau, *Le Dialogue du Sauveur*, 96.

Just before this saying of Christ, one of the disciples wants to know in what kind of garments they are to be clothed when they leave the corruptible flesh behind. In the quoted saying Christ states that fleshly clothing is temporary since it is associated with demonic forces ("The rulers and the administrative powers"). The disciples are urged not to concern themselves with fleshly reality ("these temporary garments"), but rather to get rid of such a life ("strip yourselves") in order to obtain a joyful heavenly existence so "that you will become bles[se]d (ⲙⲁⲕⲁ[ⲣⲓ]ⲟⲥ)."

The question here is whether this blessedness is achievable only in the future or already in the present. Fourth- or fifth-century readers would probably vote for both possibilities. Attaining blessedness by stripping oneself of the fleshly garments would be the same as fighting back fleshly inclinations and temptations which were thought to equal the battle against demonic powers. The only other occurrence of ⲙⲁⲕⲁⲣⲓⲟⲥ in the *Dialogue of the Savior* actually strengthens such an interpretation: "[Bl]essed ([ⲙⲁ]ⲕⲁⲣⲓⲟⲥ) is the person who has encountered the w[ar; he sa]w the contest with his eyes [and neither] did he kill nor was [he] killed but came forth triumphant" (141.23–142.4).[92] Accordingly, we again have encountered a main theme in Codex III, namely the immovability of the elect race as being uncontrolled by dark emotions and powers.

The term ⲙⲁⲕⲁⲣⲓⲟⲥ in Codex III is mostly applied to divine figures, and primarily to God who is described as the provider of such blessedness.[93] But earthly persons also partake in divine blessedness when they strip themselves of fleshly inclinations, when they win the battle against demons, and when they die, as seems to be the case in the *Dialogue of the Savior*. Actually, two such persons in Codex III are called "blessed" and probably thought to be role models for scribe and readers: The first is John the apostle in the *Apocryphon of John*.[94] The other is Eugnostos, know from the title of "Eugnostos the Blessed (ⲙⲁⲕⲁⲣⲓⲟⲥ)" (70.1; 90.12–13).[95] Both of them seem to be referred to in the colophon, the latter directly, the former indirectly, and they may even be one and the same person.

---

92 Translated from Coptic text in Létourneau, *Le Dialogue du Sauveur*, 92–94.
93 ⲙⲁⲕⲁⲣⲓⲟⲥ as referring to divine figures (21.23–24; 39.11; 119.9), and to the godhead (6.8; 24.25; 72.19; 73.1; 95.12, 16–17) who also is the giver of blessedness (6.8–9).
94 "But he (= the Saviour) rejoiced [when I (= John)] asked him; he said to me: 'Blessed (ⲙⲁⲕⲁⲣⲓⲟⲥ) are [you] for having followed (me)'" (35.22–25); translated from Coptic text in Barc and Funk, *Le livre des secrets de Jean*, 159.
95 Translated from Coptic text in Pasquier, *Eugnoste*, 34, 60.

Eugnostos and Gongessos in the Colophon

The colophon is only extant in Codex III and probably never existed in the other version of the *Gospel of the Egyptians* in Codex IV.[96] The whole colophon takes up lines 5–16 of page 69 (see fig. 2), but I will focus on lines 8–13, since the following analysis primarily focuses on the names of Eugnostos and Gongessos. In order to present the former interpretation of these names, the translation of Böhlig and Wisse is shown together with my new translation of that passage in the colophon.

Codex III (69.8–13)[97]	Böhlig and Wisse translation	New translation
ⲧⲉⲭⲁⲣⲓⲥ ⲧⲥⲩⲛⲣⲉⲥⲓⲥ	Grace, understanding,	Grace, sagacity,
ⲧⲉⲥⲑⲏⲥⲓⲥ ⲧⲉⲫⲣⲟⲛⲏⲥⲓⲥ	perception, prudence (be)	perception, prudence
ⲙ̅ⲛ̅ⲡⲉⲣⲥ̅ⲣⲏⲧⲥ̅·	with him who has written it,	with him who wrote it down,
ⲉⲩⲅⲛⲱⲥⲧⲟⲥ ⲡⲁⲅⲁⲡⲏⲧⲓⲕⲟⲥ	Eugnostos the beloved	Eugnostos the loving one
ⲥ̅ⲙⲡⲉⲡ̅ⲛ̅ⲁ̅ ⲥ̅ⲛ̅ⲧⲥⲁⲣⲝ̅·	in the spirit – in the flesh	in the spirit, in the flesh.
ⲡⲁⲣⲉⲛ ⲡⲉ ⲅⲟⲅⲅⲉⲥ'ⲥ'ⲟⲥ	my name is Gongessos –	– My name is Gongessos
ⲙ̅ⲛ̅ⲛⲁϣⲃⲣ̅ⲟⲩⲟⲉⲓⲛ	and my fellow lights	together with my fellow lights
ⲥ̅ⲛⲟⲩⲁⲫⲑⲁⲣⲥⲓⲁ	in incorruptibility ...	in incorruption.

The two names are extremely rare. Eugnostos is attested three times elsewhere, but of relevance here are only the two occurrences in the Codex III titles of *Eugnostos the Blessed* (70.1; 90.12).[98] Gongessos is not found anywhere else.[99] Usually, the two are thought to be one and the same person, where Eugnostos is a spiritual name and Gongessos a worldly one, in accordance with the translation of Böhlig and Wisse ("Eugnostos the beloved in the spirit – in the flesh my name is Gongessos").[100] The fact that Gongessos is not attested elsewhere has led to the suggestion that the name

---

96 Böhlig and Wisse, *Nag Hammadi Codices III,2 and IV,2*, 8–9.

97 Coptic text transcribed from fig. 2; Böhlig and Wisse translation, cf. *Nag Hammadi Codices III,2 and IV,2*, 166.

98 A person called "Eugnostos" is found in the *History of Alexander* by Arrian (86–160 AD), who briefly describes him as a "clerk in charge of the mercenaries" (γραμματέα δὲ ἐπὶ τῶν ξένων Εὔγνωστον) under the rule of Alexander the Great in Egypt; text and translation from Edgar Iliff Robson, *Arrian: Anabasis Alexandri. Books I–IV* (LCL 236; London: William Heinemann, 1967), 234–37. This reference is found in Wilhelm Pape and Gustaf Eduard Benseler, *Wörterbuch der griechischen Eigennamen. Nachdruch der dritten Auflage* (Graz: Akademische Druck- u. Verlagsanstalt, 1959). However, it would be too speculative to make a connection between the Eugnostos person in Arrian and the two Eugnostoi mentioned in *Gos. Eg.* and *Eugnostos* in Codex III.

99 Neither Pape and Benseler, *Wörterbuch*, nor the *Thesaurus Linguae Graecae* database have any entries on the name.

100 The two kinds of names, a worldly and a spiritual, are attested in monastic sources. They could refer to one and the same person, cf. Hugo Lundhaug and Lance Jenott, *The Monastic Origins of the Nag Hammadi Codices* (STAC 97; Tübingen: Mohr Siebeck, 2015), 189–93.

was a Greek transcription of the well-attested Roman name Concessus.[101] The idea that the two names refer to one person and that the last name is Concessus is widely accepted and also adopted in the latest standard translations in English, French, and German.[102]

However, when we take a paratextual element in the colophon into consideration, namely the raised dot (·), it may be argued that Eugnostos and Gongessos are thought, by the codex scribe, to be presented as two different persons: The scribe uses the raised dot just before "Eugnostos," i.e. subsequent to ⲙ̅ⲡⲉⲣⲥⲉⲏⲧⲥ̄· – "him who wrote it down(·)"– and also after ϩ̄ⲛⲧⲥⲁⲣⲝ· – "in the flesh(·)"; accordingly, the scribe's use of the dot before and after the phrasing – "(·)Eugnostos the loving one in the spirit, in the flesh(·)" – could indicate that this phrase was meant to form one semantic unity.[103] In the codex pages surrounding the colophon, we actually do find examples of a parallel use of punctuation marking similar phrases related to names.[104] Nevertheless, we still end up with an odd use of the double preposition in the saying that "Eugnostos" is a "loving one in the spirit, in the flesh (ϩ̄ⲙ-ⲡⲉⲡ̄ⲛⲁ̄ ϩ̄ⲛ-ⲧⲥⲁⲣⲝ)."[105]

---

101 Paulinus Bellet, "The Colophon of the *Gospel of the Egyptians*: Concessus and Macarius of Nag Hammadi," in *Pre-Christian Gnosticism: A Survey of the Proposed Evidences* (ed. Edwin M. Yamauchi; Grand Rapids, Mich.: Eerdmans, 1973), 46.

102 "Eugnostos the beloved in the Spirit – my worldly name is Gongessos [in note: "The Latin form of this name is Concessus"]," cf. Marvin Meyer, "The Holy Book of the Great Invisible Spirit," in *The Nag Hammadi Scriptures: The International Edition* (ed. Marvin Meyer; New York: HarperCollins, 2007), 269; "Eugnoste le charitable est mon nom spirituel, mon nom charnel est Concessus," cf. Charron, "Livre sacré du Grand Esprit invisible," 549; "dem geliebten Eugnostos im Geist – im Fleisch ist mein Name Concessus," cf. Uwe-Karsten Plisch, „Das heilige Buch des großen unsichtbaren Geistes (NHC III,2; IV,2) („Das ägyptische Evangelium")," in *Nag Hammadi Deutsch: 1. Band: NHC I,1–V,1: Eingeleitet und übersetzt von Mitgliedern des Berliner Arbeitskreises für Koptisch-Gnostische Schriften* (ed. by Hans-Martin Schenke, Hans-Gebhard Bethge, and Ursula Ulrike Kaiser; Koptisch-Gnostische Schriften II, GCS Neue Folge 8; Berlin: Walter de Gruyter, 2001), 320–21.

103 The use of the raised dot in early Coptic manuscripts is quite an under-studied phenomenon. The problem is that a consistent punctuation system did not seem to exist in the manuscript culture of Late Antiquity. The scribes basically dotted the text as they pleased; it could, for instance, have been for the sake of reading the text aloud, but we cannot know for sure. Emmel has touched upon the use of punctuation in his edition of *Dial. Sav.*, cf. Emmel, *The Dialogue of the Savior*, 31–32, and briefly says: "A raised point … is used to mark the ends of some, though not all, clauses" (p. 31).

104 E.g. "(·)The mighty Samblō and the mighty Abrasax(·)" (·ⲧⲓⲛⲟϭ ⲥⲁⲙⲃⲗⲱ ⲙ̄ⲛ̄ⲡⲛⲟϭ ⲛⲁⲃⲣⲁⲥⲁⲝ·) 64.26–65.1; "(·)The second, Oroiaēl, the place of the mighty Seth(·)" (·ⲧⲙⲉϩⲥⲛⲁⲩ ⲟⲣⲟⲓⲁⲏⲗ ⲡⲙⲁ ⲙ̄ⲡⲛⲟϭ ⲛ̄ⲥⲏⲑ·) 65.15–17; "(·)Others (say), that it is Providence(·)" (·ϩⲉⲛⲕⲟⲟⲩⲉ ⲭⲉⲟⲩⲡⲣⲟⲛⲟⲓⲁ ⲧⲉ·) 70.19–20; "(·)He is called Father of the universe(·)" (·ϣⲁⲩⲭⲟⲟⲥ ⲉⲣⲟϥ ⲭⲉⲡⲓⲱⲧ ⲙ̄ⲡⲧⲏⲣϥ·) 73.1–3; translated from Coptic text in Böhlig and Wisse, *Nag Hammadi Codices III,2 and IV,2*, 150, 152; Pasquier, *Eugnoste*, 34, 38.

105 Instead a linking entity term (ⲙ̄ⲛ-) would be preferable: ϩ̄ⲙⲡⲉⲡ̄ⲛⲁ̄ <ⲙ̄ⲛ>ⲧⲥⲁⲣⲝ ("in the spirit <and> the flesh"), or a construction with a relative: ϩ̄ⲙⲡⲉⲡ̄ⲛⲁ̄ <ⲉⲧ>ϩ̄ⲛⲧⲥⲁⲣⲝ ("in the spirit <which is> in the flesh").

But a similar double, and even triple, use of the preposition (ϩⲛ̅-) is actually witnessed three times in Codex III.[106]

The above interpretation rests upon connecting the preposition ("in the flesh") to the first person, "Eugnostos the loving one in the spirit, in the flesh," instead of the second one, i.e. "in the flesh my name is Gongessos," as it is rendered in Böhlig and Wisse's translation. This leaves us with two different persons: Eugnostos, who may possibly be regarded as the same as John the Apostle, and Gongessos, who might be the authentic scribe of Codex III, as will be argued below.

Leaving Gongessos aside for a moment, we will see that the scribe shows a similar interest in connecting the spiritual closely to the fleshly later on. In the prologue of the *Wisdom of Jesus Christ*, the Saviour appears in a spiritual, rather than a physical, form, and the implied author then says: "I will not be able to speak of his (spiritual) form, nor will any mortal flesh be able to receive it (= his spiritual form) itself, except a perfectly pure flesh (ⲥⲁⲣⲝ ⲛ̅ⲕⲁⲑⲁⲣⲟⲛ), like he taught us on the mountain ... in Galilee" (91.14–20).[107] This passage refers to the transfiguration account in the synoptic gospels ("like he taught us on the mountain ... in Galilee") where Jesus changes appearance before his disciples (Matt 17:1–8 par.). Even though it was Christ who was transfigured in the gospels, the quotation from the *Wisdom of Jesus Christ* also seems to promise that earthly persons ("mortal flesh") will be able to receive such a spiritual form, if they obtain a form of "pure flesh (ⲥⲁⲣⲝ ⲛ̅ⲕⲁⲑⲁⲣⲟⲛ)" similar to their transfigured Saviour.[108]

But who is the implied author referred to in the *Wisdom of Jesus Christ*? In the earlier analysis of the last sentence quoted from the epilogue of the *Apocryphon of John* (39.21–24), I argued that the future teaching of the Saviour mentioned there ("I will [teach yo]u, once again, about what is coming") most likely points forward to the *Wisdom of Jesus Christ*. By consequence, John is presented as the writer of the *Wisdom of Jesus Christ* in the epilogue of the *Apocryphon of John* ("for [I gave you

---

106 All parallels found in *Gos. Eg.*: The "church" was "praising, singing, giving glory *in* a single voice (ϩⲛ̅ⲟⲩⲥⲙⲏ ⲛ̅ⲟⲩⲱⲧ̅), *in* a pattern (ϩⲛ̅ⲟⲩϩⲓⲕⲱⲛ), *in* an enthusiastic mouth (ϩⲛ̅ⲟⲩⲧⲁⲡⲣⲟ ⲉⲙⲉⲥⲛ̅ⲧⲟⲛ ⲙ̅ⲙⲟⲥ)" (55.4–9); "He (= Seth) established it (= his seed) *in* the fourth realm (ⲛ̅ϩⲣⲁⲓ̈ ϩⲛ̅ⲡⲙⲉϩⲫⲧⲟⲟⲩ ⲛ̅ⲁⲓⲱⲛ), *in* the mighty light Davithe (ϩⲛ̅ⲡⲙⲉϩϣⲟⲙⲛ̅ⲧ̅ ⲛ̅ⲛⲟϭ ⲛ̅ⲟⲩⲟⲉⲓⲛ ⲇⲁⲩⲉⲓⲑⲉ)" (56.19–22); "He armed them *with* a weapon of knowledge of this truth (ϩⲛ̅ⲟⲩϩⲟⲡⲗⲟⲛ ⲛ̅ⲥⲟⲟⲩⲛ ⲛ̅ⲧⲉⲓ̈ⲁⲗⲏⲑⲉⲓⲁ), *with* an unbeatable power of incorruption (ϩⲛ̅ⲟⲩⲇⲩⲛⲁⲙⲓⲥ ⲛ̅ⲁⲧ̅ϫⲣⲟ ⲉⲣⲟⲥ ⲛ̅ⲧⲉⲧⲁⲫⲑⲁⲣⲥⲓⲁ)" (64.6–9); translated from Coptic text in Böhlig and Wisse, *Nag Hammadi Codices III,2 and IV,2*, 112, 118, 146.

107 Text translated from the Coptic text in Barry, *La Sagesse de Jésus-Christ*, 116–18. This is the only time the implied author speaks in the first person ("I") in the whole of *Soph. Jes. Chr.*

108 That it is not only intended to describe the flesh of the Saviour in the *Wisdom of Jesus Christ*, but also the flesh of mortal people, can, in a fourth century context, be confirmed in a Coptic letter by the monastic leader Pachomius: "let us in the desert keep our flesh pure (ⲥⲁⲣⲝ ⲉⲥⲟⲩⲁⲁⲃ) as well as our soul ... in order that God will remember us and dwell with us forever" (*Letter Eight* 5); translated from Coptic text in Hans Quecke, *Die Briefe Pachoms: Griechischer Text der Handschrift W. 145 der Chester Beatty Library eingeleitet und herausgegeben. Anhang: Die koptischen Fragmente und Zitate der Pachombriefe* (TPL 11; Regensburg: Friedrich Pustet, 1975), 112.

these things] to write down"). Such an assumption can be supported by the above quotation from the *Wisdom of Jesus Christ* (91.14–20), where the implied author refers to Christ's transfiguration ("*I* will not be able to speak of his form") which he and his fellow disciples saw and learned about ("like he taught *us* on the mountain"). In the synoptic gospels, these disciples are Peter, James, and John (Matt 17:1 par.), but in the context of Codex III the person behind this author's comment (i.e. the person behind the 1. pers., sing.: "I") most likely is thought to be John.[109] So, here John is presented as the writer of the *Wisdom of Jesus Christ* as well.

Likewise Eugnostos is presented as the writer of the *Gospel of the Egyptians* ("Grace, sagacity, perception, prudence with him who wrote it down, Eugnostos the loving one in the spirit, in the flesh").[110] So, if John is to be understood as the implied author of the *Wisdom of Jesus Christ*, he probably also would be understood as such an author of *Eugnostos the Blessed*, since these two texts are almost identical. And if the author of *Eugnostos the Blessed* (i.e. "Eugnostos") is supposed to be John, then Eugnostos in the colophon would be John as well.

The best argument for identifying Eugnostos with John is not simply the interrelation between the *Apocryphon of John*, the *Wisdom of Jesus Christ*, and *Eugnostos the Blessed*, but rather his attributive name in the colophon: "the loving one (ⲁⲅⲁⲡⲏⲧⲓⲕⲟⲥ)" (or: "beloved" according to Böhlig and Wisse) since it could refer to the beloved disciple, "the one whom Jesus loved (ὃν ἠγάπα ὁ Ἰησοῦς)," from the Gospel of John (13:23; 19:26; 21:7).[111] There the beloved disciple is presented as the author of the Gospel (John 21:24–25), and this author is clearly identified with John in early Christianity.[112]

Now we turn to the other person mentioned in the colophon: "My name is Gongessos together with my fellow lights in incorruption" (69.11–13). Who, then, is this Gongessos and his colleagues? This group of his "fellow lights (ⲁⲃⲣⲟⲅⲟⲉⲓⲛ)" is clearly associated with heavenly reality, being linked with the sphere of the divine ("in incorruption") and shining existence ("fellow lights").[113] Perhaps these "fellow lights" are hinted at in the epilogue of the *Apocryphon of John*, when the Saviour says to John: "[I tell the]se things to you that you may writ[e them down and give th]em to your fellow spirits (ⲣⲟⲙⲟⲡⲛ̅ⲁ̅) [secretly, for this] is the myster[y of the] immovable [race]" (39.15–18); in the nearest context the "fellow spirits" would be John's "fellow disciples

---

109 In Codex III, Peter is not mentioned; James appears in the prologue of *Ap. John* as the brother of John (1.2–[3]) and in *Gos. Eg.* (64.13), but not as a writer or transmitter of divine teachings.
110 *Gos. Eg.* 69.8–11. In a primordial mythological scheme, also Seth is presented as writer of a book (68.1–14 [twice]), which probably refers to *Gos. Eg.*, but since Seth seems to be identical with Jesus in *Gos. Eg.* (64.1–3), he can hardly be the transmitter but rather the originator of the teaching thought to be contained in such a book. In a similar manner, the Saviour is, of course, the originator of the teaching written down by John in *Ap. John* and *Soph. Jes. Chr.*
111 Translated from the Greek of NA[27].
112 Cf. note 76.
113 Cf. Lundhaug and Jenott, *The Monastic Origins*, 192–93.

(ϣⲃⲣⲙⲁⲑⲏⲧⲏ[ⲥ])" (40.7) mentioned a little later on.[114] However, in the context of the whole codex these "fellow spirits" may apply to codex readers since they also, throughout the rest of Codex III, are given "the myster[y of the] immovable [race]" of the elect (39.17–18). Accordingly, the "fellow lights" in the colophon might just as well relate to codex readers or other persons contemporary with the production of the colophon.

Since the colophon does not follow after the other version of the *Gospel of the Egyptians* in Codex IV, it was probably added to the text in Codex III.[115] The question is, of course, when it was added, and if it could have been produced by the scribe of our codex, i.e. sometime during the fourth or fifth centuries. The use of the possessive pronoun (1. pers. sing.) in the sentence – "*My* name is Gongessos together with *my* fellow lights in incorruption" – strengthens such a hypothesis. If the authentic scribe of Codex III was entitled a ⲅⲟⲅⲅⲉⲥⲥⲟⲥ, not as an indication of a personal name but rather as a title or a specific function, his associates may be *gongessoi* too ("*together with* my fellow lights in incorruption"). But what, then, is a ⲅⲟⲅⲅⲉⲥⲥⲟⲥ? And could any monastic context, whatever it might be, help to explain its meaning? The title ⲅⲟⲅⲅⲉⲥⲥⲟⲥ is based on the Greek verb γογγύζειν and thus refers to "one who whispers" (less likely: "one who murmurs").[116] From early monastic literature we know that Egyptian monks and nuns were, as part of the discipline, urged to recite and memorise prayers, rules, and scripture.[117] This was not only done while reading in a cell but also practiced in the everyday life of the monastics, who continuously mumbled and whispered passages from the Bible and other literature in order to recall earlier memorised wording.[118] Could this be the context for our ⲅⲟⲅⲅⲉⲥⲥⲟⲥ and his fellow lights, that they are mumbling monks memorising Christian literature in an Egyptian monastery?[119]

---

114 Translated from the Coptic text in Barc and Funk, *Le livre des secrets de Jean*, 169, 171.

115 Böhlig and Wisse, *Nag Hammadi Codices III,2 and IV,2*, 8–9.

116 Following the suggestion of Jean Doresse, *Les livres secrets des gnostiques d'Égypte. Introduction aux écrits gnostiques coptes découverts à Khénoboskion* (Paris: Librairie Plon, 1958), 214, who also mentions that Zoroastrians whispered prayers and content of holy books to their pupils, cf. Doresse, *Les livres secrets*, 273 n. 79a.

117 Examples are given in Hugo Lundhaug, "Memory and Early Monastic Literary Practices: A Cognitive Perspective," *JCH* 1 (2014): 98–120, 103–5.

118 "[T]he totalizing character of the [monastic] system even extends into the mind and voice of the monk when he is alone in his cell, for in this situation he is commanded to continue doing simple handiwork with his hands while he meditates ... with his brain and his vocal cords. I understand this to mean the constant recitation or mumbling of prayers and passages of Scripture. ... There is no silence in this monastery, but rather a constant buzzing sound like a flight of bees, as everyone continually mumbles prayers and passages of Scripture in a low voice." Bentley Layton, "Rules, Patterns, and the Exercise of Power in Shenoute's Monastery: The Problem of World Replacement and Identity Maintenance," *JECS* 15 (2007): 45–73, 70–71; cf. also Lundhaug, "Memory and Early Monastic Literary Practices," 105.

119 While I consider the monastic context the most plausible, another possible parallel deserves mention here, namely a third century passage from Plotinus' refutation of the magical practices of the

John as Implied Author of Codex III

In line with the above study on the use of the John and Eugnostos figures in Codex III, John is, in the epilogue of the *Apocryphon of John*, presented as the writer of both that text and the *Wisdom of Jesus Christ*. When we take the colophon into consideration he may also be construed as the author of the *Gospel of the Egyptians*, if "Eugnostos the loving one" in fact refers to the beloved disciple of the Gospel of John. If Eugnostos in the colophon is John, the author of the following text, *Eugnostos the Blessed*, can be identified with John as well. The fact that the colophon also presents Eugnostos as a spiritual person in the flesh matches a similar idea (proposed by the implied author of the *Wisdom of Jesus Christ*) in a passage referring to the transfiguration account in the synoptic gospels, where the third disciple is John. So, even if John is explicitly identified only as the author of the first text in Codex III, the scribe also seems to identify him as the author of the following three texts. An implied Johannine author is not easily found in the last text, but since the *Dialogue of the Savior* continues the revelatory discourse of the *Wisdom of Jesus Christ* with the same disciples, he may have been regarded by the scribe as the author of that text as well.[120]

That John was regarded as the author of all the texts of the codex is also indicated by the fact that the *Apocryphon of John* carries a title prominently on the back of the front flyleaf (fig. 1), as the only two lines written on that entire page.[121] In fact, two other contemporary Coptic books from the Bodmer codices, Papyrus Bodmer XXI (Joshua) and XXIII (Isaiah), also display this feature, bearing titles on the back of their

---

so-called gnostics (*Enn.* 2.9): "what are they doing except making the powers obey the word and follow the lead of people who say spells and charms and conjurations, any one of us who is skilled in the art of saying precisely the right things in the right way, songs and cries and *aspirated* (προσπνεύσεις) and *hissing sounds* (σιγμούς τῆς φωνῆς) and everything else which their writings say has magic power in the higher world?" (my cursive); translation and Greek text taken from Luc Brisson, "Plotinus and the Magical Rites Practiced by the Gnostics," in *Gnosticism, Platonism and the Late Ancient World: Essays in Honour of John D. Turner* (ed. Kevin Corrigan et al.; NHMS 82; Leiden: Brill, 2013), 445. I thank Dylan M. Burns for this reference.

120 In *Soph. Jes. Chr.* the Saviour discusses with Philip, Matthew, Thomas, Mary, Batholomew, and the whole disciple group; in *Dial. Sav.* also with this disciple group and individually with Matthew, Mary, and Judas, from early on in the Syriac tradition thought to be Thomas, cf. Helmut Koester, "Introduction [to the *Gospel of Thomas*]," in *Nag Hammadi Codex II,2–7 together with XIII,2*, Brit. Lib. Or. 4926(1), and P. Oxy. 1, 654, 655* (ed. Bentley Layton; NHS 20; Leiden: Brill, 1989), 39.

121 Perhaps Codex XI attests another instance of an entitled front flyleaf verso page, even though the text there is too damaged to know its exact content (partially visible in James M. Robinson, ed., *The Facsimile Edition of the Nag Hammadi Codices. Codex XI, XII and XIII* [Leiden: Brill, 1973], 6). A reconstruction has been suggested, though: [ⲑ]ⲉⲣ[ⲙⲏⲛⲓⲁ] ⲛ̄ⲧⲧ[ⲛⲱⲥⲓⲥ] ("[The Interpretation] of K[nowledge]"), thus corresponding to the subscript title (22.35) of the first text in Codex XI, cf. John D. Turner, "Introduction to Codex XI," in *Nag Hammadi Codices XI, XII, XIII* (ed. Charles W. Hedrick; NHS 28; Leiden: Brill, 1990), 19–20. But even if there seems to be a decorative horizontal line visible below the letter traces, we cannot be sure whether the faint letters attest a superscript title or not.

front flyleafs.[122] The latter codex' front flyleaf verso page reads: "The th[ird] p[art]of the Book of [Isai]ah the Prophet," which corresponds to the content of the whole book (= Isa 47:1–66:24).[123] The former Bodmer codex' front flyleaf verso has a double title: "The Book of Joshua, Son of Nauē. The Book of Judith" which is also meant to point to the contents of the whole codex.[124] So, it seems that the first title of Codex III may also be intended to refer to the contents of the whole Codex III, as a "Secret Book of John."

A close reading of the secondary ending of the Gospel of John opens the door for later writers who wanted to add extra-canonical accounts to the history and teaching of Jesus Christ given in the earlier witnesses of the New Testament gospels.

> Gospel of John (21:24–25)
> This is the (beloved) disciple who bears witness to this and who wrote this down (γράψας), and we know his witness is true. But there are also many other things Jesus did. If each of them were written down, I do not think the whole world could contain the books (βιβλία) that would be written.[125]

John is here presented as the author of the Gospel of John ("the [beloved] disciple ... who wrote this down"), if we follow the early tradition where John is identified with this disciple. Notice that these final verses of the text are not thought to be written by John himself, but by a later transmitter ("*I* do not think") to subsequent readers of the Gospel ("*we* know his [= John's] witness is true"). The door opened for our scribe is the saying that the Gospel does not present everything taught or done by Christ ("there are also many other things, Jesus did"), thus leaving room for later apocryphal accounts to emerge. Our scribe seemingly imagined Codex III to be one of these numerous "books that would be written," namely another book by John the Apostle or, as the flyleaf title of the codex puts it, "The Secret Book of John."

---

122 Both codices have been dated to the fourth century, cf. Rodolphe Kasser, *Papyrus Bodmer XXI: Josué VI,16–25, VII,6–XI,23, XXII,1–2,19–XXIII,7,15–XXIV,23 en sahidique* (Cologny–Genève: Bibliotheca Bodmeriana, 1963), 5; Rodolphe Kasser, *Papyrus Bodmer XXIII: Esaïe XLVII,1–LXVI,24 en sahidique* (Cologny–Genève: Bibliotheca Bodmeriana, 1965), 5. I thank Hugo Lundhaug and Alin Suciu for bringing these two codices to my attention.
123 Translated from Coptic text in Kasser, *Papyrus Bodmer XXIII*, 38.
124 Translated from Coptic text in Kasser, *Papyrus Bodmer XXI*, 8. The problem with this double title is that only the Joshua text is extant (in the first three quires) and not the Judith text, but instead there remain a single folio, which Kasser suggests to be from a fifth quire, attesting the end of the Book of Tobit; and therefore he suggests that "Judith" from the back of the front flyleaf is a misspelling of "Tobit," cf. Kasser, *Papyrus Bodmer XXI*, 26–28. However, this problem has no influence on my interpretation of the intended use of the entitled back of the front flyleaf.
125 Translated from Greek text in NA[27].

Summary

Applying the methodology of new philology, the present contribution has, from the outset, viewed Nag Hammadi Codex III as a fourth- or fifth-century artifact being part of a manuscript culture that was most likely monastic. Thus the codex was analysed as the product of a creative scribe who selected, modified, and inscribed the five texts into the codex in order to present the whole codex as an apocryphal work of John the Apostle.

The study of the amount of inscribed text and its variance within the Codex III columns suggested that a deliberate choice was made by the scribe regarding texts and their sequence within the codex. As witnessed in other Nag Hammadi codices, the *Apocryphon of John* was preferred as the first text in Codex III and arguably the main work to which the other four texts were thematically related.

Analyses of the prologue and epilogue of the *Apocryphon of John* suggested that the text was closely related to the Gospel of John, that it relied on creating an atmosphere of secrecy, and that the two overall main themes concerned a race of elect people and a myth of Wisdom's fall related to the deficiency of femininity. These two themes were closely interwoven and basically thought to arm the readers in a battle against demonic forces that threatened the well-being of their souls. Armoury in such a battle was primarily presented as the divine Spirit providing the readers with full control over their emotions and protection against influence from demonic powers. Reminiscences of these ideas were clearly detectable in the four other texts in the codex, but also common among fourth- and fifth-century monastics in Egypt.

We have seen that the scribe used paratextual elements for both aesthetical and communicative purposes. Focus was especially on the communicative purpose, which means information given from scribe to the readers of the codex, e.g. by the use of *paragraphi cum corone* or super- and subtitles.

The scribe used the *paragraphus* in three different ways. Most important was the third use, which marked the running text of Codex III four times. Three of these paragraphs marked with *paragraphus* agree with the overall themes of the codex as a whole. The fourth *paragraphus* marked the colophon where the scribe may have presented himself: "My name is Gongessos together with my fellow lights in incorruption," a name that perhaps refers to the activities of both the scribe and the readers of the codex, while memorising texts in their monastery.

As for the scribe's use of titles, the first one, "The Secret Book of John," aims to designate the whole Codex III as the Saviour's mystical teaching given to John the Apostle, but ultimately made accessible by the scribe to the readers of the whole codex. The second title, "The Holy Book of the Great Invisible Spirit," present the godhead as Spirit and thus the spiritual principle needed by the readers to battle demons and control dark emotions. The third title, "Eugnostos the Blessed," refers to John as role model for readers who should strive to reach such divine blessedness themselves. The fourth title, "The Wisdom of Jesus [Christ]," presents the main divinities in the myth of Wisdom's fall in a pedagogical dialogue between the Saviour and his disciples. That text was most likely related to the final text in the codex, "The Dialogue of the Savior," since the same disciples there simply continued the dialogue with their Lord. For fourth- and fifth-century readers, the three revelation dialogues (*Apocryphon of John*, *Wisdom of Jesus Christ*, and *Dialogue of the Savior*) concerned ethical teachings, which were relevant in a monastic context too.

Bibliography

Barc, Bernard, and Wolf-Peter Funk. *Le livre des secrets de Jean. Recension brève (NH III,1 et BG,2)*. Bibliothèque copte de Nag Hammadi, Section "Textes" 35. Québec: Les presses de l'Université Laval, 2012.

Barns, John W. B., Gerald M. Browne, and John C. Shelton. *Nag Hammadi Codices: Greek and Coptic Papyri from the Cartonnage of the Covers*. Nag Hammadi Studies 16. Leiden: Brill, 1981.

Barry, Catherine. *La Sagesse de Jésus-Christ (BG,3; NH III,4). Texte établi, traduit et commenté.* Bibliothèque copte de Nag Hammadi, Section "Textes" 20. Québec: Les presses de l'Université Laval, 1993.

Bellet, Paulinus. "The Colophon of the *Gospel of the Egyptians*: Concessus and Macarius of Nag Hammadi." Pages 44–65 in *Pre-Christian Gnosticism: A Survey of the Proposed Evidences.* Edited by Edwin M. Yamauchi. Grand Rapids, Mich.: Eerdmans, 1973.

Böhlig, Alexander, and Frederik Wisse, eds. *Nag Hammadi Codices III,2 and IV,2. The Gospel of the Egyptians (The Holy Book of the Great Invisible Spirit)*. Nag Hammadi Studies 4. Leiden: Brill, 1975.

Brisson, Luc. "Plotinus and the Magical Rites Practiced by the Gnostics." Pages 443–58 in *Gnosticism, Platonism and the Late Ancient World: Essays in Honour of John D. Turner*. Edited by Kevin Corrigan, Tuomas Rasimus, Dylan M. Burns, Lance Jenott, and Zeke Mazur. Nag Hammadi and Manichaean Studies 82. Leiden: Brill, 2013.

Broek, Roelof van den. "[Review of] Nag Hammadi Codices III,2 and IV,2. The Gospel of the Egyptians (The Holy Book of the Great Invisible Spirit), eds. A. Böhlig, F. Wisse, P. Labib, Leiden: Brill 1975." *Vigiliae Christianae* 31 (1977): 231–34.

Charron, Régine. *Concordance des textes de Nag Hammadi. Le codex III*. Bibliothèque copte de Nag Hammadi: Section "Concordances" 3. Sainte–Foy, Québec: Les presses de l'Université Laval, 1995.

–. "Livre sacré du Grand Esprit invisible (NH III,2; IV,2)." Pages 509–70 in *Écrits gnostiques: La bibliotèque de Nag Hammadi*. Edited by Jean-Pierre Mahé and Paul-Hubert Poirier. Bibliothèque de la Pléiade 538. Paris: Gallimard, 2007.

Crum, Walter E. *A Coptic Dictionary*. Oxford : Clarendon Press, 1939.

Doresse, Jean. "Trois livres gnostiques inedits: Evangelie des Egyptiens. – Epître d'Eugnoste. – Sagesse de Jésus Christ." *Vigiliae Christianae* 2 (1948): 137–60.

–. *Les livres secrets des gnostiques d'Égypte. Introduction aux écrits gnostiques coptes découverts à Khénoboskion*. Paris: Librairie Plon, 1958.

Emmel, Stephen. "A Fragment of Nag Hammadi Codex III in the Beinecke Library: Yale Inv. 1784." *Bulletin of the American Society of Papyrologists* 17 (1980): 53–60.

–. ed. *Nag Hammadi Codex II I,5: The Dialogue of the Savior*. Nag Hammadi Studies 26. Leiden: Brill, 1984.

Falkenberg, René. "Matthew 28:16–20 in the Nag Hammadi Library: Reception of the Great Commission in the *Sophia of Jesus Christ*." Pages 93–104 in *Mark and Matthew II: Comparative Readings: Reception History, Cultural Hermeneutics, and Theology*. Edited by Eve-Marie Becker and Anders Runesson. Wissenschaftliche Untersuchungen zum Neuen Testament 304. Tübingen: Mohr Siebeck, 2013.

Fallon, Francis T. *The Enthronement of Sabaoth: Jewish Elements in Gnostic Creation Myths*. Nag Hammadi Studies 10. Leiden: Brill, 1978.

Funk, Wolf-Peter. "The Linguistic Aspect of Classifying the Nag Hammadi Codices." Pages 107–47 in *Les textes de Nag Hammadi et le problem de leur classification: Actes du colloquetenu à Québec du 15 au 19 septembre 1993*. Edited by Louis Painchaud and Anne Pasquier. Bibliothèque copte de Nag Hammadi, Section "Études" 3. Québec: Les presses de l'Université Laval, 1995.

–. "Die ersten Seiten des Codex III von Nag Hammadi." Pages 99–104 in *Divitiae Aegypti: Koptologische und verwandte Studien zu Ehren von Martin Krause*. Edited by Cäcilia Fluck, Lucia Langener, Siegfried Richter, Sophia Schaten, and Gregor Wurst. Wiesbaden: Reichert, 1995.

Genette, Gérard. *Palimpsests: Literature in the Second Degree*. Translated by C. Newman and C. Doubinsky. Stages 8. Lincoln: University of Nebraska Press, 1997 [1982].

–. *Paratexts: Thresholds of Interpretation*. Translated by J. E. Lewin. Literature, Culture, Theory 20. Cambridge: Cambridge University Press, 1997 [1987].

Johnson, William A. "The Function of the Paragraphus in Greek Literary Prose Texts." *Zeitschrift für Papyrologie und Epigraphik* 100 (1994): 65–68.

Kasser, Rodolphe. *Papyrus Bodmer XXI: Josué VI,16–25, VII,6–XI,23, XXII,1–2,19–XXIII,7,15–XXIV,23 en sahidique*. Cologny–Genève: Bibliotheca Bodmeriana, 1963.

–. *Papyrus Bodmer XXIII: Esaïe XLVII,1–LXVI,24 en sahidique*. Cologny–Genève: Bibliotheca Bodmeriana, 1965.

Koester, Helmut. "Introduction [to the *Gospel of Thomas*]." Pages 38–49 in *Nag Hammadi Codex II,2–7 together with XIII,2*, Brit. Lib. Or. 4926(1), and P. Oxy. 1, 654, 655*. Edited by Bentley Layton. Nag Hammadi Studies 20. Leiden: Brill, 1989.

Kohlenberger III, John R., Edward W. Goodrick, and James A. Swanson. *The Greek-English Concordance to the New Testament*. Zondervan Greek Reference Series. Grand Rapids, Mich.: Zondervan, 1997.

Layton, Bentley. "Rules, Patterns, and the Exercise of Power in Shenoute's Monastery: The Problem of World Replacement and Identity Maintenance." *Journal of Early Christian Studies* 15 (2007): 45–73.

Létourneau, Pierre. *Le Dialogue du Sauveur (NH III,5): Texte établi, traduit et présenté*. Bibliothèque copte de Nag Hammadi, Section "Textes" 29. Québec: Les presses de l'Université Laval, 2003.

Lundhaug, Hugo. "Memory and Early Monastic Literary Practices: A Cognitive Perspective." *Journal of Cognitive Historiography* 1 (2014): 98–120.

Lundhaug, Hugo, and Lance Jenott. *The Monastic Origins of the Nag Hammadi Codices*. Studien und Texte zu Antike und Christentum 97. Tübingen: Mohr Siebeck, 2015.

Meyer, Marvin. "The Holy Book of the Great Invisible Spirit." Pages 252–69 in *The Nag Hammadi Scriptures: The International Edition*. Edited by Marvin Meyer. New York: HarperCollins, 2007.

Mina, Togo. "Le papyrus gnostique du Musee Copte." *Vigiliae Christianae* 2 (1948): 129–36.

Muehlberger, Ellen. "Ambivalence about the Angelic Life: The Promise and Perils of an Early Christian Discourse of Asceticism." *Journal of Early Christian Studies* 16 (2008): 447–78.

Painchaud, Louis. "The Use of Scripture in Gnostic Literature." *Journal of Early Christian Studies* 4 (1996): 129–46.

Pape, Wilhelm, and Gustaf Eduard Benseler. *Wörterbuch der griechischen Eigennamen: Nachdruch der dritten Auflage*. Graz: Akademische Druck- u. Verlagsanstalt, 1959.

Parrott, Douglas M., ed. *Nag Hammadi Codices III,3–4 and V,1 with Papyrus Berolinensis 8502,3 and Oxyrhynchus Papyrus 1081*. Nag Hammadi Studies 27. Leiden: Brill, 1991.

Pasquier, Anne. *Eugnoste. Lettre sur le Dieu transcendant (NH III,3 et V,1): Texte établi et présenté*. Bibliothèque copte de Nag Hammadi, Section "Textes" 26. Québec: Les presses de l'Université Laval, 2000.

Petersen, Theodore. "The Paragraph Mark in Coptic Illuminated Ornament." Pages 295–330 in *Studies in Art and Literature for Belle da Costa Greene*. Edited by Dorothy Miner. Princeton, N. J.: Princeton University Press, 1954.

Plisch, Uwe-Karsten. "Das heilige Buch des großen unsichtbaren Geistes (NHC III,2; IV,2) („Das ägyptische Evangelium")." Pages 293–321 in *Nag Hammadi Deutsch: 1. Band: NHC I,1–V,1. Eingeleitet und übersetzt von Mitgliedern des Berliner Arbeitkreises für Koptisch-Gnostische Schriften*. Edited by Hans-Martin Schenke, Hans-Gebhard Bethge, and Ursula Ulrike Kaiser. Koptisch-Gnostische Schriften II, Die griechische christliche Schriftsteller der ersten Jahrhunderte, Neue Folge 8. Berlin: Walter de Gruyter, 2001.

Quecke, Hans. *Die Briefe Pachoms: Griechischer Text der Handschrift W. 145 der Chester Beatty Library eingeleitet und herausgegeben. Anhang: Die koptischen Fragmente und Zitate der Pachombriefe*. Textus patristici et liturgici 11. Regensburg: Friedrich Pustet, 1975.

Rasimus, Tuomas. "Introduction." Pages 1–16 in *The Legacy of John: Second-Century Reception of the Fourth Gospel*. Edited by Tuomas Rasimus. Supplements to Novum Testamentum 132. Leiden: Brill, 2010.

Robinson, James M., ed. *The Facsimile Edition of the Nag Hammadi Codices. Codex XI, XII and XIII*. Leiden: Brill, 1973.

–. ed. *The Facsimile Edition of the Nag Hammadi Codices. Codex III*. Leiden: Brill, 1976.

–. ed. *The Facsimile Edition of the Nag Hammadi Codices. Introduction*. Leiden: Brill, 1984.

–. *The Nag Hammadi Story, Volume I: The Discovery and Monopoly*. Nag Hammadi and Manichaean Studies 86. Leiden: Brill, 2014.

Robson, Edgar Iliff. *Arrian: Anabasis Alexandri. Books I–IV*. Loeb Classical Library 236. London: William Heinemann, 1967.

Turner, John D. "Introduction to Codex XI." Pages 3–20 in *Nag Hammadi Codices XI, XII, XIII*. Edited by Charles W. Hedrick. Nag Hammadi Studies 28. Leiden: Brill, 1990.

–. "The Johannine Legacy: The Gospel and the *Apocryphon of John*." Pages 105–44 in *The Legacy of John: Second-Century Reception of the Fourth Gospel*. Edited by Tuomas Rasimus. Supplements to Novum Testamentum 132. Leiden: Brill, 2010.

Waldstein, Michael, and Frederik Wisse, eds. *The Apocryphon of John. Synopsis of Nag Hammadi Codices II,1; III,1; and IV,1 with BG 8502,2*. Nag Hammadi and Manichaean Studies 33. Leiden: Brill, 1995.

Williams, Michael Allen. *The Immovable Race: A Gnostic Designation and the Theme of Stability in Late Antiquity*. Nag Hammadi Studies 29. Leiden: Brill, 1985.

–. "Interpreting the Nag Hammadi Library as Collection(s) in the History of "Gnosticism(s)"." Pages 3–50 in *Les textes de Nag Hammadi et le problem de leur classification: Actes du colloquetenu à Québec du 15 au 19 septembre 1993*. Edited by Louis Painchaud and Anne Pasquier. Bibliothèque copte de Nag Hammadi, Section "Études" 3. Québec: Les presses de l'Université Laval, 1995.

–. *Rethinking "Gnosticism": An Argument for Dismantling a Dubious Category*. Princeton N. J.: Princeton University Press, 1996.

Wisse, Frederik. "Nag Hammadi Codex III: Codicological Introduction." Pages 225–38 in *Essays on the Nag Hammadi Texts: In Honour of Pahor Labib*. Edited by Martin Krause. Nag Hammadi Studies 6. Leiden: Brill, 1975.

Katrine Brix*

Two Witnesses, One Valentinian Gospel? The *Gospel of Truth* in Nag Hammadi Codices I and XII

Scholars have traditionally regarded NHC I,*3* and XII,*2* as two witnesses to the Valentinian text known as the *Gospel of Truth*. Soon after the discovery of NHC I,*3* scholars related its initial words ⲡⲉⲩⲁⲅⲅⲉⲗⲓⲟⲛ ⲛ̄ⲧⲙⲏⲉ· to an ancient Valentinian "Gospel of Truth" mentioned by Ireneaus in his second-century work *Against the Heresies* (III.9.11). Meanwhile, for NHC XII,*2* these initial words are lost due to the fragmentary state of the manuscript. From the few preserved words and phrases of the fragments it has however been possible to identify NHC XII,*2* as a Sahidic version of NHC I,*3*. This identification has encouraged restoration of the fragments according to the version of I,*3*. Behind this restoration lies the expectation that NHC I,*3* and XII,*2* preserve versions of the fifth Valentinian gospel through which we can gain insight into second century Valentinianism. In this article I wish to challenge this view by shedding light on the differences between NHC I,*3* and XII,*2*. Even if NHC I,*3* and XII,*2* may be related to the Valentianian *Gospel of Truth*, their differences reveal a level of textual fluidity that problematizes the notion that we may regard the two manuscripts as a single window through which we may gain insight into second-century Valentinianism.

In order to evaluate the hypothesis that the two manuscripts could be used as a more or less uniform gateway to one second-century Valentinian *Gospel of Truth*, it is necessary to scrutinize the variations between the manuscripts. I shall suggest that there is a risk of overly harmonizing the two witnesses when NHC I,*3* serves as the foundation for reconstructing NHC XII,*2*. If we read and reconstruct NHC XII,*2* in light of NHC I,*3*, reconstruction rather becomes modification and rewriting. In this article I instead read the two witnesses on their own terms and ask what we can learn from the differences between them.

Before presenting a synopsis of NHC I,*3* and XII,*2* it is worth remembering that, as Frederik Wisse has stated, the condition of NHC XII,*2* is too poor to allow for a full comparison with NHC I,*3*.[1] Yet, his comprehensive reconstruction of NHC XII,*2* constitutes an attempt to harmonize it with the text of NHC I,*3*. The reconstructions are not mere reconstruction of lacunae, but suggestions of how the manuscript of NHC XII,*2* would have read if it agreed with NHC I,*3*. In this article I shall compare the two

---

* A sincere thanks to the NEWCONT-group, in particular Hugo Lundhaug and Lance Jenott, for their improvements on this article. For its correctness I am alone responsible.
1 Frederik Wisse, "NHC XII,*2*: The Gospel of Truth," in *Nag Hammadi Codices XI, XII, XIII* (ed. Charles W. Hedrick; NHS 28; Leiden: Brill, 1990), 330.

manuscripts with a critical perspective on this assumed harmony, starting with a brief presentation of them in the context of their respective codices.

The Codices

While Nag Hammadi Codex I is a well-preserved manuscript, with all the original pages of the *Gospel of Truth* extant, the situation is very different with Codex XII. Wisse estimated that this was the Nag Hammadi codex in the "poorest state of preservation,"[2] and it probably suffered most of its damage in the years after its discovery.[3] While Codex I consists of five well-preserved tractates, we must speak of Codex XII as a collection of fragments. The papyrus pages have no pagination, and the right and left margins are lost, a fact that complicates a calculation of the original number of pages in the codex. Even the number of tractates within Codex XII is uncertain. The major part of what has been preserved of the codex has been identified as the *Sentences of Sextus* and fragments of the *Gospel of Truth*. The codex also included at least one additional unknown tractate, since two larger fragments can neither be assigned to the *Sentences of Sextus* (NHC XII,*1*) nor the *Gospel of Truth* (XII,*2*).[4]

In Codex I, scholars have observed thematic and genealogical coherence between the tractates. Four of the five manuscripts are labeled Valentinian: the *Prayer of the Apostle Paul* (I,*1*), the *Gospel of Truth* (I,*3*), the *Treatise on the Resurrection* (I,*4*), and the *Tripartite Tractate* (I,*5*), while it is disputed whether the *Apocryphon of James* belongs to this Valentinian tradition. Francis E. Williams comments that the *Apocryphon of James* (I,*2*) bears too few Valentinian notions to be classified as Valentinian,[5] while other scholars, e.g. Henri-Charles Puech, Gilles Quispel,[6] and

---

2 Wisse, "Introduction to Codex XII," in *Nag Hammadi Codices XI, XII, XIII* (ed. Charles W. Hedrick; NHS 28; Leiden: Brill, 1990), 289.
3 Wisse, "Introduction to Codex XII," 290. On the circumstances around the discovery of the Nag Hammadi texts cf. James M. Robinson, "Nag Hammadi: The First Fifty Years," in *The Nag Hammadi Library After Fifty Years. Proceedings of the 1995 Society of Biblical Literature Commemoration* (ed. John D. Turner and Anne McGuire; NHMS 44; Leiden: Brill, 1997), 3–13, and Wisse, "Introduction to Codex XII," 289.
4 Wisse, "Introduction to Codex XII," 290 and Frederik Wisse, "NHC XII,*3*: Fragments," in *Nag Hammadi Codices XI, XII, XIII* (ed. Charles W. Hedrick; NHS 28; Leiden: Brill, 1990), 349.
5 Francis E. Williams, "The Apocryphon of James," in *Nag Hammadi Codex I: The Jung Codex* (ed. Harold W. Attridge; NHS 22; Leiden: Brill: 1985), 22: "The only clear resemblance between its teaching and the Valentinian is its tripartite division of the human being, with the place of honor accorded to the spirit; but this is found in the teachings of various Gnostic schools. Otherwise, the mythology typically associated with Valentianism is missing."
6 Henri-Charles Puech and Gilles Quispel, "Les Écrits Cnostiques Du Codex Jung," *VC* 8 (1954): 20–22.

more recently John Painter,[7] regard the *Apocryphon of James* within the Valentinian tradition.[8] Whether Codex I is Valentinian or not, the texts indeed appear homogeneous. Not only do we find common theological features between them, but also the Subachmimic/Lycopolitan dialect (L6) is a common characteristic of the texts in this codex.[9] Among the Nag Hammadi codices only Codex I, X and XI,*1* and *2* are written in the L6 dialect. John Turner notes that the subachmimic dialect of XI,*1* and *2* resembles the first three manuscripts of Codex I,[10] while Birger A. Pearson observes that the language of Codex X resembles in particular the *Gospel of Truth* (I,*3*) and the other texts of Codex I, except I,*5* (the *Tripartite Tractate*).[11]

Synoptic Passages

If we assume that NHC XII,*2* once encompassed the whole of the *Gospel of Truth* as known from Codex I,*3*, there is indeed much that has been lost. Whereas NHC I,*3* begins at the bottom of page 16, it is not before page 30.27–31.6 that the text finds a parallel in NHC XII,*2*. This means that we have no idea of how NHC XII,*2* would have narrated the initial cosmogonic myth and the subsequent crucifixion of Jesus, or if these episodes were included in the manuscript at all. Neither do the fragments in Codex XII include the remarkable section on the book (par. NHC I,*3* 22.38–23.18), nor the paraenetic section at NHC I,*3* 32.31–33.34. The sections of Codex I,*3* to which the fragments of Codex XII,*2* offer parallels are:

---

7 John Painter, *Just James: The Brother of Jesus in History and Tradition* (Columbia, S. Car.: University of South Carolina Press, 1997), 164: "Thus, like the documents in the *Jung Codex*, the *Apocryphon of James* is Gnostic, and the ending resembles the ending of the *Gospel of Truth*."

8 Also Judith Hartenstein and Uwe-Karsten Plisch suggest a Valentinian origin behind I,*2*, cf. Judith Hartenstein and Uwe-Karsten Plisch, "Der Brief des Jakobus," in *Nag Hammadi Deutsch* (ed. Hans-Martin Schenke et al.; 2 vols.; GCS, Neue Folge 8; Berlin: Walter de Gruyter, 2001–2003), 1:16: "Es kann also gut sein, daß die EpJac die ApcJac, eine eindeutige gnostisch-valentinianische Schrift, voraussetzt und hochschätzt, ja sich als ihre Fortsetzung versteht."

9 Regarding the various Subachmimic dialects cf. Wolf Peter Funk, "How closely related are the Subakhmimic dialects?" *ZÄS* 112 (1985): 124–39.

10 John D. Turner, "Introduction to Codex XI," in *Nag Hammadi Codices XI, XII, XIII* (ed. Charles W. Hedrick; NHS 28; Leiden: Brill, 1990), 11.

11 Birger A. Pearson, "Introduction to codex X," in *Nag Hammadi Codices IX and X* (ed. Birger A. Pearson; NHS 15; Leiden: Brill, 1981), 23.

Fragment 1 (NHC XII 53.19–29): Jesus' revelation of the Father and the form of Jesus at NHC I 30.27–31.6.[12]

Fragment 2 (NHC XII 54.19–28): Jesus' work and the parable of the lost sheep at NHC I 31.25–32.3.[13]

Fragment 3 (NHC XII 57.1–29): Manifestation of the fragrances and proclamation of the Word at NHC I 34.4–35.4.[14]

Fragment 4 (NHC XII 58.1–29): The realm of the Father and the return to him from deficiency at NHC I 35.5–35.[15]

Fragment 5 (NHC XII 59.18–30): Unction and jars at NHC I 36.13–26.[16]

Fragment 6 (NHC XII 60.17–30): The depth of the Father and the Word proceeding from it at NHC I 37.7–21.[17]

The Fragments

Fragment 1

Let us start with the first fragment of NHC XII 53.19–29[18] and see how it relates to its parallel at NHC I 30.276–31,6.

NHC XII,2 53.19–29

(19) [6±] … [	
(20) [ⲁⲩⲱ] ⲛⲉⲧⲥⲱⲧⲙ̅ ⲉⲣⲟ[ϥ]	[And] those who heard [him]
(21) [ⲛⲉϥ]ϯ ⲛⲁⲩ ⲛ̅ϯ†ⲡⲉ [ⲙⲛ̅ ⲡⲓⲥⲧⲟⲓ ⲛ̅]	[he] gave them the taste [and smell of]
(22) [ⲟⲩⲥ]ⲙⲟⲧ ⲛ̅ⲧⲁϥ ⲡϣ[ⲏⲣⲉ ⲙ̅ⲙⲉⲣⲓⲧ]	his [f]orm. [The beloved] so[n]
(23) [ⲁϥⲟ]ⲩⲱⲛϩ̅ ⲛⲁⲩ ⲉⲃⲟⲗ [ⲁϥⲧⲁⲙⲟⲟⲩ]	[re]vealed to them. [He told them]
(24) [ⲉⲡⲉⲓ]ⲱⲧ ̀ ⲡⲁⲧϣⲁϫⲉ [ⲙ̅ⲙⲟϥ ⲉ]	[about the Fa]ther, the unspeakable, [as]
(25) [ⲁϥⲛⲓϥⲉ]ⲉ ⲙ̅ⲡⲉϥⲙⲉⲉⲩⲉ ⲉ[ϩⲣⲁⲓ ⲉⲣⲟ]	[he blew] his thought i[nto]
(26) [ⲟⲩ ⲁϥⲉⲓⲣ]ⲉ ⲙ̅ⲡⲉϥⲟⲩⲱϣ[ϣ· ⲁϩⲁϩ ϭⲉ]	[them. He di]d his wil[l. Many then]
(27) [ϫⲓ ⲙ̅ⲡⲟⲩ]ⲟⲉⲓⲛ ⲛⲉϥϩⲛ̅ ⲡⲥ[ⲙⲟⲧ ⲛ̅ⲥⲁ]	[received the li]ght. It was in t[he carnal f]orm.
(28) [ⲡⲝ̅ ⲛⲉ]ⲩϩⲟ ⲛ̅ϣⲙ̅ⲙⲟ ⲡⲉ [ⲉⲣⲟⲟⲩ]	He was a strange appearance [to them.]
(29) [4–5] ⲉⲛⲉϥⲕⲧⲁⲉⲓⲧ ⲙ̅. [	[…] He was turned […].

---

12 Wisse, "Gospel of Truth," 345.

13 Wisse, "Gospel of Truth," 345.

14 Wisse, "Gospel of Truth," 345.

15 Wisse, "Gospel of Truth," 346.

16 Wisse, "Gospel of Truth," 346.

17 Wisse, "Gospel of Truth," 346.

18 All Coptic qoutations of NHC XII,2 in this article are from Wisse, "Gospel of Truth." Translations are my own.

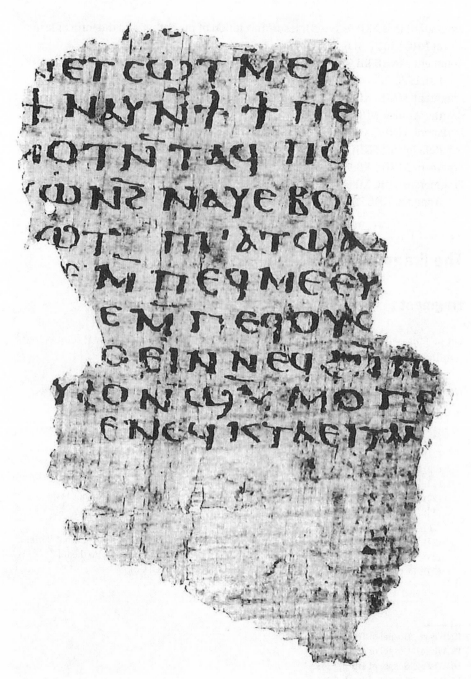

Fig. 6: The *Gospel of Truth* (NHC XII 53).

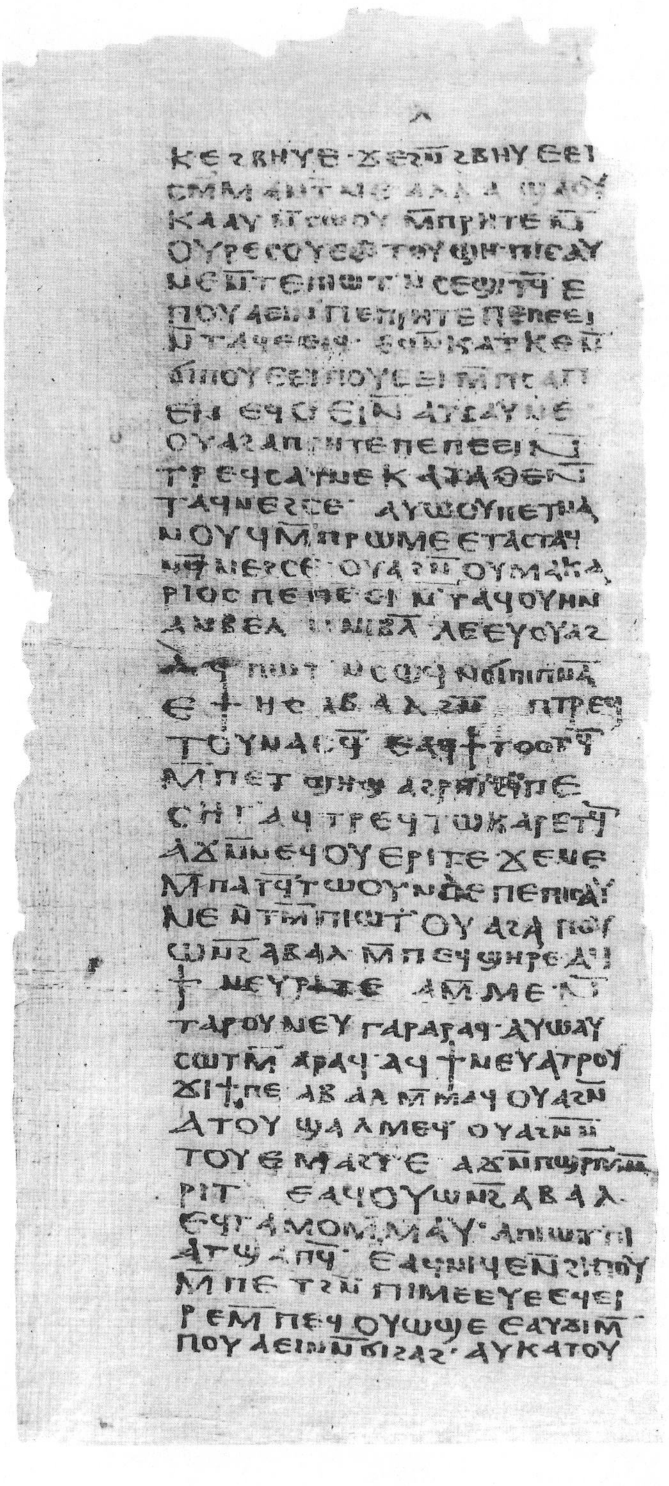

Fig. 7:
The *Gospel of Truth*
(NHX I 30).

NHC I,3 30.27–31.6[19]

(27)	ⲁⲩⲱ ⲁⲩ	And they
(28)	ⲥⲱⲧⲙ̅ ⲁⲣⲁϥ· ⲁϥϯ ⲛⲉⲩ ⲁⲧⲣⲟⲩ	heard him, and he allowed them
(29)	ϫⲓ ϯⲡⲉ· ⲁⲃⲁⲗ ⲙ̅ⲙⲁϥ ⲟⲩⲁϩⲛ̅	to taste from him and
(30)	ⲁⲧⲟⲩⲱⲗⲙⲉϥ· ⲟⲩⲁϩⲛ̅ⲛ ⲧⲟⲩⲉⲙⲁϩⲧⲉ ⲁ.ⲭⲛ̅	smell him and grasp[21] the beloved Son.
	ⲡ.ⲱ̅ⲣ̅ⲙⲛ̅	
(31)	ⲣⲓⲧ· ⲉⲁϥⲟⲩⲱⲛϩ̅ ⲁⲃⲁⲗ·	And he appeared,
(32)	ⲉϥⲧⲁⲙⲟ ⲙ̅ⲙⲁⲩ· ⲁⲡⲓⲱⲧ ⲡⲓ	telling them about the Father, the
(33)	ⲁⲧⲱⲁⲡ.ϥ̅· ⲉⲁϥⲛⲓϥⲉ ⲛ̅ϩⲏⲧⲟⲩ	incomprehensible. He blew into them
(34)	ⲙ̅ⲡⲉⲧϩⲛ̅ ⲡⲓⲙⲉⲉⲩⲉ ⲉϥⲉⲓ	that which is in the thought, doing
(35)	ⲣⲉ ⲙ̅ⲡⲉϥⲟⲩⲱⲱⲉ ⲉⲁⲩⲭⲓ ⲙ̅	his will. Many received
(36)	ⲡⲟⲩⲁⲉⲓⲛ ⲛ̅ϭⲓ ϩⲁϩ· ⲁⲩⲕⲁⲧⲟⲩ	the light and turned
(1)	ⲁⲣⲁϥ ϫⲉ ⲛⲉⲩⲟⲉⲓ ⲛ̅ϣⲙ̅ⲙⲟ ⲡⲉ	to it since they were strangers.
(2)	ⲁⲩⲱ ⲛⲉⲩⲛⲉⲩ ⲁⲡⲉϥⲉⲓⲛⲉ ⲉⲛ	They did not see his image
(3)	ⲡⲉ ⲁⲩⲱ ⲛⲉⲙ̅ⲡⲟⲩⲥⲟⲩⲱ	and those belonging
(4)	ⲛϥ̅ ⲛ̅ϭⲓ ⲑⲩⲗⲏ ϫⲉ	to[22] matter (ⲑⲩⲗⲏ)
(5)	ⲛ̅ⲧⲁϥⲉⲓ ⲁⲃⲁⲗ ϩⲓ̈ⲧⲟⲟⲧⲥ̅ ⲛ̅ⲟⲩⲥⲁⲣⲝ ⲛ̅	did not know him, because he came in a fleshly
(6)	ⲥⲙⲁⲧ·	form.

This juxtaposition of NHC I,3 and XII,2 supports the widespread assumption that the version of the *Gospel of Truth* in Codex XII is a shorter and more condensed version of the one in Codex I. The word "flesh," ⲥⲁⲣⲝ, at NHC XII 53.27–28 is reconstructed according to the expression at NHC I 31.5–6: ⲛ̅ⲧⲁϥⲉⲓ ⲁⲃⲁⲗ ϩⲓ̈ⲧⲟⲟⲧⲥ̅ ⲛ̅ⲟⲩⲥⲁⲣⲝ ⲛ̅ⲥⲙⲁⲧ. The editors probably find evidence for the expression ⲡⲥ[ⲙⲟⲧ ⲛ̅ⲥⲁⲣⲝ] because of the ⲥ of ⲡⲥ[ⲙⲟⲧ at NHC XII 53.27. The ⲥ is read as the initial letter of the Coptic word ⲥⲙⲟⲧ to which the qualification ⲛ̅ⲥⲁⲣⲝ is added. As the word ⲥⲁⲣⲝ is theologically loaded, one may ask whether the extant ⲥ legitimates reconstructing the expression ⲡⲥ[ⲙⲟⲧ ⲛ̅ⲥⲁⲣⲝ]. This reconstruction assumes that the *Gospel of Truth* interprets John 1:14. NHC I,3 uses the expression ⲥⲱⲙⲁ and not ⲥⲁⲣⲝ at NHC I 26.4–8 when speaking about the coming of the Word.[22] Still, the use of ⲥⲁⲣⲝ at NHC I 31.5 legitimates the reconstruction of this word at XII 53.27–28. A comparison of the two manuscripts illustrates that their sequences

---

19 All Coptic qoutations of NHC I,3 in this article are from Harold W. Attridge and George W. MacRae, "The Gospel of Truth," in *Nag Hammadi Codex I; The Jung Codex* (ed. Harold W. Attridge; NHS 22; Leiden: Brill, 1985). Translations are my own.

20 Walter E. Crum, *A Coptic Dictionary* (Oxford: Clarendon Press, 1939), 10a translates "ⲁⲙⲁϩⲧⲉ ⲉϫⲛ-" as "rule," "have power over."

21 The subject marker ⲛ̅ϭⲓ at NHC I,3 31.4 is unexpected and complicates the integration of ⲑⲩⲗⲏ into the sentence. Attridge and MacRae notes that the editio princeps emends the text, inserting the possessive pronoun "ⲛⲁ" before "ⲑⲩⲗⲏ." Cf. Attridge and MacRae, "Gospel of Truth," 100.

22 NHC I,3 26.4–8: ⲉⲁϥⲓ ⲁⲧⲙⲏⲧⲉ ⲛ̅ϭⲓ ⲡⲓϣⲉϫⲉ· ⲉⲧⲛ̅ϩⲣⲏⲉⲓ ϩⲛ̅ ⲡϩⲏⲧ· ⲛ̅ⲛⲉⲧϣⲉϫⲉ ⲙ̅ⲙⲁϥ ⲟⲩϩⲣⲁⲩ ⲟⲩⲁⲉⲉⲧϥ̅ ⲉⲛ ⲡⲉ ⲁⲗ·ⲗⲁ ⲁϥⲣ̅ ⲟⲩⲥⲱⲙⲁ· Cf. Kendrick Grobel, *The Gospel of Truth: A Valentinian Meditation on the Gospel* (New York: Abingdon Press, 1960), 105.

appear in reverse order. At NHC XII 53.28 the word ⲛ̄ϣⲙ̄ⲙⲟ, "foreign," follows the phrase about the Son's fleshly form and describes his ϩⲟ, "face" or "appearance," as foreign to those to whom he appeared (ⲛⲉ]ⲩϩⲟ ⲛ̄ϣⲙ̄ⲙⲟ ⲡⲉ). In NHC I,3 it is not the Son who appears foreign, ⲛ̄ϣⲙ̄ⲙⲟ, but some beings/existences: ⲛⲉⲩⲟⲉⲓ ⲛ̄ϣⲙ̄ⲙⲟ ⲡⲉ (NHC I 31.1), who appear foreign to the Son. These foreign existences at NHC I,3 are the strangers who turn to the light. Thereafter the image is mentioned at NHC I 31.2, and it is said that those who belonged to matter were ignorant (NHC I 31.3–4). At NHC XII,2 the order is either reversed or the ⲛ̄ϣⲙ̄ⲙⲟ is omitted in the first statement about those turning to the light, while it is included in the later description of the light's, i.e. the Son's, appearance.

Nevertheless, the comparison of the two manuscripts reveals an interchange in the sequences, and that the "light" in the fragment (NHC XII,2) is the object of the strangers' striving, while "the light" in the other manuscript (I,3) figures as a synonym for the Son, describing his form and appearance. While NHC I,3 in this section seems focused on the question of Jesus' form, NHC XII,2 seems to have joined the topics of the revelation of the Father's will with the question of Jesus' form. In this way the section appears more compact in Codex XII.

With regard to Fragment 1 and its equivalent at NHC I 30.27–31.6, the difference between the two manuscripts increases towards the end of the fragment. Having stated that the version in Codex XII "is significantly different" from that of Codex I, Wisse points to the intended *vacat* at the beginning of XII 53.29.[23] It is difficult to estimate how we should interpret this *vacat*, but whereas the verb ⲕⲧⲟ in Codex I,3 is integrated into the sentence about the reception of light and the strangers turning to Jesus, it is remarkable that in Codex XII the verb ⲕⲧⲟ appears after the statement about the reception of light and the foreign appearances, and therefore may not have anything to do with this passage. Furthermore, the stative form ⲕⲧⲁⲉⲓⲧ in XII,2 probably refers to Jesus, who has in some way turned or changed. The plural affirmative past ⲁⲩⲕⲁⲧⲟⲩ ⲁⲣⲁϥ of the same verb in I,3 indicates that it is those who receive the light who turn to Jesus. We do not know how XII,2 continues from there. We can only conclude that the discrepancies between NHC XII,2 and NHC I,3 toward the end of fragment 1 do not simply represent an abbreviated and thus more concise version of the *Gospel of Truth*, but rather an independent turn taken by the version in NHC XII,2. At the last line of this fragment, at NHC XII 53.29, the version in Codex XII appears obscure compared to that of Codex I.

Another notable variation between the two manuscripts in this section is the use of two different predicates about the Father in a passage that is otherwise quite similar. With the use of ⲡⲓⲁⲧϣⲁϫⲉ̣, "unspeakable," at NHC XII 53.24 instead of ⲁⲧϣⲁⲡϥ̄, "incomprehensible," at NHC I 30.33, we see that the difference between the manuscripts is not only a stylistic matter. What we have here are two different

23 Wisse, "Gospel of Truth," 345.

descriptions of the highest principle. If one undertook the experiment of analyzing the text from the perspective of a hypothetical Greek *Vorlage* the differences between the manuscripts appear even more distinct. The translating scribe behind XII,*2* would then have written another word than the translating scribe behind I,*3*, and we can not tell whether the Greek text read ἀλάλητος or ἀχώρητος. The idea of a common Greek *Vorlage* behind NHC I,*3* and XII,*2* is accompanied by the idea that this Greek *Vorlage* would be in accord with Irenaeus' description of the fifth Valentinian gospel. About the Valentinians Irenaeus declares in *Adversus Haereses* I.1.1 that they regard the highest divine principle as ὑπάρχοντα δ' αὐτὸν ἀχώρητον καὶ ἀόρατον[24]. Here the word ἀχώρητον corresponds to ⲁⲧⲱⲁⲡ̄ⲏ̄ in NHC I,*3*,[25] whereas none of the other words in the *via negationis* with which Irenaeus describes the highest principle of Ptolemy's pleroma, ἀόρατον, ἀκατονομάστον, ἀγέννητον,[26] are directly equivalent to ⲡⲓⲁⲧⲱⲁϫⲉ in NHC XII,*2* 53,24. Of the predicates, which Irenaeus mentions, the one that comes closest to ⲡⲓⲁⲧⲱⲁϫⲉ is ἀκατονομάστον, but this is not an equivalent and we would rather expect the Coptic ⲁⲧ† ⲣⲁⲛ. However, regardless of the original language[27] of the *Gospel of Truth* and whether the scribe behind the recension attested

---

24 Adelin Rousseau and Louis Doutreleau, eds., *Irénée De Lyon: Contre Les Hérésies I* (SC 264; Paris: Cerf, 2008), 28.

25 Crum, *Coptic Dictionary*, 576a.

26 English: "invisible, unnameable, ungenerated."

27 In 1961 Gerhardt Fecht argued for a Coptic original behind the *Gospel of Truth*: "Von dem hier behaupteten koptischen Originalcharakter des EV zeugen weiterhin die mehrfach auftretende und nur als literarisches Mittel verständliche Variation in der Wortwahl, die nicht den Wortlaut eines griechischen Originals widerspiegeln kann, und ein ebenso deutliches wie sinnvolles Wortspiel, das einen koptischen Urtext voraussetzt. 3) Schliesslich ist noch zu bemerken, dass die im EV zu konsta-tierende Art einer sorgfältig gegliederten Textdarbietung für die ältere ägyptische Literatur bezeich-nend ist." Gerhardt Fecht, "Der erste 'Teil' des sogenannten Evangelium Veritatis," *Or* 30 (1961): 373. Fecht's thesis was refuted by among others Peter Nagel: "Dann ist G. Fecht als einziger dem Chorus der Ἑλληνισταί entgegengetreten mit der Behauptung, das EV sei von vornherein koptisch konzipiert und formuliert worden. Die Antithese Fechts, die sich vorwiegend auf prosodische und stilistische Merkmale beruft, vermochte sich bislang nicht durchzusetzen." Peter Nagel, "Die Herkunft des Evan-gelium Veritatis in sprachlicher Sicht," *OLZ* 61, (1966): 6. Peter Nagel also refers to the analysis of the language of the *Gospel of Truth* in Erich Lüddeckens, "Beobachtungen zu Schrift und Sprach des 'Evangeluim Veritatis,'" *ZÄS* 90 (1963): 81–89. There Lüddeckens states: "Auf die koptische Poesie scheint mir in der von Fecht angenommenen metrischen Gliederung des Ev. Ver. Nichts hinzuweisen." Lüddeckens, "Beobachtungen," 85, note 2. Still, Lüddeckens does not refute the possibility of a Coptic original behind Gospel of Truth and concludes: "... daß der Text des Ev. Ver. – ob er nun koptischer oder griechischer Herkunft ist – im Gegensatz zu dem unordentlichen Eindruck der uns vorliegenden Niederschrift bewußt in eine bestimmte stilistische Form gegeben wurde unter Nutzung von Möglich-keiten, die uns bereits in einem genuin ägyptischen Literaturwerk koptischer Sprache nachgewiesen worden sind." Lüddeckens, "Beobachtungen," 89. Nagel's suggestion for a Syriac original did not gain more approval than Fecht's suggestion of a Coptic original and today Nagel regards the question of the original language behind Gospel of Truth unsolved, cf. Peter Nagel, *Codex apocryphus gnosticus Novi Testamenti* (WUNT 326, Tübingen: Mohr Siebeck, 2014), 35. Here I shall not opt for a solution to

in NHC XII deliberately changed the text or only had an inattentive moment, their variant descriptions of the highest principle tell us that NHC I,*3* and NHC XII,*2* differ, regardless of whether they stem from the same *Vorlage* or not. Their variant readings tell us that they cannot be regarded as homogeneous evidence of a fifth Valentinian Gospel. Also the correspondence between the predicate ἀχώρητον in Irenaeus' account and ⲁⲧϣⲁⲡϥ in NHC I,*3* cannot alone testify to a relationship between an assumed Greek *Vorlage*, Irenaeus' account and NHC I,*3*. Instead it is problematic to reconstruct the hypothetical Greek *Vorlage* from NHC I,*3* or XII,*2* or the process of transmission and redaction from the hypothetical original into the two versions known today. This process is often illustrated as two parallel redaction lines springing from the same Greek source that at some point in history were translated into the two Coptic versions we now possess. For these redaction lines or even the Greek *Vorlage* we have no evidence.

Fragment 2

We shall now proceed to the next synoptic passage, which displays even greater variation between the two versions. This second fragment of NHC XII,*2* has been assigned page number 54 by its editor, who identifies NHC I 31.25–32.3 as a parallel.[28] Since the preceding lines at NHC I 31.22–24 contribute to our evaluation of the relationship between the two witnesses, I shall include them here:

NHC XII,2 54.19–28

(19) [ⲙⲣ̄ⲣⲉ ⲉⲧⲟⲗ]ⲙ̄ ⲗⲟⲙⲧ ⲁϥⲡⲟⲣ[ⲕⲟⲩ	He destro[yed the twisted bonds ...]
(20) [9±] ⲛ̄ⲃⲣ̄ⲣⲉ ⲁϥⲥⲟⲟ[ⲣ̄ⲉ ⲉ]	[9±] young. He raised
(21) [ⲉⲣⲁⲓ ⲇⲉ ⲛ̄ⲛⲁⲉ]ⲓ ⲛ̄ⲧⲁⲩⲥⲗⲁⲁⲧⲉ ⲟ[ⲩⲙⲟ]	[those] who had stumbled.
(22) [ⲉⲓⲧ ⲁϥϣⲱⲡ]ⲉ ⲛ̄ⲛⲁⲉⲓ ⲉⲧⲥⲟⲣ[ⲙ̄· ⲟⲩ]	[He became a way for thos]e who had gone astra[y.]
(23) [ⲥⲟⲟⲩⲛ ⲁϥϣ]ⲱⲡⲉ ⲛ̄ⲛⲁⲉⲓ ⲉⲧ[ⲟ ⲛ̄ⲁⲧ]	[He becam]e [knowledge] for those who [were]
(24) [ⲥⲟⲟⲩⲛ· ⲟ]ⲩⲙⲛ̄ⲧⲁⲧⲙⲟⲩ ⲁⲥϣ[ⲱⲡⲉ]	[ignorant.] Immortality came
(25) [ⲛ̄ⲛⲁⲉⲓ ⲉⲧⲙ]ⲟⲟⲩⲧ ⲡⲁⲉⲓ ⲡ[ⲉ ⲡϣⲱⲥ]	[to those who were m]ortal. He is [the shepherd]
(26) [ⲉϥⲕⲱ ⲉⲣⲣ]ⲁ̣[ⲓ] ⲙ̄ⲡⲡ̄ⲧⲁⲉⲓⲟ̣[ⲩ ⲙⲛ̄ ⲯⲓⲥ]	[that left] [behin]d the ninet[y-nine]
(27) [ⲛ̄ⲉⲥⲟⲟⲩ] ⲛⲁⲉⲓ ⲉⲧⲉ ⲙ̄ⲡⲟⲩⲥⲱ[ⲣ̄ⲙ̄ ⲁϥ]	[sheep], these that had not gone astr[ay. He]
(28) [ϣⲓⲛⲉ ⲛ̄ⲥ]ⲁ ⲡⲁⲓ̈ ⲛ̄ⲧⲁϥⲥⲱⲣ̄ⲙ̄ [	[sought af]ter the one that had gone astray.

---

the language of the original *Gospel of Truth*. All that is certain is that NHC I,*3* and XII,*2* are written in Coptic and were as such used by one or more Coptic communities.

28 Wisse, "Gospel of Truth," 345.

NHC I,3 31.22–32.3[29]

(22)	ⲭⲉ ⲛ̄ⲧⲁⲩ ⲡⲉⲧⲉ·	For they were
(23)	ⲛⲉⲩⲥⲁⲣⲙ̄· ⲛ̄ⲉ̄ⲣⲉⲩ ⲛ̄ⲛⲓⲣⲁⲉⲓⲛⲉ·	leading astray from his face those
(24)	ⲛ̄ⲧⲁⲩⲣ̄ ⲉ̄ⲁⲉ ⲙ̄ⲡⲓⲛⲁⲉ ⲛ̄ⲉ̄ⲣⲏ̄ⲓ̈ ⲉ̄ⲛ̄	who were in need of mercy below
(25)	ϯⲡⲗⲁⲛⲏ ⲟⲩⲁⲉ̄ⲛ ⲉ̄ⲛ̄ⲥⲛⲉⲩⲉ̄	in error and bonds.
(26)	ⲁⲩⲱ ⲙ̄ⲛ̄ ⲟⲩϭⲁⲙ· ⲁⲩⲃⲁⲗⲟⲩ ⲁ	And with great power he released
(27)	ⲃⲁⲗ ⲁⲩⲱ ⲁⲩⲭⲡⲓⲁⲩ ⲉ̄ⲛ̄ ⲡⲥⲁⲩⲛⲉ	and upbraided them by knowledge.
(28)	ⲡⲉ· ⲁⲩϣⲱⲡⲉ ⲉⲩⲟⲉⲓ ⲛ̄ⲟⲩ	He became a
(29)	ⲙⲁⲉⲓⲧ· ⲛ̄ⲛⲉⲉⲓ ⲉⲛⲉⲩⲥⲁⲣⲙ̄	way for those who had gone astray,
(30)	ⲁⲩⲱ ⲟⲩⲥⲁⲩⲛⲉ· ⲛ̄ⲛⲉⲉⲓ ⲉⲧⲟⲓ̈	knowledge for those who were
(31)	ⲛ̄ⲁⲧⲥⲁⲩⲛⲉ· ⲟⲩϭⲓⲛⲉ ⲛ̄ⲛⲉⲉⲓ ⲉ	ignorant, discovery for those who were
(32)	ⲛⲉⲩϣⲓⲛⲉ· ⲟⲩⲁⲉ̄ⲛ· ⲟⲩⲧⲁⲭⲣⲟ	seeking and strength
(33)	ⲛ̄ⲛⲉⲉⲓ ⲉⲧⲉⲛⲉⲩⲛⲁⲉⲓⲛ ⲁⲣⲁⲩ	for those who were shaken,
(34)	ⲟⲩⲙⲛ̄ⲧⲁⲧⲭⲱⲉ̄ⲙ̄ ⲛ̄ⲛⲉⲉⲓ ⲉⲧⲉ	and purity for those who
(35)	ⲛⲉⲩⲭⲁⲉ̄ⲙ̄ ⲉⲛⲧⲁⲩ ⲡⲉ ⲡϣⲱⲥ	were defiled. He was a shepherd
(36)	ⲉⲛⲧⲁⲣⲕⲱⲉ ⲛ̄ⲥⲱⲩ· ⲙ̄ⲡⲓⲡⲥⲧⲉ	who left behind the ninety-
(1)	ϯⲓⲥ ⲛ̄ⲉⲥⲁⲩ ⲉⲧⲉⲙ̄ⲡⲟⲩⲥⲱⲣⲙ̄	nine sheep that had not gone astray.
(2)	ⲁϥⲉⲓ ̄ ⲁⲩϣⲓⲛⲉ ⲛ̄ⲥⲁ ⲡⲉⲉⲓ ⲛ̄ⲧⲁⲩ	He went and sought after the one that had
(3)	ⲥⲱⲣⲙ̄	gone astray.

Here too the text of Codex XII is in such poor condition that it is difficult to compare it to the text in Codex I. Still, a few theologically loaded words are preserved and reveal notable differences from the version of Codex I. The first statement about the destruction of the twisted bonds (ⲙⲣ̄ⲣⲉ ⲉⲧⲟ̄ⲗ̄ⲙ̄ⲗⲟⲙⲧ) is reconstructed in NHC XII 54.19, and even though this is a plausible restoration, the two manuscripts express different statements. NHC XII,2 describes destruction of "the twisted bonds," while NHC I,3 simply mentions the bonds as a circumstance for those who have been led astray. Furthermore, the statement about knowledge and ignorance in the fragment relies on reconstruction from Codex I,3 and therefore cannot serve as an argument for agreement between the two manuscripts.

On the other hand, the two preserved words, ⲥⲗⲁⲁⲧⲉ (NHC XII 54.21) and ⲙⲛ̄ⲧⲁⲧⲙⲟⲩ (NHC XII 54.24), show that the description of Jesus in Codex XII differs from Codex I. A similar expression ⲧⲁⲭⲣⲟ ⲛ̄ⲧⲟⲩⲣⲓⲧⲉ ⲛ̄ⲛⲉⲉⲓ ⲛ̄ⲧⲁⲉ̄ⲥⲗⲁⲧⲉ·, "make firm the feet of those who have stumbled" at NHC I 33.1–2 appears in the paraenetic section (NHC I 32.31–33.32) following the parable of the lost sheep. Even if the phrase at NHC I 33.1–2 is not identical with NHC XII,2's ⲁⲩⲥⲟⲟⲩ[ⲉ̄ⲉ̄ ⲉ̄ⲉ̄ⲣⲉⲓ̈ ⲇⲉ ⲛ̄ⲛⲁⲉ]ⲓ̣ ⲛ̄ⲧⲁⲩⲥⲗⲁⲁⲧⲉ, "he raised [those, who had] stumbled," the similarities reveal that what in NHC I,3 is put forward as an exhortation to the audience is in NHC XII,2 a statement about Jesus. The contexts of these two statements are simply not the same and we must conclude that NHC I,3 and XII,2 introduce their interpretation of Matthew's parable of the lost sheep differently.

---

29 Attridge and MacRae, "Gospel of Truth," 100, 102.

Another difference worthy of notice is the appearance of the word "immortality," ⲙⲛⲧⲁⲧⲙⲟⲩ, at NHC XII 54.24. Not only is this word absent from the corresponding passage in NHC I,*3*, it does not even appear anywhere in NHC I,*3* at all. There are passages in NHC I,*3* that teach that the death of Jesus is life for many (ⲡⲓⲙⲟⲩ ⲛ̄ⲧⲟⲟⲧϥ̄ ⲟⲩⲱⲛϩ̄ ⲛ̄ϩⲁϩ ⲡⲉ, NHC I 20.13–14), and that Jesus was dressed in eternal life during his descent to death (ⲉϥⲥⲱⲕ ⲙ̄ⲙⲁϥ ⲁⲡⲓⲧⲛ̄ ⲁⲡⲙⲟⲩ ⲉⲣⲉⲡⲓⲱⲛϩ̄ ⲛ̄ⲁⲛⲏϩⲉ ⲧⲟ ϩⲓⲱⲱϥ, NHC I 20.28–30), but these are in the section about the crucifixion of Jesus while dressed in a book. The turn from death to life is also described at NHC I 25.18–19 and 42.17–18, but in both passages it refers to the attainment of life by believers. In contrast to Codex I, the fragments in Codex XII preserve no reference to the crucifixion. While one can suggest that the version of NHC XII,*2* might have taught a message like that in Codex I, based on the words "immortality," "ⲙⲛⲧⲁⲧⲙⲟⲩ" (NHC XII 54.24) and "[m]ortal," "[ⲉⲧⲙ]ⲟⲟⲩⲧ" (NHC XII 54.25), the position of these words between the description of Jesus and the parable of the lost sheep is peculiar. To what "immortal" and "mortal" in NHC XII,*2* actually refer is unclear. In this same section NHC XII,*2* leaves out the three statements about Jesus as "finding," "strength," and "purity." The preceding section at NHC I 31.21–22 makes a brief allusion to the crucifixion with the statement ⲉⲁϥⲧⲣⲟⲩⲱϫⲛ̄ ⲛ̄ϭⲓ ⲛⲓⲕⲟⲗⲁⲥⲓⲥ· ⲙⲛ ⲛⲓⲙⲁⲥⲧⲓⲅⲝ, "He caused the punishments and tortures to cease," but again, this is not a passage preserved in the fragments of Codex XII. Wisse comments that ⲙⲛⲧⲁⲧⲙⲟⲩ (NHC XII 54.24) and ⲙⲛⲧⲁⲧⲭⲱⲣⲙ̄ (NHC I 31.34) may both derive from the Greek ἀφθαρσία.[30] Still, about the wording of a hypothetical Greek *Vorlage* behind NHC I,*3* and XII,*2* we can only guess. The fact is that ⲙⲛⲧⲁⲧⲙⲟⲩ in the fragment of Codex XII is absent from the parallel text in NHC I,*3*. This absence illustrates an example of individual development in the case of each version and that NHC XII,*2* is not only an abbreviated version of I,*3*.

NHC I,*3* and XII,*2*'s reception of Matthew's parable of the lost sheep (Matt 18:12) only shows minor discrepancies. The fragment in Codex XII does not preserve the arithmetic speculation which NHC I,*3* combines with this parable. On the basis of what is preserved of this parable in XII,*2*, we can estimate that the passage was shorter than the version in Codex I,*3*. This further supports the impression that Codex XII's version of the *Gospel of Truth* was more concise than that of Codex I.

Fragment 3

In their discussion of NHC XII,*2* fragment 3, the editors observe more discrepancies than similarities between it and NHC I,*3*. The fragment encompasses twenty-nine

---

30 Wisse, "Gospel of Truth," 345. This thesis could agree with Lampe's definition of the Greek noun as meaning both immortality and incorruption, cf. Geoffrey W. H. Lampe ed., *A Patristic Greek Lexicon*, (Oxford: Claredon Press, 1961), 274–75.

lines, but each line has only a word or two preserved, while the last line is missing. The fragment has been identified as a parallel to NHC I 34.4–35.4[31] on the basis of the words ⲡⲙⲁⲁⲝ[ⲉ] (NHC XII 57.5; ⲙ̄ⲙⲉϣϫⲉ NHC I 34.9),[32] ⲥⲧ̄ⲛⲟⲩϥⲉ (NHC XII 57.8,11; ⲥⲧⲁⲉⲓ NHC I 34.4,6,10,10,14,17,26),[33] ⲯⲩⲭⲓⲕⲟⲛ (NHC XII 57.13; NHC I 34.19),[34] ⲁⲣⲟϣ (NHC XII 57.20); ⲁⲣⲁϣ (NHC I 34.32)[35] and [ⲡⲟ]ⲩϫⲁⲉ[ⲓ] (NHC XII 57.24,[26]; ⲡⲟⲩϫⲉⲉⲓ· (NHC I 35.1).[36] These words suggest that NHC XII,2 may have taught a message about procession and manifestation of the divine fragrance/spirit which agreed with NHC I,3, or at least used similar imagery. The editors observe that parts of NHC I,3 are absent from NHC XII 57.1–29, despite the fact that they see it as a parallel to NHC I 34.3–35.2. Wisse comments that NHC I 34.13–14 and 34.20–26 appear to be absent from NCH XII,2[37] and that the wording of NHC XII 57.23–29 "differs considerably from Codex I."[38] The beginning of the fragment also reads differently than the parallel passage in NHC I, and as the syntax at NHC I 34.10–21, which ought to correspond to NHC XII 57.6–15,[39] is itself unclear, this disagreement complicates the reconstruction of NHC XII,2 and the comparison of the two manuscripts. What can be compared to the text in NHC I,3 is NHC XII 57.16–22. The editors reconstruct this passage as follows:

NHC XII,2 57.16–22

(16)	[12± ⲉ]ⲧⲃⲉ [ⲡⲁⲓ ⲁϥⲉⲓ ⲛ̄]	The[refore it came,]
(17)	[ϭⲓ ⲡⲛⲁ̅ϩⲧⲉ ⲁϥⲃⲱⲗ] ⲉⲃⲟⲗ ⲙ̄[ⲡⲓⲙⲉ]	[namely the faith. It resolved the di-]
(18)	[ⲣⲓⲥⲙⲟⲥ ⲁⲩⲱ ⲁϥⲉ]ⲓ ⲉⲡϫⲱ[ⲕ ⲉⲃⲟⲗ]	[vision and it ca]me to the completi[on,
(19)	[ⲉⲧϩⲙⲙ ϫⲉ]ⲕ[ⲁⲁⲥ ⲛ̄]ⲛⲉϥϣⲱ[ⲡⲉ]	[which is hot], s[o that] the cold [would not]
(20)	[ⲉϥⲥⲱⲧ] ⲉⲉⲓ ⲛ[ⲁϥ ⲛ̄]ϭⲓ ⲡⲓⲁⲣⲟϣ [ⲁⲩ]	[again] come t[o it.]
(21)	[ⲱ ϥⲛ]ⲁ̅ⲃⲱⲗ ϩ[ⲙ̄ ⲡ]ⲧⲱⲧ ⲛ̄[ϩⲏⲧ ⲉⲧ]	[It shall] dissolve in a harmony [that is]
(22)	[ϫⲏⲕ]	[perfect].

---

31 Wisse, "Gospel of Truth," 345.

32 English: "Ear"/"ears."

33 ⲥⲧ̄ⲛⲟⲩϥⲉ means "good smell" or "parfume," cf. Crum, *Coptic Dictionary*, 362b, and Wolfhart Westendorf, *Koptisches Handwörterbuch: Bearbeitet auf der Grundlage des Koptischen Handwörterbuchs von Wilhelm Spiegelberg* (Heidelberg: Universitätsverlag Winter, 2008), 200–1.

34 English: "physical."

35 English: "cold."

36 English: "Salvation."

37 Wisse, "Gospel of Truth," 345–46.

38 Wisse, "Gospel of Truth," 346.

39 Wisse, "Gospel of Truth," 345.

NHC I,3 34.28–34

(28)	ⲉⲧⲃⲉ ⲡⲉⲉ̣ⲓ ⲁ̣ϥⲓ ⲛ̄ϭⲓ ⲡ̄ⲛⲁ̣ⳉ	Therefore faith came.
(29)	ⲧⲉ· ⲁϥⲃⲱⲗ ⲙ̄ⲡ̣ⲓⲡⲱϣⲉ ⲁⲃⲁⲗ	It dissolved the division
(30)	ⲁ̣ⲩⲱ ⲁϥⲉⲓⲛⲉ ⲙ̄ⲡⲓⲡⲗⲏⲣⲱⲙⲁ	and it brought the fullness (Pleroma),
(31)	ⲉⲧⳉⲏⲙ̄· ⲛ̄ⲧⲉ ϯⲁⲅⲁⲡⲏ ϫⲉⲕⲁⲥⲉ	that is warm of love, so that
(32)	ⲡⲁⲣⲁϣ· ⲛⲉϥⲥⲱⲧⲉ ⲁϣⲱⲡⲉ	the cold will not again occur,
(33)	ⲁⲗⲗⲁ ϯⲙⲛ̄ⲧⲟⲩⲉⲉⲓ ⲧⲉ· ⲛ̄ⲧⲉ	but it is the unity of
(34)	ⲡⲓⲙⲉⲉⲩ ⲉⲧϫⲏⲕ ⲁⲃⲁⲗ·	thought that is perfect.

The reconstruction of these lines is thought provoking. As mentioned above only a few words are preserved in each line of the fragment from Codex XII. This means that the meaning of these lines relies on reconstruction. If we did not have the text of NHC I,3, we would have no idea how to fill out the lacunae, and all that would remain would be:

> Concerning [...] from [...] to the complet[...] he/it/his was/would not [...] to come to [...] the cold [...] dissolve [...] join/agree/mingle/agreement/mingling [...]

As we can see, the many reconstructions inevitably tend towards harmonization of the fragment from Codex XII with the text preserved in Codex I. A comparison of Codex XII fragment 3 and its parallel in NHC I,3 reveals that the fragment has a significantly different wording despite the editors' attempt to harmonize the two versions; the editors reconstruct the fragment by adding the phrase of NHC I 34.28–29, ⲁϥⲓ ⲛ̄ϭⲓ ⲡⲛⲁⳉⲧⲉ·, and they also identify the ⲡϫⲱ of NHC XII 57.18 as ⲡϫⲱ[ⲕ ⲉⲃⲟⲗ], which translates the Greek πλήρωμα and accordingly figures as a parallel to the ⲡⲗⲏⲣⲱⲙⲁ of NHC I 34.30.[40] The fragment does not translate the Greek term πλήρωμα with ⲡϫⲱⲕ ⲉⲃⲟⲗ elsewhere, but preserves it as ⲡⲗⲏⲣⲱⲙⲁ (NHC XII 58.3, 24). Even if the editors' reconstruction of NHC XII 57.16–22 restored its original wording, NHC I,3 and XII,2 would feature different interpretations of the concept of the pleroma here. Concerning the pleroma, NHC I,3 states that it is brought by faith (34.28–30). In XII,2, faith comes to the completion, which is understood as the pleroma (NHC XII 57.16–18). These different statements illustrate that NHC I,3 sees the pleroma as a result of faith, while NHC XII,2 understands the pleroma as a sphere or space at which faith arrives. This significant difference is glossed over when the editors harmonize NHC XII,2 with I,3. Accordingly the reconstruction of fragment 3 paves the way for an interpretation of the Valentinian myth within XII,2.

That the XII,2 differs from I,3 also becomes evident in its use of ⲧⲱⲧ ⲛ̄[ⳉⲏⲧ] (NHC XII 57.21), here translated as "harmony." NHC I 34.28–34 does not employ this phrase,

---

40 Wisse, "Gospel of Truth," 346: "ⲡϫⲱⲕ ⲉⲃⲟⲗ translates πλήρωμα. Elsewhere in the fragments πλήρωμα has not been translated."

but rather ϯⲙⲛ̄ⲧⲟⲩⲉⲉⲓ ⲧⲉ· ⲛ̄ⲧⲉ ⲡⲓⲙⲉⲉⲩ (NHC I 34.33–34), meaning "unity of thought." NHC I,3 teaches that a unity of perfect thought occurs where the cold had been. NHC XII,2, on the other hand, teaches that the cold dissolves in perfect harmony. While the vocabulary of the two manuscripts agrees on the surface, minor deviations suggest independent development of their respective texts. The restoration of the lacunae according to NHC I,3 creates the impression that NHC XII,2 simply replaces the phrase "unity of perfect thought" with "perfect harmony." Such an impression contributes to an understanding of XII,2 as an abbreviate version of I,3, and neglects an independent process of development in the case of each version. It is not clear whether the phrase "unity of perfect thought" was abbreviated to "perfect harmony" or rather developed from it. In NHC I,3 the paternal thoughts are a central theme for its metaphysics. The expression "unity of perfect thought" agrees well with this metaphysics of I,3, while the expression "perfect harmony" of XII,2 fits better into a setting that seeks to distance itself from this metaphysics. If the scribe had not transmitted the word ⲙⲉⲉⲩⲉ at XII,2 53.25 and 60.19,23 one could assume that he deliberately sorted out this word in order to harmonize XII,2 with his own conviction. This might not be the case.

Fragment 4

We shall now proceed to fragment 4, which appears to be parallel to NHC I 35.5–35.[41] Fragment 4 has been assigned with page number 58, it is the other side of fragment 3 and has, naturally, suffered the same damages. Of twenty-nine identified lines, only a few words of each line are preserved. The preservation of a few theologically loaded words and phrases reveals that also this side of the fragments could be in accord with NHC I,3. These theologically loaded words and phrases are: ⲡⲓⲡⲗⲏⲣⲱ[ⲙⲁ] (NHC XII 58.3, 24, [29–30]; NHC I 34.36; 35.8, 29, 35–36), [ⲡⲓ]ϣⲧⲁ (NHC XII 58.4, 28, [28]; ϣⲧⲱ/ϣⲧⲁ NHC I 35.9, 33), ⲡⲗⲁⲛⲏ (NHC XII 58.5; NHC I 35.18), [ⲡⲃⲁ]ⲑⲟⲥ ⲙ̄ⲡⲉⲓⲱ[ⲧ] (NHC XII 58.11; ⲡⲓⲃⲁⲑⲟⲥ ⲛ̄ⲧⲉ ⲡⲓⲱⲧ NHC I 35.15–16), ⲡⲛⲟⲃⲉ (NHC XII 58.20, ⲛⲁⲃⲓ NHC I 35.26) and ϣⲱⲛⲉ (NHC XII 58.26; NHC I 35.31).[42] The preserved keywords of fragment 3 correspond to NHC I,3's description of the manifestation of the divine fragrance. Likewise the preserved words of fragment 4 follow NHC I,3 with clarification of how the manifestation of this fragrance causes salvation and leads to unity with the Father. This agreement is undeniable and prompts the conclusion that the versions are similar at this point. Still, harmonization may hinder us from understanding NHC XII,2 as an independent witness. Understanding NHC XII,2 on its own terms requires an evaluation of the respective contexts of the preserved keywords. There the use of the word ⲡⲓϣⲧⲁ at NHC XII 58.4 and ⲡⲗⲁⲛⲏ at NHC XII 58.5 causes confusion.

---

41 Wisse, "Gospel of Truth," 346.
42 English: "Pleroma," "deficiency," "error," "depth of the Father," "sin," and "disease."

Concerning ⲡⲗⲁⲛⲏ, meaning "error" NHC XII 58.3–7 mentions this as not being the cause behind the occurrence of deficiency, ⲡⲓϣⲧⲁ:

NHC XII,2 58.3–7

(3)	ⲁⲩⲱ ⲙ̄ⲡⲉ]	[And]
(4)	[ⲡⲓ]ϣⲧⲁ ϣⲱⲡⲉ [ⲉⲃⲟⲗ ϩⲓⲧⲟⲟⲧ̄ⲥ̄]	[the] deficiency [did not] occur [through]
(5)	[ⲛ̄ϯ]ⲡⲗⲁⲛⲏ· ⲁⲩⲱ ⲁ[ⲥϣⲱⲡⲉ ⲉⲧⲃⲏ	[the] error and [it came about because of]
(6)	[ⲏⲧⲥ̄ ⲛ̄ϯⲙ̄ⲛ̄ⲧⲛⲟ[ⲩⲧⲉ ⲙ̄ⲡⲉⲓⲱⲧ ⲛ̄]	[the Father's di]vinity [that is]
(7)	[ⲁⲧ]ϣⲓⲧⲥ	[im]measurable

While, however, NHC I 35.8–11, appears as a parallel to this statement with its:

NHC I,3 35.8–11

(8)	ⲉⲛⲧⲁϥϣⲱⲡⲉ ⲉⲛ	It did not occur,
(9)	ⲛ̄ϭⲓ ⲡⲓϣⲧⲱ̄ ⲛ̄ϯϩⲩⲗⲏ ⲁⲃⲁⲗ ϩ̄ⲓⲧⲟ	the deficiency of matter, through
(10)	ⲟⲧⲥ̄ ⲛ̄ϯⲙ̄ⲛ̄ⲧⲁⲧⲁⲣⲏⲭⲥ̄ ⲛ̄ⲧⲉ	the limitlessness of
(11)	ⲡⲓⲱⲧ·	the Father.

It is notable that the word ⲡⲗⲁⲛⲏ is not present within this context of NHC I,3. Instead we find the word ⲡⲗⲁⲛⲏ a few lines below, where NHC I,3 states:

NHC I,3 35.14–18

(14)	ⲁⲗⲗⲁ ⲁϥⲁ	But
(15)	ϣⲉ{ⲉ}ⲉⲓ ⲛ̄ϭⲓ ⲡⲓⲃⲁⲑⲟⲥ ⲛ̄ⲧⲉ ⲡⲓ	the depth of the Father
(16)	ⲱⲧ· ⟦ϩⲁ`ϩ´ⲧⲏϥ ⲉⲛ·⟧ ⲁⲩⲱ ⲛⲉϥϣⲟⲟⲡ	was multiplied ⟦not with him⟧ and within him
(17)	ϩⲁϩ̄ⲧⲏϥ ⲉⲛ ⲛ̄ϭⲓ ⲡⲓⲙⲉⲩⲉ ⲛ̄ⲧⲉ	was not the thought of
(18)	ϯⲡⲗⲁⲛⲏ·	error.

Both NHC I,3 35.28 and XII,2 58.5 employ the word ⲡⲗⲁⲛⲏ in the sense of "error" and not as a personified character as in the beginning of NHC I,3. Yet the word appears in two different contexts. NHC XII,2 explains that deficiency did not occur because of ⲡⲗⲁⲛⲏ. NHC I,3 on the other hand teaches that "the thought of error was not within him," i.e. the Father. NHC I,3's expression ⲡⲓⲙⲉⲩⲉ ⲛ̄ⲧⲉ ϯⲡⲗⲁⲛⲏ· appears more developed than the simple ⲡⲗⲁⲛⲏ of NHC XII,2. The relationship between the expression [ⲡⲃⲁ]ⲑⲟⲥ ⲙ̄ⲡⲉⲓⲱ[ⲧ], "depth of the Father" and the word ⲡⲗⲁⲛⲏ in the two versions demonstrates the different contexts. In NHC XII,2 [ⲡⲃⲁ]ⲑⲟⲥ ⲙ̄ⲡⲉⲓⲱ[ⲧ] follows after the explanation of why deficiency did not come about appearing in another context six lines later. In NHC I,3 the expression "depth of the Father," ⲡⲓⲃⲁⲑⲟⲥ ⲛ̄ⲧⲉ ⲡⲓⲱⲧ, appears two lines prior to the mention of ⲡⲗⲁⲛⲏ, and introduces what is said about error. This means that NHC I 35.14–18 can not be a parallel to NHC XII 58.3–7, despite their common use of the word ⲡⲗⲁⲛⲏ. Instead NHC I,3 35.8–11 appears to parallel NHC

XII 58.3–7, where the expression ⲡⲓⲱⲧⲱ̄, the deficiency, is the point in common rather than ⲡⲗⲁⲛⲏ. NHC I,*3*'s ⲡⲓⲱⲧⲱ̄ ⲛ̄ⲧⲉ̄ⲩⲗⲏ, instead of NHC XII,*2*'s simple ⲡⲓⲱⲧⲱ, shows that NHC I,*3* here uses the longer formula specifying deficiency as related to matter. Apart from a common employment of the word ⲱⲧⲁ/ⲱⲧⲱ the equivalence between NHC XII,*2* 58.3–7 and NHC I,*3* 35.8–11 lies in the predicates "immeasurable," [ⲛ̄ⲁⲧ] ⲱⲓⲧⲥ (NHC XII 58.6–7), and "limitlessness," ⲙⲛ̄ⲧⲁⲧⲁⲣⲏⲭⲥ̄ (NHC I 35.11) attributed to the Father. However, again NHC I,*3* and XII,*2* use different predicates about the Father as was the case with XII,*2* 53.24 and I,*3* 30.33. From the theologically loaded keywords of fragment 3 and 4 and their equivalences at I,*3* it is possible to recognize coherence between the Valentinian myth and the manuscripts, in particular if the concept of ⲡⲗⲁⲛⲏ refers to the fallen Sophia.[43] However, from the few preserved words of NHC XII,*2* we can not estimate if I,*3* and XII,*2* agree in their interpretation of the myth. From I,*3* we can assume that the Father at this stage of the text expands, dissolving the deficiency. The state of XII,*2* does however not allow us to draw this conclusion. Even the reconstruction does not provide an answer to this problem. The only sure conclusion we can draw from the analysis of the few preserved words is that the contexts of NHC I,*3* and XII,*2* differ here, and that I,*3* and XII,*2* use different predicates about the Father. Even if the texts teach the same message they certainly depict it differently.

Fragment 5

Fragment 5 follows fragment 4 as page number 59 according to the codicological restoration of NHC XII. This restoration is based on a few essential words that correspond to NHC I 36.13–27. These words are: ⲱⲧⲣ̄ⲧⲱⲣ (NHC XII 59.20; ⲱⲧⲁⲣⲧⲣ̄ NHC I 36.16), ⲡⲓⲧⲱ̄ⲣⲥ̄ (NHC XII 59.21, 27, [30]; NHC I 36.16, 17, 17, 19, 22, 23, 26), ⲡⲛⲁⲉ ⲛ̄ⲧⲉ ⲡⲉ⳿ⲓ⳿ⲱ[ⲧ] (NHC XII 59.22; ⲡⲛⲁⲉ ⲙ̄ⲡⲓⲱⲧ NHC I 36.18), and ⲧⲗⲟⲉⲓⲥⲉ (NHC XII 59.28; ⲧⲗⲁⲉⲓⲥⲉ NHC I 36.24–25).[44] The first seventeen lines of page 59 are lacking. Therefore, even if there are a few well preserved lines, they are too few to evaluate the fragment's relationship to NHC I,*3*. From these few phrases, ⲉⲧⲱⲧⲣ̄ⲧⲱⲣ (NHC XII 59,19 "who were disturbed," ⲉ.ⲭⲓ ⲙ̄ⲡⲓⲧⲱⲣⲥ (XII 59,21) "receiving the ointment, ⲛⲁⲉ ⲟⲉ ⲛⲁⲩ (XII 59,23) "mercy on them" we may assume that NHC XII,*2* used imagery similar to NHC I,*3* when describing the state of disconnection from the Father as a state of unstableness, while paternal mercy is received as or along with an ointment.

---

43 Attridge and MacRae, "Gospel of Truth," 77–78. Bentley Layton, *The Gnostic Scriptures* (New York: ABRL, Doubleday, 1995), 253: "'error': a feminine personification corresponding to both wisdom and Ialdabaōth in gnostic myth."

44 English: "Disturbed," "ointment," "mercy of the Father," and "reason."

Fragment 6

The manuscript page constituting the sixth fragment of Codex XII has also lost nearly the first half of the page as the first sixteen lines are missing. Of the remaining lines, only a few theologically loaded words are preserved. These words, for which the editors have identified parallels in NHC I 37.7–21, are ⲙⲉⲉⲩⲉ (NHC XII 60.19, 23; ⲙⲉⲩⲉ/ ⲙⲉⲉⲩⲉ NHC I 37.8, 13), ⲡⲗⲟⲅⲟ[ⲥ] (NHC XII 60.19, 21; NHC I 37.8, 11), ⲁϥⲟⲩⲟⲛϩⲟⲩ ⲉⲃⲟⲗ (NHC XII 60.20; ⲁϥⲟⲩⲱⲛϩ ⲙ̄ⲙⲁⲩ ⲁⲃⲁⲗ/ⲉⲙⲡⲟⲩⲟⲱⲛⲉϩ ⲁⲃⲁⲗ NHC I 37.9–10, 14–15), [ⲡ]ⲉϩⲟⲟⲩ (NHC XII 60.22),[45] ⲡⲟⲩⲱϣ (NHC XII 60.27, 28; ⲡⲟⲩⲱϣⲉ NHC I 37.17–18, 18, 19) ⲡⲉϥϩⲏⲧ (NHC XII 60.29),[46] and [ⲡⲉ]ⲓⲱⲧ (NHC XII 60.30; ⲡⲓⲱⲧ NHC I 37.19). The missing lines and the fragmentary context of the few preserved words make this fragment just as fragile a witness for comparison with NHC I,3 as fragment 5. Still, it does feature an example of variation between the two versions. This is seen at the last lines of fragment 6, which states ⲡⲟⲩⲱϣ [ⲡⲉⲧϥ̄ⲙⲟⲧⲛ̄ ⲙ̄]ⲡⲉϥϩⲏⲧ ⲧⲏ[ⲣϥ̄ ⲛ̄ϩⲏⲧϥ̄ ⲛ̄ϭⲓ ⲡⲉ]ⲓⲱⲧ ⲁⲩⲱ ⲡ[ⲉⲧϥⲉⲩⲇⲟⲕⲉⲓ], "The will, in this [the] Father [rests] his whole heart and [is pleased]" (NHC XII 60.28–30). The parallel at NHC I 37.7–21 lacks the expression ⲡⲉϥϩⲏⲧ ⲧⲏ[ⲣϥ̄ ⲛ̄ϩⲏⲧϥ̄]. Instead NHC I,3 37.19–21 reads ⲡⲟⲩⲱϣⲉ ⲇⲉ ⲡⲉⲧⲉ ⲡⲓⲱⲧ ⲙⲁⲧⲛ̄ ⲙ̄ⲙⲁϥ· ⲛ̄ϩⲏⲧϥ̄ ⲟⲩⲁϩⲛ̄ ⲡⲉⲧⲣ̄ ⲉⲛⲉϥ·, "the will, the Father rests in it and is pleased." This difference comes unexpected because NHC XII,2, which is the shorter version, uses a longer expression. In the other examples illustrated above we observed that NHC I,3 generally used longer expressions. In I,3 the Father simply rests, while XII,2 describes how the Father rests his whole heart or mind. While one can speculate of the addition or omission of the phrase "his whole heart" we should be careful in overloading this phrase with theological meaning. It is interesting that the phrase "his whole heart" reveals a clear statement that does not appear in the text of NHC I,3 and that XII,2 therefore had another wording.

Conclusion

Having compared NHC XII,2 with NHC I,3 it becomes apparent that both manuscripts express an individual development. While I would still argue that these extant witnesses to the *Gospel of Truth* transmit ancient Valentinian teaching[47] it is problem-

---

45 NHC I,3 does not employ the word "ϩⲟⲟⲩ" within NHC I,3 37.7–21, but at NHC I,3 32.27 and 32.

46 NHC I,3 does not employ the word "ϩⲏⲧ" at NHC I,3 37.19–21 in the sense of "heart" or "mind," but only once as the preposition "in" at I,3 37.20. Otherwise the word "ϩⲏⲧ" in the sense of "heart" or "mind" appears several times throughout NHC I,3.

47 It would go beyond the scope of this article to discuss the Valentinian features within the *Gospel of Truth*. In short I would argue that *Gos. Truth* reveals a middle-platonic fourfold ontological structure that among others Hans Joachim Krämer finds significant for Gnostic Valentinian texts, cf. Hans Joachim Krämer, *Die Ursprung der Geistmetaphysik: Untersuchungen zur Geschichte des Platonismus*

atic to talk about either NHC I,3 or XII,2 as versions of the "fifth Valentinian Gospel." The discovery of the *Gospel of Truth* is not the discovery of the text mentioned in the second century work of Irenaeus. While NHC I,3 features a version of a Christian philosophical tractate that may or may not have taken its departure from the ancient unknown Gospel mentioned by Irenaus, all we can say about XII,2 is that it is similar to I,3, but appears to be an independently transmitted version of the work.

The state of NHC XII,2 is so fragmentary that only distinct keywords and phrases can be used to identify parallels in NHC I,3. Within this fragile frame of reference important differences emerge, while it is difficult to determine which version is the earlier. Nevertheless, NHC I,3 has served as the basis for the identification of the fragments of NHC XII,2. These fragment are assumed to belong to a shorter and abbreviated version of the *Gospel of Truth*, and this shines through in the reconstruction of the fragments. As plausible as these reconstructions may be, it should not lead to the conclusion that the two witnesses necessarily express a similar theology. Regarding NHC I,3 and XII,2 as two voices speaking the same message implies a view of Valentinianism as a more static and homogeneous Christian philosophy and belief system that was even transmitted unchanged over centuries. The attempt of modern scholars to harmonize NHC I,3 and XII,2 assumes a uniformity of the two texts' theologies. Instead, Valentinianism may have had borders at least as blurred as what came to be mainstream Christianity. It is possible that these versions have undergone a journey of different turns before they ended up in NHC I and XII. But it is also possible that only one of them, possibly I,3, was transmitted over a longer period of time, while XII,2 was produced on the basis of the version found in I,3 at a later stage of development. The analysis of the differences between NHC I,3 and XII,2 reveals that the texts are not mere copies, but differ significantly from each other. These differences may not be a product of casual developments, but may be intended. When we reconstruct one manuscript from the other, this possibility of an editorial/redactional intention is ignored. The attempt to fit the wording of NHC I,3 into the fragments of NHC XII,2 may thus give rise to a misleading impression of NHC XII,2 as basically the same as I,3. The editors of NHC XII,2 have done an excellent work illustrating the affinities between NHC I,3 and XII,2. Now that these affinities have been identified and acknowledged it is time to disregard the reconstructions in the square brackets in order to gain a more nuanced and independent picture of NHC XII,2.

---

zwischen Platon und Plotin (Amsterdam: B. R. Grüner, 1967), 238–54. Also the arithmetic speculation of NHC I,3 32.4–16, can be related to the marcosian teaching of Irenaeus, *Haer.* I.16.2.

Bibliography

Attridge, Harold W. and George W. MacRae. "The Gospel of Truth." Pages 55–117 in *Nag Hammadi Codex I: The Jung Codex*. Edited by Harold W. Attridge. Nag Hammadi Studies 22. Leiden: Brill, 1985.

Crum, Walter E. *A Coptic Dictionary*. Oxford: Clarendon Press, 1939.

Fecht, Gerhardt. "Der erste 'Teil' des sogenannten Evangelium Veritatis," *Orientalia* 30 (1961): 371–90.

Funk, Wolf-Peter. "How closely related are the Subakhmimic dialects?" *Zeitschrift für ägyptische Sprache und Altertumskunde* 112 (1985): 124–39.

Grobel, Kendrick. *The Gospel of Truth: A Valentinian Meditation on the Gospel*. New York: Abingdon Press, 1960.

Hartenstein, Judith and Uwe-Karsten Plisch. "Der Brief des Jakobus." Pages 11–26 in *Nag Hammadi Deutsch* 1. Edited by Hans-Martin Schenke, Hans-Gebhard Bethge and Ursula Ulrike Kaiser. Die Griechischen Christlichen Schriftsteller der Ersten Jahrhunderte 8. Berlin: Walter de Gruyter, 2001.

Krämer, Hans Joachim. *Die Ursprung der Geistmetaphysik: Untersuchungen zur Geschichte des Platonismus zwischen Platon und Plotin*. Amsterdam: B. R. Grüner, 1967.

Lampe, Geoffrey W. H. *A Patristic Greek Lexicon*. Oxford: Claredon Press, 1961.

Layton, Bentley. *The Gnostic Scriptures: A New Translation with Annotations and Introductions*. New York: Doubleday, 1995.

Lüddeckens, Erich. "Beobachtungen zu Schrift und Sprach des "Evangeluim Veritatis." *Zeitschrift für ägyptische Sprache und Altertumskunde* 90 (1963): 81–89.

Nagel, Peter. "Die Herkunft des Evangelium Veritatis in sprachlicher Sicht." *Orientalische Literaturzeitung* 61 (1966): 5–14.

–. *Codex apocryphus gnosticus Novi Testamenti*. Wissenschaftliche Untersuchungen zum Neuen Testament 326. Tübing: Mohr Siebeck, 2014.

Painter, John. *Just James: The Brother of Jesus in History and Tradition*. Columbia, S. Car.: University of South Carolina Press, 1997.

Pearson, Birger A. "Introduction to codex X." Pages 211–27 in in *Nag Hammadi Codices IX and X*. Edited by Birger A. Pearson. Nag Hammadi Studies 15. Leiden: Brill, 1981.

Puech, Henri-Charles and Quispel, Gilles. "Les Écrits Gnostiques du Codex Jung." *Vigiliae Christianae* 8 (1954): 1–51.

Robinson, James M. "Nag Hammadi: The First Fifty Years." Pages 4 – 33 in *The Nag Hammadi Library After Fifty Years: Proceedings of the 1995 Society of Biblical Literature Commemoration*. Edited by John D. Turner and Anne McGuire. Nag Hammadi and Manichaean Studies 44. Leiden: Brill, 1997.

Rousseau, Adelin and Louis Doutreleau. *Irénee De Lyon: Contre Les Hérésies I*. Sources Chrétiennes 264. Paris: Cerf, 2008.

Turner, John D. "Introduction to Codex XI." Pages 3–20 in *Nag Hammadi Codices XI, XII, XIII*. Edited by Charles W. Hedrick. Nag Hammadi Studies 28. Leiden: Brill, 1990.

Westendorf, Wolfhart. *Koptisches Handwörterbuch: Bearbeitet auf der Grundlage des Koptischen Handwörterbuchs von Wilhelm Spiegelberg*. Heidelberg: Universitätsverlag Winter, 2008.

Williams, Francis E. "The Apocryphon of James." Pages 13–53 in *Nag Hammadi Codex I: The Jung Codex*. Edited by Harold W. Attridge. Nag Hammadi Studies 22. Leiden: Brill: 1985.

Wisse, Frederik. "Introduction to Codex XII." Pages 289–94 in *Nag Hammadi Codices XI, XII, XIII*. Edited by Charles W. Hedrick. Nag Hammadi Studies 28. Leiden: Brill, 1990.

–. "NHC XII,2: The Gospel of Truth." Pages 329–47 in *Nag Hammadi Codices XI, XII, XIII*. Edited by Charles W. Hedrick. Nag Hammadi Studies 28. Leiden: Brill, 1990.

–. "NHC XII,3: Fragments." Pages 349–55 in *Nag Hammadi Codices XI, XII, XIII*. Edited by Charles W. Hedrick. Nag Hammadi Studies 28. Leiden: Brill, 1990.

Lillian I. Larsen*

Monastic Paideia: Textual Fluidity in the Classroom

In introducing his compendium of *Greek Textbooks of Prose Composition and Rhetoric* (*Progymnasmata*), George Kennedy likens the formulaically fixed and infinitely fluid praxis that defined ancient/late-ancient classroom settings to the "structural features of classical architecture."[1] He emphasizes that not only the secular literature of the Greeks and Romans, but also the writing of early Christians, is best understood in light of "the habits of thinking and writing learned in schools."[2] Following Kennedy, one can argue the particular importance of examining the textual fluidity endemic to ancient/late-ancient source material through a pedagogical lens. Within this frame, monastic texts and artifacts offer something of a microcosm for understanding emergent praxis. Effectively elucidating the persistent character of adoptive classroom protocol, they simultaneously afford a suggestive exploratory locus for identifying the structures that govern fluid adaptation of established models.

* Thanks to Hugo Lundhaug and Liv Ingeborg Lied for suggesting inclusion of this essay in the current volume. In the early stages of this work, identifying monastic school exercises often seemed most akin to looking for a needle in a haystack. Sincere thanks are due Professor Cribiore for her generous assistance and astute direction in guiding these initial phases. Thanks are likewise due the Metropolitan Museum of Art in New York City, which afforded generous access to their extensive monastic archive, and an outstanding photographer to document select school artifacts included in this collection. These images have proved essential, not only to identifying a number of the pieces addressed in this preliminary survey, but also to broader, ongoing work aimed at identifying and cataloguing evidence for monastic school practice. Subsequent research has been generously supported by the University of Redlands, through research leaves and successive faculty grants. Complementary resources have been made available through the Riksbanken Jubileumsfond under the auspices of the Monasticism and Classical Paideia Project at Lund University, Sweden. In early May 2014, project monies likewise covered costs for travel and closer examination of the contexts that inform a understanding number of the artifacts included in this essay. This 'expedition', aimed at better sketching the contours of "Monastic Education in Egypt," was jointly organized and sponsored by the MOPAI and NEWCONT research teams. Per this frame, warm thanks are due Hugo Lundhaug for use of the Beni Hasan photos taken during that journey. Most recently, the rich resources of the Saint Shenouda Archimandrite Coptic Library, in Los Angeles, have proved essential in identifying and locating publications related to the more dispersed range of artifacts, referenced here in the footnotes. Hany Takla's assistance, and good humored 'sleuthing', has likewise made this culminating research phase a particular pleasure.

1 George A. Kennedy, ed. and trans., *Progymnasmata: Greek Textbooks of Prose Composition and Rhetoric* (Atlanta: Scholars Press, 2003), ix
2 Kennedy, *Progymnasmata*, ix.

Reversing scholarly assessment that has iteratively framed,[3] and more recently named, monasticism "a missing chapter in the history of education,"[4] this essay reads descriptions of the Graeco-Roman curriculum – as outlined in the first century *Institutes* of Quintilian,[5] in conversation with the shifts in content commended in late antique delineations of monastic pedagogical practice – as articulated in guidelines attributed to Jerome, Basil and Pachomius.[6] It then examines a select subset of monastic material remains in light of these descriptions. As overt continuity and fluid shifts link literary articulation with material manifestation (and vice versa), each affirms that monastic students – like their Graeco-Roman counterparts – moved from learning letters and manipulating alphabets, to articulating syllables, forming words, and copying phrases. At a more advanced stage, classroom practice in reformulation of gnomic sentences, sayings, and stories is as patent.[7] From Cappadocia to Palestine to Egypt, what remains distinctive is not the absent, or even the exceptional, character of such praxis, but rather the degree to which monastic pedagogues are both adopting, and fluidly adapting, established forms.

---

3 Cf., e.g., Henri I. Marrou, *History of Education in Antiquity* (trans. G. Lamb; Madison: University of Wisconsin Press, 1956, 1982), 330–33.

4 Sara Rappe, "The New Math: How to Add and Subtract Pagan Elements in Christian Education" in *Education in Greek and Roman Antiquity* (ed. Yun Lee Too; Leiden: Brill, 2001), 77; cf. Lillian I. Larsen, "'On Learning a New Alphabet': The Sayings of the Desert Fathers and the Monostichs of Menander" in *Early Monasticism and Classical Paideia* (ed. Samuel Rubenson; vol. 3 of *Papers Presented at the Sixteenth International Conference on Patristic Studies held in Oxford 2011*, ed. Markus Vinzent; StPatr 55; Leuven: Peeters, 2013), 59–63.

5 Quintilian, *Institutio Oratoria* (*Inst.*) (Russell, LCL).

6 The most detailed monastic curriculum is that outlined by Jerome, *Epistle* (*Epist.*) 107 in *Select Letters of Jerome* (Wright, LCL), 338–70. Alternately descriptive is Basil's *Regula Fusius Tractate* (*Reg. Fus.*) 15 in *The Ascetic Works of Saint Basil* (trans. W. K.L. Clarke; London: SPCK, 1925), 175–78 [PG 31.952–57]. Arguably affirming commensurate practice is the more cryptic regulation of Pachomius' *Praecepta* (*Praec.*) 139–40 in Amand Boon, ed., *Pachomiana Latina: Règle et épitres de S. Pachôme, épitre de S. Théodore et "Liber" de S. Orsiesius: Texte latin de S. Jérôme* (BRHE 7; Leuven: Bureaux de la Revue, 1932), 50–51; Armand Veilleux, trans., *Pachomian Koinonia: The Lives, Rules, and Other Writings of Saint Pachomius and His Disciples* (3 vols.; CS 45–47; Kalamazoo, Mich.: Cistercian Publications, 1980–82), 2:166; cf. Larsen, "On Learning a New Alphabet," 59–67.

7 Lillian I. Larsen, "Ørkenfedrenes *Apophthegmata* og den klassiske Retoriske Tradisjon." *MCPL* 16 (2001): 26–35; idem, "Pedagogical Parallels: Re-Reading the *Apophthegmata Patrum*" (Unpublished diss.; Columbia University, 2006); idem, "The *Apophthegmata Patrum* and the Classical Rhetorical Tradition," in *Historica, Biblica, Ascetica et Hagiographica: Papers Presented at the Fourteenth International Conference on Patristic Studies held in Oxford 2003* (ed. Frances M. Young, Mark J. Edwards, and Paul M. Parvis; StPatr 39; Leuven: Peeters, 2006), 409–15; idem, "The *Apophthegmata Patrum*: Rustic Rumination or Rhetorical Recitation" *MCPL* 23 (2008): 21–30; idem, "Early Monasticism and the Rhetorical Tradition: Sayings and Stories as Schooltexts" in *Education and Religion in Late Antiquity* (ed. Peter Gemeinhardt and Peter Van Nuffelen; Farnham: Ashgate, 2016), 13–33.

Letters and Alphabets

In the ancient world, as in the contemporary, elementary instruction began with learning letters and alphabets. Registering forms current within a first-century, Grae-co-Roman frame,[8] Quintilian suggests that foundational pedagogical investments be introduced with the practice of "giving [children] ivory letters to play with" in order to stimulate learning.[9] He recommends that once the letters have been sufficiently fixed in a child's mind in "their usual order," that teachers "reverse that order or rearrange it in every kind of combination," so that young pupils "learn to know the letters by their appearance and not from the order in which they occur."[10]

Outlining curricular guidelines appropriate to an emergent Christian frame, late-ancient monastic pedagogues commend practice that employs corresponding forms and content. In this instance, the most detailed descriptions are delineated by Jerome in a letter aimed at convincing Laeta, a wealthy Roman householder, to send her young daughter to Bethlehem – to be educated in a monastery.[11] There is little that distinguishes Jerome's pedagogical models from those articulated generations earlier. Commending exercises appropriate to the elementary formation of a "virgin,"

---

8 While Egypt, even *sans* a monastic frame, has often been treated as exceptional, Raffaella Cribi-ore's seminal work has clearly demonstrated that with respect to "educational practices, Egypt was in close touch with the rest of the Mediterranean" (*Gymnastics of the Mind: Greek Education in Hellenistic and Roman Egypt* [Princeton: Princeton University Press, 2001], 6); cf. idem, *Writing, Teachers, and Students in Graeco-Roman Egypt* (Atlanta: Scholars Press, 1996); Teresa Morgan, *Literate Education in the Hellenistic and Roman Worlds* (Cambridge: Cambridge University Press, 1998).

9 Quintilian, *Inst.* 1.1.26 (Russell, LCL); *Non excludo autem, id quod est inventum irritandae ad discendum infantiae gratia eburneas etiam litterarum formas in lusum offerre.*

10 Quintilian, *Inst.* 1.1.25 (Russell, LCL); *Quae causa est praecipientibus, ut etiam, cum satis adfixisse eas pueris recto illo quo primum scribi solent contextu videntur, retro agant rursus et varia permutatione turbent, donec litteras qui instituuntur facie norint non ordine.*

11 Jerome, *Epist.* 107.4 and 13 (Wright, LCL); Paula, Laeta's young daughter, is the granddaughter and namesake of the wealthy Roman founder and patron of the monastery from whence Jerome is writing. In administering this community, the elder Paula is also assisted by Laeta's sister, Eustochium. In making his case, Jerome explicitly offers his own services as tutor. As Paula's ideal instructor, a man of "approved years, life, and learning," he advertises his proposed role as akin to that of Aristotle's teaching Alexander "his first letters" (4; *Magister probae aetatis et vitae atque eruditionis est eligendus nec, puto, erubescit doctus vir id facere vel in propinqua vel in nobili virgine, quod Aristoteles fecit in Phlippi filio, ut ipse librariorum vilitate initia ei traderet litterarum*). As the letter concludes, Jerome reiterates his offer to serve as young Paula's "tutor" and "foster-father." Carrying her on his shoulders, he suggests that he will "train her stammering lips ... tak[ing] more pride in [his] task than ... the worldly philosopher [Aristotle]; for ... [rather than] teaching a Macedonian king, destined to die by poison in Babylon, [he will instruct] the handmaid and bride of Christ who one day [will] be presented to the heavenly throne" (13; *Ipse, si Paulam miseris, balbutientia senex verba formabo multo gloriosior mundi philosopho, qui non regem Macedonum Babylonio periturum veneno, sed ancillam et sponsam Christi erudiam regnis caelestibus offerendam*).

Jerome suggests that his prospective student be provided "a set of letters made ... of boxwood or of ivory," and be told their proper names.[12] Echoing Quintilian, he recommends that young Paula "not only [be made to] grasp the right order of the letters and remember their names in a simple song, but also frequently upset their order and mix the last letters with the middle ones, the middle with the first."[13]

Both Quintilian and Jerome likewise emphasize the importance of developing fluency in writing the alphabet. Quintilian notes that while some might deem "the art of writing well and quickly ... unimportant," learning to efficiently shape letters is essential to later study because "a sluggish pen delays thoughts."[14] To these ends, he commends practice be structured so that students develop a steady hand by following "fixed outlines" with increasing "frequency and speed."[15] Jerome's instructions are less detailed, but commensurate. He suggests that when young Paula "begins with uncertain hand to use the pen," her fingers should be guided to "follow outlines" until she is able to form the letters on her own "without straying away."[16]

A sample of four exercises – respectively associated with three Egyptian sites – suggests, at once, routine adoption and measured adaptation of established norms. The first, provenanced to the Monastery of Epiphanius in Thebes, preserves a Greek alphabet in "the right order" (Jerome, *Epist.* 107). Formed to fit the shape of an irregular ostracon, and penned in an informal, but practiced hand, the alphabet's twenty-four characters are spread over four horizontal lines. Affirming monastic, if not explicitly pedagogical purpose, this content is followed by a brief line of text: θεοφιλεστατοι μοναχοι ("... monks most beloved of God") (Fig. 8).[17]

---

12 Jerome, *Epist.* 107.4 (Wright, LCL); *Fiant ei litterae vel buxeae vel eburneae et suis nominibus appellentur.*

13 Jerome, *Epist.* 107.4 (Wright, LCL); *... et non solum ordinem teneat litterarum, ut memoria nominum in canticum transeat, sed ipse inter se crebro ordo turbetur et mediis ultima, primis media misceantur ut eas non sonu tantum, sed et visu noverit.*

14 Quintilian, *Inst.* 1.1.28 (Russell, LCL); *Non est aliena res, quae fere ab honestis negligi solet, cura bene ac velociter scribendi ... tardior stilus cogitationem moratur*[!]

15 Quintilian, *Inst.* 1.1.27 (Russell, LCL); *... et celerius ac saepius sequendo certa vestigia firmabit articulos ...*

16 Jerome, *Epist.* 107.4 (Wright, LCL); *Cum vero coeperit trementi manu stilum in cera ducere, vel alterius superposita manu teneri regantur articuli vel in tabella sculpantur elementa, ut per eosdem sulcos inclusa marginibus trahantur vestigia et foras non queant evagari.*

17 O.MMA 12.180.107; *ed. pr.* Walter E. Crum and Hugh G. Evelyn White, *The Monastery of Epiphanius at Thebes* (2 vols.; New York: Metropolitan Museum of Art, 1926), 2:136 and 322 no. 620; cf. Cribiore, *Writing, Teachers and Students*, 189 no. 67; Although such an alphabet might routinely meet designation as a 'school' artifact, in discussions of monastic remains, assignation of pedagogical purpose has proved less consistent. While debates about what differentiates scribal from school practice remain significant, it is arguable that, per Quintilian (*Inst.* 1.1.27–8) and Jerome (*Epist.* 107.4), both pre-suppose pedagogical investment – albeit, perhaps, to alternate ends. Diverse perspectives on this question are respectively captured in the essays of Bagnall, Larsen, Lundhaug/Jenott, and Maravela, in *Monastic Education in Late Antiquity: The Transformation of Classical Paideia* (ed. Lillian I. Larsen and

Fig. 8: Greek Alphabet, Monastery of Epiphanius, O.MMA 12.180.107

A second exercise survives only in fragments. As re-assembled, it is formed of iteratively patterned letters organized in successive horizontal rows. Each row is comprised of nine letters. The four initial, and the four final are *betas*. These precede and follow an alphabetically sequenced central letter, thus: ΒΒΒΒΑΒΒΒΒ / ΒΒΒΒΒΒΒΒΒ / ΒΒΒΒΓΒΒΒΒ / ΒΒΒΒΔΒΒΒΒ, etc. Again, of Epiphanian provenance, both patterned content,

Samuel Rubenson; Cambridge: Cambridge University Press, forthcoming); cf. Scott Bucking, "Scribes and Schoolmasters? On Contextualizing Coptic and Greek Ostraca Excavated at the Monastery of Epiphanius" *JCoptS* 9 (2007): 21–47.

Fig. 9: Writing Exercise, Monastery of Epiphanius, O.MMA 14.1.188

and rough execution suggest monastic pedagogical practice, aimed not only at recognizing the letters, but also tracing them with "frequency," and eventually, "speed" (Quintilian, *Inst.* 1.1.28) (Fig. 9).[18]

An exercise preserved on both sides of a third ostracon is as interesting. Generally provenanced to Thebes, and provisionally associated with the Monastery of Phoibammon, included content consists of five alphabets, penned in horizontal lines, in a less than practiced hand (Table 1). As transcribed by Anneliese Biedenkopf-Ziehner, the ostracon's first and third alphabets – two of three included on the *recto* – follow the "usual order" in which the letters are commonly written. The second alphabet variously "reverse[s] that order." In turn, a fourth alphabet – the first of two preserved on the *verso* – presents a "rearranged" sequence of letters (Quintilian, *Inst.* 1.1.25; cf. Jerome, *Epist.* 107.4). The first letter of this alphabet is paired with the last, the second

18 O.MMA 14.1.188; *Ed pr.* Crum and Evelyn White, *Monastery of Epiphanius*, 2:118 and 298 no. 576; O.BM 19082, 18816, 18798, 18972; *ed. pr.* R. M. Hall, *Coptic and Greek Texts of the Christian Period from Ostraka, Stelae, etc. in the British Museum* (London: British Museum, 1905), 36 pl. 29, no. 2; cf. Cribiore, *Writing, Teachers, and Students*, 181 no. 34, pl. I; Monika R. M. Hasitzka, *Neue Texte und Dokumentation zum Koptisch-Unterricht* (2 vols.; MPER 18; Vienna: Österreichische Nationalbibliothek, 1990), 42 no. 39; Lillian I. Larsen, "Re-drawing the Interpretive Map: Monastic Education as Civic Formation in the *Apophthegmata Patrum*" *Coptica* 12 (2013): 17 and 26 fig. 3; idem, "Sayings and Stories as Schooltexts," 17 fig. 1.1. Although respective shards have been variously categorized, there is good evidence to support both pedagogical purpose and Epiphanian provenance; cf. idem, "Excavating the Excavations of Early Monastic Education," in *Monastic Education in Late Antiquity*, forthcoming.

with the second to last, the third with third to last, thus: ⲁ ⲱ, ⲃ ⲯ, ⲅ ⲭ … ⲙ ⲛ. The ostracon's fifth alphabet is incomplete. Adhering to an overall pattern of interspersed sequencing, however, like the first and third, it appears to follow the "usual order." Four of the five alphabets begin with a chrism, a symbol which additionally serves to separate one iteration from the next. Although these alphabets were presumably executed without the aid of letter-sets "made … of boxwood or ivory" (Jerome, *Epist.* 107.4; cf. Quintilian, *Inst.* 1.1.26), both content and execution suggest pedagogical practice, which encouraged "not only … grasp[ing] the right order of … letters" but also routinely "upset[ting] their order and mix[ing] the last letters with the middle ones, the middle with the first" (Jerome, *Epist.* 107.4; cf. Quintilian, *Inst.* 1.1.25).[19]

Table 1: Mixed Alphabets

(V) ⲣ	ⲁ ⲃ ⲅ ⲇ ⲉ ⲍ ⲏ ⲑ ⲓ ⲕ ⲗ
	ⲙ ⲛ ⲝ ⲟ ⲡ ⲣ ⲥ ⲧ ⲩ ⲫ ⲭ
	ⲯ ⲱ
ⲣ	ⲱ ⲯ ⲭ ⲫ ⲩ ⲧ ⲥ ⲣ ⲡ ⲟ
	ⲝ ⲟ ⲡ ⲣ ⲥ ⲧ ⲩ ⲫ ⲭ ⲯ ⲱ
[ⲣ]	ⲁ ⲃ ⲅ ⲇ ⲉ ⲍ ⲏ ⲑ ⲓ ⲕ ⲗ
	ⲙ ⲛ ⲝ ⲟ ⲡ ⲣ ⲥ
(R) ⲣ	ⲁ ⲱ ⲃ ⲯ ⲅ
	ⲭ ⲇ ⲫ ⲉ ⲩ ⲍ
	ⲧ ⲏ ⲥ ⲑ ⲣ ⲓ ⲡ
	ⲕ ⲟ ⲗ ⲝ ⲙ ⲛ
ⲣ	ⲁ ⲃ ⲅ ⲇ ⲉ

A fourth example is preserved, not on an ostracon, but rather the plastered wall of a re-used tomb. It is provenanced not to Thebes, but to the middle-Egyptian Pharaonic site of Beni Hasan (Fig. 10). Faintly visible – in a space variously identified by its use as a pedagogical locus,[20] and/or occupation by Late Ancient monks[21] – it is comprised of a series of three alphabets arranged in squarish sectors (Table 2). As transcribed, the first sector includes an alphabet sequenced in conventional order; the second, an alphabet in reverse order; the third, a mixed alphabet. Like the interspersed, iterative sequences preserved in the student exercise examined above, the model appears to be aimed at encouraging practice with "learn[ing] to know letters by their appear-

---

19 AM 21 (C. O. 16); As published in Anneliese Biedenkopf-Ziehner, *Koptische Ostraka: Ostraka aus dem Ashmolean Museum in Oxford* (Wiesbaden: Harrassowitz Verlag, 2000), 137–44, Taf. 17.
20 Cribiore, "Gymnastics of the Mind," 23–24.
21 Bucking, "Scribes and Schoolmasters," 40.

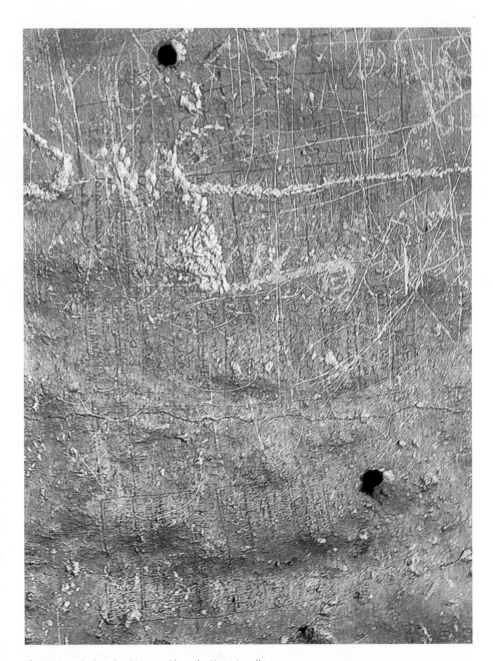

Fig. 10: Inscription, Beni Hasan, Photo by Hugo Lundhaug

ance and not [solely] from the order in which they occur" (Quintilian, *Inst.* 1.1.25; cf. Jerome, *Epist.* 107.4).[22] While these exercises are of disparate provenance, one might argue that each respectively offers something of an instructional counterpart to the other. Whether placed in conversation or viewed separately, however, both affirm monastic use of the conventional strategies described in extant literary sources.[23]

Table 2: Mixed Alphabets Beni Hasan

ⲁ ⲃ ⲅ ⲇ ⲉ ⲍ	ⲱ ⲧ ⲝ ⲫ ⲩ ⲧ	ⲁ ⲱ ⲃ ⲩ ⲅ ⲭ
ⲏ ⲑ ⲓ ⲕ ⲗ ⲙ	ⲥ ⲣ ⲡ ⲟ ⲝ ⲛ	ⲁ ⲫ ⲉ ⲩ ⲍ ⲧ
ⲛ ⲝ ⲟ ⲡ ⲣ ⲥ	ⲙ ⲗ ⲕ ⲓ ⲑ ⲏ	ⲏ ⲣ ⲫ ⲡ ⲓ ⲟ ⲥ
ⲧ ⲩ ⲫ ⲭ ⲧ ⲱ	ⲑ ⲉ ⲇ ⲅ ⲃ ⲁ	ⲕ ⲝ ⲗ ⲛ ⲏ

Syllables

Moving from letters to syllables, there is little to suggest that pedagogical habits became any less formulaic. Quintilian emphasizes the role of repetition at this stage, noting that with respect to syllables "no short cut is possible: they must all be [thoroughly] learnt." He additionally warns that "there is no good in putting off ... the most difficult ... [for] the sole result is bad spelling."[24] Urging caution in "placing ... blind

---

22 Cf. Percy E. Newberry, *Beni Hasan* (4 vols.; Archaeological Survey of Egypt; London: Kegan Paul, 1893–1900), 2:76–77, pl. XXV; The alphabets are not included in Jean François Champollion's initial publication of the site, *Monuments de l'Égypte et de la Nubie: Tome II: Autographié en entier* (ed. Gaston Maspero; Paris: Didot, 1889). Instead, the three sectors are simply described as *"Compose' des Lettres de l'alphabet, voyelles et consonnes melées sans ordre"* (459). It is perhaps for that reason that the alphabets have likewise remained peripheral to broader scholarly discussion of this body of school evidence. While Newberry's 1893 publication includes the alphabets, their distinctive character is not mentioned; cf. Larsen, "Sayings and Stories as Schooltexts," 17 and 18 fig. 1.3; idem, "Excavating the Excavations."
23 Recurring narrative reference to such classroom detail within monastic *apophthegmatic* sources invites new appreciation for the 'apt' wit that characterizes assertions like that attributed to Arsenius, who with all his "Latin and Greek education" does not yet "know the "alphabet" of an Egyptian ἀγροῖκος (AP/G Arsenius 6 [PG 65:87–90]; τὴν μὲν Ῥωμαϊκὴν καὶ Ἑλληνικὴν ἐπίσταμαι παίδευσιν τὸν δὲ ἀλφάβητον τοῦ ἀγροίκου τούτου οὔπω μεμάθηκα). Perhaps as noteworthy is the irony inherent in the fact that it is precisely such 'sayings' that have long been used to argue against monastic investment in literate pursuits; cf. Larsen, "Rustic Rumination or Rhetorical Recitation," 21–30; idem, "Re-drawing the Interpretive Map," 1–30.
24 Quintilian, *Inst.* 1.1.30–31 (Russell, LCL); *Syllabis nullum compendium est; perdiscendae omnes nec, ut fit plerumque, difficillima quaeque earum differenda, ut in nominibus scribendis deprehendantur.*

confidence in a child's memory," he instead commends repetition – and adjusting the pace while reading – so that "clear and obvious sequence[s] of letters can suggest [themselves] without [it] being necessary for [a] child to stop to think."[25]

Albeit less detailed, allusions to the repetitive rehearsal that Quintilian commends also surface in monastic source material. Jerome offers little further discussion. However, the Pachomian *Praecepta* arguably affirm the premise that "no short cut is possible" (Quintilian, *Inst*. 1.1.30), explicitly mandating that each newly entering monk, if "ignorant of letters," should with all gratitude "go at the first, third and sixth hour to someone who can teach" in addition to letters, "the fundamentals of a syllable."[26] What is known of the auditory dimension of such practice adds meaningful resonance to Basil's suggestion that the living quarters of adults and children be kept separate, so that "the house of the monks ... not be disturbed by ... repetition of lessons necessary for the young."[27]

A rough chart of syllabic combinations that adjoins and follows the mixed Beni Hasan alphabets discussed above (Fig. 10), brings such literary descriptions to life.[28] Framed as an organized series of bi-literal and tri-literal sequences, both form and content align with examples encountered in a broader array of extant school artifacts.[29] Bi-literal syllables are constructed of sequences that pair a single consonant with each respective vowel, thus: ва, ве, вн, ви, во, ву, вⲱ through ϯⲁ, ϯⲉ, ϯн, ϯι, ϯо, ϯу, ϯⲱ. These are followed by a series of tri-literal combinations: ваⲃ, веⲃ, внⲃ, виⲃ, воⲃ, вуⲃ, вⲱⲃ, through ваⳅ. Subsequent permutations, while less legible, appear predictable. One group is formed using г (*gamma*), the following, ⲇ (*delta*). Each suggests repetitive practice aimed at "impress[ing]" syllables "on the memory," to facilitate ready recall while reading and/or writing (Figs. 10 and 11) (Quintilian, *Inst*. 1.1.30–31).[30]

---

25 Quintilian, *Inst*. 1.1.31 (Russell, LCL); *Quin immo ne primae quidem memoriae temere credendum; repetere et diu inculcare fuerit utilius, et in lectione quoque non properare ad continuandam eam vel accelerandam, nisi cum inoffensa atque indubitata litterarum inter se coniunctio suppeditare sine ulla cogitandi saltem mora poterit.*

26 Pachomius, *Praec.* 139 (Boon, *Pachomiana Latina*; trans. Veilleux, *Pachomian Koinonia*); *Et si litteras ignorabit hora prima et tertia et sexta uadet ad eum qui docere potest et qui ei fuerit delegatus, et stabit ante illum, et discet studiosissime cum omni gratiarum actione. Postea uero scribentur ei elementa syllabae ...*

27 Basil, *Reg. Fus.* 15 (PG 31.953; trans. Clarke, *Ascetic Works of Saint Basil*); καὶ ἅμα οὐδὲ θόρυβον ἕξει ὁ οἶκος τῶν ἀσκητῶν ἐν τῇ μελέτῃ τῶν διδαγμάτων ἀναγκαίᾳ οὔσῃ τοῖς νέοις; cf. Cribiore, *Gymnastics of the Mind*, 23–24.

28 Newberry, *Beni Hasan*, 2:76–77, pl. XXV; cf. Champollion, *Monuments*, 459–60.

29 Evidence for broader practice is well documented; cf., e.g., Cribiore, *Reading, Writing, and Teachers*, 191–96 nos. 78–97; Hasitzka, *Neue Texte*, 1.55–63 nos. 73–82.

30 Two wooden tablets, loosely provenanced to the Fayyum – both now owned by the University of Michigan – are particularly interesting. Neither has been explicitly named monastic; however, each reaffirms the non-exceptional character of the combinations preserved at Beni Hasan. The first tablet combines a syllabary on its *recto* face with three alphabets on its *verso*. The syllabary is comprised

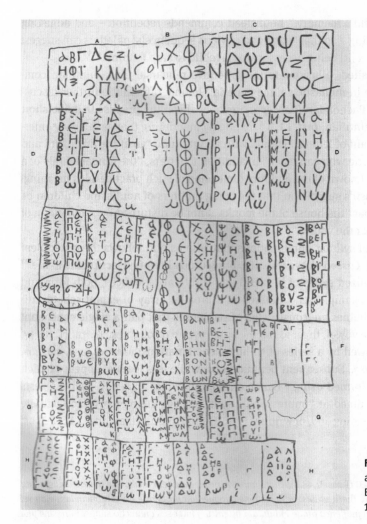

Fig. 11: Alphabets and Syllabary, Beni Hasan, Newberry 1893, Pl. XXV

of triliteral combinations through *lambda*. The three alphabets are, again, sequenced in convention-al, reversed, and mixed order (T.Mich. 763; *ed. pr.* Arthur Edward Romilly Boak, "Greek and Coptic School Tablets at the University of Michigan," *CP* 16:2 [1921]: 189–94; cf. Cribiore, *Writing, Teachers, and Students*, 192–93 no. 83, pl. VII). The *recto* and *verso* faces of a second Michigan tablet likewise preserve a syllabary. Here sequences are rendered solely in Coptic, and develop a full slate of bilit-eral and triliteral combinations, each formed using the letter ϣ (*shai*) (T.Mich. N. 765; *ed. pr.* Arthur Edward Romilly Boak, "A Coptic Syllabary at the University of Michigan" *Aegyptus* 4:4 [1923]: 296–97; cf. Hasitzka, *Neue Texte*, 59–60 no. 78). Published by Elinor Mullet Husselman, a third syllabary in the Michigan collection is preserved within a classroom codex, comprised of a range of school related content (P.Mich. 926; *ed. pr.* Husselman, "A Bohairic School Text on Papyrus," *JNES* 6:3 [1947]: 129–51; cf. Hasitzka, *Neue Texte*, 133–38 no. 20 ff. 1v–5r). Husselman identifies the syllabary's combination of Greek and Bohairic as particularly significant. While, again, no secure monastic provenance is claimed, in passing, Husselman suggests possible links to "a [monastic] settlement on the edge of the desert to the south of Theadelphia" (129).

Fig. 12: *Xalinos*, Monastery of Epiphanius, T.MMA 14.1.219

The Beni Hasan syllabary also includes a set of Coptic letters (ϣ ϥ ϩ ϭ ϫ ϯ) written across the lower portion of two segments of its bi-literal combinations.[31] This blending of Coptic and Greek has led to suggestion that assigning the inscription a pedagogical purpose is, perhaps, premature.[32] While the function of the letters is not immediately clear, one could as readily argue that inclusion of Coptic letters strengthens the case for school provenance.[33] In fact, given the syllabary's fifth to sixth century date, the absence of distinctly Coptic characters might be similarly noteworthy.[34]

An exercise preserved on a wooden board, provenanced to the Monastery of Epiphanius, is as distinctive. Apparently aimed at affording practice with articulation of syllabic sequences and words "of studied difficulty" (Quintilian, *Inst.* 1.1.37), the board's content is framed as a maxim that includes every letter of the Greek alphabet (Fig. 12):

ἀβροχίτων δ'ὁ φύλαξ θηραζυγοκαμψιμετώπος.

Softly dressed is the guard who bends under the yoke the head of the wild beasts.[35]

---

31 These letters are circled in blue on Newberry's transcription, pictured above (Fig. 11). A similar juxtaposition is preserved on an ostracon of Theban provenance. Here, following a Greek alphabet organized vertically in a regular arrangement comprised of six columns and four rows (α β γ δ / ε ζ η θ / ι κ λ μ / ν ξ ο π / ρ σ τ υ / φ ψ χ ω), a fifth horizontal row of Coptic letters (ϣ ϥ ϩ ϭ ϫ ϯ) is penned (O.BM 31663; *ed. pr.* Hall, *Coptic and Greek Texts*, 35 pl. 28 no. 4; cf. Cribiore, *Writing, Teachers, and Students*, 190 no. 72, pl. VI; Hasitzka, *Neue Texte*, 1.51 no. 64).
32 Cf. Bucking, "Scribes and Schoolmasters," 40.
33 Cf. Cribiore, *Gymnastics of the Mind*, 24–25.
34 Cf. Larsen, "Excavating the Excavations." A full Coptic alphabet would, of course, likewise include the characters that comprise the Greek alphabet.
35 T.MMA 14.1.219; *ed. pr.* Crum and Evelyn White, *Monastery of Epiphanius*, 2:136 and 321 no. 616; cf. Paulinus Bellet, "*Anthologia Palatina* 9.538: The Alphabet and the Calligraphic Examination in the Coptic Scriptorium" *BASP* 19 (1982), 1–8; Cribiore, *Writing, Teachers, and Students*, 188–189 no. 66; Scott Bucking, *Practice Makes Perfect: P.Cotsen-Princeton 1* (Los Angeles: Cotsen Occasional Press,

It presents what is perhaps the earliest extant example of a χαλινός, a syllabic exercise "formed of a number of syllables which go ill together and [are] harsh and rugged in sound." Quintilian commends use of such sequences for improving "pronunciation and distinctness of utterance."[36]

Words

With respect to forming words, the structural parallels that link Graeco-Roman and monastic practice remain as patent. In his first century curriculum, Quintilian's instructions are succinct. He recommends that once the syllables have been learned, "students begin to construct words with them."[37] He additionally advises that "in accordance with the usual practice" students not "waste [their] labour in writing out common words of everyday occurrence," but rather "learn ... explanations ... of ... more obscure words" in order to "acquire [knowledge that] would otherwise demand special time ... be devoted to it" later on.[38]

Affirming parallel practice, Jerome recommends that the words used in forming sentences not be selected "haphazard[ly]," but instead, "chosen and arranged on purpose." To this end, he suggests that as an aid in training both tongue and memory, young Paula's wordlists include "the names of the prophets and the apostles, and the whole list of patriarchs from Adam downwards, as [given by] Matthew and Luke."[39] Basil, too, commends work with "names taken from the Scriptures."[40] Promoting instruction explicitly aimed at even the most recalcitrant student, Pachomius enjoins that, along with "the fundamentals of a syllable, ... verbs, and nouns [should also] be written."[41]

2011), 57–58; Larsen, "Redrawing the Interpretive Map," 18 and 29 fig. 6; idem, "Sayings and Stories as Schooltexts," 19 and 20 fig. 1.6.

36 Quintilian, *Inst.* 1.1.37 (Russell, LCL); *Non alienum fuerit exigere ab his aetatibus, quo sit absolutius os et expressior sermo, ut nomina quaedam versusque adfectatae difficultatis ex pluribus et asperrime coëun- tibus inter se syllabis catenatos et velut confragosos quam citatissime volvant;* χαλινοὶ *Graece vocantur.*

37 Quintilian, *Inst.* 1.1.31 (Russell, LCL); *Tunc ipsis syllabis verba complecti ...*

38 Quintilian, *Inst.* 1.1.34–35 (Russell, LCL); *Illud non poenitebit curasse, cum scribere nomina puer (quemadmodum moris est) coeperit, ne hanc operam in vocabulis vulgaribus et forte occurrentibus perdat. Protinus enim potest interpretationem linguae secretioris ... dum aliud agitur, ediscere et inter prima elementa consequi rem postea proprium tempus desideraturam.*

39 Jerome, *Epist.* 107.4 (Wright, LCL); *Ipsa nomina, per quae consuescet verba contexere, non sint for- tuita, sed certa et coacervata de industria, prophetarum videlicet atque apostolorum, et omnis ab Adam patriarcharum series de Matheo Lucaque descendat, ut, dum aliud agit, futurae memoriae praeparetur.*

40 Basil, *Reg. Fus.* 15 (PG 31.953); ... καὶ ὀνόμασιν αὐτοὺς τοῖς ἐκ τῶν Γραφῶν κεχρῆσθαι.

41 Pachomius, *Praec.* 139 (Boon, *Pachomiana Latina*; Veilleux, *Pachomian Koinonia*); The *precept* continues: "and even if [s/]he does not want to, [s/]he shall be compelled to read" (... *Postea uero scribentur ei elementa syllabae, uerba ac nomina, et etiam nolens legere compelletur*).

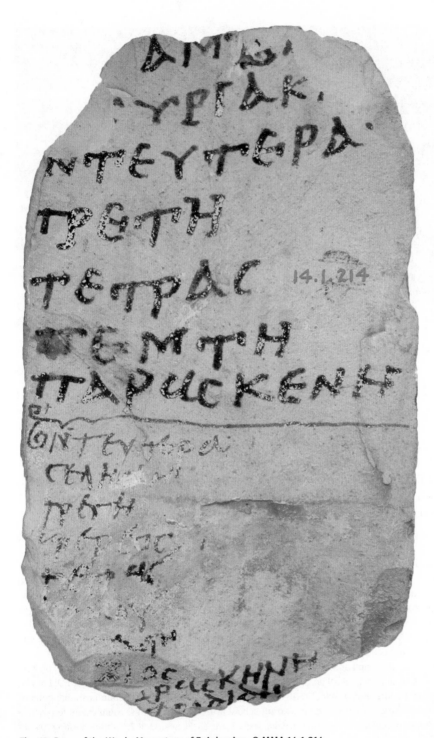

Fig. 13: Days of the Week, Monastery of Epiphanius, O.MMA 14.1.214

Fig. 14: Word List, Beni Hasan, Photo by Hugo Lundhaug

Affirming the flexible character of established models, it is, arguably, here that one begins to gain a clearer sense of the degree to which monastic practice registers (and monastic artifacts attest), at once, the adoption and fluid adaptation of familiar forms. For example, a papyrus fragment, provenanced to the Monastery of Epiphanius, displays a list of bird names, enumerated in Greek with Coptic equivalents.[42] A second Epiphanian artifact preserves a wordlist comprised of the days of the week, in various combinations of Christian and "pagan," or more accurately "planetary," nomenclature (Fig. 13).[43]

---

42 O.MMA 14.1.549; *ed. pr.* Crum and Evelyn White, *Monastery of Epiphanius*, 2:137 and 323 no. 621; As originally published in the excavation's catalogue, this piece is categorized as "miscellaneous." Attendant commentary suggests that it may have functioned as a Greek-Coptic "glossary" of which the Greek is preserved, but "the presumed Coptic equivalents [have] broken away (323); cf. Hasitzka, *Neue Texte*, 173 no. 247; Cribiore names the list "an exercise, not a glossary" (*Writing, Teachers, and Students*, 202 no. 123, pl. XI).

43 O.MMA 14.1.214; Crum and Evelyn White, *Monastery of Epiphanius*, 2:136 and 322 no. 618, pl. XIV; cf. Hasitzka, *Neue Texte*, 178–79 no. 252; Cribiore, *Writing, Teachers, and Students*, 202 no. 122; Larsen, "Redrawing the Interpretive Map," 17–18 and 28 fig. 4. It is not unusual to encounter similar content in broader classroom archives. In fact, extant school artifacts readily attest commensurate practice across a range of school settings (Cf. Hasitzka, *Neue Texte*, 63–74 nos. 83–107; Cribiore, *Writing, Teachers, and Students*, 196–203 nos. 98–128). Bucking suggests the juxtaposition of Greek and Coptic in

The sequences encountered in a set of inscriptions – again preserved *in situ* at Beni Hasan – are alternately suggestive.[44] Arranged in small clusters, and in variously dispersed combinations, extant wordlists are comprised of biblical names: ⲛⲱϩ[ⲉ] (Noah), ⲁⲃⲣⲁϩⲁⲙ (Abraham), ⲓ[ⲥⲁ]ⲕ (Isaac), [ⲓⲁⲕⲱ]ⲃ (Jacob), ⲓⲱⲥⲏⲫ (Joseph), ... ⲓⲱϩⲁⲛⲛⲏⲥ (John), ⲇⲁⲛⲓⲏⲗ (Daniel), ⲁⲛⲁⲛⲓⲁⲥ (Ananias), ⲙⲓⲥⲁ[ⲏⲗ] (Michael),[45] and ⲁⲍ[ⲁ] ⲣⲓⲁⲥ (Azarias) (Fig. 14).[46] Elsewhere, the term ⲁⲡⲁ is repeated ten times[47] Fluidly infused with biblical and monastic content, this nomenclature brings to mind Jerome's commendation that Paula rehearse names of the "prophets ... apostles ... [and] patriarchs ... from Adam downwards" (*Epist.* 107.4). Placement proximate with the linked alphabets and syllabary discussed above, lends interesting context to Pachomius' cryptic injunction that with the letters, and "the fundamentals of a syllable ... verbs and nouns" should also be written (*Praec.* 139).[48]

---

the first wordlist invites consideration of what subset of monastic instruction may have been aimed at facilitating fluency across languages (Bucking, "Scribes and Schoolmasters," 23 ff). In turn, the inclusion of both 'Christian' and 'planetary' nomenclature, likewise, raises interesting questions about the degree to which extant artifacts mark, and bridge, the melding of disparate cultures and source material.

44 Newberry, *Beni Hasan*, 2:65–68.

45 Hugo Lundhaug notes the re-construction of ⲙⲓⲥⲁ[ⲕ] (Meshak) as alternately plausible.

46 These lists were first transcribed by Champollion (*Monuments*, 384); then re-published by Newberry (*Beni Hasan*, 2:68 no. 75); cf. Larsen, "Excavating the Excavations."

47 Newberry, *Beni Hasan*, 2:67 no. 69.

48 On comparative grounds, a wordlist included in the Greek-Bohairic codex published by Husselman is particularly interesting (P.Mich. 926). The list appears on the *verso* of the fifth folio of the codex. It follows the lengthy Greek-Bohairic syllabary, discussed above. Constituted primarily of biblical names, the wordlist begins with ⲃⲁⲣⲛⲁⲃⲟⲥ (Barnabus), then turns to a broader range of characters: ... ⲁⲛⲇⲣⲉⲁⲥ (Andreas), ⲥⲟⲗⲟⲙⲟⲛ (Solomon), ⲁⲇⲁⲙ (Adam), ⲛⲟⲉ (Noah), ⲁⲃⲣⲁϩⲁⲙ (Abraham), ⲓⲥⲁⲕ (Isaac), ⲓⲁⲕⲱⲃ (Jacob), ⲙⲱⲩⲥⲏⲥ (Moses), ⲇⲁⲩⲓⲇ (David), ⲥⲉⲧⲣⲁⲕ (Shadrach), ⲙⲉⲥⲁⲕ (Meshak), ⲉⲃⲑⲉⲛⲁⲅⲅⲱ (Abednego), ⲇⲁⲛⲓⲏⲗ (Daniel). It is positioned adjacent to a copying exercise, comprised of the greetings that introduce Paul's letter to the Romans, and in close proximity to a bi-syllabic pronunciation exercise comprised of ⲃⲁⲗⲗⲟⲥ, ⲃⲉⲗⲗⲟⲥ, ⲃⲏⲗⲗⲟⲥ, ⲃⲓⲗⲗⲟⲥ, ⲃⲟⲗⲗⲟⲥ, ⲃⲩⲗⲗⲟⲥ, ⲃⲱⲗⲗⲟⲥ – combinations phonetically akin to Paul's name (Husselman, *"Bohairic School Text,"* 129–35, 147–48; Hasitzka, *Neue Texte*, 138–39 no. 207 ff. 5v–6r). One of the two school tablets published by Boak likewise combines practice with syllables and words. Here, the included wordlist is comprised of both biblical and monastic names (Boak, "A Coptic Syllabary," 296–97; cf. Hasitzka, *Neue Texte*, 59–60 no. 78). As has been repeatedly affirmed in broader work on ancient school practice, parallel patterns persist across linguistic and geographical borders; cf. Adam H. Becker, *Fear of God and the Beginning of Wisdom: The School of Nisibis and Christian Scholastic Culture in Late Antique Mesopotamia* (Philadelphia: University of Pennsylvania Press, 2006); David Carr, *Writing on the Tablet of the Heart* (New York: Oxford University Press, 2003). Liv Ingeborg Lied has noted the presence of fluidly re-shaped pedagogical content in Syriac material.

Sentences

Like the static rehearsal that distinguishes late-ancient manipulation of alphabets, syllables and words, classroom work with sentences followed set protocol. Again, Quintilian's directives are straightforward. He suggests that once syllables have been learned, students "begin construct[ing] words with them and sentences with the words."[49] In selecting content – as with wordlists – he commends taking the longer view. Even at the early stage of copying texts, he advises that the lines set before young students "should not express thoughts of no significance, but convey some sound moral lesson."[50] His stated rationale is simple. At a later point in life, such subject matter might still be remembered, "and the impression made upon [an] unformed mind [also] contribute to the formation of ... character."[51]

Outlining parallel parameters for monastic work with sentences and short passages, Jerome advises that even as a small child, young Paula's "tongue ... be imbued with the sweet music of the Psalms,"[52] and that she progressively move to "lessons of life in the proverbs of Solomon."[53] Commending a lengthy list of biblical texts,[54] he promotes repetition of Scripture as a fixed daily task – with "verses" learned first in Greek," then in Latin.[55] In turn, he urges avoidance of all "apocryphal books."[56] As Paula matures, Jerome suggests that rather than "jewels or silks," her treasures ought to be "manuscripts of the holy scriptures." Even here, however, she should "prefer correctness and accurate arrangement to gilding and Babylonian parchment with elaborate decorations."[57] Like Jerome, Basil too promotes classroom use of "maxims

---

49 Quintilian, *Inst.* 1.1.31–32 (Russell, LCL); *Tunc ipsis syllabis verba complecti et his sermonem connectere incipiat.*

50 Quintilian, *Inst.* 1.1.35–6 (Russell, LCL); *... ii quoque versus, qui ad imitationem scribendi proponentur, non otiosas velim sententias habeant, sed honestum aliquid monentis.*

51 Quintilian, *Inst.* 1.1.36 (Russell, LCL); *Prosequitur haec memoria in senectutem et impressa animo rudi usque ad mores proficiet.*

52 Jerome, *Epist.* 107.4 (Wright, LCL); *... adhuc tenera lingua psalmis dulcibus inbuator.*

53 Jerome, *Epist.* 107.12 (Wright, LCL); *Discat primum Psalterium ... et in Proverbiis Salomonis erudiatur ad vitam.*

54 Jerome, *Epist.* 107.12 (Wright, LCL); Jerome's list progresses from Ecclesiastes and Job, to the Gospels, the Acts of the Apostles, and the Epistles. Selections from Hebrew Scriptures are extensive. Beyond the biblical canon, Jerome commends the works of "Cyprian ... the letters of Athanasius and the treatises of Hillary" (*Cypriani opuscula semper in manu teneat, Athanasii epistulas et Hilarii libros inoffenso decurrat pede.*)

55 Jerome, *Epist.* 107.9 (Wright, LCL); *Reddat tibi pensum cotidie scripturarum certum. Ediscat Graecorum versuum numerum. Sequatur statim et Latina eruditio.*

56 Jerome, *Epist.* 107.12 (Wright, LCL); *...* because "it requires great skill to look for gold in mud" (*grandis esse prudentiae aurum in luto quaerere*).

57 Jerome, *Epist.* 107.12 (Wright, LCL); *Pro gemmis aut serico divinos codices amet, in quibus non auri et pellis Babyloniae vermiculata pictura, sed ad fidem placeat emendata et erudita distinctio.*

[drawn] from Proverbs,"[58] and suggests replacing "myths" with Christian stories "of wonderful deeds."[59] Pachomius mandates that "whoever enters the monastery uninstructed" be given "twenty Psalms or two of the Apostle's Epistles, or some other part of Scripture."[60]

The material record of monastically provenanced 'sentences', again attests both adoptive and adaptive praxis. For example, four of the ten artifacts categorized as "school pieces" in the Monastery of Epiphanius catalogue preserve lines drawn from Homer. These extracts are rendered in Greek, and like the mixed alphabets discussed above, each is introduced by Christian symbolism – in this instance, a cross. Of the two ostraca that remain extant, one preserves a portion of the first two lines of the *Iliad* (1.1–2) (Fig. 15).[61] A second, records iterative rehearsal of the initial line (*Il.* 1.1), "in varying stages of completeness" – followed by a portion of less readily identifiable Coptic text.[62] Crum and Evelyn White identify the contents of the two additional ostraca as likewise comprised of "recurring Homeric tag[s]."[63] These, however, are no longer extant. Whether the four ostraca should be broadly classified as school related, solely "scribal," or both, remains a topic of debate.[64] It bears noting, however, absent a monastic frame, the inclusion of Homeric content is often named a marker of pedagogical provenance.[65]

---

58 Basil, *Reg. Fus.* 15 (PG 31.953; trans. Clarke, *Ascetic Works of Saint Basil*); ... καὶ γνώμαις παιδεύειν ταῖς ἐκ τῶν Παροιμιῶν; cf. Gregory of Nyssa, *Vita Macrina* 962D.

59 Basil, *Reg. Fus.* 15 (PG 31.953; trans. Clarke, *Ascetic Works of Saint Basil*); ... καὶ ἀντὶ μύθων τὰς τῶν παραδόξων ἔργων ἱστορίας αὐτοῖς διηγεῖσθαι.

60 Pachomius, *Praec.* 139 (Boon, *Pachomiana Latina*; Veilleux, *Pachomian Koinonia*); *Qui rudis monasterium fuerit ingressus ... dabunt ei uiginti psalmos uel duas epistulas apostoli, aut alterius scripturae partem.*

61 O.MMA 14.1.139; *ed. pr.* Crum and Evelyn White, *Monastery of Epiphanius*, 2:135 and 320 no. 612, pl. XIV; cf. Cribiore, *Writing, Teachers, and Students*, 225 no. 225; Larsen, "Re-drawing the Interpretive Map," 17 and 27 fig. 4; idem, "Sayings and Stories as Schooltexts," 19 fig. 1.4.

62 O.MMA 14.1.140; *ed. pr.* Crum and Evelyn White, *Monastery of Epiphanius*, 2:135 and 320 no. 611, pl. XIV; cf. Cribore, *Writing, Teachers, and Students*, 213 no. 168.

63 One preserves *Il.* 1.201: "And to him speaking he addressed winged words" (και μιν φων- / ησας επεα π- / τεροεντα π- / ροσηυδα); *ed. pr.* Crum and Evelyn White, *Monastery of Epiphanius*, 2:135 and 320 no. 613; cf. Cribiore, *Writing, Teachers, and Students*, 225 no. 226; the other, *Il.* 1.22: "Then indeed all the others ..." (ενθ αλλοι μ[εν] / παντες); *ed. pr.* Crum and Evelyn White, *Monastery of Epiphanius*, 2:135 and 320 no. 614; cf. Cribiore, *Writing, Teachers, and Students*, 226 no. 227.

64 Bucking, "Scribes and Schoolmasters," 21–47.

65 Homeric school material has likewise been identified among the *New Finds at Sinai*, here provenanced to the monastic community at St. Catherine's; cf. P. G. Nikopoulos, et al., *Holy Monastery and Archdiocese of Sinai. The New Finds* (Athens: Mount Sinai Foundation, 1999), 124–28. Warm thanks to Sebastian Brock for calling my attention to these material remains, and to the Metropolitan Museum of Art for providing library access to this publication. On broader use of Homeric content, see Cribiore, *Gymnastics of the Mind*, 140–43 and Morgan, *Literate Education*, 105 ff. Referencing the unpublished dissertation of M. Handy Ibrahim, Morgan notes that Homer was used for "reading, dictation, copy-

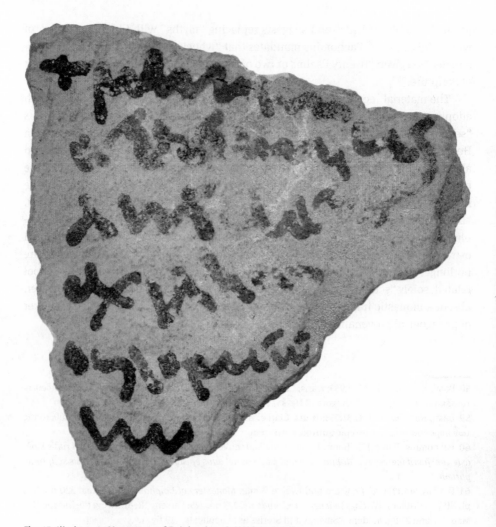

Fig. 15: Iliad 1.1–2, Monastery of Epiphanius, O.MMA 14.1.139

---

ing, composing, 'calligraphy' and 'higher education'" (105 n. 57); cf. Ibrahim, "Ἡ Ἑλληνορρωμαϊκή Παιδεία ἐν Αἰγύπτῳ" (Unpublished diss.; University of Athens, 1972), 187 ff. This, of course, matches the use of gnomic maxims, sentences and sayings, more generally. Cribiore notes that students first encountered excerpts and *sententiae* in exercises of penmanship and memorization. At every succeeding educational level, they rehearsed the same sentences "chew[ing them] over and over," making collections, then expanding, paraphrasing and contracting their content, until they could (at an opportune moment, or in a well-turned phrase) incorporate a given articulation into everyday speech and writing (*Gymnastics of the Mind*, 178–79). Morgan observes that "more texts of gnomic sentences survive [in schoolhands] than fragments of any other literature or any other kind of exercise." Displaying a full range of expertise, they "appear to have been used at every stage [of learning] ... from elementary reading and writing to rhetorical exercises" (*Literate Education*, 122); cf. Ibrahim, 187 ff.

Fig. 16: Sentences of Menander, Monastery of Epiphanius, O.MMA 14.1.210

As pedagogically suggestive is a larger Epiphanian ostracon that preserves a sizable collection of the "Sentences of Menander." Adhering to a format familiar across a range of school settings, the sentences are organized alphabetically from α (*alpha*) through φ (*phi*) (Fig. 16).[66] The artifact's first, partially legible line enjoins "fear of God" ([...]φοβὸς θεοῦ); the second assigns "the beginning [of great wisdom" to "learning] letters" (Ἀρχὴ μ[εγίστη τοῦ φρονεῖν τὰ] γράμματα).[67] Given that this

---

66 Cribiore, *Gymnastics of the Mind*, 178–79; Morgan, *Literate Education*, 120 ff; cf. Carr, *Writing on the Tablet of the Heart*.

67 O.MMA 14.1.210; *ed. pr.* Crum and Evelyn White, *Monastery of Epiphanius*, 2:135 and 320–21 no. 615; cf. Cribiore, *Writing, Teachers, and Students*, 252 no. 319, Pl. XLIV; Larsen, "Pedagogical Parallels," 67–69; idem, "On Learning a New Alphabet," 59–77; idem, "Re-drawing the Interpretive Map," 18 and 34, fig. 7; idem, "Sayings and Stories as Schooltexts," 19 and 20 fig. 1.5. Again, a broader array of classroom examples is well documented. Particularly interesting, however, is a lengthy Greek-Coptic codex

content is recorded in a relatively practiced hand, Cribiore suggests that the collected maxims may have served as a teacher's model,[68] manifesting practice that marks routine classroom use of lines that "convey some sound moral lesson" (Quintilian, *Inst.* 1.1.35).

Sayings, Stories (and Sermons)

The iterative progressions that link work with alphabets, syllabaries, words, and sentences, are further expanded in the set pedagogical sequences that govern reformulation of maxims and *sententiae* into sayings, stories, and a broader range of derivatively malleable source material. While traditional readings have named this "simple" content core evidence in arguments that premise the absence of monastic investment in pedagogical pursuits,[69]extant collections of sayings and stories present a particularly provocative (and productive) locus for exploring the fluid adjustments endemic to classroom use. In fact, the essential role assigned such classroom content, is described, not only in the practice delineated by Quintilian – and his monastic counterparts – but more explicilty in ancient/late-ancient handbooks of elementary exercises (*progymnasmata*), aimed at delivering students "to the threshold of rhetoric." Extant manuals delineate sequences that remained the conduit of formulaically fixed, and infinitely fluid strategies of literary redeployment, from the hellenistic period, through byzantium, and beyond.[70]

Both Quintilian and Basil link sentences with 'sayings' that report the names, words and actions of illustrious individuals.[71] Both likewise commend the use of games and rewards as enticement to enhance the pleasurable value of such practice; counting "entertainment" an immediate impetus for core competency in "learning the sayings of famous men [as well as] ... selections from the poets."[72] Like rehearsal of gnomic sentences, the long-term usefulness of work with this content was implicit. Iterative re-framing of moral maxims/sentences into sayings, and exemplary stories, was aimed not only at attaining fluid command of established compositional forms,

---

included in Hasitzka, *Neue Texte*, 1.202–10 no. 269, 2.95–96; cf. Dieter Hagedorn and Manfred Weber, "Die griechisch-koptische Rezension der Menandersentenzen" *ZPE* 3 (1968), 15–50.

68 Cribiore, *Writing, Teachers and Students*, 252 no. 319; Larsen, "On Learning a New Alphabet," 59–77; cf. Bucking, "Scribes and Schoolmasters," 34–35 for an alternate reading.

69 See Robert L. Wilken's *Global History of Christianity: The First Thousand Years* (New Haven: Yale University Press, 2012), 99–108, for what is perhaps the most recent articulation of this premise.

70 Kennedy, *Progymnasmata*, ix.

71 *Reg. Fus.* 15 (PG 31.953; trans. Clarke, *Ascetic Works of Saint Basil*); ... καὶ ἆθλα μνήμης ὀνομάτων τε καὶ πραγμάτων αὐτοῖς προτιθέναι; cf. Larsen, "Ørkenfedrenes Apophthegmata," 26-35.

72 Quintilian, *Inst.* 1.1.36 (Russell, LCL); *Etiam dicta clarorum virorum et electos ex poetis maxime (namque eorum cognitio parvis gratior est) locos ediscere inter lusum licet.*

but also insuring "that the soul ... be lead to practise (*sic*) good immediately and from the outset, [and] while ... still plastic and soft, pliable as wax, [be] ... molded by the shapes pressed upon it."[73]

Again, a series of monastic exercises elucidates the stable fluidity of emergent practice in useful ways. For example, faintly visible on two faces of a small 'Epiphanian' ostracon is content comprised of two 'sentences' and a 'saying'. As identified in Crum and Evelyn White's early transcription, the *verso* preserves Proverbs 13:7 and 13 (Fig. 17a):

ογν νετειρε μμοογ νρμμαο εμντογ λααγ αγω ογν νε[τ]θββιο μμοογ εγ?νογνοσ μμντρ[μμαο]

There are those who make themselves rich, having nothing, and there are those who humble themselves, while being very [wealthy] (Prov 13:7).

πετκαταφρονει νογ?ωβ σενακαταφρονε μμοϥ πετρ?ωβ ⲇε ?ητⲥ ντεντολη [παι] πε ετογοχ [μ] νλααγ ναγαθο[ν] να϶ωπ[ε.

He who despises a matter, he will be despised; the one who acts according to the commandment, [this one] is safe; nothing good will happen [(to a deceitful son)] (Prov 13:13).[74]

---

73 Basil, *Reg. Fus.* 15 (PG 31.956; trans. Clarke, *Ascetic Works of Saint Basil*); Εὔπλαστον οὖν ἔτι οὖσαν καὶ ἀπαλὴν τὴν ψυχήν, καὶ ὡς κηρὸν εὔεικτον, ταῖς τῶν ἐπιβαλλομένων μορφαῖς ῥᾳδίως ἐκτυπουμένην, πρὸς πᾶσαν ἀγαθῶν ἄσκησιν εὐθὺς καὶ ἐξ ἀρχῆς ἐνάργεσθαι χρή; Here Basil is echoing not only Quintilian, but an assertion that recurs across generations of school curricula. This is the premise that each iteration of a moral extract retained implicit capacity to promote virtue and shape character. Writing in the fourth century BCE, Plato recommends that the end result of "compil[ing] anthologies of the poets and mak[ing] collections of whole passages, which ... must be committed to memory" is not only that a student gain wide familiarity with literature, but also "to make [one] a good and wise [individual]" (*Leg.* 810e–12a [Bury, LCL]; οἱ δὲ ἐκ πάντων κεφάλαια ἐκλέξαντες καί τινας ὅλας ῥήσεις εἰς ταὐτὸν συναγαγόντες, ἐκμανθάνειν φασὶ δεῖν εἰς μνήμην τιθεμένους, εἰ μέλλει τις ἀγαθὸς ἡμῖν καὶ σοφὸς ἐκ πολυπειρίας καὶ πολυμαθίας γενέσθαι). In his pedagogical treatise *Ad Demonicum*, Pseudo-Isocrates suggests that noble behavior results from a mind "fraught with many noble maxims; for, as it is the nature of the body to be developed by appropriate exercises, it is the nature of the soul to be developed by moral precepts (*Ad Demonicum* 12 [Norlin, LCL]; Οὕτω δὲ τὴν γνώμην οὐ δυνατὸν διατεθῆναι τὸν μὴ πολλῶν καὶ καλῶν ἀκουσμάτων πεπληρωμένον· τὰ μὲν γὰρ σώματα τοῖς συμμέτροις πόνοις, ἡ δὲ ψυχὴ τοῖς σπουδαίοις λόγοις αὔξεσθαι πέφυκε). Plutarch premises that teachers be selected by virtue of their ability to set "precepts and exhortations beside the young, in order that [children's] characters [might] grow to be upright (*Lib. ed.* 4C [Babbitt, LCL]; οἱ νόμιμοι τῶν διδασκάλων ἐμμελεῖς τὰς ὑποθήκας καὶ παραινέσεις παραπηγνύουσι τοῖς νέοις, ἵν᾿ ὀρθὰ τούτων βλαστάνῃ τὰ ἤθη); cf. Teresa Morgan, *Popular Morality in the Early Roman Empire* (Cambridge: Cambridge University Press, 2007); Larsen, "On Learning a New Alphabet," 67–69; idem, "Re-drawing the Interpretive Map," 1–34; idem, "Sayings and Stories as Schooltexts," 13–33.
74 Cairo 44674.118 (*verso*); *ed. pr.* Crum and Evelyn White, *Monastery of Epiphanius*, 2:5 and 157 no. 22; cf. Larsen, "Re-drawing the Interpretive Map," 18–19, 32 fig. 9; idem, "Excavating the Excavations."

Figs. 17a and b: Proverbs and Saying, Monastery of Epiphanius, Cairo 44674.118.
Photos Courtesy of Kent Brown

The *recto*, contains what appears to be a paraphrase of this content, here attributed to Basil, but otherwise, "unattested" (Fig. 17b):

ⲁⲡⲁ ⲃⲁⲥⲓⲗⲓⲟⲥ ⲛⲓⲙ ⲅⲁⲣ ⲉⲛⲉϩ ⲡⲉⲛⲧⲁⲩⲙⲁⲕⲁⲣⲓⲍⲉ ⲙⲙⲟϥ ⲭⲉⲟⲩⲛⲧϥ ⲭⲣⲏⲙⲁ ⲏ ⲛⲓⲙ ⲡⲉⲛⲧⲁϥⲟⲩⲭⲁⲓ ⲉϥϩⲛⲟⲩⲙⲧⲟⲛ
ⲛⲥⲱⲙⲁ

Apa Basilios – For who has ever been blessed because he had property, or who has been saved while in bodily rest[75]

If one places Jerome's (and Basil's) commendation of iterative work with "lessons of life [from] the proverbs of Solomon" (Jerome, *Ep.* 107.12; cf. Basil, *Reg. Fus.* 15) in conversation with Quintilian and Basil's commendation of "pleasurable" word play with the "words/names and actions" of illustrious men (and women), both adoptive form and adaptive content is distinctive (Basil, *Reg. Fus.* 15; cf. Quintilian, *Inst.* 1.1.36).[76]

---

75 Cairo 44674.118 (*recto*); *ed. pr.* Crum and Evelyn White, *Monastery of Epiphanius*, 2:12 and 163 no. 52; cf. Larsen, "Re-drawing the Interpretive Map," 18–19, 32 fig. 10; idem, "Excavating the Excavations." Thanks to Hugo Lundhaug and Lance Jenott for expert consultation on these respective Coptic translations.

76 While these three sentences could simply be viewed as the record of a small personal collection of maxims and a saying, placed in conversation, the trio as readily elucidates transformation of "lessons ... from the Proverbs of Solomon" into a saying or a *chreia* – that is, a maxim aptly attributed to an illustrious "named or anonymous protagonist" (Theon, "Περὶ Χρείας" 1–4, et al.); Examined in light of well-documented elementary exercises (προγυμνάσματα) that governed classroom re-shaping of gnomic source material, this combined re-working elucidates the types of shifts that reflect practice so routine that, as noted above, George Kennedy likens its established forms to the "structural features of classical architecture," *Progymnasmata*, ix; cf. Ronald F. and Edward N. O'Neil, eds., *The Chreia in*

Although by virtue of traditional cataloguing, Coptic school content has long escaped categorization as school related, the combination of two "moral maxims" – gleaned from Proverbs, and a "saying" – attributed to a famous monk – appears pedagogically provocative.[77]

Three "sayings"/*apophthegms* included in the recently published P.Cotsen-Princeton school codex are as interesting.[78] As catalogued by Scott Bucking, the codex, as a whole, preserves a compendium of pedagogically focused content. Echoing, by now, familiar sequences, it includes an extensive syllabary, variously configured wordlists, the names of letters that comprise a full Coptic alphabet, and collections of "nonsensical words" – arguably akin to those used in structuring extant χαλινοί. Short sets of admonitory phrases and/or 'sentences' are interspersed throughout. Three additional "sayings" – of fluid length and content – serve as something of a coda in this progression.[79] Although, described by Bucking as elsewhere "unattested", they appear in guises similar to those which structure the "sayings" included in more familiar, published compilations of monastic *apophthegmata*.[80] In short, like the 'paraphrase' of Proverbs, attributed to Basil (Fig. 17b), each is rendered in classic pedagogical form.[81]

As transcribed, the first *apophthegm* opens with a sentence, that retains thematic emphases reminiscent of those preserved on the two-sided ostracon discussed above (Fig. 17a/b): "Apa Basilios said that it is appropriate for the monk to lead a life of poverty" (ⲁϥϫⲟⲟⲥ ⲛϭⲓ ⲁⲡⲁ ⲃⲁⲥⲓⲗⲓⲟⲥ ϫⲉ ϣϣⲉ ⲉⲡⲙⲟⲛⲁⲭⲟⲥ ⲉⲭⲡⲟ ⲛⲁϥ ⲛ̄ⲟⲩⲃⲓⲟⲥ ⲙ̄ⲙⲛ̄ⲧϩⲏⲕⲉ).[82] This 'saying' is followed by a lengthy narrative elaboration. Not unlike the fluid varia-

Ancient Rhetoric: The Progymnasmata (Atlanta: Scholars Press, 1986); idem, *The Chreia and Ancient Rhetoric: Classroom Exercises* (Atlanta: Scholars Press, 2002); Craig A. Gibson, ed. *Libanius's* Progymnasmata: *Model Exercises in Greek Prose, Composition and Rhetoric* (Atlanta: Scholars Press, 2008); Larsen, "Pedagogical Parallels," 74–115; idem, "Rustic Rumination," 21–30; idem, "On Learning a New Alphabet," 67–77; idem, "Sayings and Stories as Schooltexts," 13–33.

77 Cf. Larsen, "Excavating the Excavations"; Happily, this situation is beginning to change. Monika Hasitzka's catalog of school artifacts is devoted almost solely to Coptic remains (*Neue Texte*). Raffaella Cribiore and Jennifer Cromwell are currently working on the Coptic Epiphanian ostraca owned by Columbia University (as noted in e-mail correspondence of May 17, 2015). Scott Bucking's work, albeit sometimes tendentious, marks an important contribution to the field, particularly with respect to bilingualism.

78 P.Cotsen-Princeton 1, pp. 157–176; *ed. princ.* Bucking, *Practice Makes Perfect*, 197–214 plates 83–100.

79 Cf. Bucking, *Practice Makes Perfect*, 45–70 for more detailed discussion.

80 Bucking, *Practice Makes Perfect*, 68.

81 Cf. Larsen, "Ørkenfedrenes *Apophthegmata*"; idem, "The *Apophthegmata Patrum* and the Classical Rhetorical Tradition"; idem, "Pedagogical Parallels"; idem, "Rustic Rumination"; idem, "On Learning a New Alphabet"; idem, "Sayings and Stories as Schooltexts"; idem, "Re-drawing the Interpretive Map."

82 P.Cotsen-Princeton 1, pp. 157–169; *ed. princ.* Bucking, *Practice Makes Perfect*, 68–69 and 197–207 plates 83–93; Perhaps as surprising is the commonality of attribution and thematic content that raises additional questions about the shape of what might be named an emergent monastic 'core curriculum'.

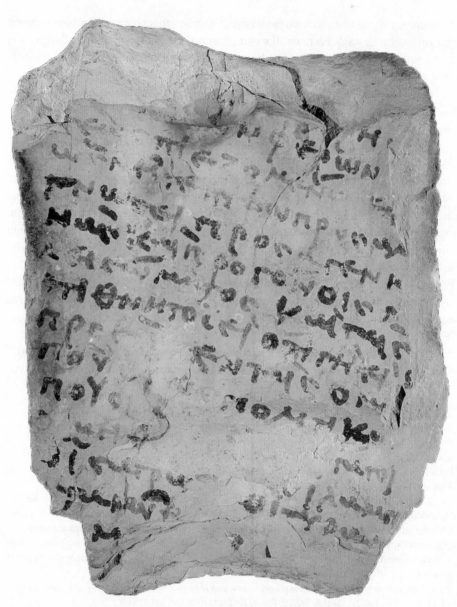

Fig. 18: Copying Exercise – Homily of Basil, Deir el Bahri, O.Col.inv.766

tion refracted in more familiar – and more stable – published collections, the second *apophthegm* is briefly formulated, and comprised of only three lines of text. A third *apophthegm* commences with what is perhaps the most classic of monastic (and pedagogical) formulae: "An old man said that …" (ⲁϥϫⲟⲟⲥ ⲛ̄ϭⲓ ⲟⲩϩⲗⲗⲟ ϫⲉ). This 'saying', again, introduces a narrative elaboration of some length.[83]

A final example – identified by Raffaella Cribiore as a copying exercise – is alternately provocative. Cribiore suggests that extracted content may have served as a vehicle for classroom practice with accents and lexical signs. Here, preserved on an ostracon of Theban provenance, it is drawn from a sermon elsewhere attributed to Basil of Caesarea (Fig. 18).[84] Richly elucidating the static forms and fluid texts that shaped both classroom practice and derivative compositional "habits", the homily is, itself, emblematic of a 'textbook' elaboration of the familiar maxim: "Give heed to yourself" (πρόσεχε σεαυτῷ). Traditionally attributed to one (or more) of the 'seven sages', not unlike the Sentences of Menander, this short maxim is representative of a larger core of conventional source material, routinely deployed in classroom settings.[85]

Conclusions

The artifacts examined in this essay, of course, raise as many questions as they answer. However, it is clear that the structures Quintilian commends in delineating repetitive "lessons necessary for the young" (Basil, *Reg. Fus.* 15), were as familiar to pedagogues, writing in the fourth through sixth centuries CE, as they were in the first. Exercises that, in elite settings, may have required organized sets "of letters made of boxwood … or ivory" (Jerome, *Ep.* 107.4; cf. Quintilian, *Inst.* 1.1.26) are here rendered on less refined – but arguably as serviceable – surfaces of stone, pottery, plaster, and wood.[86] Nonetheless, the juxtaposition of adopted forms, with readily

---

83 P.Cotsen-Princeton 1, pp. 170–176; Cf. *ed. princ.* Bucking, *Practice Makes Perfect*, 68–69 and 208–214 plates 94–100.

84 O.Col. inv. 766; cf. Raffaella Cribiore, "A Fragment of Basilius of Caesarea," in *Akten des 21. Internationalen Papyrologenkongresses, Berlin, 13.–19. 8. 1995* (ed. Bärbel Kramer et al.; APF.B 3; Stuttgart: Teubner, 1997), 187–93; cf. Basil, *Homilia in illud: "Attende tibi ipsi"* (CPG 2847). Marking what is arguably a quintessential model of fluidly mundane, pedagogical and textual re-use, the layered character of this final school-related exercise, must give pause.

85 O.Col. inv. 766; cf. Cribiore, "An Unidentified Fragment." It offers provocative elucidation of Morgan's assertion that "more sentences survive in schoolhands than fragments of any other artifact …" As demonstrated here, such content is derivatively manifested in the treatises, sermons and storylines that more advanced application facilitated and encouraged Interpretive.

86 In his early discussions of *Ancient Literacy* (Cambridge: Harvard University Press, 1989), William Harris persuasively argues that within late Roman society, broadly construed, the breakdown between *literati* and ἀγράμματοι fell largely along class lines. Premising three criteria, each derivative of

adaptable content, effectively nuances debates about pedagogical purpose.[87] Both literary descriptions and material remains affirm that monastic students practiced alphabetic sequences in conventional, reversed and mixed order (Quintilian, *Inst.* 1.1.25; Jerome, *Epist.* 107.4). They appear to have engaged few "shortcut[s]" in formulaic repetition of consonant-vowel combinations, so insuring that syllables were "all learned [by heart]" (Quintilian, *Inst.* 1.1.30–31). Patterned strings of letters, along with extant word lists, attest ample opportunity to work with "difficult to pronounce" nomenclature (Quintilian, *Inst.* 1.1.37). Extant collections of selected sentences and 'sayings' register continued emphasis on "impressing" both "mind" and "character" with "sound moral lessons" (Quintilian, *Inst.* 1.1.35–36; cf. Jerome, *Epist.* 107.12; Basil, *Reg. Fus.*15).

As Jerome and his contemporaries infuse familiar structures with Christian and monastic content, the changes they commend are relatively cosmetic. In fact, at the most basic levels of instruction, modifications are hardly perceptible. Particularly striking are exemplars attesting monastic practice with patterned strings of letters, and/or χαλινοί. However, even where the monastic curriculum has been fluidly adapted to better accommodate and/or incorporate new content, underlying structures remain familiar. Extant inscriptions (and artifacts) attest the bible's particular suitability as a source for difficult to pronounce words (Quintilian, *Inst.* 1.1.37; cf.

---

social position, Harris posits that in acquiring literate skills, financial resources would have primarily determined an individual's 1) access to education, 2) the availability and affordability of materials for reading and writing, and 3) a 'felt need' for the cultural assets and opportunities that literacy could provide. Harris also notes, however, that such delineations were hardly absolute. Blurring the boundaries between elite *literati* and the unlettered was a class of individuals with the technical skills of literacy. Often, comprised of literate slaves and artisans, who made a living by the written word, this group of individuals performed the functions of reading and, more importantly, writing for others in society. Here, economic and/or practical goals served as impetus for literate investment.

Harris' arguments remain persuasive. However, the criteria upon which his analysis is grounded can be used to support an inverse line of reasoning within a monastic frame. Extant material evidence suggests that embedded structures may have served to relativize the determinative role played by social class, and attendant financial advantage. In fact, if one accords serious weight to the protocol outlined by Basil, Jerome, and Pachomius, access to education arguably emerges as a defining feature of monastic life across conventional demographic lines. Here, (1) one's status as a community member may have afforded institutional access to "[individuals] who could teach" (Pachomius, *Praec.* 139). (2) In turn, the broad corpus of biblical texts, combined with a ready supply of ostraca, plastered surfaces, and wooden tablets, offered ample material support for acquiring skills in reading and writing. (3) Finally, ongoing involvement in mundane correspondence, reading scripture, and copying texts, appears relatively consonant with Harris' criterion of "felt need" for the skills that acquisition of literacy could provide. Such 'democratization' of education lends interesting nuance to narrative sequences that repeatedly frame acquisition of literate skills as a point of communal tension.

87 As noted above, perhaps the most significant debates address the distinctions used in designating a particular exercise scribal, pedagogical, or both; cf., e.g., Bucking, "Scribes and Schoolmasters," 21–47; Cribiore, *Writing, Teachers, and Students*, 75–118.

Jerome, *Epist.* 107.4; Basil, *Reg. Fus.* 15). Whether aimed at reading Euripides, Homer, or the letters of Paul, wordlists invite work with purposefully chosen nomenclature – and derivatively, absorption of knowledge, that might otherwise require "additional [investments of] time later on" (Quintilian, *Inst.* 1.1.34–35; cf. Jerome, *Epist.* 107.4; Basil, *Reg. Fus.* 15). Lines from the Psalms and Proverbs, by definition, exclude commerce in thoughts and sentences "of no significance" (Quintilian, *Inst.* 1.1.35–36). Excerpts attributed to biblical or monastic figures appear easily as serviceable for fluid re-framing as those assigned their broader civic and/or philosophical counterparts.[88] As the patriarchs of Hebrew Scripture displace classical heroes, prophets and apostles oust Greek gods and goddesses, and illustrious *abbas* and *ammas* effectively double as philosophers and/or civic leaders, alternate content melds with established forms, and imbues well-honed structures with a Christian and/or monastic veneer.

This 'fluidly' stable register introduces a comic element into Pachomius' enjoinder that upon entering the monastery every "unlettered" monk – even if he (or she) does not want to – should, with "all gratitude," receive mandated instruction in the skills requisite for reading Scripture (Pachomius, *Praec.* 139–140). As excerpts of Euripides cede ground to "the Psalms, a letter of Paul, or some other portion of Scripture" (Pachomius, *Praec.* 139), one needs little imagination to transpose the caricature of a recalcitrant schoolchild mirrored in Herodas' Διδάσκαλος into a late-antique frame.[89] In fact, there is little that mitigates against situating Herodas' protagonist within a monastic frame, and thus, envisioning a Pachomian monk/pupil – stammering out a biblical text – word by word, or syllable by syllable, until able to read fluently, without it being necessary "... to stop [and] think" (Quintilian, *Inst.* 1.1.31).

Not only does the context afforded by such pedagogical confluence, usefully balance debates traditionally grounded in reading adoptive and adaptive 'habits' in isolation – or more recently, as categories of contest. It also renders patent the fluidly normative character of a broader spectrum of monastic source material. For example, as illustrated here, like alphabets, syllabaries, word lists, and sentences, monastic 'sayings', *apophthegms*, and sermons (Figs. 17a/b and 18), register fluid use of standard pedagogical protocol.[90] Their predictable deployment of the "structural features" of classical composition, likewise render visible the formulaic strategies used in infusing (and cloaking) classic configurations with an alternate canon of biblical and monastic content. Along curricular trajectories that simultaneously coalesce and diverge, as lines from scripture meet passages from Homer, the Proverbs of Solomon

---

88 Cf. Larsen, "On Learning a New Alphabet," 59–77.

89 Herodas, *Didaskalos*, I. C. Cunningham, tr. and ed. in *Theophrastes: Characters, Herodas: Mimes, Cercidas and the Choliambic Poets*, LCL 225 (Cambridge, Mass.: Harvard University Press, 1929, 1993), 242–53.

90 Kennedy, *Progymnasmata*, ix; cf. Hock and O'Neil, *Chreia in Ancient Rhetoric*; Hock and O'Neil, *Classroom Exercises*; Larsen, "On Learning a New Alphabet," 59–77; idem, "Excavating the Excavations."

align with the Sentences of Menander, and wisdom drawn from classical 'sages' is transformed into 'sayings' (and sermons) of illustrious *abbas* (and *ammas*), extant artifacts elucidate the static forms that structure monastic school practice, and hint at the fluid manipulations that ultimately shaped emergent texts.[91] Offering scant support for dismissing monastic involvement in pedagogical pursuits,[92] the residue of classroom investment instead supplies a missing link in connecting Egyptian praxis, with the pedagogical 'habits of thinking and writing' that shape a wider spectrum of texts and contexts.[93] Adopted structures, and adapted content, finally refract not only the contours of educational practice in Egypt, but the fluid stability that guides pedagogical – and derivatively, literary – investment across a broad swathe of the 'monastic'[94] Mediterranean.[95]

---

91 Examined in light of the adaptive shifts commended by Jerome and Basil, resulting praxis is, to a great degree, *pro forma*. Extant exemplars register practice that remains, at once, implicitly fluid and surprisingly stable (Quintilian, *Inst.* 1.1.35–36). Whether re-working "maxims [drawn] from Proverbs" (Basil, *Reg. Fus.* 15; cf. Jerome, *Epist.* 107.12) into a saying assigned an illustrious individual – be this a philosopher, civic leader and/or monk – or rehearsing lexical syntax using Basil's homiletic exposition of a saying attributed to the seven sages, the protocol employed is emblematic of that encountered across a broad spectrum of school settings.

92 Wilken, *First Thousand Years*, 99–108; Marrou, *History of Education*, 330–33; cf. Larsen, "*Orkenfedrenes Tankesprak*," 26–37; idem, "Pedagogical Parallels"; idem, "The Apophthegmata Patrum and the Classical Rhetorical Tradition," 409–15; idem, "Rustic Rumination," 21–31; idem, "On Learning a New Alphabet," 59–77; idem, "Redrawing the Interpretive Map," 1–34; idem, "Excavating the Excavations"; idem, "Sayings and Stories as Schooltexts," 13–33.

93 The inclusion of monastic *apophthegmata* among the routine pedagogical exercises that structure the recently published P. Cotsen-Princeton School Codex adds provocative weight to such a reading (Bucking, *Practice Makes Perfect*, plates 83–100; cf. Larsen, "On Learning a New Alphabet," 59–77).

94 The terminology employed in designating emergent communal structures 'monastic' has been increasingly problematized. Here, Mariachiara Giorda's voice is one of the most significant. The questions Giorda raises add further nuance to discussions of education within a monastic frame; cf. Mariachiara Giorda, *"Il Regno di Dio in terra": I monasteri come fondazioni private, Egitto V–VII secolo* (Rome: Edizioni di Storia e letteratura, 2011).

95 Cf. Larsen, "On Learning a New Alphabet," 59–77.

Bibliography

Primary Sources

Apophthegmata Patrum. Greek Alphabetical Collection (AP/G). Edited by Jean Baptiste Cotelier. Reprinted in Patrologia Graeca [PG 65.72–440]. Edited by Jaques-Paul Migne.

Basil. *Regula Fusius Tractate (Reg. Fus.)* [PG 31:952–57]. "Longer Rules." Trans. William K. L. Clarke. *The Ascetic Works of Saint Basil*. New York: SPCK, 1925.

Herodas. *Didaskalos*. In *Theophrastes: Characters, Herodas: Mimes, Cercidas and the Choliambic Poets*, trans. and ed. Ian C. Cunningham, 242–53. Loeb Classical Library. Cambridge, Mass.: Harvard University Press, 1929, 1993.

Pseudo-Isocrates. *Ad Demonicum*. In *Isocrates* 1, trans. George Norlin, 2–35. Loeb Classical Library. Cambridge, Mass.: Harvard University Press, 1928.

Jerome. *Epistle* 107 *(Epist)*. In *Jerome: Select Letters*, trans. Frank A. Wright, 338–71. Loeb Classical Library. Cambridge, Mass.: Harvard University Press, 1933, 1991.

Pachomius. *Praecepta (Praec)*. Latin on pages 13–52 in Amand Boon, ed. *Pachomiana Latina: Règle et épitres de S. Pachôme, épitre de S. Théodore et "Liber" de S. Orsiesius: Texte latin de S. Jérôme*. Bibliothèque de la Revue d'histoire ecclésiastique 7. Leuven: Bureaux de la Revue, 1932. English trans. on pages 2:175–95 in Armand Veilleux, *Pachomian Koinonia: The Lives, Rules, and Other Writings of Saint Pachomius and His Disciples*. 3 Vols. Cistercian Studies 45–47. Kalamazoo, Mich.: Cistercian Publications, 1980–82.

Plato. *Legates (Leg)*. In *Laws*, trans. Robert Gregg Bury. Loeb Classical Library. Cambidge, Mass.: Harvard University Press, 1926, 1967.

Plutarch. *De liberis educandis*. In *Moralia* 1, trans. Frank Babbitt, 2–69. Loeb Classical Library. Cambridge, Mass.: Harvard University Press, 1927, 1949.

Quintilian. *Institutio Oratoria (Inst)*. In *The Orator's Education* 1, trans. Donald A. Russell. Loeb Classical Library. Cambridge, Mass.: Harvard University Press, 2001.

Theon. "Περὶ Χρείας." In *The Chreia in Ancient Rhetoric: The Progymnasmata*, trans. Ronald F. Hock and Edward N. O'Neil, 82–112. Atlanta: Scholars Press, 1986.

Secondary Sources

Bagnall, Roger. "The Educational and Cultural Background of Egyptian Monks." In *Rethinking Monastic Education in Late Antiquity: The Transformation of Classical Paideia*, edited by Lillian I. Larsen and Samuel Rubenson. Cambridge: Cambridge University Press, Forthcoming.

Becker, Adam H. *Fear of God and the Beginning of Wisdom: The School of Nisibis and Christian Scholastic Culture in Late Antique Mesopotamia*. Philadelphia: University of Pennsylvania Press, 2006.

Bellet, Paulinus. "*Anthologia Palatina* 9.538: The Alphabet and the Calligraphic Examination in the Coptic Scriptorium." *Bulletin of the American Society of Papyrologists* 19 (1982): 1–8.

Biedenkopf-Ziehner, Anneliese. *Koptische Ostraka: Ostraka aus dem Ashmolean Museum in Oxford*. Wiesbaden: Harrassowitz Verlag, 2000.

Boak, Arthur Edward Romilly. "Greek and Coptic School Tablets at the University of Michigan." *Classical Philology* 16:2 (1921): 189–94.

–. "A Coptic Syllabary at the University of Michigan." *Aegyptus* 4:4 (1923): 296–97.

Bucking, Scott. "Scribes and Schoolmasters? On Contextualizing Coptic and Greek Ostraca Found at the Monastery of Epiphanius." *Journal of Coptic Studies* 9 (2007): 21–47.

–. *Practice Makes Perfect*: P.Cotsen-Princeton 1 and the Training of Scribes in Byzantine Egypt. Los Angeles: Cotsen Occasional Press, 2011.

Carr, David. *Writing on the Tablet of the Heart: Origins of Scripture and Literature.* New York: Oxford University Press, 2005.

Champollion, Jean François. *Monuments de l'Égypte et de la Nubie: Tome II: Autographié en entire.* Edited by Gaston Maspero. Paris: Didot, 1889.

Cribiore, Raffaella. *Writing, Teachers and Students in Graeco-Roman Egypt.* Atlanta: Scholars Press, 1996.

—. "A Fragment of Basilius of Caesarea." Pages 187–93 in *Akten des 21. Internationalen Papyrologenkongresses, Berlin, 13.–19. 8. 1995.* Edited by Bärbel Kramer, Wolfgang Luppe, Herwig Maehler and Günther Poethke. Archiv für Papyrusforschung und Verwandte Gebiete, Beiheft 3. Stuttgart: Teubner, 1997.

—. *Gymnastics of the Mind: Greek Education in Hellenistic and Roman Egypt.* Princeton: Princeton University Press, 2001.

Crum, Walter E., Hubert E. Winlock, and Hugh G. Evelyn White. *The Monastery of Epiphanius at Thebes.* 2 Vols. New York: Metropolitan Museum of Art, 1926.

Gibson, Craig A., ed. *Libanius's* Progymnasmata: *Model Exercises in Greek Prose, Composition and Rhetoric.* Atlanta: Scholars Press, 2008.

Giorda, Mariachiara. *"Il Regno di Dio in terra": I monasteri come fondazioni private, Egitto V–VII secolo.* Rome: Edizioni di Storia e letteratura, 2011.

Hagedorn, Dieter, and Manfred Weber. "Die griechisch-koptische Rezension der Menandersentenzen." *Zeitschrift für Papyrologie und Epigraphik* 3 (1968): 15–50.

Hall, Harry Reginald. *Coptic and Greek Texts of the Christian Period from Ostraka, Stelae, etc. in the British Museum.* London: British Library, 1905.

Harris, William V. *Ancient Literacy.* Cambridge, Mass.: Harvard University Press, 1989.

Hasitzka, Monika R. M. *Neue Texte und Dokumentation zum Koptisch-Unterricht.* Mitteilungen aus der Sammlung der Papyrus Erzherzog Rainer 18. Vienna: Österreichische Nationalbibliothek, 1990.

Hock, Ronald F. and Edward N. O'Neil, eds. *The Chreia in Ancient Rhetoric: The Progymnasmata.* Atlanta: Scholars Press, 1986.

—. *The Chreia and Ancient Rhetoric: Classroom Exercises.* Atlanta: Scholars Press, 2002.

Husselman, Elinor Mullet. "A Bohairic School Text on Papyrus." *Journal of Near Eastern Studies* 6:3 (1947): 129–51.

Ibrahim, M. Handy. "Ἡ Ἑλληνορρωμαϊκὴ Παιδεία ἐν Αἰγύπτῳ." Ph.D. diss.; University of Athens, 1972.

Kennedy, George A. *Progymnasmata: Greek Textbooks of Prose Composition and Rhetoric.* Atlanta: Scholars Press, 2003.

Larsen, Lillian I. "Ørkenfedrenes *Apophthegmata* og den klassiske Retoriske Tradisjon." *Meddelanden från Collegium Patristicum Lundense* 16 (2001): 26–35.

—. "Pedagogical Parallels: Re-reading the *Apophthegmata Patrum*." Ph.D. diss.; Columbia University, 2006.

—. "The *Apophthegmata Patrum* and the Classical Rhetorical Tradition." Pages 409–15 in *Historica, Biblica, Ascetica et Hagiographica: Papers Presented at the Fourteenth International Conference on Patristic Studies held in Oxford 2003.* Edited by Frances M. Young, Mark J. Edwards, and Paul M. Parvis. Studia Patristica 39. Leuven: Peeters, 2006.

—. "The *Apophthegmata Patrum*: Rustic Rumination or Rhetorical Recitation." *Meddelanden från Collegium Patristicum Lundense* 22 (2008): 21–30.

—. "'On Learning a New Alphabet': The Sayings of the Desert Fathers and the Monostichs of Menander." Pages 59–77 in *Early Monasticism and Classical Paideia.* Edited by Samuel Rubenson. Vol. 3 of *Papers Presented at the Sixteenth International Conference on Patristic Studies held in Oxford 2011.* Edited by Markus Vinzent. Studia Patristica 55. Leuven: Peeters, 2013.

–. "Re-drawing the Interpretive Map: Monastic Education as Civic Formation in the *Apophtheg-mata Patrum*." *Coptica* 12 (2013): 1–34.
–. "Excavating the Excavations of Early Monastic Education." In *Monastic Education in Late Antiquity: The Transformation of Classical Paideia*. Edited by Lillian I. Larsen and Samuel Rubenson. Cambridge: Cambridge University Press, Forthcoming.
–. "Early Monasticism and the Rhetorical Tradition: Sayings and Stories as Schooltexts." Pages 13–33 in *Education and Religion in Late Antiquity*. Edited by Peter Gemeinhardt and Peter Van Nuffelen. Farnham: Ashgate, 2016.
Larsen, Lillian I., and Samuel Rubenson, eds. *Monastic Education in Late Antiquity: The Transformation of Classical Paideia*. Cambridge: Cambridge University Press, Forthcoming.
Lundhaug, Hugo, and Lance Jenott. "Production, Distribution, and Ownership of Books in the Monasteries of Upper Egypt: The Evidence of the Nag Hammadi Colophons." In *Monastic Education in Late Antiquity: The Transformation of Classical Paideia*. Edited by Lillian I. Larsen and Samuel Rubenson. Cambridge: Cambridge University Press, Forthcoming.
Maravela, Anastasia. "Homer and *Menandri Sententiae* in Upper Egyptian Monasticism." In *Monastic Education in Late Antiquity: The Transformation of Classical Paideia*. Edited by Lillian I. Larsen and Samuel Rubenson. Cambridge: Cambridge University Press, Forthcoming.
Marrou, Henri. I. *A History of Education in Antiquity*. Translated by George Lamb. Madison: University of Wisconsin, 1956, 1982.
Morgan, Teresa. *Literate Education in the Hellenistic and Roman Worlds*. Cambridge: Cambridge University Press, 1998.
–. *Popular Morality in the Early Roman Empire*. Cambridge: Cambridge University Press, 2007.
Newberry, Percy E. *Beni Hasan*. 4 Vols. Archaeological Survey of Egypt. London: Kegan Paul, 1893–1900.
Nikopoulos, Panagiôtès G., et al. *Holy Monastery and Archdiocese of Sinai: The New Finds*. Athens: Mount Sinai Foundation, 1999.
Rappe, Sara. "The New Math: How to Add and to Subtract Pagan Elements in Christian Education." Pages 405–32 in *Education in Greek and Roman Antiquity*. Edited by Yun Lee Too. Leiden: Brill, 2001.
Wilken, Robert L. *The First Thousand Years: A Global History of Christianity*. New Haven: Yale University Press, 2012.
Wimbush, Vincent L. "Interpreting Resistance, Resisting Interpretations." *Semeia* 79 (1997): 1–27.

Samuel Rubenson
Textual fluidity in early monasticism: Sayings, Sermons and Stories

The study of early Egyptian monasticism has made tremendous progress in the last decades. This is not only due to the analysis of hitherto neglected early monastic texts in Coptic as well as Greek, and to evolving studies of material remains, architectural, artistic and textual, but also to new theoretical perspectives and new methods.[1] As a result we now see the rise of monasticism in Egypt as less detached from its surrounding society, less uniform and orthodox, and more closely related to ecclesiastical, theological, educational and cultural developments in the late Roman society. The profiles of Antony, and Pachomius, just to mention the two most well-known so-called founders of monasticism in the early fourth century, are no longer identical with what their biographers tell us, but more vague, complex, and debated, as are their relations to the ecclesiastical leadership, a rich variety of Christian traditions, an evolving Coptic culture, and varieties of pagan ritual and literary traditions.[2]

In these debates, as well as in any attempt to evaluate new material, we still depend, however, on the tradition established by a set of very influential early monastic texts copied throughout the centuries, in particular the well-known biographies of the founding fathers, a number of collections of anecdotes and sayings, as well as rules and sermons.[3] The critical editions of these and their translations into modern languages remain a standard against which new texts and material remains are generally measured. Single sayings and rules, individual anecdotes or passages from letters or biographies, remain the material used to corroborate or to dismiss new material evidence or new texts.

A major problem, most often ignored, is that the editions of these texts depend on the results of a history of transmission that has in many cases been extremely fluid. Many of the standard editions still used, such as the early modern editions of the

---

1 For an overview and bibliography see Samuel Rubenson, "Mönchtum," *RAC* 24 (2012): 1009–63.

2 The rereading of early Egyptian monasticism has been greatly influenced by the monographs on Pachomius. See Philip Rousseau, *Pachomius: The Making of a Community in Fourth Century Egypt* (Berkeley: University of California Press, 1986) and on Antony (see Samuel Rubenson *The Letters of St. Antony: Origenist Theology, Monastic Tradition, and the Making of a Saint* (Lund: Lund University Press, 1990); rev. ed. with English translation of the letters of Antony published as *The Letters of St. Antony: Monasticism and the Making of a Saint* (SAC; Minneapolis: Fortress Press, 1995).

3 The most influential are still the *Vita Antonii*, the *Vita Pachomii* and related texts, the *Apophthegmata Patrum*, the *Historia Monachorum* and the *Historia Lausiaca*. The works by Evagrius, the only prolific Egyptian monastic author of the fourth century, are still generally regarded as not representative.

Latin systematic and the Greek alphabetic versions of the *Apophthegmata Patrum*, are based on single, or few, rather late manuscripts that represent one branch in a late stage in a cumulative and living tradition. But also for more recent editions, where the editors have been acutely aware of the significant discrepancies between the manuscripts, the use of the Lachmannian method of edition has resulted in editions that hide the transmission and give us texts that correspond to ideals, but that actually never existed. In an attempt to include as much as possible of the material found in the manuscripts the editions conceal the actual transmission.[4] In choosing which witness to follow the editor is easily influenced by ideals about what ought to have been the original, that is his or her own preconception. This is in particular the case with texts that are transmitted as anonymous or attributed to different authors, as is the case with much of the early monastic material. Lacking authorial control and a generally accepted authorial legitimacy, and transmitted to be edifying in shifting settings, a large number of early monastic texts were constantly reused and adapted to new circumstances and needs. As was observed by Jean-Claude Guy, usefulness was more important than faithfulness.[5]

My concern here is not the minute details of fluidity between single manuscripts of a text in a fixed collection, visible in differences in style, vocabulary or orthography, but on fluidity on a structural level between texts and collections of texts, often across linguistic boundaries, where entire passages are organized differently, attributed to different persons, missing or included. This is a fluidity that cannot be reduced to a critical apparatus of an edition, but manifests the necessity of respecting each manuscript as a unique edition of a living tradition.

I will focus on three examples but also try to put them in a wider context. Finally I will propose some reasons for the extraordinary fluidity in the collections of early monastic texts. The examples are taken first from the *Apophthegmata Patrum*, secondly from the *Historia Monachorum* and the *Historia Lausiaca,* and finally from the collections of letters by Antony and Ammonas.

---

4 This is for example evident in the edition of the Greek systematic collection of the *AP.* For critical remarks see Samuel Rubenson, "The Formation and Reformations of the Sayings of the Desert Fathers," in *Early Monasticism and Classical Paideia* (ed. Samuel Rubenson; vol. 3 of *Papers Presented at the Sixteenth International Conference on Patristic Studies held in Oxford 2011,* ed. Markus Vinzent; StPatr 55; Leuven: Peeters, 2013), 14–16.
5 See Jean-Claude Guy, *Recherches sur la tradition grecque des Apophthegmata Patrum* (SHG 36; Brussels: Societé des Bollandistes, 1962), 232.

The Apophthegmata Patrum

The most obvious and bewildering case of textual fluidity is, no doubt, the transmission of several thousand sayings attributed to the desert fathers, and in a few cases mothers, preserved in hundreds of manuscripts in all the languages of early and medieval Christianity in a great variety of collections.[6] This fluidity, although well known, is, however, often forgotten when scholars use the editions of them as the most authentic and reliable sources for emergent Egyptian monasticism. In spite of the emphasis on textual fluidity in the major studies by Wilhelm Bousset and Jean-Claude Guy, and more recently by Chiara Faraggiana, Britt Dahlman, and Bo Holmberg, the published editions are used as if the text presented is reliable witness to monastic life at the end of the fourth century.[7] But what the large Greek, Latin, Syriac and Armenian printed collections present is rather the end result of a long transmission in which material from a variety of backgrounds and periods has been collected and adapted to new needs. Even when the text of a single saying remains fairly stable in the manuscript tradition, its context and the title under which it appears, and thus the meaning for a reader, varies.

Already a comparison between the edited versions shows what is evident if one looks closely at the manuscripts, namely that paragraphs were added and excluded, and that the texts were constantly rearranged, reattributed, rephrased, divided and recombined. Sayings were culled from other texts, and material from sermons, letters and hagiographical texts were "apophthegmatized," i.e. made into sayings.[8] Among the sayings attributed or related to Antony, we find, for example, quotations from his letters, from the *Vita Antonii*, sayings otherwise attributed to other fathers and parallels in texts like the letters of Ammonas, the *Pratum Spirituale* of John Moschos,

---

6 For a survey, see Rubenson, "Formation and Reformations." For the editions, see the bibliography.
7 Wilhelm Bousset, *Apophthegmata: Studien zur Geschichte des ältesten Mönchtums* (Tübingen: J.C.B. Mohr, 1923); Guy, *Recherches*; Chiara Faraggiana di Sarzana, "Apophthegmata Patrum: Some Crucial Points of Their Textual Transmission and the Problem of a Critical Edition" in *Biblica et Apocrypha, Ascetica, Liturgica: Papers Presented at the Twelfth International Conference on Patristic Studies held in Oxford 1995* (ed. Elizabeth A. Livingstone; StPatr 30; Leuven: Peeters, 1997), 455–67; Britt Dahlman, "The Collectio Scorialensis Parva: An Alphabetical Collection of Old Apophthegmatic and Hagiographic Material," in *Early Monasticism and Classical Paideia* (ed. Samuel Rubenson; vol. 3 of *Papers Presented at the Sixteenth International Conference on Patristic Studies held in Oxford 2011*, ed. Markus Vinzent; StPatr 55; Leuven: Peeters, 2013), 23–33; Bo Holmberg, "The Syriac Collection of Apophthegmata Patrum in MS Sin. syr. 46," in *Early Monasticism and Classical Paideia* (ed. Samuel Rubenson; vol. 3 of *Papers Presented at the Sixteenth International Conference on Patristic Studies held in Oxford 2011*, ed. Markus Vinzent; StPatr 55; Leuven: Peeters, 2013), 35–57.
8 See the conclusions of the preliminary remarks by Faraggiana, "Apophthegmata Patrum," 467, also evident in the last column in the tables of Lucien Regnault, *Les sentences des Pères du desert: Troisième recueil & tables* (Solesmes: Abbaye Saint-Pierre, 1976), 201–89.

and the writings of Evagrius.[9] One extract from the *Vita Antonii* is for example found in a number of collections of the *Apophthegmata Patrum*, where it in a few collections have been divided into two sayings, one of which has then in one case been united with a different saying.[10]

An example of the variation in composition and the fluidity of a series of sayings are the sayings connected with the death of Abba Arsenius. Unlike most of the collections of sayings attributed to a certain abba in the alphabetic Greek collection, the sayings of abba Arsenius are arranged in a biographical sequence, indicating that the sayings are actually based on a biographical collection.[11] At the end of the Arsenius chapter of the Greek and Georgian alphabetic collections have six sayings related to his death following a series of sayings related to his illness. Except for the two last, these sayings also appear in the edition of the Greek systematic collection, as well as in the edited Latin and Old Slavonic systematic collections.[12] The Syriac edition gives us five of the six, although one is abbreviated.[13] The Armenian has two full and parts of one of the six.[14] The Arabic version preserved in MS Strasb. 4225 has parts of two of them,[15] and the edited Ethiopic versions only one.[16] Three and parts of the fourth are also preserved in a smaller Latin collection, and four and parts of one more in an important old Latin manuscript unrelated to any edited version.[17] If we restrict ourselves to these it is important to see that the parallel pieces are ordered differently in different collections, as illustrated in the table below. The exact parallels are shaded in grey and changes in order are marked in bold.[18]

---

9 See Rubenson, *The Letters of St. Antony*, 145–62 and 193–95 (tables).

10 *Vita Antonii* 85.3–4 rephrased in AP/G Antonius 10, AP/GS II.1 and AP/PJ II.1. Sayings are here and in the following referred to by sigla. For these and the editions, see bibliography. The extract is discussed in Rubenson, *Letters of St. Antony*, 161–62. The saying is divided into two separate sayings in the edited Syriac collection, AP/SS I.20 and XVI.92, the first of these is in the small Latin collection, AP/PA 32.7 then combined with a saying otherwise attributed to Abba Moyses (AP/G Moyses 6).

11 This was first observed and discussed by Faraggiana, "Apophthegmata Patrum," 455–60, who argued for the probability that large parts of the *AP* collections are actually culled from small biographic collections of edifying stories and teachings.

12 AP/G in PG 65, 105–108; AP/IA in Dvali, *Šua saukunet'a novelebis*, 15–17; AP/PJ in PL 73, 954B–955C; AP/GS in SC 474, 288–94; and AP/OS in Veder, *Scete Paterikon*, 2:441–46.

13 AP/SS in Bedjan, *Acta martyrum*, 493, 498, 572, 636, 650.

14 AP/HS in Sargissian, *Vark' srbots' harants'*, 2:288–89.

15 MS Strasbourg 4225, f. 75b, 115a–115b. For a comparative analysis see Jean-Marie Sauget, "La collection d'Apophtegmes du ms. 4225 de la Bibliothèque de Strasbourg," *OCP* 30 (1974): 485–509, for an edition see Jean Mansour, *Homelies et légendes religieuses: Un florilège arabe chrétien du Xe siècle (Ms Strasbourg 4225): Introduction et édition critique (thèse dactylographiée inédite)* (Strasbourg: Université de Strasbourg 1972).

16 AP/EP in Victor Arras, *Patericon Aethiopice* (CSCO 277–8; Leuven: Peeters, 1967), 42.

17 AP/PA in Freire, *Versão latina*, 263–64, 308. 312. 319, and AP/LD in MS Darmstadt 1953, ff. 76r–77r, 94r–94v.

18 For the abbreviations of the collections see the Bibliography.

G-PG 65	IA-Dvali	PJ PL 73	GS-Guy	OS-Veder	SS-Bedjan	HS-Sarkiss.	Strasb. 4225	EP-Arras	PA-Freire	Darm. 1953
5.1	-	XV.9a	XV.9	15.9	I.105a	I.39a	-	-	-	
32	10	XV.9b	XV.10a	15.10a	-	-	-	-	-	
-	-	-	-	-	-	-	-	-	-	
39	16	X.9	X.10	10.10	I.497	XV.31	-	-	52.5a	I.86a
40a	17a	XV.9c	XV.10b	15.10b	I.542	-	-	-	52.5b	I.86b
40b	17b	XV.9e	XV.10d	15.10d	I.543	-	VIII.330b	-	88.5	I.81a
40c	17c	XV.9d	XV.10c	15.10c	I.145	-	VIII.330a	-	52.5d	II.167
41a	18a	III.1	III.3	3.3	-	III.31	VIII.81	-	52.5c	I.168a
41b	18b	XV.9f	XV.10e	15.10e	I.146	-	VIII.331	-	52.5e	I.168b
42a	19a	XV.10a	XV.11a	15.11a	I.339	XV.32	-	89	84.1	-
42b	19b	XV.10b	XV.11b	15.11b	I.159b	XV.33b	-	90	93.7	I.166b
42c	19c	XV.10c	XV.11c	15.11c	I.159c	XV.34a	-	91a	-	-
42d	19d	XV.10d	XV.11d	15.11d	I.159d	XV.34b	-	91b	-	-
42e	19e	-	-	-	-	-	-	-	-	-
43	20	-	-	-	I.113	-	-	-	-	I.56
44	21	-	II.11	-	-	-	-	-	-	-

What we can observe from this general table are a number of interesting differences: The biographical sequence of the six sayings in the alphabetic Greek and Georgian collections is missing in the systematic collections, a consequence of these being organized according to themes. The two last sayings are, except for the Greek and Georgian alphabetic, only attested in one or two collections each. In the Latin, Greek, and Old Slavonic systematic collections one saying represents the same material as sayings 40 and the last part of 41, albeit in different sequence and beginning with sayings that have parallels earlier in the Greek and Georgian alphabetic collections (shaded above). The first segment of saying 41 is here, as in Armenian and Arabic an independent saying placed in another context. The Syriac systematic version joins like the other systematic collections, the last segment of saying 40 with the second segment of saying 41, but without the previous segments and drops the beginning of saying 42. The Armenian version gives us saying 39 and 42 in sequence, although the last is divided into several sayings. The Arabic has the last two segments of saying 40 in the same reversed order compared to the Greek, as do the Latin, Greek and Old Slavonic systematic collections. The Ethiopian only has saying 42, albeit divided into three sayings. The small Latin collection edited by Freire has a very different arrangement joining saying 39 and the first and last segments of 40 with the first two segments of 41, albeit again in different order, and further has the first two segments of 42 as independent sayings in another context. And finally the old Latin manuscript of Darmstadt is the only one that agrees with the alphabetic collections in having saying 41 as one single saying.

A survey of a number of manuscripts in Greek and Latin shows that the variation in order and presence of segments of sayings is not only between the various traditions, but also within the same tradition and collection. In the Greek alphabetic tradition, as well as in the Greek and Latin systematic traditions, which are the only ones for which a significant number of manuscripts have been analyzed, several manuscripts combine the sayings in a way different from the edition.[19] It is obvious, as Jean-Claude Guy states in his survey of the Greek traditions, that the scribes handing down the material operated with great freedom.[20]

Some of the disorder of the previous table may, however, be dissolved if we instead of the Greek alphabetic collections use the Latin systematic as our base. The result is the table below. The two last sayings have here been omitted and sayings placed in a different context are replaced by ~. The exact parallels in sequence are again shaded in grey:

PJ PL 73	GS- Guy	OS- Veder	SS Bedjan	HS Sarkiss	Ara- Mansour	EP- Arras	PA- Freire	Darm. 1953	G- PG 65	IA-Dvali
XV.9a	XV.9	15.9	~	~	-	-	-	-	29/1	-
XV.9b	XV.10a	15.10a	-	-	-	-	-	-	32	10
~	~	~	~	XV.31	-	-	52.5a	I.86a	39	16
XV.9c	XV.10b	15.10b	I.542	-	-	-	52.5b	I.86b	40a	17a
XV.9d	XV.10c	15.10c	~	-	VIII.330a	-	52.5d	II.167	40c	17c
XV.9e	XV.10d	15.10d	I.543	-	VIII.330b	-	~	~	40b	17b
~	~	~	-	~	~	-	52.5c	I.168a	41a	18a
XV.9f	XV.10e	15.10e	~	-	VIII.331	-	52.5e	I.168b	41b	18b
XV.10a	XV.11a	15.11a	~	XV.32	-	89	~	-	42a	19a
XV.10b	XV.11b	15.11b	I.159b	XV.33b	-	90	~	I.166b	42b	19b
XV.10c	XV.11c	15.11c	I.559c	XV.34a	-	91a	-	-	42c	19c
XV.10d	XV.11d	15.11d	I.159d	XV.34b	-	91b	-	-	42d	19d
-	-	-	-	-	-	-	-	-	42e	19e

The text of the edited versions of some of the segments noted above illustrates how this affects the text. The passages that come in different order in comparison to the AP/G text are marked by italics:

---

19 See the survey of Guy, *Recherches*, 20, 42, 164 and Columba Batlle, *Die 'Adhortationes sanctorum Patrum' im lateinischen Mittelalter: Überlieferung, Fortleben und Wirkung* (BGAM 31; Münster: Aschendorffsche Verlagsbuchhandlung, 1972), 16–138, and the research tool *Monastica* at the website monastica.ht.lu.se.
20 Guy, *Recherches*, 232.

G Arsenius 40–41b[21]	PJ XV.9c-f	PA 52.5b-d	SS tr. Budge I.548–549 + I.151–152.
a) Μέλλοντος τελευτᾶν τοῦ ἀββᾶ Ἀρσενίου, ἐταράχθησαν οἱ μαθηταὶ αὐτοῦ. Καὶ λέγει αὐτοῖς· Οὔπω ἦλθεν ἡ ὥρα· ὅτε δὲ ἔλθη ὥρα, λέγω ὑμῖν. Κριθῆναι δὲ ἔχω μεθ᾽ ὑμῶν ἐπὶ τοῦ βήματος τοῦ φοβεροῦ, ἐὰν δῶτε τὸ λείψανόν μού τινι. Οἱ δὲ εἶπον· Τί οὖν ποιήσομεν, ὅτι οὐκ οἴδαμεν ἐνταφιάσαι; Καὶ λέγει αὐτοῖς ὁ γέρων· Οὐκ οἴδατε βαλεῖν σχοινίον εἰς τὸν πόδα μου, καὶ ἆραί με εἰς τὸ ὄρος;	c) Qui cum moreretur, turbati sunt valde. Et dixit eis: Nondum venit hora; cum autem venerit, dicam vobis. Iudicari autem habeo vobiscum ante tribunal Christi, si permiseritis cuiquam de corpore meo aliquid facere. Et illi dixerunt: Quid ergo faciemus, quia nescimus mortuum vestire vel sepelire? Et dixit senex: Nescitis mittere funem in pede meo, et trahere me in montem?	b) Turbatis autem discipulis eius quasi iam tempore propinquante, dicit eis: Necdum uenit hora mea. Cum autem uenerit non tacebo. Sed tamen stabitis mecum in diuino iudicio ante tribunal Christi, si alicui de meo corpusculo aut rebus aut reliquias dederitis. Illis autem respondentibus «et quid faciemus, pater, quia nescimus hominem sepelire?», respondit: Numquid nescitis funem in pedibus meis mittere et ita ad montem trahere?	Now, when he was about to die Alexander and Zoilus, his brethren and disciples, were greatly disturbed, and he said unto them, Why are ye troubled? The hour hath not yet come. They said unto him, We are not troubled about thee, father. And he said unto them, When the hour hath come I will tell you, for it will be for me to rise up against you before the throne of Christ if ye give my bones to any man. Then they said unto him, What shall we do then? For we do not know how to bury [thee]. The old man said unto them, Do ye not know how to throw a cord round my legs and to carry me outside the mountain?
b) Οὗτος δὲ ὁ λόγος τοῦ γέροντος ἦν· Ἀρσένιε, διὸ ἐξῆλθες; λαλήσας, πολλάκις μετεμελήθην, σιωπήσας δὲ οὐδέποτε.	d) Cum autem traditurus esset spiritum, viderunt eum flentem, et dicunt ei: In veritate et tu times mortem, Pater? Et dixit eis: In veritate. Timor enim qui in hac hora est mihi semper fuit in me, ex quo factus sum monachus, et timeo valde; atque ita in pace dormivit.	...	
c) Ὡς δὲ ἐγγὺς ἦν τοῦ τελευτᾶν, εἶδον αὐτὸν οἱ ἀδελφοὶ κλαίοντα· καὶ λέγουσιν αὐτῷ· Ἐν ἀληθείᾳ καὶ σὺ φοβῇ, Πάτερ; Καὶ εἶπεν αὐτοῖς· Ἐν ἀληθείᾳ, ὁ φόβος ὁ νῦν μετ᾽ ἐμοῦ ἐν τῇ ὥρᾳ ταύτῃ, μετ᾽ ἐμοῦ ἐστιν ἀφ᾽ οὗ ἐγενόμην μοναχός. Καὶ οὕτως ἐκοιμήθη.	e) Ille autem sermo semper erat in ore Arsenii, Propter quid existi? loqui me semper poenituit, tacere nunquam ...	c) Pili autem oculorum eius ex iugi fletu ceciderunt. Nam omne tempus uitae suae sedens et operans pannum habebat sinu suo propter lacrimas defluentes ex oculis eius. Dum ergo moreretur coepit flere.	I.549. And his word at all times was this, Arsenius, because thou didst go forth; and he used to repeat this saying, That I have spoken I have many times repented; that I held my peace I have never repented.
41a) Ἔλεγον δὲ ὅτι ὅλον τὸν χρόνον τῆς ζωῆς αὐτοῦ,	f) Audiens autem abbas Pastor, quia ex Arsenius, lacrymatus	d) Et cum fratres eum requisissent dicentes: Quid fles, pater? Numquid et tu times? Ait: In ueritate timeo et iste timor qui nunc mecum est semper in Ille fuit ex quo factus sum monachus	I.151 When the blessed Arsenius was about to deliver up his spirit the brethren saw him

καθεζόμενος εἰς τὸ ἐργόχειρον αὐτοῦ, ῥάκκος εἶχεν ἐν τῷ κόλπῳ, χάριν τῶν δακρύων τῶν πιπτόντων ἀπὸ τῶν ὀφθαλμῶν αὐτοῦ.

41b) Ἀκούσας δὲ ὁ ἀββᾶς Ποιμὴν ὅτι ἐκοιμήθη, δακρύσας εἶπε· Μακάριος εἶ, ἀββᾶ Ἀρσένιε, ὅτι ἔκλαυσας ἑαυτὸν εἰς τὸν ὧδε κόσμον. Ὁ γὰρ μὴ κλαίων ἑαυτὸν ὧδε, αἰωνίως ἐκεῖ κλαύσεται. Εἴτε οὖν ὧδε ἑκών, εἴτε ἐκεῖ ἀπὸ βασάνων, ἀδύνατον μὴ κλαῦσαι.

est, et dixit: Beatus es, abba Arseni, quia flevisti temetipsum in saeculo isto; qui enim se in hoc saeculo non fleverit, sempiterne plorabit illic; sive igitur hic voluntarie, sive illic tormentis cogentibus, impossibile est non flere

e) Cum autem uidisset abbas Poemen quia transiit dixit: Beatus es, abba Arseni, quia te in hoc saeculo planxisti. Qui enim se hic non planxerit, illic in perpetuo lugebit. Aut hic ergo ex uoluntate aut illic pro tormentis, inpossibile est hominem non plangere.

weeping, and they said unto him, Art thou also afraid, O father? And he said unto them, The dread of this hour hath been with me in very truth from the time when I became a monk, and was afraid. And so he died.

...

152. And when Abba Poemen heard that he was dead, that is to say, that Abba Arsenius had gone to his rest, he said, Blessed art thou, O Abba Arsenius, for thou didst weep over thyself in this world. For he who weepeth not for himself in this world must weep for ever in the next. He may weep here voluntarily, or there because of the punishments [which he will receive], but it is impossible for a man to escape weeping either here or there.

---

21 "When Abba Arsenius was at the point of death, his disciples were troubled. He said to them, 'The time has not yet come; when it comes, I will tell you. But if ever you give my remains to anyone, we will be judged before the dreadful seat of judgment.' They said to him, 'What shall we do'? We do not know how to bury anyone.' The old man said to them, 'Don't you know how to tie a rope to my feet and drag me to the mountain?' The old man used to say to himself: 'Arsenius, why have you left the world? I have often repented of having spoken, but never of having been silent.' When his death drew near, the brethren saw him weeping and they said to him 'Truly, Father, are you also afraid?' 'Indeed', he answered them, 'the fear which is mine at this hour has been with me ever since I became a monk'. Upon this he fell asleep. It was said of him that he had a hollow in his chest channelled out by the tears which fell from his eyes all his life while he sat at his manual work.1b) When Abba Poemen learned that he was dead, he said weeping, 'Truly you are blessed, Abba Arsenius, for you wept for

A thorough analysis of the text of all versions, including the Arabic, Armenian, Ethiopic, Georgian and Old Slavonic and the manuscripts of all collections will reveal even greater variation and fluidity in attribution, emphasis, and concepts. Since printed editions are unable to present the extensive variation in the tradition a research tool based on a database of the material has been developed.[22]

The Journey of Abba Macarius

Turning from the single sayings in the *Apophthegmata Patrum* to the texts in the various collections of early monastic edifying stories, texts such as the *Historia Monachorum*, the *Historia Lausiaca* and the collections attributed to John Moschos and Anastasius Sinaita, we encounter fluidity on a larger scale. The same, or a similar, story can be found in a variety of versions both within a linguistic tradition and between traditions. As is obvious already from the printed editions, the manuscripts differ considerably in order and content, and a closer study of the manuscript traditions shows that sections and chapters included in the main collections are often found independently and joined to sayings and other texts. These chapters do, moreover, often contain a text that is quite different from the standard text of the editions.

An interesting example of this, studied by Britt Dahlman, shows how a collection of sayings, the so called *Scorialensis Parva*, has integrated parts of the chapter on Macarius found in the *Historia Lausiaca*, but in a shorter version and with a different sequence of the paragraphs that both have in common.[23] As suggested by Dahlman it is clear that the *Scorialensis* version is unlikely to be a revision of the text as edited by Butler and Bartelink, but rather an independent witness to one of its sources.[24] In this case a possible explanation, forwarded by Dahlman, is that the author first wrote the version which is attested in the sayings collection, and then revised and augmented the text to fit the larger framework of the full *Historia Lausiaca*.[25] If so, the fluidity is here caused by an authorial revision of an original text that survived also in an unrevised version. The fact that other versions of the *Historia Lausiaca*, such as the Syriac and the Coptic differ considerably from the

---

yourself in this world! He who does not weep for himself here below will weep eternally hereafter; so it is impossible not to weep, either voluntarily or when compelled through suffering.'" (Eng. trans. of AP/G by Benedicta Ward, *The Sayings of the Desert Fathers: The Alphabetical Collection* [London: Mowbray, 1975], 15–16.)

22 See *Monastica* (monastica.ht.lu.se).
23 Dahlman, "Collectio Scorialensis Parva."
24 Dahlman, "Collectio Scorialensis Parva," 30.
25 Dahlman, "Collectio Scorialensis Parva," 30.

edited Greek text, indicates that not all textual fluidity in the case of *Historia Lausiaca* can be attributed to authorial revision.[26] It seems likely that we do have both a fluidity in the material once used by the collector, and a fluidity in the transmission of the collections. It is even possible that the later transmission of the collections has in some cases been "contaminated" by the circulation of versions of an earlier stage.

One of the passages not found in the collection of Macarian stories of the *Scorialensis,* does, for example appear independently, but in a very different form both in collections of the *Apopthegmata Patrum* and in the *Historia Monachorum.* This is the story about how Abba Macarius travelled to the inner desert.[27] The story is first referred to by Evagrius, who in his *Antirrhetikos* 4.23 briefly mentions Macarius, travel to the garden of Jannes and Jambres and his reply to a sword-carrying demon as an example of how to respond to threatening demons.[28] The text tradition has at least three completely different versions of the story, preserved in the *Apophthegmata Patrum,* in the *Historia Monachorum* and in the *Historia Lausiaca,* and furthermore significant differences between the versions of these in different languages and collections. As has been pointed out by David Brakke, the different versions are not simply dependent on one another, but are deliberate revisions of a common story where it is unclear if, and in what way, they have used the text of one another.[29] Instead of searching for the origin of the story and the interdependence between the versions, I will here confine myself to a demonstration of the fluidity of the material.

The version of the story in *Historia Lausiaca* as edited by Butler and by Bartelink is considerably longer than the other two versions, while the *Apophthegmata Patrum* version as edited in the PG is considerably shorter. It for example does not mention the garden-tomb of Jannes and Jambres, nor the arduous journey to and from the inner desert, and the tricks of the demons. Although shorter, the *Apoph-*

---

26 The different versions of *HL* are discussed in Adelheid Wellhausen, *Die lateinische Übersetzung der Historia Lausiaca des Palladius* (Berlin: Walter de Gruyter, 2003), 42–53 and in Gabriel Bunge, *Quatre ermites égyptiens d'après les fragments coptes de l'Histoire Lausiaque* (SpOr 60; Solesmes: Abbaye de Bellefontaine, 1994), 17–80.

27 The story is analysed in David Brakke, "Macarius's Quest and Ours: Literary Sources for Early Egyptian Monasticism," *CSQ* 48 (2013): 239–51 with comments by Samuel Rubenson, "Response: To tell the Truth: Fact and Fiction in early Monastic Sources," *CSQ* 48 (2013): 317–24.

28 "Against the demon that appears carrying a sword – we should, as in a hostile manner, answer back with a phrase, just as our blessed father Macarius answered it when he saw it carrying a sword and coming to attack him when he had travelled to see the paradise that Jannes and Jambres made: *You come to me with a sword and a spear and a shield, but I come to you in the name of the Lord God of hosts (1 Kings 17:45)*" (Evagrius, *Antirrhetikos* 4.23, trans. David Brakke, *Evagrius Ponticus, Talking Back: A Monastic Handbook for Combating Demons* [Collegeville, Minn.: Cistercian Publications, 2009]).

29 Brakke, "Macarius's Quest and Ours," 248–51.

thegmata Patrum version does include an encounter with two naked men in the garden, a feature lacking in the *Historia Lausiaca* version in which the garden is desolate. In order to illustrate the fluidity in the story-telling, three passages of the story are given in the published English translations. Passages that are parallel are shaded in grey:[30]

The setting

HM 21.5, tr. Ward, p. 108	AP/G Macarius 2, tr. Ward p. 106	HL 18.5, tr. Meyer, p. 59
Another time after much fasting and prayer he asked God to show him the paradise which Jannes and Jambres had planted in the desert in their desire to make a copy of the true paradise.	... One day when I was sitting in my cell, my thoughts were troubling me, suggesting that I should go to the desert and see what I could see there. I remained for five years, fighting against this thought, saying, perhaps it comes from the demons. But since the thought persisted, I left for the desert.	He once wished, so he told us, to enter the garden-tomb of Jannes and Jambres. Now this garden-tomb had belonged to the magicians who had power along with Pharaoh back in the old days. Since they held power for a long time they built the work with stones four feet square. They erected their monument there and put away much gold. They even planted trees there, for the spot was damp and they dug a well too.

Whereas the *Apophthegmata Patrum* version continues directly with a description of the place Macarius reached and the *Historia Monachorum* briefly mentions his trouble and the angelic assistance offered him, the edited version of the *Historia Lausiaca* continues with a detailed description of his travel. This description has several features in common with the description of Macarius' return in the *Historia Monachorum*.

---

30 *Historia Monachorum* as translated by Benedicta Ward, *The Lives of the Desert Fathers* (London: Mowbray, 1980), 108–9; *Apophthegmata Patrum* as translated by Ward, *Sayings of the Desert Fathers*, 106; and *Historia Lausiaca* as translated by Robert Meyer, *Palladius: The Lausiac History* (New York: Paulist Press, 1964), 59–61.

The travel

HM 21.9, tr. Ward, p. 109	HL 18.6–7, tr. Meyer, p. 60
When he had stayed with them for seven days, Macarius asked if he could go back to the settled region and bring the monks with him. But those holy men said to him that he could not do this. For the desert was a vast trackless waste, and there were many demons in every part of it who made monks lose their way and destroyed them, so that many other who had often wished to come had perished. But Macarius could not bear to remain here any longer and said, "I must bring them here so that they can enjoy this delight." He set off in haste for the settled region, carrying some of the fruit as proof. And taking with him a large bundle of palm branches, he planted them as markers in the desert so that he should not lose his way when he came back. Then he slept for a while in the desert, and when he woke up he found that all the palm branches had been gathered up by the demons and placed by his head. Then, getting up, he said to them, If it is the will of God, you cannot prevent us from entering into the garden.	Since the holy man did not know the road, he followed the stars, traversing the desert as though it were the sea. Taking a bundle of reeds, he placed one at every mile, leaving a mark so that he might find the way back on his return. After travelling for nine days, he reached the place. Then the demon who ever acts in opposition to the athletes of Christ collected all the reeds and put them by his head as he slept near the garden-tomb. He found the reeds upon arising. God had permitted this for his own future training, so that he may not place trust in reeds, but rather in the pillar of cloud that led Israel for forty years in the desert. He used to say: "Seventy demons rushed from the garden-tomb to meet me, shouting and fluttering like crows in front of me saying, What do you wish Macarius? What do you want monk? Why did you come to our place? You cannot stay here. I told them, he said, Let me but go in and look about, and then leave.

Both the *Historia Lausiaca* and the *Historia Monachorum* give a detailed description of Macarius' journey, his care not to lose his way and the cunningness of the demons destroying his plan, but whereas the *Historia Lausiaca* version reports that this happened on the way to the inner desert, the *Historia Monachorum* version has it happen on the way back. However, the last sentence in this latter account indicates that the story about the demons did not belong to the return in a previous version.

The garden

HM 21.6–7, tr. Ward, p. 108	AP/G Macarius 2, tr. Ward, p. 106	HL 18.8, tr. Meyer, p. 60
The garden was very large, covering an enormous area. After he had prayed he made a bold effort and succeeded in entering. Inside the garden he found two holy men. They had entered by the same means themselves, and had already spent a considerable time there.	There I found a sheet of water and an island in the midst, and the animals of the desert came to drink there. In the midst of these animals I saw two naked men, and my body trembled, for I believed they were spirits.	Upon entering he found a hanging brass jar and an iron chain near the well, already consumed by time; the pomegranates had nothing inside, so dried out were they by the sun.

Textual fluidity is here clearly not only a case of a certain freedom on the part of the copyist, or the person ordering the copy, but a complete retelling of the same material, where it is impossible to deduct an original version, if there even ever was one. As suggested by Brakke it is quite possible that two stories, perhaps related to two different Macarii, one about the encounter with the demons and one about the garden-tomb were attached to one or several monks called Macarius and combined in different ways.[31] But it is also possible that several motives from folk tradition were re-used to create different versions of a story that was then attributed to one or several Macarii. The different versions we possess and the different redactions of each of them, should caution us against attempts to try to identify and edit an archetype. Here again each collection and even each manuscript is a text of its own and as such a witness to a living tradition. Instead of attempting to present the original, our task as scholars should be to study the variations and development of the tradition as evidence to shifting interests, circumstances and lines of communication at the time of the writing of the manuscript.

The Letters of Ammonas

Textual fluidity is not limited to sayings and stories that appear in totally different forms and can easily be apophthegmatized, divided, recombined and reorganized in different ways according to need and preference. We often find the same fluidity in monastic rules, sermons and letter collections. The Arabic corpus of writings attributed to Antony, a corpus for which a Coptic model is attested, although only partly

---

31 Brakke, "Macarius's Quest and Ours," 248–51

preserved, gives us several examples of this.[32] A number of passages and parts of texts in the corpus are attested elsewhere but in other settings and combined with other texts.

An interesting case is the text labeled "The Teachings of Antony". Two separate paragraphs of this Arabic text have been found in Coptic on the two sides of a fragment of a medieval Coptic codex, also here attributed to Antony.[33] The preserved Coptic text is obviously not a witness to the direct model for the Arabic, but an independent witness to the circulation of parts of the text as sayings by Antony. One of these passages is, moreover, also included as part of the text known as the *Teachings of Silvanus* in one of the Nag Hammadi Codices.[34] According to the analysis by Wolf-Peter Funk, the two Coptic versions of the text, the fragment attributed to Antony and the version of the *Teachings of Silvanus*, cannot easily be reconciled into being dependent on one another, but rather seem to be independent translations of the same text into Coptic, or, if the original is Coptic, a retranslation into Coptic from a Greek translation.[35] We thus have the same text transmitted in three ways, as a separate saying, and included in two different works, the *Teachings of Silvanus* and of Antony, and another as a separate saying and included in one of these. The question is, are the separate sayings extracts from longer works, or are these works compilations of loose words of wisdom? Since one of the sayings is present in rather different contexts in the two works, this seems unlikely. It is, to my mind, much more plausible that the teachings of Antony and of Silvanus include material from other texts, probably sayings, letters and sermons, that circulated separately in the early monastic setting before their inclusion into the texts present in Nag Hammadi Codex VII and in the Copto-Arabic corpus of Antonian material.

Included in the Copto-Arabic corpus attributed to Antony are also twenty letters, seven of which are identical with the seven regarded as authentic by most scholars.[36] The remaining fourteen letters are closely related to the letters attributed to

---

32 For the Copto-Arabic collection of texts attributed to St. Antony, see Samuel Rubenson, "Arabic Sources for the Theology of the Early Monastic Movement in Egypt," *ParOr* 16 (1991): 33–47; George Farag, "Les lettres attribuées à Antoine dans la deuxième collection arabes (letters 8 à 20): Sont-elles d'Antoine ou d'Ammonas? Étude comparée des différentes version et interprétation théologique" (Ph.D. diss., Strasbourg: Faculté théologie catholique, 2012), 61–64; Jacques Chollet, "Le Corpus arabicum de saint Antoine," *Mikhtav* 67 (2013): 26–54. Farag concludes that the Copto-Arabic collection has been compiled from a variety of sources (Farag, "Les lettres," 140).

33 BL Or. 6003, Walter Ewing Crum, *Catalogue of the Coptic Manuscripts in the British Museum* (London: British Museum, 1905), 407 (no. 979).

34 Wolf-Peter Funk, "Ein doppelt überliefertes Stück spätägyptischer Weisheit," *ZÄS* 103 (1976): 8–21.

35 Funk, "Ein doppelt überliefertes Stück," 16–17.

36 For these letters, see Rubenson, *Letters of St. Antony*, the summary of the debate and criticism by Dimitrij Bumazhnov, *Visio Mystica im Spannungsfeld frühchristlicher Überlieferungen: Die Lehre der sogenannteen Antoniusbriefe von der Gottes- und Engelschau und das Problem unterschiedlicher*

Ammonas, known in Syriac and Georgian and partly in Greek, Armenian and Ethiopic.[37] The differences between the versions are considerable both in number, sequence and content. Here I will confine myself to the Greek and Syriac versions, and the fluidity of the text is obvious from a comparison of them.[38] Both versions were published already a century ago, the Greek under the name of Augoustinos Iordanites in Jerusalem in 1911, and the Syriac by Michael Kmosko in Paris in 1915. The Greek text was then republished by François Nau in a revised version taking more manuscripts as well as the Jerusalem edition into account.[39] An additional Greek letter was published by G. L. Marriott in 1918 as part of a series of seven homilies attributed to Macarius.[40]

The relation between the Syriac and the Greek versions, as edited, is illustrated in the table below, albeit somewhat simplified:

S	1	2	3	4	5	6	7	8+9+10a	10b	11	12	13+14
G	-	2	6	3	-	-	-	4	8	5	1	7

or

G	1	2	3	4	5	6	7	8
S	12	2	4	9+8+10a	11	3	13+14	10b

The Georgian and Arabic versions, none of which has received a critical edition – except for one Georgian letter[41] – include most of the Syriac letters not preserved in Greek and with some important exceptions, especially as regards the first letter in

---

spiritueller Traditionen im frühen ägyptischen Mönchtum (STAC 52; Tübingen: Mohr Siebeck, 2009), 1–5, 12–17, and Samuel Rubenson, "Antony and Ammonas: Conflicting or Common Tradition in Early Egyptian Monasticism?" in *Bibel, Byzanz und Christlicher Orient: Festschrift für Stephen Gerö* (ed. Dimitrij Bumazhnov et al.; OLA 187; Leuven: Peeters, 2011), 185–201.

37 For a discussion of the letters attributed to Ammonas and their relations to the letters of Antony, see Rowan Williams, *Faith and Experience in Early Monasticism: New Perspectives on the Letters of Ammonas: Laudatio und Festvortrag anlässlich der Ehrenpromotion von Rowan Douglas Williams durch die Theologische Fakultät der Universität Erlangen-Nürnberg am 02. 07. 1999 in der Aula des Erlanger Schlosses* (ARKEN 20; Erlangen-Nürnberg: FAU University Press, 2002), 19–36, Rubenson, "Antony and Ammonas," and Farag, "Les lettres."

38 A thorough analysis of the Arabic corpus is found in Farag, "Les lettres."

39 Augoustinos Iordanites (Αυγουστινος Ιορδανιτης), *ΤΟΥ ΟΣΙΟΥ ΗΜΩΝ ΑΒΒΑ ΑΜΜΩΝΑ ΕΠΙΣΤΟΛΑΙ ΠΕΝΤΕ* (Jerusalem, 1911); Michael Kmosko, *Ammoni Eremitae Epistolae* (PO 10.6; Paris: Librairie de Paris, 1915). François Nau, *Ammonas, successeur de saint Antoine* (PO 11; Paris: Libraire de Paris 1915).

40 George Leicester Marriott, *Macarii Anecdota: Seven Unpublished Homilies of Macarius* (HTS 5; Cambridge, Mass.: Harvard Divinity School, 1918), 47–48 (where it appears as Macarius, Homily 57).

41 Gérard Garitte, "De unius ex Ammonae epistolis versione iberica," *Mus* 52 (1939): 11–31. The Arabic text is printed in Andraus Al Raheb, *Kitab Rawdat al nufus fi rasa'il al- qiddis Antuniyus* (The Garden of the Soul in the Letters of Saint Antony) (Cairo: 1899). An unpublished version of the Georgian text has, moreover, been used for the French translation. See Bernard Outtier et al., ed., *Lettres des Pères*

each of the collections, and in particular the fourth Greek letter, they support the sequence in the Syriac edition. It has thus generally been argued that the Syriac version best represents the original letters, whether written in Coptic or Greek, and that the preserved Greek version is a late and heavily revised text. It is however important to note that not all Syriac manuscripts have the same number of letters and the same sequence as the edition.[42] The difference in number of letters included, and in their sequence, between, as well as within, the versions shows that the letters were not transmitted as a fixed collection, but adapted to the needs and interests at the place and time of the writing of the manuscripts.[43]

The fluidity of the material becomes more obvious if we look more closely at an example of the difference in the text transmission between the Syriac and the Greek. The most obvious case is the letter designated as letter 4 in Greek which corresponds to letter 9 and parts of letter 10 and 8 in the Syriac version. The letter, in Greek (no. 4) as well as Syriac (no. 9), starts without any of the greetings otherwise common to the letters. Most probably an original greeting has been lost, but it is also possible that the letter is actually a part of a longer text. The Syriac letter 9 ends without any of the customary phrases or greetings, which has made the translators include it in the first parts of letter 10, which has a passage that is more akin to a final word. But where the Syriac text then continues with a pargaraph quoted by Besa as a word by Antony, and very akin to his letters, the Greek text includes the latter part of what in Syriac is letter 8, in Syriac preceded by what seems to be the end of a letter. A brief table illustrates the correspondence between Greek letter 4 and the Syriac letters:

G 4.1	G 4.2	G 4.3	G 4.4	G 4.5	G 4.6	G 4.7	G 4.8	G 4.9
S 9.1	S 9.2	S 9.3	S 9.4	S 9.5	S 10.1	S 10.2	S 8.2	S 8.3

Since the first part of G 4 corresponds very closely to letter 9 in Syriac there is no need to quote the entire text. The general theme is the necessity of trials for progress and the need to pray and persist in order to receive the Holy Spirit back after its initial withdrawal. The text then continues:

---

du désert: Ammonas, Macaire, Arsène, Sérapion de Thmuis (SpOr 42; Bégrolles: Abbaye de Bellefontaine, 1985), 1–60.

42 Of the ten Syriac manuscripts used by the editor it is only one that has the fourteen letters edited (BL Add. 12,175). The other manuscripts have less, or in some cases more letters, and in several of them the order is different. See the introduction to the edition by Kmosko, *Ammoni Eremitae Epistolae*, 555–56.

43 For a discussion of early monastic letter collections, see Rubenson, "The Letter-Collections of Antony and Ammonas: Shaping a Community," in *Collecting Early Christian Letters: From the Apostle Paul to Late Antiquity* (ed. Bronwen Neil and Pauline Allen; Cambridge: Cambridge University Press, 2015), 68–79.

G 4, ed. Nau

G 4.5 Ἐὰν οὖν αἰσθανθῶσι τῆς βαρύτητος παρὰ τὸ ἔθος, καὶ τὴν προϋπάρξασαν χαρὰν, καὶ αἰτήσωσι τὸν Θεὸν μετὰ δακρύων καὶ νηστείας, τότε ὁ ἀγαθὸς Θεὸς, ἐὰν ἴδῃ ὅτι ἐν εὐθύτητι καὶ ἐξ ὅλης καρδίας αἰτοῦσι καὶ ἀρνοῦνται τὰ θελήματα αὐτων πάντα, δίδωσι αὐτοῖς χαρὰν μείζονα παρὰ τὴν πρώτην. καὶ στηρίζει αὐτοὺς πλέον. Τοῦτό ἐστι τὸ σημεῖον, ὃ ποιεῖ μετὰ πάσης ψυχῆς ἐκζητούσης τὸν Θεόν.

G 4.6 Ὅτε οὖν ἡ ψυχὴ ἀναφέρεται ἐκ τοῦ ἄρδου, ὅσον ἀκολουθεῖ τῷ Πνεύματι τοῦ Θεοῦ, κατὰ τοσοῦτον ἐπιφέρονται αὐτῇ κατὰ τόπους πειρασμοὶ παρερχομένη δὲ τοὺς πειρασμοὺς γίνεται διορατικὴ καὶ ε'θηρέπειαν ἄλλην λαμβάνει. Ὅτεδ˜ε ἔμελλεν ὁ Ἡλίας ἀναλαμβάνεσθαι, ἐλθὼν εἰς τὸν πρῶτον οὐρανὸν ἐθαύμασεν αὐτοῦ τὸ φῶς. ὅτε δὲ ἐπέβη τὸν δεύτερον τοσοῦτον ἐθαύμασεν, ὡς εἰπεῖν, ὅτι ἐνόμισα ὡς σκότος εἶναι τὸ φῶς τοῦ πρώτου ο'θρανοῦ, καὶ οὕτω τὸν καθ' ἕνα οὐρανὸν τῶν οὐρανῶν. Ἡ ψυχὴ οὖν τῶν τελείων δικαίων προκόπτςι καὶ προβαίνει, ἕως οὗ ἀναβῇ εἰς τὸν οὐρανὸν τῶν οὐρανῶν.

G 4.7 Ταῦτα γράφη ὑμῖν, ἀγαπητοὶ, ἵνα στηριχθῆτε καὶ μάθητε, ὅτι οἱ πειρασμοὶ τοῖς πιστοῖς ἐπέρχονται οὐκ εἰς ζημίαν, ἀλλ' εἰς κέρδος, καὶ χωρὶς τοῦ ἐπενεχθῆναι πειρασμὸν τῇ ψυχῇ, οὐ δύναται ἀναβῆναι εἰς τὸν τόπον τοῦ κτίσαντος αὐτήν.

G 4.8 Ἐὰν δὲ θέλετε χάρισμα πνευματικὸν ἀναλαβεῖν, παράσχητε ἑαυτοὺς εἰς μόχθον σωματικὸν, καὶ μόχθον καρδίας, καὶ τοὺς

S 9 + 10 + 8, tr. by Brock

S 9.5 If, however, they perceive this unaccustomed heaviness, in contrast with the joy that they had before, and they ask Goid with tears and fasting, then, if He sees that thye are asking in uprightness from their whole heart and are denying all their own self-will, God in his grace will give them a greater joy than the first, and establish them more firmly. This is the sign that he gives to every soul that seeks God.

— — —

S 10.1 After I had written my letter I remembered a certain word, and am moved to write to you about the trial of soul of the man who is advanced, and who goes down to the depths of hell from the rank of spiritual perfection. It is of such a one that the Prophet cries, saying, "You have delivered my sould from the depths of Sheol". Trials will attach themselves to everyone who attaches himself to the Spirit of God, but as a result he acquires discernment and a different sort of splendour. Thus, when the prophet was going to be taken up, coming to the first heaven he wondered at its light; but when he came to the second he wondered so greatly as to say, "I considered the light of the fisrt to be as darkness", and so on until the final stage of perfection. Therefore the soul of the perfectly righteous progresses and goes forward until it mounts to the heaven of heavens. If you have attained this you have passed all trilas. And there are even now men on earth who have eached this stage.

S 10.2 I write this to you, beloved, so that you may firmly recognize that trials come upon the faithful not for their loss but for their advantage; and without trials being brought upon the soul it cannot mount to the place of Life, that is, of him who created it.

S 10.3 The Spirit breathes where it wills …

— — —

S 8.1 … Farewell in peace with the father of mercies, that you may receive the gift that your fathers bore.

S 8.2 Now, if you desire to receive it, you will give yourselves to bodily toil and toil of heart, and stretch your thoughts up to heaven night and day,

λογισμοὺς ὑμῶν ἀνατείνατε εἰς οὐρανὸν νυκτὸς καὶ ἡμέρας. αἰτοῦντες ἐν ὅλῃ καρδίᾳ τὸ Πνεῦμα τοῦ πυρὸς καὶ δοθήσεται ὑμῖν.

asking with all your heart for the Holy Spirit, and this will be given to you, for such was in Elijah the Tishbite and Elisha and all the other prophets.

G 4.9 Βλέπετε δὲ μήποτε εἰσέλθωσιν εἰς τὴν καρδίαν ὑμῖν λογισμοὶ διψυχίας λέγοντες 'τίς δυνήσεται τοῦτο δέξασθαι' μὴ οὖν συγχωρήσετε τοῖς λογισμοῖς τούτοις κατακυριεῦσαι ὑμῶν, ἀλλ' αἰτήσασθε ἐν εὐθύτητι καὶ λήψεσθε. Κἀγὼ δὲ ὁ πατὴρ ὑμῶν, αἰτοῦμαι, ἵνα λάβητε αὐτὸ ὁ γὰρ ποιῶν τὴν γεωργίαν αὐτοῦ κατὰ γενεὰν καὶ γενεάν, αὐτὸς λήψεται αὐτό. Ἐκεῖνο δὲ τὸ πνεῦμα, τοῖς εὐθέσι τῇ καρδίᾳ κατοικεῖ, μαρτυρῶ δὴ καὶ ὑμῖν, ὅτι μετ' εὐθείας καρδίας ἐκζητεῖτε τὸν Θεόν. Ἐπὰν δὲ δέξησθε αὐτό, ἀποκαλύψει ὑμῖν τὰ μυστήρια τοῦ οὐρανοῦ πολλὰ γὰρ ἀποκαλύψει, ἃ οὐ δύναμαι ἐν χάρτῃ γράψαι. Ἄφοβοι δὲ γενήσεσθε τότε ἀπὸ παντὸς φόβου, καὶ χαρὰ οὐράνιος ἀπολήψεται ὑμᾶς, καὶ οὕτως ἔσεσθε ὡς ἤδη μετατεθέντες εἰς τὴν βασιλείαν, ἔτι ὄντες ἐν σώματι, καῖ οὐκέτι χρῄζετε εὔξασθαι ὑπὲρ ἑαυτῶν, ἀλλ' ὑπὲρ ἑτέρων. Δόξα τῷ ἀγαθῷ Θεῷ, τῷ τοιούτων μυστηρίων καταξιοῦντι τοὺς γνησίως δουλεύοντας αὐτῷ ᾧ πρέπει δόξα αἰώνιος.

– – –

S 8.3 And see that there never enter into your hearts thoughts of doubt saying, "Who will be able to receive this?" Therefore permit not these thoughts to enter your minds, but ask in uprightness and you will receive. And I, your father, will pray on your behalf, that you may receive it; for I know that you have denied yourselves in order to do so. For he who toils in every generation will receive this same Spirit, which dwells in those who are upright of heart. And I bear witness of you, that you seek God with an upright heart. And when you receive this spirit, he will reveal to you the mysteries of heaven. For he will reveal many things which I cannot write on paper. But you will become free from every fear, and heavenly joy will overtake you: and so you will be as men already translated to the kingdom while you are still in the body, and you will no longer pray for yourselves but for others.

S 8.4 For Moses, having received the spirit, prayed for the people, saying to God, ...

This is not the place to discuss or try to explain the differences in detail. Even though there is a general agreement that the text was written in Greek or Coptic, scholars have generally regarded the Syriac version as preserving the original structure and content of the letters arguing both from the Georgian and Arabic witnesses and from internal arguments of cohesion.[44] A recent attempt to argue for the preserved Greek version by Cherubini has been refuted by Farag.[45] What is important here is to demonstrate how letters could be cut up and reunited in order to fit a specific context or tradition or reorganized and enlarged for another context. Whereas this is more clearly the case in

---

44 See Franz Klejna, "Antonius und Ammonas, eine Untersuchung über Herkunft und Eigenart der ältesten Mönchsbriefe," *ZKT* 62 (1938): 318–19; Sebastian Brock, "Introduction," in Derwas J. Chitty and Sebastian Brock, *The Letters of Ammonas: Successor of Antony* (Oxford: SLG Press, 1979), ii; Williams, *Faith and Experience*, 24. For a discussion see Bumazhnov, *Visio Mystica*, 211–14; Rubenson, "Antony and Ammonas," 187–91.
45 Roberto Cherubini, *Conoscere Dio: Lettere e altri scritti di Ammonas* (Rome: Urbaniana University Press, 2011), 46–47, and Farag, *Les lettres*, 153–55.

the letters of Ammonas, Richard Shaw has, in a recent article, made it plausible that some of the problems in the interpretation of the letters by Antony raised by Dimitri Bumazhnov are due to reorganization of the material, or what he terms textual disorder.[46]

Conclusion

As shown by the examples given above, the transmission of early monastic texts, whether sayings, stories or treatises, was very fluid. As is evident in the case of the *Apophthegmata Patrum* or the letters of Antony, and most probably also for the *Historia Monachorum* and the *Historia Lausiaca*, this fluidity goes back to the very first generation of transmission. Sayings were included in other texts, were embedded in or united into anecdotes, and variously combined with other sayings shaping collections that were, in their turn, reorganized, enlarged or reduced. Sayings were, moreover, attributed to a famous abba, reattributed to another or made anonymous. Paragraphs in hagiographical writings, sermons and letters were apophthegmatized and inserted into collections of sayings where they could be combined with material from a different source. Letters were united into collections that were later restructured, but also transmitted separately and joined to other texts from a similar background or on a similar theme. Letters could be abbreviated or enlarged. Some were copied only partially and extracts from letters were combined with extracts from other letters. For many of the monks engaged in the transmission, textual unity and authorial composition was less important than edifying value. Interesting evidence for this is the concern expressed by Evagrius to preserve *his* writings intact.[47]

Since most of our manuscripts represent the transmission several centuries after the origin and the first translation of the texts into the various languages, and a very limited number of the manuscripts preserved have been placed in their context and analyzed in detail, we cannot, with very few exceptions, know the reasons for and stages of the reshaping of the texts in the individual cases. We can, however, make some reasonable assumptions about the causes for the exceptional fluidity in early monastic material. I would like to end this paper by suggesting three different reasons related to authorship, function and ways of transmission respectively:

---

46 See Richard Shaw, "Textual Disorder in the Letters of St. Antony: An Analysis and Partial Reconstruction," *DRev* 462 (2013): 1–14, 463, 59–130. If he is right, this is another example of the textual fluidity characteristic of early monastic texts, a disorder due to lack of interest in a precise transmission.
47 In some of the manuscripts of Evagrius, *Praktikos*, the text is introduced by a note instructing the copyists to see to it that they copy the text so that no one can rearrange it. See Evagrius, *Praktikos*, ed. Antoine et Claire Guillaumont, *Évagre le Pontique. "Traité Pratique" ou "Le Moine"* (2 vols.; SC 170–71; Paris: Cerf, 1971), 496–98.

1) In contrast to literary texts composed by a known author, most early monastic material lack an identifiable author and thus also the interest of an author, or his disciples, in preserving it intact. When a name of an author is transmitted with the text it is often a later attribution, such as the attribution of the *Historia Monachorum* to Rufinus or Hieronymus. In other cases, such as the *Historia Lausiaca* or the *Pratum Spirituale*, it seems likely that the "authors", Palladius and John Moschos, used previous material, and thus acted as collectors as much as authors. The material included by them may well have been transmitted independently without necessarily having been extracted from their writings. Where we do have a clearly identifiable author, like Evagrius or Shenoute, or a community interested in preserving a specific heritage, like the Pachomians, the material is likely to be less fluid, although we, in most cases, lack sources to prove this.

2) Early monastic writings were in most cases transmitted as educational material to be used by and for novices and to be read for the spiritual progress of the reader. Since the circumstances and the needs changed the texts were revised and rearranged. Since there was not one origin and one linear development in early monasticism, and since all attempts to create a unified structure and rule remained rather limited both geographically and historically, the eastern monastic tradition never developed a fixed canon of texts.

3) Textual transmission in early eastern monasticism does not seem to have been dependent on large scriptoria were texts were copied under control and for organized distribution. The manuscripts were rather written individually either on a specific request by someone, or for use in the local monastery or by the individual himself. When large collections emerge they seem to have been the result of an accumulation of useful texts.[48] The attempts visible in the organization of sayings alphabetically or thematically, did have some success, but sayings continued to be transmitted both totally unorganized and reorganized according to other ideas. The same is, albeit to a lesser extent, true for stories, sermons and letters.

In view of the fluidity of much of the early monastic material that has come down to us, including some of the most used sources in historical studies, there is a great need for revising earlier scholarship on the emergence of the monastic tradition, its background, its social context, its motives and views and its early development. We have to realize that the sources we have preserved in the manuscripts are, like the manuscripts themselves, shaped by the tradition to which they belong. They are not prior to, but part of the development, and are primarily sources for the people and

---

48 This is obviously, as shown above, the case for the large Arabic corpus of writings attributed to Antony. The widely disparate transmission of the writings attributed to Macarius and to Evagrius in a variety of languages indicates the same. An exception is the Coptic collection of writings by Shenoute, which does not seem to have had a larger reception outside the community.

communities that wrote the manuscripts, which does not at all diminish their value. The tradition is by no means less important than its origins.

Bibliography

Primary Sources

Apophthegmata Patrum,
AP/AM Mansour, Jean. *Homélies et légendes religieuses: Un florilège arabe chrétien du Xe siècle (Ms Strasbourg 4225): Introduction et édition critique (thèse dactylographiée inédite).* Strasbourg: Harissa Seminaire Saint-Paul, 1972.
AP/EP Arras, Victor. *Patericon Aethiopice.* Corpus Scriptorum Christianorum Orientalium 277–78. Leuven: Peeters, 1967.
AP/G Migne, Jacques Paul. Patrologia Graeca 65. Paris: 1858, 75–440.
AP/GS Guy, Jean-Claude. *Les apophthegmes des Pères* I–III. Sources chrétiennes 387, 474, 498. Paris: Cerf, 1993–2005.
AP/HS Sargissian, Nerses. *Vark' srbots' harants' ew k'aghak'avarut'iwnk' nots'in* (Vies et pratiques des saints pères selon la double traduction des anciens). Vols. 1–2. Venice: I Tparani Srboyn Ghazaru, 1855.
–. Latin Translation: Leloir, Louis, *Paterica armeniaca a P. P. Mechitaristis edita (1855) nunc latine reddita.* Vols. 1–4. Corpus Scriptorum Christianorum Orientalium 353, 361, 371, 379. Leuven: Peeters, 1974–76.
AP/IA Dvali, Manana. Šua saukunet'a novelebis jveli k'art'uli t'argmanebi. 2, Anbanur-anonimuri paterikebi (*The Old Georgian Translation of the Novels of Middle Ages. 2, Alphabetical-Anonymous Patericon*), T'bilisi: Mec'niereba, 1974.
AP/OS Veder, William. *The Scete Paterikon – Patericon Sceticum – Skitskiĭ paterik.* 3 Vols. Pegasus Oost-Europese Studies 12–14. Amsterdam: Pegasus, 2012.
AP/PA Freire, J. Geraldes. *A versão latina por Pascásio de Dume dos Apophthegmata Patrum.* Vols. 1–2. Coimbra: Instituto de Estudos Clássicos, 1971.
AP/PJ Rosweyde, Heribert. *Vitae Patrum* V–VI, Antwerpen: 1615. Reprinted in: Migne, Jacques Paul. Patrologia Latina 73. Paris, 1849, 851–1024.
AP/SS Bedjan, Paul. *Acta martyrum et sanctorum Syriace 7.* Paris: 1897. Reprinted Hildesheim: Olms, 1968.
Evagrius Ponticus, *Antirrhetikos.* Translated by Brakke, David. *Evagrius Ponticus, Talking Back: A Monastic Handbook for Combating Demons.* Collegeville, Minn.: Cistercian Publications, 2009.
Evagrius Ponticus, *Practicus.* Edited and Translated by Guillaumont, André. *Évagre le Pontique, Traité Pratique.* 2 Vols. Sources chrétiennes 170–71. Paris: Cerf, 1971.
Historia Lausiaca. Edited by Bartelink, Gerard J. M. *Palladio, La storia Lausiaca. Testo critico e comment.* Vite dei Santi 2, Milano: Fondazione Lorenzo Valla, 1974.
–. Translated by Meyer, Robert. *Palladius: The Lausiac History.* New York: Paulist Press, 1964.
Historia Monachorum. Edited by Festugière, André-Jean. *Historia Monachorum in Aegypto.* Subsidia Hagiographica 53. Brussels: Société des Bollandistes, 1971.
–. Translated by Ward, Benedicta. *The Lives of the Desert Fathers.* London: Mowbray, 1980.
Vita Antonii. Edited by Bartelink, Gerard J. M. *Vie d'Antoine.* Sources chrétiennes 400. Paris: Cerf, 1994.

Secondary Literature

Batlle, Columba. *Die 'Adhortationes sanctorum Patrum' im lateinischen Mittelalter: Überlieferung, Fortleben und Wirkung*. Beiträge zur Geschichte des alten Mönchtums und des Benediktinerordens 31. Münster: Aschendorffsche Verlagsbuchhandlung, 1972.

Bousset, Wilhelm. *Apophthegmata: Studien zur Geschichte des ältesten Mönchtums*. Tübingen: J. C.B. Mohr, 1923.

Brakke, David. "Macarius's Quest and Ours: Literary Sources for Early Egyptian Monasticism." *Cistercian Studies Quarterly* 48 (2013): 239–51.

Brock, Sebastian. "Introduction." Pages i–iii in Derwas J. Chitty and Sebastian Brock, *The Letters of Ammonas: Successor of Antony*. Oxford: SLG Press, 1979.

Bumazhnov, Dimitrij. *Visio Mystica im Spannungsfeld frühchristlicher Überlieferungen: Die Lehre der sogenannteen Antoniusbriefe von der Gottes- und Engelschau und das Problem unterschiedlicher spiritueller Traditionen im frühen ägyptischen Mönchtum*. Studien und Texte zu Antike und Christentum 52. Tübingen: Mohr Siebeck, 2009.

Bunge, Gabriel. *Quatre ermites égyptiens d'après les fragments coptes de l'Histoire Lausiaque*. Spiritualité Orientale 60. Solesmes: Abbaye de Bellefontaine, 1994.

Cherubini, Roberto. *Conoscere Dio: Lettere e altri scritti di Ammonas*. Rome: Urbaniana University Press, 2011.

Chollet, Jacques. "Le Corpus arabicum de saint Antoine." *Mikhtav* 67 (2013): 26–54.

Crum, Walter Ewing. *Catalogue of the Coptic Manuscripts in the British Museum*. London: British Museum, 1905.

Dahlman, Britt. "The Collectio Scorialensis Parva: An Alphabetical Collection of Old Apophthegmatic and Hagiographic Material." Pages 23–33 in *Early Monasticism and Classical Paideia*. Edited by Samuel Rubenson. Vol. 3 of *Papers Presented at the Sixteenth International Conference on Patristic Studies held in Oxford 2011*. Edited by Markus Vinzent. Studia Patristica 55. Leuven: Peeters, 2013.

Farag, George. "Les lettres attribuées à Antoine dans la deuxième collection arabes (letters 8 à 20): Sont-elles d'Antoine ou d'Ammonas? Étude comparée des différentes version et interprétation théologique." Ph.D. diss. Strasbourg: Faculté théologie catholique, 2012.

Faraggiana di Sarzana, Chiara. "Apophthegmata Patrum: Some Crucial Points of Their Textual Transmission and the Problem of a Critical Edition." Pages 455–67 in *Biblica et Apocrypha, Ascetica, Liturgica: Papers Presented at the Twelfth International Conference on Patristic Studies held in Oxford 1995*. Edited by Elizabeth A. Livingstone. Studia Patristica 30. Leuven: Peeters, 1997.

Funk, Wolf-Peter. "Ein doppelt überliefertes Stück spätägyptischer Weisheit." *Zeitschrift für ägyptische Sprache und Altertumskunde* 103 (1976): 8–21.

Garitte, Gérard. "De unius ex Ammonae epistolis versione iberica." *Le Muséon* 52 (1939): 11–31.

Holmberg, Bo. "The Syriac Collection of Apophthegmata Patrum in MS Sin. syr. 46." Pages 35–57 in *Early Monasticism and Classical Paideia*. Edited by Samuel Rubenson. Vol. 3 of *Papers Presented at the Sixteenth International Conference on Patristic Studies held in Oxford 2011*. Edited by Markus Vinzent. Studia Patristica 55. Leuven: Peeters, 2013.

Iordanites, Augoustinos. *ΤΟΥ ΟΣΙΟΥ ΗΜΩΝ ΑΒΒΑ ΑΜΜΩΝΑ ΕΠΙΣΤΟΛΑΙ ΠΕΝΤΕ*. Jerusalem: 1911.

Klejna, Franz. "Antonius und Ammonas, eine Untersuchung über Herkunft und Eigenart der ältesten Mönchsbriefe." *Zeitschrift für katholische Theologie* 62 (1938): 309–48.

Kmosko, Michael. *Ammoni Eremitae Epistolae*. Patrologia Orientalis 10.6. Paris: Libraire de Paris, 1915.

Mansour, Jean. *Homelies et légendes religieuses: Un florilège arabe chrétien du Xe siècle (Ms Strasbourg 4225): Introduction et édition critique (thèse dactylographiée inédite)*. Strasbourg: Harissa Seminaire Saint-Paul, 1972.

Marriott, George Leicester. *Macarii Anecdota: Seven Unpublished Homilies of Macarius*. Harvard Theological Studies 5. Cambridge, Mass.: Harvard Divinity School, 1918.

Meyer, Robert. *Palladius: The Lausiac History*. New York: Paulist Press, 1964.

Nau, François. *Ammonas, successeur de saint Antoine*. Patrologia Orientalis 11. Paris: Libraire de Paris 1915.

Outtier, Bernard et al., ed., *Lettres des Pères du désert: Ammonas, Macaire, Arsène, Sérapion de Thmuis*. Spiritualité Orientale 42. Bégrolles: Abbaye de Bellefontaine, 1985.

Raheb, Andraus Al. *Kitab Rawdat al nufus fi rasa'il al- qiddis Antuniyus*. Cairo: 1899.

Regnault, Lucien. *Les sentences des Pères du désert. Troisième recueil & tables*. Solesmes: Abbaye Saint-Pierre, 1976.

Rubenson, Samuel. "Arabic Sources for the Theology of the Early Monastic Movement in Egypt." *Parole de l'Orient* 16 (1991): 33–47.

–. *The Letters of St. Antony: Origenist Theology, Monastic Tradition, and the Making of a Saint*. Lund: Lund University Press, 1990. Revised edition: *The Letters of St. Antony: Monasticism and the Making of a Saint*. Studies in Antiquity and Christianity. Minneapolis: Fortress Press, 1995.

–. "Antony and Ammonas: Conflicting or Common Tradition in Early Egyptian Monasticism?" Pages 185–201 in *Bibel, Byzanz und Christlicher Orient: Festschrift für Stephen Gerö*. Edited by Dimitrij Bumazhnov, Emmanouela Grypeou, Timothy B. Sailors, and Alexander Toepel. Orientalia Lovaniensia Analecta 187. Leuven: Peeters, 2011.

–. "Mönchtum." *Reallexikon für Antike und Christentum* 24 (2012): 1009–63.

–. "The Formation and Reformations of the Sayings of the Desert Fathers." Pages 5–22 in *Early Monasticism and Classical Paideia*. Edited by Samuel Rubenson. Vol. 3 of *Papers Presented at the Sixteenth International Conference on Patristic Studies held in Oxford 2011*. Edited by Markus Vinzent. Studia Patristica 55. Leuven: Peeters, 2013.

–. "Response: To Tell the Truth: Fact and Fiction in Early Monastic Sources." *Cistercian Studies Quarterly* 48 (2013): 317–24.

–. "The Letter-Collections of Antony and Ammonas: Shaping a Community." Pages 68–79 in *Collecting Early Christian Letters: From the Apostle Paul to Late Antiquity*. Edited by Bronwen Neil and Pauline Allen. Cambridge: Cambridge University Press, 2015.

Rousseau, Philip, *Pachomius: The Making of a Community in Fourth Century Egypt*. Berkeley: University of California Press, 1986.

Sauget, Jean-Marie. "La collection d'Apophtegmes du ms. 4225 de la Bibliothèque de Strasbourg." *Orientalia Christiana Periodica* 30 (1974): 485–509.

Shaw, Richard. "Textual Disorder in the Letters of St. Antony: An Analysis and Partial Reconstruction," *Downside Review* 462 (2013): 1–14, 463, 59–130.

Ward, Benedicta. *The Sayings of the Desert Fathers: The Alphabetical Collection*. London: Mowbray, 1975.

–. *The Lives of the Desert Fathers*, London: Mowbray, 1980.

Wellhausen, Adelheid. *Die lateinische Übersetzung der Historia Lausiaca des Palladius*. Berlin: Walter de Gruyter, 2003.

Williams, Rowan. *Faith and Experience in Early Monasticism: New Perspectives on the Letters of Ammonas: Laudatio und Festvortrag anlässlich der Ehrenpromotion von Rowan Douglas Williams durch die Theologische Fakultät der Universität Erlangen-Nürnberg am 02. 07. 1999 in der Aula des Erlanger Schlosses*. Akademische Reden und Kolloquien: Friedrich-Alexander-Universität Erlangen-Nürnberg 20. Erlangen-Nürnberg: FAU University Press, 2002.

J. Gregory Given*

Four Texts from Nag Hammadi amid the Textual and Generic Fluidity of the "Letter" in Late Antique Egypt

Among the Nag Hammadi Codices, there are at least four texts that scholars agree exhibit the characteristics, in whole or in part, of a letter.[1] The *Letter of Peter to Philip* is the sole text that bears the title of an ⲉⲡⲓⲥⲧⲟⲗⲏ ("letter"), but only the very beginning of the text resembles a letter in form; the eponymous letter from Peter to Philip clearly ends about 18 lines into the text and a brief narrative interlude segues into a dialogue between Jesus, Peter, and the other apostles. But as is indicated by the decorated titles in both NHC VIII and Codex Tchacos, it is the whole treatise that is referred to as an ⲉⲡⲓⲥⲧⲟⲗⲏ.[2] Similar in form to the *Letter of Peter to Philip* is the untitled treatise

---

* An earlier version of this essay was presented at the NEWCONT-conference, "The Nag Hammadi Codices as Monastic Books," at the University of Oslo, December 15th–17th, 2015. I wish to thank the organizers and participants for their collegial and incisive feedback, particularly Hugo Lundhaug, René Falkenberg, and Samuel Rubenson.

1 While scholars can and have analyzed the ways in which some of the texts discussed here exhibit the stylistic features of certain established types of ancient epistolary composition, for the purposes of the present analysis, only the most rudimentary epistolary characteristics are necessary for inclusion in the discussion: either the explicit designation, in title or incipit, as a "letter" (ⲉⲡⲓⲥⲧⲟⲗⲏ, ἐπιστολή), an opening epistolary prescript, and/or a closing epistolary greeting. On these standard letter components, see Hans-Josef Klauk, *Ancient Letters and the New Testament: A Guide to Context and Exegesis* (trans. Daniel P. Bailey; Waco, Tex.: Baylor University Press, 2006), 17–21, 24–25. I agree with his basic judgment, "The clearest sign that we have a letter before us is its so-called prescript" (17). For the sake of heuristic expediency, I exclude *Hypostasis of the Archons* from my analysis here, although it may be possible to analyze the text as a letter. Such an analysis would be based upon a single line, which seems to state the occasion for which the text has been penned: "[I] sent these things because you asked about the reality of the authorities." [ⲁⲉⲓ]ϫⲉⲛⲉ ⲛⲁⲉⲓ ⲉⲕϣⲓⲛⲉ ⲉⲧⲃⲉ ⲑⲩⲡⲟⲥⲧⲁ[ⲥⲓⲥ ⲛ̅]ⲉⲝⲟⲩⲥⲓⲁ (*Hyp. Arch.* 86.26–27; Coptic from Bentley Layton, ed., "The Hypostasis of the Archons," in *Nag Hammadi Codex II, 2–7 together with XIII,2*, Brit. Lib. Or. 4926(1), and P.Oxy. 1, 654, 655* [ed. Bentley Layton; 2 vols.; NHS 20–21; Leiden: Brill, 1989], 1:234). However, the lack of any other epistolary features raises the question of whether this text would be recognizable to readers as a sort of "letter" or, instead, as a sort of occasional treatise. The extent to which such a distinction can be made, to be sure, merits further consideration.

2 There is a possibility that the superscript title in NHC VIII (ⲧⲉⲡⲓⲥⲧⲟⲗⲏ ⲙ̅ⲡⲉⲧⲣⲟⲥ ⲉⲧⲁϥϫⲟⲟⲩⲥ ⲛ̅ⲫⲓⲗⲓⲡⲡⲟⲥ) (132.10–11) may be a sort of "title-ization" of the letter's incipit (à la *Gospel of Truth*), set off by the scribe from the main text and lightly decorated (so Jacques É. Ménard, *La Lettre de Pierre à Philippe: Texte établi et présenté* [BCNH.T 1; Quebec: Les Presses de l'Université Laval, 1977], 6). The title in the Tchacos Codex, however, is far less ambiguous; it is presented in an elaborately decorated subscript (occupying fully half a page!), in simplified form ([ⲧ]ⲉⲡⲓⲥⲧⲟⲗⲏ ⲙ̅ⲡⲉⲧⲣⲟⲥ ϣⲁⲫⲓⲗⲓⲡⲡⲟⲥ); see facsimile and transcription in Rudolph Kasser and Gregor Wurst, eds. *The Gospel of Judas together with the Letter of*

commonly referred to as the *Apocryphon of James*, which also begins as a letter and lapses into a dialogue, although here the break between the "letter" portion of the text and the "dialogue" is more obscure – the crucial segue is riddled with lacunae at the beginning of the text's second page.[3] It is clear in any case that the account of the dialogue between Christ and the apostles, as well as its revelatory content, is reported within the overarching frame of a letter. The text which appears in NHC III and V that we call *Eugnostos the Blessed* (based on the subscript title in the NHC III version) is identifiable as a letter insofar as it opens with a standard epistolary pre-script, beginning in the NHC III version, "Eugnostos, the Blessed, to those who are his" (III.70.1–2).While NHC V's incipit is highly fragmentary, the standard epistolary "greetings!" (ⲭⲁⲓⲣⲉ, which is absent in NHC III) is clearly visible (V.1.3). The generic[4] form of *Eugnostos* is not itself particularly unusual, but its relationship with another Nag Hammadi text certainly is: most of the content of *Eugnostos* can also be found in *Wisdom of Jesus Christ*, here placed in the mouth of Christ, in conversation with his disciples. Why is the content of this letter open to such transgeneric reappropriation? And how does this unique relationship between a letter and a dialogue relate to the letter-dialogues attributed to James and Peter? Finally, the *Treatise on the Resurrection* (ⲡⲗⲟⲅⲟⲥ ⲉⲧⲃⲉ ⲧⲁⲛⲁⲥⲧⲁⲥⲓⲥ) lacks a letter's requisite introductory formula, but is explic-itly directed to an individual interlocutor, specifies an inquiry from this interlocutor as an occasion for writing, and closes with a typical epistolary blessing.[5] So why is it called a ⲗⲟⲅⲟⲥ – a "treatise" or "discourse" – instead of an ⲉⲡⲓⲥⲧⲟⲗⲏ ("letter")?[6] Many scholars have casually set aside this topical title as evidently secondary, and refer to the text instead as the *Epistle to Rheginos*. While this ad hoc titling convention has some practical upside, it avoids, rather than reckons with, the question of how or why a "letter" might end up labeled as a ⲗⲟⲅⲟⲥ.

In what sense do all of these texts function as "letters"? The character and extent of their involvement with the literary form of the "letter," at least as we have

---

Peter to Philip, James, and a Book of Allogenes from Codex Tchacos: Critical Edition (Washington, D. C.: National Geographic, 2007), 108–9.

3 See *Ap. Jas.* 1.30–2.8. Coptic text in Francis E. Williams, ed. "The Apocryphon of James," in *Nag Hammadi Codex I (The Jung Codex): Introductions, Texts, Translations, Indices* (ed. Harold W. Attridge; NHS 22; Leiden: Brill, 1985).

4 Throughout this essay I use the adjective "generic" in the sense "of or relating to genre," rather than the more common sense, "of or relating to genus," i.e. "general," "collective," "common."

5 *Treat. Res.* 44.3–11: ⲁⲗⲗⲁ ⲉⲡⲉⲓⲇⲏ ⲉⲕϣⲓⲛⲉ ⲙ̄ⲙⲁⲛ ⲁⲡⲉⲧⲉϣϣⲉ ϩⲛ̄ ⲟⲩϩⲗⲁ6 ⲉⲧⲃⲉ ⲧⲁⲛⲁⲥⲧⲁⲥⲓⲥ †ⲥϩⲉⲉⲓ ⲛⲉⲕ ⲭⲉ ⲟⲩⲁⲛⲁⲅⲕⲁⲓⲟⲛ ⲧⲉ ⲁⲩⲱ ⲟⲩⲛ ϩⲁϩ ⲙ̄ⲙⲉⲛ ⲟⲉⲓ ⲛ̄ⲁⲡⲓⲥⲧⲟⲥ ⲁⲣⲁⲥ ϩⲛ̄ⲕⲟⲩⲉⲓ ⲛ̄ⲇⲉ ⲛⲉⲧ6ⲓⲛⲉ ⲙ̄ⲙⲁⲥ ⲉⲧⲃⲉ ⲡⲉⲉⲓ ⲙⲁⲣⲉⲡⲗⲟⲅⲟⲥ ϣⲱⲡⲉ ⲛⲉⲛ ⲉⲧⲃⲏⲧⲥ "But since you asked us sweetly about what is proper on the subject of the resur-rection, I write to you that it is necessary and that there are many of us who do not believe in it, but a few find it. For this reason, let us discuss the matter." Coptic from Malcolm L. Peel, ed. "The Treatise on the Resurrection," in *Nag Hammadi Codex I (The Jung Codex): Introductions, Texts, Translations, Indices* (ed. Harold W. Attridge; NHS 22; Leiden: Brill, 1985).

6 On the title of this text, see discussion in Peel, "Treatise on the Resurrection," 128–30.

heretofore understood it, appears varied and, at times, haphazard. The most manifestly epistolary text is called a "treatise" (λογος), the only text labeled explicitly as a "letter" (επιστολη) looks something like an excerpt from an apocryphal Acts narrative,[7] and the epistolary framework of James' "secret book," seems like an afterthought compared to the actual secret revelatory content.[8] Could it be, though, that it is not the texts themselves that are bizarre in this regard, but the generic categories that we are using to analyze them? Is it possible that we have simply selected the wrong comparanda? Insofar as these letters have been contextualized in the genre of the "letter," they have primarily been compared to letters supposedly in use among so-called Gnostics in antiquity (such as Ptolemy's *Letter to Flora* and the reported letters of Valentinus) or the letters among the New Testament Apocrypha (the letter of Peter in the Pseudo-Clementine literature, 3 Corinthians, etc.).[9]

A different set of comparanda now presents itself. Inspired by a New Philological impulse to account for the lives of these manuscripts in their *material* historical setting, Hugo Lundhaug and Lance Jenott have convincingly argued that these codices were produced – and therefore presumably used – in an Egyptian monastic milieu.[10] Now that we can begin to consider the codices as monastic books, we can seize the opportunity to contextualize these letter-like texts within the diverse world of late antique Egyptian, and particularly monastic, epistolarity.[11] We can now ask: how would a fourth- or fifth-century Egyptian reader, particularly a monastic reader, understand these "letters" from Nag Hammadi? In what sense would they be recognizable to her or him as "letters"?

In this essay I aim to take a first step towards answering these questions by situating the four Nag Hammadi "letters" within the variegated world of the "letter" in late antique Egyptian literature. I begin by surveying some recent studies illustrating the textual and generic instability of the letter within the manuscripts transmitting early Egyptian monastic letter collections, before turning to consider, in particular,

---

7 So Ménard's "hypothèse de travail;" see *La Lettre de Pierre à Philippe*, 5–6.

8 As Williams claims ("The Apocryphon of James," 16). See further discussion of this assessment below.

9 See, for example, the comparanda adduced by Marvin Meyer, "NHC VII, 2: The Letter of Peter to Philip," in *Nag Hammadi Codex VIII* (ed. John H. Sieber; NHS 31; Leiden: Brill, 1991), 227–28 and Peel, "Treatise on the Resurrection," 129–30.

10 Hugo Lundhaug and Lance Jenott, *The Monastic Origins of the Nag Hammadi Codices* (STAC 97; Tübingen: Mohr Siebeck, 2015). Lundhaug and Jenott's contributions to the present volume further explore the ramifications of this approach, particularly in light of the fact of textual fluidity in a manuscript culture.

11 While focusing on a different monastic genre, the "catechesis," Philip Rousseau has amply demonstrated just how fruitful such literary comparison between Nag Hammadi texts and early monastic literature can be. Philip Rousseau, "The Successors of Pachomius and the Nag Hammadi Codices: Exegetical Themes and Literary Structures," in *The World of Early Egyptian Christianity* (ed. James E. Goehring et al.; Washington, D. C.: The Catholic University of America Press, 2012), 140–57.

the somewhat enigmatic use of the term ⲉⲡⲓⲥⲧⲟⲗⲏ in manuscripts of Shenoute's writings. I then introduce three lengthier texts surviving from late antique Egypt which also incorporate the letter form, to varying degrees, within generically hybrid (but nevertheless unified) textual wholes. Finally returning to the four "letters" from Nag Hammadi, I briefly explore the extent to which several of the recurring interpretive issues surrounding the titles and literary forms of these texts can be resolved when set alongside these other "letters" from late antique Egypt.

Textual and Generic Fluidity in Early Monastic Letter Collections

Responding to the call of Samuel Rubenson and Bernadette McNary-Zak to take letters more seriously in writing the history of early Egyptian monasticism,[12] Malcolm Choat has, in a number of recent articles, forwarded and developed a robust defense of the centrality of the "letter" as "the most important ... literary phenomen[on] of the monastic movement."[13] In an attempt to account for the vibrant complexity of this "epistolary culture," Choat strives to nuance the classic scholarly bifurcation between the so-called "documentary" letter on papyrus or ostracon and the so-called "literary" letter, the Deissmannian "epistle."[14] He adopts only "one principle classification," which he roots in the material mode of transmission: the distinction between an "autograph" and a "manuscript copy."[15] By organizing the data in this way, he hopes to open up "a dialogue between the literary and documentary sources, to move beyond the dichotomy into the space between literary and documentary sources."[16] Once we actually venture into this space, however, it turns out that the situation is quite messy.

---

12 Samuel Rubenson, "Argument and Authority in Early Monastic Correspondence," in *Foundations of Power and Conflicts of Authority in Late-Antique Monasticism* (ed. Alberto Camplani and Giovanni Filoramo; OLA 157; Leuven: Peeters, 2007), 75–87; Bernadette McNary-Zak, *Letters and Asceticism in Fourth-Century Egypt* (Lanham, Md.: University Press of America: 2000).
13 Malcolm Choat, "The Epistolary Culture of Monasticism between Literature and Papyri," *CSQ* 48:3 (2013): 228.
14 Scholarly squabbles over the relationship between "real" letters and "literary" letters go back at least as far as the rigid bifurcation proposed by Deissmann between the private, personal "letter" and the public, literary "epistle." Adolf Deissmann, *Light from the Ancient East: The New Testament Illustrated by Recently Discovered Texts of the Graeco-Roman World* (trans. Lionel R. M. Strachan; New York: Hodder & Stoughton, 1910), 217–21.
15 Choat, "Epistolary Culture of Monasticism," 230.
16 Choat, "Epistolary Culture of Monasticism," 237.

A recent volume titled *Collecting Early Christian Letters* itself collects a number of important new studies on the phenomenon of the letter collection in antiquity. Contributions by Rubenson, Choat, and Brent Nongbri shed light on the remarkable degree of generic and textual fluidity that is to be found in monastic letter collections, one frontier in which the shaky transition between an "autograph" and a "manuscript copy" of a letter would seem to play out. What emerges in these concise yet highly instructive studies is a picture of a literary world in which neither arrangement, nor attribution, nor textual integrity, nor even genre remains stable.

Rubenson's chapter surveys the difficulties in parsing the manuscript traditions that preserve the letter collections attributed to Antony and Ammonas. As he covers in greater detail in his epochal monograph on Antony's letters, the seven letters thought to be authentically composed by Antony are preserved entirely only in Arabic, Georgian, and Latin translations, each version arranging the letters in a different order, with the Arabic manuscripts also including an additional thirteen letters attributed to Antony. The presumably original Coptic only survives in a fragmentary seventh-century codex, which preserves one full letter and parts of two others, matching the ordering in the Arabic tradition.[17] All three of the translations have the same first letter, but this letter differs significantly in style and content from the other six, and is independently preserved in a number of Syriac manuscripts, "without any trace of its being part of a collection."[18] The oldest of these Syriac manuscripts presents Antony's letter alongside material attributed to Evagrius, Macarius, and Ammonas "as part of" what Rubenson describes as "a very early collection of sayings."[19] Part of this first letter can also be found excerpted in the Greek *Apophthegmata* manuscripts.[20] Among the other six letters, there is a fair degree of structural and verbal similarities – or you might say repetition – as well as what appear to be misplaced introductory and final greetings. These features have recently led Richard Shaw to argue in a three-part series of articles for a "textual disorder" in the manuscript tradition that could hypothetically be solved by reshuffling some of the material to reconstruct at least one additional complete, previously "lost" letter of Antony.[21]

---

17 Specifically, this manuscript preserves the end of one letter, a full letter numbered as the fourth, and the beginning of another letter numbered as the fifth. See Samuel Rubenson, *The Letters of St. Antony: Monasticism and the Making of a Saint* (SAC; Minneapolis: Fortress Press, 1995), 15.
18 Samuel Rubenson, "The Letter-Collections of Antony and Ammonas: Shaping a Community," in *Collecting Early Christian Letters: From the Apostle Paul to Late Antiquity* (ed. Bronwen Neil and Pauline Allen; Cambridge: Cambridge University Press, 2015), 71.
19 Rubenson, *Letters of St. Antony*, 16 n. 6.
20 Rubenson, "Letter-Collections," 71 n. 12.
21 Shaw specifically argues that Letter IV and Letter VIIB were originally combined as a single document. Richard Shaw, "Textual Disorder in the Letters of St. Antony: An Analysis and Partial Reconstruction. Part I: Disorder in the Canon," *DRev* 131.462 (Jan. 2013): 1–14; "Part II: The Likelihood of

The corpus of letters attributed to Ammonas, Antony's disciple, displays perhaps an even higher degree of variance in order and number across Arabic, Syriac, Georgian, Armenian, and Greek manuscript traditions. To briefly list only some of the difficulties: each of these versions preserves a different number and order of letters attributed to Ammonas; most of the thirteen extra letters attributed to Antony in the Arabic manuscripts are found attributed to Ammonas in these other versions;[22] the oldest manuscripts, those in Syriac, themselves present the letters in varying number and sequence, with sometimes obscure attribution and delineation between different letters; one of the Greek letters comprises three paragraphs found in three different Syriac letters; one of the letters appears in Greek manuscripts as a homily attributed to Macarius; another can be found in the Ethiopic sayings of Abba Isaiah.[23] While Rubenson does hold open the possibility that, at the core of these two dizzyingly complex manuscript traditions, there are indeed authentic letters written by Antony and Ammonas, when it comes to their means of collection and transmission, he argues that

> they should be regarded as similar ... to the anecdotes, instructions, and sayings found in a variety of monastic florilegia. ... It is as part of such collections, including the *Sayings of the Desert Fathers*, that our letters are generally preserved, and most probably the process of collection of them has been similar and had a similar purpose.[24]

In this same volume, Choat characterizes the generic situation of the monastic letter collection in this way:

> When we attempt to study early monastic epistolography within the manuscript tradition, then we must reckon with a situation in which genre boundaries are blurred and porous, where there are different imperatives for different sorts of collections, and different priorities in the way the letters are presented in different contexts.[25]

If Rubenson amply demonstrates how such generic blurring operates in the letter collections attributed to Antony and Ammonas, Choat and Nongbri offer the letters of Pachomius as a paradigmatic example of this textual and generic fluidity. While

---

Disorder – The Letters in Context," 131.463 (Apr. 2013): 59–68; "Part III: Possibilities of Reconstruction – A Lost Letter of St. Antony?" 131.464 (Jul. 2013): 117–30.

22 For a detailed comparative study of these letters across the different versions, see George Farag, "Les Lettres attribuées à Antonie dans la deuxième collection arabe (Lettres 8 à 20): sont-elles d'Antoine ou d'Ammonas? Étude comparée des différentes versions et interprétation théologique" (PhD diss., University of Strasbourg, 2012).

23 Rubenson, "Letter-Collections," 73–75.

24 Rubenson, "Letter-Collections," 78.

25 Malcolm Choat, "From Letter to Letter-Collection: Monastic Epistolography in Late-Antique Egypt," in *Collecting Early Christian Letters: From the Apostle Paul to Late Antiquity* (ed. Bronwen Neil and Pauline Allen; Cambridge: Cambridge University Press, 2015), 88.

Jerome's Latin translation of these letters (which survives only in Medieval manuscripts) appears to preserve information about the addressees and the occasions for the letters in expanded introductory formulae that take on the role of a title,[26] the oldest witnesses – fragmentary Coptic and Greek manuscripts, which are paleographically datable to the fourth–sixth centuries – include neither introductory nor concluding epistolary formulae and, in fact, no explicit attribution to Pachomius at all.[27] Nongbri notes that these earlier manuscripts also *divide* the letters differently: One, an early Greek parchment roll, contains neither attribution nor titles for the texts upon it, but in terms of Jerome's enumeration, it marks no division between Pachomius' letters 1 and 2, and otherwise only includes letters 3, 7, 10, and the first half of letter 11 as an independent text. In a Coptic codex dating perhaps to the sixth century we find (again following Jerome's enumeration) the second half of letter 11, letter 10, the first half of letter 11, and finally letter 9, clearly split into two independent texts.[28]

Nongbri marshals these examples from the manuscripts of letters attributed to Pachomius as possible evidence for the editorial combination of multiple letters into larger textual wholes, the formation of 'composite letters' of the type that many New Testament scholars believe 2 Corinthians to be. In the context of Nongbri's other examples from the papyrological record, this evidence is indeed convincing. But taken alongside the previous examples from Antony's and Ammonas' corpora, I would suggest that the Pachomian material could also be read as evidence for precisely the opposite editorial tendency: the practice of *breaking up* letters into smaller textual units and recombining them again in other situations.[29] The disarray of the textual record also raises questions about whether all of these Pachomian materials were always transmitted as *letters* of Pachomius: some of the titles found in manuscripts of Jerome's translations (including those for letters 9 and 11, which on Nongbri's account are composite letters) refer not to an *epistula* but *verba* of Pachomius, "words" which, presumably, could have been spoken on some occasion or written in some other type of text.[30] We also find material from Pachomius' letters attributed

---

26 See the example given in Choat, "From Letter to Letter-Collection," 83: "Letter of our father Pachomius to the holy man Cornelius, who was father of the monastery of Mochansis, in which he speaks a language given to both of them by an angel, and the sound of which we have heard without being able to understand."

27 Choat, "From Letter to Letter-Collection," 83–84.

28 Brent Nongbri, "*2 Corinthians* and Possible Material Evidence for Composite Letters in Antiquity," in *Collecting Early Christian Letters: From the Apostle Paul to Late Antiquity* (ed. Bronwen Neil and Pauline Allen; Cambridge: Cambridge University Press, 2015), 59.

29 Nongbri himself briefly acknowledges the possibility that "letters 1 and 2 were originally a single letter that was later divided," but he finds it "more likely" that "the two were originally independent and later combined to form a composite letter in some manuscripts" (Nongbri, "*2 Corinthians* and Possible Material Evidence," 59). In the context of the present discussion, it seems far less clear to me which of the two options is "more likely."

30 Nongbri, "*2 Corinthians* and Possible Material Evidence," 58.

to others elsewhere: In a recent monograph, Christoph Joest notes that significant portions of one of Pachomius' letters are closely paralleled by a saying attributed to Isidore in some *Apophthegmata* collections.[31]

Taking all of these examples together, we see that in addition to a high degree of textual fluidity that seems to have stemmed from basic editorial activity – rearrangement, removal of opening and concluding formulae, addition or removal of titles, and the combination of multiple letters into a single, seamless text – we also see a consistent fluidity in attribution, as well as fluidity between what is presented as a physically inscribed "letter" and what is reported as spoken discourse. Excerpts of letters float into *Apophthegmata* and vise-versa, the names associated with these letters/sayings shift, and texts called "letters" carry along with them paratextual information about the occasions on which they were spoken by the attributed writer.

"Letter" and/as "Logos" in Shenoute's Corpus

In the manuscripts transmitting Shenoute's writings, we see a different manifestation of the generic fluidity of the letter in the somewhat enigmatic use of the term ⲉⲡⲓⲥⲧⲟⲗⲏ (*epistolê*: "letter") as a title for treatises in this corpus.[32] The majority of texts compiled in the *Canons* of Shenoute bear the title of an ⲉⲡⲓⲥⲧⲟⲗⲏ (often in the colophon or subscript of a volume) and, indeed, many present themselves as literal dispatches on specific occasions from Shenoute's hermitage.[33] One of the texts in *Canon 7* (*If Every-*

---

31 Christoph Joest, *Die Pachom-Briefe: Übersetzung und Deutung* (CSCO 655, Subsidia 133; Leuven: Peeters, 2014), 71–75.

32 While Shenoute lived and wrote in the late fourth and early fifth centuries, his work is almost exclusively preserved in the extant manuscripts from the White Monastery, which are datable to the ninth-eleventh centuries (Tito Orlandi, "The Library of the Monastery of Saint Shenute at Atripe," in *Perspectives on Panopolis: An Egyptian Town from Alexander the Great to the Arab Conquest* [ed. Arthur Egberts et al.; Leiden: Brill, 2002], 220.) Although it is impossible to account for the fluidity of these texts over the five centuries between their composition and their extant preservation, where multiple copies of the same work can be compared, the extant manuscripts display a remarkable degree of textual stability. This stability is owed in large part, no doubt, to the extreme localization of the manuscripts' preservation in Shenoute's own monastery.

33 Stephen Emmel, *Shenoute's Literary Corpus* (2 vols.; CSCO 599–600, Subsidia 111–112; Leuven: Peeters, 2004), 2:556: "... most of the works in the nine volumes of *Canons* are to be categorized as 'letters,' which Shenoute called ⲉⲡⲓⲥⲧⲟⲗⲏ." Within the *Canons* themselves there are numerous references to tablets (ⲡⲓⲛⲁⲕⲓⲥ), papyrus sheets (ⲭⲁⲣⲧⲏⲥ), letters (ⲉⲡⲓⲥⲧⲟⲗⲏ), and books (ⲭⲱⲱⲙⲉ), as well as explicit discussion of writing on tablets being compiled into sheets (at the beginning of Canon 9) and sheets being compiled into books (at the end of Canon 1; see Emmel, 2:553–54). The extent to which these extant so-called ⲉⲡⲓⲥⲧⲟⲗⲏ have themselves been cobbled together through such a process "requires reevaluation," Emmel notes, "Possibly we have – albeit fragmentarily – more of the corpus to which he refers than was previously thought" (2:558).

one Errs), however, presents itself instead as a λογος (*logos*: "speech," "discourse"), leading Stephen Emmel to conjecture that, given the subject matter ("the physical improvement of the monastery") this text was perhaps delivered by Shenoute in person on one of his visits to the monastery.[34] Yet, as Choat points out, even though Shenoute calls it λογος within the text itself, when he quotes from this same text in another treatise, he refers to the source as an επιϲτολη.[35]

Manuscript titles elsewhere in Shenoute's corpus trouble the generic distinction between επιϲτολη and λογος even further. In two separate articles Choat discusses the evident practice of White Monastery scribes in "labeling some works among She-noute's Discourses as *epistolai* when they were clearly other sorts of productions."[36] The most striking instance of this practice is found in the codex designated XH, one of only two extant manuscripts of the fourth volume of Shenoute's *Discourses*. The subscript title at the end of the volume reads ·ⲇ· επιϲτολη ·ι·, which Emmel interprets as "4(th volume): 10 epistles." On the following page, the colophon indicates that the present manuscript is a copy of "the fourth old book of *logoi* of our holy prophetic father Apa Shenoute."[37] So in two side-by-side scribal descriptions of the contents of this codex, we see these contents referred to as *epistolai* and *logoi*. In the super- and subscript titles within the codex itself, the picture gets even more complicated: XH titles one work as ϲⲓⲛοⲩθⲓοⲩ λοⲅοϲ ("*logos* of Shenoute"),[38] another as ϲⲓⲛοⲩθⲓοⲩ επιϲτολη ("letter of Shenoute"),[39] another as simply ϲⲓⲛοⲩθⲓοⲩ ("of Shenoute"),[40] before introducing three additional texts as "*Logoi* in the presence of some dignitaries who came to him with their retinues."[41] Each of these final three texts has a further introductory heading, noting the specific dignitary whose visit was the occasion for

---

34 Emmel, *Shenoute's Literary Corpus*, 2:557, 582–84.

35 Malcolm Choat, "Monastic Letter Collections in Late Antique Egypt: Structure, Purpose, and Transmission," in *Cultures in Contact: Transfer of Knowledge in the Mediterranean Context. Selected Papers* (ed. Sofía Torallas Tovar and Juan Pedro Monferrer-Sala; Cordoba: CNREU-CEDRAC, Oriens Academic, 2013), 81.

36 Choat, "Epistolary Culture of Monasticism," 229. Cf. discussion in Choat, "Monastic Letter Collections in Late Antique Egypt," 81–82.

37 ⲡⲙⲉϩϥⲧοοⲩ ⲛ̄ϫⲱⲱⲙⲉ ⲛ̄ⲁⲣⲭⲁⲓοϲ ⲛ̄ⲗοⲅοϲ ⲙ̄ⲡⲉⲛⲉⲓⲱⲧ ⲉⲧοⲩⲁⲁⲃ ⲙ̄ⲡ̄ⲣοϕⲏⲧ(ⲏϲ) ⲁⲡⲁ ϣⲉⲛοⲩⲧⲉ. Emmel, *Shenoute's Literary Corpus*, 2:614.

38 *A Beloved Asked Me Years Ago.* In this and the following two cases, Emmel notes decorated titles between texts; in each case, it is ambiguous whether these titles are superscript titles referring to the following treatise, subscript titles referring to the preceding treatise, or some combination thereof. In the other manuscript preserving the fourth volume of the *Discourses*, DU, this text bears the super-script title ϲⲓⲛοⲩθⲓοⲩ. See Emmel, *Shenoute's Literary Corpus*, 2:620.

39 *Because of You Too, O Prince of Evil.* DU gives the subscript ϲⲓⲛοⲩθⲓοⲩ επιϲτολη. Emmel, *Shenoute's Literary Corpus*, 2:621–22.

40 *Not Because A Fox Barks.* DU gives the superscript ϲⲓⲛοⲩθⲓοⲩ επιϲτολη. Emmel, *Shenoute's Literary Corpus*, 2:622.

41 See Emmel, *Shenoute's Literary Corpus*, 2.623–626.

the (presumably spoken) discourse.[42] In short, at least in these manuscripts of Shenoute's writings, λογος and επιϲτολη appear to be interchangeable, virtually synony-
mous, designations – there is no indication that the compilers, copiers, or readers of
these codices imagined that all texts bearing the title επιϲτολη must have been written
on a particular occasion as a "real letter," or that an επιϲτολη could not also have been
a spoken or written λογος.

"Letters" Among Generic Hybrids From Late Antique Egypt

The letter's dynamic generic flexibility in late antique Egypt also extends into continuous prose narratives. Three texts, in particular, demonstrate the range of ways
that the letter form interacted with lengthier generic hybrids. The *Letter of Ammon*,
which has its earliest attestation accompanying the Greek *Life of Pachomius* in two
eleventh-century manuscripts,[43] presents itself in the incipit as "The Letter of the
Bishop Ammon concerning the Conduct and Life of Pachomius and Theodore" but
largely comprises an autobiographical narrative tracking Ammon's conversion to
Christianity and education as a Pachomian monk. In this regard it has some formal
similarities to Athanasius' famous *Life of Antony*, which also presents itself as a letter.
Most interesting for my purposes, however, is the manner in which discrete, seemingly independent textual units with different generic forms are incorporated as part
of the larger textual whole. Ammon nests amid his first-person narrative secondary
accounts, given to him from others, pertaining to the life of his abbot, Theodore, and
his own training under Pachomius. Stretches of the text, such as Theodore's catechesis and his encounters with Pachomius, read as essentially loosely-narrativized
sayings collections (e.g. *Ep. Amm.* § 3, § 9–14). We also find letters embedded within
the text: in the course of the story, letters arrive from Antony and Theodore that are
then included, in whole, in the middle of the narrative (*Ep. Amm.* § 29, § 32). A reply
from Theophilus, evidently the addressee of the *Letter of Ammon*, is finally appended
at the end (*Ep. Amm.* § 37). So what in eleventh-century manuscripts is called a singular ἐπιστολή is in fact a narrative assemblage that could be analyzed as a variety
of independent texts, of different generic forms. The greatest difficulty for our comparative enterprise is the question of dating: given the fluidity of Pachomian *vitae*
traditions to which the *Letter of Ammon* is closely related, which James Goehring care-

---

42 E.g. "In the presence of Jovinus ..." "Likewise in the presence of Flavianus ..." "Likewise in the
presence of Heraklammon ..." Emmel, *Shenoute's Literary Corpus*, 2.623–25.
43 James E. Goehring, *The Letter of Ammon and Pachomian Monasticism* (PTS 27; Berlin: De Gruyter,
1986), 34. All references to the *Letter of Ammon* follow Goehring's translation and section numbering.

fully analyzes in his foundational study of the text, it could, in a way, contravene the purposes of a 'New Philological' approach to the Nag Hammadi Codices to attempt too close a comparison between this text's final literary form in eleventh-century manuscripts and the Nag Hammadi manuscripts in the fourth–fifth centuries. But close formal similarities to two other texts, which are actually physically attested in Coptic manuscripts from late antique Egypt, suggest that the *Letter of Ammon* could plausibly have taken shape in this milieu.

Perhaps the closest formal parallel to the *Letter of Ammon* is a Coptic text preserved in a sixth–seventh-century papyrus codex[44] and two seventh–eighth-century fragments from Medinet Madi.[45] This text stands untitled in both the codex and Crum's edition, but Tito Orlandi has proposed that scholars refer to it as the *Historia Horsiesi*.[46] While clearly delimited by scribal decorations as a textual unity, like the *Letter of Ammon* it appears to be an assemblage of several independent texts. It begins with a letter, headed by the introductory title: "A letter of Apa Theophilos the Archbishop of Rakote [i.e. Alexandria] to Apa Horsiesios the Archimandrite."[47] A narrative follows, recounting the journey of two deacons from Alexandria to Upper Egypt, searching for Horsiesios in order to deliver the letter, and then back to Alexandria with the archimandrite. The narrative continues, recounting the happenings of Horsiesios' visit to Alexandria, including two embedded dialogues between Horsiesios and the Archbishop Theophilos. Another letter, from Theophilos to the monks in Horsiesios' charge, is then incorporated in full within the text, followed by a brief conclusion reporting Horsiesios' safe passage back to the Thebaid with this document. The text then continues, "These are the questions of Faustos and Timotheos, deacons of the church of Rakote [i.e. Alexandria], before the holy Horsiesios the Archimandrite, which they posed to him on the boat when they were travelling to Rakote,"[48] kicking off a question-and-answer dialogue which constitutes the final third of the text. As is the case with the *Letter of Ammon*, then, in the so-called *Historia Horsiesi* we also find letters and dialogues strung together with a rudimentary narrative into a textual unity.

---

44 Walter E. Crum, *Der Papyruscodex saec. VI–VII der Philippsbibliothek in Cheltenham: Koptische theologische Schriften* (SWGS 18; Strasbourg: Trübner, 1915), 12–21. (Codex pages 38–73.) I thank Hugo Lundhaug for drawing my attention to this text.

45 Tito Orlandi, "Due fogli papiracei da Medinet Madi (Fayum): L'historia Horsiesi," *EVO* 13 (1990): 109–26, see esp. codicological and paleographical description on 109.

46 Orlandi, "Due fogli papiracei," 110–11.

47 Crum, *Der Papyruscodex*, 12.18–19: ογεπιστολη ⲛⲧⲉ ⲁⲡⲁ ⲑⲉⲟⲫⲓⲗⲟⲥ ⲡⲁⲣⲭⲓⲉⲡⲓⲥⲕⲟⲡⲟⲥ ⲛ̅ⲣⲁⲕⲟⲧⲉ ϣⲁⲁⲡⲁ ϩⲱⲣⲥⲓⲉⲥⲓⲟⲥ ⲡⲁⲣⲭⲓⲙⲁⲛⲇⲣⲓⲧⲏⲥ.

48 Crum, *Der Papyruscodex*, 17.31–33: ⲛⲁ̈ⲓⲛⲉ ⲛ̅ⲍⲏⲧⲏⲙⲁ ⲙ̅ⲫⲁⲩⲥⲧⲟⲥ ⲙⲛ̅ⲧⲓⲙⲟⲑⲉⲟⲥ ⲛ̅ⲇⲓⲁⲕ<ⲟⲛⲟⲥ> ⲛ̅ⲧⲉⲕⲕⲗⲏⲥⲓⲁ ⲛ̅ⲣⲁⲕⲟⲧⲉ ⲛ̅ⲛⲁϩⲣⲙ̅ⲡ̅ⲡⲉⲧⲟⲩⲁⲁⲃ ϩⲱⲣⲥⲓⲉⲥⲓⲟⲥ ⲡⲁⲣⲭⲓⲙⲁⲛⲇⲣⲓⲧⲏⲥ (ⲍ̄) ⲉⲛⲧⲁⲩϫⲛⲟⲩϥ ⲉⲣⲟⲟⲩ ϩⲙ̅ⲡⲉⲥⲕⲁⲫⲟⲥ ⲉⲩⲃⲏⲕ ⲉⲣⲁⲕⲟⲧⲉ.

A third, more well-known text surviving from late antique Egypt also attests to the close association between the letter and the dialogue. The *Epistula Apostolorum* (also untitled in the ancient manuscripts) bills itself in the incipit as "What Jesus Christ revealed to his disciples as a letter, and how Jesus Christ revealed the letter of the council of the apostles ..." and is then undersigned by the apostles themselves and addressed to "churches of the East and West, towards North and South."[49] After this epistolary introduction, the remainder of the text is a revelation dialogue between Jesus and the apostles, strikingly similar to such dialogues as are found among the Nag Hammadi Codices.[50] Like these codices, the *Epistula Apostolorum* is also physically attested in fourth- or fifth-century Egypt in the form of a miniature papyrus codex, which preserves most of the text in Coptic.[51] It is important to note, however, that the all-important beginning of the text is missing in the Coptic manuscript, so we must rely on the later Ethiopic manuscripts for the genre-signifying incipit.[52] And unlike the Nag Hammadi Codices, the *Letter of Ammon*, and the *Historia Horsiesi*, it is also not certain that we should count on a specifically *monastic* audience for the *Epistula Apostolorum*. Nevertheless, alongside these other examples, it is valuable as yet another representative of the generic potential of the "letter" in the literary milieu of late antique Egypt.

Reassessing the Nag Hammadi "Letters"

In this rapid survey I have highlighted only a few examples of the generic fluidity surrounding the title and form of the "letter" in late antique Egyptian, and particularly monastic, literature. Against this background, we can now turn back to the Nag Hammadi Codices and, considering them as monastic books, finally ask: how would a reader who is accustomed to this range of generic potential for the

---

49 Carl Schmidt, ed., *Gespräche Jesu mit seinen Jüngern nach der Auferstehung: ein katholisch-apostolisches Sendschreiben des 2. Jahrhunderts* (TUGAL 43; Leipzig: Hinrichs, 1919). English translation in C. Detlef G. Müller, ed., "Epistula Apostolorum," in *New Testament Apocrypha* (ed. Wilhelm Schneemelcher; trans. Robert McL. Wilson; 2 vols.; Louisville, Ky.: Westminster John Knox Press, 2003), 1:252.

50 On the *Epistula Apostolorum* as a possible "orthodox" representative of (and rejoinder to) the genre of the "Gnostic dialogue," see discussion and bibliography in Julian V. Hills, *Tradition and Composition in the* Epistula Apostolorum (HTS 57; Cambridge: Harvard University Press, 2008), 10–36. For further discussion of this genre in light of the comparisons drawn in the present essay, see note 60 below.

51 Cairo, IFAO P. 416 (LDAB 107969).

52 However, because the pages of the Coptic manuscript are numbered, it is possible to judge that the original length of the Coptic text matches the extant Ethiopic version. Hills, *Tradition and Composition*, 7.

"letter" understand the letter-like texts within these codices? Would the features that appear bizarre or inexplicable to a modern scholar make more sense to a fifth-century monk?

Lundhaug and Jenott have already demonstrated just how fruitful a close comparison between the Nag Hammadi Codices and early monastic letter collections can be. In their convincing analysis of the Nag Hammadi colophons, many of the parallels in vocabulary that they adduce for the colophon in NHC III are found in the same letter collections surveyed here, particularly those of Antony and Ammonas.[53] Similarly, the strongest parallel to (and most promising avenue for comparative interpretation of) the cryptogram in NHC VII is found in the cryptography of the letters attributed to Pachomius.[54] If, as Lundhaug and Jenott cautiously suggest, these parallels at minimum illuminate the possible interpretations of a fourth- or fifth-century reader familiar with such monastic letters,[55] it seems only reasonable to ask further: would such a reader recognize any other similarities between these letter collections and the texts available to her or him in the Nag Hammadi Codices?

The first and most basic observation to make is that such a monastic reader would likely not be troubled in the slightest by a text which clearly exhibits features of the letter-form but is titled ⲡⲗⲟⲅⲟⲥ ⲉⲧⲃⲉ ⲧⲁⲛⲁⲥⲧⲁⲥⲓⲥ, "The *logos* on the resurrection." As previously mentioned, scholars have long been content to understand this title as a designation which gives information about the topical content, if not the genre, of the text.[56] Alongside the clear evidence in Shenoute's corpus of ⲗⲟⲅⲟⲥ and ⲉⲡⲓⲥⲧⲟⲗⲏ being used interchangeably, as well as Jerome's titling of some Pachomian letters as *epistula* and others as *verba*, the monastic literary milieu now presents itself as at least one plausible context in which a letter could come to be titled as a ⲗⲟⲅⲟⲥ, as opposed to ⲉⲡⲓⲥⲧⲟⲗⲏ or some other designation.

Another striking parallel between these corpora is in the tight association and fluidity between epistolary discourse and what is reported as spoken discourse. If in the monastic letter collections we see the same textual material floating between letters, florilegia, and *Apophthegmata*, at Nag Hammadi we find a clear fluidity between the letter and the dialogue. The most glaring example of this association is the distinctive literary relationship between *Eugnostos* and the *Wisdom of Jesus Christ*. The specific nature of this relationship – and especially between the multiple versions of each of these two texts – is exceptionally complicated. While the scholarly consensus today

53 Lundhaug and Jenott, *Monastic Origins*, 193.
54 Lundhaug and Jenott, *Monastic Origins*, 194.
55 Lundhaug and Jenott, *Monastic Origins*, 197.
56 "Virtually all scholars agree that this title ... is a secondary addition, appended either by the Coptic translator or a subsequent copyist-collector to facilitate identification or indexing of the writing. ... the title describes the content rather than the literary form of the document." Peel, "Treatise on the Resurrection," 128.

holds that the *Wisdom of Jesus Christ* is secondary to *Eugnostos*,[57] the nature of the variants between the version of *Eugnostos* in NHC V and the version in NHC III suggests a significant degree of editorial intervention, perhaps, in some instances, displaying awareness of the *Wisdom of Jesus Christ*.[58] Regardless of how one might chart the precise contours of this complex intertextual relationship, this much is clear: the very same material that is presented as a continuous letter in *Eugnostos* is broken up and placed in the mouth of Jesus in the dialogue staged in the *Wisdom of Jesus Christ*. In other words, from the perspective of the *Wisdom of Jesus Christ*, in *Eugnostos* we find a remarkably literal example of Artemon's conceptualization of letter composition, as reported by Demetrius sometime in the late Roman period: "a letter should be written in the same manner as a dialogue; the letter, he says, is like one of the two sides of a dialogue" (Demetrius, *Eloc.* 223 [Innes, LCL, slightly modified]).

This does not necessarily mean that we should confidently imagine Egyptian monks as the redactors who composed one of these texts out of the other (although it is certainly possible). Such an argument about the composition history would also need to account for the fourth-century papyrus codex fragment from Oxyrhynchus containing an excerpt from the *Wisdom of Jesus Christ* in Greek (P. Oxy. 1081). What we can now say, though, is that the type of textual practice in which one would take material from a letter, break it up, re-attribute it, and cast it as direct discourse – or in which one would take sayings of a revered figure and consolidate them into a text that would be recognizable as a "letter" – would be familiar to monastic readers in late antique Egypt. This context may well nuance how we evaluate, from a reader-response perspective, the curious fact that these two texts sit side-by-side in NHC III. Additionally, the high degree of fluidity in attribution that we have observed in the monastic letter collections – particularly in the textual material that floats between a "letter" form and "spoken" discourse – should add an additional note of caution against confidently reconstructing the name ⲉⲩⲅⲛⲟⲥⲧⲟⲥ in the incipit and subscript title of the NHC V version of text, which in both cases could theoretically fit ⲉⲩⲅⲛⲟⲥⲧⲟⲥ but definitely not his title ⲡⲙⲁⲕⲁⲣⲓⲟⲥ.[59]

If in the literary relationship between *Eugnostos* and the *Wisdom of Jesus Christ* we have a clear-cut example of a letter being literally transformed into a dialogue (or vice-versa), we find a different manifestation of this curious relationship between the letter and the dialogue in the *Letter of Peter to Philip* and the so-called *Apocryphon*

---

57 Pasquier, *Eugnoste (NH III,3 et V,1): lettre sur le Dieu transcendant* (BCNH.T 26; Québec: Les Presses de l'Université Laval; Leuven: Peeters, 2000), 1.

58 See discussion in Douglas M. Parrott, ed., *Nag Hammadi Codices III,3–4 and V,1 with Papyrus Berolinensis 8502,3 and Oxyrhynchus Papyrus 1081: Eugnostos and Sophia of Jesus Christ* (NHS 27; Leiden: Brill, 1991), 3–5.

59 See discussion of this possibility in Parrott, *Nag Hammadi Codices III,3–4 and V,1*, 2 and Pasquier, *Eugnoste*, 13–16.

of James.[60] As discussed above, both texts begin with a letter and then give way to a dialogue. In the *Letter of Peter to Philip*, the "letter" portion is clearly delimited as a self-contained document within the narrative. Formally speaking, given the clear titling of the *whole* text as "letter" and the incorporation of a complete document alongside a narrative episode and a dialogue, the *Letter of Ammon* represents a strong potential generic parallel, although the revelation dialogue portion of the text is closer to what we see in the *Epistula Apostolorum*.[61] It is the *Historia Horsiesi*, however, which presents the most striking formal parallel: both texts begin with the "cold open" of a supposedly private letter, presented in full, which is only retrospectively tied into the text's narrative frame;[62] both texts then rapidly proceed into a loosely-narrativized dialogue. (In fact, given these tight formal parallels, perhaps we should refer to this untitled Coptic text not as the *Historia Horsiesi* but as the *Letter of Apa Theophilos*.) Our monastic reader, then, would not need to assume that the *Letter of Peter to Philip* is a fragment of some larger Acts narrative; the attested form of the text fits well within the generic potential of the "letter" in early Egyptian monastic literature.

---

60 On the dialogue as a genre among the Nag Hammadi Codices, see Kurt Rudolph, "Der gnostische Dialog als literarische Genus," in *Probleme der koptischen Literatur* (ed. Peter Nagel; Halle: Martin-Luther-Universität, 1968), 85–107; Pheme Perkins, *The Gnostic Dialogue: The Early Church and the Crisis of Gnosticism* (New York: Paulist Press, 1980), 25–73; and Hills, *Tradition and Composition*, 10–36. In light of Lundhaug and Jenott's approach to the Nag Hammadi Codices and the analysis presented in this essay, it would be worth taking a closer look at the relationship between the "revelation dialogues" (formerly known, to some, as "Gnostic dialogues") in the Nag Hammadi treatises and the genres of *quaestiones, zetemata,* and/or *erotapokriseis* among early monastic literature. If the "revelation dialogues" found at Nag Hammadi and in the *Epistula Apostolorum* do, in fact, represent a distinct literary genre (as distinct from, for example, "classical" Platonic dialogues; see discussion in Hills, *Tradition and Composition*, 15–17), is it possible that this genre has its origins – or at least its *floruit* – in a monastic literary milieu? Would this particular type of narrativized teaching from Christ have enjoyed an especially warm reception among Egyptian monks?

61 Unlike the other comparanda adduced here, scholars of the Nag Hammadi Codices have long recognized the *Epistula Apostolorum* as a point of comparison with the Nag Hammadi texts – no doubt in large part because it too can be analyzed as a "New Testament Apocryphon." See, e.g., Ménard, *La Lettre de Pierre à Philippe*, 5; Peel, "Treatise on the Resurrection," 129.

62 This moment of transition between the end of the letter and the narrative interlude has only recently become available to scholars in the Codex Tchacos version, through the unpublished fragments shared online by Gregor Wurst. Lance Jenott is in the process of preparing a new synoptic edition of *Letter of Peter to Philip*, incorporating these newly available fragments. While the writing on the first page is, admittedly, very difficult to make out, one interesting feature of the Tchacos version is that ink traces suggest the possibility that the scribe may have filled out the line at the end of the opening letter with one or two diplai, gently but clearly setting it apart from the rest of the treatise. Such a subtle divider is reminiscent of what we see in the *Historia Horsiesi* manuscript (see Crum, *Der Papyruscodex*, 13).

As for the so-called *Apocryphon of James*, the clear formal parallels with the *Letter of Peter to Philip*, the *Letter of Ammon*, the *Historia Horsiesi*, and the *Epistula Apostolorum* suggest that English speakers should finally side with Michel Malinine, Donald Rouleau, and Dankwart Kirchner in referring to this text as the *(Apocryphal) Letter of James*.[63] I would argue that, by referring to the text as the "Apocryphon of James," we have undervalued the role of the letter form in relation to the secret teaching that it contains. In his introduction to the *Coptic Gnostic Library* edition of the text, Francis Williams argues for the title "Apocryphon of James," reasoning,

> The term "apocryphon" is taken from the document itself, and the alleged "apocryphon" ... is of far greater importance than the "letter." "*Epistula Apocrypha*," the *editio princeps'* choice for a title, seems inappropriate, since, while the recipient is directed to keep the "apocryphon" secret from all but a chosen few, the prohibition is not extended to the letter.[64]

While Williams himself notes the structural similarities between the two texts, he is evidently unmoved by the fact that the closest parallel, in terms of form and content, is clearly titled in NHC VIII the *Letter of Peter to Philip*.[65] I would argue that, based on the monastic context of the codex in which it is contained, not only is it plausible that a reader could understand the entire text as a "letter," but also that the generic status of this text as a letter is crucial to its esotericizing rhetorical posture.

In a 2010 article in the *Journal of Early Christian Studies*, Lance Jenott and Elaine Pagels demonstrated extensive thematic parallels between the letters of Antony and NHC I within the context of religious conflicts in fourth-century Egypt. They make a convincing case that Codex I cultivates within its readers the sensation of "belonging to a privileged group," a spiritual elite – precisely the same rhetorical strategy that Samuel Rubenson identifies as operative in the letters of Antony and other monastic letter collections.[66] As (what Jenott and Pagels refer to as) the *Secret Book of James* effectively opens NHC I after the brief *Prayer of the Apostle Paul*, Jenott and Pagels see it playing a pivotal role in establishing this rhetorical posture, which carries on throughout the rest of the codex. I find Jenott and Pagels' assessment quite convincing. But I would suggest further that the *letter form* of the *(Apocryphal) Letter of James* is a key component of the text's (and, therefore, the codex's) rhetorical strategy.

---

63 Michel Malinine, *Epistula Jacobi apocrypha: Codex Jung F. Ir-F.VIIr* (Zurich: Rascher, 1968). Donald Rouleau, *L'Épître apocryphe de Jacques (NH I,2)* (BCNH.T 18; Quebec: Les Presses de l'Université Laval, 1987). Dankwart Kirchner, *Epistula Jacobi Apocrypha: die zweite Schrift aus Nag-Hammadi Codex I* (TUGAL 136; Berlin: Akademie-Verlag, 1989).
64 Williams, "The Apocryphon of James," 16.
65 Although he himself notes the literary relationship: Williams, "The Apocryphon of James," 18.
66 Lance Jenott and Elaine Pagels, "Antony's Letters and Nag Hammadi Codex I: Sources of Religious Conflict in Fourth–Century Egypt," *JECS* 18 (2010): 588. See also Rubenson, "Argument and Authority," 80–81.

One consistent function of the "letter" that we see across the monastic and Nag Hammadi examples is the clear signaling to the reader that she or he is gaining access to privileged information.[67] As Rubenson has argued, letters rhetorically create an in-group, populated by the inscribed author of the letter and the addressees. But letters also, very frequently, explicitly anticipate interlopers, either taking evasive action to forestall their interpretive efforts (as in the case of the cryptography in Pachomius' letters) or inviting the third party to join the ranks of the addressees (as in the closing blessing of the *Treatise on the Resurrection*, "Many are looking into this which I have written to you. To these I say: peace (be) among them and grace."[68]) The *(Apocryphal) Letter of James* hits the rhetorical-esoteric sweet spot: openly sharing the content of an explicitly secret teaching from Jesus, but shrouding it in the intimate form of a letter, supposedly for the eyes of the addressee only. Any interloping reader (that is, *any* reader) is dramatically assured that she or he is gaining access to truly exclusive knowledge.

Conclusions

The observations collected here only scratch the surface of the interpretive possibilities occasioned by attentive contextualization of these four texts from the Nag Hammadi Codices within the literature of late antique Egypt. I have shown how the peculiar dynamics of the generic fluidity of the letter within this milieu can enrich our understanding of several of the more unfamiliar generic features of these texts, but this hardly exhausts the comparative work to be done. I hope that I have laid the groundwork here for more fine-grained and systematic analyses. While the primary focus of this essay has been the exegetical payoff for readers of the Nag Hammadi Codices, it is equally important to recognize the reciprocal implications of the New Philological turn in the study of the Nag Hammadi texts: these texts can also now expand our understanding of the literary world of early Egyptian monasticism. In other words, not only are the Nag Hammadi "letters" illuminated by these new monastic comparanda, they also represent "new" data in the lively analysis of early monastic epistolarity.

To be sure, letters are not the only way to rhetorically carve out an elite in-group, nor are they the only genre appropriate for transmitting esoteric knowledge. But perhaps because of the special association they seem to have with the spoken word, letters are a popular and effective strategy in early Egyptian monastic literature for

---

67 The same could no doubt also be said of the role of the letter in other literary and philosophical discourses, in other times and places in antiquity. This merits a closer look.

68 *Treat. Res.* 50.12–15: ογη ϩⲁϩ ϭⲱϣⲧ ⲁϩⲟγη ⲁⲡⲉⲉⲓ ⲡⲉⲉⲓ ⲛ̄ⲧⲁⲉⲓⲥϩⲉⲉⲓ ⲙ̄ⲙⲁϥ ⲛⲉⲕ ⲛⲉⲉⲓ ϯⲧⲁⲙⲟ ⲙ̄ⲙⲁγ ⲁϯⲣⲏⲛⲏ ⲛ̄ϩⲏⲧⲟγ ⲙ̄ⲛ ⲧⲉⲭⲁⲣⲓⲥ. Translation Peel.

accomplishing both of these goals, and the generic flexibility of the "letter," I would argue, is both a result and a facilitator of these goals. If within the monastic milieu, at the very least, such a rhetorical function is one of the primary purposes of the literary letter, this may help us understand the reasons why the letter enjoys such diverse generic possibilities. It is clearly not the case that all "letters" must ultimately derive from "real" letters and their transmitters had no choice but to faithfully convey them as such.[69] Writers, editors, and scribes cast religious teachings as a letter – whether in title or form – for specific rhetorical purposes. In so doing, they have signaled to us that they are not particularly concerned with policing the generic borders that we modern scholars have tried to build for them.

Bibliography

Choat, Malcolm. "Monastic Letter Collections in Late Antique Egypt: Structure, Purpose, and Trans-
    mission." Pages 73–90 in *Cultures in Contact: Transfer of Knowledge in the Mediterranean
    Context: Selected Papers*. Edited by Sofía Torallas Tovar and Juan Pedro Monferrer-Sala.
    Cordoba: CNREU-CEDRAC, Oriens Academic, 2013.
–. "The Epistolary Culture of Monasticism between Literature and Papyri," *Cistercian Studies
    Quarterly* 48.3 (2013): 227–37.
–. "From Letter to Letter-Collection: Monastic Epistolography in Late-Antique Egypt." Pages 80–93
    in *Collecting Early Christian Letters: From the Apostle Paul to Late Antiquity*. Edited by Bronwen
    Neil and Pauline Allen. Cambridge: Cambridge University Press, 2015.
Crum, Walter E. *Der Papyruscodex saec. VI–VII der Philippsbibliothek in Cheltenham: Koptische
    theologische Schriften*. Schriften der Wissenschaftlichen Gesellschaft in Straßburg 18. Stras-
    bourg: Trübner, 1915.
Deissmann, Adolf. *Light from the Ancient East: The New Testament Illustrated by Recently Discovered
    Texts of the Graeco-Roman World*. Translated by Lionel R. M. Strachan. New York: Hodder &
    Stoughton, 1910.
Demetrius. *On Style*. Translated by Doreen C. Innes. Loeb Classical Library 199. Cambridge, Mass.:
    Harvard University Press, 1995.
Emmel, Stephen. *Shenoute's Literary Corpus*. 2 Vols. Corpus Scriptorum Christianorum Orientalium
    599–600, Subsidia 111–12. Leuven: Peeters, 2004.
Farag, George. "Les Lettres attribuées à Antonie dans la deuxième collection arabe (Lettres 8 à 20):
    sont-elles d'Antoine ou d'Ammonas? Étude comparée des différentes versions et interpretation
    théologique." PhD diss., University of Strasbourg, 2012.
Goehring, James E. *The Letter of Ammon and Pachomian Monasticism*. Patristiche Texte und Studien
    27. Berlin: Walter de Gruyter, 1986.
Hills, Julian V. *Tradition and Composition in the Epistula Apostolorum*. Harvard Theological Studies
    57. Cambridge, Mass.: Harvard University Press, 2008.

---

69 Samuel Rubenson strikes a brilliant note of caution against the scholarly assumption that it is possible to parse "real," "factual" letters from "fictional," "literary" ones in his essay, "To Tell the Truth: Fact and Fiction in Early Monastic Sources," *CSQ* 48:3 (2013): 317–24.

Jenott, Lance, and Elaine Pagels. "Antony's Letters and Nag Hammadi Codex I: Sources of Religious Conflict in Fourth-Century Egypt." *Journal of Early Christian Studies* 18 (2010): 557–89.

Joest, Christoph. *Die Pachom-Briefe: Übersetzung und Deutung.* Corpus Scriptorum Christianorum Orientalium 655, Subsidia 133. Leuven: Peeters, 2014.

Kasser, Rudolph, and Gregor Wurst, eds. *The Gospel of Judas together with the Letter of Peter to Philip, James, and a Book of Allogenes from Codex Tchacos: Critical Edition.* Washington, D. C.: National Geographic, 2007.

Kirchner, Dankwart. *Epistula Jacobi Apocrypha: die zweite Schrift aus Nag-Hammadi Codex I.* Texte und Untersuchungen zur Geschichte der altchristlichen Literatur 136. Berlin: Akademie-Verlag, 1989.

Klauk, Hans-Josef. *Ancient Letters and the New Testament: A Guide to Context and Exegesis.* Translated by Daniel P. Bailey. Waco, Tex.: Baylor University Press, 2006.

Layton, Bentley, ed. "The Hypostasis of the Archons." Pages 1:234–59 in *Nag Hammadi Codex II, 2–7 together with XIII,2*, Brit. Lib. Or. 4926(1), and P.Oxy. 1, 654, 655.* Edited by Bentley Layton. 2 Vols. Nag Hammadi Studies 20–21. Leiden: Brill, 1989.

Lundhaug, Hugo, and Lance Jenott. *The Monastic Origins of the Nag Hammadi Codices.* Studien und Texte zu Antike und Christentum 97. Tübingen: Mohr Siebeck, 2015.

Malinine, Michel. *Epistula Jacobi apocrypha: Codex Jung F. Ir-F.VIIr.* Zurich: Rascher, 1968.

McNary-Zak, Bernadette. *Letters and Asceticism in Fourth-Century Egypt.* Lanham, Md.: University Press of America: 2000.

Ménard, Jacques É. *La Lettre de Pierre à Philippe: Texte établi et présenté.* Bibliothèque Copte de Nag Hammadi, Section "Textes" 1. Quebec: Les Presses de l'Université Laval, 1977.

Meyer, Marvin, ed. "NHC VII, 2: The Letter of Peter to Philip." Pages 227–51 in *Nag Hammadi Codex VIII.* Edited by John H. Sieber. Nag Hammadi Studies 31. Leiden: Brill, 1991.

Müller, C. Detlef G., ed. "Epistula Apostolorum." Pages 1:249–84 in *New Testament Apocrypha.* Edited by Wilhelm Schneemelcher. Translated by Robert McL. Wilson. 2 Vols. Louisville, Ky.: Westminster John Knox Press, 2003.

Nongbri, Brent. "2 Corinthians and Possible Material Evidence for Composite Letters in Antiquity" Pages 54–67 in *Collecting Early Christian Letters: From the Apostle Paul to Late Antiquity.* Edited by Bronwen Neil and Pauline Allen. Cambridge: Cambridge University Press, 2015.

Orlandi, Tito. "Due fogli papiracei da Medinet Madi (Fayum): L'historia Horsiesi." *Egitto e Vicino Oriente* 13 (1990): 109–26.

–. "The Library of the Monastery of Saint Shenute at Atripe." Pages 211–30 *Perspectives on Panopolis: an Egyptian Town from Alexander the Great to the Arab Conquest.* Edited by Arthur Egberts, Brian Paul Muhs, and Joep van der Vliet. Leiden: Brill, 2002.

Parrott, Douglas M., ed. *Nag Hammadi Codices III,3–4 and V,1 with Papyrus Berolinensis 8502,3 and Oxyrhynchus Papyrus 1081: Eugnostos and Sophia of Jesus Christ.* Nag Hammadi Studies 27. Leiden: Brill, 1991.

Pasquier, Anne. *Eugnoste (NH III,3 et V,1): lettre sur le Dieu transcendant.* Bibliothèque Copte de Nag Hammadi, Section "Textes" 26. Quebec: Les Presses de l'Université Laval; Leuven: Peeters, 2000.

Peel, Malcolm L., ed. "The Treatise on the Resurrection." Pages 123–57 in *Nag Hammadi Codex I (The Jung Codex): Introductions, Texts, Translations, Indices.* Edited by Harold W. Attridge. Nag Hammadi Studies 22. Leiden: Brill, 1985.

Perkins, Pheme. *The Gnostic Dialogue: The Early Church and the Crisis of Gnosticism.* New York: Paulist Press, 1980.

Rouleau, Donald. *L'Épître apocryphe de Jacques (NH I,2).* Bibliothèque Copte de Nag Hammadi, Section "Textes" 18. Quebec: Les Presses de l'Université Laval, 1987.

Rousseau, Philip. "The Successors of Pachomius and the Nag Hammadi Codices: Exegetical Themes and Literary Structures." Pages 140–57 in *The World of Early Egyptian Christianity*. Edited by James E. Goehring, Janet A. Timbie, and D. W. Johnson. Washington, D. C.: The Catholic University of America Press, 2012.

Rubenson, Samuel. The Letters of St. Antony: Monasticism and the Making of a Saint. Studies in Antiquity and Christianity. Minneapolis: Fortress Press, 1995.

–. "Argument and Authority in Early Monastic Correspondence." Pages 75–87 in *Foundations of Power and Conflicts of Authority in Late-Antique Monasticism*. Edited by Alberto Camplani and Giovanni Filoramo. Orientalia Lovaniensia Analecta 157. Leuven: Peeters, 2007.

–. "To Tell the Truth: Fact and Fiction in Early Monastic Sources." *Cistercian Studies Quarterly* 48:3 (2013): 317–24.

–. "The Letter-Collections of Antony and Ammonas: Shaping a Community." Pages 68–79 in *Collecting Early Christian Letters: From the Apostle Paul to Late Antiquity*. Edited by Bronwen Neil and Pauline Allen. Cambridge: Cambridge University Press, 2015.

Rudolph, Kurt. "Der gnostische Dialog als literarische Genus." Pages 85–107 in *Probleme der koptischen Literatur*. Edited by Peter Nagel. Halle: Martin-Luther-Universität, 1968.

Schmidt, Carl, ed. *Gespräche Jesu mit seinen Jüngern nach der Auferstehung: ein katholisch-apostolisches Sendschreiben des 2. Jahrhunderts*. Texte und Untersuchungen zur Geschichte der altchristlichen Literatur 43. Leipzig: Hinrichs, 1919.

Shaw, Richard. "Textual Disorder in the Letters of St. Antony: An Analysis and Partial Reconstruction. Part I: Disorder in the Canon." *Downside Review* 131.462 (Jan. 2013): 1–14. "Part II: The Likelihood of Disorder – The Letters in Context." 131.463 (Apr. 2013): 59–68. "Part III: Possibilities of Reconstruction – A Lost Letter of St. Antony?" 131.464 (Jul. 2013): 117–30.

Williams, Francis E., ed. "The Apocryphon of James." Pages 13–53 in *Nag Hammadi Codex I (The Jung Codex): Introductions, Texts, Translations, Indices*. Edited by Harold W. Attridge. Nag Hammadi Studies 22. Leiden: Brill, 1985.

Michael Philip Penn
Know Thy Enemy:
The Materialization of Orthodoxy in Syriac
Manuscripts

Even among early Christians, a group renown for their downright cantankerousness, the ancient Syriac churches stood out in their ability not to get along. Particularly contentious were the Christological controversies that quickly divided Syriac Christianity into several competing factions. By the end of the seventh century, these ongoing debates over how to best express Christ's humanity and Christ's divinity resulted in no less than four separate Syriac churches: 1) the East Syrians who more strongly emphasized Christ's dual nature and rejected the 431 CE Council of Ephesus that had anathematized the Greek theologian Nestorius (often called by their opponents Nestorians); 2) the Chalcedonians who supported the 451 CE decisions of the Council of Chalcedon and were thus theologically aligned with the imperial Byzantine church (often called Melkites from the Syriac word malkā, that is king or emperor); 3) the Miaphysites who opposed the Council of Chalcedon and instead stressed Christ's single nature (often called by their opponents monophysites or Jacobites); and 4) the Maronites who supported the Council of Chalcedon but in the late seventh century broke away from their fellow Chalcedonians over monothelitism, the belief that though Christ had two natures, he had a single will.[1]

---

1 The scholarly literature on the Christological controversies is unbelievably vast. A standard reference remains Alois Grillmeier, *Jesus der Christus im Glauben der Kirche* (2 vols.; Freiburg im Breisgau: Herder, 1979–1990). For some more recent (and concise) discussions that focus on the controversies' impact on Syriac Christianity especially, see Wilhelm Baum and Dietmar W. Winkler, *Die Apostolische Kirche des Ostens: Geschichte der sogenannten Nestorianer* (Klagenfurt: Verlag Kitab, 2000), 25–34, translated in Wilhelm Baum and Dietmar W. Winkler, *The Church of the East: A Concise History* (New York: Routledge, 2003), 21–32; Sebastian P. Brock, "The 'Nestorian' Church: A Lamentable Misnomer," *BJRL* 78 (1996): 32–35; Susan Ashbrook Harvey, *Asceticism and Society in Crisis: John of Ephesus and the Lives of the Eastern Saints* (Berkely: University of California Press, 1990), 21–27; Andrew Louth, "Why Did the Syrians Reject the Council of Chalcedon?" in *Chalcedon in Context: Church Councils, 400–700* (ed. Richard Price and Mary Whitby; Liverpool: Liverpool University Press, 2009), 107–16; Gerrit J. Reinink, "Tradition and the Formation of the 'Nestorian' Identity in Sixth- to Seventh-Century Iraq," *CHRC* 89 (2009): 217–50; Lucas Van Rompay, "The East (3): Syria and Mesopotamia," in *The Oxford Handbook of Early Christian Studies* (ed. Susan Ashbrook Harvey and David G. Hunter; Oxford: Oxford University Press, 2008), 376–78; Lucas Van Rompay, "Society and Community in the Christian East," in *The Cambridge Companion to the Age of Justinian* (ed. Michael Maas; Cambridge: Cambridge University Press, 2004), 239–66; Adam M. Schor, *Theodoret's People: Social Networks and Religious Conflict in Late Roman Syria* (Transformation of the Classical Heritage; Berkeley: University of California Press, 2011), 3–5; Uriel I. Simonsohn, *A Common Justice: The Legal Allegiances of Christians and Jews under Early Islam* (Philadelphia: University of Pennsylvania Press, 2011), 2–3. For a brief

Modern scholars have frequently examined how these divides affected theology, polity, social networks, and literary narratives. It may, however, be fruitful to examine these issues from a slightly different angle. Focusing on Syriac manuscript culture, I want to explore how the Christological controversies changed the ways early Christians wrote and read the manuscripts now held in the British Library, the world's largest collection of ancient Syriac texts. Among Syriac Christians, such changes became particularly prevalent when having to deal with a phenomenon I call "know thy enemy."

Due to the Christological controversies, Syriac Christians were faced with a serious dilemma. In order to debate Christological opponents they needed to have accurate copies of their adversaries' beliefs. But how could a Miaphysite preserve in good conscience writings from the Council of Chalcedon that he so adamantly opposed? How should a loyal East Syrian read the Council of Ephesus that condemned Nestorius? Extant manuscripts preserve a variety of strategies that Syriac Christians employed in such circumstances. Textualized tactics such as narrative framing, reading marks, and marginalia witness theological differences becoming material differences and suggest that surviving materials can help one better understand the social dynamics of early Christianity.

Knowing thy enemy became particularly important for Syriac Christians because the Byzantine, Sassanian, and early Islamic empires in which they dwelled were empires of disputation. In each, imperial authorities often sponsored public, theological debates.[2] For example, the courts of Justinian (d. 565) and later Byzantine rulers would patronize and help adjudicate public disputations between competing groups of Christians. The Sassanians were even fonder of such disputes, and one hears of Persian rulers sponsoring contests between Miaphysite and East Syrian Christians.

---

overview of recent research on the Christological controversies, see Averil Cameron, "Introduction," in *Chalcedon in Context: Church Councils 400–700* (ed. Richard Price and Mary Whitby; Liverpool: Liverpool University Press, 2009), 1–6

2 For a useful analysis of the various roles of public disputations in late antiquity before the sixth century, see Richard Lim, *Public Disputation, Power, and Social Order in Late Antiquity* (Berkeley: University of California Press, 1995). For a discussion of sixth- through eighth-century disputations in both the Roman and Sassanian Empires, see David Bertaina, *Christian and Muslim Dialogues: The Religious Uses of a Literary Form in the Early Islamic Middle East* (Piscataway: Gorgias Press, 2011), 10, 37, 41, 236–37, 246; Averil Cameron, "Disputations, Polemical Literature and the Formation of Opinion in the Early Byzantine Period," in *Dispute Poems and Dialogues in the Ancient and Mediaeval Near East: Forms and Types of Literary Debates in Semitic and Related Literatures* (ed. Gerrit J. Reinink and H. L. J. Vanstiphout; Leuven: Peeters, 1991), 101–4; Jamsheed K. Choksy, *Conflict and Cooperation: Zoroastrian Subalterns and Muslim Elites in Medieval Iranian Society* (New York: Columbia University Press, 1997), 31; Joel Thomas Walker, *The Legend of Mar Qardagh: Narrative and Christian Heroism in Late Antique Iraq* (Berkeley: University of California Press, 2006), 172–80.

A surviving East Syrian document was even written as preparation for just such an occasion.[3] Early Muslim rulers continued this tradition.[4]

Although only a small number of Syriac Christians would ever participate in an imperially sponsored contest, surviving Syriac manuscripts reflect this culture of disputation and are filled with texts defending each community's Christological stance while attacking the positions of their opponents. Undoubtedly, most of these texts were meant more to reassure the faithful than to help persuade outsiders. But regardless of whether Syriac authors envisioned their mission as preparing readers for public debates, serving as a ready resource to help in the composition of future theological tractates, or simply assuring the sympathetic reader of the correctness of their community's theology, all faced a similar problem. Each of these tasks required knowledge of what the opposition believed. That is, to write against the creed of the Council of Chalcedon or against the decisions of the Council of Ephesus or against Leo's *Tome* you first had to discern what these documents said in the first place. To debate the opposition you first had to know thy enemy. As a result, Miaphysite manuscripts are filled with quotations from Chalcedonian theologians, East Syrian manuscripts are filled with quotations from Miaphysite theologians, and so forth. Ironically, one needed heterogeneous manuscripts and heterodox texts in order to defend a homogenous view of orthodoxy.

The necessity of accurately preserving the texts of ones' opponents did not mean this was a pleasant or unproblematic undertaking. Pity the poor scribes who had to slowly and painstakingly copy dozens of pages they found to be theologically abhorrent. Even more disturbing, could such activity be theologically suspect? Manuscript colophons often reflected the belief that the meticulous transcription of laudatory texts provided the careful scribe with theological benefits in the world to come. Might the converse be true? And even if a Syriac scribe was not concerned about the ramification upon his own soul, what about that of his orthodox readership? Might their reading of heretical texts adversely affect their spiritual welfare? Worse yet, what if

---

3 Walker, *The Legend of Mar Qardagh*, 174–80.

4 *Maronite Chronicle* (Ignazio Guidi and E. W. Brooks, *Chronica minora* [CSCO 3, Scriptores Syri 3; Paris: L. Durbecq 1904], 70). For Islamic sources on public theological debates, see Sidney H. Griffith, "Answering the Call of the Minaret: Christian Apologetics in the World of Islam," in *Redefining Christian Identity: Cultural Interaction in the Middle East Since the Rise of Islam* (ed. Heleen L. Murre-Van den Berg, Jan J. Van Ginkel, and Theo M. Van Lint; OLA 134; Leuven: Peeters, 2005), 120–23; Sidney H. Griffith, "Answering the Call of the Minaret. The Topics and Strategies of Christian Apologetics in the World of Islam," in *Die Suryoye und ihre Umwelt* (ed. Andreas Heinz Martin Tamcke; Münster: Lit Verlag, 2005), 36; Sidney H. Griffith, "The Monk in the Emir's Majlis: Reflections on a Popular Genre of Christian Literary Apologetics in Arabic in the Early Islamic Period," in *The Majlis: Interreligious Encounters in Medieval Islam* (ed. Hava Lazarus-Yafeh et al.; SALL 4; Wiesbaden: Harrassowitz, 1999), 60–65.

future readers did not realize that the excerpt they were reading was heterodox and an inattentive reader was swayed by its content?

Narrative Framing

One strategy Syriac writers used to guard against such scenarios was the use of narrative framing. When they included a passage from a text considered particularly heretical these writers might also include a brief prologue or epilogue indicating their disagreement with what they were copying. For example, consider the eighth-century manuscript British Library Additional 14,532 that is titled "a volume of demonstrations from the holy fathers against various heresies."[5] These heresies are so various that it takes the manuscript 433 pages and no less than 334 subsections to address them! The greatest concern is Christology and the author compiled hundreds of patristic excerpts to battle theological opponents ranging from Julian of Halicarnassus to John Grammaticus. As part of its opening section, a seventy-page defense of Miaphysite Christology, the manuscript follows the typical pattern of including excerpts from the opposition and thus presents several quotations from the Council of Chalcedon. These passages are fairly accurate in content. Nevertheless, the author was particularly careful in how he framed the Chalcedonian creed. In red ink he introduces this anti-Miaphysite creed as: "The definition [of faith] that was established by the Council of Chalcedon. Having already misled the simple, they made this definition ..." (Fig. 19).[6] With such an introduction there could be little doubt as to the author's opinion about this council and how he wished his readership to view the creed as well.

Even more involved were the efforts by the anonymous Miaphysite scribe of a most likely seventh-century collection of church canons now known as British Library Additional 14,526. To create this compendium of canons the author drew upon previous documents ranging from the fourth-century *Constitution of the Holy Apostles* to canons from the various ecumenical councils.[7] Most of these he passed over without comment. But when this Miaphysite scribe (or his exemplar) reached the decisions of the Council of Chalcedon, it was too much. The extant manuscript presents an accu-

---

5 William Wright, *Catalogue of Syriac Manuscripts in the British Museum Acquired Since the Year 1838, Volume 2* (London: Cambridge University Press, 1871), 955–67.
6 BL Add. 14,532, f. 22b. The same narrative frame appears in BL Add. 14,538, f. 93a which is dependent upon this section of the most likely tenth-century BL Add. 14,532 or upon a shared exemplar.
7 Wright, *Catalogue of Syriac Manuscripts*, 1033–36. Wright dates the manuscript on paleographic grounds to the seventh century. He also notes that the manuscript includes a list of Byzantine emperors starting with Constantine the Great and ending with Constantine III. Wright suggests that since this list does not include Constantine III's successor the manuscript was most likely written during the one year Constantine III reigned which is 641 CE. It, however, certainly remains possible that BL Add. 14,526 could have itself been written at a later date and simply included an earlier king list.

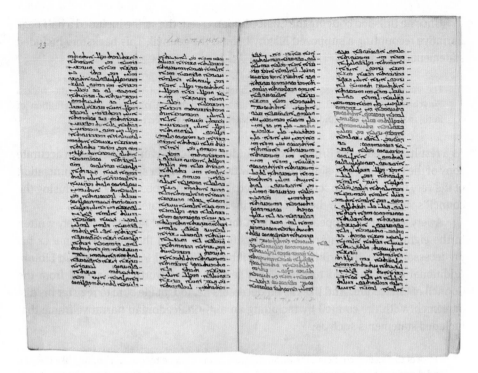

Fig. 19: British Library Additional 14,532, ff. 22b–23a. This most likely eighth-century Miaphysite manuscript includes numerous quotations from pro-Chalcedonian sources. On these two pages the scribe had to include a number of citations from the Council of Chalcedon itself. Although he copied these accurately, he added an anti-Chalcedonian narrative before and after the conciliar decisions. So, too, the page includes a number of marginal reading marks to warn future readers that these quotations were to be considered heterodox. © The British Library Board, Add 14,532.

rate transcription of the Chalcedonian creed but frames it with a particularly extensive set of comments. These begin with an incipit stating:

> Next, the creed or indeed the new definition [of faith] of the council that was gathered in Chalcedon on whose account there arose divisions and strife among [all] the churches under heaven. Its confession is like that of the iniquitous Nestorius and like that of Leo of Rome.[8]

The claim that the Christology of the council of Chalcedon and its supporter Pope Leo were essentially the same as the "arch-heretic" Nestorius' is a common diatribe found among Miaphysite theological tractates. Now a Miaphysite scribe repurposed it as a topic heading for the council itself.

---

8 BL Add. 14,526, f. 36a.

Once he finished copying the Chalcedonian creed, the scribe included a half page narrative recounting a supposed history behind the council. This backstory included statements such as

> The council was gathered in Chalcedon allegedly because of the doctrine of the wicked Eutyches ... But as we said, in truth, it was gathered with the goal of establishing a definition [of faith] that would affirm and strengthen the teaching of the wicked Nestorius.[9]

As a result, the reader of British Library Additional 14,526 can still access an accurate copy of the Council's decision but it is now framed on either side with a denunciation of the very words that the scribe had copied. There is little possibility of confusing the council's viewpoints with those of the scribe or his anticipated audience.

A very similar tact appears in British Library Additional 14,533 most likely written in the eight or ninth century. Its Miaphysite scribe faced the same dilemma as his predecessors. Like the scribes of British Library Additional 14,532 and British Library Additional 14,526 he had to copy down several pages worth of material from the Council of Chalcedon. And like his predecessors he, too, made sure to register his disagreement with the council by including an anti-Chalcedonian narrative frame that included statements such as:

> Those of Chalcedon condemn the incarnate word being a single nature. ... Thus just like the goal and doctrine of the Nestorians, they rend Christ into two natures. They wrote with the [same] craftiness that Nestorius had used aiding him against [Saint] Cyril and tearing apart the orthodox doctrine of the single nature of God, the incarnate word.[10]

Although these manuscripts came from different hands all of these scribes confronted a similar problem: having to preserve decisions from a council they despised. And they all came up with similar solutions: framing their accurate depiction of the council's decisions with brief comments and narratives sharing their discord with those very decisions. Undoubtedly, this served to help allay the scribe's own conscience and likely, from his perspective, vouchsafed his spiritual well-being. But it also indicated for later readers how they too were to approach the preserved text. That is, these incipits and brief narratives warned future readers that what they were reading was not edifying but rather enemy territory.

---

9 BL Add. 14,526, f. 38b.
10 BL Add. 14,533, f. 13a.

Reading Marks

For many, however, the concern for how to affect a compatriot's reading experience resulted in more extensive interventions than a simple narrative frame. Particularly popular were marginal markings to help orient the reader and reinforce whether a given quotation was considered as orthodox or heretical. This textual tactic became especially prevalent among *catenae* manuscripts.

One of the most popular genre of early Syriac manuscripts were compilations of patristic quotations primarily focusing on issues of Christology. Sometimes, these *catenae* manuscripts included entire documents relevant to the topic. But often they were in the form of thousands of shorter patristic quotations compiled from hundreds of documents. As with other types of Syriac manuscripts, these collections frequently included excerpts that the compiler considered heretical so that he could present the opposition's viewpoint only later to dispute it. As a result, a single manuscript page could include dozens of quotations from those authors considered orthodox intermingled with dozens from those authors considered heretical.

Usually, scribes headed each quotation with a brief bibliographic citation, noting the excerpt's origins. Few alert Miaphysite readers would be caught unaware by a passage labeled "from Nestorius" or East Syrians by one "from the Council of Ephesus." But what about less well known figures? Or what about the many times these headings simply begin "from the same [author]"? Or, even more likely, what if after reading hundreds of such selections the reader was beginning to doze off? Wasn't there the real danger that an inattentive reader might accidentally confuse orthodox and heretical passages?

To help prevent this from happening, many Syriac manuscripts incorporated a series of marks to help even the most careless reader navigate the boundaries of orthodoxy. There never emerges a completely standardized system of such markings. They differ greatly in shape and frequency. Some appear original to the manuscript. Some may have been added later. Many show dependence upon exemplars.

It seems likely that the origin of these various markings is connected with another, even more ubiquitous annotation in Syriac manuscripts. Hundreds of extant Syriac manuscripts include marginal notations, most often angle brackets, to distinguish when the text is directly quoting from scripture. These reading marks alerted future readers to give particular regard to these extracts. In some ways they were the ancient equivalents of a "red letter bible," the practice begun in the late nineteenth century of using red print to emphasize words the gospels quote as being said by Jesus.[11] In Syriac manuscripts, marking a quotation as scriptural did not simply convey author-

---

11 Philip Sellew, "Red Letter Bible," in *The Oxford Guide to Ideas & Issues of the Bible* (ed. Michael D. Coogan and Bruce M. Metzger; Oxford: Oxford University Press, 2001), 422.

ity upon that particular citation but also upon the arguments the text's author was supporting by that extract.

Almost completely unknown in modern scholarship, however, is that Syriac scribes often used similar marks to distinguish which parts of the text they considered orthodox from which parts belonged to the enemy.[12] For example, reconsider the pages from British Library Additional 14,532 reproduced in Fig. 19. As previously noted, this eighth-century Miaphysite manuscript uses narrative framing in its presentation of the Council of Chalcedon. But in this case the scribe went one step further and throughout much of the manuscript used marginal marks to point out other passages that he also considered to be heretical. At first, the scribe used the symbol of a line, not to indicate edifying quotations from scripture, but rather "heretical" quotations such as those from Nestorius or those from the Council of Chalcedon. Often these interventions are quite extensive such as when the scribe quotes several folia worth of material from the Council of Chalcedon and marks every line of it. But this is not the only type of reading mark this scribe employed. Later in the manuscript one finds a slightly more involved set of notations. In a section concerning the Miaphysite adversary John Grammaticus the scribe not only continues to mark those passages the scribe thought were heretical. He also supplements this system with another set of reading marks, in this case an angle bracket, that he places next to those quotations coming from folks he considered orthodox, such as Basil, Athanasius, and Severus. He thus marked both the bad guys and the good guys. A similar practice of using different reading marks to distinguish orthodox quotations from heretical ones occurs in a number of other manuscripts such as the most likely eighth- or ninth-century British Library Additional 14,629.[13]

In many manuscripts, such reading marks became quite extensive. For example the most likely tenth-century British Library Additional 14,538 marks 169 passages as heretical; the most likely eighth- or ninth-century British Library Additional 14,532 marks 150; the most likely seventh-century British Library Additional 14,533 marks 89; the most likely seventh-century British Library Additional 14,603 marks 80. Some scribes, though, were much more modest such as that of the most likely eight- or ninth-century British Library Additional 14,629 who only marked 7.[14] The list of enemies was also often quite wide-ranging. For example, there are almost a dozen

---

12 The only examples I am familiar with of modern scholars who discuss these marks are a brief reference found in Wright, *Catalogue of Syriac Manuscripts*, 549, which notes reading marks in BL Add. 17,210. Over a century later George Anton Kiraz, *A Grammar of the Syriac Language: Volume 1: Orthography* (Piscataway, N. J.: Gorgias Press, 2012), 118, plate 5 cites this remark and provides a color plate of a folio from BL Add. 17,210.

13 For manuscripts' content and approximate date of composition see Wright, *Catalogue of Syriac Manuscripts*, 955–67, 754–56.

14 For manuscripts' content and approximate date of composition see Wright, *Catalogue of Syriac Manuscripts*, 1003–8, 967–76, 286–87, 754–56.

figures whom the scribe of British Library Additional 14,532 clearly disliked such as Nestorius, Leo, Theodoret, and Eunomius.

These markings show other patterns as well. Given the number of quotations that appear in these *catenae* texts, it is not surprising that scribes occasionally missed a reference.[15] But in other cases only specific works of an author would be targeted. For example, a scribe might mark passages from the *Tome of Leo* but leave some of Leo's letters unmarked.[16] Alternatively, sometimes a scribe would mark only part of a "heretical" passage; instead of marking an entire quote, only those sections he found most offensive. So too, there are several cases of where an author the scribe saw as orthodox had himself quoted someone both considered to be heretical. Here the scribe often only marked the quote within the quote for example, when Basil (considered by the scribe as orthodox) quotes Eunomius (considered by the scribe as heretical) or Peter of Anitioch quotes Damian of Alexandria.[17]

Not all manuscript copies of a given text were marked. For example, the most likely eighth-century British Library Additional 14,532 and the most likely eighth- or ninth-century British Library Additional 14,533 share much of the same text but in many of these cases only the British Library Additional 14,532 version contains reading marks.[18] Often only a few of the documents in a given manuscript were marked up. Then, even in the same manuscript, other documents from the same suspect author or other documents quoting that author had no markings at all.[19] So too various sections in extant manuscripts often contain different systems of annotation. In some cases they simply mark alleged heretics. In other cases they mark both the heretical and the orthodox. In still others they distinguish when an orthodox author is himself quoting from a heretical one or the other way around. At other points they may make no marking at all. In such cases it remains quite likely that some sections may have been compiled (either by that scribe or his predecessors) from exemplars that had different types and degrees of reading marks. In other words, just as Syriac scribes often felt certain manuscript elements such as scholia were important enough parts

---

15 For example, BL Add. 12,155 contains 46 quotations from Julian of Halicarnassus and marks 45 of them (it misses one on 75a). BL Add. 14,629 has a less impressive ratio when quoting Julian missing one out of eight (19a). Other examples of clear mistakes include BL Add. 14,532, ff. 64b, 65a which twice forgets to mark a quotation from the otherwise marked Julian and BL Add. 12,155, f. 38b that misses a passage from Probus.

16 BL Add. 12,155, ff. 37b, 50a, 52b–53a include marks next to Leo's *Tome* but BL Add. 12,155, ff. 45a–45b cite Leo's *Letters* but leave them unmarked.

17 BL Add. 14,532, f. 121b; BL Add. 14,532, ff. 132a–132b.

18 E.g. compare the same documents that appear in BL Add. 14,532, ff. 36a–79a and BL Add. 14,533, ff. 52a–73a, as well as BL Add. 14,532, ff. 94b – 133b and BL Add. 14,533, ff. 73a–89a. In both cases BL Add. 14,532 has reading marks but BL Add. 14,533 does not.

19 E.g. consider BL Add. 12,154 or BL Add. 14,533 that even breaks off reading marks part way through a section when it marks up the first thirty-two folios of a section but not the final eighteen (BL Add. 14,533, ff. 1a–32a versus ff. 32a–50a).

of an exemplar to be preserved verbatim, so too marginal markings distinguishing allegedly heretical passages from orthodox ones were frequently copied from one manuscript to another.

Marginalia

For some, such reader marks were insufficient and they instead employed a third strategy, composing more lengthy marginalia. Consider two manuscripts written in East Syrian script, British Library Oriental 2309 and British Library Oriental 4070. Each manuscript preserves the rulings of eleven church councils beginning with the fourth-century Council of Nicaea and ending with the fifteenth-century Council of Florence. The manuscripts themselves are fairly recent. On paleographic grounds British Library Oriental 2309 is dated to the seventeenth century and the colophon of British Library Oriental 4070 securely dates it to 1823 CE.[20] Their virtually identically content, however, points to an earlier, most likely shared, exemplar but these two scribes had different reactions to what they were copying especially when they came to the controversial Council of Chalcedon.

The scribe of British Library Oriental 4070 simply copied down the information he found about the Council of Chalcedon and moved on to the next council. But British Library Oriental 2309 included a material reaction to this report. When the scribe of British Library Oriental 2309 came to the Council of Chalcedon, his exemplar did not provide any narrative framing. So he added a marginal note to personally register his complaint about the text he was copying and to warn his audience about its content (Fig. 20): "Reader, when you see this statement you should condemn it. Know that its explanation should be anathematized."[21]

Almost a thousand years earlier, the Miaphysite scribe of the most likely eighth-century *catenae* text British Library Additional 12,155 copied numerous reading marks from previous exemplars to help distinguish what he considered orthodox passages from heretic ones.[22] But he supplemented the textual strategy of his exemplar with some of his own interventions, in this case a series of additional marginalia directly arguing with the authors he was copying down in the body of the

---

20 For manuscripts' content and date of composition see George Margoliouth, *Descriptive List of Syriac and Karshuni MSS. of the British Museum Aquired Since 1873* (London: Trustees of the British Museum, 1899), 7, 22.
21 BL Or. 2309, f. 38a.
22 BL Add. 12,155 consists of 534 pages of patristic quotations divded into 50 sections that make up "a volume of demonstrations from the holy fathers against various heresies." Wright, *Catalogue of Syriac Manuscripts*, 921–55. Wright dates the manuscript on paleographic grounds to the eighth century.

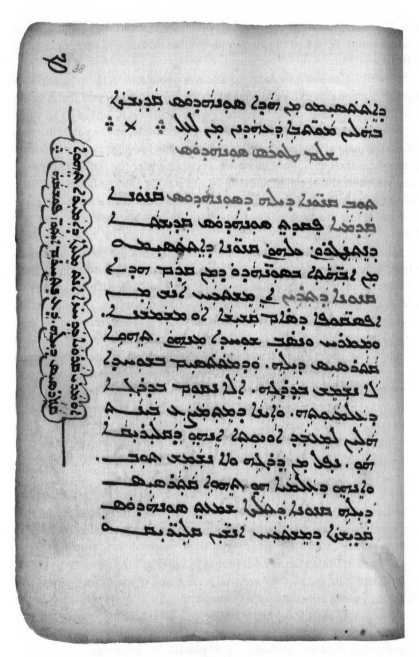

Fig. 20: British Library Oriental 2309, f. 38a. This most likely seventeenth-century collection of church councils includes an anti-Chalcedonian marginal note placed next to some of that council's rulings. It reads: "Reader, when you see this statement you should condemn it. Know that its explanation should be anathematized." British Library Oriental 4070, a nineteenth-century version of the same documents, includes the identical main text but does not have any marginalia. © The British Library Board, Or 2309.

manuscript. For example, on the very page on which he reproduces a quotation from the pro-Chalcedonian Pope Leo the Miaphysite scribes adds: "It is wickedness that Leo is putting here."[23]

The same scribe also had a tendency to discover quotations in the main text that were particularly amenable to his theological convictions and to repeat them, either verbatim or as a paraphrase, in the margins. He was particularly apt to do so when copying down conciliar decisions he did not like. For example, at one point this poor Miaphysite scribe had to copy an exemplar that contained several pages dominated with passages from the Council of Chalcedon. Fortunately for the scribe, these were interspersed with occasional pro-Miaphysite citations. This allowed him to radically shift the theological balance of the page. While he was stuck with a main text filled with objectionable text, he recopied key parts of the few pro-Miaphysite sections and repeated these in the margins.

These brief slogans served as a running argument against the preponderance of the main text. As a result, whenever anyone reads these statements from the Council of Chalcedon in the main text, they also encounter the anti-Chalcedonian arguments twice—once in the main text and more prominently in the margins. These marginal glosses began with the statement that the earlier Council of Ephesus had decreed that "there will not be a definition of faith apart from that which was at the Council of Nicaea." (As both the councils of Nicaea and Ephesus took place before the Council of Chalcedon the implication was that the Chalcedonian creed was too innovative to be considered valid). The marginalia continue by defending the pro-Miaphysite Dioscorus whom the Council of Chalcedon had deposed: "It was not because of faith that the holy Dioscorus was deposed" (Thus Dioscorus's deposition was invalid). They conclude by highlighting that the Council of Chalcedon was presented with two possible creeds, one by Dioscorus and one "by the wicked Leo."[24] (And, alas, they chose the "wrong one").

But it was not simply ancient scribes who expressed their displeasure at the texts they were accessing. A similar phenomenon occurred among later readers of these documents, especially when they thought the original scribe did not adequately mark a given passage as heretical. This tendency is particularly visible in a series of readerly interventions found in British Library Additional 14,528 (Fig. 21). The contents of this sixth-century Miaphysite manuscript are similar to many of the other manuscripts used to know thy enemy. Like these other manuscripts the original scribe preserved conciliar decisions, including those he didn't like, as well as writings from opponents to Miaphysitism such as Pope Leo. As in other manuscripts, the scribe's motive for copying oppositional texts was undoubtedly to provide the textual resources future Miaphysite readers needed to defend Miaphysite positions and attack Chalcedonian

---

23 BL Add. 12,155, f. 53a.
24 BL Add. 12,155, f. 51a.

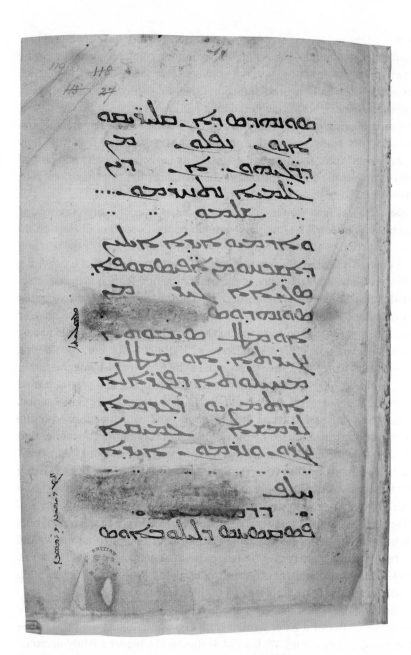

Fig. 21: British Library Additional 14,528, f. 119a. This collection of ecclesiastical documents was compiled by a Miaphysite scribe, most likely in the sixth century. The codex included a number of pro-Chalcedonian texts which the original scribe left unmodified. A later Miaphysite reader intervened making a number of changes. On this page, for example, he changed a reference to the Council of Chalcedon from "the holy Council" to "the despised Council." So, too, he changed the reference to Pope Leo who helped convene the Council of Chalcedon from "The illustrious Leo of Rome" to "Leo the wicked Roman." © The British Library Board, Add 14,528.

ones. Most likely this scribe was writing over a century before techniques such as narrative framing, reading marks, or marginalia became common practices. So he simply copied opposition literature without comment. For later Miaphysite readers, the original scribe's textually neutral stance became increasingly problematic and forced one of them to make his own material interventions.

The first modification occurs in the manuscript's incipit. Through erasure and marginal gloss a later reader changed a phrase that originally had read "the holy Council of Chalcedon" into "the despised council." As for Pope Leo who had helped convene this controversial council, the reader changed him from "the illustrious Leo" to "the wicked Leo".[25]

The reader's ire was next expressed seventeen pages later, this time against the Byzantine emperor Marcian who originally assembled the Council of Chalcedon. In this case one can actually follow the reader's various attempts to modify the text and then see him change his mind midway through.[26] Toward the bottom of a page, the reader encountered a positive reference to the zeal of the God-fearing Marcian. Disagreeing with this assessment of the Byzantine emperor, the reader produced a number of serial interventions: 1) He first erased the bottom line of the page that was initially pro-Marcian. 2) He then wanted to erase the first two words at the top of the next page, words that most likely characterized Marcian as a "fearer of God." But, considering it unwise to erase the word "God" he simply erased the first word leaving the rather enigmatic "____ of God." 3) He then returned to the bottom of the first page and tried writing a new anti-Marcian text, but in a hand that imitated that of the original scribe. The reader, however, only got as far as the first word "this" which he formed in the same script (Estrangela) as that used by the original scribe, but not in a manner that would be entirely convincing. 4) He then began to form the second word, "emperor," in the script he was more familiar with, Serto. 5) Most likely catching himself using the more contemporary script he stopped part way through the word "emperor" and crossed it out. 6) He then gave up trying to write over the erased lines in the style of the original scribe. He instead left the rest of the line blank and wrote a marginal note underneath in the Serto script he was most familiar with. Although no one would confuse this note with the hand of the original scribe, at least the later reader was now able to complete his emendation that changed an originally positive characterization of Marcian into the phrase "this faithless and Godless emperor."

Just a page later, the reader made yet another, albeit much simpler intervention, now changing the incipit of a letter written from Leo to Anatolius, the pro-Chalcedonian Bishop of Constantinople. With a quick erasure the reader slightly demoted Anatolius changing him from the "Head Bishop of Constantinople" to "a bishop of

---

25 BL Add. 14,528, f. 119a.
26 BL Add. 14,528, ff. 136b–137a.

Constantinople." Leo fared worse being transformed via erasure and marginal gloss from "Leo, the Chief Bishop of Rome" to "Leo, the Wicked Bishop of Rome."[27]

The reader's final interventions occurred toward the end of the same letter. At this point Leo's letter originally maligned Dioscorus, the Miaphysite Bishop of Alexandria. The later reader partially rejuvenated Dioscorus's legacy by erasing a negative epithet the text originally put before his name. He then ended his series of interventions with a final note at the bottom of the page that reads: "Woe upon your mouth wicked unclean Leo!" It's not everyday that one encounters marginalia cursing the pope.

• • •

To know thy enemy one needed access to their texts. But the very act of copying and reading the opposition's literature was potentially problematic. Syriac writers tried to solve this conundrum in various ways: through literary framing, through reading marks, through additional marginalia. These interventions allowed Syriac Christians to register disapproval toward a text and to warn future readers that they too were about to encounter something heretical. But these strategies were neither isolated nor idiosyncratic. What made these tactics so persuasive and pervasive was how closely they reflected other prevalent aspects of Syriac manuscript culture.

For Syriac Christians reading was anything but a passive activity. Syriac colophons abound with examples of scribes anticipating that their labors in reproducing texts would provide them with spiritual reward in the world to come. Often these same scribes would enlist the reader in this task, asking him or her to pray on behalf of the scribe who toiled in the manuscript's production.[28] Scribes would occasionally further entice readers to pray for them claiming that any reader who did so would also receive a share of these blessings.[29] Those who bound, collated, indexed, owned, and repaired manuscripts also wrote similar prayer requests.[30] Some readers, however,

27 BL Add. 14,528, f. 138a.

28 E.g. BL Add. 12,134, f. 132b; BL Add. 12,135, f. 205a; BL Add. 12,138, f. 311b; BL Add. 14,431, f. 157a; BL Add. 14,712, f. 51a; BL Add. 14,500, f. 79b; BL Add. 14,506, f. 97a; BL Add. 14,555, f. 42b; BL Add. 14,484, f. 121b; BL Add. 14,514, f. 93b; BL Add. 14,458, f. 157b; BL Add. 14,457, f. 200b; BL Add. 14,473, f. 146b; BL Add. 14,493, f. 189a; BL Add. 14,475, f. 208b; BL Add. 14,434, f. 128b; BL Add. 14,562, f. 140b; BL Add. 14,564, f. 194a; BL Add. 14,690, f. 178a; BL Add. 14,692, f. 99a; BL Add. 14,708, f. 51b; BL Add. 14,709, f. 94a; BL Add. 14,710, f. 227a; BL Add. 14,711, f. 220b; BL Add. 14,714, f. 138b; BL Add. 14,728, f. 238b; BL Add. 14,736, f. 64a; BL Add. 17,103, f. 70b; BL Add. 17,119, f. 83a; BL Add. 17,151, f. 109a; BL Add. 17,158, f. 55b; BL Add. 17,190, f. 1a; BL Add. 17,199, f. 79a; BL Add. 17,221, f. 105a; BL Add. 17,224, f. 42b; BL Add. 17,227, f. 150b; BL Add. 17,231, f. 24b; BL Add. 17,240, f. 41a, 94a; BL Add. 17,251, f. 158b; BL Add. 17,257, f. 21a; BL Add. 17,261, f. 63a; BL Add. 17,269, f. 11a; BL Add. 18,714, f. 190b.

29 BL Add. 14,702, f. 53a; BL Add. 17,299, f. 77b.

30 Binders: e.g. BL Add. 14,635, f. 5a; BL Add. 21,454, f. 230b. Collators/correctors: e.g. BL Add. 12,135, f. 42b; BL Add. 12,148, f. 233b; BL Add. 12,149, f. 84a; BL Add. 14,431, f. 157a; BL Add. 14,506, f. 76a; BL Add. 14,547, f. 236a; BL Add. 14,565, f. 164b; BL Add. 12,149, f. 84a. Indexers: e.g. BL Add. 14,432,

took the connection between written word and everlasting life a little too seriously resulting in a related phenomenon of pilfered prayers. That is, upon encounter such a prayer petition some readers erased the name of the original scribe and replaced it with their own.[31] Underlying this type of intervention was the belief that the very act of a name being read would give that person merit, even if later readers (or at the very least God) knew that this went against the prayer's original intent.

Of course, ancient scribes were aware that later readers might modify the text they were writing. Thus one often finds curses against those who changed these notices.[32] Unfortunately for their original authors, such curses were not always effective. After they changed the colophon, cautious readers also erased the curse.[33] Sometimes particularly cunning scribes tried to guard against this. For example British Library Additional 17,124 ends: "Anyone who in any way removes this notice, he will receive the curses and anathemas that we wrote above in double" (Coincidentally, this statement has remained unmodified).[34]

In other cases, scribes invited the reader to be a collaborator. That is, some scribes would complain about a poor exemplar and then directly address the reader asking that he or she correct the work as best as they were able. For example, the scribe of British Library Additional 14,576 wrote: "I, the poor Theodores, vocalized this book without an exemplar. But whoever finds a suitable exemplar, on account of love [for God], may he correctly finish whatever is lacking."[35] Similarly, when the scribe of British Library Additional 17,264 noticed that someone had erased some names from his exemplar he proclaimed: "These names were erased. O reader, upon your life, if you should come across [another] copy, correct them so that you might receive mercy."[36]

Just as scribes often felt their labors in copying a text would gain them otherworldly benefit, so too future readers felt that the act of reading would provide them with spiritual merit. This belief helps explain the large number of reader signatures found in Syriac manuscripts, places where readers recorded their name in the margins of the works they had read. Often these signatures also included a request

---

f. 3a. Owners: e.g. BL Add. 14,636, f. 56b; BL Add. 14,544, f. 113b; BL Add. 17,182, f. 99b. Repairers: BL Add. 14,491, f. 132a; BL Add. 14,565, f. 164b; BL Add. 14,635, f. 5a.

31 E.g. BL Add. 14,577, f. 130a; BL Add. 14,587, f. 136a; BL Add. 14,605, f. 139a; BL Add. 14,643, f. 60b. For a larger discussion of pilfered prayers see Michael Philip Penn, "Moving Beyond the Palimpsest: Erasure in Syriac Manuscripts," *JECS* 18:2 (2010): 281–83.

32 E.g. BL Add. 12,172, f. 195a; BL Add. 14,442, f. 48a; BL Add. 14,454, f. 1a; BL Add. 14,485, f. 121b; BL Add. 14,486, f. 81a; BL Add. 14,487, f. 71b; BL Add. 14,503, f. 178b; BL Add. 14,522, f. 26a; BL Add. 14,550, f. 1a; BL Add. 14,593, f. 2a; BL Add. 17,102, f. 59b; BL Add. 17,181, f. 136b. For a larger discussion of such anathemas and their erasure see Penn, "Beyond the Palimpsest," 283–85.

33 E.g. BL Add. 12,154 f. 1a; BL Add. 14,454, f. 1a.

34 BL Add. 17,124, f. 68a.

35 BL Add. 14,576, f. 84b.

36 BL Add. 17,264, f. 65a.

that future generations of readers pray on behalf of the earlier reader's soul.[37] As a result, when a discouraged Syriac scribe took on the persona of his codex complaining that, "we books are many but readers few," the problem was not simply that the scribe was wasting his time copying such a long codex.[38] A larger issue was that, without readers, the circulation of spiritual merit central to the manuscript enterprise would come to a screeching halt.

The strong connection between writing, reading, and salvation undoubtedly helped motivate the laborious copying of ancient manuscripts. When, for example, the scribe of British Library Additional 14,519 twice (!) complained about being bitten by flies as he was writing or the scribe of British Library Additional 12,174 bemoaned the poor quality of the velum he was forced to write upon, they could at least find some compensation knowing that they would gain a heavenly reward for having completed their task.[39] After surviving "the trials of ink" and "the trials of the pen" they would rejoice upon reaching a safe harbor.[40]

But if the copying of good words was advantageous for one's soul, what about evil ones? Concern for such spiritual demerits occasionally manifested itself in the ways Syriac scribes wrote specific names. For example, British Library Additional 14,509 begins with a song set to the melody "the priest Zacharias." As written, however, this tune would be particularly difficult to sing. Every few lines one comes across an illegible word. Illegible that is until you turn the page 180 degrees. The scribe has written upside down the names of figures such as Marcion and Mani whom he considered heretical.[41] This scribe wasn't the only one to invert his opponents. For example, the scribe of British Library Oriental 2309 carefully wrote upside-down the names of those who supported the controversial doctrine of monothelitism.[42] This was not, however, only a scribal concern. When coming across a suspect name later readers also often intervened. For example, the ninth-century lectionary British Library Additional 14,492 initially dedicated one set of readings to the Greek theologians Diodorus, Theodore of Mopsuesta, and Nestorius. When a later Miaphysite reader came across

---

37 BL Add. 12,139, f. 139a; BL Add. 12,170, f. 47a, 135b; BL Add. 14,434, f. 128b; BL Add. 14,464, f. 63a; BL Add. 14,473, f. 148b; BL Add. 14,479, f. 101a; BL Add. 14,548, f. 2a; BL Add. 14,558, f. 171a; BL Add. 14,574, f. 40b; BL Add. 14,576, f. 55b; BL Add. 14,582, f. 161a; BL Add. 14,598, f. 239b; BL Add. 14,703, f. 268b; BL Add. 17,122, f. 11b; BL Add. 17,159, f. 92b; BL Add. 17,227, f. 150b; BL Add. 17,248, f. 140a; BL Add. 18,715, f. 138a.

38 BL Add. 12,170, f. 135a.

39 BL Add. 14,519, ff. 17a, 66b. BL Add. 12,174, ff. 175a, 424b

40 BL Add. 17,185, f. 61a; 17,217, f. 63; BL Add. 14,667, f. 50. Sebastian Brock, "The Scribe Reaches Harbor," *ByzF* 21 (1995): 195–202.

41 BL Add. 14,509, f. 1a–b.

42 BL Or. 2309, f. 54b. Also consider a manuscript of Jacob of Edessa's *Hexameron* (*Lyon Syriac 2*) where one also encounters gibberish, that is until you reorient the page and realize that the scribe has written upside down the name Satan every time it appeared in Jacob's account (e.g. *Lyon Syriac 2*, f. 15a).

these references to theologians later associated with the East Syrians, he erased their names from the codex.[43]

With writing or reading a suspect name being such a concern, how much more an entire text. For example, reconsider the eighth-century manuscript British Library Additional 12,155. In addition to the marginal notes found in this 265 folia *cantena* text, there exists a strong pattern of alterations that takes place in the main text. Most of the manuscript's hundreds of references to the Miaphysite luminary Severus of Antioch have been erased and then in many cases Severus's name was later rewritten over the erasures. A marginal note sheds some light on the circumstances. It begins, "This volume fell into the hands of a heretic and he erased from it the name of the holy one and light of the whole world." That is, at some point the manuscript passed from a Miaphysite to a non Miaphysite community where a reader erased Severus' name. When the manuscript returned to Miaphysites, a later reader rewrote the original names over the erasures. The marginalia go on to state "Let the wrath of the Lord come upon him who dared this, and he even dared [to do] this many times."[44]

This reader was certainly not the only one who "dared to do this many times." Syriac manuscripts abound with this type of intervention.[45] One should thus view textual reactions to the problem of knowing thy enemy as a subset of these larger concerns regarding the power of writing, reading, and the desire to carefully patrol orthodoxy. When manuscripts had direct spiritual consequences for those who composed and read them, when folks we call readers were occasionally invited and often morally required to physically change the texts they were reading, when texts and manuscripts were frequently crossing sectarian boundaries, it became imperative to figure out how to tell a heretic when you read one.

Syriac scribes and readers appear to have modified manuscripts more frequently than any other group of early Christians. Nevertheless, modern scholarship concerning other linguistic traditions may be very helpful in contextualizing Syriac manuscript interventions. For example, consider the work of Latinist John Dagenais. In Dagenais's words, medieval reading "was above all an ethical activity. ... Texts ... engaged the reader ... They required the reader to take a stand about what he or she

---

43 BL Add. 14,492, f. 5a. So too, the original scribe of the eighteenth-century Cambridge Add. 1989 carefully followed his exemplar and included a prayer to the exactly the same East Syrian luminaries as found in the British Library lectionary. As with BL Add. 14,492, a later reader struck out each name. But, in this case, the alterations went a bit further and he replaced the struck out names with theologians he considered more respectable: Gregory, Basil of Caseseria, and John Chrysostom (Cambridge Add. 1989, f. 16b).

44 BL Add. 12,155, f. 12a.

45 For a larger discussion of Syriac manuscript changes motivated by heresiological concerns see Penn, "Beyond the Palimpsest," 285–89. For similar types of interventions, but in these cases motivated by the rise of Islam see Michael Philip Penn, "Monks, Manuscripts, and Muslims: Syriac Textual Changes in Reaction to the Rise of Islam," *Hug* 12:2 (2009): 235–57.

read."[46] Dagenais observation of what he calls "the ethics of reading in manuscript culture" is particularly useful for understanding the ways Syriac Christians altered the texts that they encountered. When a Miaphysite came across a positive reference to the Council of Chalcedon or when a Syriac Christian an East Syrian confronted a condemnation of his hero Nestorius, modifying part of the offending passage was an "ethical reading practice." The manuscript became a space where one "could take a stand" about what was being written and being read.

A recognition of these dynamics of ancient reading also affects the way we read ancient manuscripts. Dagenais's statement that "in the Middle Ages the primary 'literary' activity was not writing, and certainly not 'authoring' or 'creating,' but reading,"[47] reminds us that the works we study are not so much the product of individual authors or even of individual scribes but rather the accumulation of a series of readers. In Dagenais's words we should approach manuscripts less as "literature" than as "lecturature."[48] This paradigm shift concerning how Christians read manuscripts moves one from a type of text criticism whose primary goal is the recovery of an *Urtext* to an emphasis on transmission history where manuscripts reflect an evolving, frequently contested, multilayered process of meaning-making.[49] Such an approach puts Syriac materials, for the first time, in conversation with recent developments in emerging disciplines such as "new philology," "new medievalist," and "the history of the book."[50]

---

46 John Dagenais, *The Ethics of Reading in Manuscript Culture: Glossing the Libro de buen amor* (Princeton, N. J.: Princeton University Press, 1994), xvii.

47 Dagenais, *The Ethics of Reading*, 22.

48 Dagenais, *The Ethics of Reading*, 23.

49 For brief critiques of traditional text criticism's search for origins, see Karen L. King, *What is Gnosticism?* (Cambridge: Harvard University Press, 2003), 220–21; Stephen G. Nichols, "Introduction: Philology in a Manuscript Culture," *Speculum* 65:1 (1990): 3–7; Andrew Taylor, *Textual Situations: Three Medieval Manuscripts and Their Readers* (Material Texts; Philadelphia: University of Pennsylvania Press, 2002), 12–15.

50 The bibliography of recent works often categorized as "history of the book" is immense. Especially influential are the works of Roger Chartier and Anthony Grafton as well as the University of Pennsylvania Press's Material Texts series. Of particular import to the debate surrounding "new philology" and "new medievalism" was the January 1990 special issue of *Speculum* and the collection of essays *Towards a Synthesis? Essays on the New Philology* (ed. Keith Busby; Atlanta: Rodopi, 1993). Dagenais, *The Ethics of Reading* represents a particularly articulate critique of both "new" and "old" philology by a scholar who nevertheless remains very committed to studying medieval manuscript culture. His comments include such quotable remarks as "My dissatisfactions with New Philology arise when New Philology (and its congener, New Medievalism) begins to look like Old Theory – namely the theory of the 1960s, 1970s, and 1980s. ... The New Philology continually reveals its own origins in approaches to literature that many in the literary establishment, and especially in medievalist circles, have felt to be self-indulgent or self-serving, pointless, plagued by fundamental misunderstandings or misreadings, or just plain dull" (xv) and "On the other hand, traditional philology seems unwilling or unable to rise to the legitimate challenges to traditional ways of looking at texts raised by new approaches to

The problematic necessity of Syriac Christians preserving oppositional literature is part of a larger phenomenon of early Christian materialization of difference. As a result of the ancient requirement to know thy enemy, Syriac manuscripts now become material witnesses. They attest that many early Christians patrolled the ever con-tested boundaries of orthodoxy, not through the composition of theological tractates, but through their – quite literally – active reading of them. For these Christians, the materiality of manuscripts provided both the incentive and the opportunity to define and guard orthodoxy.

Bibliography

Baum, Wilhelm, and Dietmar W. Winkler. *Die Apostolische Kirche des Ostens: Geschichte der sogenannten Nestorianer*. Klagenfurt: Verlag Kitab, 2000.
–. *The Church of the East: A Concise History*. New York: Routledge, 2003.
Bertaina, David. *Christian and Muslim Dialogues: The Religious Uses of a Literary Form in the Early Islamic Middle East*. Piscataway: Gorgias Press, 2011.
Brock, Sebastian P. "The 'Nestorian' Church: A Lamentable Misnomer." *Bulletin of the John Rylands Library* 78 (1996): 23–35.
–. "The Scribe Reaches Harbor." *Byzantinische Forschungen* 21 (1995): 195–202.
Cameron, Averil. "Disputations, Polemical Literature and the Formation of Opinion in the Early Byzantine Period." Pages 91–108 in *Dispute Poems and Dialogues in the Ancient and Mediaeval Near East: Forms and Types of Literary Debates in Semitic and Related Literatures*. Edited by Gerrit J. Reinink and Herman L. J. Vanstiphout. Leuven: Peeters, 1991.
–. "Introduction." Pages 1–6 in *Chalcedon in Context: Church Councils 400–700*. Edited by Richard Price and Mary Whitby. Liverpool: Liverpool University Press, 2009.
Choksy, Jamsheed K. *Conflict and Cooperation: Zoroastrian Subalterns and Muslim Elites in Medieval Iranian Society*. New York: Columbia University Press, 1997.
Dagenais, John. *The Ethics of Reading in Manuscript Culture: Glossing the Libro de buen amor*. Princeton, N. J.: Princeton University Press, 1994.
Griffith, Sidney H. "The Monk in the Emir's Majlis: Reflections on a Popular Genre of Christian Liter-ary Apologetics in Arabic in the Early Islamic Period." Pages 13–65 in *The Majlis: Interreligious Encounters in Medieval Islam*. Edited by Hava Lazarus-Yafeh, Mark R. Cohen, Sasson Somekh, and Sidney H. Griffith. Studies in Arabic Language and Literature 4. Wiesbaden: Harrassowitz, 1999.
–. "Answering the Call of the Minaret: Christian Apologetics in the World of Islam." Pages 91–126 in *Redefining Christian Identity: Cultural Interaction in the Middle East Since the Rise of Islam*. Edited by Heleen L. Murre-Van den Berg, Jan J. Van Ginkel, and Theo M. Van Lint. Orientalia Lovaniensia Analecta 134. Leuven: Peeters, 2005.

---

medieval textuality. Too often the response has been shrill, or merely diversionary. The defense has rested on pronouncing the words 'trendy' or 'fashionable,' uttering 'Derrida' in a hoarse whisper, and reaching for the nearest cruciform object" (xvi). Also, see Taylor, *Textual Situations: Three Medieval Manuscripts and Their Readers*, 1–25, 197–200.

–. "Answering the Call of the Minaret: The Topics and Strategies of Christian Apologetics in the World of Islam." Pages 11–42 in *Die Suryoye und ihre Umwelt*. Edited by Andreas Heinz Martin Tamcke. Münster: Lit Verlag, 2005.

Grillmeier, Alois. *Jesus der Christus im Glauben der Kirche*. 2 Vols. Freiburg im Breisgau: Herder, 1979–1990.

Guidi, Ignazio, and Ernest W. Brooks. *Chronica minora*. Corpus Scriptorum Christianorum Orientalium 3, Scriptores Syri 3. Paris: L. Durbecq, 1904.

Harvey, Susan Ashbrook. *Asceticism and Society in Crisis: John of Ephesus and the Lives of the Eastern Saints*. Berkely: University of California Press, 1990.

King, Karen L. *What is Gnosticism?* Cambridge: Harvard University Press, 2003.

Kiraz, George Anton. *A Grammar of the Syriac Language. Volume 1. Orthography*. Piscataway, N. J.: Gorgias Press, 2012.

Lim, Richard. *Public Disputation, Power, and Social Order in Late Antiquity*. Berkeley: University of California Press, 1995.

Louth, Andrew. "Why Did the Syrians Reject the Council of Chalcedon?" Pages 107–16 in *Chalcedon in Context: Church Councils, 400–700*. Edited by Richard Price and Mary Whitby. Liverpool: Liverpool University Press, 2009.

Margoliouth, George. *Descriptive List of Syriac and Karshuni MSS. of the British Museum Aquired Since 1873*. London: Trustees of the British Museum, 1899.

Nichols, Stephen G. "Introduction: Philology in a Manuscript Culture." *Speculum: A Journal of Medieval Studies* 65:1 (1990): 1–10.

Penn, Michael Philip. "Monks, Manuscripts, and Muslims: Syriac Textual Changes in Reaction to the Rise of Islam." *Hugoye: Journal of Syriac Studies* 12:2 (2009): 235–57.

–. "Moving Beyond the Palimpsest: Erasure in Syriac Manuscripts." *Journal of Early Christian Studies* 18:2 (2010): 261–303.

Reinink, Gerrit J. "Tradition and the Formation of the 'Nestorian' Identity in Sixth- to Seventh-Century Iraq." *Church History and Religious Culture* 89 (2009): 217–50.

Rompay, Lucas Van. "Society and Community in the Christian East." Pages 239–66 in *The Cambridge Companion to the Age of Justinian*. Edited by Michael Maas. Cambridge: Cambridge University Press, 2004.

–. "The East (3): Syria and Mesopotamia." Pages 365–86 in *The Oxford Handbook of Early Christian Studies*. Edited by Susan Ashbrook Harvey and David G. Hunter. Oxford: Oxford University Press, 2008.

Schor, Adam M. *Theodoret's People: Social Networks and Religious Conflict in Late Roman Syria*. Transformation of the Classical Heritage. Berkeley: University of California Press, 2011.

Sellew, Philip. "Red Letter Bible." Page 422 in *The Oxford Guide to Ideas & Issues of the Bible*. Edited by Michael D. Coogan and Bruce M. Metzger. Oxford: Oxford University Press, 2001.

Simonsohn, Uriel I. *A Common Justice: The Legal Allegiances of Christians and Jews under Early Islam*. Philadelphia: University of Pennsylvania Press, 2011.

Taylor, Andrew. *Textual Situations: Three Medieval Manuscripts and Their Readers*. Material Texts. Philadelphia: University of Pennsylvania Press, 2002.

Walker, Joel Thomas. *The Legend of Mar Qardagh: Narrative and Christian Heroism in Late Antique Iraq*. Berkeley: University of California Press, 2006.

Wright, William. *Catalogue of Syriac Manuscripts in the British Museum Acquired Since the Year 1838, Volume 2*. London: Cambridge University Press, 1871.

Jeff W. Childers

"You Will Find what You Seek:" the Form and Function of a Sixth-Century Divinatory Bible in Syriac

A Unique Syriac Manuscript

The British Library manuscript, Add. 17,119 is remarkable for several reasons.[1] Copied in the sixth or seventh century, the codex is an important early witness to the Syriac Peshiṭta text of the Gospel of John. It contains the entire text of the Gospel on 83 parchment leaves, in a regular estrangela hand, though a few of the original leaves have been lost and the lacunae were supplemented later. Philip E. Pusey collated the manuscript's biblical text for the 1901 edition of the Peshiṭta Gospels,[2] and it has been collated again for the Greek *Editio Critica Maior* project at Münster and Birmingham. Yet among Syriac Bibles it is a curious specimen, because this fairly compact volume (about 22 × 13 cm) contains only John's Gospel, and appears not to have part of a *tetraeuangelium*. Although the first two folios have been replaced so that it is impossible to be certain about its original scope, the manuscript contains no Ammonian/Eusebian sections, no harmony at the bottom of the folios, and no ṣḥāḥē, the ancient chapter divisions commonly found in Syriac Gospel manuscripts. The absence of these typical features is striking, and it further differentiates the manuscript as unusual in its production.

Ancient volumes dedicated to a single Gospel are rare. The only other Syriac manuscript known to contain only the Gospel of John is Harvard, MS Syriac 176,[3] a manuscript having the Harklean text of John and the Harklean Masora[4]–hardly analogous to Add. 17,119. Although the Gospel text of our manuscript is not especially distinctive as a Peshiṭta witness, the volume itself, as a material object, is unique. The

---

1 See William Wright, *Catalogue of Syriac Manuscripts in the British Museum Acquired since the Year 1838*, vol. 1 (London: Trustees of the British Museum, 1870), 71–72.
2 Philip E. Pusey and G. H. Gwilliam, *Tetraeuangelium sanctum juxta simplicem Syrorum versionem ad fidem codicum, massorae, editionem denuo recognitum* (Oxford: Clarendon Press, 1901).
3 Dated to 1091/92, 1491/91, or 1591/92. See Moshe H. Goshen-Gottstein, *Syriac Manuscripts in the Harvard College Library: A Catalogue* (HSS 23; Missoula, Mont.: Scholars Press, 1979), 110–11. Digital images of this manuscript are now available at the Harvard Library website: http://pds.lib.harvard.edu/pds/view/42715137 (accessed 12 May 2014).
4 See Andreas K. Juckel, "The 'Syriac Masora' and the New Testament Peshiṭta," in *The Peshiṭta: Its Use in Literature and Liturgy. Papers Read at the Third Peshiṭta Symposium* (ed. Bas ter Haar Romeny; MPIL 15; Leiden: Brill, 2006), 107–21. I am indebted to Andreas Juckel for unpublished information on Peshiṭta and Harklean manuscripts that have been collated for the *Editio Critica Maior*.

colophon gives no clues as to the circumstances of the book's production, beyond ascribing its copying to one "unworthy George" (ܚܛܝܐ ܓܝܘܪܓܝܤ ܒܟ ܪܚܡܐ, f. 83r). The most peculiar feature of all is the manuscript's inclusion of numerous *hermeneiai*, a system of "interpretations" keyed to the Gospel text, apparently for the purpose of offering divinatory guidance to the book's users.

The idiosyncratic nature of the codex suggests it was created specifically for the practice of sortilege, i.e. the drawing of lots for the purpose of divination. This is not to say that the text of John's Gospel was incidental to the form and purpose of the manuscript. The main contents of the codex consist of the Gospel text, and as we shall see, where it was deficient or incurred damage, the Gospel text has been corrected or supplemented through the years. Indeed, various pieces of evidence, summarized below, suggest that a genre of specialized manuscripts of John's Gospel containing *hermeneiai* may once have been widespread. These artifacts resist the standard classifications. They are not merely Gospel books nor are they simply oracle collections containing scraps of biblical text. Add. 17,119 is the most complete and intact example known to exist.[5] It represents a distinct kind of book, once common, a sort of *divining gospel*, in which the text of John's Gospel and oracular material are synthesized into a single work. Though oracular, the material is also hermeneutical. Applying a mode of interpretation uniqely adapted to the genre of divining gospel, users were able to bring the divine authority of the text to bear on a seeker's questions, coaxing from the sacred book guidance for life.

In its present form, the codex Add. 17,119 tells a complex story of survival. This study focuses on the form and dynamic history of this unique Syriac manuscript, explaining the function of its divinatory content, setting it within the context of parallel materials in different languages, explicating its connections to the text of John's Gospel, and attempting to describe its history on the basis of phenomena observable in the codex itself.

Puššāqē (Hermeneiai) in Add. 17,119

The text of John's Gospel in Add. 17,119 is routinely interrupted with declarations and exhortations in another voice, occurring within the main text column and written in the same hand. The manuscript once contained 308 of these rubricated statements, though the first six are missing due to the aforementioned defect at the beginning of

---

5 For a preliminary discussion of the manuscript's features, see Jeff W. Childers, "Hermeneutics and Magic: A Unique Syriac Biblical Manuscript as an Oracle of Interpretation," in *My Lots Are in Thy Hands: Sortilege and Its Practitioners in Late Antiquity* (ed. William E. Klingshirn and AnneMarie Luijendijk; RGRW; Leiden: Brill), forthcoming.

the manuscript.[6] The statements are accompanied by numbers in the margins, and the expression, ܦܘܫܩܐ (*puššāqā*), normally prefaces the statements. This term means "interpretation," and corresponds to the Greek ἑρμηνεία (*hermeneia*). Many of the original numbers have become illegible, or nearly so, and a later set of replacement numbers regularly occurs.

The accompanying image shows folios 4v–5r. This opening contains the Peshiṭta text of John 1:38–48. It also includes the following six statements, or *puššāqē*, incorporated into the Gospel text and numbered in the margins:

4v	Jn 1:38	ܡܢ ܐܒܠܐ ܠܚܕܘܬܐ	ܝܕ
		from grief to joy	14
	Jn 1:39	[7]ܦܘܫܩܐ ܒܬܪ ܥܣܪܐ ܝܘܡܝܢ ܗܘܐ ܣܘܥܪܢܐ	ܝܗ
		Interpretation: after ten days the matter (will) happen	15
	Jn 1:42	ܦܘܫܩܐ ܡܫܟܚ ܐܢܬ ܡܕܡ ܕܒܥܐ ܐܢܬ	ܝܘ
		Interpretation: you (will) find what you seek	16
5r	Jn 1:44	ܦܘܫܩܐ ܠܐ ܗܘܐ ܘܠܐ ܫܡܥ ܐܢܬ ܠܡܠܬܐ	ܝܙ
		[8]Interpretation: it will not happen and you will not hear the word	17
	Jn 1:46	ܦܘܫܩܐ ܐܬܪܕܦ ܘܗܘܐ ܫܦܝܪ ܠܟ	ܝܚ
		Interpretation: pursue, (and) it (will) turn out well for you	18
	Jn 1:47	ܦܘܫܩܐ ܚܛܗܐ ܠܐ ܡܫܬܟܚ ܒܣܘܥܪܢܟ	ܝܛ
		Interpretation: no sin is found in your matter	19

The material is marked by inconsistencies and errors. For example, *Puššāqā* 14 lacks the prefatory term, ܦܘܫܩܐ. In *Puššāqā* 15, ܣܘܥܪܐ is written erroneously for ܣܘܥܪܢܐ ("matter;" see *Puššāqā* 19). Mistakes and confused readings occur throughout the material.

Most of the statements make little sense as direct comments on the portions of biblical text to which they are attached. Most give no moral instruction, nor do they carry obvious liturgical functions–indeed, very few of the statements have any explicit religious content at all, Christian or otherwise.[9] Although at times the language of a given statement resonates with terms and themes in the accompanying

---

6 See discussion below.

7 The text has.ܣܘܥܪܐ

8 Or, "may it not happen and may you not hear the word."

9 Apart from fairly generic encouragements to remain faithful or confident, *Puššāqē* 40, 64, 77, and 250 credit God as the source of a particular result, 30 and 94 exhort the reader to entreat God or put trust in God, 306 mentions God as an object of thanksgiving for good fortune, 307 exhorts the reader to put confidence in God rather than humans, and 19 and 237 mention "sin," though in such a way that it is unclear whether personal moral fault is the focus (see *Puššāqā* 19 above). *Puššāqā* 62 quotes a portion of John 5:14 (see below), though its meaning, like that of the rest, is not distinctly Christian.

Fig. 22: British Library Additional 17,119, ff. 4v–5r. © The British Library Board (Add. 17,119 Syriac). Image used by permission of the British Library.

biblical text,[10] the focus of the statements overall seems to lie outside Scripture. The statements are couched as responses to a person's inquiries about particular topics, with the response often occurring in the second-person masculine singular, sometimes as comments on the subjects of inquiry. Although characteristically vague, the *puššāqē* cover a range of subjects, or ܣܘܥܪ̈ܢܐ ("matters, affairs"), as indicated by the following further examples:

---

10 For further explanation of this feature, see below.

10r	Jn 3:30	ܗܕܐ ܕܝ ܒܥܘܬܐ ܡܢ ܐܠܗܐ ܝܗܝܒܐ	ܡ
		this matter is given by God	40
14r	Jn 4:42	ܦܘܫܩܐ ܡܢ ܐܟܣܢܝܐ ܐܬܐ ܛܒܐ ܫܡܥܐ.	ܢܗ
		Interpretation: from a stranger (will) come a fine report	55
26r	Jn 6:69	ܦܘܫܩܐ ܠܚܪܝܢܐ ܗܘܐ ܣܘܥܪܢܐ ܗܢܐ. ܠܚܪܬܐ ܕܝܢ ܠܛܒܬܐ ܗܘܐ.	ܨܘ
		Interpretation: this matter (will) result in conflict, but in the end it (will) turn out well	96
31v	Jn 8:16	ܦܘܫܩܐ ܝܐܝܐ ܫܘܬܦܘܬܐ	ܩܝܛ
		Interpretation: the partnership/participation is fitting	119
32r	Jn 8:20	ܦܘܫܩܐ ܠܘ ܙܒܢܐ ܗܘ ܕܬܫܪܐ.	ܩܟܒ
		Interpretation: it is not time for you to begin	122
43v	Jn 11:4	ܦܘܫܩܐ ܡܕܡ ܕܠܐ ܡܣܟܝܬ ܢܣܒܬ.	ܩܣܕ
		Interpretation: you will get something you do not expect	164
47v	Jn 11:46	ܦܘܫܩܐ ܦܘܪܩܢܐ ܛܒܐ.	ܪܟܕ
		Interpretation: a good deliverance	224
59v	Jn 14:29	ܦܘܫܩܐ ܠܐ ܕܐܢ ܠܟ ܠܐ ܬܕܚܠ	ܪܟܕ
		Interpretation: he/it (will) not judge you; do not fear	224
76v	Jn 20:5	ܦܘܫܩܐ ܣܘܥܪܢܐ ܕܒܥܝܬ ܡܫܟܚܬ	ܪܦܙ
		Interpretation: the matter that you seek you (will) find	287
79v	Jn 21:3	ܦܘܫܩܐ ܚܡܫܐ ܝܘ̈ܡܝܢ ܗܘܐ ܠܟ ܣܘܥܪܢܐ ܛܒܐ.	ܪܨܚ
		[11]Interpretation: in five days a good thing (will) happen to you	298

Apart from the problem of occasional errors and confused readings, the sense of many of the *puššāqē* is obscure.[12] Although labeled "interpretations," they are not interpretations in the usual sense, i.e. plain expositions of the text's meaning for moral or theological purposes. Instead, they function as oracular pronouncements.[13] These examples show that the codex is a specially designed tool for *sortition*, or sortilege, in which the *puššāqē* (i.e. *hermeneiai*) that accompany the biblical text constitute a system of divination by which an inquirer could receive an answer in the form of a numbered lot-oracle (*sors*) keyed to the biblical text. The method by which the user would select a particular *puššāqā* is specified nowhere in the manuscript, though the consistent numbering of the statements and their thematic distribution indicate a more elaborate system than that of simply turning to passages at random (e.g. *sortes biblicae*), such as in the examples of lot oracles discussed below. It is possible that the missing first leaves provided some clue as to the intended method by which a person's question would be linked to a particular response.

11 Or, "a good thing will be yours."

12 I am indebted to Sebastian P. Brock, for his suggestions regarding the proper translation of several of the *puššāqē*.

13 The *hermeneiai* occurring in biblical manuscripts like Add. 17,119 are rather mysterious and scholars are divided as to their original function. This matter will be discussed further below.

Sortilege

Sortilege involving the Biblical Text

Sortilege involving the biblical text enjoys a long and ancient tradition,[14] yet it has often been met with ambivalence. Augustine of Hippo criticized "those who draw lots (*sortes*) from the pages of the Gospel," on account of their using the sacred text for "worldly business and the vanity of this life."[15] Repeated canonical prohibitions indicate that practices of sortilege using the biblical text were fairly widespread. For example, the *Admonitions for Monks* attributed to Rabbula of Edessa (411–35) forbids monks from taking an oracle (ܦܬܓܡܐ) out of a book, and the rules attributed to Jacob of Edessa († 708) explicitly prohibit using the Gospels, Psalms, and "the lots of the Apostles" in this way as well.[16] In the West, Charlemagne delivers a similar proscription in 789, forbidding divination and the use of the Gospels or Psalms for sortilege.[17] These references suggest there was a sustained and lively fortune-telling industry using biblical texts in both the East and the West. They also suggest that the Gospels and Psalms were the biblical texts most commonly used in this practice.[18] Although they give no indication of familiarity with a tool precisely like Add. 17,119, the function they have in view is evidently parallel, whereby the biblical text becomes a tool for the practice of sortilege. For analogies to the apparatus of Add. 17,119, we look to other relics of ancient sortilege.

---

14 See Pieter W. van der Horst, *"Sortes*: Sacred Books as Instant Oracles in Late Antiquity," in *The Use of Sacred Books in the Ancient World* (ed. Leonard V. Rutgers et al.; CBET 22; Leuven: Peeters, 1998), 151–59; William E. Klingshirn, "Defining the *Sortes Sanctorum*," *JECS* 10 (2002): 77–130.

15 Augustine, *Letters* 55.37. See Harry Y. Gamble, *Books and Readers in the Early Church* (New Haven: Yale University Press, 1997), 240.

16 *Admonitions for Monks* 19. See Arthur Vööbus, *Syriac and Arabic Documents Regarding Legislation Relative to Syrian Asceticism* (PETSE 11; Stockholm: Estonian Theological Society in Exile, 1960), 31, 95.

17 *Duplex Legationis Edictum* 20, MGH, Capit. 2.1:64; the reference and helpful discussion are in Klingshirn, "Defining the *Sortes Sanctorum*," 110.

18 The Gospels and Psalms were also the most frequently read in public liturgy and in monasteries, and regularly copied, so it is perhaps unsurprising that extant evidence for *hermeneia* occur mainly in Gospel and Psalms manuscripts. On *hermeneia* in Armenian and Georgian Psalters, see Bernard Outtier, "Réponses oraculaires dans des manuscrits bibliques caucasiens," in *Armenia and the Bible* (ed. Christopher Burchard; ArTS 12; Atlanta: Scholars Press, 1993), 182.

Christianized Sortilege

A comparison with the *Sortes Astrampsychi* may help clarify the form and function of the *puššāqē* in Add. 17,119. Originating perhaps in the second century, this Greek tool for the practice of sortilege was originally pagan, but was subject to editing and came to circulate in at least two Christianized editions.[19] The second edition consists of 92 numbered questions on various topics, keyed to 1030 answers, arranged into 103 numbered decades.[20] Topics include business concerns, travel, the outcome of legal matters, career moves, finding lost objects, and love. Within the system, answers are grouped according to topic, yet on the page they are distributed in a seemingly random way throughout the corpus of responses. They are not actually random, however, but very carefully arranged, so that the skilled user may always produce an answer appropriate to the topic. The introduction explains an elaborate process, presumably to be kept secret from the inquirer so as to preserve the mystery. In response to an inquirer's question, the diviner would use the numbers and table provided, along with a chance number provided by the inquirer, in order to arrive at a suitable answer. For instance, if an inquirer wishes to know whether he or she will set out on a journey (εἰ ἀποδημῶ;)–question 17–through an arcane process of calculation, the *sortes* might yield the answer, "you will set out suddenly and for some time" (ἀποδημήσεις ἐξαπίνης καὶ μακράν); a different number selection on the part of the inquirer would yield, "do not set out; it is not to your advantage" (μὴ ἀποδημήσῃς· οὐ γὰρ συμφέρει σοι).[21] The tool is designed in such a way as to enable users to get answers, seemingly by the will of fate, the gods, or God, to specific questions posed by an inquirer. The Christianized form includes questions such as whether the inquirer shall remain a priest, or be appointed bishop.

The apparatus in Add. 17,119 is similar to the oracles of *Astrampsychi*. Like the latter, the *puššāqē* are brief; they also deal with some of the same topics, such as inheritance, travel, and business. Their numbering and distribution suggest that the original design may have included a system for selection not dissimilar to that governing the use of the *Sortes Astrampsychi*, though no explicit evidence for such a mechanism

---

19 Gerald M. Browne, ed., *Sortes Astrampsychi. Vol. I: Ecdosis Prior* (Leipzig: B. G. Teubner, 1983); Randall Stewart, ed., *Sortes Astrampsychi. Vol. II* (Leipzig: K. G. Saur, 2001); Kai Brodersen, ed., *Astrampsychos das Pythagoras-Orakel* (TzF 88; Darmstadt: Wissenschaftliche Buchgesellschaft, 2006). A Latin tool known as the *Sortes Sangallenses* appears to derive from the same archetype as the *Sortes Astrampsychi* (Randall Stewart, "The Textual Transmission of the 'Sortes Astrampsychi,'" *ICS* 20 [1995]: 136–38; text edited by Hermann Winnefeld, *Sortes Sangallenses* [Bonn: Max. Cohen, 1887]).

20 Stewart, "The Textual Transmission of the 'Sortes Astrampsychi,'" 135–47; see also the discussion and translation by Randall Stewart and Kenneth Morell in William Hansen, ed. *Anthology of Ancient Greek Popular Literature* (Bloomington: Indiana University Press, 1988), 285–324.

21 See Stewart, *Sortes Astrampsychi*, 9, 14, 21, 67; cf. Hansen, *Anthology of Ancient Greek Popular Literature*, 292, 294, 297, 317.

survives in Add. 17,119. Yet there are also important differences between the two–in particular, the statements in Add. 17,119 are more general than those of *Astrampsychi*;[22] the former prefer to speak in terms of ܣܘܥܪܢܐ ("thing, matter, affair"), rather than focusing on particular situations. This feature makes them more like the oracles in the *Sortes sanctorum*,[23] another ancient Christianized tool for sortition, whose statements are often longer and more florid, but also very general in focus.[24] The generic quality of the answers in Add. 17,119 resembles the statements in the *Sortes sanctorum*,[25] and suggests that specific questions were not a part of the divinatory apparatus of the Syriac manuscript.

No explicit evidence for a system of selection survives as part of the apparatus in Add. 17,119. However, vestiges of an originally topical organization occur in places where subject headings seem to have found their way into the *sortes* themselves, as in the following examples:[26]

9r	Jn 3:19	ܦܘܫܩܐ ܕܡܛܠ ܡܟܣܢܘܬܐ[27] ܫܒܘܩ ܠܐ ܬܥܒܕ	ܠܘ
		Interpretation: About reproof: leave (it and) do not do (it)	36
9v	Jn 3:25	ܦܘܫܩܐ ܕܡܛܠ[28] ܐܘܪܚܐ ܫܦܝܪܐ ܗܝ	ܠܚ
		Interpretation: about the journey: it is good	38
15r	Jn 4:53	ܦܘܫܩܐ ܕܡܛܠ ܥܘܕܪܢܐ	ܣ
		Interpretation: about help	60
22v	Jn 6:31	ܦܘܫܩܐ ܕܡܛܠ ܚܝܐ ܘܦܘܪܩܢܐ	ܦܕ
		Interpretation: about life and deliverance	84

In instances such as these, headings from what may once have been a topical arrangement of *sortes* have crept into the statements as they were transmitted, presumably by accident. These may originally have functioned like the set questions do in *Astrampsychi*. No simple pattern is immediately evident in the manuscript, yet the arcane

22 They do not share all the same topics; e.g. the *puššāqē* do not concern themselves with such things as marriage, family affairs, or childbirth; nor do they address specific clerical careers, such as appointment to the role of bishop.
23 Klingshirn has designated them according to their incipit in several manuscripts: *Post solem surgunt stellae* ("Defining the *Sortes Sanctorum*," 94–98).
24 See examples in Klingshirn, "Defining the *Sortes Sanctorum*," 97.
25 See Franziska Naether, *Die Sortes Astrampsychi. Problemlösungsstrategien durch Orakel im römischen Ägypten* (Orientalische Religionen in der Antike: Ägypten, Israel, Alter Orient 3; Tübingen: Mohr Siebeck, 2010), 303; cf. Enrique Montero Cartelle and Alberto Alonso Guardo, *Los "Libros de Suertes" medievales: Las* Sortes Sanctorum *y los* Prenostica Socratis Basilei. *Estudio, traduccíon y edición crítica* (Neuva Roma 21; Madrid: Consejo superior de investigaciones científicas, 2004), 20–26.
26 The same phenomenon occurs in codices Bezae and Sangermanensis (see below).
27 Corrected from ܡܣܟܢܘܬܐ ("poverty").
28 Corrected from.ܡܛܠ

arrangement of the topical sets of answers in *Astrampsychi* stand as a reminder that cryptic patterns of organization are to be expected, and that corruption through the transmission process is likely to have affected the ordering of the material.[29]

Another parallel is to be found in the Byzantine *Riktologion*, a tool for divination in which a numbered series of passages occur, based mostly on the Gospels, followed by the term ἑρμηνεία and an oracular pronouncement.[30] For instance, number 31 paraphrases John 15:7 ("if you remain in me and I remain in you"), after which it presents the following word of hope: Καλὸν τὸ πρᾶγμά σου ἀποκαλύψεως ἐστιν, ὦ ἄνθρωπε, καὶ βοήθειαν ἔχεις παρὰ τῷ θεῷ.[31] Like Add. 17,119, the *Riktologion* calls the statements "interpretations" (*hermeneiai*), yet it is clear that the book is a tool for sortilege, and the *hermeneiai* are in fact oracles, albeit connected to scripture.

Add. 17,119 attests to a system of sortilege with certain parallels in other surviving lot oracle collections, such as *Sortes Astrampsychi*, *Sortes sanctorum*, *Sortes Sangallenses*, and the *Riktologion*. Although the systems in these tools do not appear to be directly related to the material in Add. 17,119, they share significant features of form and function, so that further comparison will undoubtedly illuminate the nature and use of the Syriac *puššāqē*. However, a body of other texts preserve elements so closely related to the apparatus in Add. 17,119 that they must derive from the same basic system–Gospel manuscripts with *hermeneiai*.

Hermeneiai in Other Biblical Manuscripts

Though Add. 17,119 has unique features, other artifacts attest to the longevity and distribution of putting *hermeneiai* with biblical texts. These warrant full analysis, and a somewhat more detailed comparison of them with our manuscript is offered elsewhere;[32] for purposes of this study only summary information is provided.

---

29 E.g. see Stewart, "The Textual Transmission of the 'Sortes Astrampsychi,'" 136–38.

30 F. Drexl, "Ein griechisches Losbuch," *ByzZ* 41 (1941): 311–18.

31 "The matter (for which you seek) revelation is good, and you will have God's help" (ibid., 317).

32 For a more detailed comparison, see Jeff W. Childers, "Embedded Oracles: Sortilege in a Syriac Gospel Codex," in *Contemporary Examinations of Classical Languages: Valency, Lexicography, Grammar, and Manuscripts* (ed. Timothy M. Lewis, Alison Salvesen, and Nicholas Al-Jeloo; PLAL 5; Piscataway, N. J.: Gorgias), forthcoming.

Greek and Greco-Coptic Papyri and Parchment Fragments

Several Greek and Greco-Coptic papyrus and parchment fragments from the fifth–eighth centuries have portions of John's Gospel with *hermeneiai*.[33] The oracular statements in these manuscripts are typically prefaced by the term ἑρμηνεία, though the fragmentary nature of the evidence makes it difficult to categorize the materials,[34] and in a few instances the *hermeneiai* themselves are impossible to make out. The seventh- to eighth-century fragmentary papyrus P.Ness. (P.Colt) 2.3 (also known as 𝔓⁵⁹) from Nessana in southern Palestine illustrates the typical format of many of these witnesses. On each of the few surviving leaves of the codex occurs a portion of John's Gospel, under which appears the term ερμηνια and a short oracular statement. For instance, the verso of one leaf (iv.d) has John 11:49–52 in Greek, followed by blank space, then the term ερμηνια centered on the page in slightly smaller letters (in the same hand), under which is the following statement, also in smaller letters: σ]ωτηρι[α] καλη. The layout is typical of this class of witnesses. Some of them have *hermeneiai* in both Greek and Coptic beneath the biblical text, and at least one manuscript is entirely in Coptic. This manuscript was identified recently, having portions of John 3, under which occurs the heading ⲉⲣⲙⲏⲛⲓⲁ, followed by oracular statements, all written solely in Coptic.[36]

Greek Codex Bezae

The celebrated fifth-century Greco-Latin bilingual Codex Bezae includes a set of sixty-nine Greek *hermeneiai* written in a rough hand in the bottom margins of leaves containing Mark's Gospel. F. H. Scrivener published an edition of them in 1864, though

---

33 See Stanley E. Porter, "The Use of Hermeneia and Johannine Papyri Manuscripts," in *Akten des 23. Internationalen Papyrologen-Kongresses* (ed. Bernhard Palme; PV 1; Vienna: Verlag der Österreichischen Akademie der Wissenschaften, 2007), 573–80; Bruce M. Metzger, "Greek Manuscripts of John's Gospel with 'Hermeneiai,'" in *Text and Testimony. Essays on New Testament and Apocryphal Literature in Honour of A. F. J. Klijn* (ed. Tjitze Baarda et al.; Kampen: J. H. Kok, 1988), 162–69.
34 See the discussion in Stanley Porter, "Textual Criticism in the Light of Diverse Textual Evidence for the Greek New Testament: An Expanded Proposal," in *New Testament Manuscripts: Their Texts and their World* (ed. Thomas J. Kraus and Tobias Nicklas; TENTS 2; Leiden: Brill, 2006), 322–25; David C. Parker analyzes the biblical text preserved in these witnesses, "Manuscripts of John's Gospel with Hermeneiai," in *Transmission and Reception: New Testament Text-Critical and Exegetical Studies* (ed. Jeff W. Childers and David C. Parker; TS 3.4; Piscataway, N. J.: Gorgias, 2006), 48–68.
35 Lionel Casson and Ernest L. Hettich, *Literary Papyri*, vol. 2 of *Excavations at Nessana* (Princeton: Princeton University Press, 1950), 79–93 (the text is cited from p. 87).
36 Brice C. Jones, "A Coptic Fragment of the Gospel of John with *Hermeneiai* (P.CtYBR inv. 4641)," *NTS* 60 (2014): 202–14.

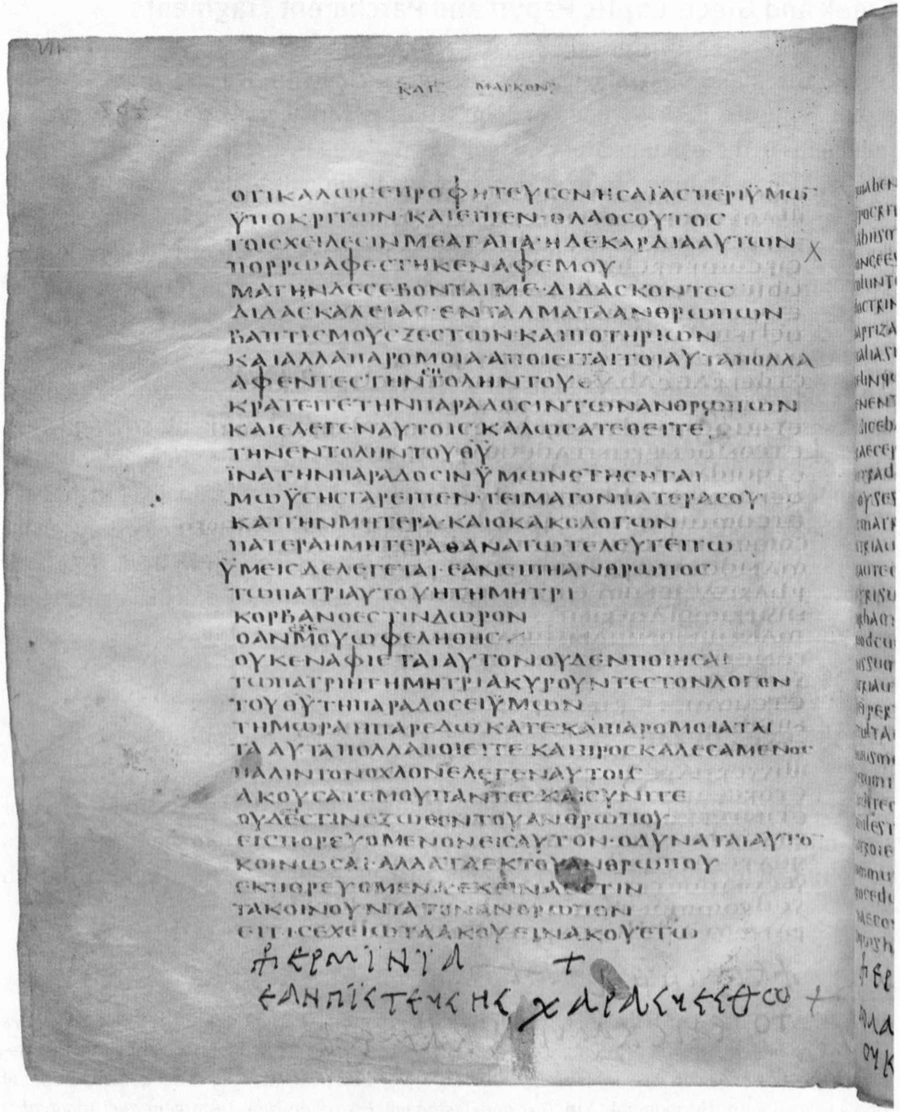

Fig. 23: Codex Bezae, f. 308v. © Cambridge University Library. Reproduced by kind permission of the Syndics of Cambridge University Library.

he did not recognize their true nature.[37] J. Rendel Harris' study in 1901 did greater justice to the material, and others have commented on it since, though Harris was the last to study Bezae's *hermeneiai* thoroughly.[38] Although the manuscript's main text is dated to the fifth century, the hand of the *hermeneiai* is later, dated to as early as 550–650 and as late as the ninth or tenth century.[39] The accompanying image shows folio 308v, with the Greek text of Mark 7:6–16. In the bottom margin the following statement occurs, marked by a staurogram (⳨): ερμϊνϊα + εαν πϊστευσησ χαρα συ εσθω +, which appears to mean: "*hermeneia* + if you believe, you will have joy +." The statement is not numbered, though it occurs forty-sixth in sequence. When we consult *Puššāqā* 46 in Add. 17,119, we find the following, at John 4:10: ܪܚܘܫ ܕܚܝܡ ܐܪ ܪܐܪܩ ܚܠ ܪܐܡ ("Interpretation: if you begin, you [will] have joy"). If we emend ܕܚܝܡ ("you begin") to ܚܝܡ, the statement becomes precisely parallel to the *hermeneia* in Bezae: "if you are confident, you (will) have joy." Codex Bezae and Add. 17,119 share many other *hermeneiai*, frequently in the same or a closely related sequence; however, they often differ in both content and sequence as well.

The correlation between the Greek *hermeneiai* in Bezae and many of the Syriac *puššāqē* in Add. 17,119 points up an important observation: much of the oracular material in the surviving witnesses of Gospel texts with *hermeneiai* is interrelated.[40] The papyrus fragment, Berlin, Staatliche Museen, Ägyptische Abteilung, P. 11914– also known as 𝔓[63] and dated to the fifth or sixth century–contains the text of John 4:10. The following Greek and Coptic statements accompany the biblical text:[41]

ερμηνια	εα[ν πι]στευσησ χαρα[σοι γ]ινεται
hermeneia	if you believe, there will be joy for you
	εκϣανπιστεγε ογṇ[ογρα]ϣε ναϣωπε νακ
	if you believe, there will be joy for you

---

37 See F. H. Scrivener, *Bezae Codex Cantabrigiensis* (Cambridge: Deighton, Bell, and Co., 1864), xxvii, 451–52.

38 See J. Rendel Harris, *The Annotators of the Codex Bezae* (London: C. J. Clay & Sons, 1901), 45–74; also Otto Stegmüller, "Zu den Bibelorakeln im Codex Bezae," *Bib* 34 (1953): 13–22; Metzger, "Greek Manuscripts of John's Gospel with 'Hermeneiai,'" 165–67; and Bernard Outtier, "Les *Prosermeneiai* du Codex Bezae," in *Codex Bezae. Studies from the Lunel Colloquium, June 1994* (ed. David C. Parker and Christian-B. Amphoux; Leiden: Brill, 1996), 74–78.

39 Parker prefers the earlier date (*Codex Bezae: An Early Christian Manuscript and its Text* [Cambridge: Cambridge University Press, 1992], 43, 49), but Metzger dates it to the ninth or tenth century ("Greek Manuscripts of John's Gospel with 'Hermeneiai,'" 165–66).

40 Harris observed and studied the close connections between the material in codex Bezae and Sangermanensis 15 (see below); Stegmüller noted the parallels between that material and the *hermeneiai* in the Johannine papyrus and parchment fragments.

41 Stegmüller, "Zu den Bibelorakeln im Codex Bezae," 17; also Metzger, "Greek Manuscripts of John's Gospel with 'Hermeneiai,'" 164.

Obviously, the material in Greek and Coptic is parallel to that of the aforementioned *Puššāqā* 46 at John 4:10 in Add. 17,119 and the forty-sixth *hermeneia* in codex Bezae. Also, like the *hermeneiai* in the Johannine papyri and parchment fragments, Bezae presents only one oracle per page, at the bottom of the page. This suggests that the structure of its ancestor may have been more like the Johannine fragments than either Add. 17,119 or Sangermanensis 15.

Latin Sangermanensis 15

Further parallels occur in another manuscript, the ninth-century Latin Bible, Sangermanensis 15 (Paris, Bibliothèque Nationale lat. 11553; i.e. g1), whose *hermeneiai*[42] Harris also studied, demonstrating that they are closely related and must draw upon the same archetype as those in codex Bezae, though neither codex Bezae nor Sangermanensis 15 show direct dependence on one another.[43] The latter includes 185 numbered statements in Latin, written in the margins alongside the text of John's Gospel and keyed to sections of the Gospel text. The hand is somewhat later than that of the main Gospel text. Many of the statements parallel those in Codex Bezae and Add. 17,119, often in a similar sequence. The accompanying image shows folio 126r. In the left margin near the bottom, the following statement occurs in connection with the text of John 4:4:

Sangermanensis 15	Jn 4:4	*xliii*	*si credideris gloria tibi*
		43	if you believe, you (will have) glory

The number and location are slightly different, but otherwise this statement nearly matches the aforementioned *hermeneiai* in both Add. 17,119 and in Codex Bezae, with the exception that "glory" stands in the place of "joy." To illustrate further: in the margin at John 11:10 (f. 130r) Sangermanensis 15 has the following: *clxxiii salus bona*. This matches the *hermeneia* mentioned above, in P.Ness. (P.Colt) 2.3 accompanying John 11:49–52, and the aforementioned *Puššāqā* 177 at John 11:46, as the following table shows:

---

42 Sangermanensis does not use the *hermeneia* formula, with perhaps one exception: the statement numbered 247 (f. 132v) reads, *interpretati causa tibi immanet* in which *interpretati* appears to correspond to ἑρμηνεία. Harris misunderstood the term *interpretati* and corrected it to *insperata* (Harris, *Annotators of the Codex Bezae*, 68).

43 See J. Rendell Harris, "The 'Sortes Sanctorum' in the St. Germain Codex (g1)," *AJP* 9 (1888): 58–63; idem, *Annotators of the Codex Bezae*, 59–74.

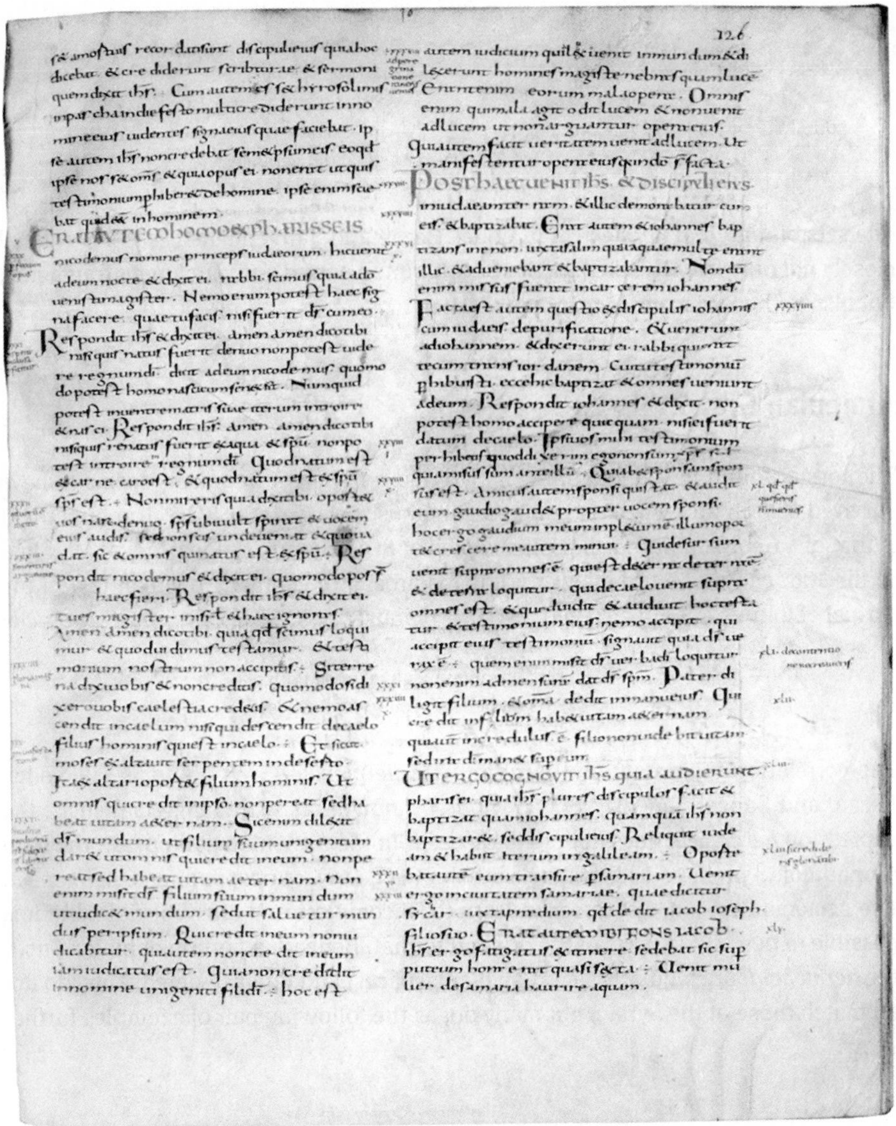

Fig. 24: Codex Sangermanensis 15, f. 126r. © Bibliothèque nationale de France. Used by kind permission of BnF.

Sangermanensis 15	Jn 11:10	*clxxiii*	*salus bona*
		173	a good salvation
P.Ness. (P.Colt) 2.3	Jn 11:49–52		σ]ωτηρι[α] καλη
			good salvation
Add. 17,119	Jn 11:46	ܡܘ	ܐܘܙܐܪ ܐܚ̈ܝܠ
		177	a good deliverance

The sets of marginal *hermeneiai* in Codex Bezae and Sangermanensis 15 are related closely not only to each other and to the Johannine papyri and parchment fragments, but also to the Syriac *puššāqē* in Add. 17,119.

Armenian Graz 2058/2

The format found in the Johannine papyri and parchment fragments seems to have survived also in an Armenian palimpsest manuscript, Graz 2058/2.[44] The upper text is that of a Georgian liturgical psalter copied at St. Catharine's monastery at Mt. Sinai in the 10th century, but the lower writing is an eighth-century Armenian text of the Gospel of John.[45] At John 4:11–14 (f. 79r), the manuscript includes the following oracle:

Graz 2058/2 Jn 4:11–14   48   թէ հաւատաս խնդութիւն լինի քեզ
                                           If you believe, you (will) have joy

The correlation in content and location with *hermeneiai* in $\mathfrak{P}^{63}$, Add. 17,119, codex Bezae, and Sangermanensis 15 is obvious. Although, as with Sangermanensis, the expression *hermeneia* does not regularly occur in the Armenian palimpsest, the term բարգմանն[...] prefaces its first oracle at John 1:1 (f. 66v), corresponding to *hermeneia*. The Armenian evidence of this manuscript is incomplete and often illegible, but it is possible to perceive aspects of the original format. Beneath a portion of biblical text, the *hermeneiai* are regularly set off by blank spaces, and often centered. They do not all match those of the Syriac, but many do, as the following pair of examples further show:

Add. 17,119	Jn 5:24	ܝܘ	ܐܦܘܟܐ ܐܒܛܐ ܐܩܫܦ
		67	Interpretation: a good change/return
Bezae	Mk 9–10	(69)	ερμϊνηα + μεταβουλη καλϊ
			herminea: a good change

---

44 In addition to Graz 2058/2, Outtier also described an 11th-century Armenian manuscript of John's Gospel with *hermeneiai* written into the margin, like *Sangermenensis*: Erevan, Matenadaran 9650 (Outtier, "Les Prosermeneiai du Codex Bezae," 76; idem, "Réponses oraculaires," 182).
45 I am indebted to Erich Renhart at the university library in Graz, who has been working to decipher the text and has kindly shared with me some of his preliminary findings.

Graz 2058/2	Jn 5:24a	73	փոփոխումս բարի
			a good change
Add. 17,119	Jn 6:11	ܒ	ܪܘܫܐ ܘܢ ܪܝܚܐܘ ܪܝܘ ܪܐܟܐ
		77	Interpretation: life and profit from God
Sangerm. 15	Jn 5:35	lxxvi[46]	*lucro et uita et do*[47]
		76	life and profit and (?) from God
Graz 2058/2	Jn 6:10–11	83	կենդանութիւն եւ շահ լայ
			life and profit f(rom) G(od)

The Place of Add. 17,119 among the Hermeneiai Witnesses

Obviously, the *hermeneia* systems in the Greek and Coptic Johannine papyri and parchments, Codex Bezae, Sangermanensis 15, and the Armenian palimpsest are all interrelated. It is evident that Add. 17,119 draws upon the same *hermeneia* tradition, and that these sources, in diverse languages and with distinct provenances, share a remarkable degree of common ancestry and influence. The archetype was probably Greek. Other points of contact include the generic character of the *sortes*. As mentioned previously, Add. 17,119 offers very general statements, often using the term ܪܝܚܐܘ. The other witnesses have the same general character. Rather than focusing on particular situations, the responses in the other witnesses routinely feature the terms πραγμα, *causa*, or ܗܢ–each of which refers generally to a "matter" or "affair" and is parallel to ܪܝܚܐܘ.

Furthermore, some *sortes* in codices Bezae and Sangermanensis 15 exhibit intrusions of topical headings like those in Add. 17,119.[48] For instance, at John 6:11, Sangermanensis 15 has the following "oracle," which is rather a heading: *lxxx. de uita et salute* (f. 127v), corresponding precisely to *Puššāqā* 84 in the Syriac text at John 6:31 (see above). In a few places, identical headings such as this one occur in the Syriac, Sangermanensis 15, and Codex Bezae. None of these witnesses provides a full list of topics, but the apparently accidental intrusions of topical headings into the material show the close interrelationship of the material and its shared ancestry.

In his research on a selection of these materials, Kevin Wilkinson compares the contents and sequences of a number of the *hermeneiai* in the fragmentary Johannine papyri and parchments, in Codex Bezae, and in Sangermanensis 15, confirming their

---

46 The manuscript has *lxxvi*, but by sequence the correct reading may be *lxxii* (Harris, *Annotators of the Codex Bezae*, 64).

47 The text of *Sangermanensis* appears garbled. Harris suggested that it may originally have been the heading of a group instead of a *sors* proper, but the Syriac and Armenian texts confirm the basic sense of the oracular statement.

48 See Harris, *Annotators of the Codex Bezae*, 70–71.

close interrelationship.[49] But whereas Codex Bezae has only sixty-nine oracles that are much later additions to the manuscript, and *Sangermanensis* has 185 oracles that constitute a somewhat later and marginal feature, the Syriac manuscript boasts a much fuller set of 308 oracles, incorporated into the biblical text in the same hand, and dating to a significantly earlier period than the other two. Like those in the Johannine papyri and parchment fragments, and the Armenian palimpsest, the *puššāqē* in Add. 17,119 were part of the original design and execution of the manuscript, not later additions. Unlike all the other extant witnesses, however, the Syriac manuscript incorporates its *puššāqē* directly into the biblical text, with minimal distinction (rubrication and marginal numbering). As the most complete and legible surviving example of a codex with *hermeneiai* from a fairly early period, Add. 17,119 must play a crucial role in understanding the *hermeneia* tradition and the role played by these remarkable books in the contexts of their production and use.

The Function of the *Hermeneiai* and the Gospel of John

Comparing the *hermeneia* witnesses suggests that the archetype for the *sortes*, presumably Greek, had a measure of structural independence from the Gospel text. This would help account for the different ways in which similar or even identical material appears in such different formats across the various witnesses. The *sortes* may once have existed as a distinct collection of statements, parallel to those of *Astrampsychi*, perhaps organized by topic. Yet their independence should not be exaggerated. One of the most striking similarities shared by the *hermeneia* witnesses is their connection to the Gospel of John. The noteworthy exception is Codex Bezae, where the *hermeneiai* occur with the Gospel of Mark instead. However, it ought to be remembered that Bezae's "Western" order of the Gospels puts Mark in the fourth position.[50] Considering their rough, unnumbered, and disconnected presentation in Bezae, it is not unlikely that the *hermeneiai* migrated to the margins of Mark's Gospel from the margins of a copy of John, or perhaps from a set of the *hermeneiai* circulating independently.

---

49 Wilkinson also shows that they exhibit meaningful connection to the Gospel of John (see below); Kevin Wilkinson, *"Hermêneiai* in Manuscripts of John's Gospel: An Aid to Bibliomancy," in *My Lots Are in Thy Hands: Sortilege and Its Practitioners in Late Antiquity* (ed. William E. Klingshirn and AnneMarie Luijendijk; RGRW; Leiden: Brill), forthcoming. I am grateful to Wilkinson for sharing his research with me.
50 Outtier, "Réponses oraculaires," 181.

Given the breadth and diversity of the evidence surveyed so far, along with the ecclesial proscriptions against bibliomantic sortilege, it is likely that specialized copies of John's Gospel having *hermeneiai* were once fairly numerous and widespread, though they faced official ambivalence, and perhaps repression. The evidence of the Greek papyri fragments suggests that such books may have been available by the fifth century, possibly before. Having established the formal characteristics of the *puššāqē* of Add. 17,119, their context amidst a wide range of other copies of tools for sortilege, and the likelihood of a broad *hermeneia* tradition from an early period, this study turns now to the following questions: What are the *hermeneiai/puššāqē* precisely, and how did they function? Why did the *hermeneiai* tend to attach themselves to books containing John's Gospel?

The Gospel of John as Host for the Hermeneiai

The present study has emphasized that the expressions *puššāqā* or ἑρμηνεία as they occur in the *hermeneia* witnesses (and the Byzantine *Riktologion*) are "interpretations" only in a highly specialized sense.[51] They are certainly not plain expositions of the biblical text; nor are they derived from biblical commentaries or homilies. They do not have obvious liturgical functions.[52] Their affinities with other lot oracles indicate that the common view is sound: they are basically oracular in function. However, the connection of the *hermeneiai* with a biblical text–and John in particular–requires explanation.[53]

As has already been mentioned, early and late antique Christianity was familiar with the bibliomantic use of scripture.[54] Particularly intensive use of the Fourth Gospel in these ways may have been prompted by the mystical qualities of John's language and the mysteries of its contents. Whatever the impetus, evidence for the

---

51 On the basis of limited exposure to the evidence, some editors of the Greek and Greco-Coptic material speculated that the materials were exegetical in nature (see Porter, "Use of Hermeneia and Johannine Papyrus Manuscripts," 575). This view has been followed by some, but not many. The common view is represented by Metzger: the *hermeneiai* are "not intended as exegetical comments on the Scripture text" ("Manuscripts of John's Gospel with 'Hermeneiai,'" 166–67).
52 Cf. Wally V. Cirafesi, "The Bilingual Character and Liturgical Function of 'Hermeneia' in Johannine Papyrus Manuscripts: A New Proposal," *NovT* 56 (2014): 45–67. Struck by the bilingual nature of some of the witnesses, Cirafesi proposes that the *hermeneiai* are liturgical tools for use in bilingual contexts. Cirafesi did not have access to the Syriac or Armenian evidence. Furthermore, clearly connecting the bulk of the material with inarguably liturgical functions remains to be done.
53 The long association of the material with John's Gospel is underscored by a unique occurrence in *Puššāqā* 62 at John 5:3, which quotes a portion of John 5:14 as the oracle: ܐܬܐ ܠܐ ܐܢܬ ܚܠܝܡ ܐܢܬ ܗܐ ("behold you are well, do not sin"). Sangermanensis 15 (f. 126v) and codex Bezae (f. 318r) have nearly identical statements. See also Harris, *Annotators of the Codex Bezae*, 64, n. 1.
54 Gamble, *Books and Readers in the Early Church*, 237–41.

mantic use of John spans the centuries. For instance, Augustine exhorts his hearers to cure headaches by sleeping with a copy of John's Gospel, rather than using amulets;[55] John's opening statements of power are used apotropaically in Syriac healing charms and Arabic amulets;[56] a late 13th-century Benedictine charm against sheep murrain begins with a recitation from the beginning of John 1;[57] and a Nottingham sorcerer is reputed to have sold copies of John's Gospel for ten shillings apiece in the early 17th century as a guard against witchcraft.[58]

Perhaps more than any other book of the Bible, the Gospel of John has been used in ways that reveal an enduring belief in its mystical power—including its role in practices of divination (e.g. Add. 17,119). By their integration into copies of John, the *puššāqē*/*hermeneiai* acquired a mystical power by association, bolstering their divinatory authority. However, it would be wrong to conclude, as some have, that the contents of John's Gospel have no substantial connection to the contents of the *sortes*.

The Meaning and Function of the Puššāqē

In 1884, M. Samuel Berger remarked that the *sortes* of Sangermanensis were "sans aucune relation avec la texte de l'Évangile;"[59] Harris echoed this assessment and others have followed. In view of the very sparse religious content of the *puššāqē*, and the process observable elsewhere (e.g. *Sortes Astrampsychi*), by which formerly pagan *sortes* are adapted to Christian use, it is not unlikely that much of the material in the *puššāqē* originated from non-Christian sources. However, in their present form they have been fitted to the context of John's Gospel. Surveying the Greek, Greco-Coptic, and Latin *hermeneia* witnesses, Porter argued against "a capricious attachment of apophthegms" to the manuscripts, describing the statements as, "certainly Johannine in flavor." He does not deny their oracular function, but highlights the resonances in vocabulary and theme between the statements and their biblical contexts. He concludes, "[t]he state-

---

55 *Tract. Ev. Jo.* 7.12.
56 For a Syriac example, see Harvard Syr 156 (Goshen-Gottstein, *Syriac Manuscripts in the Harvard College Library: A Catalogue*, 103–5); for Arabic examples, see Clifford E. Bosworth, *The Mediaeval Islamic Underworld: The Banū Sāsān in Arabic Society and Literature. Part 1, the Banū Sāsān in Arabic Life and Lore* (Leiden: Brill, 1976), 128.
57 Herbert Edward Salter, ed., *Eynsham Cartulary* (2 vols.; OHS 49–50; Oxford: Oxford Historical Society, 1907–08), 1:18.
58 Keith Thomas, *Religion and the Decline of Magic* (New York: Oxford University Press, 1997), 187, 249 (see also 31, 36, 52, 275–76); see Don C. Skemer, *Binding Words: Textual Amulets in the Middle Ages* (University Park, Penn.: Pennsylvania State University Press, 2006), 50–51, 67–68; T. Julian Brown, *The Stonyhurst Gospel of Saint John* (Oxford: The Roxburghe Club, 1969), 29–37; George Gifford, *A Dialogue Concerning Witches and Witchcrafts* (London, 1593), sig. B1v.
59 *Bulletin Critique* 5 (1884) 361–66; quoted by Harris, "The 'Sortes sanctorum' in the St. Germain Codex (*g1*)," 59.

ments are neither strictly commentary nor simply unattached oracular pronouncements, but biblically motivated and connected reflections on the biblical text, perhaps utilizing similar language."[60] Porter does not analyze the statements in detail, and his characterization of them functions more as a warning against simplistic readings of the *hermeneiai* than a precise description of their purpose. In fact, characterizing the statements as "reflections on the biblical text" may underplay their oracular function and exaggerate their ability to function as commentary or gloss on the biblical text.[61] Yet an analysis of the *puššāqē* in Add. 17,119 shows that Porter is right to raise a caution against divorcing the statements from their Johannine context too much.

Many of the *puššāqē* echo the language of the Gospel or resonate with its tone.[62] For instance, some of them talk about life or truth or glory, which are common topics in John. *Puššāqē* 9 and 33 focus on true speech and testimony, in contexts concerning accurate testimony (John 1:23; 3:11). Testimony language is common in the *puššāqē*, as it is in John's Gospel. The promise of finding what one seeks is keyed to the story of discovering the empty tomb in John 20 (*Puššāqā* 287), and an expectation of joy is expressed in the context of the resurrection narrative (*Puššāqā* 291). In the context of John 7, where Jesus is falsely accused, *Puššāqā* 105 enjoins, "do not fear slander." The oracle adjacent to Jesus' request for a drink in John 4:7 speaks of "refreshment and gain" (*Puššāqā* 44).

For some of these, the alleged connections are rather vague, but a few are so suggestive as to prompt a closer look, in which we find some connections responding even more directly to the narrative. For example, in the context of a dispute involving John the Baptist's disciples (John 3:25), *Puššāqā* 42 instructs, "do not dispute." At precisely the point where Jesus encourages his disciples, "Do not let your hearts be troubled" (John 14:1), *Puššāqā* 213 has, "do not be distressed at this matter". At John 16:33, where Jesus encourages his disciples to "take heart, for [he has] overcome the world," *Puššāqā* 246 also says, "you will overcome in judgment." Oracles regarding court decisions and judgments seem especially frequent in the scenes of Jesus' trials in John 18, and an oracle about laughter and ridicule is keyed to John 19:2 (*Puššāqā* 272), where the soldiers are taunting Jesus. Further down in the same chapter, two oracles occur about deeds being completed well and finished, using the same term (ܫܠܡ) that occurs in the immediate Gospel context more than once to speak of Jesus' completing and fulfilling his work on the cross (John 19:28, 30). In John 5, where the healed paralytic is challenged by the Jews to confess who was responsible for per-

---

60 Porter, "Use of Hermeneia and Johannine Papyrus Manuscripts," 579.

61 See Porter, "What Do We Know and How Do We Know It? Reconstructing Early Christianity from its Manuscripts," in *Christian Origins and Greco-Roman Culture: Social and Literary Contexts for the New Testament* (eds. Stanley E. Porter and Andrew W. Pitts; TENTS 9; Leiden: Brill, 2013), 60–63, in which Porter takes the *hermeneia* materials as evidence that early Christian communities were reflective and theologically constructive.

62 The following analysis of Johannine connections is adapted from Childers, "Embedded Oracles."

forming a healing on the Sabbath, *Puššāqā* 63 exhorts, "do not deny but confess." After Judas slips out to betray Jesus (John 13:30) and before Jesus speaks of his imminent glorification (13:31), *Puššāqā* 210 reads, "from want/deficiency will come glory." Where Jesus bequeathes peace (John 14:27), *Puššāqā* 223 promises, "the affair will produce peace." A few involve numbers, as in *Puššāqā* 28, where it is promised that a thing will resolve after three days, shortly after Jesus' promise to rebuild the temple in three days (John 2:19–22).

Many of these resonances are remarkable, but the pattern is far from thoroughgoing. In many instances there is no perceptible connection between the language of the oracle and that of its biblical context. Furthermore, John presents more opportunities than the *puššāqē* exploit. For instance, one wonders why John 5, with its lengthy discussion of testimony, did not attract more *puššāqē* regarding testimony. Yet where they occur, the large number of thematic parallels and shared language cannot be coincidental. Whatever the origin of the *puššāqē*, as we have them now in Johannine texts, the structure and language of the biblical narrative influenced the placement of at least many of them, and undoubtedly affected their wording as well. This is more evident in the *puššāqē* of Add. 17,119 than in Sangermanensis 15, partly because the former is a more complete set, but also because in the Syriac the placement reveals greater intentionality than we see in the Latin; the structure of the Syriac may preserve a more primitive placement of the oracular materials.

In any case, the pattern of placement shows us that for their potency, the *puššāqē* draw not only on the authority of the sacred codex and the aura of mystery and power that John's Gospel enjoyed, but even on very specific elements of the narrative itself, sometimes in sophisticated ways. In this sense, they are "interpretations," though the method by which the user connected divine scripture to the needs and concerns of inquirers exhibits a different mode of interpretation than is common in patristic and medieval commentaries or homilies. These interpretations are essentially oracular in nature and divinatory in purpose.

Just as the aforementioned proscriptions against "drawing lots" are aimed at clergy, it is likely that the users of the *hermeneia* manuscripts were clerical. Yet it is uncertain how the users of these tools would be approached by inquirers, or how the diviner would correlate the inquirer's concerns to particular responses. Clear instructions accompany the *Sortes Astrampsychi*, and practitioners of the *Sortes sanctorum* used a prescribed system of die-casting or knucklebones, but the biblical manuscripts include no such instructions. Yet Sangermanensis 15 may provide a clue. The accompanying image shows folio 89v. Prior to its presentation of the Eusebian Canons, a wheel occurs, divided into eight sections and filled with a broken series of numbers leading up to 316. Although this would appear to be a device to help the diviner select the right response,[63] the mechanism of its operation is very obscure. Many of the

---

63 See Harris, "The 'Sortes Sanctorum' in the St. Germain Codex (*g1*)," 60–61.

Fig. 25: Codex Sangermanensis 15, f. 89v. © Bibliothèque nationale de France. Used by kind permission of BnF.

numbers do not even correspond to sections in John with *sortes* (though most of them do), reminding us that the extant systems may be corrupt and "broken," and therefore very difficult to unravel or reconcile perfectly. Furthermore, no such organizational or selection device occurs in Add. 17,119 or in the other known *hermeneia* manuscripts.

History of Use

The preceding analyses and discussion show that connecting the divinatory material with the Gospel of John in a single, specialized volume was integral to the purpose of the material. We cannot know as much as we might wish to know about the circumstances of the codex's origins, its owners, or the precise manner of its use. Nevertheless, by observing alterations to the codex and attending to the testimony of the several hands that have marked its pages, it is possible to chronicle in broad outline the history of this codex.

Origins of Add. 17,119

The manuscript was created in the sixth or seventh century.[64] Notes about the codex's origins are very sparse. The scribe discloses his name on the last leaf, in slightly diminutive letters, in a conventional way that reveals nothing further about his identity, location, or circumstances: ܝܘ ܐܠ ܠܟ، ܐܬܐ، ܠܕ ܠܟܝܢܐ ܚܣ ܣܘ ܕ ܢܟܐ ܕܚܠܬ ܕܢܘܣܝ ܚܣܘܡ ܕܝܟܐ ܐܟ ܪܚܡ ("Pray, my lord, for the unworthy George, who wrote, that he may receive mercy on the day of judgment. Amen" f. 83r). Nothing is said about date or original ownership. The book that he created consists largely of the text of John's Gospel, carefully copied, though not without error, mostly in the form of a few omissions. Yet the biblical content is limited to the Gospel of John only, making it an unusual Gospel codex, as we have discussed.[65] Also as described above, the typical Gospel apparatus is missing. Instead, the scribe included the rubricated *puššāqē* and their numbers as an integrated part of the original book, incorporating the *puššāqē* into the flow of the biblical text. It is impossible to know whether the scribe simply imitated his exemplar in doing this, or modified the format of the *puššāqē* in some way. But it is clear that from its execution, the codex was intended to function as a *hermeneia* manuscript. The book may have included a title, instructions, or further apparatus related to its special content, but if so, these have not survived; the first folios (1–2) of the manuscript are missing.

The last folio includes a simple colored cross of a type common to Syriac decoration, surrounded by a bold nimbus. Before that, the original scribe included a subscription and doxology at the end of the book. The doxology is rather unusual, perhaps reflecting the special nature of the codex: ܬܫܒܘܚܬܐ ܠܐܠܗܐ ܒܡܪܘܡܐ. ܘܣܠܡܐ ܥܠ ܐܪܥܐ. ܘܣܒܪܐ ܛܒܐ ܠܒܢܝ ܐܢܫܐ ܐܡܝܢ ("Glory to God in heaven, and peace on earth, and good hope to people. Amen," f. 83v). In language reminiscent of scripture (Luke 2:14), the doxology praises God, yet invokes peace and good fortune for people.

---

64 The date is based on paleography (see Wright, *Catalogue*, 1:71).
65 See above.

The subscription is even more intriguing. It reads: ܥܠܡ ܐܘܢܓܠܝܘܢ ܕܝܘܚܢܢ ܫܠܝܚܐ ܒܪ ([Syriac text]) ([Syriac text])
("Ended is the Gospel of John the Apostle, Son of Zebedee, which was interpreted by John, Bishop of Constantinople, whom by people is customarily called Chrysostom," f. 82v). Due to this subscription, Wright presumed the *puššāqē* ("interpretations") had something to do with Chrysostom's "interpretation," or *Commentary on John*,[66] a series of exegetical homilies on John's Gospel that were very popular in Greek and Syriac.[67] However, a thorough comparison with Chrysostom's *Commentary* shows that the *puššāqē* have no particular connection to Chrysostom or his material. It is possible that the composer of the subscription connected the book to Chrysostom by mistake, though that would be surprising, in view of the fairly obvious yet special nature of the *puššāqē*, and the apparently widespread use of sortilege materials. Perhaps the composer sought to disguise the true nature of the *puššāqē*, by referring to Chrysostom's more readily approved *Puššāqā*, or Commentary. Yet the most likely explanation may be that the Chrysostom reference is merely incidental. Some West Syrian Psalters mention Athanasius' interpretation on the Psalms, yet no discernable connection exists between Athanasius' *Commentary on the Psalms* and the material of the Psalters in which the notes occur.[68] References such as these may simply reflect the popularity and use of specific commentators in monastic or ecclesial libraries. The attachment of such a subscription to John's Gospel may even predate the attachment of the *puššāqē* to the Gospel text.

Such was the codex as originally executed in the sixth or seventh century, to the extent we can reconstruct its original form.

Correction, Repair, and Loss

Over time, the book's tale continued to develop, as it changed owners and continued to manifest evidence of the sustained use of both its Gospel text and its divinatory apparatus. As for the ownership of the codex, fragmentary notes on the last folio

---

66 Wright, *Catalogue*, 1:71.

67 See Jeff W. Childers, *The Syriac Version of John Chrysostom's* Commentary on John. *I. Mêmrê 1–43* (CSCO 651, 652; Leuven: Peeters, 2013); idem, "Mapping the Syriac Chrysostom: The Topography of His Legacy in the Syriac Tradition," in *Bible, Qur'ān and Their Interpretation: Syriac Perspectives I* (ed. Cornelia Horn; EMTC 1; Warwick, Rhode Island: Abelian Academic: 2013), 129–51.

68 See David G. K. Taylor, "Psalm Headings in the West Syrian Tradition," in *The Peshiṭta: Its Use in Literature and Liturgy. Papers Read at the Third Peshiṭta Symposium* (ed. Bas ter Haar Romeny; MPIL 15; Leiden: Brill, 2006), 377; Jeff W. Childers, "Chrysostom in Syriac Dress," in *Cappadocian Writers, The Second Half of the Fourth Century* (vol. 15 of *Papers Presented at the Sixteenth International Conference on Patristic Studies held in Oxford 2011*, ed. Markus Vinzent; StPatr 67; Leuven: Peeters, 2013), 323–32.

show that at some point it came into the possession of the Monastery of Silvanus at Damascus, having been purchased for it by the abbot (f. 83r). However, it eventually became part of the great collection of old Syriac books preserved at Deir al-Suryani in the Wadi Natrun in Egypt. It may have been brought there by Mushê of Nisibis when he returned to the monastery in 932, along with the many other texts acquired on his travels, though we cannot know for certain.[69] From Deir al-Suryani the codex was acquired by the British Library in the mid-19th century, where its leaves were paginated and some leaves restored; the codex was bound, and eventually catalogued by William Wright.[70]

Long before coming into the possession of the British Library, users of the codex noticed that the text of John was defective here and there. At least three different hands are evident in the repair or completion of the Gospel text, writing in the margins at locations where they detected errors, or variant readings to be "corrected" (e.g. ff. 9v, 13v, 27r, 35v, 49v). These corrections show that the text of John's Gospel was very important to at least many of the book's users over the centuries; John was probably being read on its own terms, so that any problems with the biblical text were seen to be in need of remedy. The Gospel text is never treated as incidental to the purpose of the book.

Apart from marginal corrections, at some point in the history of the codex two leaves with portions of John 16 and 17 went missing and were replaced (f. 63, 66). Whereas the original leaves are parchment, the replacement leaves are paper, in a hand of about the twelfth century. In these replacement leaves, *puššāqē* are not written into the Gospel text, but they are included in the margins, in two or three different hands, at least one of which was later than that of the replaced Gospel text. Due to tearing and damage to the edges of the leaves, some of these marginal *puššāqē* are fragmentary. It is impossible to know where the replacement *puššāqē* came from or whether they matched the original ones from the missing leaves. What is certain is that a user of the codex found it necessary to replace the missing biblical text in folios 63 and 66, but did not incorporate *puššāqē* in doing so. However, later users deemed the *puššāqē* to be important enough to replace them also, from whatever exemplar was available, including their numbers, in sequence.[71] The continuing importance of the *puššāqē* to the users of the codex is also evident in the correction and re-inking of many of the numbers accompanying them. As numbers wore away and became illegible, correctors supplied legible ones throughout the manuscript.

---

69 See Sebastian P. Brock, "Without Mushê of Nisibis, Where Would We Be? Some Reflections on the Transmission of Syriac Literature," *JEastCS* 56 (2004): 15–24.

70 Wright, *Catalogue*, 1:71–72.

71 Ff. 63 and 66 also include a few marginal corrections to the Gospel text, showing that the Gospel text itself continued to merit attention.

In time signatures were added to the gatherings of folios, or perhaps the original signatures were restored, and a regular heading ܐܘܢܓܠܝܘܢ ܕܝܘܚܢܢ ("Gospel of John") was added to the manuscript; this normally occurs at the top of every fifth folio (verso). The original scribe had included no liturgical notations, nor did the manuscript acquire such notations or other typical Gospel apparatus over time, as biblical manuscripts often do. This suggests that the book never came into public or liturgical use, although the use and significance of the Gospel text itself is evident throughout the manuscript's history.

At some point the first two leaves went missing, and just as folios 63 and 66 had been replaced, these were also replaced with paper leaves containing John 1:1–19a, having the simple heading, ܐܘܢܓܠܝܘܢ ܕܝܘܚܢܢ ("Gospel of John," f. 1r).[72] This replacement text is in a bold and regular hand, somewhat later than the hand in the aforementioned replacements (f. 63, 66), though still judged by Wright to be of the twelfth century. This repair to the codex underscores once again the importance of the biblical text to its user–yet these replacement leaves do not include *puššāqē*, not even in the margins, so that the surviving apparatus begins with *Puššāqā* 7 (f. 3r). Why were the first six *puššāqē* not replaced? Perhaps there was no exemplar from which to take them. Or, since the hand of the first two folios is distinctive, it may be that this new user had no interest in the *puššāqē* and cared only about the biblical text. Such a user would have been like the much later reader, Philip E. Pusey, who collated the Syriac manuscript for the 1901 edition of the Peshiṭta Gospels yet made no mention of the *puššāqē*, presumably because they were of no interest to him or his purposes. By the time of the twelfth century replacement, the manuscript may have been revered as a venerable copy of scripture, worth restoring and using as such, irrespective of its original divinatory purpose. In any case, the first six *puššāqē* and any initial aids were lost to the codex and never replaced, but the manuscript's function as a complete copy of the Peshiṭta text of John's Gospel was carefully preserved.

Conclusion

Scripture has always enjoyed a central status and authority within the Christian tradition. However, the ecclesially sanctioned literary and dramatic contexts of its use–e.g. commentaries, homilies, and liturgies–provide only a partial glimpse into the diverse function of scripture within historic communities of textual practice. The analysis of ancient Bibles as material objects inhabiting a living tradition supplies another and often overlooked perspective. From a fairly early period, some commu-

---

72 The recurring heading already mentioned was added in a different hand, probably slightly earlier.

nities produced and used copies of John's Gospel that included explicit and sophisticated divinatory content. Though unconventional by sanctioned ecclesial standards, the users of these *hermeneia* materials were "interpreters," bringing scripture to bear on the pressing questions and daily lives of common Christian folk, outside the official contexts of liturgical practice and theological deliberation.

Many details of these objects' origins and use remain obscure. However, vestigial traces, in several different languages and in monuments of diverse provenances, attest to the deep and lasting impact of the *hermeneia* tradition in Christian communities. The Syriac manuscript Add. 17,119 stands as one of the most important witnesses to be so identified. The preceding analyses and discussion show that connecting the divinatory material with the Gospel of John in a single, specialized volume like Add. 17,119 was integral to the purpose of the material. Once combined, the synthesis of Gospel and *puššāqē* created a distinctive artifact, a codex that contained both a fair copy of the Peshiṭta text of John and a related set of oracular pronouncements: the *divining gospel*. The statements, by which the book's user could gain mystical guidance in response to specific questions, draw their potency from their context in a sacred material object. Yet they also draw specific language and thematic flavor from the Gospel text itself. This has made it difficult to classify the material's function in relation to the biblical text, but the fuller evidence supplied by the Syriac manuscript underscores the basically oracular function of the *puššāqē*, without denying their organic connection to John's Gospel. We are reminded that when we detach ancient texts from the concrete artifacts in which they reside, we are liable to lose critical dimensions of the text's original significance.

Add. 17,119 bears a remarkable legacy to a widespread ancient practice, inviting careful study. I am in the process of preparing an edition and full analysis of the *puššāqē* material of the Syriac manuscript, along with some of its parallels, in hopes of furthering that study. Yet even this preliminary analysis has shown that certain moments of the dynamic history of the codex are already apparent. The material characteristics of the codex situate scripture within concrete yet distinct and changing contexts of interpretation and use. As the book was used, repaired, and annotated through several centuries, it came to manifest changing views regarding the significance and validity of its original divinatory content, especially in relation to the sacred text of its context, the Gospel of John. That content never went away–and it may be that it continued to be used for its intended purpose throughout the book's history, at least until the beginning of its sojourn in London. But it was the Gospel text in particular that was especially preserved, even when some of the *puššāqē* had been lost and forgotten. A powerful reverence for an artifact bearing the Gospel text had undoubtedly been the impetus for synthesizing oracles into the codex in the first place; this reverence persevered, ensuring not only that defects in the Gospel portions of the manuscript would be redressed when encountered, but also that the book itself would be preserved through the centuries and continue to be a source of wonder today.

Bibliography

Bosworth, Clifford E. *The Mediaeval Islamic Underworld: The Banū Sāsān in Arabic Society and Literature. Part 1, the Banū Sāsān in Arabic Life and Lore.* Leiden: Brill, 1976.

Brock, Sebastian P. "Without Mushê of Nisibis, Where Would We Be? Some Reflections on the Transmission of Syriac Literature." *Journal of Eastern Christian Studies* 56 (2004): 15–24.

Brodersen, Kai, ed. *Astrampsychos das Pythagoras-Orakel.* Texte zur Forschung 88. Darmstadt: Wissenschaftliche Buchgesellschaft, 2006.

Brown, T. Julian. *The Stonyhurst Gospel of Saint John.* Oxford: The Roxburghe Club, 1969.

Browne, Gerald M., ed. *Sortes Astrampsychi. Vol. I: Ecdosis Prior.* Leipzig: B. G. Teubner, 1983.

Cartelle, Enrique Montero and Alberto Alonso Guardo. *Los "Libros de Suertes" medievales: Las Sortes Sanctorum y los Prenostica Socratis Basilei. Estudio, traduccíon y edición crítica.* Neuva Roma 21. Madrid: Consejo superior de investigaciones científicas, 2004.

Casson, Lionel and Ernest L. Hettich, ed. *Literary Papyri.* Vol. 2 of *Excavations at Nessana:* . Princeton: Princeton University Press, 1950.

Childers, Jeff W. "Chrysostom in Syriac Dress." Pages 323–32 in *Cappadocian Writers, The Second Half of the Fourth Century.* Vol. 15 of *Papers Presented at the Sixteenth International Conference on Patristic Studies held in Oxford 2011.* Edited by Markus Vinzent. Studia Patristica 67. Leuven: Peeters, 2013.

–. "Embedded Oracles: Sortilege in a Syriac Gospel Codex." Forthcoming in *Contemporary Examinations of Classical Languages: Valency, Lexicography, Grammar, and Manuscripts.* Edited by Timothy M. Lewis, Alison Salvesen, and Nicholas Al-Jeloo. Perspectives on Linguistics and Ancient Languages 5. Piscataway, N. J.: Gorgias.

–. "Hermeneutics and Magic: A Unique Syriac Biblical Manuscript as an Oracle of Interpretation." Forthcoming in *My Lots Are in Thy Hands: Sortilege and Its Practitioners in Late Antiquity.* Edited by William E. Klingshirn and AnneMarie Luijendijk. Religions in the Graeco-Roman World. Leiden: Brill.

–. "Mapping the Syriac Chrysostom: The Topography of His Legacy in the Syriac Tradition." Pages 129–51 in *Bible, Qur'ān and Their Interpretation: Syriac Perspectives I.* Edited by Cornelia Horn. Eastern Mediterranean Texts & Contexts 1. Warwick, Rhode Island: Abelian Academic: 2013.

–. ed. *The Syriac Version of John Chrysostom's* Commentary on John. *I. Mêmrê 1–43.* 2 vols. Corpus Scriptorum Christianorum Orientalium 651, 652. Leuven: Peeters, 2013.

Cirafesi, Wally V. "The Bilingual Character and Liturgical Function of 'Hermeneia' in Johannine Papyrus Manuscripts: A New Proposal." *Novum Testamentum* 56 (2014): 45–67.

Drexl, F. "Ein griechisches Losbuch." *Byzantinische Zeitschrift* 41 (1941): 311–18.

Gamble, Harry Y. *Books and Readers in the Early Church.* New Haven, Conn.: Yale University Press, 1997.

Gifford, George. *A Dialogue Concerning Witches and Witchcrafts.* London, 1593.

Goshen-Gottstein, Moshe H. *Syriac Manuscripts in the Harvard College Library: A Catalogue.* Harvard Semitic Studies 23; Missoula, Mont.: Scholars Press, 1979.

Harris, J. Rendel. *The Annotators of the Codex Bezae.* London: C. J. Clay & Sons, 1901.

–. "The 'Sortes Sanctorum' in the St. Germain Codex (*g1*)." *American Journal of Philology* 9 (1888): 58–63.

Horst, Pieter W. van der "*Sortes*: Sacred Books as Instant Oracles in Late Antiquity." Pages 142–73 in *The Use of Sacred Books in the Ancient World.* Edited by Leonard V. Rutgers et al. Contributions to Biblical Exegesis and Theology 22. Leuven: Peeters, 1998.

Jones, Brice C. "A Coptic Fragment of the Gospel of John with *Hermeneiai* (P.CtYBR inv. 4641)." *New Testament Studies* 60 (2014): 202–14.

Juckel, Andreas K. "The 'Syriac Masora' and the New Testament Peshiṭta." Pages 107–21 in *The Peshiṭta: Its Use in Literature and Liturgy. Papers Read at the Third Peshiṭta Symposium*. Edited by Bas ter Haar Romeny. Monographs of the Peshiṭta Institute Leiden 15. Leiden: Brill, 2006.

Klingshirn, William E. "Defining the *Sortes Sanctorum*." *Journal of Early Christian Studies* 10 (2002): 77–130.

Metzger, Bruce M. "Greek Manuscripts of John's Gospel with 'Hermeneiai.'" Pages 162–69 in *Text and Testimony. Essays on New Testament and Apocryphal Literature in Honour of A. F. J. Klijn*. Edited by Tjitze Baarda et al. Kampen: J. H. Kok, 1988.

Naether, Franziska. *Die Sortes Astrampsychi. Problemlösungsstrategien durch Orakel im römischen Ägypten*. Orientalische Religionen in der Antike: Ägypten, Israel, Alter Orient 3. Tübingen: Mohr Siebeck, 2010.

Outtier, Bernard. "Les *Prosermeneiai* du Codex Bezae." Pages 74–78 in *Codex Bezae. Studies from the Lunel Colloquium, June 1994*. Edited by David C. Parker and Christian-B. Amphoux. Leiden: Brill, 1996.

–. "Réponses oraculaires dans des manuscrits bibliques caucasiens." Pages 181–84 in *Armenia and the Bible*. Edited by Christopher Burchard. University of Pennsylvania Armenian Texts and Studies 12. Atlanta, Ga.: Scholars Press, 1993.

Parker, David C. *Codex Bezae: An Early Christian Manuscript and its Text*. Cambridge: Cambridge University Press, 1992.

–. "Manuscripts of John's Gospel with *Hermeneiai*." Pages 48–68 in *Transmission and Reception: New Testament Text-Critical and Exegetical Studies*. Edited by Jeff W. Childers and David C. Parker. Texts and Studies 3.4. Piscataway, N. J.: Gorgias, 2006.

Porter, Stanley E. "Textual Criticism in the Light of Diverse Textual Evidence for the Greek New Testament: An Expanded Proposal." Pages 305–37 in *New Testament Manuscripts: Their Texts and their World*. Edited by Thomas J. Kraus and Tobias Nicklas. Texts and Editions for New Testament Study 2. Leiden: Brill, 2006.

–. "The Use of Hermeneia and Johannine Papyri Manuscripts." Pages 573–80 in *Akten des 23. Internationalen Papyrologen-Kongresses*. Edited by Bernhard Palme. Papyrologica Vindobonensia 1. Vienna: Verlag der Österreichischen Akademie der Wissenschaften, 2007.

–. "What Do We Know and How Do We Know It? Reconstructing Early Christianity from its Manuscripts." Pages 41–70 in *Christian Origins and Greco-Roman Culture: Social and Literary Contexts for the New Testament*. Edited by Stanley E. Porter and Andrew W. Pitts. Texts and Editions for New Testament Study 9. Leiden: Brill, 2013.

Pusey, Philip E., and G. H. Gwilliam. *Tetraeuangelium sanctum juxta simplicem Syrorum versionem ad fidem codicum, massorae, editionem denuo recognitum*. Oxford: Clarendon Press, 1901.

Salter, Herbert Edward, ed. *Eynsham Cartulary*. 2 vols. Publications of the Oxford Historical Society 49–50. Oxford: Oxford Historical Society, 1907–1908.

Scrivener, Frederick H. *Bezae Codex Cantabrigiensis*. Cambridge: Deighton, Bell, and Co., 1864.

Skemer, Don C. *Binding Words: Textual Amulets in the Middle Ages*. University Park, Penn.: Pennsylvania State University Press, 2006.

Stegmüller, Otto. "Zu den Bibelorakeln im Codex Bezae." *Biblica* 34 (1953): 13–22.

Stewart, Randall. "The Textual Transmission of the 'Sortes Astrampsychi.'" *Illinois Classical Studies* 20 (1995): 135–47.

Stewart, Randall, ed. *Sortes Astrampsychi. Vol. II*. Leipzig: K. G. Saur, 2001.

Stewart, Randall and Kenneth Morell. "The Oracles of Astrampsychus." Pages 285–324 in *Anthology of Ancient Greek Popular Literature*. Edited by William Hansen. Bloomington, Ind.: Indiana University Press, 1988.

Taylor, David G. K. "Psalm Headings in the West Syrian Tradition." Pages 365–78 in *The Peshiṭta: Its Use in Literature and Liturgy. Papers Read at the Third Peshiṭta Symposium*. Edited by Bas ter Haar Romeny. Monographs of the Peshiṭta Institute Leiden 15. Leiden: Brill, 2006.

Thomas, Keith. *Religion and the Decline of Magic*. New York: Oxford University Press, 1997.

Vööbus, Arthur. *Syriac and Arabic Documents Regarding Legislation Relative to Syrian Asceticism*. Papers of the Estonian Theological Society in Exile 11. Stockholm: Estonian Theological Society in Exile, 1960.

Wilkinson, Kevin. "*Hermêneiai* in Manuscripts of John's Gospel: An Aid to Bibliomancy." Forthcoming in *My Lots Are in Thy Hands: Sortilege and Its Practitioners in Late Antiquity*. Edited by William E. Klingshirn and AnneMarie Luijendijk. Religions in the Graeco-Roman World. Leiden: Brill.

Winnefeld, Hermann, ed. *Sortes Sangallenses*. Bonn: Max. Cohen, 1887.

Wright, William. *Catalogue of Syriac Manuscripts in the British Museum Acquired since the Year 1838*. Vol. 1. London: Trustees of the British Museum, 1870.

Liv Ingeborg Lied

Between "Text Witness" and "Text on the Page": Trajectories in the History of Editing the Epistle of Baruch

The last decade has seen a rapidly growing interest in the reception history of writings from Late Antiquity and the continuing transformative impact copying, editing and reader engagement have had on the narrative contents of these writings. Thus, as the present volume bears witness to, micro and macro level changes of texts, as well as the scribal and reader practices that produced them, are finally starting to receive the attention they deserve.

This essay will address another, related, aspect of the transformation that might take place when writings circulate, which has not attracted the same level of interest: transmission and circulation of writings lead not only to changes in textual contents, but may also lead to a re-identification of the writings themselves. In other words, the cultural perceptions and identifications of writings may change too.

Traces of such historical identifications are still extant in the form of paratextual features in surviving manuscripts. Hence, we may study textual elements that served to communicate between text and reader and which are sources for the cultural perceptions of the various text units.[1] However, the potential value of these paratextual features have rarely been taken into consideration by editors of critical text editions, since the interest of editors is more commonly the narrative contents of the composition, and primarily in its earliest possible version. Other features of the manuscripts, which may tell us how those who later copied and engaged with the writings understood them, are sometimes noted, but not granted further interest. Since the focus of editors is on the early text, and since they use the copy in a manuscript primarily as a witness to that text, why should they bother with later identifications and perceptions of it?

The essay will survey the extant Syriac manuscripts that contain the so-called Epistle of Baruch and apply the outcome of this exploration to discuss the main trajectories of the editorial history of this epistle from the 17th to the 21st century, bringing the history of editing in critical dialogue with the available manuscripts. The Epistle

---

1 Cf. Gérard Genette, *Paratexts: Thresholds of Interpretation* (trans. Jane E. Lewin; Cambridge: Cambridge University Press, 1997), 2; cf. Eva Mroczek's essay in the present volume. In this essay I apply the term "paratext" to refer to texts sharing the page with the main body of text, such as titles and end titles, which were designed to communicate between the scribe/those who produced a codex and those who later read and engaged with it.

of Baruch[2] is probably most commonly known by Western scholars as the last ten chapters (chapters 78–87) of *2 (Syriac Apocalypse of) Baruch*. However, as many will also be aware, the Epistle also circulated widely in Syriac, Peshiṭta, manuscripts detached from *2 Baruch*. I will look systematically for the identification and location of the Epistle in these Syriac manuscripts and ask why, how and the extent to which these paratextual features could – and should – matter to current editorial practices. Hence, I will deal with scholarly identifications of writings, editors' assessments of the value of the material features, contexts and locations of texts in manuscripts, as well as prevailing notions in the academy of what identifiable texts and text units[3] in manuscripts can be used for. So far, the manuscripts containing the Epistle have primarily been used as witnesses[4] to older texts and text units. But, to *what* are they bearing witness, and why does it matter?[5]

The Epistle of Baruch: An Overview of Extant Manuscripts

As the first step in the discussions of the present essay, I will survey the extant manuscripts known to contain the Epistle.[6] The survey of manuscripts is based on the 1961 preliminary edition of the *List of Old Testament Peshiṭta Manuscripts*, published by

---

2 From here on called "the Epistle."

3 Inspired by Matthew J. Driscoll, in this essay I apply the term "text" for "a series of words in a particular order," and more precisely as "the words on the page." "Manuscript" I understand as "the text-bearing object," which is to say, a culturally produced material artefact that contains the text. I use the term "text unit" to denote any textual entity in manuscripts that is distinguishable within the general flow of text by textual or visible features, such as (but not limited to) titles or subtitles, paragraphing graphemes, spacing, decorations, and marginal annotations. I apply the term "work" to denote a *conceived* compositional unit. Finally, I reserve the term "book" for "biblical books", reflecting the common Syriac use of the terms *spr'* and *ktb'* to denote biblical books/writings. Cf. further Liv Ingeborg Lied, "Text – Work – Manuscript: What Is an 'Old Testament Pseudepigraph*on*?'" *JSP* 25:2 (2015): 150–65.

4 Kyle McCarter defines "witness" as, "Any manuscript (including a translation of a manuscript, a fragment of a manuscript, or a quotation from a manuscript) providing testimony to a text" (Kyle McCarter, *Textual Criticism: Recovering the Text of the Hebrew Bible* [GBS, Old Testament Series; Philadelphia: Fortress Press, 1986], 79).

5 I am indebted to Konrad D. Jenner, Bas ter Haar Romeny, Jan J. van Ginkel, Wido T. van Peursen, Gert Jan Veldman, Emidio Vergani, Matthias Henze, Eva Mroczek and Hugo Lundhaug for their kind assistance and/or response to earlier versions of this essay.

6 Cf. Liv Ingeborg Lied, "*2 Baruch* – Syriac," in *Deutero-Canonical Scriptures* (ed. Matthias Henze; vol. 2 of *The Textual History of the Bible*; ed. Armin Lange; Leiden: Brill, forthcoming).

the Peshiṭta Institute in Leiden,[7] as well as the updates in the Peshiṭta Insititute Communication, published since 1962 in *Vetus Testamentum* and continuing after 1999 in the *Journal for the Aramaic Bible/Aramaic Studies*.[8] Furthermore, the survey applies an unpublished list of lectionary manuscripts kept at and generously shared by the Peshiṭta Institute.[9] The survey also counts the Deir al-Suryan Syriac MS 14,[10] as well as the 10th/11th century Mt Sinai Arabic Codex 589.[11] To my knowledge, the number of manuscripts containing the Epistle, in full or in parts, is now 47, but there might still be more manuscripts not yet listed here.[12] It should be noted that apart from the Arabic codex, all these manuscripts are Syriac manuscripts. The oldest date from the 6th or 7th centuries, the youngest are from the 19th century.[13]

As suggested by the above introduction, today the Epistle is most often studied as an integral part of *2 Baruch*. However, there is only *one instance* in the Syriac material[14] of a manuscript preserving this Epistle as attached to the rest of *2 Baruch*. This manuscript is the 6th/7th century, so-called Codex Ambrosianus which is assumed to be the oldest extant, complete[15] Syriac Peshiṭta Old Testament codex known to

---

7 *List of Old Testament Peshiṭta Manuscripts (Preliminary Issue)* (ed. The Peshiṭta Institute [Willem Baars and M. D. Koster], Leiden University; Leiden: Brill, 1961). The list counts thirty eight manuscripts.
8 The survey of the Peshiṭta Institute Communication adds two manuscripts, designated Jerusalem 42 and Cambridge Dd 7.13 and found in the 1968 Fourth Supplement and in the 1977 Fifth Supplement.
9 This list, which was developed by Willem Baars, was generously shared with me at a research stay in Leiden in December 2013 and adds five lectionary manuscripts to the survey (BL Add 14,485, 14,486, and 14,687, a manuscripts found in Bartella, dated 1466, and Ms 2 of the Monastery of St Mark). With thanks to Konrad D. Jenner, Wido T. van Peursen and Bas ter Haar Romeny.
10 This manuscript is recorded by Sebastian P. Brock and Lucas van Rompay in the *Catalogue of Syriac Manuscripts and Fragments in the Library of Deir al-Surian, Wadi al-Natrun (Egypt)* (OLA 227; Leuven: Peeters, 2014), 64.
11 Fred Leemhuis, Albertus F. J. Klijn and Geert J. H. van Gelder, *The Arabic Text of the Apocalypse of Baruch: Edited and Translated with a Parallel Translation of the Syriac Text* (Leiden: Brill, 1986).
12 This list counts manuscripts as discrete entities. The Epistle is copied twice in the Codex Ambrosianus (cf. below). If both copies are counted separately the number would be 48.
13 This overview excludes occurrences of the Epistle in printed books. Note that manual copying of Syriac texts continued well beyond the development of print and is still a continuing practice alongside print.
14 Note, however, that the Arabic codex, which contains *2 Bar.* 3:2–25:3 and 29:4–87:1, also contains the Epistle attached to, alternatively appended to or copied in connection with, *2 Baruch* – depending on our interpretation of unit demarcation markers in this given codex. The Arabic codex will not be further discussed in the context of this essay.
15 The term "complete" here reflects the presentation of the codex in the title on folio 1v, recorded by those who were involved in copying the codex. The title presents the codex as a *pandect* (*pndqtys*), i.e., a full-bible codex, and further states that the codex contains "the whole old [testament]" (*pndqtys d'tyqt' kwlh*). For the contents and order of books in this codex, cf. Sebastian P. Brock, *The Bible in the Syriac Tradition* (Gorgias Handbooks 7, Piscataway, N. J.: Gorgias Press, 2006), 43, 116; and Philip M. Forness, "Narrating History Through the Bible in Late Antiquity: A Reading Community for the Syriac Peshiṭta Old Testament Manuscript in Milan (Ambrosian Library, B. 21 Inf)," *Mus* 127:1–2 (2014): 41–76.

us.[16] In this codex, the Epistle is recorded on folios 265v-267r as an integral part of "The Apocalypse of Baruch the son of Neriah translated from the Greek into Syriac,"[17] generally known as *2 Baruch* (folios 257r-267r).[18]

The Codex Ambrosianus is not merely the only Syriac manuscript that records the Epistle as an integral part of *2 Baruch*. This codex is also special in the present context because it records the Epistle twice: in two contexts, in the form of two text types,[19] with two names. In this particular codex, thus, the Epistle survives both attached to and detached from *2 Baruch*.[20] This other, detached Epistle is the one that circulated widely: this version of the Epistle is found in the 47 Syriac manuscripts mentioned above.

What kind of manuscripts included the detached Epistle in the Syriac context? The Epistle appears, first, in biblical manuscripts of various sorts, copied throughout the entire time span indicated above.[21] The Epistle is part of *pandects* as well as codices containing collections of prophetic books, the oldest presumably being the assumed 6th century British Library codex Add 17,105. Furthermore, the Epistle is part of composite codices containing less familiar collocations of biblical books, or biblical books and other books. After the 10th to the 12th centuries we sometimes find that the Epistle is excluded from some biblical codices, or that it appears in codices containing deuterocanonical material.[22]

Excerpted passages from the Epistle also appear in lectionaries (9th–16th centuries), and masoretic manuscripts (10th-13th centuries).[23] This means that, not only was the

---

16 Shelfmark B 21 Inf and Bis Inf of the Biblioteca Ambrosiana. Note that it is sometimes assumed that BnF Syr 341 may be just as old, or older.

17 *Ktb' dglynh dbrwk br nry' dmpq mn ywny' lswryy'* (folio 257r).

18 For the sake of clarity and convenience, I will refer to this epistle as "the attached Epistle" in the following.

19 I borrow the term "text types" from Robert H. Charles (*The Apocalypse of Baruch, Translated from the Syriac, Chapters I–LXXVII from the Sixth Cent. MS in the Ambrosian Library of Milan, and Chapters LXXVIII–LXXXVII – the Epistle of Baruch – from a New and Critical Text Based on Ten MSS and Published Herewith. Edited, with Introduction, Notes, and Indices* [London: Black, 1896], xxiv–xxv).

20 Again, for the sake of clarity and convenience, I will refer to this epistle as "the detached Epistle", not because it is devoid of a context as such, but because it circulated detached from *2 Baruch* – the context and reference which is being discussed in the present essay.

21 If nothing else is explicitly stated all mentioned Syriac manuscripts are Peshiṭta manuscripts.

22 After the 10th to the 12th century there is a growing tendency to exclude the Epistle from Syriac biblical codices, and from the 17th century onwards we sometimes find the Epistle in collections of deuterocanonical writings. However, judging from the manuscripts that have come down to us, this tendency is not dominant at any point. Apparently, the Epistle has been treated both as a part of the Old Testament, proper, and as deuterocanonical in Syriac traditions. Some bible manuscripts would include it, others would not.

23 A masora is a codex containing sample texts (excerpts, "words and readings") from the Old and New Testaments, as well as often from patristic writings. A masora is a philological, grammatical and orthographical collection with an educational purpose, with the aim of promoting correct pronunci-

Epistle part of biblical codices, it was also used and engaged with by Syriac Christians as a biblical book. Lectionary manuscripts show that lections from the Epistle were scripted to be read in worship contexts. The masoretic manuscripts show that sample passages were collected and located among other relevant biblical passages, structured in the most common order of the biblical books of the Peshiṭta Old Testament, in codices produced for grammatical, orthographical and pronunciation purposes.

Thus, the manuscripts that have survived suggest that the Epistle has been copied and used as a biblical book by Syriac Christians. It should be noted, firstly, that we have no surviving record of the Epistle before the 6th century. This does not mean that the Epistle could not have been copied in the Syriac tradition in earlier centuries, but it is worth keeping in mind that we have no secure knowledge of it, neither in Syriac nor in any other tradition for that matter, before that time. Secondly, the fact that the Epistle is, with one exception, only attested in Syriac manuscripts, also suggests that the Epistle has been read first and foremost in the Syriac tradition. We know that the Epistle was translated into Arabic, probably from Syriac[24] and, although new manuscripts in Arabic or other Christian language traditions might come to light in the future, the Epistle is at present not attested in any other tradition. In this sense, the Epistle is first and foremost a Syriac Christian writing. Again, this does not mean that the Epistle may not have circulated in other contexts, but rather that the manuscript evidence that is available to us is Syriac and Christian. Finally, in the Syriac manuscripts, the Epistle is found in two contexts. The Epistle is on the one hand part of *2 Baruch*. The only complete copy of *2 Baruch* that has come down to us includes the Epistle,[25] and there are no other attestations of *2 Baruch* that do *not* include it.[26] On

---

ation of words and avoiding grammatical misunderstandings. Cf. Marlia M. Mango, "The Production of Syriac Manuscripts, 400–700 AD," in *Scritture, libri e testi nelle aree provinciali di Bisanzio* (eds. Guglielmo Cavallo, Giuseppe de Gregorio and Marilena Maniaci; Spoleto, 1991), 161–79; Andreas K. Juckel, "The 'Syriac Masora' and the New Testament Peshiṭta," in *The Peshiṭta: Its Use in Literature and Liturgy. Papers Read at the Third Peshiṭta Sumposium* (ed. Bas ter Haar Romeny; MPIL 15; Leiden: Brill, 2006), 107–21.

24 Leemhuis et al, *Arabic Text*, vii. Cf. also Adriana Drint, "The Mount Sinai Arabic Version of IV Ezra: Text, Translation and Introduction" (PhD diss., Rijksuniversiteit Groningen, 1995), 7, 11–14.

25 The layout of the text and the codicological features in this codex suggest that the Epistle is presented as a subunit. It may be interpreted as an independent unit, but still as a unit which is integral to the larger entity *2 Baruch*. The Epistle is introduced by a heading in red ink (cf. the discussion below), but it is not separated out from the running text of the column by decorative graphemes or borders, or by skipping of lines. It is a matter of discussion how we interpret these codicological features. It is not given whether *2 Baruch* is to be understood as a single work-entity, or as a corpus that includes several work-entities. Hence the relationship of the Epistle to the rest of *2 Baruch* can be interpreted either as a separate unit attached to another unit, or as an integral part of one single unit. Ceriani describes the Epistle as the last part of *2 Baruch* ("extrema parte"), but notes that the incipit makes the Epistle appear "quae a libro separata" (*Monumenta sacra et profana V,II*, 113 and 167; *I,I*,1).

26 The Mt Sinai Arabic Codex 589 includes the Epistle as well. The hypothesis that the Epistle should be regarded an integral part of *2 Baruch* has been also been argued on the basis of shared

the other hand, the number of manuscripts containing the detached Epistle suggests that the Epistle also led an equally legitimate life apart from *2 Baruch* among Syriac Christians.[27] I would argue that the Epistle can, and should, be studied as a legitimate part of both these contexts.

Trajectories in the History of Editing of the Epistle

The modern editorial history of the detached Epistle is relatively long.[28] Early editions were part of both the Paris Polyglot (1629–45) and the London (B. Walton) Polyglot (1655–57).[29] The detached Epistle was also published by Paul de Lagarde in his *Libris Veteris Testamenti Apocryphi Syriace* in 1861, based on the manuscript Add 17,105 (mentioned above), with references to variants in the London Polyglot.[30]

---

narrative contents and the development of the narrative plot. Cf. Pierre M. Bogaert, *L'Apocalypse Syriaque de Baruch: Introduction, traduction du syriaque et commentaire* (SC 144–45; 2 vols.; Paris: Cerf, 1969) I, 67–78; Frederick J. Murphy, *The Structure and Meaning of Second Baruch* (SBLDS 78; Atlanta, Ga: Scholars Press, 1985); Mark Whitters, *The Epistle of Baruch: A Study of Form and Message* (JSPSup 42; Sheffield: Sheffield Academic Press, 2003), 35–65; Matthias Henze, *Jewish Apocalypticism in Late First Century Israel: Reading Second Baruch in Context* (TS 142; Tübingen: Mohr Siebeck, 2011), 369; and Lutz Doering, "The Epistle of Baruch and It's Role in *2 Baruch*," in *Fourth Ezra and Second Baruch: Reconstruction After the Fall* (ed. Matthias Henze and Gabriele Boccaccini; Leiden: Brill, 2013), 151–73 at 172.

27 Although drawing conclusions simply on the basis of the number of extant manuscripts can be misleading, this conclusion is still very likely based on the amount of examples of the detached compared to the attached Epistle.

28 The publications discussed in this essay are publications intended solely or primarily for an academic audience. Also, I do not deal with exegetical and interpretative studies of the Epistle. These studies are almost exclusively found in the context of more general treatments of *2 Baruch*. Cf. e.g. Mark Whitters, *The Epistle of Baruch: A Study of Form and Message* (JSPSup 42; Sheffield: Sheffield Academic Press, 2003) and Henze, *Jewish Apocalypticism*. The Syriac tradition of the detached Epistle remains largely unexplored in scholarship. In addition to the editions that will be discussed below, cf. Hans R. Bosker, "A Comparison of Parsers: Delilah, Turgama and Baruch" (Bachelor thesis, University of Leiden, 2008).

29 The Paris Polyglot is probably based on the 17th century BnF Ms Syr 6 (Pierre M. Bogaert, *Apocalypse de Baruch I*, 46). The London Polyglot is assumed to be based on the equally late Egerton 704 and Bodleian Syr 1 (Charles, *The Apocalypse of Baruch*, xxx; Bogaert, *Apocalypse de Baruch I*, 46). The 1823 edition of Samuel Lee is supposedly based primarily on the London Polyglot, and the Urmia edition (1852) is likewise applying the London Polyglot as well as the edition of Samuel Lee (Brock, *Bible*, 130).

30 Paul de Lagarde, *Libris Veteris Testamenti Apocryphi Syriace* (Lipsiae: F. A. Brockhaus, 1861), 88–93. Charles refers, somewhat sarcastically, to this edition saying: "This is merely *b* [Add 17,105] in a printed form, and not an edition of the Syriac text based on the Nitrian MSS" (Charles, *Apocalypse of Baruch*, xxx–xxxi).

The history of the editing of the Epistle as part of *2 Baruch*, however, starts only in 1865, when Antonio M. Ceriani, curator at the Biblioteca Ambrosiana in Milan, published a Latin translation of the – to date – only known Syriac manuscript folios containing the Epistle attached to the rest of *2 Baruch*. In 1868, Ceriani published an edition of the Syriac text of *2 Baruch*, and finally a photolithographic edition was published in 1883.[31]

Ceriani's publications represented a major breakthrough for the study of the Epistle and for research into *2 Baruch* in general, but it also complicated the picture – in interesting ways. With Ceriani's publication, the Epistle was made known to scholars as a writing circulating in the Syriac Church, but also as part of the larger work *2 Baruch*, generally understood as a Jewish apocalypse stemming from the 1st or 2nd centuries CE. The goal for editors and commentators from this time onwards thus became not only to provide a good edition of a Syriac biblical book. Another goal became equally important: to provide the best edition of the Epistle as an integral part of an assumed 1st/2nd century Jewish apocalypse.

Trajectory A: The Epistle as an Integral Part of *2 Baruch*

Ceriani's edition of the Epistle is part of his 1868 edition of the Syriac text of *2 Baruch*. The base text of this edition is the text of the Epistle found in the Codex Ambrosianus folios 265v-267r, where the Epistle is copied as the last part of *2 Baruch*.[32] Ceriani's edition of the Epistle is, to a large degree, faithful to the text of the manuscript. He corrects punctuation and diacritical points, but makes very few changes to the consonantal text.[33] Variants known to him from other manuscripts "qui ad manus erant" he notes in the critical apparatus.[34] The manuscripts "at hand" to Ceriani were the detached version of the Epistle in the Ambrosianus (folios 176v-177v), as well as Add

---

31 Antonio M. Ceriani, "Apocalypsis Baruch, olim de graeco in syriacum, et nunc desyriaco in latinum translate," in *Monumenta sacra et profana ex codicibus praesertim Bibliothecae Ambrosianae* 1.2 (Milan: Bibliotheca Ambrosianae Mediolani, 1865), 73–98; idem, "Apocalypsis Baruch Syriacae," in *Monumenta sacra et profana ex codicibus praesertim Bibliothecae Ambrosianae* 5.2. (Milan: Bibliotheca Ambrosianae Mediolani, 1868), 113–80; idem, *Translatio Syra Pescitto Veteris Testamenti ex codice Ambrosiano, sec. fere VI photolithographice edita* (vol. 2; Milan: Bibliotheca Ambrosianae Mediolani, 1883), 364–66. Note the confusion of dates of these volumes, both in the editions themselves and in the research literature. Fasc. 5.2 is not dated in the volume, Fasc. 5.1 is dated 1868. The catalogue in the Ambrosian Library has 1868, but the publication of the volume in its present form may well have been in 1871. Note also that the date of Fasc. 1.2 (1865) is problematic, the volume is often dated 1866 in the reserach literature. I am indebted to Stefano Serventi for his kind assistance.
32 Ceriani, *Monumenta sacra et profana 5.2*, 167–80.
33 Cf., also, Sven Dedering, "Apocalypse of Baruch," in *The Old Testament in Syriac According to the Peshiṭta Version* 4.3 (Leiden: Brill, 1973), i–iv, 1–50, at p. ii n. 1.
34 Ceriani, *Monumenta sacra et profana 5.2*, 167.

17,105, A 145 Inf of the Biblioteca Ambrosiana (dated 1615) and the lectionary manuscript Add 14,485 (dated 824) which he knew from his visits to London.

Ceriani never published a separate edition of the detached Epistle.[35] The existence of the detached Epistle is first and foremost represented in Ceriani's work by the variants noted in the critical apparatus and by the mention of it in the forewords to the Syriac text and the Latin translation.[36] It is interesting to note that the handwritten notes[37] in the margins of the photolithographical edition of the codex suggest that the attached Epistle is represented by the editor as primary. This is suggested by the fact that the detached Epistle in folios 176v-177v is identified as "Ep. Bar. Apoc."[38] and by the chapter enumeration entered by Ceriani, which starts with 78 and ends with 86[39] in line with the Epistle attached to the apocalypse in *2 Baruch*.[40]

In 1896, Robert Henry Charles published the edition that was to become the first comprehensive critical edition of *2 Baruch*, an edition that included the critical text of the Epistle, based on 13 attestations in 12 Syriac manuscripts.[41] The manuscripts applied by Charles were the Codex Ambrosianus with its two versions of the Epistle (the detached Epistle is his manuscript *a* and the attached Epistle bears the siglum *c*)[42], Add 17,105 (*b*), as well as 10 other manuscripts found in London, Oxford and

---

[35] He did publish the LXX versions of the Book of Baruch and the Epistle of Jeremiah (Ceriani, *Monumenta sacra et profana* 1,I). According to Emidio Vergani, Ceriani intended to publish a comprehensive critical edition of the Peshiṭta Old Testament, and his notes are still kept in the Ambrosian Library (B. 21 Ter Inf), but unfortunately Ceriani never completed this task (Emidio Vergani, "An Introduction to Ceriani's Reprint of the Ambrosian Manuscript B 21 Inf. (Codex Ambrosianus 7a1)," in *A Facsimile Edition of the Peshiṭto Old Testament Based on the Codex Ambrosianus (7a1)* [ed. and intro. Antonio M. Ceriani; repr. Piscataway, N. J.: Gorgias Press, 2013], VII–XIII at XIII).

[36] Ceriani, *Monumenta sacra et profana*, 1,I, 1 and 5.3, 113.

[37] The names of the books and the chapter numbers were entered by Ceriani. Cf. Vergani, "Introduction," XII.

[38] Note that the Epistle is given another name in the title and header by the scribe in the very same manuscript folios.

[39] The postscript on folio 267r is enumerated chapter 87.

[40] Ceriani, *Facsimilie Edition*, 364–66 [*Translatio Syra*, 364–66]. Note also that he comments on a marginal note written in the outer margin of folio 177v, which contains the detached Epistle, in his treatment of the attached Epistle. In other words, a *codicological feature* of the former folio is described as being relevant to the latter based on the notion that the composition is the same.

[41] Charles, *Apocalypse of Baruch*, xxiii–xxviii; 124–67. Cf. also Robert H. Charles, "II Baruch," in *The Apocrypha and Pseudepigrapha of the Old Testament in English* (vol. 2; ed. Robert H. Charles, Oxford: Clarendon Press, 1913), 470–74. As mentioned above, the Codex Ambrosianus contains two copies of the Epistle. Hence, Charles consulted 12 manuscripts, but one of them renders the Epistle twice and Charles refers to the two copies in terms of two "manuscripts," a practice not uncommon in his day. In addition to these 12 manuscripts, Charles also applied the Paris and London Polyglota.

[42] Ceriani was the first to apply the *siglum a* as a designation of Codex Ambrosianus folios 176v–177v (*Monumenta sacra et profana V,II*, 167). He also applies the sigla *B*, *d*, and *m*, and in addition *l*, *p*, *u*, and *w* which refer to the already existing editions of the text known to him (i.e. the London and Paris Polyglota, and the edition of de Lagarde).

Paris, and hence available to Charles who was working in Ireland and England at the end of the 19th century and the beginning of the 20th century.[43] Four of these manuscripts dated from the 17th century, six have been dated to the 10th to the 12th centuries. Nine can be regarded as biblical manuscripts in the sense that they contain collections of biblical books, most of them containing a complete text of the Epistle. The remaining three manuscripts are masoretic, transmitting excerpted passages. Hence, whereas the edition of Ceriani (and de Lagarde) had primarily been based on one single largely unemended manuscript, Charles' edition of the Epistle was the first to apply more manuscripts in an endeavor to create a critical text.[44] Charles' critical text can be understood as eclectic in the sense that the edited text brings in readings from different manuscripts. Charles corrects c, and his goal is express to present "the best text", in other words, the most original text.[45] And still, c is Charles' most important witness and his edition might be considered a comparative study of c with the other available manuscripts in order to "ascertain the critical value of c".[46]

Charles develops a *stemma*, depicting "two types of text."[47] c represents one type, all other manuscripts represent the other. Among the manuscripts representing this second type of text, he describes the oldest manuscripts as the most trustworthy and belonging to another subgroup than the younger manuscripts. Charles notes, furthermore, that c often stands alone, both when it attests to "the true text" and when it is corrupt, but also that this subgroup of old manuscripts preserves "the true text" much more often than c. In other words, according to Charles, manuscripts a and b (i.e. Codex Ambrosianus folios 176v-177v and Add 17,105) contain the oldest text more often than c.[48] He also proposes that both types of text derive from a common ancestor, but that the two types were already developed in the 6th–7th centuries. He suggests that they had been circulating independently for a while, possibly since the 4th century.[49]

Based on this analysis, Charles concludes: "As a further result of this examination, we have come to feel that so long as we follow its guidance, we can nowhere greatly err from the sense of the Hebrew original."[50] In other words, when the Codex

---

43 For a complete list, cf. Charles, *Apocalypse of Baruch*, xxiii–xxiv.

44 Otto F. Fritzsche published an emended edition of Ceriani's Latin translation of the Epistle, not the manuscripts, in 1871 (*Libri Apocryphi Veteris Testamenti Graece* [Lipsiae: F. A. Brockhaus, 1871], 690–99). He records the emendations of his predecessors Walton, de Lagarde and Ceriani in the footnotes. Fritzsche's work is not discussed any further here. Cf. Charles, *Apocalypse of Baruch*, xxiii.

45 Charles, *Apocalypse of Baruch*, ix, xxiii.

46 Charles, *Apocalypse of Baruch*, xxiii.

47 Charles, *Apocalypse of Baruch*, xxiv–xxv.

48 Note that Charles does not say which *manuscript* he considers the oldest (a/c or b): he talks about the age of *texts* and *compositions* in circulation.

49 Charles, *Apocalypse of Baruch*, xxii–xxx.

50 Charles, *Apocalypse of Baruch*, xxix.

Ambrosianus version of the attached Epistle is corrected and checked by comparing it with the other available manuscripts of the detached Epistle, the road to the assumed Hebrew 1st/2nd century text of the Epistle and, by implication, *2 Baruch*, is considered safe to travel. In yet other words, the differences between the preserved texts aside; Charles assumed the existence of a single, hypothetical original.

Charles' choice of manuscripts and the *stemma* he developed have had great influence on all later studies of the attached Epistle. Early translators, such as Michael Kmosko and Bruno Violet, followed Charles to a large degree.[51] Likewise, in a critical edition and translation published as late as in 2009, Daniel M. Gurtner chose to reproduce the text of folios 265v-267r of the Codex Ambrosianus as the base text with only a few corrections, listing Charles' manuscripts in the introduction and noting variants found in them in the apparatus.[52]

For Pierre M. Bogaert, the main post-1960s translator and commentator on the attached version of the Epistle, Charles' study also served as an important point of departure, although Bogaert both expanded and sometimes challenged his points of view. Bogaert's 1969 commentary on *2 Baruch*, Epistle included, benefitted greatly from the publication of the Peshiṭta Institute's *List of Old Testament Peshiṭta Manuscripts* in 1961. This list counted 38 manuscripts containing the Epistle, Bogaert added yet another one,[53] and hence his list of manuscripts included 27 more manuscripts than the list presented by Charles. Bogaert develops the *stemmae* of Charles and Violet, adding four important manuscripts, the BnF Syr 6, 64, and 341, as well as Ms Oo I.1,2 (Cambridge).[54] And just like Charles before him, Bogaert observes that the Codex Ambrosianus contains two copies of the Epistle, that the detached Epistle enjoyed an autonomous circulation among Syriac Christians apart from *2 Baruch*, and that the text of the Epistle attached to the apocalypse (i.e., *2 Baruch*) is different to

---

51 Michael Kmosko, "Apocalypsis Baruch filii Neriae, translatus de graeco in syriacum," in *Patrologia syriaca* (vol. 2; 3 vols; ed. René Graffin; Paris: Firmin-Didot et Socli, 1907), 1068–300 at 1210; Bruno Violet, *Die Apokalypsen des Esra und des Baruch in deutscher Gestalt* (GCS 32; Leipzig: Hinrichs, 1924), LVI–LXII. Violet makes some small adjustments to Charles' *stemma* (*Apokalypsen*, LVIII).

52 Daniel M Gurtner, *Second Baruch: A Critical Edition of the Syriac Text, with Greek and Latin Fragments, English Translation, Introduction, and Concordances* (JCTCRS 5; New York: T&T Clark/Continuum, 2009), 9–10, 124–47.

53 Add 14,485, which was already applied by Ceriani.

54 Bogaert, *Apocalypse de Baruch* I, 43–46. Note that none of Charles, Kmosko, or, Gurtner, use the 7th/8th century manuscript BnF Syr 341, or the 12th century Oo I.1,2 (The so-called "Buchanan Bible," kept at the Cambridge University Library). These manuscripts could all be considered highly important, early witnesses. Likewise, they do not apply Add 14,485 (even though Ceriani had already made use of it), nor manuscripts known to us at least from 1961 from collections and libraries in, e.g., Rome and the Middle East. It should be noted that BnF Syr 341 and Oo I.1,2 are the manuscripts that are most similar to the Codex Ambrosianus. They are all complete bibles, and the earliest ones known to us. However, the primary interest of the editors was assumedly not the types of manuscripts. They were interested in the type and age of copied texts, conceived of as witnesses to older texts.

the text of the Epistle in all the other manuscripts. However, Bogaert too holds that it is still likely that both stem from a common earlier Syriac version and, partly in contrast to Charles, he judges the attached Epistle to contain the oldest Syriac tradition, seeing the autonomous circulation of the detached version in the Syriac tradition as a secondary phenomenon.[55]

As we can see, all the editors of the attached Epistle have treated it primarily as an integrated part of *2 Baruch*. They all acknowledge two types of Epistle text, they see the attached version as an early, sometimes the earliest, version of the Epistle, and apply manuscripts containing both the attached and detached version of the Epistle as witnesses to an assumed common ancestor – a hypothetical original Epistle text.

Trajectory B: The Detached Epistle

In 1973, Sven Dedering published his edition of *2 Baruch* (chapters 1–77), based on the text in the Codex Ambrosianus. Here Dedering chose not to publish the Epistle since, "the usual form of this text is that found with the Epistle of Jeremiah and Baruch."[56] Dedering thus aimed to publish the Epistle together with these other two books as a part of the larger Leiden-project of editing and publishing the texts of the Peshiṭta Old Testament, taking the text in Codex Ambrosianus folios 176v-177v as his base text. Unfortunately, Dedering died before he could finish his edition of the Epistle. However, his unpublished preliminary work on that edition still exists in the form of a handwritten manuscript kept by the Peshiṭta Institute,[57] making it clear that he indeed regarded the detached version of the Epistle as the default text of the Epistle. He describes the attached version as, "a derivation from the basic text."[58] "The basic text" he identifies as the type of text found in folios 176v-177v of

---

55 Bogaert does not claim that the Epistle was necessarily "originally" part of *2 Baruch* in its, according to Bogaert, Greek original. He notes that the Epistle is thoroughly integrated into the composition as we have it in the sole Syriac witness to the complete version of *2 Baruch*, but also that the one who once authored *2 Baruch* before it was translated into Syriac could have made use of an earlier independently circulating text (Bogaert, *Apocalypse de Baruch*, 72–73, 78).

56 Dedering, "Apocalypse of Baruch," iv. Some later translations and studies present *2 Baruch* without the Epistle. Cf. e.g. Gwendolyn B. Sayler, *Have the Promises Failed? A Literary Analysis of 2 Baruch* (SBLDS 72; Chico, Calif: Scholars Press, 1984); Adam H. Becker, "2 Baruch," in *Outside the Bible: Ancient Jewish Writings Related to Scripture* (vol 2; eds. Louis H. Feldman, James L. Kugel and Lawrence H. Shiffman; Lincoln: University of Nebraska Press, 2013), 1565–85.

57 Dedering's handwritten manuscript is unfortunately still not published, but was generously made available to me at the Institute in Leiden.

58 Note, however, that he adapts Ceriani's chapter enumeration (78–86), which is based on the enumeration of the attached Epistle as an integral part of *2 Baruch*.

the Codex Ambrosianus as well as in other manuscripts that preserve the detached version of the Epistle.[59]

Dedering's judgment is, in this regard, different from that of Charles and Bogaert, probably, and at least partly, because the planned edition of the Epistle was part of the larger Leiden Peshiṭta project. Still, and on the other hand, it remains interesting to note that Dedering's choice is in fact similar to the choice of Charles and Bogaert in another regard: he also chose to edit the Epistle as one, single, text unit. He edited *2 Baruch* without the Epistle in his above mentioned 1973 edition, despite the fact that the Leiden Peshiṭta project was based on the Codex Ambrosianus, the earliest complete Peshiṭta Old Testament, where the Epistle at folios 265v-267r is codicologically and content-wise an integral part of *2 Baruch*. In other words, just as Charles and Bogaert before him, Dedering explicitly acknowledges the two versions of the Epistle as autonomous, "different textual traditions,"[60] but he still treats the two basically as one unit, editing the Epistle where it is normally found in the Syriac tradition, and disregarding it in the other, despite the manuscript information to the contrary. Where Charles and Bogaert let the interest in the hypothetical older, Greek or Hebrew text of *2 Baruch* guide their choices, Dedering lets the default context of the Syriac tradition guide his. In other words, although the Epistle bears many signs of being two units in the history of Syriac use, only one is acknowledged in the planned edition.

The edition of the Epistle published by Donald M. Walter, Gillian Greenberg, George A. Kiraz and Joseph Bali in 2013 is another edition that identifies the detached Epistle as a text belonging to the Syriac Christian tradition. It includes Lamentations, the Epistle of Jeremiah and the two Epistles of Baruch, with the aim of making these texts – fully vocalised – available to the religious communities that still use them.[61] While the edition is based on the 1887–91 Peshiṭta Mosul text, it also includes two appendices listing variant readings from Codex Ambrosianus. Appendix 2 lists variant readings in the detached Epistle (folios 176v-177v). Appendix 4, part 2, lists the variants of both versions of the Codex Ambrosianus, referring to the text of folios 265v-267r as the "Apocalypse of Baruch," seeing the Epistle there as part of the larger apocalypse.[62] In a footnote the editors describe the attached Epistle as a "variant version" and yet, unlike Dedering, as a variant that still fully belongs to *2 Baruch* in the codex context in which it is found.[63] As such, this is the only edition that acknowledges the two contexts of the Epistle as equally legitimate.

---

59 Dedering, "Epistle of Baruch," no pages [ms page 2]. Dedering based his edition on the Codex Ambrosianus version of the Epistle, but consults 26 other manuscripts (i.e., he chose not to consult the masoretic manuscripts).

60 Dedering, "Apocalypse of Baruch," iv.

61 Walter et al, *Lamentations*, VII.

62 Walter et al, *Lamentations*, XLI –XLVII.

63 Walter et al, *Lamentations*, XXXIV n. 2.

Trajectories and Editorial Choices

As we have seen, the editors of the Epistle have largely treated it in two different ways. To the editors of the detached Epistle (trajectory B, above) it is seen as a work integral to the tradition of the Syriac Church and treated as such, while the attached version is seen as a variant to the common text. This view stands in some contrast to that of the group of editors who have treated it as an integral part of *2 Baruch* (trajectory A, above).[64]

As pointed out above, the editors in trajectory A are all aware of the differences between the detached and the attached versions of the Epistle in the Syriac tradition. They point to the fact that the titles, end titles and postscripts are different, and that the two types of Epistle text display many, but not necessarily content-changing, variants.[65] Editors also point out that the differences between the two are probably due to the fact that they have been transmitted separately and thus belong to different chains of transmission in the Syriac tradition. This has been acknowledged ever since the first critical edition of the Epistle was published by Charles in 1896.

An important difference between the two trajectories is that Charles, Kmosko, Violet, Bogaert, Gurtner and other editors and commentators on the Epistle are not primarily interested in the Epistle as a text belonging to the Syriac manuscript tradition in which it is found. They are instead interested in the history of the hypothetical text of the composition *Epistle of Baruch*, a history that is assumed to stretch back until the time before it was supposedly translated into Syriac. Hence, they apply the Syriac manuscripts primarily as "witnesses to" *2 Baruch* and the Epistle integral to it. In other words, and notably with varying degrees of caution, they value these occurrences of the Epistle text in Syriac manuscripts as good or bad witnesses to the hypothetical earlier, attached Epistle text. Although the manuscripts do not take us beyond the Syriac copies from the 6th/7th century, the idea of the early text that can be derived through procedures of textual criticism warrants a study of both Syriac textual traditions of the Epistle as basically witnesses to one and the same textual unit.

While this procedure makes sense when the assumed early text guides the editorial choices, it must be acknowledged that it is a highly paradigmatic choice, and certainly not the only possible one. In the following, I would like to show how other, admittedly equally paradigmatic, choices may produce additional knowledge, helping us answer different questions.

---

64 Although with some interesting paradoxes in its own right, in the following discussion I will comment upon trajectory B only when it brings trajectory A into perspective.

65 This is the aspect of the Epistle that is best researched, and thus not included here. See, e.g., the convenient lists in Walter et al, *Lamentation*, XXXIV – XXXVI, and XLII–XLVII (but note the mistake in the rendering of verse 9:3 in the third column). Note, also, that I do not comment on the location of the rosettes in the two versions. They are placed differently in the two types of the Epistle indicating, possibly, that they have been read differently.

"The First Epistle of Baruch": Identifications and Collocations

The alternative choice, guided by the perspective of New Philology, involves making the extant manuscripts and the identification and material contextualisation of the Epistle the object of analysis. In the following I focus on both the attached and the detached Epistle as parts of Syriac Christian literary culture and its physical media.

The following study explores the order and collocations of text units in extant manuscripts, as well as paratextual features associated with the text units in these manuscripts.[66] The object of study is, firstly, the titles written in red ink in the columns, marking the beginning of a text unit. Secondly, I study the end titles, also mostly recorded in red ink, marking the end of a single text unit or a text corpus, i.e., a group of units assumed to belong together. Thirdly, I survey short title annotations in the upper margins of the manuscript pages. These annotations in the top margins would typically appear in the first folio of each new quire of a codex, and/or occasionally at the end of a quire.[67]

The study of these paratextual features will give us an indication as to how those who copied and otherwise took part in the production of the manuscripts would have named and identified the text units. It also gives us a sense of how those who later engaged with the manuscripts, i.e., those who saw and read, or alternatively heard the rubrics read aloud,[68] could have identified the text they read or heard.

These titles and annotations cannot be studied independently of the order and collocation of text units in the manuscripts, since the components of the titles reflect the order and explicit material context of text units in the manuscripts. Furthermore, the study of collocations of texts in manuscripts indicates to us the order in which these text units were copied, and hence the culturally shared expectations about which text units were assumed to belong together.

---

66 The discussion of paratextual features and collocations of text units in the manuscripts is based on a systematic study of the Syriac manuscripts that include the Epistle. I have studied the relevant manuscripts kept in the British Library, the Bibliothèque nationale de France in Paris, The University Library in Cambridge, and the Biblioteca Ambrosiana in Milan. Other manuscripts I have studied in the form of digital copies and microfilms at the Peshiṭta Institute in Leiden. One manuscript, Ms Ds 14, is only known to me through the description of it in the Catalogue (Brock and van Rompay, *Catalogue*, 64). I have also consulted the *Peshiṭta List* and the critical apparatus in former editions of the Epistle.
67 These short titles were, among other things, an aid to binders who had to make sure that the quires were ordered correctly when binding the codices.
68 Note that it cannot be fully ascertained that rubrics were always also read when texts were recited in context of worship.

From this perspective we can explore the available remains of *cultural identification and interpretation* of the text units by those who produced and engaged with the manuscripts. How is the Epistle identified in Syriac manuscripts, and in what order and which contexts is it copied?

The Identification of the Epistle in Biblical Manuscripts and Masoretic Manuscripts

Let us return to the Codex Ambrosianus, which is the sole manuscript containing the attached Epistle, as well as the only surviving manuscript that records the Epistle in both versions. In this manuscript, the title of the attached Epistle is "The Epistle of Baruch son of Neriah which he wrote to the nine and a half tribes" (folio 265v).[69] In other words, the Epistle is identified by reference to Baruch and his genealogy, as well as by reference to the tribal identity of its recipients. The detached Epistle, on the other hand, bears the title, "The First Epistle of Baruch the Scribe, which he sent from the midst of Jerusalem to Babylon" (folio 176v).[70] This version of the Epistle is also identified as an epistle of Baruch. However, Baruch is identified by his office as scribe, rather than by his genealogy, and the title underscores geographic locations rather than the identity of the recipients. In addition and importantly, the Epistle is identified as, the "First Epistle."

The title of the detached Epistle found in the Codex Ambrosianus is particularly elaborate, and there is variation in the exact wording both across manuscripts and within single manuscripts.[71] Although the titles of the Epistle are not uniform, which is not to be expected in Syriac manuscripts,[72] we should note that the titles of the

---

69 *'grt' dbrwk br nry' dktb ltš'' šbṭyn wplgh.*

70 *'grt' qdmyt' dbrwk spr' dšdr mn gw 'wršlm lbbl.*

71 The large majority of the Syriac masoretic and biblical codices that are still extant include the three main elements in their identification of the detached Epistle. It is generally described as the "First Epistle" (*'grt' qdmyt'*) and it is identified with Baruch who is most often described as "the scribe" (*spr'*). Furthermore, the Epistle is commonly identified as the epistle "which he sent from [the midst of] Jerusalem to Babylon" (*dšdr mn gw 'wršlm lbbl*). The other 6th/7th century biblical manuscript, Add 17,105, for instance, identifies it as "The Epistle of Baruch the Scribe which he sent from Jerusalem to Babylon" (folio 116r) in the title, dropping "first", but then refers to it as the "First Epistle of Baruch the Scribe" in the end title (folio 121r). Cf. further, e.g., Add 12,172, folio 192v, Egerton 704, folio 373r (17th century) and Add 14,684, folio 24r which simply reads, "First Epistle of Baruch" (Cf. Add 14,482, folio 47r), a common short title found in the masoretic manuscripts. Cf, further, Dedering, "Epistle of Baruch," no pages [ms page 20].

72 Syriac manuscripts may often identify text units by long and short titles (e.g., titles, end titles, annotations in top margins), and also use different title identifications for the same text unit.

detached Epistle are *systematically* different to the title of the attached version.[73] They highlight Baruch's office as scribe, the geographic locations of the sending and receiving parties, as well as the place of this particular epistle in a list that counts more epistles than just one: this is the First Epistle.

Let us first deal with the ascription, "First Epistle." To understand this part of the identification, we need to address the order and context of text units in Syriac biblical manuscripts. The "First Epistle," in all probability, bears this name because it is commonly recorded together with another epistle of Baruch, appropriately named "The Second Epistle of Baruch" (*'grt' dtrtyn dbrwk*). This "Second Epistle" is, in fact, a well-known biblical book: this is the Syriac, Peshiṭta title of 1 Baruch or the Book of Baruch, which is also known to us from Greek, Latin, Coptic and other language traditions.

In order to understand the remaining two aspects of the title, "Baruch the Scribe" and "from Jerusalem to Babylon," a further and more extensive look at the context of the Epistle in Syriac codices is instructive. In the Syriac manuscript tradition, the two Baruch-epistles are commonly, although not always, grouped together with a third epistle, The Epistle of Jeremiah. These three epistles were apparently often assumed to belong together and were regularly copied together.[74] The three epistles may sometimes appear under the common heading, "The Epistles of Jeremiah and of Baruch" (*'grt' d'rmy' wdbrwk*).[75]

Moreover, when these three epistles are found together in biblical and masoretic manuscripts, they are recorded after the Book of Jeremiah and Lamentations, and appear as an integral part of, or a unit appended to, the larger Jeremiah corpus.[76] The short title of the upper margin of the folios containing the epistles sometimes read "Jeremiah," alternatively, "Jeremiah, the prophet," and, sometimes they are explicitly recorded *before* the appearance of the final end title of the Jeremiah corpus, noting,

---

73 Cf. Dedering, "Epistle of Baruch," no pages [ms page 20]. Note, however, the intriguing variant in Add 12,178, a masora from the 9th/10th centuries, referring to the Epistle as "The First Epistle of Baruch bar Neriah" (folio 111v).

74 For instance, the one who repaired BnF Ms Syr 11 extracted folios containing exactly these three epistles from another codex and put them into the codex in question. Note also the shared and continuous kephalaia-marking in A 145 Inf, suggesting that the three epistles were seen as one unit.

75 Cf., e.g., the Codex Ambrosianus folio 176r. Typically, the name of each of the three epistles will then appear in rubrics in the text column at the beginning of each text unit.

76 When the epistles are collocated with other books categorised as deuterocanonical, or when they appear in codices containing collections of deuterocanonical texts, they are recorded independently or as a tripartite unit (e.g. Ms 90 in the German State Library; Manchester Rylands Syr Ms 3). Some biblical manuscripts, for instance, Add 12,172, contain the Epistle in an uncommon context. In Add 12,172 the Epistle is copied together with Genesis and the story of Eleazar, Shamuni and the seven sons from 2 Maccabees (cf. William Wright, *Catalogue of Syriac Manuscripts in the British Museum Acquired Since the Year 1838* [Part 1; London: British Museum, 1870], 6–7).

"The end of Jeremiah."[77] This suggests that, in the Syriac biblical manuscripts containing them, these epistles could fruitfully be considered Jeremianic texts.[78]

In this context the second aspect of the title, "Baruch, the Scribe," also becomes meaningful. Baruch is, of course, widely known as the prophet Jeremiah's scribe. And when the Epistle is recorded together with these other epistles, and thus presented as written messages recorded by a scribe, and located after two other books ascribed to Jeremiah, it certainly makes sense to refer to Baruch here in his role as scribe. Also the third aspect of the title, i.e., the focus on geographical location of the sender and recipients in the title of the detached Epistle, makes sense in the context of the Jeremiah corpus. The detached Epistle is "sent from Jerusalem to Babylon."[79] The focus on Babylon is evident in both the Second Epistle and in the Epistle of Jeremiah, as well as in Jeremiah proper, e.g., in Jer 29 where it is suggested that an epistle should be sent from Jerusalem to the exiles in Babylon.

The relevance of studying the titles in their codex contexts becomes even clearer when we compare the identification of the detached Epistle with the identification of the attached Epistle. In the attached Epistle, Baruch is presented as "son of Neriah." Here the title of the attached Epistle probably reflects the general title of *2 Baruch* in the Codex Ambrosianus, cited above. In that general title, Baruch, the main protagonist and the one who receives the revelation in *2 Baruch*, is presented with reference to his own genealogy and not by mention of his role vis-à-vis another major persona, Jeremiah.[80] Moreover, the attached Epistle addresses the nine and a half tribes, it does not refer to Babylon. This is probably best understood in light of the importance of the tribes of Israel throughout *2 Baruch*. The tribes are also an issue *across* book units in the part of Codex Ambrosianus where *2 Baruch* is located.

In other words, the title of the attached Epistle reflects its work and codex context, just like the detached Epistle, but since the two contexts are different, the identification of the two types of the Epistle in Syriac manuscripts is equally different. And, in the case of the detached Epistle, the title is colored by the fact that it is commonly

---

77 There is variation between manuscripts, and sometimes codicological features, such as indentions, blank spaces and decorations, can be interpreted either way. BnF Ms Syr 64, folios 57r–77r, at folio 77r. Cf. also Add 14,684, folios 24r–25r.

78 The Book of Baruch and the Epistle of Jeremiah is commonly found attached to, or at least near, Jeremiah and Lamentation in many linguistic traditions, for instance in early Coptic, Greek and Latin codices, as well as in the Syro-Hexapla (see C 313 of the Biblioteca Ambrosiana). The feature that is special to the Syriac, Peshiṭta tradition is that it includes yet *another* epistle of Baruch, i.e., the First Epistle.

79 Note the intriguing change made in the superscript of the Syriac, Peshiṭta, version of the Second Epistle (The Book of Baruch). This text is now an Epistle that Baruch wrote *to* or *for* Babylon (*lbbl*), not *in* Babylon (*bbbl*), as other versions would have it (Cf. e.g. folio 177v of the Codex Ambrosianus; BnF Ms Syr 341, folio 160r).

80 Cf. J. Edward Wright, *Baruch ben Neriah: From Biblical Scribe to Apocalyptic Seer* (Colombia, SC: University of South Carolina Press, 2003).

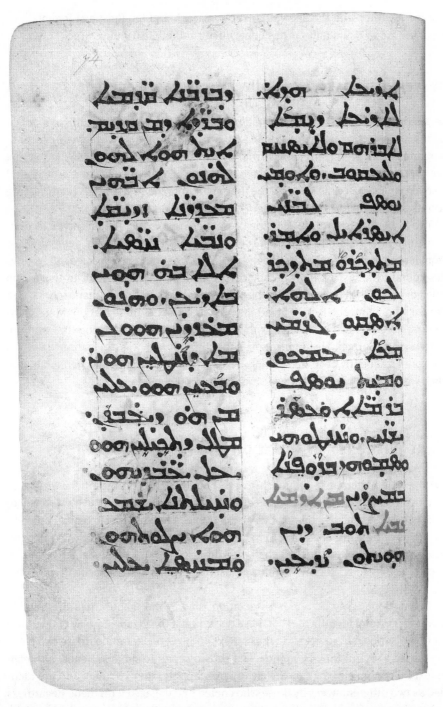

Fig. 26: British Library Additional 14,687, f. 74r. Fig. 1 shows a lection from the First Epistle of Baruch identified as "From Jeremiah the Prophet." © The British Library Board.

recorded together with the Second Epistle of Baruch and the Epistle of Jeremiah, as part of the larger Jeremianic corpus in masoretic and biblical manuscripts.

The Identification of the Epistle in Lectionary Manuscripts

The Jeremianic context and identification of the Epistle is clearly highlighted when we look at the lectionary manuscripts. As pointed out initially, five surviving lectionary manuscripts preserve readings from the Epistle. Add 14,485 includes a reading from 6:8–23 (folios 119v-120r). All other occurrences of lections from the Epistle, found in lectionary manuscripts covering the time span from the 9th to the 17th centuries, are variants of one and the same passage: 2 Bar. 8:1-[7]15.

The issue that is interesting in the present context is that the preserved lectionary manuscripts generally identify these readings as "From Jeremiah" (*mn 'rmy'*), or "From Jeremiah, the Prophet" (*mn 'rmy' nby'*). And, as could be expected, all lectionaries contain the text type of the detached Epistle. This means that, to those who copied or supervised the copying of the majority of these lectionary manuscripts, and to those who heard the lections read in worship contexts, these lections were probably first and foremost associated with Jeremiah – figure, book or corpus – and not with a book of Baruch. The implication is that this passage was drawn from a writing that would frequently be understood by Syriac Christians as integral to Jeremiah, and which was read in worship contexts as a lection from Jeremiah.

"Text Witness" or "Text on the Page"?

How does this alternative approach to the Epistle in the manuscripts add to and challenge existing perspectives? As earlier studies of the Epistle have established, the Epistle existed as two related but distinct types of text, circulated and copied in two chains of transmission in the Syriac context. The *stemmae* of Charles, Violet and Bogaert correctly reflect the fact that with the exception of the attached Epistle in Codex Ambrosianus, all other Syriac manuscripts transmit the detached type of the text.

The present essay adds the observation that in the manuscripts the explicit remains of cultural identification of these two types of the Epistle, by way of titles and unit organisation, suggest that, in the context of the Syriac tradition, these two types of text may also fruitfully be approached as two separate *entities*. Hence, although the textual contents of the two are clearly overlapping, they circulate and are identified as two different *works* by those who copied and engaged with them. Regardless of shared contents, the Epistle has two, equally legitimate, contexts and identities and, in the cultural context that preserves them, the one is not simply reducible to the other. When the Epistle is attached to the rest of *2 Baruch*, it is a legitimate and integral part of *2 Baruch*. And when the Epistle is part of the Jeremianic corpus, it is legitimately a part of that corpus as well; read, excerpted and engaged with as such by Syriac Christians. This recognition of two separate entities is likely to have already been the case in the 6th/7th centuries, when a scribe copied the Epistle(s) twice in Codex Ambrosianus, in two different contexts and with two different names. The curious fact that the Epistle is copied twice in this codex is less curious when we realise that the two types were probably already in circulation independently of each other, and were used and understood as two separate entities equally worthy of being copied into this deluxe manuscript of the Old Testament.

In addition to adding to our existing knowledge of the transmission of *2 Baruch* and the Epistle, the present analysis also challenges the text critical procedures and (implicit) paradigms represented by the scholarly editions of the attached Epistle discussed above. These challenges concern the use of "texts-on-the-page" as "text witnesses."

A first challenge is the way in which editors conceive of *textual units* and *works*. All editors of the attached Epistle presume a singular, early Jewish Epistle. However, while it is possible and even likely that the two types of the Epistle identifiable in our sources have sprung from a singular Epistle, as suggested by, e.g., Charles and Bogaert, this assumption must remain hypothetical since we have no sources to it.

This fact brings into question how editors use their source material. The editorial procedures described above presume that the editor regards a text unit as a cultural entity that is formed and identified early on and then transmitted and circulated as the same, stable, unchanged, entity throughout the centuries, regardless of later changes incurred in its transmission. The present study shows that this is not a straightforward and unproblematic practice. A text unit may be re-identified, relocated, and re-contextualised and thus become a different *work* to those who engaged with it later on than it once was or might have been. Editions of the attached Epistle have had a tendency to disregard what the unit *became*, assuming that it remained the same work that it once was or simply using it as a means to get to the assumed early text.

This first challenge does not only concern conceptions of textual units, but also editors' interpretation of text production, textual stability and variance in texts; more specifically the variance found in the two types of Epistle text, and the information that can be gleaned from it. For instance, when Charles notes that masoretic manuscripts "support" manuscript a, and not c,[81] he implies that these Syriac 10th–13th century manuscripts support a hypothesis that the readings in a are, on many occasions, more likely to bear witness to the earliest form of the text of the attached Epistle than does c; as well as to "ascertain the value of c in those chapters in which it stands alone, i.e., i–lxxvii"

---

81 Charles, *Apocalypse of Baruch*, xxvi.

(*2 Baruch*).[82] Building on the observation that the texts of masoretic manuscripts have more in common with the text unit Charles refers to as *a* than his *c*, but rephrasing it in line with new philology, I would suggest that they rather display a general tendency in the use of the Epistle in the Syriac Church. The fact that the texts in these manuscripts have more in common with the text in the detached Epistle than the text of the attached Epistle, shows us that the detached version of the Epistle was the one from which scriptural lections and sample texts were collected. We also see that this text was shaped to fit its contexts of use among Syriac Christians. In other words, these manuscripts suggest that the text of the detached Epistle was the one favored and traditionally circulated by Syriac Christians. They show us that this version was widely circulated and continued to be changed, used and adjusted to the needs of its users.

Charles's aims and procedures are legitimate within a historical-critical paradigm where the hypothetical original or early text and its early historical context is what guides the editor. From this perspective, the Syriac copies of the text are first and foremost interesting in their capacity as immaterial "witnesses" to something older. This paradigm is geared to facilitate a study of the history of the text and the original composition, and encourages us to read the available textual traditions "backwards." However, as the case of the Epistle suggests, this procedure may demand that the editor systematically reads the text detached from the material and cultural contexts in which it is found. Editors have described the fact that in these manuscripts the detached Epistle is recorded under another name, with another postscript, and in context of text units other than the attached Epistle, but they have not considered the consequences of it. In other words, they have generously applied the text in columns on folios of Syriac manuscripts, but not considered paratextual features or collocations of texts in the same manuscripts as relevant to their study. Likewise, the relevance, significance and signs of engagement by Syriac users, such as the excerption and recollection of passages from the detached Epistle in masoretic manuscripts and lectionaries, are not taken into consideration. This procedure detaches the text "proper" from other textual features of the manuscript, but the theoretical and methodological foundation legitimising this practice is not explicitly discussed.

This first challenge is intimately linked with a second challenge: with the exception of the Arabic manuscript mentioned initially, the Syriac manuscripts are the *only* empirical sources we have for the Epistle(s), and yet the Syriac Christian cultural context has not been deemed relevant to editors' assessments of their sources, since the main aim of the editions has been to provide a text that lies behind them. Although we may assume with Charles and Bogaert that the Epistle(s) has been translated from Hebrew and/or Greek, and that it might have had a history of transmission

---

82 Charles uses these other manuscripts to ascertain the "trustworthiness of the MS. *c*." I.e., he uses manuscripts to check how good a witness *c* in general is as a witness to the 2nd century CE *2 Baruch* (Charles, *Apocalypse of Baruch*, xxiii).

before our first available snapshots of it in Add 17,105 and the Codex Ambrosianus, the fact remains that the Syriac manuscripts constitute the only sources presently available.

This matters to the way we apply the sources, even if our goal is to establish the earliest possible text. As pointed out in the above discussion of the double rendering of the Epistle in the Codex Ambrosianus, there are already two developed types of the Epistle in the Syriac context in the 6th/7th centuries. We have no other sources for an earlier Epistle. This means that the Epistles are already at this time two entities in the context of the Syriac tradition, and it is likely that the Syriac transmission has either already changed both of them or, perhaps even created them. We may well discuss, with Charles and Bogaert, which type of text might be most likely to contain the oldest readings and hence be the best witness to the early text but, whatever we do, we cannot move behind the fact that both these readings are already the products of Syriac translation, copying, editing and re-copying. Logically then, this cultural transmission is both the "reference" and the "referent" of the entire argument.

The consequence of current practice is that the cultural specificity and interpretational activity of the tradition that in fact produced and used the manuscripts are not deemed as relevant or interesting. This approach could be considered problematic in its own right based on a general consideration in many other academic fields dealing with material artefacts, that the artefacts should (at least) be studied in the context of the culture that produced and engaged with them. It is particularly problematic when the Syriac source material is the only material available. Even though we know for sure that the manuscripts were produced by and for Syriac Christians, the context this usage suggests for the text has not been considered relevant, since it has been viewed as a later reception with no bearing on the analysis of the hypothetical early text. But the fact remains: these "received" texts, which are normally considered secondary, are our *only* sources and the entire discussion of the early text is based on them. What the Epistle developed into is indeed the only available source for what it might once have been.

A third challenge to the dominant editorial practice is that it creates an impression of the circulation of *2 Baruch* that is out of proportions with the actual evidence. When later editors use the spectrum of Syriac manuscripts as witnesses to the attached Epistle, these procedures may prompt a disproportionate impression of a level of popularity among Syriac Christians. On the one hand, it is probable and even likely that an entity identifiable as the "Apocalypse of Baruch" – Epistle included – was transmitted among Syriac Christians, as suggested by both the Codex Ambrosianus and the Mt Sinai Arabic Codex. However, on the other hand, and as the above discussion has shown, the transmission of the Epistle on its own is not evidence for a transmission of *2 Baruch*. Throughout their history of circulation, the forty seven occurrences of the detached Epistle in Syriac manuscripts have probably never been referred to or identified as, "a part of *2 Baruch*" by anyone other than their modern editors. The identification of the text of the detached Epistle as "witnesses to *2 Baruch*" is thus not a label that tells us what this text unit was to those who engaged with it; it tells us how modern scholars have found the occurrences of the text helpful.

Fourth and finally, when we follow traditional editorial procedures we miss out on the opportunity to study the Epistle in contexts other than the assumed original or early one. Instead of seeing these Syriac manuscripts and their texts exclusively as more or less corrupt witnesses to an earlier text, we could also see them as texts that were meaningful in the cultural context in which we find them. The Epistle of Baruch has been used in Syriac liturgy and in educational contexts, but this use has rarely been studied in its own right. If we study the text units as integral parts of their manuscripts, and study transmission of texts and text units as a process that may both transform them and let them take on a new cultural identifications as they circulate, we open up for new insights.

Concluding Remarks

This essay has provided a methodological reflection on current editorial practices and the paradigms that guide them. The study of the Syriac manuscripts containing the Epistle of Baruch illustrates how paradigmatic conceptions and models of text production and transmission, categorisations of texts and text units, and default ways of assessing available historical information from other periods than the hypothetical original or early historical context of a given writing affect what we see in our surviving historical sources.

Whereas the available manuscripts suggest that the Epistle survives in two types of text, in two chains of transmission, identified by two names, associated with two different figures, in the context of two different biblical corpora, and was therefore probably also conceived of as two different works by those who encountered it in the Syriac tradition, editors have commonly used this material to reach a singular, early text beyond and behind these manuscripts. The editors that have used manuscripts containing the detached Epistle in their quest for the most original reading of the Epistle attached to *2 Baruch*, have systematically disregarded the paratextual and codicological information in the manuscripts which suggests that to those who produced and used the manuscripts the detached Epistle was a different entity with its own history and context of interpretation than the attached Epistle. They may well have originally come from one, singular text, but our sources present them as two distinct units, and each of them already carry the marks of the literary, codicological, and cultural contexts that have preserved them.

What the present study of the Epistle shows is that we are not looking at the reception history of the Epistle as a stable part of *2 Baruch*, but rather at the complex and continuing use, transformation and engagement with writings that systematically defy editors' categorisation of what that textual entity "really is" or "once was."

Bibliography

Becker, Adam H. "2 Baruch." Pages 1565–85 in *Outside the Bible: Ancient Jewish Writings Related to Scripture*. Edited by Louis H. Feldman, James L. Kugel and Lawrence H. Shiffman. Vol. 2. Lincoln: University of Nebraska Press, 2013.

Bogaert, Pierre M. *L'Apocalypse Syriaque de Baruch: Introduction, traduction du syriaque et commentaire*. Sources chrétiennes 144–45. 2 vols. Paris: Cerf, 1969.

Bosker, Hans R. "A Comparison of Parsers: Delilah, Turgama and Baruch." Bachelor thesis, University of Leiden, 2008.

Brock, Sebastian P. *The Bible in the Syriac Tradition*. Gorgias Handbooks 7. Piscataway, NJ: Gorgias Press, 2006.

Brock, Sebastian P. and Lucas van Rompay. *Catalogue of Syriac Manuscripts and Fragments in the Library of Deir al-Surian, Wadi al-Natrun (Egypt)*. Orientalia Lovaniensia Analecta 227. Leuven: Peeters, 2014.

Ceriani, Antonio M. "Apocalypsis Baruch, olim de graeco in syriacum, et nunc de syriaco in latinum translate." Pages 73–98 in *Monumenta sacra et profana ex codicibus praesertim Bibliothecae Ambrosianae* 1.2. Milan: Bibliotheca Ambrosianae Mediolani, 1865.

–. "Apocalypsis Baruch Syriacae." Pages 113–80 in *Monumenta sacra et profana ex codicibus praesertim Bibliothecae Ambrosianae* 5.2. Milan: Bibliotheca Ambrosianae Mediolani, 1868.

–. *Translatio Syra Pescitto Veteris Testamenti ex codice Ambrosiano, sec. fere VI photolithographice edita*. 2nd vol. Milan: Bibliotheca Ambrosianae Mediolani, 1883.

Charles, Robert H. *The Apocalypse of Baruch, Translated from the Syriac, Chapters I–LXXVII from the Sixth Cent. MS in the Ambrosian Library of Milan, and Chapters LXXVIII–LXXXVII – the Epistle of Baruch – from a New and Critical Text Based on Ten MSS and Published Herewith. Edited, with Introduction, Notes, and Indices*. London: Black, 1896.

–. "II Baruch." Pages 470–74 in *The Apocrypha and Pseudepigrapha of the Old Testament in English*. Edited by Robert H. Charles. 2 vols. Oxford: Clarendon Press, 1913.

Dedering, Sven. "Apocalypse of Baruch." Pages i–iv, 1–50 in *The Old Testament in Syriac According to the Peshiṭta Version* 4.3. Leiden: Brill, 1973.

Doering, Lutz. "The Epistle of Baruch and It's Role in *2 Baruch*." Pages 151–73 in *Fourth Ezra and Second Baruch: Reconstruction After the Fall*. Edited by Matthias Henze and Gabriele Boccaccini. Leiden: Brill, 2013.

Drint, Adriana. "The Mount Sinai Arabic Version of IV Ezra: Text, Translation and Introduction." PhD diss., Rijksuniversiteit Groningen, 1995.

Forness, Philip M. "Narrating History Through the Bible in Late Antiquity: A Reading Community for the Syriac Peshiṭta Old Testament Manuscript in Milan (Ambrosian Library, B. 21 Inf)." *Le Muséon* 127/1–2 (2014): 41–76.

Fritzsche, Otto F. *Libri Apocryphi Veteris Testamenti Graece*. Lipsiae: F. A. Brockhaus, 1871.

Genette, Gérard. *Paratexts: Thresholds of Interpretation*. Translated by Jane E. Lewin. Cambridge: Cambridge University Press, 1997.

Gurtner, Daniel M. *Second Baruch: A Critical Edition of the Syriac Text, with Greek and Latin Fragments, English Translation, Introduction, and Concordances*. Jewish and Christian Texts in Contexts and Related Studies 5. New York: T&T Clark/Continuum, 2009.

Henze, Matthias. *Jewish Apocalypticism in Late First Century Israel: Reading Second Baruch in Context*. Texts and Studies in Ancient Judaism 142. Tübingen: Mohr Siebeck, 2011.

Juckel, Andreas K. "The 'Syriac Masora' and the New Testament Peshiṭta." Pages 107–21 in *The Peshiṭta: Its Use in Literature and Liturgy. Papers Read at the Third Peshiṭta Sumposium*. Edited by Bas ter Haar Romeny. Monographs of the Peshiṭta Institute Leiden 15. Leiden: Brill, 2006.

Kmosko, Michael. "Apocalypsis Baruch filii Neriae, translatus de graeco in syriacum." Cols. 1068–1300 in Patrologia syriaca. Vol. 2. Edited by René Graffin. Paris: Firmin-Didot et Socli, 1907.

Lagarde, Paul de. *Libris Veteris Testamenti Apocryphi Syriace*. Lipsiae: F. A. Brockhaus, 1861.

Leemhuis, Fred, Albertus F. J. Klijn and Geert J. H. van Gelder. *The Arabic Text of the Apocalypse of Baruch: Edited and Translated with a Parallel Translation of the Syriac Text*. Leiden: Brill, 1986.

List of Old Testament Peshiṭta Manuscripts (Preliminary Issue). Edited by The Peshiṭta Institute, Leiden University. Leiden: Brill, 1961.

Lied, Liv Ingeborg. "Text – Work – Manuscript: What Is an 'Old Testament Pseudepigraph*on*?'" *Journal for the Study of the Pseudepigrapha* 25:2 (2015): 150–65.

–. "*2 Baruch* – Syriac." In *Deutero-Canonical Scriptures*. Edited by Matthias Henze. Vol. 2 of *The Textual History of the Bible*. Edited by Armin Lange and Emmanuel Tov. Leiden: Brill, forthcoming.

Mango, Marlia M. "The Production of Syriac Manuscripts, 400–700 AD." Pages 161–79 in *Scritture, libri e testi nelle aree provinciali di Bisanzio*. Edited by Guglielmo Cavallo, Giuseppe de Gregorio and Marilena Maniaci. Spoleto, 1991.

McCarter, Kyle. *Textual Criticism: Recovering the Text of the Hebrew Bible*. Guides to Biblical Scholarship, Old Testament Series. Philadelphia: Fortress Press, 1986.

Murphy, Frederick J. *The Structure and Meaning of Second Baruch*. Society of Biblical Literature Dissertations Series 78. Atlanta, Ga: Scholars Press, 1985.

Sayler, Gwendolyn B. *Have the Promises Failed? A Literary Analysis of 2 Baruch*. Society of Biblical Literature Dissertations Series 72. Chico, Cal.: Scholars Press, 1984.

Vergani, Emidio. "An Introduction to Ceriani's Reprint of the Ambrosian Manuscript B 21 Inf. (Codex Ambrosianus 7a1)." Pages VII–XIII in *A Facsimile Edition of the Peshiṭto Old Testament Based on the Codex Ambrosianus (7a1)*. Edited by Antonio M. Ceriani. Reprint. Piscataway, N. J.: Gorgias Press, 2013.

Violet, Bruno. *Die Apokalypsen des Esra und des Baruch in deutscher Gestalt*. Die griechischen christlichen Schriftsteller der ersten drei Jahrhunderte 32. Leipzig: Hinrichs, 1924.

Whitters, Mark. *The Epistle of Baruch: A Study of Form and Message*. Journal for the Study of the Pseudepigrapha: Supplement Series 42. Sheffield: Sheffield Academic Press, 2003.

Wright, J. Edward. *Baruch ben Neriah: From Biblical Scribe to Apocalyptic Seer*. Colombia, S. C.: University of South Carolina Press, 2003.

Wright, William. *Catalogue of Syriac Manuscripts in the British Museum Acquired Since the Year 1838*. Part 1. London: British Museum, 1870.

Eva Mroczek

The End of the Psalms
in the Dead Sea Scrolls, Greek Codices, and
Syriac Manuscripts

It is said of David, king of Israel, peace be upon him, that when he had completed the Book of Psalms, he was flushed with conceit and said before Him: Master of the Worlds, is there a creature in existence which excels me in reciting song? At that moment a frog came along and said to him: David, be not puffed up with conceit, for I utter more songs than you. Moreover, for every song I utter, I recite 3000 proverbs, as is written, "And he spoke 3000 proverbs and his songs were 1005" (1 Kgs 5:12).[1]

How many psalms of David are there? And at what point is the Book of Psalms completed? In one sense, the answer to these questions is simple: both Jewish and Christian tradition indicates that the canonical psalter ends with Ps 150.[2] But this, as we might expect, is only one way of answering this question. Indeed, in ancient texts, David is credited with compositions far beyond 150. In the Qumran Psalms scroll, 11QPsalms[a], David is imagined to have spoken 4,050 songs. And in about 800 CE, the Patriarch Timothy I of Baghdad wrote of a report he had heard about the discovery in a cave near Jericho of numerous Hebrew manuscripts, including "over two hundred psalms of David."[3]

---

1 Malachi Beit-Arié, "Perek Shirah: Introduction and Critical Edition" (2 vols.; PhD Thesis, Hebrew University of Jerusalem, 1966). This text has been preserved in several manuscripts as early as the 10th century, but Beit-Arié argues for a much earlier origin. On this text's possible knowledge of Ps 151, see Joseph M. Baumgarten, "Perek Shira, an Early Response to Psalm 151," *RevQ* 9 (1978): 575–78. I have cited Baumgarten's translation.

2 The canons of the Council of Laodicea (363–364) are said to have limited the canonical psalms to 150, but this is problematic. Canon 59 reads Ὅτι οὐ δεῖ ἰδιωτικοὺς ψαλμοὺς λέγεσθαι ἐν τῇ ἐκκλησίᾳ, οὐδὲ ἀκανόνιστα βιβλία, ἀλλὰ μόνα τὰ κανονικὰ τῆς καινῆς καὶ παλαιᾶς διαθήκης. "Let no private psalms nor any uncanonical books be read in the church, but only the canonical ones of the New and Old Testament"; Canon 60 provides a catalogue of the canonical books (it lists Baruch and the Epistle of Jeremiah, but excludes Revelation), and includes note on the number of psalms –Βίβλος Ψαλμῶν ἑκατὸν πεντήκοντα, the book of 150 psalms. But the absence of Canon 60 from various early witnesses and from Syriac translations suggests that the catalogue was not original to the council, but rather appended later. See, e.g., Brooke Foss Westcott, *A General Survey of the History of the Canon of the New Testament* (5th ed.; Cambridge: Macmillan, 1881), 431–38; NPNF² 14:159–60.

3 Timothy I writes that the texts, both biblical and non-biblical, were found by a hunter who had followed his dog into a cave, and included many texts quoted in the New Testament but missing from the Old. He laments that he has been unable to find out any more information about the discoveries. The first publication of this letter is by Oskar Braun, "Ein Brief des Katholikos Timotheos I über biblische Studien des 9. Jahrhunderts," *OrChr* 1 (1901): 299–313. See also Raphael J. Bidawid, *Les lettres du patriarche nestorien Timothée I* (Vatican City: Biblioteca apostolica vaticana, 1956), and

This profusion of psalms beyond canonical limits, then, is a feature of the literary imagination. But if we turn to material evidence, what do manuscripts of psalm collections themselves tell us about the number and limits of the psalms? One scroll from Masada, MasPsalms[b], does end with Ps 150, showing a collection with an ending like the later Masoretic psalter did exist around the turn of the eras.[4] But even in the Masoretic tradition – even if their contents are uniform – there is some variation in how the psalms are counted: the Codex Leningradensis, the oldest complete biblical codex and the basis for the *BHS*, presents Pss 114 and 115 as one, and ends up with 149 psalms, numbered up to קמט in the middle of the column above each composition.[5] The *number* 150 itself, then, was not always the gold standard.

Things become still more complex in non-Masoretic traditions. In this essay, I present the enumeration and ending of the Book of Psalms in manuscripts from three different linguistic and religious milieus, where both the content and the numbering of the psalms are variable. I discuss the most extensive psalms scroll from Qumran, the first century manuscript 11QPsalms[a]; two major Septuagint codices, the fourth century Sinaiticus and the fifth century Alexandrinus; and 12t4,[6] a Syriac manuscript of the 12th century that contains commentaries, psalms, odes, and hymns. These material artifacts are snapshots of evolving traditions, showing how particular scribes, in different times and places, understood the shape and limits of the Book of Psalms.

Much distinguishes the three manuscript examples from one another, but despite their differing contents, languages, physical forms, and community contexts, they share two major features. First, none of these manuscripts actually contains 150 psalms; and although the later Greek and Syriac witnesses show awareness that 150 is the established number, all three, in some way, enumerate the psalms beyond 150. Second, each of the manuscripts contains some version of Ps 151, a liminal composi-

---

John C. Reeves, "Exploring the Afterlife of Jewish Pseudepigrapha in Medieval Near Eastern Religious Traditions: Some Initial Soundings," *JSJ* 30 (1999): 175–77. On Timothy's intellectual influence on the Church of the East, see Bas ter Haar Romeny, "Biblical Studies in the Church of the East: The Case of Catholicos Timothy I," in *Historica, Biblica, Theologica et Philosophica: Papers Presented at the Thirteenth International Conferenc on Patristic Studies held in Oxford 1999* (ed. Maurice F. Wiles, Edward Yarnold, and Paul M. Parvis; StPatr 34; Leuven: Peeters, 2001), 503–10.

4 Shemaryahu Talmon, "Hebrew Fragments from Masada: 1(f) MasPs[a] and (g) MasPs[b]," in *Masada VI: Yigael Yadin Excavations from 1963–1965, Final Reports* (ed. Shemaryahu Talmon and Yigael Yadin; Jerusalem: Israel Exploration Society and the Hebrew University of Jerusalem, 1999), 76–97.

5 While the Leningradensis is the basis for the *BHS*, it is not completely followed here; the psalms are numbered up to 150, with the codex's original Hebrew enumeration in small print under the large Arabic numerals. Multiple manuscripts besides Leningradensis count Pss 114 and 115 as one. On this combination see e.g. Gert T. M. Prinsloo, "Psalms 114 and 115: one or two poems?" *OTE* 16 (2003): 668–89.

6 The sigla of the Syriac manuscripts referred to in this essay follow the format of the 1961 *List of Old Testament Peshiṭta Manuscripts (Preliminary Issue)*, edited by the Peshiṭta Institute in Leiden.

tion that does not appear in the Masoretic canon. In its most familiar Greek version, the composition reads:

> [1] I was small among my brothers, and the youngest in my father's house;
> I tended my father's sheep.
> [2] My hands made a harp; my fingers fashioned a lyre.
> [3] And who will tell my Lord? The Lord himself; it is he who hears.
> [4] It was he who sent his messenger and took me from my father's sheep,
> and anointed me with his anointing-oil.
> [5] My brothers were handsome and tall, but the Lord was not pleased with them.
> [6] I went out to meet the Philistine, and he cursed me by his idols.
> [7] But I drew his own sword; I beheaded him,
> and took away disgrace from the people of Israel.[7]

The composition appears at the end of Greek, Latin, Syriac, and Arabic psalters. It is even included in an early Islamic chronicle, the ninth-century work of al-Ya'qūbī, who incorporates it into an account of David's life, placing it after Absalom's revolt.[8] Here, too, we find awareness of the idea that this psalm closes a collection, as al-Ya'qūbī introduces it with the words, "Then David said in the last psalm."

This psalm was unknown in Hebrew until the discovery of the Dead Sea Scrolls; in fact, there was doubt that it had had a Hebrew original at all.[9] But this psalm – or, more precisely, two separate compositions related to its Hebrew *Vorlage*,[10] named

---

7 NRSVA translation.

8 As observed by Reeves, "Exploring the Afterlife," 165. For the text, see al-Ya'qūbī, *Tārīkh al-Ya'qūbī* (2 vols.; Beirut: Dār Ṣādir, 1970; repr.); *Tārīkh of Ibn Abī Ya'qūb: Volume. 1* (ed. M.Th. Houtsma; Leiden: Brill, 1883), 46–60, 169. See also Rifaat Y. Ebied and Lionel R. Wickham, "Al-Ya'ḳūbī's Account of the Israelite Prophets and Kings," *JNES* 29 (1970): 82 and 90 n. 70. I am grateful to my colleague R. Kevin Jaques for his assistance with this text.

9 Martin Noth did not think Ps 151 had a Hebrew original, but ascribed its composition to Alexandrian Jewish circles; see "Die fünf syrisch überlieferten apokryphen Psalmen," *ZAW* 48 (1930): 22.

10 The relationship between the Greek and Hebrew compositions is complex, and the Hebrew text in 11QPsalms[a] cannot really be called the *Vorlage* of the Greek Ps 151. See the excellent overview by Eric Reymond, *New Idioms within Old: Poetry and Parallelism in the Non-Masoretic Poems of 11Q5 (=11QPsa)* (SBLEJL 31; Atlanta: Society of Biblical Literature, 2011), 51–74. Early studies include Patrick W. Skehan, "The Apocryphal Psalm 151," *CBQ* 25 (1963): 407–9; William H. Brownlee, "The 11Q Counterpart to Ps 151,1–5," *RevQ* 4 (1963): 379–87; André Dupont-Sommer, "Le Psaume CLI dans 11QPsa et le problème de son origine essénienne," *Sem* 14 (1964): 25–62; Jean Carmignac, "La forme poétique du Psaume 151 de la grotte 11," *RevQ* 4 (1963): 371–78; and "Précisions sur la forme poétique du Psaume 151," *RevQ* 5 (1965): 249–52; James A. Sanders, "Ps. 151 in 11QPss," *ZAW* 75 (1963): 73–86; John Strugnell, "Notes on the Text and Transmission of the Apocryphal Psalms 151, 154 (= Syr. II) and 155 (= Syr.I II)," *HTR* 59 (1966): 259–61. More recently, Menahem Haran and Mark S. Smith argued that the Greek and Syriac had a shorter Hebrew original than the expansive 11QPsalms[a] text; see Menahem Haran, "The Two Text-forms of Psalm 151," *JJS* 39 (1988): 171–82; and Mark S. Smith, "How to Write a Poem: The Case of Psalm 151 A (II QPsa 28.3–12)," in *Sirach, Scrolls, and Sages: Proceedings of a Second International Symposium on the Hebrew of the Dead Sea Scrolls, Ben Sira, and the Mishnah,*

Ps 151A and 151B – turned up in 11QPsalmsᵃ, and here, too, it is the last psalm. But while this text closes both the Qumran collection and the Greek Psalter, it does so in different ways. 11QPsᵃ, which does not presuppose a collection of 150 psalms, does not distinguish these compositions from the rest of the collection by any paratextual means. But Greek manuscripts introduce it with a superscription that call it a Davidic "idiograph," ἰδιόγραφος, but "outside the number," ἔξωθεν τοῦ ἀριθμοῦ – claiming its Davidic authenticity even as it asserts its otherness vis-a-vis an established corpus. And in the Syriac tradition, we find not one but five psalms that manuscripts present as *both* authentically Davidic *and* explicitly outside the standard collection of 150.[11]

The study of Ps 151 in its Greek, Hebrew, and Syriac versions (and the Syriac psalms 154 and 155, which also appear in the Dead Sea Psalms Scroll) is not new. But for the most part, it has been studied text-critically, to establish the relationships between the versions, to trace its textual development, and perhaps to recover its most original form. But, instead of studying the development of the text itself, I want to focus on the way it is presented and framed in the Hebrew, Greek, and Syriac witnesses. I use these versions not as sources for text-critical work on a composition, but as ends in themselves – as snapshots of the scriptural worlds inhabited by the scribes and communities who created and used them. My special focus is paratexts, specifically the scribal presentation of numbers and boundaries to textual collections.[12] Paratextual material – titles, numbers, introductions, scribal notations – give us some of the clearest indications of how scribes understood and wanted to present the material they were copying.

How do our material manuscripts and the scribal choices to which they testify help us understand the reception history of psalms, and more broadly, ideas about

---

Held at Leiden University, 15–17 December 1997 (ed. Takamitsu Muraoka and John F. Elwolde; STDJ 33; Leiden: Brill, 1997), 182–208. On the relationships between the versions of Ps 151 see also Shemaryahu Talmon, "Extra-Canonical Hebrew Psalms from Qumram–Psalm 151," in *The World of Qumran from Within: Collected Studies* (Jerusalem: Magnes Press; Leiden: Brill, 1989), 244–72; David N. Wigtil, "The Sequence of the Translations of Apocryphal Psalm 151," *RevQ* 11 (1983): 401–7; Harry F. van Rooy, *Studies on the Syriac Apocryphal Psalms* (JSSSup 7; Oxford: Oxford University Press, 1999), 57–80; Michael Segal, "The Literary Development of Psalm 151: A New Look at the Septuagint Version," *Textus* 21 (2002): 139–58.

11 As William Holladay writes, "In spite of the strong conviction, then, that the Psalms numbered 150, there was a contrary tendency to add 'just one more' or 'just a few more'!" (William L. Holladay, *The Psalms Through Three Thousand Years: Prayerbook of a Cloud of Witnesses* [Minneapolis: Augsburg Fortress, 1993], 89).

12 Gérard Genette calls paratext "a zone between text and off-text, a zone not only of transition but also of *transaction*: a privileged place of pragmatics and a strategy, of an influence on the public, an influence that ... is at the service of a better reception for the text and a more pertinent reading of it." Genette, *Seuils* (Paris: Seuil, 1987), translated as *Paratexts: Thresholds of Interpretation* (trans. Jane E. Lewin; Cambridge: Cambridge University Press, 1997), 2 (emphasis in original); see also Genette, "Introduction to the Paratext," trans. Marie Maclean, *NLH* 22 (1991): 261–72.

scripture and canon? What do the numbers and endings of the psalms in Hebrew, Greek, and Syriac manuscripts suggest about what shifted and what persisted in the centuries between them? While the idea of scripture as a coherent and delimited entity is present in the Greek and Syriac traditions to a greater extent than in the Scrolls, ultimately inspired writing continues to spill over beyond its own boundaries, even after the canon seems to be closed. This tension between a bounded collection – organized and limited by numbers – and a sense of authenticity outside its boundaries suggests something intriguing about the relationship between revelation and scripture: "authentic" revealed text and closed scriptural collections were not necessarily imagined to be identical. Even once canonical boundaries are drawn and recognized, the criteria for what they mean to include and exclude is less clear than we might expect.

Qumran

My earliest example is the Qumran Psalms Scroll, 11QPsalms[a], and the scribal handling of boundaries of the psalms. This manuscript contains about 50 compositions in a completely different order from the biblical psalms, together with 10 compositions not found in the canonical Book of Psalms.[13] These include some texts known from other sources and translations (e.g. the hymn to wisdom in Ben Sira 51, Ps 151, and Pss 154 and 155, known from Syriac translations), and previously unknown compositions (e.g. "David's Compositions," a text extolling David for his prolific psalm writing, wisdom, and prophetic inspiration, and the "Apostrophe to Zion," also found in two other Qumran manuscripts).

Other manuscripts from Qumran that have been categorized as "psalms scrolls" present a diverse range of scopes, orders, and inventories. As I have argued elsewhere, none of them are representations of our "Book of Psalms" per se, a textual unity and bibliographic concept that did not exist either materially or as a concept in the second temple textual imagination.[14] And in these collections, there is to be no boundary

---

13 The *editio princeps* is James A. Sanders, *The Psalms Scroll of Qumrân Cave 11 (11QPs[a])* (DJD 4; Oxford: Clarendon, 1965). See also Peter Flint, *The Dead Sea Psalms Scrolls and the Book of Psalms* (STDJ 17; Leiden: Brill, 1997).

14 On the non-existence of a "Book of Psalms" as a concept in the second temple period, and alternative ways of conceptualizing how psalms collections were categorized and imagined, see my monograph, *The Literary Imagination in Jewish Antiquity* (New York: Oxford University Press, 2016), chapter 1, as well as Mroczek, "Thinking Digitally About the Dead Sea Scrolls: Book History Before and Beyond the Book," *BH* 14 (2011): 241–69; "Psalms Unbound: Ancient Concepts of Textual Tradition in 11QPsalms[a] and Related Texts" (PhD diss., University of Toronto, 2012), esp. 29–36; and "The Hegemony of the Biblical in Biblical Studies," *JAJ* 6:1 (2015): 2–35. See also the complementary work by Mika Pajunen, who has come to similar conclusions about the lack of a particular "Book of Psalms"

between what we would call the "canonical" and "non-canonical" compositions – texts that are found in the later entity, the biblical Psalter – are collected together, undifferentiated, with texts not included in the Masoretic canon.

Psalm 151A and B

Among the "non-canonical" texts is a Hebrew text related to our marginal Greek Ps 151:

הללויה לדויד בן ישי קטן הייתי מואחי וצעיר מבני אבי וישימני 3
רועה לצונו ומושל בגדיותיו ידי עשו עוגב ואצבעותי כנור 4
ואשימה ל**** כבוד אמרתי אני בנפשי ההרים לוא יעידו 5
לו והגבעות לוא יגידו עלו העצים את דברי והצואן את מעשי 6
כי מי יגיד ומי ידבר ומי יספר את מעשי אדון הכול ראה אלוה 7
הכול הוא שמע והוא האזין שלח נביאו למושחני את שמואל 8
לגדלני יצאו אחי לפראתו יפי התור ויפי המראה הגבהים בקומתם 9
היפים בשערם לוא בחר **** אלוהים בם וישלח ויקחני 10
מאחר הצואן וימשחני בשמן הקודש וישימני נגיד לעמו ומושל בבני 11
בריתו 12
תחלת גב[ ]רה ל[ ]יד משמשחו נביא אלוהים אזי רא[ ]תי פלשתי 13
[ ] מחרף ממ[ ] אנוכי [ ] את 14

3 A Halleluia of David, son of Jesse. I was smaller than my brothers and the youngest of my father's sons; he made me
4 shepherd of his flock and ruler over his kid goats. My hands made a flute, my fingers a lyre,
5 and I gave glory to YHWH. I said to myself: the mountains do not witness
6 to me, nor do the hills proclaim on my behalf, the trees my words and the flock my deeds.
7 Who, then, is going to announce and who will speak and who will recount my deeds? The Lord of all saw, the God
8 of all, he heard, and he listened. He sent his prophet to anoint me, Samuel
9 to make me great. My brothers went out to meet him, handsome of figure and handsome of appearance. Though they were tall of stature,
10 handsome *Blank* by their hair, YHWH God did not choose them, but sent to fetch me
11 from behind the flock and anointed me with holy oil, and made me leader of his people /and ruler/ over the sons of
12 his covenant. *Blank*

through analysis of manuscript variety at Qumran in "Perspectives on the Existence of a Particular Authoritative Book of Psalms in the Late Second Temple Period," *JSOT* 39 (2014): 139–63. On the variety and fluidity of collections see also Armin Lange, "Collecting Psalms in Light of the Dead Sea Scrolls," in *A Teacher for All Generations: Essays in Honor of James C. VanderKam* (ed. Eric F. Mason et al.; JSJS 153; Leiden: Brill, 2012), 297–308. Most recently, see David Willgren, "Like A Garden Of Flowers: A Study Of The Formation Of The 'Book' Of Psalms" (Ph.D. Dissertation, Lund University, 2016).

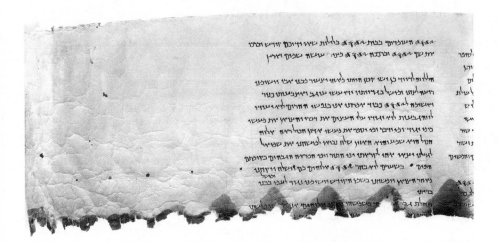

Fig. 27: 11QPsalms[a] column 28–29. Courtesy of the Israel Antiquities Authority.

[13] Beginning of David's power, after God's prophet had anointed him. Then I saw a Philistine
[14] threatening from the ra[nks of the Philistines.] I [...]

See Fig. 27, the last column of 11QPsalms[a]. As in the Septuagint psalter, this text appears at the very end of the collection. But while the Septuagint Ps 151 is "outside the number," beyond the established 150, in the Qumran Psalms Scroll, the corresponding text is simply designated as a Halleluia of David, without differentiation. No number 150 is presupposed here, and the text does not stand outside of any border. The DJD editor of the scroll, James A. Sanders, observes that "Ps 151 in 11QPs[a] is in no wise supernumerary. Far from being 'rider' or something extra it is placed, with the psalm that follows it, in a climactic position to the whole scroll."[15]

"David's Compositions"

Although Ps 151A and B closes the collection, there is another text that has often been called its "colophon," even though it comes a column earlier. This is a text Sanders called "David's Compositions" – a description of David as a scribe, sage, and luminous, perfect man, who wrote psalms: 4,050 songs in total, prophetically revealed and calendrically arranged (see Fig. 28, on the left column):

---

[15] Sanders, *The Psalms Scroll*, 58. The translation given is from DJD, though a range of readings is possible; for alternatives see Reymond, *New Idioms*, 54–65.

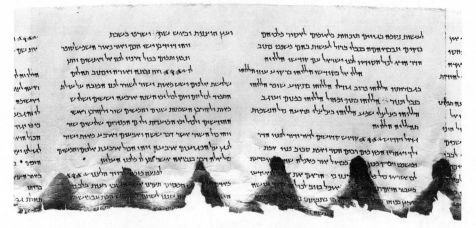

Fig. 28: 11QPsalmsᵃ column 6–27. Courtesy of the Israel Antiquities Authority.

ויהי דויד בן ישי חכם ואור כאור השמש וסופר ²

ונבון ותמים בכול דרכיו לפני אל ואנשים ויתן ³

לו **** רוח נבונה ואורה ויכתוב תהלים ⁴

שלושת אלפים ושש מאות ושיר לשורר לפני המזבח על עולת ⁵

התמיד לכול יום ויום לכול ימי השנה ארבעה וששים ושלוש ⁶

מאות ולקורבן השבתות שנים וחמשים שיר ולקורבן ראשי ⁷

החודשים ולכול ימי המועדות ולים הכפורים שלושים שיר ⁸

ויהי כול השיר אשר דבר ששה וא(ר)בעים וארבע מאות ושיר ⁹

לנגן על הפגועים ארבעה ויהי הכול ארבעת אלפים לחמשים ¹⁰

כול אלה דבר בנבואה אשר נתן לו מלפני העליון ¹¹

² *Blank* And David, son of Jesse, was wise, and luminous like the light of the sun, and a scribe,

³ *Blank* and discerning, and perfect in all his paths before God and men. And

⁴ *Blank* YHWH gave him a discerning and enlightened spirit. And he wrote psalms:

⁵ three thousand six hundred; and songs to be sung before the altar over the perpetual

⁶ offering of every day, for all the days of the year: three hundred

⁷ and sixty-four; and for the Sabbath offerings: fifty-two songs; and for the offerings of the first days of

⁸ the months, and for all the days of the festivals, and for the Day of Atonement: thirty songs.

⁹ And all the songs which he spoke were four hundred and forty-six. And songs

¹⁰ to perform over the possessed: four. The total was four thousand and fifty.

¹¹ All these he spoke through prophecy which had been given to him from before the Most High.[16]

This reckoning does not place limits on collections or try to enumerate specific compositions. Unlike later enumerations of 150, it does not actually count particular psalms. Instead, it uses numbers to emphasize the correct liturgical calendar, and for

---

16 11QPsalmsᵃ, col. 27. For the text and translations, I am relying on Sanders, *The Psalms Scroll*.

poetic and affective impact – that is, to create a composition about David's prolific psalmody and inspiration.[17] They link David to an earlier tradition about Solomon's 4,005 sayings and songs (1 Kgs 5:12; David, with a total of 4,050, comes out ahead).

The publication of "David's Compositions" puts some of the concerns of New Philology into sharp relief. The DJD volume of 11QPsalms[a] obscures the material aspects of this text, and this has implications for how we understand its genre and significance. First, the text – called in DJD "the only prose composition in the scroll"[18] is printed in prose format, while all the other texts are printed stichometrically. But this does not reflect the form of the manuscript itself. In the *physical* manuscript, *every* composition is in prose format, except for the acrostic Psalm 119.[19] Second, the critical edition presents the transcriptions, translations, and notes to the "Apocryphal Compositions" separately at the end (Pages 53–93), with "David's Compositions" as the final text. But this is not the way that the manuscript itself is organized: the non-Masoretic psalms are not set apart from the rest of the collection, and "David's Compositions" is not the final piece; rather, it is followed by Pss 140, 134, and 151A and B. Thus, the organization and formatting of the compositions in the printed edition is at odds with the physical manuscript.

The material context of "David's Compositions," then, is quite different from what the critical edition might suggest. What implications does it have for how we understand the text? Scholars have invariably understood it not as a text, but as a paratext: it is not part of the collection itself, but instead tells us something *about* it, communicating information about how it is to be received. Variously called a "prose insert," an authorial note, a catalogue, a colophon, an epilogue, or a scribal notation, it is understood as something heteronomous to and in the service of the text proper.[20] In this case, scholars agree that its purpose is to stake a claim for the Davidic

---

17 James Kugel writes that the text "seeks to overwhelm us with numbers" (Kugel, "David the Prophet," in *Poetry and Prophecy: The Beginnings of a Literary Tradition* [ed. James L. Kugel; Ithaca: Cornell University Press, 1990], 54). On this composition see my article "'David did not ascend into the heavens' (Acts 2:34): Early Jewish Ascent Traditions and the Myth of Exegesis in the New Testament," *Judaïsme ancien – Ancient Judaism* 3 (in press); and earlier, "Moses, David, and Scribal Revelation: Preservation and Renewal in Second Temple Jewish Textual Traditions," in *The Significance of Sinai: Traditions about Sinai and Divine Revelation in Judaism and Christianity* (ed. George J. Brooke, Hindy Najman, and Loren T. Stuckenbruck; Themes in Biblical Narrative 12; Leiden: Brill, 2008), 91–115.
18 Sanders, *The Psalms Scroll*, 91.
19 This is not the case for all psalms manuscripts. Flint lists nine mss that are arranged stichometrically, twenty-one in prose, and at least two – 4QPs[c] and 11QPs[a] – with both; *Psalms Scrolls*, 49.
20 James A. Sanders, *The Dead Sea Psalms Scroll* (Ithaca: Cornell University Press, 1967), 133–35 ("prose insert," a term that has been widely repeated in the scholarship); Eugene Ulrich, "The Text of the Hebrew Scriptures at the Time of Hillel and Jesus," *Congress Volume: Basel 2001* (ed. Andre Lemaire; VTSup 92; Leiden: Brill, 2002), 104 ("colophon," another popular designation); Flint, *Dead Sea Psalms Scrolls*, 224 ("a prose piece with the function of an extended superscription"); James C. VanderKam, "Studies on 'David's Compositions,'" *ErIsr* 26 (1999): 212* –20*.

authorship of the psalms in the scroll – giving this collection scriptural and prophetic authority.[21]

To be sure, the text does share traits with typical scribal colophons, such as the enumeration of a set of compositions and a statement about their origins. But both the literary and material features of this text suggest that the scholarly tendency to read this text as functional, referential, and set apart from the rest of the collection go too far. Materially, in its placement and layout in the manuscript, "David's Compositions" is not distinctly paratextual or "functional"; it does not stand outside the collection, but is part of it. While it is distinctively formatted in prose in the DJD edition, this distinguishing feature does not exist in the manuscript, where nearly all the compositions are in prose.[22] Further, the publishing decision to place the text at the end of the edition – even though in the manuscript, it is followed by several other compositions – bolsters the interpretation that the text stands outside of and refers back to the collection itself, like a stereotypical colophon.[23] This oversimplifies its role in the collection, obscuring other, more complex aspects of its relationship with the other texts on the scroll. Indeed, its richly allusive literary texture and evocative praise of an ideal figure suggests it

---

21 For example: "The prose 'epilogue' 'David's Compositions' must ... be considered as functionally oriented. Its purpose is clearly to exalt David as the author of a myriad of pss for a variety of occasions. It may well intend to extend Davidic authorship and authority to all the works of the scroll." (Gerald Henry Wilson, *The Editing of the Hebrew Psalter* (SBLDS 78; Chico, CA: Scholars Press, 1985], 137; Jed Wyrick: "the real intent of this list is to validate a body of liturgical and poetic works in as many ways as possible" (*The Ascension of Authorship: Attribution and Canon Formation in Jewish, Hellenistic, and Christian Traditions* [Cambridge, Mass.: Harvard University Press, 2004], 93). Among many others, see Sanders, *The Psalms Scroll*, 63–64, 92; Alan M. Cooper, "The Life and Times of King David According to the Book of Psalms," in *The Poet and the Historian: Essays in Literary and Historical Biblical Criticism* (ed. Richard E. Friedman; HSS 26; Chico, Cal.: Scholars Press, 1983), 117–31; Kugel, "David the Prophet," esp. 46, 55.

22 While the large indent in the first three lines of the composition might suggest a special scribal choice, no evidence from other scrolls suggests that such a layout is meant to indicate a generic distinction; rather, scar tissue on the scroll's surface likely caused the scribe to avoid inscribing that part of the parchment (see Sanders, *The Psalms Scroll*, 93, and Emanuel Tov, *Scribal Practices and Approaches Reflected in the Texts Found in the Judean Desert* [STDJ 54. Leiden: Brill, 2004], 137), as it has in several other places on the Psalms scroll (see Sanders, *The Psalms Scroll*, 14); see, for instance, the clearly visible surface defect and indentation in col. 15 2–3. Tov (*Scribal Practices*, 115) lists other examples of scrolls where scribes have avoided writing on a poor surface, including the multiple indented lines in 4QRP[b] (4Q364) 9a–b 5–7 and 4QInstr[b] (4Q416) 2 ii 19–21.

23 To be sure, colophons in later codex-based traditions sometimes do appear in places other than at the very end of a manuscript, and sometimes more text is added after a colophon. The fact that the composition in 11QPsalms[a] col. 27 is not at the end of the manuscript does not, by itself, mean it is not a colophon. But to place it at the end in the published edition, in a distinct format, and to define it as always functional and heteronomous, sets up an overly rigid distinction between this text and the other compositions and obscures its literariness.

may not be as generically distinct from the other compositions in the scroll as most scholars assume. As I have argued elsewhere, the composition itself makes no claim to functionality or auxiliary status either: the 4,050 psalms are an ideal number that inscribes itself into the tradition of Solomonic wisdom (1 Kgs 5:12, where Solomon is responsible for 4,005 proverbs and songs[24]); it does not enumerate anything in particular, and certainly not the compositions on this scroll.[25] Rather than a functional paratext that tells us about the scroll's authorship and does the other instrumental work we expect a colophon to do, we have a literary composition, a paean about David that includes praise of his character, his prolific psalm-writing, and his prophetic inspiration.[26]

At Qumran, then, we do not have distinct paratextual material that would frame the Psalms for us in any clear way, and no specific number of psalms is presupposed or used. The number 4,050 in the so-called "colophon" is a symbolic choice embedded in a literary composition, not a scribal paratext. While other Qumran psalms manuscripts display various contents and scopes, this particular collection ends with Hebrew versions related to the *Vorlage* to Ps 151, but without any indication of boundaries drawn around the collection.

Septuagint Codices

Things change when we move to Greek manuscripts – there, we do find distinct, heteronomous paratexts that frame the texts themselves, and these paratexts do show awareness of a limited psalms collection of 150 compositions. That number draws boundaries, and actually refers to identifiable, specific compositions that are numbered using Greek letters in the margins. But even as 150 is the established number, Greek psalms manuscripts in fact contain 151 compositions. Psalm 151 has the following superscription:

οὗτος ὁ ψαλμὸς ἰδιόγραφος εἰς δαυιδ
καὶ ἔξωθεν τοῦ ἀριθμοῦ
ὅτε ἐμονομάχησεν τῷ γολιαδ.

---

24 On this parallel see Noam Mizrahi, "Comparison of the List of 'David's Compositions' (11QPs a 27 2–11) to the Characterization of David and Solomon in Kings and Chronicles," *Meghillot: Studies in the Dead Sea Scrolls 5-6. A Festschrift for Devorah Dimant* (Jerusalem: Bialik Institute, 2008), 167-96 (Hebrew). See also the tradition in Perek Shirah, quoted in the epigraph to this essay.

25 See Mroczek, "Moses, David, and Scribal Revelation"; "The Hegemony of the Biblical." There is no demonstrative that refers directly to the text, the way that, for example, we read in Proverbs ("these too are proverbs of Solomon that the men of Hezekiah, wrote," Prov 25:1).

26 I discuss the genre and function of this text fully in my monograph, *The Literary Imagination in Jewish Antiquity.*

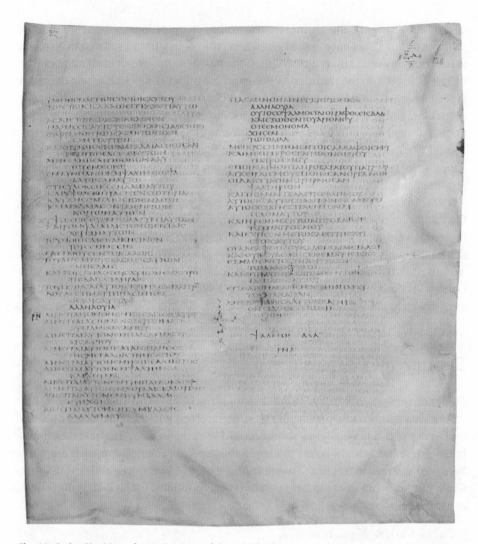

Fig. 29: Codex Sinaiticus, f. 128. Courtesy of the British Library.

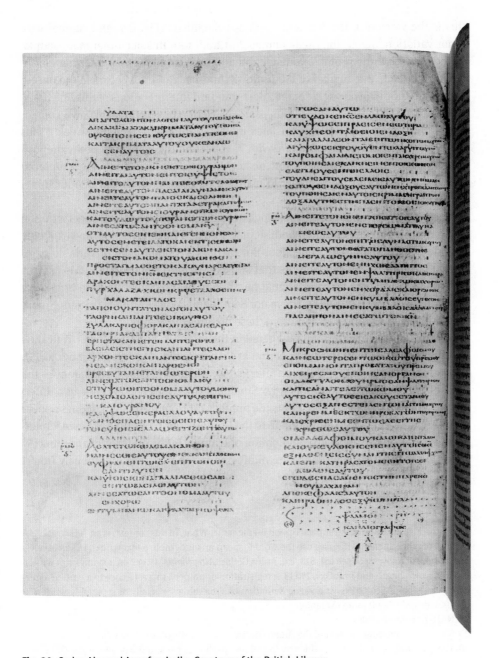

Fig. 30: Codex Alexandrinus facsimile. Courtesy of the British Library.

This is the version in the 4th century Codex Sinaiticus (Fig. 29), and shared, with minor variation, across the Greek manuscript tradition. In some other manuscripts, the notation that the psalm is "outside the number" is followed by a further clarification – "outside the number of 150 psalms." Another variation occurs in the phrase οὗτος ὁ ψαλμὸς ἰδιόγραφος εἰς δαυιδ. Most standard interpretations of this line translate comparably to the NRSV – "This psalm is ascribed to David as his own composition."[27] Pietersma, however, translates more faithfully to the literal Greek: "This psalm is autographical. Regarding David,"[28] reflecting the ambiguity of the preposition εἰς, whose basic meaning is "for" or "to." In Codex Alexandrinus, εἰς is replaced with the genitive τοῦ,[29] seemingly to clarify a possessive, authorial relationship – a writing *of* David.[30]

Despite these variations, the ἰδιόγραφος and ἔξωθεν τοῦ ἀριθμοῦ superscription is a shared paratextual layer that both signal Ps 151 as a Davidic writing, and explicitly exclude it from a standard collection. But there is a second layer of variable paratextual features in the manuscripts that shows how scribes negotiated this psalm's ambiguous status: the actual marginal numbering of the psalm, and the brief colophons at the end of the Psalter. The major Septuagint codices – the Vaticanus, Sinaiticus, and Alexandrinus – each present these features differently.

While the other psalms are numbered in the margins, both the Codex Vaticanus and the Sinaiticus stop their numbering at Ps 150, without giving a number to 151. Vaticanus (4ᵗʰ c.) includes a notation after Ps 150, which says Βιβλος ψαλμων ρν' – the Book of 150 Psalms. The scribe of Codex Sinaiticus (4ᵗʰ c.; see Fig. 29) gives us a different presentation: while he, too, omits the number 151 from the margin, it does appear after the composition, in the colophon to the Psalter: "the 151 psalms of David." Interestingly, we find the opposite combination of features in the Codex Alexandrinus (5ᵗʰ c; see Fig. 30). There, the psalms are numbered in the margins continuously from 1

---

27 The precise meaning of the superscription is enigmatic. What, in this context, is an "idiograph"? A handful of other ancient witnesses use the word to mean an autograph, a text written in somebody's own hand. For ἰδιόγραφος see LSJ, 818, e.g. Aulus Gellus, *Attic Nights*, 19.14.7 on a manuscript written in Virgil's own hand, and in P. Oxy. 250.13, a registration of propety, in a reference to a written agreement. Liddell and Scott also list a vague definition of something "specially or separately written" – but provide only Ps 151 as an example.

28 NETS translation, 2007.

29 See Fig. 30, although the text of the superscription is nearly illegible on the folio.

30 The εἰς δαυιδ is analogous to the לדוד in Hebrew psalms superscriptions, which the Old Greek translates also with the dative, τῷ; later recensions change τῷ to τοῦ to clarify the authorial relationship. On this move see Albert Pietersma, "Exegesis and Liturgy in the Superscriptions of the Greek Psalter," in *X Congress of the International Organization for Septuagint and Cognate Studies, Oslo, 1998* (ed. Bernard A. Taylor; SBLSCS 51; Atlanta: Society of Biblical Literature, 2001), 103. The variant in Alexandrinus – τοῦ δαυιδ for εἰς δαυιδ – seems to reflect a similar impulse to move from an ambiguous relationship of association to one of authorship.

through 151. But the colophon, rather than referring to 151 psalms, retains the primacy of 150, referring instead to "150 Psalms of David and the idiograph."

From the paratextual features in these two codices, we can see that there was some variation in how the psalms were conceived of as a unit, and disagreement about how to treat this marginal psalm. What is shared is that it was worth copying in luxury codices across the tradition, and its superscription accorded it Davidic authenticity. Codex Alexandrinus also contains a letter of Athanasius, who speaks unequivocally about this psalm as a Davidic composition that should be recited in times of strife, further bolstering its authority and importance, even encouraging its usage. And yet, the psalm always occupies an outsider position.

Syriac Manuscripts

Psalm 151 in Syriac

The Syriac tradition presents us with new complications: not only Ps 151 but also four more compositions fit the category of authentically Davidic, but outside a standard number. I begin with a brief look at manuscripts that contain Ps 151, but not the other four apocryphal psalms. Psalm 151 can be found in Syro-Hexaplaric manuscripts, which follow the Septuagint, and some Peshiṭta versions as well. Its earliest known Syriac version, however, is in manuscript 6h22 (6th c),[31] a translation of Athanasius' Psalms commentary. There, we find a subscription after Ps 150, which signals that "the one hundred and fifty Psalms of the Prophet David are completed, with the commentary on them by Athanasius the Archbishop of Alexandria."[32] And yet, Ps 151

---

[31] This is earlier than the Syro-Hexapla, but closely related to that text. See Willem Baars, "Apocryphal Psalms," in *The Old Testament in Syriac according to the Peshiṭta version: Part IV Fasc. 6: Canticles or Odes; Prayer of Manasseh; Apocryphal Psalms; Psalms of Solomon; Tobit I(3) Esdras* (Leiden: Brill, 1972), viii; Strugnell, "Notes," 269–70; Robert J. V. Hiebert, *The "Syrohexaplaric" Psalter, Septuagint and Cognate Studies* 27 (Atlanta: Scholars Press, 1989), 235; van Rooy, *Studies*, 74; Schneider, "Biblische Oden im syrohexaplarischen Psalter," *Bib* 40 (1959): 199–209. The text of Ps 151 in 6h22, together with its superscriptions and subscriptions, were published by Strugnell, "Notes," 270–72; for 6h22 see Robert W. Thomson, *Athanasiana Syriaca Part IV. Expositio in Psalmos. 1. Abbreviated Version. 2. Longer Version* (CSCO 386, Scriptores Syri 167; Leuven: Peeters, 1977). It also appears in two other commentary manuscripts besides 6h22: the Scholia of Bar Hebraeus, published by Paul de Lagarde, *Praetermissorum libri duo* (Göttingen: Dieterich, 1879), 244; and an unpublished manuscript of various psalms commentaries at the British Museum, Oriental 9354, f. 16v; see Lucas Van Rompay, *Théodore de Mopsueste. Fragments syriaques du Commentaire des Psaumes (Psaume 118 et Psaumes 138–148)* (CSCO 436, Scriptores Syri 190; Leuven: Peeters, 1982). See van Rooy, *Studies*, 64.
32 Van Rooy, *Studies*, 66.

follows. It is not accompanied by any commentary, but its text is presented together with its number and its superscription, which closely follows the LXX version:

ܕܡܐܐ ܘܚܡ̈ܫܝܢ ܘܚܕ܂ ܗܢܐ ܡܙܡܘܪܐ ܕܝܠܗ ܕܕܘܝܕ܂ ܡܟܬܒ ܘܠܒܪ ܡܢ ܡܢܝܢܐ ܗܘ܀

The one hundred and fifty-first. This Psalm was written by David himself and is outside the number.

After the text of the psalm, another colophon signals for a second time that the psalms commentary has ended.[33]

Harry van Rooy describes in detail all the superscriptions to Ps 151 in both Syro-Hexaplaric and Peshiṭta manuscripts. The Syro-Hexaplaric tradition is more uniform when it comes to the paratextual handling of Ps 151. Most manuscripts follow the Ambrosian Syro-Hexapla, manuscript 9SH1, more or less closely:

ܩܢܐ ܗܢܐ ܡܙܡܘܪܐ ܕܝܠܗ ܡܢ ܕܘܝܕ܂ ܡܟܬܒ ܘܠܒܪ ܡܢ ܡܢܝܢܐ ܗܘ. ܠܐ ܕܝܢ ܒܟܠܗܘܢ ܝ ܣ̈ܝܡܐ ܡܫܬܟܚ.

151. This Psalm was written by David himself and is outside the number. It is not found in all the books.

The major difference between this Syro-Hexaplaric heading and the one in 6h22 is that the Syro-Hexapla adds the note about the psalm's absence from other manuscripts. In addition, in 9SH1, a decoration across the whole column separates Ps 151 from the other 150 – adding another layer of paratextual distinction.

Many Peshiṭta psalms manuscripts – classified as liturgical books – include Ps 151 after the canonical collection, usually followed by the Odes. These display greater variety in terms of the paratextual handling of Ps 151: some include a colophon signifying completion after Ps 150 *and* Ps 151; some after Ps 150 only; and some after Ps 151 only.[34] Van Rooy provides a complete list of the superscriptions and subscriptions in these manuscripts; here, I will highlight only two examples from his study that illustrate the ambiguity in how Syriac scribes imagined the number and ending of the Psalms. The oldest Peshiṭta manuscript with Ps 151, 12t2 (written in 1189/90 CE

33 Van Rooy (*Studies*, 66–68) describes the position of Ps 151 in the other two commentaries. In Bar Hebraeus, there is no indication that the commentary ends at Ps 150, but Ps 151 follows directly. In Oriental 9354, Ps 151 appears after a commentary on Psalms by Nathaniel of Zirzor and is introduced as "spoken by David." Van Rooy notes that the copyist had some space left on the folio, and used the psalm as "filler material" (67).

34 Van Rooy, *Studies*, 69. Such variation in the placement of subscriptions is not uncommon in Syriac manuscripts. When several Jeremianic texts appear in one manuscript, a subscription might mark the end of Jeremiah either after Jeremiah-Lamentations or after the Epistles of Baruch and Jeremiah or only after Jeremiah itself. A similar variability exists in manuscripts of the Book of Daniel and Bel and the Dragon. I thank Liv Lied for this important point.

according to its colophon),[35] has two subscriptions. After Ps 150, it tells us that the psalms *within the number 150* are completed. Psalm 151 follows, introduced with the heading "another psalm" and followed by the subscription "the 151 psalms are completed." This manuscript, then, preserves two numbers and two moments of completion for the psalms. Another manuscript, 10t1 (cf. 10t4 and 10t5), paratextually frames Ps 151 in a completely different way: Psalm 150 is followed by a decoration the width of the folio, then Ps 151. The final subscription, before the Odes begin, tells us that the *150 praises of David are completed*. Here, the subscript refers to the 150 psalms – even as it follows Ps 151!

Five Syriac Apocryphal Psalms

Psalm 151, then, appears in many Syriac manuscripts as a marginal text – both a Davidic composition and an outsider. The variability of its paratextual features testifies to the fact that the proper way to draw the boundaries of the psalms was not quite settled – but it also reflects a broader tendency in Syriac manuscripts, which commonly allow for this kind of variance in how textual boundaries are marked.

Things become even more variable, however, when we consider those manuscripts that contain not only Ps 151, but also another four psalms. Conventionally titled the "five Syriac apocryphal psalms," these compositions have long been known from medieval manuscripts.[36] With the discovery of 11QPsalms[a], Ps 151 and two more of these five Syriac compositions turned up in Hebrew originals, which had been lost for centuries. In the Qumran manuscript, these compositions do not appear as a unit, although their numbering and arrangement in the DJD version may be somewhat misleading – they are numbered Syriac Psalms I–III and presented together as a group, even though this is not the way they appear in the manuscript. Sanders argues that,

> The fact that these three psalms appear in 11QPs[a] says nothing about their ultimate origin. ... the three are interspersed among the thirty-six canonicals (in Cols. xviii, xxiv, and xxviii) in such a way as to cast no doubt on their "canonicity" at Qumran, or to suggest any relationship among them. They have no more special relationship of origin one to another than do Pss 141, 133, and 144, which in 11QPs[a] appear (in that order) on the same column.[37]

---

35 Van Rooy, *Studies*, 69.

36 Stephano Evodio Assemani and Guiseppe Simone Assemani, *Bibliothecae Apostolicae Vaticanae Codicum Manuscriptorum Catalogus Partis Primae. Tomus Tertius* (Rome: Ex typographia linguarum orientalium Angeli Rotilii, 1756), 385–86. See the edition of Noth, "Apokryphen Psalmen." Prior to Noth's edition, the Apocryphal Psalms were published by William Wright, "Some Apocryphal Psalms in Syriac," in *Proceedings of the Society of Biblical Archaeology* 9 (1886–87): 257–58, 264–66, and Alphonse Mingana, "Some Uncanonical Psalms," in *Woodbrooke Studies: Volume 1* (Cambridge: W. Heffer & Sons, 1927), 288–92. See also Baars, "Apocryphal Psalms"; van Rooy, *Studies*.

37 Sanders, *The Psalms Scroll*, 75.

These psalms are in no way distinguished from the other psalms, either scribally or thematically, but are simply collected, undifferentiated, with other psalmic compositions.

But the Syriac manuscripts, whose producers are working with a model of a 150-psalm collection, invariably consider the five compositions as a separate group, framing them as a group of five "outsider" psalms of David. These texts, published in Baars' 1972 critical edition in the Leiden Peshiṭta series, can be found in three manuscript traditions: manuscript 12t4, which contains commentaries, psalms, odes, and hymns that I will discuss more fully below; manuscript 19d1, a manuscript of the Prophets with the Apocryphal Psalms at the end; and a handful of manuscripts of a work of Elias of al-Anbar (10th c.) entitled *Ktaba d-Durrasha* (*Book of Instruction*, also known as the *Book of Centuries*.) The Elias manuscripts are dated from the 14th to the 19th century, and are fairly uniform. The text of the Apocryphal Psalms in 19d1, the Prophets manuscript, seems to be based on the Elias text.[38] The Elias manuscripts introduce the five apocryphal psalms with the following introduction:

ܬܘܒ ܘܗܢܘܢ ܟܡܫܐ ܡܙܡܘܪ̈ܐ ܕܠܐ ܟܬܝܒܝܢ ܒܣܕܪ̈ܐ ܕܡܙܡܘܪ̈ܐ

Next, five Psalms of David that are not written in the series of the Psalms.

These psalms are their own collection, lacking from the standard ܣܕܪܐ, series or order – a distinction probably based on liturgical usage.

Manuscript 12t4

Our richest source for the five apocryphal psalms is manuscript 12t4, also the most important witness to the East Syrian psalms and their headings. Before I describe how the boundaries of the Psalter are handled in this source, it is necessary to say something about the unpublished manuscript itself, since it opens up a new set of problems when approached from the perspective of New Philology. The manuscript was first described in 1907 by Addai Scher as part of the collection of the Chaldean archbishop in Diyarbakır.[39] It made its way to Mosul, known also by the siglum Mosul 1113, and was last noted in Baghdad at the library of the Chaldean Patriarchate. It is now partially available on microfilm as part of the Leiden Peshiṭta Institute's collection.[40] The four rolls of microfilm contain negative photos of someone

---

38 Baars, "Apocryphal Psalms," ii–vii.
39 Addai Scher, "Notice sur les manuscrits syriaques et arabes conservés à l'archevêché chaldéen de Diarbéker," *JA* 10th ser., 10 (1907): 331–62, 385–431.
40 I thank Bas ter Haar Romeny for allowing me to view and digitize the microfilm at the Peshiṭta Institute, and Maya Goldberg for her assistance in Leiden.

Fig. 31: Ms Baghdad/Mosul 1113 (12t4). Microfilm roll 4, image 8. Courtesy of the Leiden Peshiṭta Institute.

holding the codex open for the camera – the man's hands and shirt visible in every picture (see Fig. 31). Some of the photos are beautifully clear, but others are completely illegible.

The current state and whereabouts of the actual manuscript are unknown.[41] The best source for information about this important manuscript is the work of van Rooy, who has done extensive research with the microfilm.[42] But as van Rooy also notes, Scher's 1907 description makes it abundantly clear that there is or was more to the codex than what is now available on microfilm. While the "t" in 12t4 designates it as a Psalms manuscript, the psalms are preceded by five treatises by Hippolytus, Basil, Eusebius, Athanasius, and Origen, and Epiphanius' treatise *On Weights and Measures*. Each psalm is accompanied by introductions by Athanasius, Eusebius, and The-

---

41 At the time of writing, the manuscript has not been noted by the Center for the Digitization of Oriental Manuscripts, founded by Fr. Najeeb Michaeel. Many manuscripts of the Chaldean Patriarchate have been damaged or lost. I am grateful to Adam McCollum for this information.

42 van Rooy, *Studies*, especially Chapter 3, "The Syriac Manuscript 12t4 – And Important Manuscript from the Twelfth Century," 11–25, and Chapter 4, "The Syriac Apocryphal Psalms in the Manuscript 12t4," 26–42, and van Rooy, "The Marginal Notes to the Syriac Apocryphal Psalms in Manuscript 12t4," *VT* 48 (1998): 542–54.

odore; where no introduction exists in the work of these commentators, the scribe has indicated its absence (e.g. "it is not in the work of Athanasius the Interpreter"), in an attempt to be exhaustive. Psalm 150 is followed by Ps 151 and then the four other non-canonical psalms, introduced by number, in a different order from the Elias manuscripts. Typically for East Syrian Psalters, the Psalms are followed by the Odes: three songs of Moses (Exod 15, Deut 32) and the Song of Isaiah. But here, the Psalms are followed not only by the Odes, but also by eighteen sections of other material, including hymns for Sundays, ordinary days, and martyrs' feast days. The parts of the manuscript that were photographed and microfilmed in the early days of the Peshiṭta project were those that had a bearing on Old Testament textual criticism, narrowly defined (and so, the Odes did make it in because they reflect text from other parts of the canonical Bible). Scholars organized and privileged the material in ways the medieval scribes themselves did not.

What is missing, then, is the context in which these bible-related materials were preserved, which gives us a sense of what they meant for the scribes who transmitted them and for the communities who used them. And the practice of isolating biblical texts obscures the seeming lack of boundaries between different sorts of materials that have been collected in one manuscript. Given its contents and its pretensions to exhaustiveness, manuscript 12t4 appears to be a scholarly compilation whose major goal was preservation and comprehensiveness. Besides texts like Epiphanius' *On Weights and Measures*, the scribes have included psalm introductions from all three of their main authorities, even when they present conflicting information (for example, attributing the same psalm to different tradents, like David and Hezekiah).

In 12t4, the five apocryphal psalms are written continuously, with no formal distinction, after the 150 "standard" ones. The compilers of 12t4 are more forthcoming about how they understand the Davidic-but-not-canonical compositions. The introduction to Ps 151 reads:

> The one hundred and fifty first. It does not occur in the Hebrew. Neither is there an introduction to the Psalm in the work of Eusebius. And in Athanasius, who makes known the words of glory in the Lord: But when you were the smallest, you were chosen to be of some use to your brothers. You were not raised above them. But sing, while giving the glory to God who chose you. The blessed lord Theodore the commentator did not write an introduction either. In the Syriac manuscripts this is its notation [ܘܢܐܘ]. Of David, when he fought alone against Goliath.[43]

---

43 The quotation of Athanasius' words about Ps 151 is from a letter of Athanasius to Marcellinus (PG 27:37), where Athanasius recommends the recitation of different psalms in different circumstances. Dependence on Athanasius is discussed in van Rooy *Studies*, 48, and Strugnell, "Notes," 258. The Syriac is from Baars, "Apocryphal Psalms," 1 (12t4).

The scribe has noted that 151 does not occur in the Hebrew, and gone on to provide the same information for these psalms as for the 150 previous: the commentaries by Athanasius (which exists) and by Eusebius and Theodore (which do not). The repertoire of information provided is the same as for the canonical psalms.

An additional note appears at the beginning of Ps 152 that indicates different layers of liminality. There, we read that none of the three fathers commented on it, "but these four psalms are written here"; the text then continues to enumerate those four psalms, 152–155. 152 and 153 are "spoken by David" on the occasion of his fight with a lion and a bear; 154 is listed as a prayer of Hezekiah for deliverance from Assyria, and a prayer of the people when Cyrus let them return; and 155 is connected once again to the return under Cyrus. But after 155, we see that the scribe has considered the *five* psalms beyond 150 as their own unit, and all psalms of David:

> ܥܠ ܡܥܕܪܢܘܬܗ ܕܡܪܢ ܫܠܡ ܟܬܒܐ ܕܡܙܡܘܪ̈ܐ ܕܛܘܒܢܐ ܕܘܝܕ ܢܒܝܐ ܘܡܠܟܐ. ܥܡ ܚܡܫܐ ܡܙܡܘܪ̈ܐ ܕܠܝܬܝܗܘܢ ܡܢ ܡܢܝܢܐ ܝܘܢܝܐ
> ܘܠܐ ܥܒܪܝܐ܀ ܒܪܡ ܐܝܟ ܕܐܡܪܝܢ ܐܫܬܟܚܘ ܒܣܘܪܝܝܐ ܘܟܬܒܢ ܐܢܘܢ ܠܗܘ ܕܫܐܠ.

> With the help of our Lord the book of psalms of the blessed David, prophet and king, is completed, together with five Psalms, not of the number, Greek or Hebrew, but, as they say, they are found in Syriac and we wrote them for the one who asked.

Although the additional psalms – apparently copied here by request, in an effort to be exhaustive – are "not of the number," they are not beyond numbering. After the "final" Ps 150, the numbering picks up where it left off – one hundred and fifty-one through one hundred and fifty-five. The psalms are not "of the number," but, as the colophon tells us, they still *complete* the "Book of Psalms of the blessed David."

One of the interesting paratextual features of this psalm is the presence and absence of marginalia. Pss 151, 154, and 155 all have copious marginal notes with variant readings, some of which are based on textual variants known from other extant manuscripts. But there are no marginalia for Pss 152 and 153. Psalms 151, 154, and 155 are all found at Qumran in Hebrew, but Pss 152 and 153 exist only in Syriac. The lack of marginalia is unusual, and the evidence of different scribal handling in the manuscript may indicate a different history of transmission for 152–153 on the one hand and 151, 154, and 155 on the other.[44]

What do the notations in 12t4 tell us about the way the boundaries of the Book of Psalms were imagined? First, we know that the scribes saw these psalms as a separate group. Such self-conscious recognition of the "otherness" of these (or any other) compositions as distinct from an established Psalms collection is absent from the Qumran Psalms Scroll; rather, these texts are scattered and woven into the collection. In the

---

44 On this see van Rooy, "Marginal Notes," 546. On the origins of 152 and 153, which are only known in Syriac, see *Studies*, 110–32.

Syriac (and in the Greek), on the other hand, there is a sense of an established number of psalms beyond which additional compositions are somehow different.[45] But how are they different, exactly? How is their "otherness" understood? Their exclusion from the number of 150 does not appear to depend on any judgment about their inspiration or authenticity. These psalms are presented as no less authentic, no less Davidic, than the rest. Rather, their connection to David is spelled out explicitly, both in the superscriptions to the individual psalms that link them to events in his life, and in the general introductions and conclusions to the group. They are presented as authentic writings ascribed to a biblical figure – and at least Ps 151, via a reference to Athanasius, is recommended for prayer.

So what are these boundaries, and what *does* distinguish the "outside" texts from the "inside" ones? Syriac scribes differentiate these psalms from the Psalter "proper" in several ways. The common brief introduction gives pragmatic information about scribal convention and the manuscript tradition, saying simply that these five psalms of David are "not written in the series ('order') of the psalms," possibly making a distinction based on liturgical use. 12t4 gives more distinguishing features, like language (Ps 151 does not exist in Hebrew; the other four are found in neither Hebrew nor Greek, but "they are found in Syriac") and the availability of patristic commentaries (no major commentators introduce Ps 151 except Athanasius, who recommends it for recitation; the other four are not discussed by Athanasius, Eusebius, or Theodore). Finally, the number in excess of a conventional 150 places these psalms in a separate category. The distinction between canonical and non-canonical compositions is not presented as a difference between sacred and profane, or authentic and spurious. Rather, it is based on pragmatic scholarly observations, the concerns of a librarian – where and in what languages the compositions are found, commentators' attention, and number.

Conclusion

I have presented snapshots of three evolving traditions of counting psalms and ending psalm collections in Hebrew, Greek, and Syriac. While these examples come from different geographical and religious milieus, they not only differ from one another, but also show unmistakable evidence of instability and development within their own traditions. As we can see from the paratextual handling – the numbers and

---

45 As van Rooy writes, "this distinction applies even to Psalm 151, that does appear in the Septuagint. [The scribe] knows the five Apocryphal Psalms as a distinct unit in Syriac and included them upon request in his manuscript. Although he knows the five as a unit, he distinguishes Psalm 151 from the other four, as indicated by the separate introduction to Psalm 151 and the new introduction before Psalm 152" (van Rooy, *Studies*, 50).

notations – around the final compositions, the end of the Book of Psalms remains something of a shape-shifter, never completely settled.

The Dead Sea Scrolls psalms manuscripts do not presuppose a standard number of 150 psalms – rather, the number 4,050 serves to throw open the imagined corpus of psalms beyond any identifiable collection. In the Septuagint and the Syriac manuscripts, on the other hand, numbers set boundaries. But as the Greek and Syriac evidence shows, even when the number 150 is recognized, it often remains an imagined boundary that the manuscripts themselves transgress, presenting collections that exuberantly spill over such borders. What do these borders want to contain, and what do they want to exclude? It seems clear that even when the limits of a normative collection have been set, this does not mean that everything outside those boundaries is considered spurious. Texts can be explicitly marked as ancient, authentic, Davidic – but remain outsiders. Whatever the boundaries of canon limit and exclude, the ancient evidence tells us that inspired and authentic writings could still be imagined to exist outside them.

Bibliography

al-Yaʿqūbī. *Tārīkh al-Yaʿqūbī*. 2 vols. Beirut: Dār Ṣādir, 1970.

Assemani, Stephano Evodio, and Guiseppe Simone Assemani. *Bibliothecae Apostolicae Vaticanae Codicum Manuscriptorum Catalogus Partis Primae. Tomus Tertius*. Rome: Ex typographia linguarum orientalium Angeli Rotilii, 1756.

Baars, Willem. "Apocryphal Psalms." Pages i–x, 1–12 in *The Old Testament in Syriac according to the Peshiṭta version: Part IV, Fasc. 6: Canticles or Odes; Prayer of Manasseh; Apocryphal Psalms; Psalms of Solomon; Tobit I(3) Esdras*. Leiden: Brill, 1972.

Baumgarten, Joseph M. "Perek Shira, an Early Response to Psalm 151." *Revue de Qumran* 9 (1978): 575–78.

Beit-Arié, Malachi. "Perek Shirah: Introduction and Critical Edition." 2 vols. PhD Thesis, Hebrew University of Jerusalem. Jerusalem, 1966.

Bidawid, Raphael J. *Les lettres du patriarche nestorien Timothée I*. Vatican City: Biblioteca apostolica vaticana, 1956.

Braun, Oskar. "Ein Brief des Katholikos Timotheos I über biblische Studien des 9. Jahrhunderts." *Oriens Christianus* 1 (1901): 299–313.

Brownlee, William H. "The 11Q Counterpart to Ps 151,1–5." *Revue de Qumran* 4 (1963): 379–87.

Carmignac, Jean. "Précisions sur la forme poétique du Psaume 151." *Revue de Qumran* 5 (1965): 249–52.

–. "La forme poétique du Psaume 151 de la grotte 11." *Revue de Qumran* 4 (1963): 371–78.

Cooper, Alan M. "The Life and Times of King David According to the Book of Psalms." Pages 117–31 in *The Poet and the Historian: Essays in Literary and Historical Biblical Criticism*. Edited by Richard E. Friedman. Harvard Semitic Studies 26. Chico, Cal.: Scholars Press, 1983.

Dupont-Sommer, André. "Le Psaume CLI dans 11QPsa et le problème de son origine essénienne." *Semitica* 14 (1964): 25–62.

Ebied, Rifaat Y., and Lionel R. Wickham. "Al-Yaʿḳūbī's Account of the Israelite Prophets and Kings." *Journal of Near Eastern Studies* 29 (1970): 80–98.

Flint, Peter. *The Dead Sea Psalms Scrolls and the Book of Psalms*. Leiden: Brill, 1997.
–. "Unrolling the Dead Sea Psalms Scrolls." Pages 229–50 in *The Oxford Handbook of the Psalms*. Edited by William P. Brown. New York: Oxford University Press, 2014.
Genette, Gérard. *Seuils*. Paris: Seuil, 1987.
–. "Introduction to the Paratext." Translated by Marie Maclean. *New Literary History* 22 (1991): 261–72.
–. *Paratexts: Thresholds of Interpretation*. Translated by Jane E. Lewin. Cambridge: Cambridge University Press, 1997.
Haran, Menahem. "The Two Text-forms of Psalm 151." *Journal of Jewish Studies* 39 (1988): 171–82.
Hiebert, Robert J. V. *The "Syrohexaplaric" Psalter*. Atlanta: Scholars Press, 1989.
Holladay, William. *The Psalms Through Three Thousand Years: Prayerbook of a Cloud of Witnesses*. Minneapolis: Augsburg Fortress, 1993.
Kugel, James L. "David the Prophet." Pages 45–55 in *Poetry and Prophecy: The Beginnings of a Literary Tradition*. Edited by James L. Kugel. Ithaca: Cornell University Press, 1990.
Lagarde, Paul de. *Praetermissorum libri duo*. Göttingen: Dieterich, 1879.
Lange, Armin. "Collecting Psalms in Light of the Dead Sea Scrolls." Pages 297–308 in *A Teacher for All Generations: Essays in Honor of James C. VanderKam*. Edited by Eric F. Mason et al. Leiden: Brill, 2012.
List of Old Testament Peshiṭta Manuscripts (Preliminary Issue). Edited by the Peshiṭta Institute, Leiden University. Leiden: Brill, 1961.
Mingana, Alphonse. "Some Uncanonical Psalms." Pages 288–92 in *Woodbrooke Studies: Volume 1*. Cambridge: W. Heffer & Sons, 1927.
Mizrahi, Noam. "Comparison of the List of 'David's Compositions' (11QPs a 27 2–11) to the Characterization of David and Solomon in Kings and Chronicles." Pages 167-96 in Meghillot: *Studies in the Dead Sea Scrolls 5-6: A Festschrift for Devorah Dimant*. Edited by Moshe Bar-Asher and Emmanuel Tov. Jerusalem: Bialik Institute, 2008 (in Hebrew).
Mroczek, Eva. "Moses, David, and Scribal Revelation: Preservation and Renewal in Second Temple Jewish Textual Traditions." Pages 91–115 in *The Significance of Sinai: Traditions about Sinai and Divine Revelation in Judaism and Christianity*. Edited by George J. Brooke et. al. Leiden: Brill, 2008.
–. "Thinking Digitally About the Dead Sea Scrolls: Book History Before and Beyond the Book." *Book History* 14 (2011): 241–69.
–. "Psalms Unbound: Ancient Concepts of Textual Tradition in 11QPsalmsᵃ and Related Texts." PhD diss., University of Toronto, 2012.
–. "'David did not ascend into the heavens' (Acts 2:34): Early Jewish Ascent Traditions and the Myth of Exegesis in the New Testament." *Judaïsme ancien – Ancient Judaism* 3 (2015): 261–94.
–. "The Hegemony of the Biblical in Biblical Studies," *Journal of Ancient Judaism* 6:1 (2015): 2–35.
Noth, Martin. "Die fünf syrisch überlieferten apokryphen Psalmen." *Zeitschrift für die alttestamentliche Wissenschaft* 48 (1930): 1–23.
Pajunen, Mika S. "Perspectives on the Existence of a Particular Authoritative Book of Psalms in the Late Second Temple Period." *Journal for the Study of the Old Testament* 30 (2014): 139–63.
Pietersma, Albert. "Exegesis and Liturgy in the Superscriptions of the Greek Psalter." Pages 99–138 in *X Congress of the International Organization for Septuagint and Cognate Studies, Oslo, 1998*. Edited by Bernard A. Taylor. Society of Biblical Literature Septuagint and Cognate Studies 51. Atlanta: Society of Biblical Literature, 2001.
Prinsloo, Gert T. M. "Psalms 114 and 115: One or Two Poems?" *Old Testament Essays* 16 (2003): 668–89.

Reeves, John C. "Exploring the Afterlife of Jewish Pseudepigrapha in Medieval Near Eastern Religious Traditions: Some Initial Soundings." *Journal for the Study of Judaism in the Persian, Hellenistic, and Roman Periods* 30 (1999): 148–77.

Reymond, Eric D. *New Idioms within Old: Poetry and Parallelism in the Non-Masoretic Poems of 11Q5 (=11QPsa)*. Society of Biblical Literature Early Judaism and Its Literature 31. Atlanta: Society of Biblical Literature, 2011.

Romeny, Bas ter Haar. "Biblical Studies in the Church of the East: The Case of Catholicos Timothy I." Pages 503–10 in *Historica, Biblica, Theologica et Philosophica: Papers Presented at the Thirteenth International Conferenc on Patristic Studies held in Oxford 1999*. Edited by Maurice F. Wiles, Edward Yarnold, and Paul M. Parvis. Studia Patristica 34. Leuven: Peeters, 2001.

Rooy, Harry F. van. "The Marginal Notes to the Syriac Apocryphal Psalms in Manuscript 12t4." *Vetus Testamentum* 48 (1998): 542–54.

–. *Studies on the Syriac Apocryphal Psalms*. Journal of Semitic Studies Supplement. Oxford: Oxford University Press, 1999.

Van Rompay, Lucas. *Théodore de Mopsueste. Fragments syriaques du Commentaire des Psaumes (Psaume 118 et Psaumes 138–148)*. Corpus Scriptorum Christianorum Orientalium 436, Scriptores Syri 190; Leuven: Peeters, 1982.

Sanders, James A. "Ps. 151 in 11QPss." *Zeitschrift für die alttestamentliche Wissenschaft* 75 (1963): 73–86.

–. *The Psalms Scroll of Qumrân Cave 11 (11QPsᵃ)*. Discoveries in the Judean Desert 4. Oxford: Clarendon, 1965.

–. *The Dead Sea Psalms Scroll*. Ithaca: Cornell University Press, 1967.

Schaff, Philip, and Henry Wace, eds. *A Select Library of Nicene and Post-Nicene Fathers of the Christian Church: Second Series*. 14 Vols. Buffalo, N. Y.: Christian Literature Publishing Co., 1890–1900.

Scher, Addai. "Notice sur les manuscrits syriaques et arabes conservés à l'archevêché chaldéen de Diarbéker." *Journal Asiatique* 10 (1907): 331–62, 385–431.

Schneider, Heinrich. "Biblische Oden im syrohexaplarischen Psater." *Biblica* 40 (1959): 199–209.

Segal, Michael. "The Literary Development of Psalm 151: A New Look at the Septuagint Version." *Textus* 21 (2002): 139–58.

Skehan, Patrick W. "The Apocryphal Psalm 151." *Catholic Biblical Quarterly* 25 (1963): 407–9.

Smith, Mark S. "How to Write a Poem: The Case of Psalm 151 A (11 QPsa 28.3–12)." Pages 182–208 in *Sirach, Scrolls, and Sages: Proceedings of a Second International Symposium on the Hebrew of the Dead Sea Scrolls, Ben Sira, and the Mishnah, Held at Leiden University, 15–17 December 1997*. Edited by Takamitsu Muraoka and John F. Elwolde. Leiden: Brill, 1997.

Strugnell, John. "Notes on the Text and Transmission of the Apocryphal Psalms 151, 154 (= Syr. II) and 155 (= Syr.I II)." *Harvard Theological Review* 59 (1966): 259–61.

Talmon, Shemaryahu. "Extra-Canonical Hebrew Psalms from Qumram-Psalm 151." Pages 244–72 in *The World of Qumran from Within: Collected Studies*. Jerusalem: Magnes Press; Leiden: Brill, 1989.

–. "Hebrew Fragments from Masada: 1(f) MasPsᵃ and (g) MasPsᵇ." Pages 76–97 in *Masada VI: Yigael Yadin Excavations from 1963–1965, Final Reports*. Edited by Shemaryahu Talmon and Yigael Yadin. Jerusalem: Israel Exploration Society and the Hebrew University of Jerusalem, 1999.

Thomson, Robert W. *Athanasiana Syriaca Part IV. Expositio in Psalmos. 1. Abbreviated Version. 2. Longer Version*. Corpus Scriptorum Christianorum Orientalium 386, Scriptores Syri 167. Leuven: Peeters, 1977.

Tov, Emanuel. *Scribal Practices and Approaches Reflected in the Texts Found in the Judaean Desert*. Studies on the Texts of the Desert of Judah 54. Leiden: Brill, 2004.

Ulrich, Eugene. "The Text of the Hebrew Scriptures at the Time of Hillel and Jesus." Pages 85–108 in *Congress Volume: Basel 2001*. Edited by Andre Lemaire. Leiden: Brill, 2002.

VanderKam, James C. "Studies on 'David's Compositions.'" *Eretz Israel* 26 (1999): 212* –20*.

Westcott, Brooke Foss. *A General Survey of the History of the Canon of the New Testament*, 5th ed. Cambridge: Macmillan, 1881.

Wigtil, David N. "The Sequence of the Translations of Apocryphal Psalm 151." *Revue de Qumran* 11 (1983): 401–7.

Willgren, David. "Like a Garden of Flowers: A Study of The Formation of The 'Book' of Psalms." Ph.D. Dissertation, Lund University, 2016.

Wilson, Gerald H. *The Editing of the Hebrew Psalter*. SBL Dissertation Series 78. Chico, Cal.: Scholars Press, 1985.

Wright, William. "Some Apocryphal Psalms in Syriac." *Proceedings of the Society of Biblical Archaeology* 9 (1886–87): 257–58, 264–66.

Wyrick, Jed. *The Ascension of Authorship: Attribution and Canon Formation in Jewish, Hellenistic, and Christian Traditions*. Cambridge, Mass.: Harvard University Press, 2004.

James R. Davila

Translating the Hekhalot Literature: Insights from New Philology

The New Philology needs little introduction to the readers of this volume. In his short book published in 1989, Bernard Cerquiglini highlighted some concerns about scholarly approaches to the study of manuscripts.[1] These concerns were not new, and are not without their own difficulties,[2] but around them as collected by Cerquiglini there coalesced a conscious perspective to look beyond the traditional search for an original text behind the manuscripts to an appreciation of the individual manuscripts as artifacts and texts in their own right, giving full attention to a manuscript's text, physical characteristics, layout, marginalia, etc.[3] Cerquiglini questioned whether the Lachmannian aim to reconstruct an *Urtext* from a corpus of manuscripts through textual criticism and stemmatic analysis was methodologically viable and he argued in particular that medieval works in vernacular languages were not suited to such an approach. The scribes who copied these works did not hesitate to revise and improve on the text, making the production of a stemma problematic. He also questioned the validity of determining manuscript affiliations on the basis of shared errors, given that scribes can make the same mistakes independently, can consult multiple manuscripts, and can rewrite works on their own to an unpredictable extent.[4]

The pre-Kabbalistic Jewish mystical texts in Hebrew and Aramaic which comprise the "Hekhalot literature" (the literature of the celestial "palaces") provide a concrete case for which many of the concerns of New Philology are potentially relevant. In 1981 Peter Schäfer and his colleagues published a synoptic edition of seven medieval and early modern manuscripts of the main texts of the Hekhalot corpus.[5] These manuscripts were not always the earliest ones available for every text, but they included all complete copies of a number of the texts and a range of manuscripts of various origins and dates for the others. Schäfer's *Synopse* was followed in 1984 by an edition of all fragments of Hekhalot texts preserved in the Cairo Geniza which were known at

---

1 Bernard Cerquiglini, *In Praise of the Variant: A Critical History of Philology* (trans. Betsy Wing; Baltimore: Johns Hopkins University Press, 1999 [orig. pub. 1989]).
2 Taken up, for example, in the articles published in *Towards a Synthesis? Essays on the New Philology* (ed. Keith Busby; Faux titre 68; Amsterdam: Rodopi, 1993).
3 The articles "On the New Philology" edited by Stephen G. Nichols in *Speculum* 65:1 (1990) were something of a manifesto for this perspective.
4 Cerquiglini, *In Praise of the Variant*, chapter three.
5 Peter Schäfer, with Margarete Schlüter and Hans Georg von Mitius, *Synopse zur Hekhalot-Literatur* (TSAJ 2; Tübingen: Mohr Siebeck, 1981), hereafter the *Synopse*.

the time.[6] These ranged in date from before the ninth century to the fourteenth, with most originating in the eleventh and twelfth centuries, a period earlier than any of the complete medieval and later manuscripts. These two editions revitalized the field of Hekhalot studies by making the major texts available in reliable editions.

Schäfer's editions were published before New Philology emerged as an independent perspective, and to my knowledge he has not interacted with it specifically, but in these editions and in a series of subsequent publications he raised very similar concerns about the texts and manuscripts of the Hekhalot literature. The synoptic presentation of the manuscripts in the *Synopse* was a carefully considered strategy to deal with the challenges posed by the texts in the manuscripts. Likewise, the multi-volume German translation of the material was produced with a diplomatic format for the same reasons. If I may quote my own summary of his position:

> Schäfer and his colleagues have produced their German translations of the Hekhalot texts on a diplomatic basis: they translate one manuscript (usually O), occasionally emending it when its readings are incoherent, and they collate variants in the other manuscripts in the notes. The notes also consistently flag incoherent readings as corrupt and sometimes, but far from always, indicate that one reading is better than the others. This is a coherent approach that arises naturally from the assumptions behind the presentation of the manuscripts themselves in synoptic format in the *Synopse*. This format in turn was chosen as the best means of presentation for the Hekhalot macroforms,[7] given their nature. They are generally loosely redacted, without a clear overall plan and sometimes with little sense of order at all; often their beginning and ending are not clearly or consistently marked internally either within their own content or in the layout of the manuscripts; the text of some of the macroforms varies widely even among the complete medieval and later manuscripts, suggesting that no canonical form was ever established; and the much earlier Geniza fragments sometimes confront us with very different and obviously better readings and even redactions than that of the late complete manuscripts, demonstrating that the texts continued to be redacted for centuries after their original production. Presentation of these texts in synoptic format with diplomatic translations allowed Schäfer and his colleagues to make them available while sidestepping many of the difficult, if not intractable, problems with conceptualizing the texts that lie behind the manuscripts.[8]

6 Peter Schäfer, *Geniza-Fragmente zur Hekhalot-Literatur* (TSAJ 6; Tübingen: Mohr Siebeck, 1984), hereafter, *Geniza-Fragmente*.
7 Two technical terms coined by Schäfer are especially important for this discussion. A "microform" is a short unit of text that stands on its own. A "macroform" is a larger work that is built up of numerous microforms. The Hekhalot texts that go under the standard titles discussed below are macroforms, while the individual paragraphs numbered in the *Synopse* would generally count as microforms.
8 James R. Davila, *Hekhalot Literature in Translation: Major Texts of Merkavah Mysticism* (SJJTP 20; Leiden: Brill, 2013), 20–21 (hereafter abbreviated *HLIT*). I explain briefly why I judge some of the concerns about the delineation of the boundaries of the Hekhalot macroforms to be exaggerated in the following paragraph of ibid., 21. Even those who have expressed concerns about such delineations continue to refer to the same macroforms and titles as used here. Schäfer has explained his position in detail in numerous works. See, first, the introductions to the four volumes in which he and his colleagues have translated the Hekhalot texts into German: Peter Schäfer and Klaus Hermann, *Übersetzung der Hekhalot-Literatur I §§ 1–80* (TSAJ 46; Tübingen: Mohr Siebeck, 1995); Peter Schäfer et al.,

Recently Michael Swartz has explicitly connected the work of Schäfer and his colleagues on the Hekhalot texts with New Philology.[9] The article ranges widely over Jewish literature from Late Antiquity to the Middle Ages, but its ultimate focus is the Hekhalot literature and Swartz draws his case studies from two of these texts, the *Ma'aseh Merkavah* and the *Hekhalot Zutarti*. Summarizing his own earlier work on the *Ma'aseh Merkavah*, he finds it to survive in multiple recensions that are in turn built up from shorter units. He writes,

> The case of Ma'aseh Merkavah shows us that diachronic analysis of a Hekhalot text is possible. It can be done by paying attention to the relationship between the distribution of units in the manuscripts and the form and substance of those units. However, diachronic analysis does not require that the history of a text begin with a single, original source that was "corrupted" or "emended" by later scribes; rather, it attests to the editorial activity of scribes over the years who compiled discrete components into larger structures.[10]

His second example is a more traditional comparison of the opening paragraphs of the *Hekhalot Zutarti* in the complete medieval manuscripts with a somewhat earlier fragment from the Cairo Geniza, drawing provisional conclusions about possible manuscript affiliations and redactional development of the material.

Swartz concludes with some reflections about the limitations and benefits of the "synoptic method," which parallels in many ways the approaches of New Philology.

> This approach acknowledges that Hekhalot literature begins with a wide variety of smaller units rather than unitary texts of individual authorship. It links manuscript evidence to form (*gattung* [sic]) and content, showing that fissures in the manuscript evidence can be seen as demarca-

---

Übersetzung der Hekhalot-Literatur II §§ 81–334 (TSAJ 17; Tübingen: Mohr Siebeck, 1987); *Übersetzung der Hekhalot-Literatur III §§ 335–597* (TSAJ 22; Tübingen: Mohr Siebeck, 1989); *Übersetzung der Hekhalot-Literatur IV §§ 598–985* (TSAJ 29; Tübingen: Mohr Siebeck, 1991). In addition see Schäfer, "Tradition and Redaction in Hekhalot Literature," in *Hekhalot-Studien* (TSAJ 19; Tübingen: Mohr Siebeck, 1988), 8–16; "Prolegomena zu einer kritischen Edition und Analyse der *Merkava Rabba*," in *ibid.*, 17–49; "Aufbau und redaktionelle Identität der *Hekhalot Zutarti*," in *ibid.*, 50–62; "Zum Problem der redaktionellen Identität von *Hekhalot Rabbati*," in *ibid.*, 63–74; "Ein neues Fragment zur Metoposkopie und Chiromantik," in *ibid.*, 84–95; "Ein neues *Hekhalot Rabbati*-Fragment," in *ibid.*, 96–103. See also David J. Halperin, "A New Edition of the Hekhalot Literature," *JAOS* 104 (1984): 543–52. In the late 1980s Schäfer and Chaim Milikowsky debated the nature of the rabbinic literature in the *Journal of Jewish Studies* and this discussion also touched on the Hekhalot literature: Schäfer, "Research into Rabbinic Literature: An Attempt to Define the Status Quaestionis," *JJS* 37 (1986): 139–52, esp. p. 149; Milikowski, "The Status Quaestionis of Research in Rabbinic Literature," *JJS* 39 (1989): 201–11; Schäfer, "Once Again the Status Quaestionis of Research in Rabbinic Literature: An Answer to Chaim Milikowsky," *JJS* 40 (1989): 89–94.

9 Michael Swartz, "Three-Dimensional Philology: Some Implications of the *Synopse zur Hekhalot-Literatur*," in *Envisioning Judaism: Studies in Honor of Peter Schäfer on the Occasion of his Seventieth Birthday* (ed. Ra'anan Boustan et al.; 2 vols.; Tübingen: Mohr Siebeck, 2013), 529–50.

10 Swartz, "Three-Dimensional Philology," 545.

tions of independent units. It privileges the microform over the macroform. And finally, it treats the synoptic method as an invitation to think historically about the evolution of this complex literature.[11]

My own approach to the Hekhalot texts since the mid-1990s has been somewhat different, but perhaps not in principle incompatible with the perspective of Schäfer, Swartz, and their colleagues. A 1994 article of mine focused on another specific work, the *Hekhalot Rabbati*, the longest work in the corpus.[12] I argued that the evidence supported the possibility of reconstructing an *Urtext* behind the complete European manuscripts of this work using traditional Lachmannian (although I did not use that term) methods for the production of an eclectic critical edition. At the same time I acknowledged the possibility that the Geniza fragments reflected an earlier stage of textual diversity before the text became relatively fixed.

Then in 2013 I published an English translation of most of the major Hekhalot texts as I reconstructed them based on the seven manuscripts published in the *Synopse* and those published in the *Geniza Fragmenta*, along with two other complete manuscripts of the *Hekhalot Rabbati* which I collated from microfilms.[13] For the most part, the translations were based on Hebrew and Aramaic texts that were eclectically reconstructed from the manuscripts more or less on Lachmannian lines. The purpose of this article is to reflect, especially in the light of New Philology, on the theoretical background to this translation and some of the practical issues involved in producing it.[14]

---

11 Swartz, "Three-Dimensional Philology," 549.

12 James R. Davila, "Prolegomena to a Critical Edition of the Hekhalot Rabbati," *JJS* 45 (1994): 208–26.

13 Davila, *HLIT*. The seven manuscripts published in the *Synopse* are as follows. MS New York, Jewish Theological Seminary 828/8128 (hereafter, "N") is an Ashkenazic manuscript dating probably to the end of the fifteenth or the beginning of the sixteenth century, heavily interpolated with magical, liturgical, and even apocalyptic materials. MS Oxford, Bodleian Library, Michael 9 (Neugebauer 1531) (hereafter, "O") is an Ashkenazic manuscript dating to around 1300. MS Munich, Bayerische Staatsbibliothek, Cod. hebr. 40 (hereafter, "M40") is an Italian manuscript written by multiple scribes. The section containing the Hekhalot texts translated here is dated to the end of the fifteenth century. MS Munich, Bayerische Staatsbibliothek, Cod. hebr. 22 (hereafter, "M22") is an Italian manuscript that was also written by multiple scribes, but the section containing the Hekhalot texts translated in *HLIT* is dated to the middle of the sixteenth century. MS Dropsie, Philadelphia, Dropsie University 436 (hereafter, "D") is a Sephardic manuscript dated to the fifteenth century. MS Vatican, Biblioteca Apostolica, Vaticana, Vat. ebr. 228 (hereafter, "V") is a Byzantine manuscript dated to the fifteenth century. MS Budapest, Rabbinic Seminary, Kaufman 238 (hereafter, "B") is an Italian manuscript dated to the fifteenth century. The other two manuscripts are MS Florence Laurenziana Plut. 44/13 (hereafter, "F"), an Italian manuscript dating to the fourteenth century, and MS Leiden Or. 4730 (hereafter, "L"), an Italian manuscript that may date to the sixteenth or seventeenth century. Cf. Davila, *HLIT*, 19, 38–39.

14 Recent publications that deal with some related issues are Ra'anan Boustan, "The Study of Heikhalot Literature: Between Mystical Experience and Textual Artifact," *CurBR* 6 (2007): 130–60;

Theoretical considerations

In undertaking my translation of the Hekhalot texts I found it necessary to balance the theoretical issues that arose from dealing with the manuscripts with the practical constraints involved with producing a comprehensible and useful translation. Although I was not thinking specifically in terms of New Philology, it is highly relevant to the main issues that arose. The fundamental problem was that, although manuscripts are rightly regarded as individual artifacts of interest in themselves, producing a translation of a text preserved in multiple manuscripts requires the translator to make decisions about how best to interpret and arrange the information in the manuscripts. Broadly speaking, the possibilities were (1) to translate the individual manuscripts in synoptic format;[15] (2) to translate a single manuscript judged to be the best, correcting only obvious corruptions and giving the variant readings of the other manuscripts in an apparatus;[16] or (3) to translate an eclectic text, critically reconstructed from the manuscripts. The third option was the approach I used. None of these approaches would be in principle wrong or right, but I found this one to be most amenable due both to theoretical and practical considerations.

On the theoretical level, some reflections on the nature of the manuscripts data for the Hekhalot texts are in order, particularly in light of some broader considerations concerning the scribal transmission of manuscripts. We have two major sources for the text of the Hekhalot literature. The first consists of forty-seven mostly complete and mostly European (a few late ones are "Oriental") manuscripts in Hebrew and Aramaic dating from c. 1300 to the seventeenth century.[17] These contain complete texts of the chief macroforms of the Hekhalot literature as well

---

Daniel Abrams, "Critical and Post-Critical Textual Scholarship of Jewish Mystical Literature: Notes on the History and Development of Modern Editing Techniques," *Kabbalah* 1 (1996): 17–71; Daniel Abrams, with a foreword by David Greetham, *Kabbalistic Manuscripts and Textual Theory: Methodologies of Textual Scholarship and Editorial Practice in the Study of Jewish Mysticism* (SSLJM 26; Jerusalem: Hebrew University Magnes Press, 2010), 37–47, 475–89.

15 This would parallel the approach chosen by Schäfer in his arrangement of the seven manuscripts in the *Synopse*, as well as the approach generally used for the layout of the parallel material in synopses of the New Testament Gospels. The standard such synopsis is Kurt Aland, *Synopsis of the Four Gospels: Greek-English Edition of the Synopsis Quattuor Evangeliorum* (Stuttgart: United Bible Societies, 1980).

16 This approach was used by Schäfer and his colleagues in their German translation of the *Synopse*, for which see n. 8 above.

17 These manuscripts are surveyed by Schäfer in "Handschriften zur Hekhalot-Literatur," in *Hekhalot-Studien*, 154–233, and by Klaus Herrman in *Massekhet Hekhalot: Traktat von den himmlischen Palästen. Edition, Übersetzung und Kommentar* (TSAJ 39; Tübingen: Mohr Siebeck, 1994), 22–65. Although the actual texts of most of them remain unpublished, these works survey their contents in detail down to the level of individual paragraph units as delineated in the *Synopse*.

as some smaller macroforms, and other odds and ends.[18] Some of the macroforms survive in multiple recensions, but arguably these manuscripts go back to something not far from a single recension and perhaps even a single manuscript of that recension. In the introduction to my translation I suggested that this putative *Urtext* could have been a recension produced by the Ḥaside Ashkenaz sometime in the thirteenth century. The reality may be more complex,[19] but the data still point toward these manuscripts descending from an *Urtext*, one that in principle may be subject to text-critical reconstruction. I will refer to this text from now on as the European *Urtext*.

The second source consists of something over a dozen highly fragmentary Middle Eastern ("Oriental") manuscripts recovered from the Cairo Geniza.[20] These have been

---

18 The chief macroforms, with their paragraph enumeration in the *Synopse*, are *Hekhalot Rabbati* (§§ 81–121, 152–73, 189–277), "The Greater (Book of the Heavenly) Palaces"; *Sar Torah* (§§ 281–306), "The Prince of Torah"; *Hekhalot Zutarti* (approximately §§ 335–75, 407–26), "The Lesser (Book of the Heavenly) Palaces"; *Maʿaseh Merkavah* (§§ 544–96), "The Working of the Chariot"; *Merkavah Rabba* (§§ 655–708), "The Greater (Book of the) Chariot"; and *Sefer Hekhalot* (§§ 1–79), "The Book of the Palaces," also known as *3 Enoch*. Another rather complex macroform, the *Shiʿur Qomah* was not fully represented in the *Synopse* and was not included in my translation, although part of it is found in one of the macroforms that I did translate. The *Shiʿur Qomah* consists of traditions about the size of and esoteric names for the various gigantic body parts of God. See discussion below. The relevant shorter macroforms and fragments are *The Chapter of R. Nehuniah ben HaQanah* (§§ 307–14); the incantation prayers in *The Great Seal-Fearsome Crown* (§§ 318–21//§§ 651–54); a brief account of *The Ascent of Elisha ben Avuyah* (§ 597); the *Sar Panim* ("The Prince of the Presence") (§§ 623–39), and *The Youth* (*hanaʿar*). Apart from the Geniza fragment G12 (see below) I did not translate *3 Enoch* in *HLIT*. There is an excellent English translation of *3 Enoch* by Philip Alexander in *Apocalyptic Literature and Testaments*, vol. 1 of *The Old Testament Pseudepigrapha* (ed. James H. Charlesworth; Garden City, N.Y.: Doubleday, 1983), 223–315.

19 In a recent article Schäfer has made a preliminary comparison of the text of the published Geniza fragments to that of the complete European manuscripts listed in n. 13 above and concluded that the Geniza fragments are generally more closely affiliated to the Italian and Byzantine manuscripts than to the Ashkenazic ones ("The Hekhalot Geniza" in *Hekhalot Literature in Context: Between Byzantium and Babylonia* [ed. Raʿanan Boustan, Martha Himmelfarb, and Peter Schäfer; TSAJ 153; Tübingen: Mohr Siebeck, 2013], 179–211). If upheld, this conclusion would imply that the European *Urtext* originated outside of Ashkenaz, perhaps in Byzantine-Italian circles, and the Ashkenazic form of the text is a somewhat later development. The European *Urtext* behind the Ashkenazic and Byzantine-Italian manuscripts may well be older than the thirteenth century.

20 Most of these were published in *Geniza Fragmente*. For full publication information on the relevant fragments see chapter eight of *HLIT*. Some relevant material from these fragments is discussed below. Happily, Gideon Bohak has recently reported that his research in the Geniza collection of the Cambridge University library has brought to his attention "a few dozen additional Geniza fragments of the Hekhalot literature." A dozen belong to *Tefillat Rav Hamnuna Sava* ("The Prayer of Rav Hamnuna the Elder"), which Bohak includes in the Hekhalot corpus but which was not published in the *Synopse* and which I did not translate in *HLIT*. See Bohak, "Observations on the Transmission of the Hekhalot Literature in the Cairo Geniza" in *Hekhalot Literature in Context* (ed. Boustan et al.), 213–29, esp. pp. 214 (quoted) and 219.

paleographically dated to from before the ninth century to the fourteenth century, with most falling in the eleventh to twelfth centuries. They include manuscripts of the *Hekhalot Rabbati*, the *Hekhalot Zutarti*, the *Shiʿur Qomah*, and texts that include material known also from the *Sar Torah*, the *Sar Panim*, and from *3 Enoch*, as well as individual copies of otherwise lost Hekhalot works. The Geniza texts of the previously known macroforms are generally closely related to the later complete manuscripts, but the former are often quite corrupt, but with a pattern of corruptions independent of the complete manuscripts and thus sometimes preserving early readings lost in them. The Geniza manuscripts also have some more significant redactional differences from the complete manuscripts.

The first observation that arises from these data is that if we begin with the methodological working hypothesis that there is a reconstructable *Urtext* behind the complete manuscripts, our efforts at textual criticism are to a large extent rewarded with what looks like a reconstructed *Urtext*. This is especially true for the *Hekhalot Rabbati*, the *Sar Torah*, the *Hekhalot Zutarti*, and the briefer macroform the *Sar Panim*. The *Maʿaseh Merkavah* and the *Merkavah Rabba*, which seem to be later compositions than the other macroforms, survive with some recensional variation that seems to indicate they were built up out of earlier blocks of text, but *Urtexts* behind these easily-isolated blocks of text themselves remain reconstructable and were not difficult to incorporate into the English translation of their longer recensions, especially given my particular concern, explained below, with reconstruction of the text of the microforms.

All this having been said, the evidence of both the complete manuscripts and the Geniza fragments is not fully explained with the reconstruction of this European *Urtext*. On the contrary, the *Urtext* appears to be a recension that imperfectly preserves and understands its *Vorlage* and, even more disquietingly, which suppresses an earlier textual variety. Two lines of evidence point in these directions, both in the text of the *Hekhalot Rabbati* in the section containing the teaching of R. Nehuniah ben HaQanah concerning the "descent" (i.e., visionary ascent) to God's celestial throne chariot (§§ 198–237). First, the section includes conversations with the angels of the sixth celestial palace which contain a number of Greek phrases transliterated into Hebrew letters (§§ 230 [2x], 233, 236).[21] In the text of all of the nine manuscripts consulted (which include the two earliest complete ones, O and F) the Greek text is badly corrupted and cannot be reconstructed from any surviving readings, although Yohanan Levy convincingly reconstructed this Greek material by means of judicious conjectural emendation.[22] In the surviving recension of the

---

21 The passage concerning the angel ʿAnaphiʾel may also contain a Greek phrase in § 242. For details see Davila, *HLIT*, 116–17 (§ 230 nn. c, l); 119 (§ 233 n. l); 121 (§ 236 n. m); 126 (§ 242 n. m).
22 Yohanan Levy, "Remnants of Greek Sentences and Names in 'Hekhalot Rabbati,'" *Tarbiz* 12 (1941): 163–67 (in Hebrew). Gideon Bohak has registered skepticism toward many of Levy's recon-

Hekhalot Rabbati, these phrases are treated as divine names in the form of corrupt *nomina barbara*, but the meaning of the Greek of at least one of these indicates that it was originally part of the conversation. In § 233 the transliterated Greek phrase, followed by "God of Israel," is inserted into the narrative flow as a divine name, without reference to the context. But the Greek phrase means something like "Excellent day, excellent prayer (or "luck")! Show the sign! Peace!" This makes good sense as a greeting to the ascending mystic by the angel Dumi'el in the immediately following sentences and it is difficult to escape the conclusion that a scribe who did not realize the phrase was Greek has moved it from its original context in the mouth of Dumi'el and made it into a contextually incongruous divine name.[23] This is evidence for an earlier text, one lacking the incongruity, behind the recension of our surviving European *Urtext* as preserved in the Ashkenazic, Sephardic, and Byzantine-Italian manuscripts.

The second piece of evidence comes from a Geniza manuscript. In the same nine complete manuscripts, the teaching of R. Nehuniah about the descent to the chariot is interrupted by an odd interlude in which he makes a perplexing comment about the angels at the entrance of the sixth palace and his disciples make use of an obscure magical rite to call him back from the fifth palace in order to explain the comment (§§ 224–228). As had been recognized before the discovery of the Geniza fragment, the passage is clearly secondary: it misunderstands R. Nehuniah's explanatory narrative about the process of the descent to be an on-the-scene description by him in a trance state of a descent he is actually undergoing. The text of the end of § 233 is corrupt and the narration of the ideal descent resumes in § 229 without transition. The Geniza fragment Oxford Heb. f. 56, fol. 125a 1–15 (GO56), in an Oriental script of the twelfth to fourteenth centuries and thus perhaps originating in Iraq, preserves an earlier version of the text whose chief difference from the complete manuscripts is that it moves smoothly from § 223 to § 229 without the interpolated passage. Again

---

structed Greek phrases, but in the case of § 233 he does allow that "Levy probably was right in detecting a dialogue between the mystic and the angelic guard" even though the specifics of the dialogue cannot now confidently be reconstructed, and this suffices to make my point ("Remains of Greek Words and Magical Formulae in Hekhalot Literature," *Kabbalah* 6 [2001]: 121–34, quotation from p. 132).

23 The divine name in § 242 which apparently contains a Greek phrase is also contextually incongruous, but the Greek has not been deciphered, so we do not know what it originally meant or how it may originally have appeared in context. The reconstructed meaning of the other Greek phrases in § 230 (first phrase) and § 236 make sense in context as divine names. The second Greek phrase in § 230, which seems to mean roughly "the God of heaven, fire, earth, is silence" could make sense in its current context as a divine name, although it is possible that this context is secondary and it was originally a reference, perhaps in the mouth of the angel Dumi'el, to the meaning of his Hebrew name ("God is my silence") in the immediately following lines. See Davila, *HLIT*, § 230 n. l. Unfortunately, none of these phrases survive in any of the published Geniza manuscripts.

this gives us access to an earlier text than that which can be reconstructed from the complete manuscripts.[24]

These examples give us good reason to infer that the medieval European manuscripts that contain complete texts of the major macroforms represent only one recension of the Hekhalot literature and behind them lie lost textual traditions that existed in the Geonic period. The surviving fragments of these earlier textual traditions are too sparse to tell us if they too represent a lost *Urtext* that could be recovered with the recovery of complete manuscripts of the Geonic era. The transmission of the Hekhalot materials in some of these manuscripts gives us pause concerning the latter possibility, in that they indicate that transmission of the texts in the earliest manuscripts showed at least as much interest in the smaller units of Hekhalot traditions as in the macroforms known from the later manuscripts.[25]

The earliest surviving Hekhalot manuscript (G1, likely before the ninth century) contains a collection of Merkavah hymns also found in the *Hekhalot Rabbati* and elsewhere, but in a different order, in a somewhat different textual form, and with material found also in some manuscripts of the *Sar Torah* and in the *Sar Panim*.[26] According to a new interpretation of the manuscript fragments of G4 (twelfth century or a little later), it arguably preserves a version of the culmination of the ascent account of the *Hekhalot Rabbati* (§§ 246–50) which was followed by an adjuration introducing a *Shi'ur Qomah* text that describes God's gigantic body, thus giving the material a very different climax from that of the later manuscripts, which at this point introduce a corpus of hymns sung daily by the throne of God, which hymns are recited by the arriving adept.[27] In G6 (no earlier than the thirteenth century), material also known from *Hekhalot Rabbati* §§ 213–14 is incorporated into an adjuration.[28] A passage

---

24 For the passage see Davila, *HLIT*, 111–16 and for bibliography see p. 112 (§ 224 n. a.). The Geniza fragment was published by Schäfer in "Ein neues *Hekhalot Rabbati*-Fragment." It could conceivably be possible to argue that §§ 224–28 originally belonged to the text and was deleted, but to my knowledge no one has done so. The secondary nature of this passage was recognized on redaction-critical grounds even before the discovery of GO56 and it would be very difficult to argue that the passage is more original than the text in GO56 or to affect a neutrality between them, when the secondary nature of §§ 224–28 has been so clearly demonstrated. For detailed argumentation see Schäfer's article as well as the bibliography cited in *HLIT*.
25 Even the reconstructed European *Urtext* of the complete macroforms in the later manuscripts shows that individual microforms and briefer episodes could find a home in more than one place. For example, the story of the Four Who Entered Paradise, whose text is itself quite varied, is found both in the *Hekhalot Zutarti* (§§ 338–45) and the *Merkavah Rabba* (§§ 671–74). Indeed, a paean to the powers of the Hekhalot practitioner appears in slightly variant forms twice in the same macroform, the *Hekhalot Zutarti* (§ 349–50a//§ 361). Such examples could be multiplied. The implication is that at least some microforms circulated independently before being subsumed into the text of a macroform.
26 Schäfer, "The Hekhalot Geniza," 183–86.
27 Schäfer, "The Hekhalot Geniza," 191–94; Bohak, "Observations," 216–17.
28 Schäfer, "The Hekhalot Geniza," 194–96.

about an ascent of R. Ishmael and the angel ʿAnaphiʾel found in *Hekhalot Zutarti* §§ 420–21 appears in somewhat different forms in an otherwise unknown Hekhalot text preserved in G8 2b 36b–49a, eleventh century) and in G75 (eleventh century), an incantation text.[29] What seems to be a redactionally early version of the opening of *3 Enoch* and some material found later in the book (§§ 1–2, 61–62//1:12, 43:2–44:4, as found in the late manuscripts) is found in G12 (eleventh or twelfth centuries) followed by physiognomic material that does not appear in the complete macroforms of the late manuscripts.[30] In addition, Reimund Leicht and Joseph Yahalom have argued plausibly that this was the opening of an esoteric midrash on the individual Hebrew letters of Genesis 5:1, another manuscript of which they have identified.[31]

It is possible that the composers of all of the Geniza texts noted in the preceding paragraph were aware of more or less the same macroforms as the *Hekhalot Rabbati*, the *Hekhalot Zutarti*, the *Sar Torah*, the *Sar Panim*, and *3 Enoch* as known in the late manuscripts and excerpted them for the composers' own purposes. But we need not conclude this. The scribal culture indicated in these fragments points toward a perspective in which the basic unit is the microform. And this may be the original scribal culture that produced the Hekhalot texts; one in which the microform – often no more than a paragraph – was the original unit of composition, with longer episodes created in individual manuscripts using the microforms as building blocks, and macroforms then constructed out of multiple episodes. If this be the case, the further back we penetrate behind the European *Urtext*, the greater variety we would find, going back to strata that consist mainly of microforms that were only later constructed into the surviving macroforms of the *Urtext*.

The original textual variety of the Hekhalot traditions suggested by this evidence is quite similar to the textual variety known from medieval European literary tradition written in vernaculars, such as the *Chanson de Roland* and the *Percevals*, discussed by Cerquiglini in chapter three of *In Praise of the Variant*, and supports his reservations about the concept of a Lachmannian critical text,[32] as well as Schäfer's reservations about reconstructing an *Urtext* for the Hekhalot literature. At the same time, Cerquiglini acknowledges an important exception to the norm of textual variety in medieval literature:

---

29 Davila, *HLIT*, 375, 376, 401–2, 411–12. G75 was originally published by Peter Schäfer and Shaul Shaked et al. in *Magische Texte aus der Kairoer Geniza*, vol. 3 (TSAJ 72; Tübingen: Mohr Siebeck, 1999), 184–90.
30 Schäfer, "Ein neues Fragment zur Metoposkopie und Chiromantik."
31 Reimund Leicht and Joseph Havalom, "*Sefer Zeh Sefer Toledot Adam*: An Unknown Esoteric Midrash on Genesis 5:1 from the Geonic Period," *GQ* 4 (2008): 9–82. I was not aware of this article when I wrote my treatment of G12 in *HLIT*, 375, 402–4.
32 Cerquiglini, *In Praise of the Variant*, 48–52, 66, 67, 77.

There was only one text in the Middle Ages. Du Cange notes that, starting in the eleventh century (i.e., at the moment when the written word attained full development), *textus* was used more and more exclusively to designate the *codex Evangilorum*. Attested around 1120, the French word *tiste*, changed then to *texte* (a scholarly word), means "the book of the gospels." This text was the Bible, the immutable word of God that may, of course, be annotated, but not rewritten.[33]

In other words, the norm in Europe of the Middle Ages was a literature characterized by textual variety, with the exception of the Bible, whose divine and canonical authority was associated with a fixed text subject to commentary but not revision. These parallel tracks of vernacular textual variety and canonical textual stability suggest a possible analogy to the textual situation we find in the Hekhalot manuscripts. The Geniza manuscripts, which generally reflect the textual variety of the Hekhalot literature in the Geonic era are comparable to the vernacular literature transmitted in a scribal tradition that did not distinguish copying, revision, and rewriting. But at some point early in the transmission of these traditions in European circles a single recension (or perhaps a narrow range of recensions) of the Hekhalot texts was formulated and acquired a quasi-canonical status which led to a comparative textual fixity and the purging of variant textual traditions. The analogy is suggestive, but imperfect, since medieval vernacular literature did not evolve a canonical status that led to even comparative textual fixity. Likewise, the European Hekhalot tradition did not develop a divine authority or a textual fixity on the level of scripture, although a comparatively fixed *Urtext* (by medieval standards) can be discerned behind them.

One could perhaps find a better analogy in the historical development of the biblical texts themselves. Source criticism of the Pentateuch makes it abundantly clear that this work developed out of smaller units that once had a life of their own and there is broad agreement on the presence of Deuteronomic and Priestly strata incorporated into the text. But efforts to recover further or in any greater detail the development of earlier source material into our Pentateuch have largely reached a stalemate, with no comprehensive reconstruction of Pentateuchal origins commanding anything resembling a consensus. In the Second Temple period the Pentateuch had achieved a fixed form overall, with putative earlier recensions almost entirely suppressed but with a great many individual textual variants surviving from manuscript to manuscript along with a scribal tradition that felt free to expand and develop the text in a continuum that ranged from careful copying to substantial rewriting. The textual state of the European *Urtext* of the Hekhalot literature is similar in many ways to this stage of the development of the Pentateuch. But unlike the Hekhalot literature, the text of the Pentateuch was further winnowed in the Jewish tradition, with nearly all textual variations suppressed, leaving us with the narrowly fixed Masoretic Text. This analogy supports the idea that textual variety is the norm in manuscript transmission

---

33 Cerquiglini, *In Praise of the Variant*, 34–35.

unless this variety is deliberately suppressed in a canonical version, and it may be worth exploring further in future research.[34]

Practical issues regarding the translation

This then is the theoretical context for understanding the Hekhalot literature as texts. Our earliest evidence for some of the major macroforms consists of fragments of what look like these macroforms, but in some cases with significant redactional differences, as well as formulations of Hekhalot material which place some of the microforms known from the later macroforms in entirely different contexts as parts of previously unknown works. It is possible that fuller access to currently unavailable Geonic manuscripts would allow us to reconstruct an earlier *Urtext* of Hekhalot macroforms, but it is equally possible that earlier evidence would lead us back to more and more varied collections of microforms which only later were fused into the more stable macroforms. The later, complete European manuscripts present us with a group of macroforms which in some cases show some recensional variety, but overall can reasonably be traced back to an *Urtext* that was in existence by the thirteenth century and there is sufficient evidence to reconstruct this European *Urtext* with a significant degree of confidence. Where does this state of affairs leave us? What do we translate and how do we present the translation?

As noted above, a translation could be crafted as either a synoptic presentation of each manuscript (i.e., essentially translating the seven manuscripts of the *Synopse* and perhaps others using the same layout as in the *Synopse*), or as a diplomatic arrangement using a single, "best" manuscript as the base text, or on the basis of eclectic, critically reconstructed Hebrew and Aramaic texts.[35] The synoptic

---

34 For the current state of the question on Pentateuchal source criticism, see Reinhard G. Kratz, "The Pentateuch in Current Research: Consensus and Debate," in *The Pentateuch: International Perspectives on Current Research* (ed. Thomas B. Dozeman, Konrad Schmid, and Baruch J. Swartz; FAT 78; Tübingen: Mohr Siebeck, 2011), 31–61. For the use and transmission of the text of the Pentateuch (and other books of the Hebrew Bible) in the Second Temple period, with special attention to how the Dead Sea Scrolls further our understanding, see Eugene Ulrich, *The Dead Sea Scrolls and the Origins of the Bible* (Grand Rapids, Mich.: Eerdmans, 1999); Ronald S. Hendel, "Assessing the Text-Critical Theories of the Hebrew Bible after Qumran," in *The Oxford Handbook of the Dead Sea Scrolls* (ed. Timothy H. Lim and John J. Collins; Oxford: Oxford University Press, 2010), 281–302; Molly M. Zahn, "Rewritten Scripture," in ibid., 323–36.
35 The ideal would be to create a hypertext edition that combines the advantages of all three approaches. It would have as its basis a transcription of each manuscript which could be viewed on its own or in synoptic columns with other manuscripts or in a diplomatic format with just the variants of the other manuscripts. But the edition would also be viewable as an eclectic text reconstructed from all the manuscripts with an apparatus of variants. Ideally photographs of the manuscripts would be

arrangement is the only one which treats each manuscript as a text in its own right, but this arrangement is impractical for a translation of the Hekhalot literature, both because the multiple columns of translated text would take up a great deal of expensive space and because the individual manuscripts are at times so corrupt that the text would defy translation. No one has attempted a comprehensive synoptic translation, although I have used similar principles to translate the Geniza fragments of the major macroforms (see below).

The German translation was on a diplomatic basis and produced good results. It treated the base manuscript (generally O) as a text in its own right, correcting only obvious corruptions in it, but giving variants from the other manuscripts in an apparatus much like an apparatus for an eclectic reconstructed text. It has the advantage of translating a real text that exists in a manuscript, and MS O often preserves a text that makes good sense. But its text is far from flawless and not infrequently it requires considerable emendation on the basis of the other manuscripts to produce a sensible text and, even when its text makes sense in itself, it is sometimes not the most original that can be reconstructed from all the manuscripts – if and when the early or original text is what we are aiming for. Manuscript F preserves a still better text of the *Hekhalot Rabbati*, but even it has many imperfections that would have required correction if it had been used as the base text.[36] Ultimately, a diplomatic translation is a compro-

---

included, tagged to each word of each transcribed manuscript. Translations of the diplomatic format of each manuscript as well as of the eclectic reconstructed text could be included, with each translation unit tagged to the text of the original. Computer technology is not far from the point where it will become practical to produce such editions. Cf. the comments of Cerquiglini in *In Praise of the Variant*, 79–82, as well as my comments in "Prolegomena," 220.

36 The "hymns of the throne" in *Hekhalot Rabbati* §§ 251–57//§§ 260–66 (translated in *HLIT*, 133–42), are a good example. They appear in the manuscripts in multiple contexts and the text of any single manuscript is more or less corrupt, although text-critical reconstruction can at least frequently suggest a plausible *Urtext*. I have discussed the textual reconstruction of § 253 in detail in "Prolegomena," 210–13. The *Partiturtext* of eleven manuscripts of the paragraph given on pp. 223–26, with secondary readings underlined, shows that although F preserves the text of the hymn with the highest density of more original readings, even it is far from pristine. Indeed two lines of the poem are missing entirely from it. The German translation translates the text as two to three synoptic columns, with the first (of MS O) heavily annotated with variants and corrections from the other manuscripts (Schäfer, *Übersetzung*, 2:225–38).

A similar example in the *Hekhalot Zutarti* is the section on the four living creatures in the heavenly throne room in §§ 353–56, *HLIT*, 208–14. Manuscript O preserves the best text, but it is still imperfect and needs correction on the basis not only of G7, but at times other manuscripts as well. For examples of readings in the European manuscripts which make sense in themselves but can be improved on with reference to a Geniza manuscript, see the passage on the four faces engraved on God's throne in *Hekhalot Rabbati* § 273, *HLIT*, 149–50, esp. nn. o, p, discussed below.

The case of § 253 is a stark reminder of the limitations of the diplomatic and synoptic approaches. They maintain the integrity of the individual manuscripts with their damaged text of the hymn, but forgo the opportunity offered by judicious textual criticism to reconstruct this beautiful poetic work

mise: it treats the base manuscript as a real text on its own terms, but demotes the other manuscripts to sources of textual variants which are relegated to an apparatus not unlike one for an eclectic reconstructed text.

My English translation was of an eclectic reconstructed text whose basis was the seven manuscripts published in the *Synopse*, two other complete manuscripts of the largest macroform, the *Hekhalot Rabbati*, and such Geniza fragments as were available. The text was reconstructed using the traditional canons and criteria of textual criticism, but without any particular attempt to construct a stemma of the manuscripts. Three of the main macroforms (the *Hekhalot Zutarti*, *Ma'aseh Merkavah*, and *Merkavah Rabba*) are extant complete in only five manuscripts, while the briefer macroforms (translated in chapter seven) survive in fewer than these. One can occasionally note alignments of manuscripts in a group this small, but the textual criticism is best undertaken simply by evaluating each individual reading. The other two major macroforms (the *Hekhalot Rabbati* and *Sar Torah*) survive in considerably more manuscripts than used in the translation. The five complete manuscripts already mentioned were selected mainly because they contained all the complete texts of the three aforementioned macroforms rather than for anything special about their texts of the *Hekhalot Rabbati* and the *Sar Torah*. Following Schäfer's lead in the German translation, I included the text of the Florence manuscript (F) as a particular good text of the *Hekhalot Rabbati*, and that of the Leiden manuscript (L) as an example of a particularly freely transmitted late copy thereof. Any effort to construct stemmata for the manuscripts of the *Hekhalot Rabbati* and the *Sar Torah* will require the collation of the variants in the many other surviving complete manuscripts of those two macroforms. For some of the macroforms the sparse evidence of the Geniza fragments produces suggestive patterns of alignment with the later complete manuscripts but, again, it is mainly the individual readings of the Geniza texts which help us reconstruct the earliest available text which was the goal of my translation.

As with the other two options, this one had its own disadvantages and advantages. The chief disadvantage is that the reconstruction of the main text demands a judgment call for an original reading in every variation unit, even in the many cases where it is difficult using the normal text-critical criteria to choose an original reading among two or more variants. But this problem is to some degree ameliorated by the fact that in such cases the sense of the variants is generally not greatly different and one choice or another does not significantly affect the meaning of the passage. Still, once internal criteria and consideration of the characteristics of the individual manuscripts have been considered and found inconclusive, a reading still has to be chosen for the main text and in such cases I have generally accepted the reading of the majority of manuscripts. Undoubtedly in some of these cases this resulted in a less

---

in something at least approaching its original form. This is a real esthetic and literary loss. The loss is less in other passages, but it is pervasive and its cumulative effect is real.

original reading being chosen over a more original one, but a diplomatic approach makes the same sort of decision simply by using one manuscript as the main text and, even using manuscript that has a high density of more original readings, that approach must also sometimes result in the preference of a less original reading. The main advantage of a critical eclectic reconstruction is that in many, many cases, the use of textual criticism can isolate original (or at least more original) and secondary readings and place the (more) original readings in the main text, producing a text that overall is closer to the sought-after *Urtext*.

That said, in the case of this translation two other factors created additional complexities for reconstructing a main text. The first is the evidence that the basic unit of the Hekhalot literature is the microform rather than the macroform. The evidence for the primacy of the microforms has been reviewed above and it led me to proceed with the principle that, if a choice became necessary, the text being reconstructed was that of the individual microforms and short episodes rather than the text of the macroforms or any specific recension of a macroform. The second factor is the surviving fragments from the Cairo Geniza, which preserve evidence for an earlier text, and apparently an earlier textual variety, than the text of the later complete Hekhalot manuscripts.

The Geniza manuscripts comprise our earliest evidence for the Hekhalot literature, preserving fragments of the *Hekhalot Rabbati*, the *Sar Torah*, the *Hekhalot Zutarti*, the *Sar Panim*, *3 Enoch*, and the *Shiʿur Qomah*, as well as a number of previously unknown Hekhalot works. These fragments have value for textual criticism as sources for early readings, but also value as the earliest witnesses to the form of the Hekhalot traditions, sometimes varying significantly from the arrangement of the later complete manuscripts. In order to give full weight to both of these factors, I collated the relevant text for my translations of the *Hekhalot Rabbati* (chapter two), the *Sar Torah* (chapter three), the *Hekhalot Zutarti* (chapter four), and the *Sar Panim* (chapter seven),[37] but I also translated the Geniza Hekhalot fragments as texts in their own right in chapter eight.[38]

As demonstrated above, the range of textual variation in the Hekhalot literature exists across a continuum, one pole of which is represented by the existence of variant recensions of the macroforms. The *Maʿaseh Merkavah* survives in a long and a short

---

37 For the *Shiʿur Qomah* material, see below.

38 For the most part I chose not to translate other, non-Hekhalot material found in the same codex (e.g., the *Shiʿur Qomah* material in G6) or even in the same context (e.g., the adjurational material in G4), this on the ground that my focus was on the Hekhalot text and thus it was unnecessary to translate associated material, especially when the latter was itself fragmentary or its placement in the codex in relation to the Hekhalot passage was unclear. The exception is G75, a fully preserved adjuration containing material found in the *Hekhalot Zutarti*, which I translated in its entirety. One could legitimately debate how much contextual material to translate in these situations, and others might have proceeded differently.

recension, the latter of which lacks a substantial section (§§ 579–91) found in the former. The *Merkavah Rabba* also survives in a short (§§ 665–70) and long recension (§§ 655–708). In both cases it is possible that the two recensions were transmitted independently for some time, but I have chosen to translate the long recension, using the manuscripts of both recensions to reconstruct the text where it overlaps, and indicating clearly in the notes and introductions what the boundaries of the two recensions are. By proceeding this way it is possible that in some places I have reconstructed a text somewhat different from what was found in the putative *Urtext* of each recension, because I have reconstructed the earliest possible text of the individual macroforms. But the textual apparatus, when used with the Hebrew text of the *Synopse*, provides sufficient information for a reader to reconstruct a text of either recension, using only the manuscripts or manuscript that contain that recension, should that be necessary for some specific inquiry about the transmissions of the texts.

The opposite pole on the continuum of textual variation in the Hekhalot texts is that of individual variation units within a microform. My aim of reconstructing the earliest possible text of each microform was to a large degree achievable using the standard canons of textual criticism, which in theory should give us the earliest possible text of the European *Urtext* overall. But the Geniza fragments added a note of complexity to this process, since not infrequently they preserved what I judged to be better readings that had not survived in any of the later manuscripts descended from the *Urtext*. For example the text of G1 C 1b–14 allows us to improve on the text of the description of the faces of the celestial living creatures (man, ox, lion, and eagle) engraved on the throne of God found in *Hekhalot Rabbati* § 273, preserving readings such as "They have the face of the ox. They low like an ox and the vision of them is like an ox" (§ 273 nn. o, p), recovering material that corresponds to the pattern of the parallel paragraphs while applying specifically to the ox and is thus superior to the reading "They run like an ox" (miscopied by reminiscence from the paragraph on the man) in all the European manuscripts ("They run" being missing in M22). Likewise, "They have the face of a lion" (n. y), corrects the contextually inappropriate and bewildering "They have the face of a man" in all the European manuscripts (except a marginal note in L). Again, the latter reading was miscopied from the paragraph on the man by reminiscence. The result is that we have an earlier text of this microform, but this text probably did not ever exist in the European *Urtext* that is being reconstructed overall. To put it bluntly, the text of the *Hekhalot Rabbati* as a whole never existed in exactly the form I have reconstructed and translated it. I can think of any number of ways I might have proceeded differently, such as reconstructing the *Urtext* based on the complete manuscripts and flagging possible original variants in the Geniza texts in the notes. But I judged it more important to privilege the best text of the microforms and, again, anyone specifically interested in the European *Urtext* will have the resources to reconstruct it from the apparatus and the text of the *Synopse*.

Between the poles of variant recensions of the macroforms and individual variation units in the microforms lies a continuum of variation within larger or smaller units, some sense of which can be given in the following. As noted above (n. 25), some microforms are found in more than one macroform or even more than once in a given macroform. I have translated the doublet of §§ 349–50a and § 361 in the *Hekhalot Zutarti* individually in both places, reconstructing each from the manuscript evidence in its place, but collating the variants between the two in the notes to §§ 349–50a. In this case it was not possible using textual criticism to reach back to an earlier text behind the two versions of the microform, so I have treated them as separate texts. The textual complexities of the story of the Four Who Entered Paradise were such that I was tempted to resort to a synoptic presentation in this one case, but in the end I chose to translate the episode once, using all the evidence from all manuscripts of both the *Hekhalot Zutarti* (including the somewhat idiosyncratic version in the Geniza fragment of this macroform, G7) and the *Merkavah Rabba*. This required some subjective decisions about what to put in the main text and what to relegate to the apparatus and I have explained in my introduction to the chapter what my reasoning was for reconstructing the form of the main text as I did. As with the recensions of the *Ma'aseh Merkavah*, those who wish to reconstruct the best form of the text of the Four Who Entered Paradise in the *Hekhalot Zutarti* or the *Merkavah Rabba* will find sufficient information to do so in the apparatus of my translation and the Hebrew text in the *Synopse*. As already noted, I also translated the full text of G7 in chapter eight.

More complicated cases abound. The list of the names of Metatron in the closing paragraph of the *Hekhalot Rabbati* (§ 277) is also found with considerable variation in the complexly parallel collection G1 (F 12–21), *The Chapter of R. Nehuniah ben HaQanah* § 310, *Merkavah Rabba* § 682, and the Geniza macroform G19 1a 25b–1b 2a. The Geniza sources containing variant versions of the account of 'Anaphi'el in *Hekhalot Zutarti* § 420–21 have already been noted above. The second prayer in *Sar Torah* § 306 appears also in G1 (B 6b–15) and the Geniza macroform G8 (2b 27b–30a). These three microforms thus appear repeatedly in completely different contexts within different macroforms and often each instantiation of the microform shows its own redactional integrity and can be reasonably treated as a text on its own. For the most part I have treated them as such, reconstructing each on the basis of the manuscript evidence for it in a given macroform and translating the Geniza fragments individually as texts in their own right in chapter eight. At the same time, I have occasionally noted variants from versions of the same microform in other macroforms when I thought they were of interest for reconstructing the earliest possible text of a microform.

One passage in the *Hekhalot Zutarti* (§§ 362, 364–65) had a significant overlap with a magical handbook known as the *Havdalah di-R. Akiva*, which was transmitted in its own manuscript tradition and an edition of which was published by Gershom Scholem.[39] A Geniza fragment of the latter work (G18) has since been recovered and it

---

39 Scholem, "*Havdala De-Rabbi 'Aqiva*. A Source for the Tradition of Magic During the Geonic Period," *Tarbiz* 50 (1980–1981): 243–81 (in Hebrew).

includes material in the overlap. To make matters more complicated, another Geniza fragment (G16) also preserves material from the overlap but it is uncertain to which macroform, if either, it might have belonged. In this case I collated the relevant material from Scholem's edition and G18 in my translation of the *Hekhalot Zutarti* and also translated G16 in chapter eight (as a possible manuscript of the *Hekhalot Zutarti*), but did not translate G18, since it belonged to a text outside the Hekhalot corpus.

The *Shi'ur Qomah* tradition offers a special challenge to the textual critic and it is not clear to me that an *Urtext* can be recovered for it. Since its content is at best tangentially related to that of the main Hekhalot macroforms and considerable work remains for establishing the history of its transmission, I did not translate the *Shi'ur Qomah* as a macroform on its own terms.[40] But a recension of some *Shi'ur Qomah* material is incorporated as part of the *Merkavah Rabba* (§§ 695–704), and this I did translate. For this section of *Shi'ur Qomah* traditions I proceeded on the principle of attempting to reconstruct the earliest form of the individual microforms, drawing not only on the manuscripts of the *Merkavah Rabba*, which I collated fully, but also on *Shi'ur Qomah* material found elsewhere in the *Synopse* and on the Geniza *Shi'ur Qomah* fragments. In the case of the latter two sources, I limited citation of variants to those that seemed interesting. As before, this may result in some places in the reconstruction of a text that is not identical to the *Urtext* of the *Merkavah Rabba*, although such a text can be worked out from the apparatus, but which includes earlier readings in the individual macroforms.

We also find that individual manuscripts sometimes include microforms or short episodes that are found in few or no other manuscripts of the same Hekhalot macroform, although these smaller units often appear elsewhere outside the Hekhalot traditions. Such passages appear frequently in N but also occasionally in other manuscripts. Some notable examples of such smaller units that appear in a small number of manuscripts of the *Hekhalot Rabbati* include the *David Apocalypse* (§§ 122–26), which appears in different places in this macroform; a passage found also in *Seder Rabba di-Bereshit* (§§ 175–88 or some part thereof); *Aggadat R. Ishmael* (§§ 130–38); the *Messiah Aggada* (§§ 140–45); and in the *Sar Torah*, a passage involving a test of the Sar Torah praxis (§§ 304–05). Cases where a small unit is found only in a single manuscript of a Hekhalot macroform include one about Metatron's intercession for the repentant (§§ 147–49, N) in the *Hekhalot Rabbati* and another about Metatron and the heavenly throne room in the *Sar Torah* (§§ 295–96, B). Almost all such passages appear elsewhere either in another Hekhalot manuscript or in some other type of work and many of them are translated elsewhere. I have noted their existence at the relevant place in the Hekhalot macroform, but have not translated them. The "Throne

---

40 The manuscript evidence for the *Shi'ur Qomah*, apart from some Geniza fragments published in *Geniza-Fragmente*, has been edited and translated by Martin Samuel Cohen in *The Shi'ur Qomah: Texts and Recensions* (TSAJ 9; Tübingen: Mohr Siebeck, 1985).

Midrash" in *Hekhalot Zutarti* §§ 368–75 is a special case. §§ 368b–73a and § 375 appear only in N, but the entire passage has been argued to be either very early and potentially part of the *Urtext*, or a very late addition, so I have translated it all to facilitate consideration of the question of its date and origin.

In a number of cases, longer episodes, essentially shorter macroforms, survive only in a single manuscript of a macroform, such as *The Chapter of R. Nehuniah ben HaQanah*, which appears only in V, although elements of it find parallels in other Hekhalot texts. I have translated it as a separate macroform in chapter seven. A version of the large episode revolving around the heavenly Youth appears in the middle of the *Hekhalot Zutarti* (§§ 375–405) only in manuscript N, although various forms of the passage are known from the *Shiʿur Qomah* tradition. I have omitted *The Youth* from the *Hekhalot Zutarti* but translated another version of it in chapter seven for reasons indicated there.

Finally, it was necessary to make a number of other decisions about how to handle details of the texts and manuscripts which are of some interest for New Philology. I have already referred to the Greek sentences and phrases transliterated into Hebrew letters which appear in the *Hekhalot Rabbati* in now hopelessly corrupt form. In the main text of the translation I have transliterated these into English letters, following the reconstruction of Levy, which does not appear in any surviving manuscript. I have explained their apparent meaning and the basis of the text in notes in the apparatus. Otherwise, where transliterated Greek words or phrases appear in any of the macroforms I have transliterated these into English letters as well as was possible and explained their possible original form and meaning in notes in the apparatus. The representation of divine names and *nomina barbara* represented a challenge because they too were frequently very corrupt in the manuscripts. I judged that any benefit of giving a full account of the variant forms was outweighed by the corresponding necessity of a considerable increase in the size of the apparatus, so for these I simply used the reading of a single good manuscript – O whenever possible, otherwise another, clearly designated manuscript. When I judged that a more intelligible text of these could be reconstructed, I have translated this better text and explained the grounds for it in a note in the apparatus. In general I ignored abbreviations (treating them as the unabbreviated text) and division marks and punctuation in the individual manuscripts, punctuating the translation according to its best sense in my judgment and indicating other possible punctuations in the notes in the apparatus. The Tetragrammaton appears in many forms in the manuscripts. I have given it as YHWH in the main text and apparatus, unless I am translating or giving a reading of a single manuscript, in which case I transliterated the form used in that manuscript. Following Schäfer's practice in the *Synopse*, I indicated manuscript corrections and erasures in the apparatus on the grounds that they can sometimes be of interest for the history of interpretation.

One criticism laid against the *Synopse* is that its transcription of the Hebrew and Aramaic texts did not indicate certain physical features of the manuscripts such as variations in letter size, including enlarged chapter headings and the like.[41] In at least one case such a variation may matter for the reconstruction of a Geniza text. In G3 2a 9 most of the line, apart from the last word and a half, is destroyed, but we can reconstruct that it began *Hekhalot Rabbati* § 152. The space available, however, is considerably more than would be needed to fill in the missing text. A chapter heading is probably missing, but this in itself does not seem to be enough to fill in the lacuna. In manuscript F (98b 20), however, this paragraph opens with the Hebrew for "Chapter Seven" (פירקא שביעיתא) in lettering of about one-and-a-half times the normal size.[42] A similarly enlarged chapter heading with the same text and comparable space on either side would fill the lacuna in the Geniza manuscript nicely. Although the latter manuscript does use Hebrew letters to mark paragraph divisions, not enough of it survives to tell us whether it likewise inserted enlarged chapter headings. My reconstruction of this line of the Geniza fragment is speculative, but remains an interesting example of how the layout of one manuscript can potentially help us to reconstruct lost text in another.[43]

Conclusion

The New Philology provides a useful theoretical perspective for understanding the manuscript transmission of the Hekhalot literature and I have drawn on it in this essay to explore some of the issues I faced when producing an English translation of these texts, drawing on the canons and criteria of textual criticism. The nature of the Hekhalot texts necessitates that any translation of any sort – whether of a synoptic arrangement of the individual manuscripts, of a diplomatic arrangement of a good manuscript as base text with an apparatus of variants from other manuscripts, or of a critically reconstructed eclectic text with an apparatus of variants – will be a complicated affair that requires some effort and care to use. Each of the possible approaches has its advantages and disadvantages, but I found it best for my purposes to translate a traditional eclectic critical text, focusing on reconstructing the best possible text of the individual microforms, and giving some special attention to the early Geniza manuscripts by both collating them in the apparatuses and translating them as individual texts in a separate chapter.

---

41 Abrams, "Critical and Post-Critical Textual Scholarship," 38–39.
42 The thirteen letters of the chapter heading take up the same space as eighteen letter spaces in the line above it and nineteen letter spaces in the line below it. The second word of this chapter heading in manuscript F has been transcribed incorrectly as *šby'ytyt* in *HLIT* § 152 n. a, p. 77. I am grateful to the Biblioteca Mediceo Laurenziana for permission to publish material from manuscript F.
43 Davila, *HLIT*, 393 and n. s.

To sum up, a close analysis of the textual evidence for the Hekhalot literature points to an earlier period, perhaps in the Geonic era, in which the scribal tradition focused on shorter textual units – "microforms" – which were mixed and matched to produce widely varying larger combinations of microforms. Many of the Geniza fragments reflect this stage of development. But in Europe by the thirteenth century this earlier textual diversity was purged in favor of much more stable larger combinations of the smaller units – "macroforms" – and something approaching an informal canon of these macroforms, and the complete manuscripts copied from this point on reflect this narrower textual tradition. Any attempt to reconstruct an *Urtext* for the material in the earlier stage would be futile, frustrated by the instability and diversity of the manuscript tradition, but the texts of the later complete manuscripts (at least the ones I have studied closely) by and large do go back to a textual archetype that existed by the thirteenth century and the application of traditional textual criticism leads us back to a reconstructable European *Urtext*.

Such levels of textual variation are recognized by New Philology: the norm for medieval vernacular literature is a textual diversity of the sort we find in the Hekhalot Geniza fragments. But Cerquiglini has acknowledged that the Bible, because of its canonical status, was an exception to this norm and was transmitted (apart from accidental scribal errors) as a fixed text. I have argued here that the European *Urtext* is at least partially analogous to the medieval biblical text in that it consisted of a quasi-canonical collection of macroforms transmitted in the manuscripts with a relatively fixed text whose *Urtext* is susceptible to reconstruction. It is this reconstructed *Urtext* that I have translated into English and the full force of my argument can only be evaluated by close attention to the reconstructed main text and the critical apparatus of thousands of variants.

The clearest application of New Philology to my translation project is thus to the Geniza fragments of the Hekhalot literature. New Philology gives us an explanatory and methodological framework that allows us to understand these texts on their own terms as a fluid textual tradition that does not admit to reconstruction of an archetype or *Urtext* through traditional textual criticism. I have accordingly gathered these fragments into a single chapter in my translation and translated each individually.

At the same time, the later, complete European manuscripts of the Hekhalot literature are of a somewhat different nature and do invite the application of traditional textual criticism to reconstruct an approximation of an (at latest) thirteenth-century European *Urtext*, which I have translated into English. As with any such reconstruction, the results are to some degree hypothetical and doubtless imperfect. But any historical endeavor is in the same sense a hypothetical reconstruction, yet that does not excuse the historian from undertaking it.

My translation project, of course, in no way precludes application of New Philology to the Hekhalot manuscripts to study their individual texts and physical characteristics, a highly desirable project that is barely begun.

New Philology has shown that the application of traditional textual criticism to many manuscript traditions is of questionable value and indeed is often counterproductive. It also offers to refocus our attention on the individual manuscripts, their texts, and their physical features, opening up a very fruitful pathway to harvesting historical details that would otherwise have eluded us. But in certain cases, including the case of the complete European Hekhalot manuscripts, traditional textual criticism nevertheless remains an essential tool in our scholarly toolbox.

Bibliography

Abrams, Daniel. "Critical and Post-Critical Textual Scholarship of Jewish Mystical Literature: Notes on the History and Development of Modern Editing Techniques." *Kabbalah* 1 (1996): 17–71
—. *Kabbalistic Manuscripts and Textual Theory: Methodologies of Textual Scholarship and Editorial Practice in the Study of Jewish Mysticism*. Foreword by David Greetham. Sources and Studies in the Literature of Jewish Mysticism 26. Jerusalem: Hebrew University Magnes Press, 2010.
Aland, Kurt. *Synopsis of the Four Gospels: Greek-English Edition of the Synopsis Quattuor Evangeliorum*. Stuttgart: United Bible Societies, 1980.
Alexander, Philip. "3 (Hebrew Apocalypse of) Enoch." Pages 223–315 in *Apocalyptic Literature and Testaments*. Vol. 1 of *The Old Testament Pseudepigrapha*. Edited by James H. Charlesworth. Garden City, N. Y.: Doubleday, 1983.
Bohak, Gideon. "Remains of Greek Words and Magical Formulae in Hekhalot Literature." *Kabbalah* 6 (2001): 121–34.
—. "Observations on the Transmission of the Hekhalot Literature in the Cairo Geniza." Pages 213–29 in *Hekhalot Literature in Context: Between Byzantium and Babylonia*. Edited by Ra'anan Boustan, Martha Himmelfarb, and Peter Schäfer. Texte und Studien zum antiken Judentum 153. Tübingen: Mohr Siebeck, 2013.
Boustan, Ra'anan. "The Study of Heikhalot Literature: Between Mystical Experience and Textual Artifact." *Currents in Biblical Research* 6 (2007): 130–60.
Busby, Keith, ed. *Towards a Synthesis? Essays on the New Philology*. Faux titre 68. Amsterdam: Rodopi, 1993.
Cerquiglini, Bernard. *In Praise of the Variant: A Critical History of Philology*. Translated by Betsy Wing. Baltimore: Johns Hopkins University Press, 1999 [orig. pub. 1989].
Cohen, Martin Samuel. *The Shi'ur Qomah: Texts and Recensions*. Texte und Studien zum antiken Judentum 9. Tübingen: Mohr Siebeck, 1985.
Davila, James R. "Prolegomena to a Critical Edition of the Hekhalot Rabbati." *Journal of Jewish Studies* 45 (1994): 208–26.
—. *Hekhalot Literature in Translation: Major Texts of Merkavah Mysticism*. Supplements to the Journal of Jewish Thought and Philosophy 20; Leiden: Brill, 2013.
Halperin, David J. "A New Edition of the Hekhalot Literature." *Journal of the American Oriental Society* 104 (1984): 543–52.
Hendel, Ronald S. "Assessing the Text-Critical Theories of the Hebrew Bible after Qumran." Pages 281–302 in *The Oxford Handbook of the Dead Sea Scrolls*. Edited by Timothy H. Lim and John J. Collins. Oxford: Oxford University Press, 2010.
Herrman, Klaus. *Massekhet Hekhalot: Traktat von den himmlischen Palästen. Edition, Übersetzung und Kommentar*. Texte und Studien zum antiken Judentum 39. Tübingen: Mohr Siebeck, 1994.

Kratz, Reinhard G. "The Pentateuch in Current Research: Consensus and Debate." Pages 31–61 in
    The Pentateuch: International Perspectives on Current Research. Edited by Thomas B. Dozeman,
    Konrad Schmid, and Baruch J. Swartz. Forschungen zum Alten Testament 78. Tübingen: Mohr
    Siebeck, 2011.
Leicht, Reimund, and Joseph Havalom. "*Sefer Zeh Sefer Toledot Adam*: An Unknown Esoteric Midrash
    on Genesis 5:1 from the Geonic Period." *Ginzei Qedem* 4 (2008): 9–82.
Levy, Yohanan. "Remnants of Greek Sentences and Names in 'Hekhalot Rabbati.'" *Tarbiz* 12 (1941):
    163–67.
Milikowski, Chaim. "The Status Quaestionis of Research in Rabbinic Literature." *Journal of Jewish
    Studies* 39 (1989): 201–11.
Schäfer, Peter. *Geniza-Fragmente zur Hekhalot-Literatur*. Texte und Studien zum antiken Judentum 6.
    Tübingen: Mohr Siebeck, 1984.
–. "Research into Rabbinic Literature: An Attempt to Define the Status Quaestionis." *Journal of
    Jewish Studies* 37 (1986): 139–52.
–. "Aufbau und redaktionelle Identität der *Hekhalot Zutarti*." Pages 50–62 in *Hekhalot-Studien*.
    Texte und Studien zum antiken Judentum 19. Tübingen: Mohr Siebeck, 1988.
–. "Ein neues Fragment zur Metoposkopie und Chiromantik." Pages 84–95 in *Hekhalot-Studien*.
    Texte und Studien zum antiken Judentum 19. Tübingen: Mohr Siebeck, 1988.
–. "Ein neues *Hekhalot Rabbati*-Fragment." Pages 96–103 in *Hekhalot-Studien*. Texte und Studien
    zum antiken Judentum 19. Tübingen: Mohr Siebeck, 1988.
–. "Handschriften zur Hekhalot-Literatur." Pages 154–233 in *Hekhalot-Studien*. Texte und Studien
    zum antiken Judentum 19. Tübingen: Mohr Siebeck, 1988.
–. "Prolegomena zu einer kritischen Edition und Analyse der *Merkava Rabba*." Pages 17–49 in
    Hekhalot-Studien. Texte und Studien zum antiken Judentum 19. Tübingen: Mohr Siebeck, 1988.
–. "Tradition and Redaction in Hekhalot Literature." Pages 8–16 in *Hekhalot-Studien*. Texte und
    Studien zum antiken Judentum 19. Tübingen: Mohr Siebeck, 1988.
–. "Zum Problem der redaktionellen Identität von *Hekhalot Rabbati*." Pages 63–74 in *Hek-
    halot-Studien*. Texte und Studien zum antiken Judentum 19. Tübingen: Mohr Siebeck, 1988.
–. "Once Again the Status Quaestionis of Research in Rabbinic Literature: An Answer to
    Milikowsky." *Journal of Jewish Studies* 40 (1989): 89–94.
–. "The Hekhalot Geniza." Pages 179–211 in *Hekhalot Literature in Context: Between Byzantium
    and Babylonia*. Edited by Ra'anan Boustan, Martha Himmelfarb, and Peter Schäfer. Texte und
    Studien zum antiken Judentum 153. Tübingen: Mohr Siebeck, 2013.
Schäfer, Peter, Hans-J. Becker, Klaus Hermann, Claudia Rohrbacher-Sticker, and Stefan Siebers.
    Übersetzung der Hekhalot-Literatur II §§ 81–334. Texte und Studien zum antiken Judentum 17.
    Tübingen: Mohr Siebeck, 1987.
–. *Übersetzung der Hekhalot-Literatur III §§ 335–597*. Texte und Studien zum antiken Judentum 22.
    Tübingen: Mohr Siebeck, 1989.
–. *Übersetzung der Hekhalot-Literatur IV §§ 598–985*. Texte und Studien zum antiken Judentum
    29. Tübingen: Mohr Siebeck, 1991.
Schäfer, Peter, and Klaus Hermann. *Übersetzung der Hekhalot-Literatur I §§ 1–80*. Texte und Studien
    zum antiken Judentum 46. Tübingen: Mohr Siebeck, 1995.
Schäfer, Peter, and Shaul Shaked, with Reimund Leicht, Bill Rebiger, and Irina Wandrey. *Magische
    Texte aus der Kairoer Geniza*, vol. 3. Texte und Studien zum antiken Judentum 72. Tübingen:
    Mohr Siebeck, 1999.
Schäfer, Peter, with Margarete Schlüter and Hans Georg von Mitius. *Synopse zur Hekhalot-Literatur*.
    Texte und Studien zum antiken Judentum 2. Tübingen: Mohr Siebeck, 1981.
Scholem, Gershom. "*Havdala De-Rabbi ʾAqiva*. A Source for the Tradition of Magic during the Geonic
    Period." *Tarbiz* 50 (1980–1981): 243–81.

Swartz, Michael. "Three-Dimensional Philology: Some Implications of the *Synopse zur Hekhalot-Literatur*." Pages 529–50 in *Envisioning Judaism: Studies in Honor of Peter Schäfer on the Occasion of his Seventieth Birthday*. Edited by Raʿanan Boustan, Klaus Herrmann, Reimund Leicht, Annette Yoshiko Reed, and Guiseppe Veltri. 2 vols. Tübingen: Mohr Siebeck, 2013.

Ulrich, Eugene. *The Dead Sea Scrolls and the Origins of the Bible*. Grand Rapids, Mich.: Eerdmans, 1999.

Zahn, Molly M. "Rewritten Scripture." Pages 323–36 in *The Oxford Handbook of the Dead Sea Scrolls*. Edited by Timothy H. Lim and John J. Collins. Oxford: Oxford University Press, 2010.

Index

Index of Ancient Works and Discrete Units

In alphabetical order

Index of Manuscripts, Fragments, and Ostraca

Page numbers in **boldface** script indicate the presence of an image.